Research Anthology on Usage, Identity, and Impact of Social Media on Society and Culture

Information Resources Management Association
USA

Volume II

IGI Global
PUBLISHER of TIMELY KNOWLEDGE

Published in the United States of America by
IGI Global
Information Science Reference (an imprint of IGI Global)
701 E. Chocolate Avenue
Hershey PA, USA 17033
Tel: 717-533-8845
Fax: 717-533-8661
E-mail: cust@igi-global.com
Web site: http://www.igi-global.com

Library of Congress Cataloging-in-Publication Data

Names: Information Resources Management Association, editor.
Title: Research anthology on usage, identity, and impact of social media on
  society and culture / Information Resources Management Association,
  editor.
Description: Hershey, PA : Information Science Reference, [2022] | Includes
  bibliographical references and index. | Summary: "This reference set
  discusses the impact social media has on an individuals' identity
  formation as well as its usage within society and cultures, exploring
  new research methodologies and findings into the behavior of users on
  social media as well as the effects of social media on society and
  culture as a whole"-- Provided by publisher.
Identifiers: LCCN 2022016910 (print) | LCCN 2022016911 (ebook) | ISBN
  9781668463079 (hardcover) | ISBN 9781668463086 (ebook)
Subjects: LCSH: Social media--Psychological aspects. | Identity
  (Psychology) | Social media and society.
Classification: LCC HM742 .R46783 2022 (print) | LCC HM742 (ebook) | DDC
  302.23--dc23/eng/20220509
LC record available at https://lccn.loc.gov/2022016910
LC ebook record available at https://lccn.loc.gov/2022016911

British Cataloguing in Publication Data
A Cataloguing in Publication record for this book is available from the British Library.

The views expressed in this book are those of the authors, but not necessarily of the publisher.

For electronic access to this publication, please contact: eresources@igi-global.com.

Editor-in-Chief

Mehdi Khosrow-Pour, DBA
Information Resources Management Association, USA

Associate Editors

Steve Clarke, *University of Hull, UK*
Murray E. Jennex, *San Diego State University, USA*
Ari-Veikko Anttiroiko, *University of Tampere, Finland*

Editorial Advisory Board

Sherif Kamel, *American University in Cairo, Egypt*
In Lee, *Western Illinois University, USA*
Jerzy Kisielnicki, *Warsaw University, Poland*
Amar Gupta, *Arizona University, USA*
Craig van Slyke, *University of Central Florida, USA*
John Wang, *Montclair State University, USA*
Vishanth Weerakkody, *Brunel University, UK*

List of Contributors

Table of Contents

Section 2
Development and Design Methodologies

Volume II

Section 3
Tools and Technologies

Section 4
Utilization and Applications

Volume III

Section 5
Organizational and Social Implications

Section 6
Critical Issues and Challenges

Preface

Over the years, social media has blossomed from a leisure tool used by a select pool of younger individuals to an essential form of communication for everyone. It has connected individuals globally and has become an essential practice in marketing, advertising, broadcasting news stories, conducting research, and more. The internet has quickly become a new hub for communication and community development. In most communities, people develop new cultural norms and identity through social media usage. However, while these new lines of communication are helpful to many, challenges such as social media addiction, cyberbullying, and misinformation lurk on the internet and threaten forces both within and beyond the internet.

Staying informed of the most up-to-date research trends and findings is of the utmost importance. That is why IGI Global is pleased to offer this three-volume reference collection of reprinted IGI Global book chapters and journal articles that have been handpicked by senior editorial staff. This collection will shed light on critical issues related to the trends, techniques, and uses of various applications by providing both broad and detailed perspectives on cutting-edge theories and developments. This collection is designed to act as a single reference source on conceptual, methodological, technical, and managerial issues, as well as to provide insight into emerging trends and future opportunities within the field.

The *Research Anthology on Usage, Identity, and Impact of Social Media on Society and Culture* is organized into six distinct sections that provide comprehensive coverage of important topics. The sections are:

1. Fundamental Concepts and Theories;
2. Development and Design Methodologies;
3. Tools and Technologies;
4. Utilization and Applications;
5. Organizational and Social Implications; and
6. Critical Issues and Challenges.

The following paragraphs provide a summary of what to expect from this invaluable reference tool.

Section 1, "Fundamental Concepts and Theories," serves as a foundation for this extensive reference tool by addressing crucial theories essential to understanding the usage, identity, and impact of social media. The first chapter of this section, "The Dark Side of Engaging With Social Networking Sites (SNS)," by Profs. Eileen O'Donnell and Liam O'Donnell of Technological University Dublin, Ireland, explores the dark side of social networking sites. The final chapter of this section, "The Facebook Me: Gender, Self-Esteem, and Personality on Social Media," by Profs. Robert Andrew Dunn and Heng Zhang of East Tennessee State University, USA, examines the influence of gender, personality, and self-esteem on social media presentation.

Section 2, "Development and Design Methodologies," presents in-depth coverage of the design and development of social media assessment and research. The first chapter of this section, "Psychological Impact and Assessment of Youth for the Use of Social Network," by Profs. Sapna Jain and M. Afshar Alam of Jamia Hamdard, India and Prof. Niloufer Adil Kazmi of Independent Researcher, India, dissects the effect of online life on each youngster in both the negative and positive bearing of their development utilizing the social impact hypothesis. The final chapter of this section, "At the Mercy of Facebook: A Meta-Analysis on Impact of Social Networking Sites, Teen Brain on Teenage Pregnancies," by Prof. Nirupama R. Akella of Wichita State University, USA, is a meta-analysis of teen brain research and social media technology such as Facebook that could result in spiraling rates of teenage pregnancy. The author discusses contemporary theories of brain circuitry including teen brain structure and function as one of the plausible reasons for rising teenage pregnancy rates.

Section 3, "Tools and Technologies," explores the various tools and technologies used in communications and research on social media. The first chapter of this section, "Collaborative Social Networks: Effect of User Motivation, Cognition, and Behavior on User Participation," by Prof. Yulin Chen of Tamkang University, New Taipei City, Taiwan, investigates the relationships between the motivation, cognition, and behavior of knowledge management. It analyzes university students preparing to share content on the Tamshui Humanities Knowledge Collaboration System to determine whether different participation motivation dimensions (community motivation and personal motivation) affected their knowledge management cognition and behavior. The final chapter of this section, "The Important Role of the Blogosphere as a Communication Tool in Social Media Among Polish Young Millennials: A Fact or a Myth?" by Profs. Sylwia Kuczamer-Kłopotowska and Anna Kalinowska-Żeleźnik of University of Gdańsk, Poland, proposes and discusses the hypothesis that the blogosphere is a relatively well-developed and independent social media communication tool used by millennials.

Section 4, "Utilization and Applications," describes the interactions between users on social media. The first chapter of this section, "Adolescents, Third-Person Perception, and Facebook," by Prof. John Chapin of Pennsylvania State University, USA, documents the extent of Facebook use and cyberbullying among adolescents. It is based on a study theoretically grounded in third-person perception (TPP), the belief that media messages affect other people more than oneself. The final chapter of this section, "Facebook Communities of African Diasporas and Their U.S. Embassies: A Content Analysis Study," by Prof. Hesham Mesbah of Rollins College, USA and Prof. Lauren Cooper of Florida House of Representatives, USA, explores how the Nigerian, Ethiopian, and Egyptian diasporas in the United States use their Facebook groups to create their imagined communities. It also draws a parallel between their use of Facebook and how the embassies of their countries of origin use the same platform in performing their official duties.

Section 5, "Organizational and Social Implications," includes chapters discussing the impact of social media usage and interpersonal interaction on society. The first chapter of this section, "Understanding Social Media Addiction Through Personal, Social, and Situational Factors," by Prof. Asli Elif Aydin of Istanbul Bilgi University, Turkey and Prof. Ozge Kirezli of Yeditepe University, Turkey, gains an in-depth understanding of the social media addiction construct. The final chapter of this section, "Transformation of China's Most Popular Dating App, Momo, and Its Impact on Young Adult Sexuality: A Critical Social Construction of Technology Analysis," by Prof. Weishan Miao of Chinese Academy of Social Sciences, China and Prof. Jian Xu of Deakin University, Australia, explores China's most popular dating app 'Momo' and its impact on young adult sexuality.

Section 6, "Critical Issues and Challenges," presents coverage of academic and research perspectives on the critical issues imposed by social media on its users, communities, and society. The first chapter of this section, "Positive vs. Negative Emotions and Network Size: An Exploratory Study of Twitter Users," by Prof. Yeslam Al-Saggaf of Charles Sturt University, Australia, examines the relationship between the expression of positive and negative emotions in Twitter and users' network size. The final chapter of this section, "The Tipping Point: A Comparative Study of U.S. and Korean Users on Decisions to Switch Social Media Platforms," by Prof. Soo Kwang Oh of Pepperdine University, USA; Prof. Seoyeon Hong of Rowan University, USA; and Prof. Hee Sun Park of Korea University, South Korea, focuses on why users quit certain social media and change their favorite platforms, such as the current shift from Facebook to Twitter to Instagram and Snapchat. Furthermore, this exploratory study builds an understanding of social media usage and motivations for switching from a cross-cultural perspective by comparing findings from Korean and U.S. users.

Although the primary organization of the contents in this multi-volume work is based on its six sections, offering a progression of coverage of the important concepts, methodologies, technologies, applications, social issues, and emerging trends, the reader can also identify specific contents by utilizing the extensive indexing system listed at the end of each volume. As a comprehensive collection of research on the latest findings related to social media, the *Research Anthology on Usage, Identity, and Impact of Social Media on Society and Culture* provides social media analysts, communications specialists, computer scientists, online community moderators, sociologists, psychologists, business leaders and managers, marketers, advertising agencies, government officials, libraries, students and faculty of higher education, researchers, and academicians with a complete understanding of the applications and impacts of social media. Given the vast number of issues concerning usage, failure, success, strategies, and applications of social media, the *Research Anthology on Usage, Identity, and Impact of Social Media on Society and Culture* encompasses the most pertinent research on the applications, impacts, uses, and research strategies of social media.

Section 3
Tools and Technologies

Chapter 22
Collaborative Social Networks:
Effect of User Motivation, Cognition, and Behavior on User Participation

Yulin Chen
Tamkang University, New Taipei City, Taiwan

ABSTRACT

This article investigates the relationships between the motivation, cognition, and behavior of knowledge management. It analyzes university students preparing to share content on the Tamshui Humanities Knowledge Collaboration System (hereafter referred to as the Tamshui Wiki) to determine whether different participation motivation dimensions (community motivation and personal motivation) affected their knowledge management cognition and behavior. The stimulus–organism–response theory is adopted to assess the relationships between several intrinsic cognition (knowledge management and community reputation) and behavior (attention, interest, action, and share) dimensions. A total of 364 valid samples are collected. Correlation analysis and regression analysis are adopted for statistical calculation. Findings reveal that the participation willingness and community motivation of the students had a greater effect on their knowledge management cognition than personal motivation. Frequent users of Wikipedia were approving of knowledge collaboration and able to link cognition with behavior.

1. INTRODUCTION

Wikipedia contains vast amounts of user-generated content and comprehensive knowledge management structures (Parameswaran & Whinston, 2007). The platform aims to promote knowledge management through continuous user contribution (Koh et al. 2007; Farzan & Brusilovsky 2011; Butler 2001). User participation is voluntary. Researchers agree that participatory media or Wikipedia can build communities of knowledge as an intermediary to generate positive interactions between users and participatory media (Larson & Watson, 2011). In this process, the contents and the format of communication are critical (Barwise & Meehan, 2010; Wang, Jiao, Abrahams, Fan, & Zhang, 2013), for example, content co-creation and content involvement (Clark & Melancon, 2013; Goh, Heng, & Lin, 2013) or media envi-

DOI: 10.4018/978-1-6684-6307-9.ch022

ronment (distinction of content, value delivery and opportunity development) and platform requirements (Larson & Watson, 2011; Khajeheian, Esmaeilkhoo, & Yousefikhah, 2012). Salamzadeh considered the co-working space and the short creation period for shortening of the learning curve by start-up accelerators (Salamzadeh & Markovic, 2018).

Regretfully, previous studies on knowledge management largely focused on evaluating management efficacy or validating user experiences (Parboteeah, Valacich, & Wells, 2009). To the authors' knowledge, no case studies have evaluated user cognition and behavior based on their participation motivations, and none have independently validated or discussed the knowledge management systems of educational institutions (Jiang, Chan, Tan, & Chua, 2010). Therefore, this study selected the Tamshui Humanities Knowledge Collaboration System (hereafter referred to as the "Tamshui Wiki") as the research sample and users' motivations for participating in knowledge management as the research variables in order to analyze users' pre-participation intrinsic cognition and behavioral responses. The findings of this study serve as a reference for improvement efforts of participatory media management. Several suggestions are also made concerning community and team recognition and contribution.

The Tamshui Wiki was established on 13th September 2013 to consolidate information on Tamshui, including local features, history, culture, customs, lifestyle, travel and tourism, and attractions. The system comprises four major segments, namely history, events, names, and records. The system was co-created by university students and local scholars. The purpose of the system is to motivate students in voluntarily participating in cultural and historical knowledge creation and to share and impart local knowledge. In this study, a questionnaire survey and statistical analysis were used for comprehensive validation and analysis of results. This was employed to investigate the relationships between the motivations, cognitions, and behaviors of Tamshui Wiki users. The study endeavored to determine users' motivations for participating in knowledge management prior to content creation and the possible effects of intrinsic cognition and overt behaviors on users' motivations. Findings indicated that students developed a high regard for knowledge and organization on the platform prior to participation, validating the feasibility of using Tamshui Wiki as a means to motivate students in participating in knowledge management.

This study wanted to solve three research problems. First, a group of university students with experience of knowledge collaboration was surveyed to examine their perceptions and behaviors concerning humanities knowledge collaboration system. In addition to analyzing their basic understanding of knowledge management, the study also validated the effects of participation motivation on user cognition. Second, although extant literature has undoubtedly expanded our understanding of user motivation (Nambisan & Baron, 2007), the study aimed to provide more concrete definitions and elucidate the demands and views of university students without knowledge management experience, thereby effectively improving educational institutions, highlighting the significance of humanities knowledge collaboration systems, and demonstrating improper operations (Kaysers & Eul, 2018). Third, an extensive evaluation of users' experiences with using knowledge management systems was performed to formulate approaches to reinforce their participatory willingness, help students effectively gain community recognition, and prompt them to willingly and actively participate in knowledge contribution (Kohler, Fueller, Matzler, & Stieger, 2011). The proposed framework can be effectively implemented into relevant educational institutions to maximize benefits by merging higher education and knowledge creation/management.

Section 2 briefly discusses participation motivation, knowledge management, community reputation, stimulus–organism–response (SOR) theory, and attention–interest–search–action–share (AISAS) theory. In Section 3, a number of hypotheses are proposed to evaluate the relationships between motivation, cognition, and behavior. Sections 4 and 5 explain the research procedures and perform data analysis.

Finally, results are discussed and conclusions are drawn, and several suggestions are made on how to use the proposed model, thereby adding professional value to knowledge collaboration systems.

2. THEORETICAL BACKGROUND

2.1. Participation Motivation of Wikipedia

Wikipedia is an online collaborative editing website that transcends conventional knowledge transfer, replication, and storage (Lee, Lee & Kang, 2005). Many studies on knowledge contribution have shown that motivation directly affects users' attitude in participating in knowledge contribution (He & Wei, 2009). Motivation can be analyzed in two dimensions, namely community motivation and personal motivation (Yang & Lai, 2011; Peddibhotla & Subramani, 2007). Wikipedia users are a group who actively establish and maintain common interests. They identify with the community and enhance their sense of belonging through knowledge sharing and member interaction. Walther (1996) analyzed Wikipedia and found that the commitment of community members stimulated the participatory willingness of other users (Walther, 1996). Compared to other social media platforms, such as Twitter and Facebook, Wikipedia has a greater emphasis on knowledge contribution and sharing, rather than serving as a channel for expressing personal emotions. Wikipedia is also not suited for circulating news or posting comments. Therefore, Wikipedia operates on the collective contributions and efforts of knowledgeable strangers or like-minded groups (Bock & Kim, 2001; Bock et al., 2005). Therefore, users' experiences or perceptions of a community, including speculation and personal experiences also influence user participation motivation (Oreg & Nov, 2008; Prasarnphanich & Wagner, 2009).

In previous studies on personal participation motivation, common factors for motivation include users' habits and satisfaction. Yan and Davison (2013) mentioned that Wikipedia adopts two strategies, specifically, initial sharing and continued sharing strategies (Yan & Davison, 2013). Factors that affect initial sharing strategies include tangible, extrinsic rewards or satisfaction, such as money or status. Those that affect continued sharing strategies are intangible, including social norms and social connections. Lerner and Tirole (2002) found that extrinsic rewards trigger greater satisfaction than do intrinsic rewards (Lerner & Tirole, 2002). These rewards include skills and learning (Lakhani & Von Hippel, 2003), as well as the acquisition of professional or useful knowledge (Lakhani & Wolf, 2005; Wasko & Faraj, 2005). Intrinsic satisfaction is correlated to a sense of achievement (Bryant, Forte & Bruckman, 2005), interest and enjoyment (Torvalds & Diamond, 2001), reciprocal relationships, fulfillment of duties and responsibilities (Ryan & Deci, 2000), and satisfying others' needs. These factors are all intrinsic motivations (Wasko & Faraj, 2005).

Community motivation comprises many dimensions, including cultural characteristics, management and support, and structural reinforcement (Wang & Noe, 2010). Among the various dimensions, the most widely discussed dimension is subjective norms and co-working space (Nejati, Salamzadeh, & Salamzadeh, 2011; Salamzadeh & Markovic, 2018). Drucker (2001) mentioned that to enhance the value of knowledge (Drucker, 2001), it should be expanded and used as the key resource to foster organization competitiveness (Cho, Chen & Chung, 2010). The transfer of information and experiences triggers the exchange of knowledge in communities or organizations and promotes member interactions (Lin, Hung & Chen, 2009).

First, users' community (Nov, Naaman & Ye, 2010), and personal participation motivations were surveyed (Koh & Kim, 2003; Wasko & Faraj, 2005; Cho et al., 2010). Then, users' understanding of knowledge management and community reputation are investigated (Spinellis & Louridas, 2008; Biswas, Hussain & O'Donnell, 2009; Miller & Laczniak, 2011). Finally, users' behavioral responses were measured based on the dimensions of attention, interest, action, and share (Hall, 1924; Davis, Bagozzi & Warshaw, 1992; Wasko & Faraj, 2005). Therefore, users' participation motivation and intrinsic cognition undoubtedly have an interactive relationship.

2.2. Knowledge Management and Community Reputation

Knowledge management can be defined as the transfer of assets or the sharing of knowledge (Prasarnphanich & Wagner, 2009). Knowledge is the conversion of information into tangible and intangible assets (Stvilia et al., 2008). Chen et al. (2006) developed an empirical model and proposed a set of criteria concerning users' perceptions of knowledge sharing to explain different cognitive relationships during the conversion process (Chen et al., 2006). Martz and Shepherd (2003) asserted that knowledge transfer could be achieved through demonstration and education, helping people gain a better understanding of knowledge management (Martz & Shepherd, 2003). Matsumoto et al. (2009) analyzed the knowledge consolidation of a group of experts and found that the management of different platforms helped users gain a better understanding of management (Matsumoto et al., 2009). Knowledge management encourages knowledge association and motivates users to immerse themselves directly and indirectly into the community (Forte, Larco & Bruckman, 2009). This is extremely beneficial for knowledge integration within the community. Therefore, various tools (Hou & Li, 2011; Mason, 2005) and empirical models for managing knowledge have emerged in recent years (Dixon, 2000; Housel & Bell, 2001).

Nambisan and Nambisan (2008) asserted that community participation motivation is achieved through the co-creation of community members (Nambisan & Nambisan, 2008). Therefore, managing vast amounts of knowledge is a challenge for communities. Utilizing the professional consensus within communities to garner member recognition and trust (Schroeder & Wagner, 2012) is possibly the single most important factor in knowledge management (Chiu et al., 2006). If successful, the reputation of the community can automatically generate professional recognition and trust. Zeithmal (1988) defined store reputation as a type of image recognition that affects customers' interest in the store and their purchase intentions (Zeithaml, 1988). Community reputation refers to the overall evaluation of people within and outside the community (Bergami & Bagozzi, 2000). This type of reputation is based on users' perceptions. Bhattacharya et al. (1995) found that members are more willing to trust and recognize communities that strive to establish a positive reputation (Bhattacharya, Rao & Glynn, 1995). A professional and trustworthy community image also enhances users' satisfaction (Arazy et al., 2011). These findings remind us not to underestimate the importance of community reputation in community knowledge management (Carillo & Okoli, 2011; Arazy, Yeo & Nov, 2013). Anderson et al. (2007) found that organizations and communities affect the behaviors and performance of their members, consequently promoting different intrinsic cognition and overt behaviors (Anderson, Winett & Wojcik, 2007). Therefore, the study endeavored to examine the cognitive effects of knowledge management and community reputation and to explore relationships between the intrinsic cognition and overt behaviors of users of knowledge collaboration systems.

2.3. Relationship Between Intrinsic Cognition and Overt Behavior

The SOR model used in environmental psychology is applied to analyze the effects of environmental stimuli (S) on users' emotions and cognition (O) and how stimuli trigger or influence users' behavioral responses (R) (Mehrabian & Russell, 1974). Emotional responses refer to the emotional and cognitive states of consumers, including cognition, experience, and evaluation (Jiang et al., 2010; Parboteeah et al., 2009). Nambisan provided an empirical framework for a virtual environment, including pragmatic experience, social experience, available experience, and entertainment experience (Nambisan & Baron, 2009). Kohler et al. explained the motivation of users to participate in information creation. Combined with the interactive advantages of the virtual environment, users gain cognitive benefits, community integration benefits, personal integration benefits, and also enjoy these benefits. Kohler et al. also validated the importance of pragmatic experience, social experience, and pleasure experience, and explained that the level of pleasure included mental stimulation, recreation, and a pleasant experience (Kohler et al., 2011; Nambisan & Baron, 2007).

In addition, this study used the AISAS model to analyze behavior. The AISAS model was introduced by American marketing expert Mr. Samuel Roland Hall in the 1920s (Hall, 1924). He used the model to evaluate consumers' psychological processes. The model is now widely used to examine consumer behaviors, namely "attention", "interest", "search", "action", and "share", in the age of the Internet (Davis, Bagozzi & Warshaw, 1992). Users are more likely to form a proactive attitude towards an enterprise when they support the products or services of the enterprise. Conversely, they exhibit a reserved attitude when they question the enterprise's products and services (Sumita & Isogai, 2009). Therefore, the model measures the behavioral responses of the users analyzed in this study, namely "attention", "interest", "action", and "share". The attention and interest dimensions of the model entail the attraction of users. Then, through action and sharing, users meet and interact with like-minded individuals (Wasko & Faraj, 2005). Therefore, these four dimensions can be adopted as observation variables to measure users' overt behavior.

3. RESEARCH MODEL AND HYPOTHESES

This study developed a research model to analyze participation motivation, intrinsic cognition, and overt behavior.

3.1. Effects of Community Motivation on Intrinsic Cognition and Overt Behavior

This study proposes a number of hypotheses concerning knowledge management and community reputation to test intrinsic cognition. The content on Wikipedia is entirely established and edited by users. The website encourages users with the relevant knowledge to contribute to the website, such as using various themes to enhance the meaning and enjoyment of knowledge management (Abrahams et al., 2012) Skyrme and Amidon (1999) verified that the knowledge establishment process in communities reinforced knowledge management (Skyrme & Amidon, 1999). Alsadhan et al. (2008) developed a knowledge management process based on the factors of acceptance and application (Alsadhan, Zairi & Keoy, 2008). Mas-Machuca and Martínez (2012) adopted enterprises as research samples to test knowledge management strategies, technical literacy, and cultural standards. These studies validated that, with the

Figure 1. Research model.

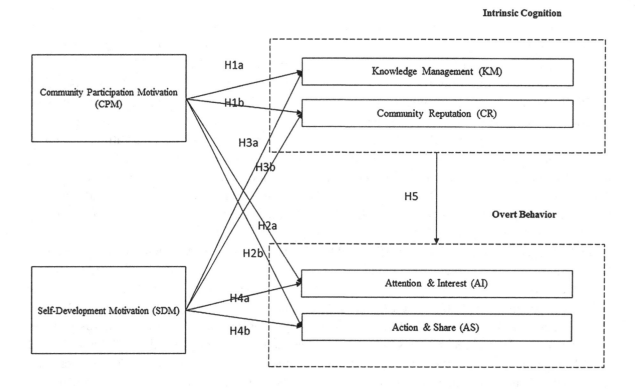

use of appropriate technologies (Mas-Machuca & Martínez Costa, 2012), knowledge effectively improves management effectiveness. Knowledge and management must satisfy community requirements in order to reinforce users' cognition of the management system (Figure 1).

The cognitive establishment of community professionalism and trust relies on the strengthening and reconstruction of community reputation. Empirical results of previous studies have validated the importance of trust in community management (Ridings, Gefen & Arinze, 2002). Consequently, professionalism is based on trust and the establishment of trustworthy attitudes and behaviors (Misztal, 1996). From the perspective of the community, trust symbolizes the confidence that users have in the community and its members and the belief that their personal and community interests are not at risk (Tsai, Huang & Chiu, 2012). Nahapiet and Ghoshal (1998) validated that when a high level of trust was present in communities, members were more willing to participate, interact, and collaborate (Nahapiet & Ghoshal, 1998).

Based on empirical results, Erez (1990) proposed that professionalism and trust are the fundamental elements of social reciprocity (Erez, 1990). When members are willing to help other members resolve their problems, they are confident that they will receive assistance from others when they are in need. In other words, community members' concerns of being exploited decrease concurrently with an increase in trust between community members (Tsai & Ghoshal, 1998), and their willingness to contribute to the community and share with others increases (Ring & Van de Ven, 1992). Communities that value professionalism and trust enhance the willingness of their members to engage in knowledge contribution (Chang & Chuang, 2011). Therefore, this study hypothesizes that community participation motivation is correlated to the users' identity with knowledge management and community reputation:

H1a: Community participation motivation is correlated to the intrinsic cognition of knowledge management (knowledge and management).

H1b: Community participation motivation is correlated to the intrinsic cognition of community reputation (professionalism and trust).

This study analyzed overt behavior based on the attention, interest, action, and share dimensions of the AISAS model. Motivation affects both user cognition and overt behaviors. For example, communities that value innovation generally encourage their members to share (Bakker et al., 2006). Conversely, overly competitive communities may induce a negative perception of knowledge sharing, damaging team spirit (Schepers & Van Den Berg, 2007) and dampening participatory willingness within the community. Darr et al. (1995) and Reagans et al. (2005) asserted that learning from knowledge management processes and encouraging cooperation between members, knowledge contribution, and even productivity, within communities can be enhanced (Darr, Argote & Epple, 1995; Reagans, Argote & Brooks, 2005). Taylor and Wright (2004) reported that the learning culture of communities affected knowledge contribution behavior (Taylor & Wright, 2004). Therefore, this study hypothesizes that participation motivation affects users' attention, interest, action, and sharing behaviors:

H2a: Community participation motivation is correlated to users' overt behaviors of attention and interest.

H2b: Community participation motivation is correlated to users' overt behaviors of action and sharing.

3.2. Effects of Personal Motivation on Intrinsic Cognition and Overt Behavior

Knowledge management stimulates people's willingness to share their knowledge with strangers and continue to participate and share (Chiu et al., 2006). Members impart their knowledge to other members through sharing (Senge, 1997; Chang & Chuang, 2011). Therefore, knowledge management and sharing can be viewed as using the exchange of information between members to help others acquire knowledge. In addition to the aforementioned influences of the community, users' personal habits also lead to differences in the understanding of knowledge management. Common personal participation motivation factors include the exercise and understanding of knowledge ownership, perceived personal gain, and establishment of community trust. Solely observing personal participation motivation, Lin found that personal supportive attitude had a positive influence on the extent and quality of knowledge contribution (Lin, Fan & Chau, 2014). The reciprocity between members also influences other members. Therefore, this study hypothesizes that users' personal motivation affects their knowledge and community cognition:

H3a: Personal participation motivation is correlated to the intrinsic cognition of knowledge management (knowledge and management).

H3b: Personal participation motivation is correlated to the intrinsic cognition of community reputation (professionalism and trust).

Users with positive attitudes and strong curiosity generally prefer to actively partake in knowledge contribution. Cabrera and Cabrera (2005) found that people with an open attitude or strong curiosity were more likely to exchange their views with others and generate interest (Cabrera & Cabrera, 2005). Similarly, people that are confident in imparting knowledge are more willing to voluntarily contribute knowledge to society. Social exchange theory categorizes individual perceptions into perceived welfare and perceived cost: perceived welfare refers to intrinsic motivations, such as reward, respect, reputation, and incentive, while perceived cost refers to emotional investment (Wang & Noe, 2010). Social exchange prompts a sense of belonging, personal obligation, gratitude, trust, and loyalty.

Previous studies also found a correlation between knowledge management and the willingness to share. Jabr et al. (2014) found that the sense of presence affected knowledge contribution behavior and participation (Jabr et al., 2014). Therefore, users opt to frequently participate in their communities and contribute knowledge to maintain a strong sense of presence within the community (Chen, 2007). The theory of reasoned action indicated that people are more willing to contribute when they feel needed (Bock et al., 2005). Coincidently, it is the exact opposite for monetary remuneration, suggesting that the benefits acquired from social exchange cannot entirely be measured through physical exchange. From the perspective of personal psychology, users largely anticipate receiving an expected return (Clary et al., 1998), engage in learning or practicing a skill (Bonaccorsi & Rossi, 2003), achieving knowledge sharing (Lakhani & Von Hippel, 2003), or co-managing a project for their participation (Nov & Ye, 2008). Generating interesting behavioral responses helps members in a community to get to know one another (Hakansson & Ford, 2002). Complex knowledge transactions generate member interactions and help members acquire or exchange knowledge. Therefore, this study hypothesizes that users' personal participation motivation affects their overt behavior:

H4a: Personal participation motivation is correlated to overt behavior (attention and interest).
H4b: Personal participation motivation is correlated to overt behavior (action and share).

3.3. Effects of Intrinsic Cognition on Overt Behavior

The use of emotional elements, such as care, understanding, and empathy, can often be seen on enterprise-operated social media (Liang, Ho, Li, & Turban, 2011) to trigger users' support and reinforce corporate image (Schau, Muñiz Jr., & Arnould, 2009)). Many studies have analyzed and validated the effects of emotional responses on users' cognition and behavior. These effects include stimulating user interaction or expanding the influence of social networks (Liang & Turban, 2011; Ren et al., 2012). Positive cognition, such as corporate satisfaction, trust, and brand awareness(Wang, Hernandez, & Minor, 2010; Wells, Parboteeah, & Valacich, 2011), can be used to help users accurately evaluate an organization and enhance marketing performance (Wang, Hernandez, & Minor, 2010; Wells, Parboteeah, & Valacich, 2011).

Referencing the behavioral responses of the AISAS model, this study categorized the four behavior dimensions into two stages. Attention and interest were categorized into the early stage, and action and share were categorized into the late stage. The attention and interest dimensions focus on attracting like-minded users. In addition, users with similar preferences also attract one another (Hall, 1924). The action and share dimensions focus on user exchange (Sumita & Isogai, 2009). The action and share dimensions affect users' pre-participation interest. Users are typically hesitant and exchange opinions with others before making decisions (Kankanhalli et al., 2005). Therefore, this study hypothesizes that users' intrinsic cognition affects the dimensions of attention, interest, action, and share:

H5a: Intrinsic cognition of knowledge management (knowledge and management) is correlated to users' overt behavior (attention and interest).
H5b: Intrinsic cognition of knowledge management (knowledge and management) is correlated to users' overt behavior (action and share).

H5c: Intrinsic cognition of community reputation (professionalism and trust) is correlated to users' overt behavior (attention and interest).

H5d: Intrinsic cognition of community reputation (professionalism and trust) is correlated to overt behavior (action and share).

4. RESEARCH METHODOLOGY

To ensure content validity, this study consolidated research theories based on the three variables (Nambisan & Baron, 2009): participation motivation (community and personal)(Koh & Kim, 2003; Wasko & Faraj, 2005; Cho et al., 2010; Nov, Naaman & Ye, 2010), intrinsic cognition (knowledge management and community reputation)(Spinellis & Louridas, 2008; Biswas et al., 2009; Cho et al., 2010; Miller & Laczniak, 2011), and overt behavior (attention, interest, action, and share)(Mehrabian & Russell, 1974a; Davis et al., 1992; Hall, 1924; Wasko & Faraj, 2005). The survey period was between 10th and 15th April 2017. Written and online questionnaires served as the media for collecting data on the university students who were invited to partake in the content creation of the Tamshui Wiki. A total of 372 questionnaires were administered, and 364 valid questionnaires were collected. Among the valid recipients, 27% were men, and 73% were women; 125 were first-year university students, 153 were second-year university students, and 86 were third-year university students. The questionnaires were used to determine whether the recipients' participation motivation affected their knowledge collaboration cognition and behavior before they participated in knowledge management and creation (Table 1).

5. DATA ANALYSES AND RESULTS

5.1. Reliability and Validity

We performed a factor analysis and a reliability analysis to evaluate the reliability and validity of the data. The Cronbach's α values for intrinsic cognition of knowledge management (knowledge), intrinsic cognition of knowledge management (management), intrinsic cognition of community reputation (professionalism), intrinsic cognition of community reputation (trust), overt behavior (attention and interest), and overt behavior (action and share) were 0.745, 0.793, 0.852, 0.767, 0.919, and 0.914, respectively (Table 2).

Indicating that the data is appropriate factor analysis (Kaiser, 1974). The factor load is close to or higher than 0.7, indicating good convergence and discriminant validity (Chin, 1998). Two statistical analyses, namely simple correlation analysis and linear regression analysis, are performed in this study. First, simple correlation analysis can show the degree of correlation between variables. The value is mainly related to the Pearson correlation coefficient. This part of the study analyzed and compared the relationships between the variables. Second, the use of regression analysis was employed for further evaluation. It was found that the load of the main variable was significant at the $P < 0.001$ level, and that no commonly used factor load was significant. In addition, this study conducted multiple tests to examine the correlation between independent variables. A Variance Inflation Factor (VIF) exceeding 10 indicates multiple collinearity problems. In this study, the value of VIF is exclusively lower than 10, indicating that there was no multicollinearity.

*Figure 2. The results of the research model: *p < 0.05, **p < 0.01, ***p < 0.001.*

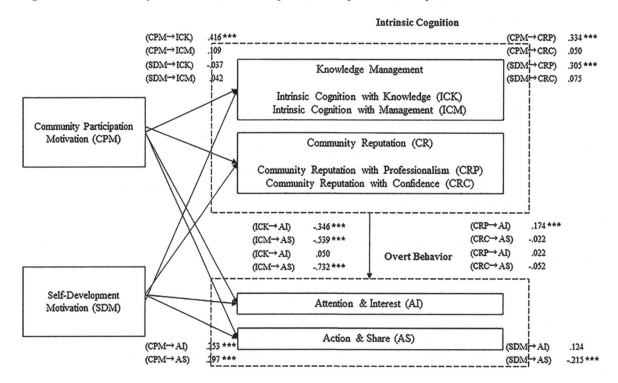

5.2. Hypothesis Testing

This study formulated five hypotheses based on the participation motivation, intrinsic cognition, and overt behavior concerning humanities knowledge collaboration systems (Figure 2). For H1a, the β-values for intrinsic cognition (knowledge) and intrinsic cognition (management) were 0.416 (p <0.001) and 0.109, respectively. For H1b, the β-values for intrinsic cognition (knowledge) and intrinsic cognition (management) were 0.334 (p < 0.001) and 0.05. These results validate that community motivation affected the intrinsic cognition of knowledge and the intrinsic cognition of management. For H2a, the β-value for overt behavior (attention and interest) was 0.254 (p < 0.001). For H2b, the β-value for overt behavior (action and share) was 0.297 (p < 0.001). These results validate that community motivation affected the overt behavior dimensions of attention, interest, action, and share.

For H3a, the β-values for intrinsic cognition (knowledge) and intrinsic cognition (management) were −0.037 and 0.042. For H3b, the β-values for intrinsic cognition (professionalism) and intrinsic cognition (trust) were 0.306 (p < 0.001) and 0.075. These results validate that personal motivation significantly affected knowledge cognition, but failed to affect the other cognition dimensions. For H4a, the β-value for overt behavior (attention and interest) was 0.124. For H4b, the β-value for overt behavior (action and share) was −0.215 (p < 0.001). These results validate that when users became more familiar with the Tamshui Wikipedia, the effects of personal motivation on users' actions and sharing became stronger.

For H5a, the β-values for the effects of intrinsic cognition (knowledge) on overt behavior (attention and interest) and overt behavior (action and share) were −0.346 (p < 0.001) and −0.539 (p < 0.001), respectively. The β-values for the effects of intrinsic cognition (management) on overt behavior (attention and interest) and overt behavior (action and share) were 0.05 and −0.732 (p < 0.001), respectively. These results validate that intrinsic cognition (knowledge and management) affected users' overt behavior dimensions of attention, interest, action, and share. For H5b, the β-values for the effects of intrinsic cognition (professionalism) on overt behavior (attention and interest) and overt behavior (action and share) were 0.174 (p < 0.001) and −0.022, respectively. The β-values for the effects of intrinsic cognition (trust) on overt behavior (attention and interest) and overt behavior (action and share) were 0.022 and −0.052, respectively. These results validated that the intrinsic cognition (professionalism) of community reputation generated users' attention and interest. However, frequent users of the Tamshui Wikipedia should be more familiar with the sharing of knowledge.

5.3. Discussion of Findings

Interesting findings were revealed in this study. Results showed that the effects of pre-participation community motivation were stronger than personal motivation in Tamshui Wiki users. Users with increased knowledge management cognition typically had increased considerations, which influenced their willingness to share knowledge (Table 3).

For H1, results showed a moderate correlation between community motivation and knowledge management cognition. Specifically, community motivation positively affected knowledge management cognition (H1b) and community reputation cognition (H1b). This hypothesis confirmed that community motivation of knowledge collaboration systems influences member cognition. Members that are more familiar with the community tend to have a higher value for the professionalism of the content in the system (Miller & Laczniak, 2011). Therefore, educational institutions that aspire to foster community recognition through knowledge management can aim to enhance the professional image of the community (Chevalier & Mayzlin, 2006) and users' appreciation of the knowledge collaboration system.

For H2, results showed a moderate correlation between community motivation and users' behavioral responses. Specifically, community motivation positively affected overt behavior (attention and interest; H2a) and overt behavior (action and share; H2b). These findings demonstrate that the Tamshui Wiki promotes community concepts successfully. Even students that have not yet participated in knowledge management held a positive regard towards the platform, exhibiting interest and attention. The essential aspects of establishing a successful collaboration platform are to validate whether the correct community concepts are delivered and whether effective member relationships have been established before promoting knowledge management (Clemons, Gao & Hitt, 2006).

For H3, results showed a low correlation between personal motivation and community reputation cognition. Specifically, personal motivation positively affected intrinsic cognition (professionalism), suggesting that frequent users of the Tamshui Wikipedia generated a higher affirmation towards the collaboration system and acknowledgment of the professionalism and support provided by the platform (Mudambi & Schuff, 2010).

For H4, results showed a moderate correlation between personal motivation and users' behavioral responses. Specifically, personal motivation negatively affected overt behavior (action and share), suggesting that the personal motivation of frequent users of the Tamshui Wikipedia negatively impacted their perception of other users. In other words, although frequent users of the Tamshui Wikipedia may acknowledge content quality, they also acknowledge the inadequacies in content management and promotion of the Tamshui Wikipedia (Agarwal & Karahanna, 2000), causing them to form a reserved attitude toward content promotion on collaboration systems.

For H5, results showed that intrinsic cognition (knowledge) negatively influenced overt behavior (attention and interest) and overt behavior (action and share; H5a); intrinsic cognition (management) negatively influenced overt behavior (action and share; H5b); and intrinsic cognition (professionalism) negatively influenced overt behavior (attention and interest). These results suggest that, in the Tamshui Wiki, users with increased knowledge management cognition are more aware of the internal management and application functions of the platform (La Ferle & Choi, 2005). That is, although they accept the knowledge and the community (Davis, Bagozzi & Warshaw, 1992), they maintained a reserved attitude towards publicity and sharing. They were fully aware that collaboration systems are not effective tools for propaganda and exposure (Wang & Zhang, 2012). In this context, managers should flexibly utilize different social platform functions to complement the inadequacies in management and interaction of the Tamshui Wikipedia .

6. CONCLUSION

6.1. Research Implications and Findings

Users typically have different motives for participating in different knowledge collaboration systems (Wasko & Faraj, 2005), leading to differences in intrinsic cognition and overt behavior. Previous studies on user experiences have identified three common characteristics of user experiences. First, user experiences transcend simple tool orientations and working space (Salamzadeh & Markovic, 2018); second, user emotions must be taken into account (Law, Roto, Hassenzahl, Vermeeren, & Kort, 2009); and third, user experiences and user subjective norms are factors that should be considered together, the subjective norms significantly influenced ecological intentions and behaviour (Nejati et al., 2011). These observations prompted research into a magnitude of variables, including emotions, experiences, enjoyment, and aesthetics (Hassenzahl & Tractinsky, 2006; Hassenzahl & Roto, 2007).

These observations are consistent with the argument proposed in this study that brand identity and emotional behaviors are stimuli. Information not only connects users (Muniz Jr. & O'Guinn, 2001), but also consolidates user needs (Nambisan & Baron, 2009). Previous studies repeatedly emphasized the effects of emotions and behaviors in user experiences(Pullman & Gross, 2004), such as how to proactively stimulate users' perceptions and emotions and enhance their revisitation and repurchase intentions (Koufaris, 2002), or how to enhance user loyalty and maintain positive relations (Pullman & Gross, 2004). The theoretical contributions of this study expanded on the aforementioned studies, emphasizing that brand identity and user habits have a complementation effect on user experiences (Pine & Gilmore, 1999).

Furthermore, these findings showed that community motivation effectively promoted member participation and reinforced their pre-participation knowledge management and acceptance of community reputation. Personal motivation is more applicable to the exploitation of users' reliance on Wikipedia to increase management and cross-platform promotion (Sumita & Isogai, 2009). Members with a sound understanding of knowledge management are more likely to identify with community reputation when they acknowledge the professionalism of the collaboration system (Koh & Kim, 2003). Hence, for communities aspiring to establish knowledge management systems, managers should focus on reinforcing knowledge management and community reputation cognition (Meng & Agarwal, 2007).

These two dimensions significantly and positively affect the management and trust of knowledge management systems. Management training should be provided to members who are unfamiliar with the Tamshui Wikipedia, such as university students (Fallis, 2008; Lim, 2009; Okoli et al., 2014). When members trust the professionalism of the community, and to maintain and strengthen the modified community pattern (Khajeheian et al., 2012), platform usability and usefulness become the motivating factors for sharing knowledge (Wasko & Faraj, 2005). Therefore, managers should endeavor to enhance the application value of knowledge collaboration systems according to different knowledge requirements during the system development stage.

This study primarily evaluated the users of the Tamshui Wiki. It made the following research contributions to the field of knowledge management: First, it categorized users' knowledge management dimensions into community motivation. The pre-participation motivation requirements of knowledge management uncovered in this study served as variables for analyzing knowledge management. Second, it referenced the SOR and AISAS theories to extensively investigate the correlation between intrinsic cognition and overt behavior. Empirical results showed that community reputation had an immense influence on knowledge management cognition. Third, it examined users' definitions and perceptions of pre-participation knowledge management. Amidst the trend of social media diversification, it is imperative that knowledge management be reinforced by integrating knowledge sharing and knowledge promotion. Managers should consider how to maximize platform categories, particularly for university students who frequently use Wikipedia, facilitating the promotion and dissemination of humanities knowledge (Agarwal & Karahanna, 2000).

Finally, it evaluated the feasibility of integrating educational institutions and knowledge management. The purpose of the Tamshui Wiki is not only to accumulate and impart local humanities knowledge, but also to enhance the contribution and development of humanities knowledge of educational institutions by encouraging collaboration between university students and local scholars. The findings of this study demonstrate that community reputation is a significant factor affecting knowledge management (Davis, Bagozzi & Warshaw, 1992) and highlighted the necessity of strengthening community cognition (Kaysers & Eul, 2018). The findings of this study can serve as a reference for educational institutions in their efforts to promote knowledge management.

6.2. Limitations and Recommendations

Based on the limitations of this study, three suggestions are made for future research. First, the effects of the content of a collaboration system on cognition and behavior were not analyzed. Future researchers can consider evaluating the different messages that exist in knowledge management systems (Cho et al., 2010), such as the effects of text, image, and video content on user emotions and behavior or how to adjust content based on user demand to enhance their willingness to actively share and promote content.

Second, different knowledge collaboration platforms can be developed using the proposed theoretical model or by analyzing the effectiveness of knowledge management in different educational institutions (Nov, Naaman & Ye, 2010). These efforts can enhance members' understanding of knowledge contribution and knowledge sharing (Spinellis & Louridas, 2008) and the visibility of humanities collaborative content creation in educational institutions (Biswas, Hussain & O'Donnell, 2009).

Finally, this study only analyzed the Tamshui Wiki to target single-system performance. Therefore, the findings of this study may not be reproducible to all user demands. Therefore, it is suggested that future studies adjust the variables of user motivation, cognition, and behavior to determine collaborative relationships across all collaboration systems.

ACKNOWLEDGMENT

This study was funded by the Ministry of Science and Technology – Digital Humanities Program (No. 0510234) (No. 0610234).

REFERENCES

Agarwal, R., & Karahanna, E. (2000). Time flies when you're having fun: Cognitive absorption and beliefs about information technology usage. *MIS Quarterly: Management Information Systems, 24*(4), 665–694. doi:10.2307/3250951

Anderson, J. C., & Gerbing, D. W. (1988). Structural equation modeling in practice: A review and recommended two-step approach. *Psychological Bulletin, 103*(3), 411–423. doi:10.1037/0033-2909.103.3.411

Arazy, O., Nov, O., Patterson, R., & Yeo, L. (2011). Information quality in wikipedia: The effects of group composition and task conflict. *Journal of Management Information Systems, 27*(4), 71–98. doi:10.2753/MIS0742-1222270403

Arazy, O., Yeo, L., & Nov, O. (2013). Stay on the wikipedia task: When task-related disagreements slip into personal and procedural conflicts. *Journal of the American Society for Information Science and Technology, 64*(8), 1634–1648. doi:10.1002/asi.22869

Baker, J., Grewal, D., & Parasuraman, A. (1994). The influence of store environment on quality inferences and store image. *Journal of the Academy of Marketing Science: Official Publication of the Academy of Marketing Science, 22*(4), 328–339. doi:10.1177/0092070394224002

Barwise, P., & Meehan, S. (2010). The one thing you must get right when building a brand. *Harvard Business Review, 88*(12).

Bock, G., Zmud, R. W., Kim, Y., & Lee, J. (2005). Behavioral intention formation in knowledge sharing: Examining the roles of extrinsic motivators, social-psychological forces, and organizational climate. *MIS Quarterly: Management Information Systems, 29*(1), 87-111.

Carillo, K., & Okoli, C. (2011). Generating quality open content: A functional group perspective based on the time, interaction, and performance theory. *Information & Management, 48*(6), 208–219. doi:10.1016/j.im.2011.04.004

Chin, W. W. (1998). The partial least squares approach to structural equation modeling. *Modern Methods for Business Research,*, 295-336.

Cho, H., Chen, M., & Chung, S. (2010). Testing an integrative theoretical model of knowledge-sharing behavior in the context of wikipedia. *Journal of the American Society for Information Science and Technology, 61*(6), 1198–1212.

Clark, M., & Melancon, J. (2013). The influence of social media investment on relational outcomes: A relationship marketing perspective. *International Journal of Marketing Studies, 5*(4), 132–142. doi:10.5539/ijms.v5n4p132

Davis, F. D., Bagozzi, R. P., & Warshaw, P. R. (1992). Extrinsic and intrinsic motivation to use computers in the workplace. *Journal of Applied Social Psychology*, 22(14), 1111–1132. doi:10.1111/j.1559-1816.1992. tb00945.x

Eroglu, S. A., Machleit, K. A., & Davis, L. M. (2003). Empirical testing of a model of online store atmospherics and shopper responses. *Psychology and Marketing*, 20(2), 139–150. doi:10.1002/mar.10064

Fallis, D. (2008). Toward an epistemology of wikipedia. *Journal of the American Society for Information Science and Technology*, 59(10), 1662–1674. doi:10.1002/asi.20870

Forte, A., Larco, V., & Bruckman, A. (2009). Decentralization in wikipedia governance. *Journal of Management Information Systems*, 26(1), 49–72. doi:10.2753/MIS0742-1222260103

Goh, K., Heng, C., & Lin, Z. (2013). Social media brand community and consumer behavior: Quantifying the relative impact of user- and marketer-generated content. *Information Systems Research*, 24(1), 88-107.

Hassenzahl, M., & Roto, V. (2007). Being and doing: A perspective on user experience and its measurement. *Interfaces*, 72, 10–12.

Hassenzahl, M., & Tractinsky, N. (2006). User experience - A research agenda. *Behaviour & Information Technology*, 25(2), 91–97. doi:10.1080/01449290500330331

Jiang, Z., Chan, J., Tan, B. C. Y., & Chua, W. S. (2010). Effects of interactivity on website involvement and purchase intention. *Journal of the Association for Information Systems*, 11(1), 34–59. doi:10.17705/1jais.00218

Kaiser, H. F. (1974). An index of factorial simplicity. *Psychometrika*, 39(1), 31–36. doi:10.1007/BF02291575

Kaysers, F., & Eul, E. (2018). *Start-ups' perception of collective learning in accelerators*. Academic Press.

Khajeheian, D., Esmaeilkhoo, H., & Yousefikhah, S. (2012). Information technology and media convergence: An entrepreneurial approach towards media matrix management. *African Journal of Business Management*, 6(29), 8483–8489.

Koh, J., Kim, Y., & Kim, Y.-G. (2003). Sense of virtual community: A conceptual framework and empirical validation. *International Journal of Electronic Commerce*, 8(2), 75–93. doi:10.1080/10864415 .2003.11044295

Kohler, T., Fueller, J., Matzler, K., Stieger, D., & Füller. (2011). CO-creation in virtual worlds: The design of the user experience. *MIS Quarterly: Management Information Systems*, 35(3), 773–788. doi:10.2307/23042808

Koufaris, M. (2002). Applying the technology acceptance model and flow theory to online consumer behavior. *Information Systems Research*, 13(2), 205–223. doi:10.1287/isre.13.2.205.83

Larson, K., & Watson, R. T. (2011). The value of social media: Toward measuring social media strategies. *Thirty Second International Conference on Information Systems*, 1-18.

Law, E. L. (2009). Understanding, Scoping and Defining User Experience. Academic Press.

Liang, T., Ho, Y.-T., Li, Y.-W., & Turban, E. (2011). What drives social commerce: The role of social support and relationship quality. *International Journal of Electronic Commerce, 16*(2), 69–90. doi:10.2753/JEC1086-4415160204

Liang, T., & Turban, E. (2011). Introduction to the special issue social commerce: A research framework for social commerce. *International Journal of Electronic Commerce, 16*(2), 5–13. doi:10.2753/JEC1086-4415160201

Lim, S. (2009). How and why do college students use wikipedia? *Journal of the American Society for Information Science and Technology, 60*(11), 2189–2202. doi:10.1002/asi.21142

Liu, B. Q., & Goodhue, D. L. (2012). Two worlds of trust for potential e-commerce users: Humans as cognitive misers. *Information Systems Research, 23*(4), 1246–1262. doi:10.1287/isre.1120.0424

Mehrabian, A., & Russell, J. A. (1974). *An Approach to Environmental Psychology.* Academic Press.

Meng, M., & Agarwal, R. (2007). Through a glass darkly: Information technology design, identity verification, and knowledge contribution in online communities. *Information Systems Research, 18*(1), 42–67. doi:10.1287/isre.1070.0113

Muniz, A. M. Jr, & O'Guinn, T. C. (2001). Brand community. *The Journal of Consumer Research, 27*(4), 412–432. doi:10.1086/319618

Nambisan, S., & Baron, R. A. (2007). Interactions in virtual customer environments: Implications for product support and customer relationship management. *Journal of Interactive Marketing, 21*(2), 42–62. doi:10.1002/dir.20077

Nambisan, S., & Baron, R. A. (2009). Virtual customer environments: Testing a model of voluntary participation in value co-creation activities. *Journal of Product Innovation Management, 26*(4), 388–406. doi:10.1111/j.1540-5885.2009.00667.x

Nejati, M., Salamzadeh, Y., & Salamzadeh, A. (2011). Ecological purchase behaviour: Insights from a middle eastern country. *International Journal of Environment and Sustainable Development, 10*(4), 417–432. doi:10.1504/IJESD.2011.047774

Nov, O. (2007). What motivates wikipedians? *Communications of the ACM, 50*(11), 60–64. doi:10.1145/1297797.1297798

Nov, O., Naaman, M., & Ye, C. (2010). Analysis of participation in an online photo-sharing community: A multidimensional perspective. *Journal of the American Society for Information Science and Technology, 61*(3), 555–566.

Okoli, C., Mehdi, M., Mesgari, M., Nielsen, F. Å., & Lanamäki, A. (2014). Wikipedia in the eyes of its beholders: A systematic review of scholarly research on wikipedia readers and readership. *Journal of the Association for Information Science and Technology, 65*(12), 2381–2403. doi:10.1002/asi.23162

Parboteeah, D. V., Valacich, J. S., & Wells, J. D. (2009). The influence of website characteristics on a consumer's urge to buy impulsively. *Information Systems Research, 20*(1), 60–78. doi:10.1287/isre.1070.0157

Peddibhotla, N. B., & Subramani, M. R. (2007). Contributing to public document repositories: A critical mass theory perspective. *Organization Studies*, *28*(3), 327–346. doi:10.1177/0170840607076002

Pine, B. J., & Gilmore, J. H. (1999). *The Experience Economy: Work is Theatre and Every Business a Stage*. Academic Press.

Prasarnphanich, P., & Wagner, C. (2009). The role of wiki technology and altruism in collaborative knowledge creation. *Journal of Computer Information Systems*, *49*(4), 33–41.

Pullman, M. E., & Gross, M. A. (2004). Ability of experience design elements to elicit emotions and loyalty behaviors. *Decision Sciences*, *35*(3), 551–576. doi:10.1111/j.0011-7315.2004.02611.x

Ren, Y., Harper, F. M., Drenner, S., Terveen, L., Kiesler, S., Riedl, J., & Kraut, R. E. (2012). Building member attachment in online communities: Applying theories of group identity and interpersonal bonds1. *MIS Quarterly: Management Information Systems*, *36*(3), 841–864. doi:10.2307/41703483

Salamzadeh, A., & Markovic, M. R. (2018). Shortening the learning curve of media start-ups in accelerators: Case of a developing country. In Evaluating media richness in organizational learning (pp. 36-48). IGI Global.

Schau, H. J., Muñiz, A. M. Jr, & Arnould, E. J. (2009). How brand community practices create value. *Journal of Marketing*, *73*(5), 30–51. doi:10.1509/jmkg.73.5.30

Schroeder, A., & Wagner, C. (2012). Governance of open content creation: A conceptualization and analysis of control and guiding mechanisms in the open content domain. *Journal of the American Society for Information Science and Technology*, *63*(10), 1947–1959. doi:10.1002/asi.22657

Spinellis, D., & Louridas, P. (2008). The collaborative organization of knowledge. *Communications of the ACM*, *51*(8), 68–73. doi:10.1145/1378704.1378720

Stvilia, B., Twidale, M. B., Smith, L. C., & Gasser, L. (2008). Information quality work organization in wikipedia. *Journal of the American Society for Information Science and Technology*, *59*(6), 983–1001. doi:10.1002/asi.20813

Wang, C., & Zhang, P. (2012). The evolution of social commerce: The people, management, technology, and information dimensions. *Communications of the Association for Information Systems*, *31*(1), 105–127.

Wang, G. A., Jiao, J., Abrahams, A. S., Fan, W., & Zhang, Z. (2013). ExpertRank: A topic-aware expert finding algorithm for online knowledge communities. *Decision Support Systems*, *54*(3), 1442–1451. doi:10.1016/j.dss.2012.12.020

Wang, Y. J., Hernandez, M. D., & Minor, M. S. (2010). Web aesthetics effects on perceived online service quality and satisfaction in an e-tail environment: The moderating role of purchase task. *Journal of Business Research*, *63*(9-10), 935–942. doi:10.1016/j.jbusres.2009.01.016

Wasko, M. M., & Faraj, S. (2005). Why should I share? examining social capital and knowledge contribution in electronic networks of practice. *MIS Quarterly: Management Information Systems*, *29*(1), 35–57. doi:10.2307/25148667

Wells, J. D., Parboteeah, D. V., & Valacich, J. S. (2011). Online impulse buying: Understanding the interplay between consumer impulsiveness and website quality. *Journal of the Association for Information Systems*, *12*(1), 32–56. doi:10.17705/1jais.00254

Yang, H., & Lai, C.-Y. (2011). Understanding knowledge-sharing behaviour in wikipedia. *Behaviour & Information Technology*, *30*(1), 131–142. doi:10.1080/0144929X.2010.516019

This research was previously published in the Journal of Media Management and Entrepreneurship (JMME), 1(1); pages 57-72, copyright year 2019 by IGI Publishing (an imprint of IGI Global).

Chapter 23
Delete, Delete, Hang-Up:
On Social Media

Bruce L. Mann
Memorial University, Canada

ABSTRACT

Whereas most members of social media are enthusiastically exercising their legal right to express themselves freely, some seem unwilling or incapable of assessing the high risk of disclosing information about their most private thoughts, interests, opinions, work, and health status, particularly in times of psychological distress or personal tragedy. This chapter updates criminal activity associated with frequent use of social media. Some believe that the conceptual elasticity of the term "cyberbullying" has been used to push for a tougher crime agenda, while obscuring tragedy of the suicides in Canadian federal parliamentary debates.

A COALITION OF THE WILLING

Social networks like *Instagram* (Facebook Inc, 2020), *Facebook* (Facebook Inc, 2020), *Twitter* (Twitter, 2020), *Tumblr* (Automattic, 2020), *SnapChat* (SnapChat Inc, 2020), and others (Mann, 2009), are in fact, *global villages* (McLuhan, 1962) or at least, *town squares* (Zuckerberg, 2019), where the young and not so young eagerly share their opinions and personal data. These young and not so young comprise a coalition of the willing.

The *Canadian Charter of Rights and Freedoms* is complicit in providing platforms for the willing. Section 2 is a collection of fundamental freedoms - of expression, of religion, of thought, of belief, of peaceful assembly and of association. "Everyone has the freedom of thought, belief, opinion and expression, including freedom of the press and other media of communication" (Charter, 1982, at S2). Similar language appears in a much older document, "Everyone has the right to freedom of opinion and expression; to hold opinions without interference, and to seek, receive and impart information and ideas through any media and regardless of frontiers" (UDHR, 1948, at 19).

DOI: 10.4018/978-1-6684-6307-9.ch023

So what's the problem? The problem is that many seem unwilling or incapable of assessing the high risk of disclosing information about their most private thoughts, interests, opinions, work and health status on social media, particularly in times of psychological distress or personal tragedy. It's a form of *non compos mentis* and is no argument for breach of confidence, which begs the question, why do they do it? The answer, according to Danah Boyd (2006) is to provide their personal data with 'context, context context':

- To be nice to people that they hardly know (like the folks in their classes)
- To keep face with people that they know but don't care for
- As a way of acknowledging someone they think is interesting
- To look cool because that link has status
- To keep up with someone's posts, bulletins or other such bits
- To circumnavigate the privacy problem that they were forced to use by their parents
- As a substitute for bookmarking or 'favouriting'
- It's easier to say yes than no when they're not sure

When you know the effects of a medium, you can take steps to shape those effects, or restrict them (McLuhan, 1978), because ignoring or forgetting to read critical information in communication media may eventually cause harm, an act of omission that denotes *actus reus* or acting badly without thinking (Mann, 2009). Frequent users of social media invariably ignore or forget to read important feedback and instruction presented in text and other visual displays regardless of their intended function, even when they are explicitly told to do so (Mann, 2015, p.496; Mann, 2009, p.5). The consequence is tacit agreement to release personal data and preferences to third parties that effectively absolves those parties and the Internet Service Provider of any liability stated in the license (Mann, 2009). It's not just social media however, but *any* media with instructional or informational text (Alessi & Trollip, 2001; Edwards, 2005; Huff & Finholt, 1994; Pettersson, 1990; Ragsdale, 1988; Reinking, 1987; Wah, 2008).

Two years after Jonathan Abrams submitted an application to the U.S. Patent and Trademark Office for *Friendster*, "a system, method, and apparatus for connecting users in an online computer system based on their relationships within social networks" (OUT-LAW News, 2006), there was no shortage of social media in which to share personal information and opinions. It soon became clear however, that hands-off legislation, toothless policy statements, unknowing parents, uncaring participants, and unwilling social network intermediaries had helped to cause impersonation, denigration, sexual and aggressive solicitation, and cyberbullying to children and youth who were active users of social media (Mann, 2009). Years later, the situation is still serious - serious because the user-generated content displayed on-screen is still destroying users' lives; serious too, because of the volume of users at risk from posting their content, without intervention by the social network intermediary. The changing social interactions that this technology brought about, has out-paced our values and attitudes, an anthropological condition known as *cultural lag* (Mann, 1993).

"IS YOUR LIFE JUST WORTH ONE PHOTO?"

More than 250 people across the world have died in the pursuit of the perfect selfie since 2011 (Schetzer, 2019). The majority of these "killfies" were caused either by drowning, being hit by a car or train, or from falling from a great height. All around the world, selfie and photo deaths have increased (Baker, 2017). In 2011, Tom Ryaboi dangled his feet over the edge of a tall building in Toronto and took a picture straight down, figure 1. He posted it on Flickr, Reddit, and 500px. The picture became a viral hit.

Figure 1. Tom Ryaboi's selfie of his feet dangling over the edge of a tall building in Toronto.
Image: Tom Ryaboi, 2011.

After that event, a new generation of Instagrammers, YouTubers, and members of other social networks began to cultivate the craft of risking life and limb to post heart-pounding pictures and videos of dangerous stunts. Risk-taking social media photography deaths and injuries roughly tripled in number from the beginning of 2014 to the end of 2015, according to a media analysis conducted by medical researchers in Turkey (Dokur Petekkaya & Karadağ, 2018).

A subculture has emerged in the past eight years of people who seek out death-defying situations; they do it for the likes, followers, and adulation of fans on social media. Figure 2 shows an Instagram post of Meenakshi sitting on the edge of a rock over the Grand Canyon taken by her husband Vishnu. The caption, read, "A lot of us, including yours truly, is a fan of daredevilry attempts of standing at the edge of cliffs and skyscrapers. Is our life just worth one photo?" Months later, they would both be dead. They were killed from an 800-foot fall at Yosemite National Park, an accident that occurred while they were on the edge of a cliff and taking pictures for their Instagram account (Elgan, 2019).

"I HOPE I AM DEAD WHEN U GET HOME"

So said Courtney Brown, 17, in a text to her mother, moments before her parents found her hanging in the basement (Scott, 2015). Emily McNamara, 14, hanged herself in the garage of their family home after being bullied online and at school. Rehtaeh Parsons, 17, attempted suicide by hanging herself, which put her in a coma and ended eventually the decision to switch-off her life support. Her death was attributed to online distribution of photos of an alleged gang rape that occurred 17 months prior to her suicide.

Figure 2. A posting to an Instagram account showing a photo of Meenakshi Moorthy taken by her husband Vishnu. Months later, they would both be dead from a fall (Elgan, 2019).
Image: Vishnu Moorthy, 28 March 2018.

Amanda Todd, 15, posted a video on YouTube before she took her own life that described how she had been tormented by persistent bullying online (Leung & Bascaramurty, 2012). Jenna Bowers-Bryanton, 15, killed herself after being bullied and cyberbullied by her peers at school and on social media (CBC News, 2011). Todd Loik, 15, committed suicide because students hounded him. His phone files had pages of taunts and abuse. Jamie Hubley, 15, son of Ottawa City Councillor Allan Hubley, had been suffering from depression and died after months of suicidal musings on his blog and social-media. He left a suicide note on his blog site, "It's so hard, I'm sorry, I can't take it anymore" (Edwards, 2011). This is a sample of suicides of youths bullied by peers on social media (Weisblott, 2011). The connection between social media and suicide is most prevalent among youths, a group with both a high suicide rate and dominance on sites such as Facebook, Twitter, and Instagram (Coyle, 2014).

CYBERBULLYING

Although contemptible, there is still no consensus on a clear and working definition of "cyberbullying", in either the scholarly, or the criminal context (Arntfield, 2015). By all accounts, "cyberbullying" is an omnibus term comprising several possible criminal offenses, not all relevant in every case. The conceptual elasticity of cyberbullying has been used to push for a tougher crime agenda, while obscuring tragedy of the suicides in Canadian federal parliamentary debates (Bailey, 2014).

Bill C-13

Bill C-13 came into force in Canada on March 10, 2015 impacting domestic and international criminal search powers. *Bill C-13 the Protecting Canadians from Online Crime Act*, ostensibly aimed at prosecuting cyberbullying, more accurately increased new police powers – especially warrantless search of members' personal files held by the Internet Service Provider. Most of Bill C-13 was about lawful access, not defeating cyberbullying. However, increasing police powers was not necessary since Canada already had rules to deal with cyberbullying. Bill-13 and Bill S-4 were *ex post facto* laws, and as such, would do nothing for the many thousands of teenagers and their parents who were experiencing cruelty from their peers. One possible solution would have been to repeal Bill-13 or at least modify it. Another solution would have been to recommend educational initiatives for coping with social media.

Privacy Commissioner Daniel Therrien characterized Bill C-13 as going well beyond cyber-intimidation (OpenMedia, 2015). It grants immunity to telecom providers who disclose private information about their customers to law enforcement without a warrant. The Bill also makes it far easier for government to obtain deeply revealing metadata on targets, based merely on suspicion. Despite being promoted as an anti-cyberbullying bill, C-13 could in fact make things worse for teens online by undermining their right to privacy.

Under Bill C-13, a wide range of government officials and public officers could access Canadians' personal information without their knowledge or consent. The officers obtaining that information without a warrant could be anyone from a local Police Officer, a Tax Agent, a Justice of the Peace, a CSIS Agent, or even the Mayor (Ling, 2014). Whereas Bill C-13 provided these officials with substantial power over your information, it left the targets of such surveillance with little by way of legal recourse, not least because they are not even informed that their privacy has been breached.

This kind of overreach by government isn't unique. The UK's *Investigatory Powers Act 2016* (aka Snoopers' Charter), which gives vast spying powers to virtually all public bodies, has caused numerous controversies over the last decade — including a 2008 incident where it came to light that Dorset City Council was using state surveillance powers to snoop on the families of children that they suspected were attending the wrong schools (Investigatory Powers Act 2016). Provisions in the Act permits police and intelligence agencies to carry out targeted equipment interference, that is, hacking into computers or devices to access their data and bulk equipment interference for national security matters related to foreign investigations. Material derived from equipment interference can then be used in evidence. Catching online bullying, in all its forms, shouldn't require government overreach.

CYBERBULLYING AND THE CRIMINAL CODE

On their website entitled *Cyberbullying and the Non-Consensual Distribution of Intimate Images,* the Department of Justice (DOJ) compiled a list of twelve Criminal Code offences that the DOJ says "may apply to instances of cyberbullying" (Department of Justice Canada, 2017):

S 163.1 Child pornography

S 319 Inciting Hatred

S 264 Criminal Harassment

S 261.1 Uttering Threats

S 423(1) Intimidation

S 403 Identity Fraud

S 346 (S)extortion

S 372 False Messages, Indecent or Harassing Telephone Calls

S 241. Counselling Suicide

S 298-301. Defamatory Libel

S 430(1.1) Mischief In Relation To Data

S 342.1 Unauthorized Use Of a Computer

S **163.1 Child Pornography**

According the Department of Justice Canada, child pornography is a criminal offence that appears to fit cyberbullying behaviors. Child pornography, as defined by s. 163.1(1) of the Criminal Code, is inherently harmful to children and to society. The harm exists independently of dissemination or of any risk of dissemination and flows from the existence of the pornographic representations, which on their own violate the dignity and equality rights of children *(R. v. Sharpe, 2001)*. Section 163.1 (1) defines *child pornography* as: A photographic, film, video or other visual representation, whether or not it was made by electronic or mechanical means, that shows a person who is or is depicted as being under the age of eighteen years and is engaged in or is depicted as engaged in explicit sexual activity, or the dominant characteristic of which is the depiction, for a sexual purpose, of a sexual organ or the anal region of a person under the age of eighteen years. It is any written material, visual representation or audio recording that advocates or counsels sexual activity with a person under the age of eighteen years that would be an offence under this act. It is any written material whose dominant characteristic is the description, for a sexual purpose, of sexual activity with a person under the age of eighteen years that would be an offence under this act; or any audio recording that has as its dominant characteristic the description, presentation or representation, for a sexual purpose, of sexual activity with a person under the age of eighteen years that would be an offence under this act.

R. v. Sharpe (2001) was a constitutional rights case pitting the societal interest to regulate child pornography against the right to freedom of expression. John Sharpe was charged with two counts of possession of child pornography under s. 163.1(4) of the Criminal Code and two counts of possession of child pornography for the purposes of distribution or sale under section 163.1(3). First, the court considered the Charter under freedom of expression, and whether possession of expressive material (child pornography) was protected by right to freedom of expression in accordance with *Canadian Charter of Rights and Freedoms,* section 2(b). The crown conceded that Criminal Code prohibition of possession of child pornography had infringed freedom of expression.

Second, the court considered the Charter under the right to liberty, and whether the Criminal Code's prohibition of possession of child pornography infringed his right to liberty. Third, the court considered the scope of the definition of "child pornography" under section 163.1 of the *Criminal Code of Canada*, where "child pornography" includes visual representations that show a person who is depicted as under the age of 18 years and is engaged in explicit sexual activity, and visual representations. The dominant characteristic is the depiction, of a sexual organ for a sexual purpose, or the anal region of a person under the age of 18 years.

Counseling Underage Sex. Child pornography that includes written material or visual representations that advocate or counsel sexual activity with a person under the age of 18, is an offence under the *Criminal Code of Canada.* Prior to his trial, the accused brought a preliminary motion challenging the constitutionality of s. 163.1(4) of the Code, alleging a violation of his constitutional guarantee of freedom of expression. The Crown conceded that section 163.1(4) had infringed section 2(b) of the *Canadian Charter of Rights and Freedoms*, but argued that the infringement was justifiable under s. 1 of the Charter.

Both the trial judge and the majority of the *British Columbia Court of Appeal* ruled that the prohibition of the simple possession of child pornography as defined under s. 163.1 of the Code was not justifiable in a free and democratic society. John Robin Sharpe was given a four-month conditional sentence for his conviction of possessing child pornography. After sentencing, Lorna Dueck with the *National Coalition of Concerned Mothers,* said that this was a "hugely symbolic case" that was a missed opportunity to protect children. A child advocacy group says the sentence made Sharpe the champion for people who want to engage in sex with children (CBC News, 2002).

S 172.1 Internet Luring

Section 172.1 Internet luring is not on the DOJ's list but should be added. In *R. v. S.H., 2018,* Jonathan Regan, was acquitted of the offence of Internet luring. The Crown appealed the acquittal on the basis that the Trial Judge erred in his interpretation of the elements of the offence, by requiring the Crown to prove that the Respondent had the intention to commit the underlying offence of which the alleged luring was intended to facilitate. The acquittal was set aside and the matter remitted to Provincial Court for a new trial. Three elements of the offence under Section 172.1(1)(c) had been established from the previous case *R. v. Legare (2009)*:

An intentional communication by computer, with a person whom the accused knows or believes to be under 14 years of age, and for the specific purpose of facilitating the commission of the a specified offence as mentioned in Section 172.1(1)(c)

In *R. v. Dragos (2012),* Bogdan Dragos was convicted of Internet luring, sexual interference, indecent exposure, sexual assault, invitation to sexual touching and possession of child pornography. The accused met the 13-year-old complainant on an Internet chat room site and asked her how old she was. She told him that she was 14. He never again inquired about her age notwithstanding many comments she made which should have caused him to make additional inquiries about her age, including a statement that she was in grade 9. When the complainant's mother discovered the accused's telephone number on her telephone bill and learned that the complainant had met the accused in a chat room, the mother called the accused, told him that the complainant was "way underage" and warned him that she would call the police if the contact persisted. The accused and the complainant continued to communicate over the Internet, and the accused arranged a clandestine meeting with the complainant at a hotel, where they engaged in various sexual acts, short of sexual intercourse. The accused was 24 years old at the time of the offences and had no criminal record. He was sentenced to a total of 23 months' incarceration (18 months for Internet luring, four months consecutive for sexual interference, one month consecutive for possession of child pornography and one month concurrent for indecent exposure), followed by three years' probation.

S 319. Inciting Hatred

Incitement of hatred would seem to be an obvious characteristic of the cyberbully's method of engagement; communicating statements in any public place, and inciting hatred against any identifiable group, which is likely to lead to a breach of the peace.

One example is the case *R. v. Topham* in which Mr. Topham was charged under section 319(2) with promoting hatred to the students in his high school class through his website by re-publishing materials from the Internet. Topham's lawyer noted that the circumstances of this case were different from those in *R. v. Keegstra* who similarly had been charged under section 319(2) of the Criminal Code with promoting hatred through communications to the students in his high school class. In the Keestra case, the accused, an Alberta high school teacher, was charged under section 319(2) of the Criminal Code with willfully promoting hatred against an identifiable group by communicating anti-semitic statements to his students. That court dismissed the application on the ground that section 319(2) of the Code did not violate freedom of expression as guaranteed by section 2(b) of the Canadian Charter of Rights and Freedoms. Here too, although Mr. Topham alleged to have promoted hatred through his website by re-publishing materials which were widely available on the Internet, the defence application was dismissed. "Incitement of hatred" seems to be part of a perpetrator's method of engagement for the purposes of cyberbullying.

S 264 Criminal Harassment

Section 264 of the *Criminal Code of Canada* describes "criminal harassment" as a person causing another person to fear for their safety or for the safety of someone known to them. The conduct comprises repeatedly following the person from place to place; repeatedly communicating with, either directly or indirectly; besetting or watching where the other person resides, works, carries on business; or engages in threatening conduct directed at them or any member of their family.

In *R. v Gardner (2018)* for example, Shane Gardner plead guilty to one count of criminal harassment for sending a series of violent and chilling threats to Terry Murphy via Facebook. The threats caused Terry Murphy to fear for his safety. The Court held that general deterrence and denunciation are paramount considerations when social media is used to criminally harass another person.

S 261.1 Uttering Threats

Uttering a threat is a statement of intent to cause bodily harm or death to a person - to burn, destroy or damage real or personal property; or to kill, poison or injure an animal or bird that is the property of the person. In December 2018 for example, the entire Lord Selkirk School Division north of Winnipeg closed all 15 of its schools due to threats on social media (CBC News, 2018). The RCMP released the name of one of young perpetrators charged in connection with the threats to Selkirk-area schools. The School Division put the schools into a "hold-and-secure" status and sent email to families to alert them of their new security measures.

In January 2019, two boys aged 12 and 13, were arrested for allegedly threatening three Winnipeg schools on social media. The boys had no access to weapons, and likely didn't think they'd get caught (CBC News, 2019). Police urged parents to use the arrests as a learning opportunity to talk to their children about the effects of social media, after the anonymous online threats resulted in a $45,000 police investigation, and heightened security at the schools.

S 423(1) Intimidation

Intimidation describes a preliminary form of cyberbullying behaviour. Intimidation is characterized in the Criminal Code as stopping another person from doing something that he or she has a lawful right to do, or uses violence or threats of violence to them or their spouse or children, or injures his or her property. Intimidation further describes persistently following that person; and hiding or depriving him or her of their property. For example, a worker alleged that she had been bullied by her co-workers both in the workplace, and through social media. The worker further alleged that her employer's failure to respond to her complaints of bullying and harassment contributed to her mental disorder. The worker filed a claim with the *British Columbia Workers' Compensation Board* for compensation for a mental disorder under that Act (1996). In her application for compensation, the worker said that she had been bullied by three co-workers. The worker described silent bullying, being ridiculed in front of her co-workers, and being threatened on a social media platform. The worker wrote that she felt humiliated, intimidated, offended, and psychologically unsafe.

The worker reported that she had informed her Manager of the co-workers' behaviours around the time that they occurred, but did not file a formal written complaint with her employer until October 2016. The worker believed that the social media posts were about her as they were posted on the same day of interactions at work. The worker felt threatened by a "punch in the throat" comment. She was humiliated, intimidated and offended. The worker felt psychologically unsafe. The Chair denied the worker's appeal finding that the worker was not entitled to compensation for a mental disorder, and that the significant stressors of online bullying and harassment did not arise out of, and in the course of, the worker's employment. Perhaps on this case, section 423 was too narrowly defined.

S 403 Identity Fraud

Not everyone thinks identity fraud or scamming, and cyberbullying, fit the same category because cases of cyber-blackmail are less prominent than cyberbullying but can have the same devastating impact on victims (Kiss, 2013). The position taken here is that cyberbullying becomes the new *modus operandi* once the victims become aware of the scam. They may harass you, intimidate you, threaten you, blackmail, or extort you.

Romance scammers fraudulently impersonate another person with intent to gain advantage for themselves, consistent with section 403 of the Criminal Code. Romance scammers take advantage of people looking for romantic partners, often through dating websites, mobile apps, or social media, by pretending to be prospective companions with intent to cause disadvantage to the person being personated or person being victimized. They play on emotional triggers to get them to send money, gifts or personal details (Scamwatch, 2019). Conversations between scammers and victims often go on for months. The con artists will find different ways to ask for money. In some cases, they pretend they are flying to see the women, but got stuck in an airport with no passport and need to ask for some quick money. In one instance a woman in Brazil took out a $500 loan to help the man she thought she was dating (Cassidy CBC News, 2014).

For many years, scammers have been using the photos of Dr. Alec Couros and his family, to commit identity fraud, figure 3. Dr. Couros is a Professor of Educational Technology and Media at the University of Regina (Couros, 2015). Couros hears from new scam victims on a daily basis as they frequently find the "real" him through his own writings on the topic. Unfortunately, many victims find out too late, often after they have already sent significant amounts of money to these scammers and have developed a significant emotional attachment. Complex crime that relies on a victim's capacity for love, trust, and good will for the execution of fraud (Scamwatch, 2019).

Figure 3. Romance scam showing false identity of Dr. Alec Couros, a Canadian Professor at the University of Regina.
Used by permission of Dr. Couros.

S 346. (S)extortion

Extorting sexually explicit material online, or "sextortion", is a form of cyberbullying that uses threats, accusations, menaces or violence. *R v McFarlane* describes a case of sextortion heard in a Manitoba court *(R v McFarlane, 2018)*. The complainant was a friend of a sister of the accused, Blair McFarlane.

In 2010, McFarlane (then age 19) surreptitiously video recorded the complainant (then age 17) undressing and showering when she was in the bathroom of his family home in Winnipeg. In a different relationship five years later, McFarlane decided to attempt to extort sexually explicit material from the complainant by threatening to disseminate intimate images of her. To carry out his sextortion plan, McFarlane created multiple email accounts under pseudonyms, he extracted several nude or semi-nude still images from the recording and manipulated the images using software to hide their source. He sent emails from the fake accounts with the intimate images to the complainant and her sister. The emails were menacing. The emails said that cooperation with his demands was the only way to avoid Internet publication. The complainant's sister replied to an email, asking what he wanted. McFarlane said, to start, he wanted a picture of the complainant in a bra. The complainant did not acquiesce to the demand.

The gravity of the extortion offence was serious. The judge called the crimes "cold and calculating" and imposed 18 months' imprisonment allocated as 12 months on the extortion offence, six months concurrent on the distribution-of-an-intimate-image-without-consent offence, and six months consecutive on the voyeurism offence.

S 372. False Messages, Indecent or Harassing Telephone Calls

Cyberbullying can also include false messages, with the intent to injure or alarm someone by conveying information that they know is false. In *R. v. J.M.D* (2018). The complainant was a highly accomplished nurse who worked in a palliative care facility and taught nursing on a part time basis. Mr. J.M.D. was a single father of two teenage children. Mr. J.M.D. was charged with harassing the complainant by repeatedly text messaging her, and engaging in conduct that reasonably caused the complainant to fear for her safety. In spite of clear instruction not to contact the complainant, Mr. J.M.D. texted or e-mailed the complainant ten or more times over the course of a few days. He chided the complainant telling her that the school authorities considered her treatment of his children to be abuse. This statement was completely fabricated as on inquiries being made with the school authorities it was apparent that Mr. J.M.D. had not even spoken to the school authorities about the break up.

As expected, however, it did cause the complainant anxiety. Judge McKimm surmised that Mr. J.M.D's complaint had threatened the livelihood of a professional woman pregnant with her first child. Even without the earlier references to threatening her reputation or taking her child, Judge McKimm found Mr. J.M.D. guilty on both counts.

S 241. Counselling Suicide

Counseling, encouraging or assisting a person to die by suicide may be considered an extreme form of cyberbullying. Counselling suicide is an indictable offence and liable to imprisonment for a term of up to 14 years.

The Momo Challenge. Police in U.K. have issued a warning about the "Momo Challenge", that is urging kids to commit self-harm. Figure 4 shows the bug-eyed girl with women's breasts and chicken legs known as "Momo" that has been popping up on social media since 2018, urging kids to kill themselves, or else, "Momo's going to kill you".

The suicide 'challenge' called "Momo" has raised concern in multiple countries and is serving as a warning to parents about the dangers of your child's media consumption. There are numerous variations. For example, while watching the British preschool animated television series *Peppa Pig,* or playing the popular video game *Fortnite,* children have encountered the Momo image with an ominous voice telling the child to take a knife to their own throat. Another version threatens their family if the challenge is not completed.

R. c. Morin, 2014. In this case, the Crown accused Jonathan Morin of counselling X to commit suicide and thereby committing an indictable offence (R. c. Morin, 2014). On September 27, 2012, the victim and Y were chatting on Facebook and trading insults. Y sent some excerpts from their conversation to her boyfriend, Jonathan Morin. Angry about the comments the victim had made to his girlfriend, the accused sent her a number of insults and told her that she should kill herself. Y too, suggested that the victim should hang herself. Sadly, after this interchange, the victim attempted suicide. Before this conversation on September 27, she had felt fine and had not been thinking about suicide. The dialogue she had on Facebook with Y and Jonathan Morin is what triggered her suicide attempt.

Figure 4. Screenshot of Momo, Image from Police Service of Northern Ireland in Craigavon (Facebook, 2018).

S 298-301. Defamatory Libel

Defamatory libel, under certain conditions (i.e., published online, using one or more communication technologies,) can be considered cyberbullying. A defamatory libel is a text or other media that is published to a chat room or social media site that is likely to injure the reputation of any person by exposing him to hatred, contempt or ridicule, or that is designed to insult the person of or concerning whom it is published. Concerning the mode of expression, a defamatory libel may be expressed directly or by insinuation or irony, either in words legibly marked on any substance; or by any object signifying a defamatory libel other than by words.

For example, the appellant in *R. v. Simoes, 2014* heard at the Ontario Court of Appeal was a restaurant owner. The complainant repeatedly called the appellant's restaurants to complain, and posted negative reviews on an online restaurant review site. This triggered a flurry of online postings, e-mails and letters from the appellant, the complainant and her lawyer. E-mails inviting sexual activity were sent to the complainant's employer from fake e-mail accounts set up in the complainant's name. The same sexually explicit message was posted on an adult cyber-dating website. That posting also included the complainant's photo. At trial, counsel conceded that the e-mails to the complainant's employer and the posting on the cyber-dating website amounted to defamatory libel as defined in s. 298 of the Criminal Code.

CRIMINAL ACTS, BUT NOT CYBERBULLYING

Cyberbullying requires a computer or cell phone, as an instrument of a crime. Two other categories of computer-related offences have been defined by the U.S. Department of Justice (1989) however, that do not seem to constitute cyberbullying behavior or intent: the computer is the "object" of the crime (e.g., the theft of computer hardware or software); and the computer as the "subject" of the crime (viruses, worms, etc.), that incapacitate normal computer functioning)

S 430(1.1) Mischief In Relation To Data

Section 430 covers offenses in which a computer was the "subject" of the crime, where computer data was destroyed or altered, or where the transmission was obstructed, interrupted or interfered with the lawful use of computer data; or denies access to computer data to a person who is entitled to access to it. Typically, the offender will advance an attack in five phases: reconnaissance, scanning, gaining access, maintaining access, and covering tracks (Chatterjee, 2019). A Trojan Horse for example, is a malicious computer program that pretends to be a benign application. A Trojan Horse will purposefully do something to the user's computer that the user does not expect; from a variety of temporary harmful effects, to permanent damage, such as logging keystrokes to steal information passwords or credit card numbers (Wikipedia, 2019). They are distinct from viruses.

With a Trojan horse on a compromised computer, you would be able to do whatever you wanted. That computer would be as good as your own. You would own it. Now imagine that you owned 100,000 such computers, scattered all over the world, each one running and being looked after in someone's home, office, or school. Imagine that with just one command, you could tell all of these computers to do whatever you wanted (Solomon & Evron, 2006).

In the court of appeal for Ontario, in the case *United States v. Baratov,* the United States sought to prosecute Mr. Karim Baratov for conduct that corresponded to the Canadian offence of unauthorized use of a computer, contrary to s. 342.1 of the Criminal Code, R.S.C. 1985, c. C-46. He is alleged to have worked as a hacker-for-hire to gain unauthorized access to email accounts *(United States v. Baratov, 2017).* Since the offender in this case may have been more interested in the behaviours of the machine rather than the reactions of the machine owner. It should not be considered a case of intentional cyberbullying.

S 342.1 Unauthorized Use of a Computer

Unauthorized use of a computer is a criminal offence where the computer itself is *the subject,* not the instrument of a crime. Four separate offences can be identified under Section 342.1 as follows: (1) the obtaining offence, (2) the interception offence, (3) the user offence, and (4) the enabling offence. In order to trigger the application of this section, the unauthorized acts must have been committed fraudulently. It is important to note that these two elements are cumulative and therefore must both be present in order for a court to find the accused guilty of any of the four offences mentioned above.

In *R. c. Paré,* the Court of Quebec, a police officer was charged with having acted fraudulently in obtaining computer services *(R. c. Paré, 1987).* The accused admitted to his absence of right in obtaining the services, however he denied acting fraudulently. The Court had to establish that the act was not qualified as fraudulent simply because it was not authorized. The Defendant's conduct must also have been dishonest and morally wrong. The Defendant tried to minimize the gravity of his actions by conceding that his superiors knew, and had tolerated the situation. However, the Court found his conduct to be equivalent to willful blindness, and disregard, and that his attempt to justify his use did not remove his fraudulent intentions.

A Final Word

Social media entices young and not-so-young participants to put themselves in harm's way for admiration and respect from their peers. Active members of social media ignore or forget to read critical information in privacy policies and end-user licence agreements, which constitutes acts of omission and denotes *actus reus* or acting badly without thinking. This chapter updates the criminal activity associated with frequent use of social media, and highlights twelve Criminal Code offences associated with cyberbullying behavior and offers discussion on relevant court cases testing each offense. The recommendation taken in this chapter is that the cyber-solution is in the hands of the cyber-victims, who need to "put down the mouse and step away from the computer, and no one will get hurt" (Aftab. 2016).

REFERENCES

Aftab, P. (2016). Put down the mouse and step away from the computer...and no one will get hurt! Stop Cyberbullying, *WiredSafety.org.* Retrieved 29 March 2019, http://www.stopcyberbullying.org/teens/index.html

Alessi, S., & Trollip, S. R. (2001). *Multimedia for Learning: Methods and Development* (3rd ed.). Pearson.

Automattic Inc. (2020). *Tumblr blog.* Retrieved 16 February 2020, https://www.tumblr.com/

Bailey, J. (2014). Time to unpack the juggernaut? Reflections on the Canadian federal parliamentary debates on cyberbullying. *Dalhousie Law Journal, 37*(2), 662–707. doi:10.2139srn.2448480

Baker, E.-R. (2017). People are literally dying and injuring themselves for the perfect Insta Snap. *Vice Media Group.* retrieved 15 February 2020, https://www.vice.com/en_ca/article/evd85n/people-are-literally-dying-and-injuring-themselves-for-the-perfect-insta-snap

Bill C-13 - Historical. (2018). *Protecting Canadians from Online Crime Act.* Retrieved 24 April 2019, https://openparliament.ca/bills/41-2/C-13/

Boyd, D. (2006). Facebook's privacy trainwreck: Exposure, invasion, and drama. *Apophenia Blog.* Retrieved 15 August 2019, http://www.danah.org/papers/FacebookAndPrivacy.html

British Columbia Workers Compensation Act, RSBC 1996, c 492. (n.d.). Retrieved 11 May 2019, https://www.canlii.org/en/bc/laws/stat/rsbc-1996-c-492/latest/rsbc-1996-c-492.html

Cassidy, T. (2014). Regina man's identity used in online romance scamming. *CBC News*. retrieved 11 May 2019, https://www.cbc.ca/news/canada/saskatchewan/regina-man-s-identity-used-in-online-romance-scamming-1.2800046

CBC News. (2002). *Sharpe sentenced in B.C. child pornography case*. Retrieved 11 May 2019, https://www.cbc.ca/news/canada/sharpe-sentenced-in-b-c-child-pornography-case-1.315991

CBC News. (2011). *Bullied teen's death sparks campaign*. Retrieved 28 April 2019, https://www.cbc.ca/news/canada/nova-scotia/bullied-teen-s-death-sparks-campaign-1.996424

CBC News. 2018). *RCMP release name of youth charged in connection with threats to Selkirk-area schools*. Retrieved 30 April 2019, https://www.cbc.ca/news/canada/manitoba/selkirk-school-threats-students-return-1.4931490

CBC News. (2019). *Children, ages 12 and 13, charged for allegedly threatening Winnipeg schools: Incredibly complex investigation had police working with overseas social media company to identify anonymous users*. Retrieved 22 May 2019, https://www.cbc.ca/news/canada/manitoba/winnipeg-school-threats-arrests-1.4989564

Charter (1982). Canadian Charter of Rights and Freedoms, retrieved 26 March 2020, https://laws-lois.justice.gc.ca/eng/const/page-15.html

Chatterjee, A. (2019). The 5 Phases of Hacking. *Geeks for Geeks*. Retrieved 12 March 2019, https://www.geeksforgeeks.org/5-phases-hacking/

Couros, A. (2015). *Romance Scams Continue and I Really Need Your Help*. Retrieved 11 May 2019, http://educationaltechnology.ca/couros/2627

Coyle, S. (2014). Social media and suicide prevention, Social Work Today, 14, 1, retrieved 14 November 2018, http://www.socialworktoday.com/archive/012014p8.shtml

Criminal Code of Canada. retrieved 26 March 2020, https://laws-lois.justice.gc.ca/eng/acts/c-46/?wbdisable=false

Department of Justice Canada. (2017). *Cyberbullying and the non-consensual distribution of intimate images*. Retrieved 30 April 2019, https://www.justice.gc.ca/eng/rp-pr/other-autre/cndii-cdncii/p4.html

Dokur, M., Petekkaya, E., & Karadağ, M. (2018). Media-based clinical research on selfie-related injuries and deaths. *Ulusal Travma ve Acil Cerrahi Dergisi*, *24*, 129–135. PMID:29569684

Dragos, R. v. 2012 ONCA 538. (n.d.). Retrieved 3 May 2019, http://canlii.ca/t/fs9ps

Edwards, L. (2005). Articles 12-15 ECD: ISP liability – The problem of intermediary service provider liability. In L. Edwards (Ed.), *The new legal framework for e-commerce in Europe*. Hart Publishing.

Edwards, B. (2011). 'I wish I could be happy', Ottawa East News, retrieved 28 April 2019, https://www.insideottawavalley.com/news-story/3800605--i-wish-i-could-be-happy-/

Facebook Inc. (2020). *Instagram*. Retrieved 16 February 2020, https://www.instagram.com/

Facebook Inc. (2020). *Facebook*. Retrieved 16 February 2020, https://www.facebook.com/

Flanagan, R. (2019). Police in U.K. issue warning about 'Momo Challenge' urging kids to self-harm. *CTV News*. Retrieved 9 February 2020, https://www.ctvnews.ca/sci-tech/police-in-u-k-issue-warning-about-momo-challenge-urging-kids-to-self-harm-1.4313148

Gov.uk. (2016). Investigatory Powers Act 2016, retrieved 14 November 2018, http://www.legislation.gov.uk/ukpga/2016/25/pdfs/ukpga_20160025_en.pdf

Huff, C., & Finholt, T. (1994). *Social issues in computing: Putting computing in its place*. McGraw Hill.

Industry Canada. (2014). The Personal Information Protection and Electronic Documents Act' (S.C. 2000, c. 5) (PIPEDA), retrieved 27 April 2019, http://laws-lois.justice.gc.ca/eng/acts/P-8.6/index.html

Kiss, J. (2013). Cyber scams take advantage of hope and trust. The Guardian, retrieved 27 April 2019, https://www.theguardian.com/society/2013/aug/16/cyber-scams-take-advantage-hope-trust

Legare, R. v. [2009] 3 SCR 551, 2009 SCC 56. (n.d.). Retrieved 11 September 2019, https://www.canlii.org/en/ca/scc/doc/2009/2009scc56/2009scc56.html?resultIndex=1

Leung, W., & Bascaramurty, D. (2012). Amanda Todd tragedy highlights how social media makes bullying inescapable. *The Globe and Mail Inc*. Retrieved 27 April 2019, https://www.theglobeandmail.com/news/national/amanda-todd-tragedy-highlights-how-social-media-makes-bullying-inescapable/article4611068/

Ling, I. (2014). How federal bill C-13 could give CSIS agents — or even Rob Ford — access to your personal online data, National Post, retrieved 28 April 2019, https://nationalpost.com/news/politics/how-a-new-federal-bill-c-13-could-give-csis-agents-or-even-rob-ford-access-to-your-personal-online-data

Mackie, R. v. (D.T.), (2014) 588 A.R. 1. (n.d.). Retrieved 23 April 2019, https://ca.vlex.com/vid/r-v-mackie-d-680752897

Mann, B. L. (2009). Social networking websites: A concatenation of impersonation, denigration, sexual and aggressive solicitation, cyber-bullying and happy slapping videos. *International Journal of Law and Information Technology*, *17*(3), 252–267. doi:10.1093/ijlit/ean008

Mann, B. L. (2015). Social networking websites, In P. Leith (Ed.), Privacy in the Information Society (pp. 493–503). London, UK: Ashgate Publishing.

McLuhan, M. (1962). *The Gutenberg Galaxy: The Making of Typographic Man*. London: Routledge & Kegan Paul.

McLuhan, M. (1978). The Brain and the Media: The "Western" Hemisphere. *Journal of Communication*, *28*(4), 54–60.

Morin, R. c. 2014 QCCQ 1609. (n.d.). Retrieved 11 August 2019, https://www.canlii.org/en/qc/qccq/doc/2014/2014qccq1609/2014qccq1609.html?resultIndex=1

OpenMedia. (2015). Great to see Privacy Commissioner Daniel Therrien welcoming our community's Privacy Plan, retrieved 26 March 2020, https://openmedia.org/en/cbc-great-see-privacy-commissioner-daniel-therrien-welcoming-our-communitys-privacy-plan

OUT-LAW News. (2006). *Friendster patents social networking.* http://www.out-law.com/default.aspx?page=7092

Paré, R. v. [1987] 2 SCR 618, 1987. (n.d.). Retrieved 14 September 2019, https://www.canlii.org/en/ca/scc/doc/1987/1987canlii1/1987canlii1.html?resultIndex=1

Pengelley, R. v. 2009 19936 (ON SC). (n.d.). Retrieved 1 May 2019, http://canlii.ca/t/239jh

Pettersson, R. (1990). Teachers, students and visuals. *Journal of Visual Literacy*, *10*(1), 45–62. doi:10.1080/23796529.1990.11674450

Police Service of Northern Ireland in Craigavon. (2018). *Momo Image: Facebook.* Retrieved 8 February 2020, https://www.facebook.com/PSNI.Craigavon/photos/a.3904412376583321/2097736956928732/?type=3

R. v. J.M.D., 2018 BCPC 211. (n.d.). Retrieved 3 May 2019, http://canlii.ca/t/htm3x

McFarlane, R. v. (2018). MBCA 48, retrieved 26 March 2020, <http://canlii.ca/t/hrwh1>, retrieved on 2020-03-26

R. v. S. H., 2018 NLSC 218. (n.d.). Retrieved 11 October 2019, https://www.canlii.org/en/nl/nlsc/doc/2018/2018nlsc218/2018nlsc218.html?searchUrlHash=AAAAAQAZUi4gdi4gUy5ILiwgMjAxOCBOT FNDIDIxOAAAAAAB&resultIndex=1

Topham, R. v. (2017), BCSC 551, retrieved 26 March 2020, http://canlii.ca/t/h3cv5

Ragsdale, R. G. (1988). *Permissible computing in education: Values, assumptions and needs.* New York: Praeger Books.

Reinking, D. (1987). Computers, reading and a new technology of print. In D. Reinking (Ed.), Reading and computers: Issues for theory and practice (3-23). New York: Teachers College Press.

Reinking, D. (Ed.). (1987). Reading and computers: Issues for theory and practice. NY: Columbia University Scamwatch. *Australian Competition and Consumer Commission.* Retrieved 3 May 2019, https://www.scamwatch.gov.au/types-of-scams/dating-romance

Schetzer, A. (2019). Why is India the world capital for selfie deaths, and what's being done to stop it? *ABC News.* Retrieved 15 February 2020, https://www.abc.net.au/news/2019-03-08/selfie-deaths-india-world-capital-killfies/10874536

Scott, J. P. (2015). Courtney Brown's suicide and the tragic effects of bullying. *Canadian Living.* Retrieved 26 April 2019, http://www.canadianliving.com/life/community/courtney_browns_suicide_and_the_tragic_effects_of_bullying.php#.UQ12Imtij9g.twitter

Senate of Canada. (2014). Standing Senate Committee on Legal and Constitutional Affairs. *Bill C-13 The Protecting Canadians from Online Crime Act.* Retrieved 10 October 2019, https://sencanada.ca/en/committees/lcjc/

Sharpe, R. v. [2001] 1 SCR 45, 2001 SCC 2. (n.d.). Retrieved 5 August 2019, https://scc-csc.lexum.com/scc-csc/scc-csc/en/item/1837/index.do

Simoes, R. v. 2014 ONCA 144. (n.d.). Retrieved 11 October 2019, https://www.canlii.org/en/on/onca/doc/2014/2014onca144/2014onca144.html

SnapChat Inc. (2020). SnapChat, retrieved 26 March 2020, https://www.snap.com/en-US/privacy/privacy-center/

Solomon, A. & Evron, G. (2006). *The world of botnets*. Academic Press.

Spencer, R. v. [2014] 2 SCR 212, 2014 SCC 43. (n.d.). Retrieved 13 October 2019, https://www.canlii.org/en/ca/scc/doc/2014/2014scc43/2014scc43.html?resultIndex=1

Staff. (2014). *MacKay says feds' Online Crime Act to help justice system combat cyber-bullying*. Hill Times Publishing.

Twitter (2020). Twitter, retrieved 26 March 2020, https://twitter.com/home

UDHR. (1948). Universal Declaration of Human Rights, retrieved 26 March 2020, https://www.ohchr.org/EN/UDHR/Documents/UDHR_Translations/eng.pdf

United States Patent & Trade Mark Office. June 16, 2003, Application No. 10/462,142. (n.d.). http://patft.uspto.gov/netacgi/nph-Parser?Sect1=PTO2&Sect2=HITOFF&p=1&u=%2Fnetahtml%2FPTO%2Fsearch-bool.html&r=1&f=G&l=50&col=AND&d=PTXT&s1=7,069,308.PN.&OS=PN/7,069,308&RS=PN/7,069,308

United States v. Baratov, 2017 ONCA 481. (n.d.). Retrieved 21 May 2019, http://canlii.ca/t/h46t7

U.S. Department of Justice, National Institute of Justice. (1989). *Computer Crime: Criminal Justice Resource Manual*. Author.

R. v Gardner 2018 ONCA 584. (n.d.). Retrieved 23 April 2019, https://www.ontariocourts.ca/decisions/2018/2018ONCA0584.pdf

v Vu, R. [2013] 3 SCR 657 [Vu], 2013 SCC 60. (n.d.). Retrieved 3 March 2019, https://scc-csc.lexum.com/scc-csc/scc-csc/en/item/13327/index.do

Wah, B. W. (Ed.). (2008). *Wiley Encyclopedia of Computer Science and Engineering*. Hoboken, NJ: John Wiley & Sons, Inc.

Weisblott, M. (28 March 2011). Social media website Formspring under fire following teen suicides, retrieved 30 April 2019, https://ca.news.yahoo.com/blogs/dailybrew/social-media-website-formspring-under-fire-following-teen-20110328-100022-281.html

Wikipedia. (2019). *Trojan horse*. Retrieved 12 August 2019, https://en.wikipedia.org/wiki/Trojan_horse_(computing)

Zuckerberg, M. (2019). A privacy-focused vision for social networking, Facebook Inc., retrieved 26 March 2020, https://www.facebook.com/notes/mark-zuckerberg/a-privacy-focused-vision-for-social-networking/10156700570096634/

This research was previously published in Applying Internet Laws and Regulations to Educational Technology; pages 51-76, copyright year 2020 by Information Science Reference (an imprint of IGI Global).

Chapter 24
Facebook and the Interaction of Culture and Conflict

Godfrey A. Steele
The University of the West Indies, Trinidad and Tobago

ABSTRACT

The intersection of culture and conflict is relatively understudied in communication, focusing on mass-self communication and power relations and new media scholarship. Conflict and the cultural dimensions in media coverage are well documented, but with less attention to new media cultural settings, often limited to use as one-way broadcasting media or as audiencing participants in social media marketing. Potentially more interactive communication exists within a closed community, especially because Facebook has defining cultural, psychological, and psychosocial characteristics. Conflict message interactions facilitate studying the intersection of culture and conflict within a new media setting. This chapter focuses on conflict within the cultural context of Facebook closed communities, theorizes about this relationship, and tests its application.

INTRODUCTION

This chapter reviews the literature on conflict and culture, focusing on their intersection. It integrates concepts from culture and conflict to analyse their mutual influence and develops a theoretical framework for studying culture and conflict. Adopting a methodological approach to investigating and understanding the intersection between culture and conflict in interactions, this chapter presents an empirical test of this methodological framework, reports the results of studying culture and conflict, discusses the thematic results and discusses their significance and implications for theorizing and testing a model of studying culture and conflict. It concludes with a commentary on the intersection of culture and conflict within online closed communities in Facebook.

DOI: 10.4018/978-1-6684-6307-9.ch024

BACKGROUND

Why Study Culture and Conflict on Facebook?

Overview

The intersection of culture and conflict is a relatively understudied area of new media communication research. Embedded within such research are paradigms of mass-self communication and power relations (Castells, 2013) and new media scholarship (Boyd & Ellison, 2008). Conflict in media coverage is well documented (Arno, 2009), but there has been less attention to conflict within a new media cultural setting or to intractable conflict (Bar-Tal, Abutbul-Selinger, & Raviv, 2014), or to imagining such communities in newer media settings (Conboy, 2006). Even when such communities exist in social media networks such as Facebook, they are often limited to being used as one-way broadcasting media, among politicians for example, without real interaction (Ross, Fountaine & Comrie, 2015) or as audience participants in social media marketing (Fisher, 2015). There is potentially more interactive communication, with resulting opportunities for the intersection of culture and conflict within a closed community, especially as research on Facebook has defining cultural (Köhl & Götzenbrucker, 2014), psychological (Anderson, Fagan, Woodnutt, & Chamorro-Premuzic, 2012) and psychosocial characteristics such as oversharing (Agger, 2015). The conflict messages in interactions among members of a community offer an opportunity to study the intersection of culture and conflict within a new media setting. This chapter focuses on conflict within the cultural context of Facebook closed communities, theorizes about this relationship and tests its application.

A SYSTEMATIC REVIEW OF THE CULTURE AND CONFLICT LITERATURE IN NEWER MEDIA SETTINGS

A systematic review of the literature derived from a search of "Facebook AND culture" published between 1978 and 2017 produced extensive results for peer-reviewed journal articles (n=19,811). Refinement of this scoping search yielded fewer, but substantially high results for peer-reviewed articles for the period 2004-2017(n=19076). Prior to the research for this chapter, extensive studies had been conducted on the definition, history, development and features of social networking sites for the period 1997-2006 (Boyd & Ellison, 2008) and a narrative review of scholarship on social support based on SNS platforms for the period 2004-2017 (Meng et al., 2017).

For the purpose of this chapter's focus on culture and conflict on Facebook and the implications for reconceptualizing new media, it was decided to narrow the search to "Facebook AND culture AND conflict". This refinement yielded 5,810 peer-reviewed articles from several databases such as ProQuest, Social Sciences Citation Index (Web of Science), Science Citation Index, Medline, Emerald, Informa, Taylor and Francis, Springer and JSTOR among the top 20. Further refinement led to 4,747 peer-reviewed articles. An additional refinement to include only 2004-2017 led to 4728 results. Another refinement for the period 2004-2017, focusing on studies yielded 956 results, of which there were experimental/theoretical (n=336), social networks (n=255), communication (n=70) items and social media (n=65).

A decision was made to restrict the search to "Facebook AND culture AND conflict" with filters focusing on experimental/theoretical and social network studies for the period 2007-2017. This strategy yielded substantially fewer results (n=97). Fifty-nine (59) were directly relevant. These articles were analysed thematically and resulted in seven major emphases. These seven themes included social business/marketing potential and threats, online communities (brand love and social identity on Facebook, members' contribution of knowledge to online communities, country of origin (COO) and image, brand loyalty, social media love and the look of the Other, social media's potential for supporting virtue friendship, collaborative learning, and intergroup intractable conflict), approaches to studying social media platforms, organization members' use of social networks, comparing young users, online privacy, and social information behaviour. These seven themes are presented as findings in the fifth section based on the systematic literature review in this section.

EXPLORING AND DEFINING CONFLICT, CONFLICT MESSAGES AND INTERACTIONS IN NEWER MEDIA AND SOCIAL NETWORKING SITES

Conflict in Newer Media and Social Networking Sites

Few studies have addressed conflict within closed social media groups. Conflict in media coverage is well documented, but there has been less attention to conflict within a new media cultural setting. For example, conflict in traditional media coverage such as daily news reporting is often presented as a conflictual anthropological phenomenon (Arno, 2009). When intergroup conflict occurs over an extended period such as a generation and is unresolvable it may be described as intractable (Bar-Tal, Abutbul-Selinger, & Raviv, 2014), but there has been less attention to this phenomenon in newer media. In an alternative media setting it may be presented as contestation (Couldry & Curran, 2003), but there has been less attention to conflict in newer media environments. Similarly, while the imagining of a community of daily newspaper audiences captures the culture of such a community (Conboy, 2006), there has been less attention to imagining such communities in newer media settings. In a study of collaborative learning in the social media environment, Borstnar (2012) explored motivation, trust, and conflict among 24 students working in groups. It was theorized that an unstructured social media environment facilitates problem solving. For example, Borstnar (2012, p. 102) argued "based on the assumption that collaborative learning can be efficiently supported in a rule-free and social media unstructured environment, and that it has a positive impact on the self-organizing of the group and thus contributes to problem solving and learning."

Studying Conflict in Facebook

Borstnar's (2012) study of collaborative learning in the social media environment noted that although the effective use of ICT to support group collaboration was well-researched, there was less understanding of what happens in a less structured, rule-free and perhaps more chaotic social media environment. Borstnar (2012) investigated whether group knowledge in the group-learning process in a social media environment could be elicited. This was done by assigning 24 students to three groups and giving them tasks, conducting naturalistic observation, and measuring attitudes towards collaborative work using a questionnaire. The study's results suggested that motivation and trust were positively associated with self-management. However, increases in conflicts were associated with a decrease in formal structure and facilitation.

The rapid increase in social network sites, and their increasing popularity have brought new concerns about conflict. Will new media provide new platforms for the staging and working out of conflicts? Will new media be transformed by enduring human issues such as conflict or will they have a transformative impact on how conflict is managed? Intergroup intractable conflict occurs when groups have mutually incompatible goals which they each regard as essential to their survival (Bar-Tal, Abutbul-Selinger, & Raviv, 2014). Bar-Tal, Abutbul-Selinger, and Raviv (2014) reviewed intergenerational intractable conflicts across nationalities, states and over the course of history. They concluded that this type of conflict is often violent, and because of their long-lasting nature, the collective impact upon groups is the creation of a culture of conflict in which the conflicts are perceived to be zero-sum in nature. The question, then, for new media, is whether they can exert a new influence over the presence of intractable conflict or merely provide new arenas and tools for the perpetuation of conflict.

EXPLORING AND DEFINING CULTURE IN NEWER MEDIA AND SOCIAL NETWORKING SITES

Facebook Communities and Group Culture

Newer media not only offer opportunities to exert cultural influences and be influenced by cultural forces, but they constitute and evolve into cultures of their own. Affordances refer to the interface between the potential for action created by newer media and their tendency to predict the intensity of usage of aspects of the newer media (Kuo, Tseng, Tseng, & Lin, 2013). It is quite feasible to consider the extent to which the availability of the means to use social networks sites such as Facebook can influence the ways in which they are used and the degree to which such facilities, as afforded by these sites, actually predict user behavior.

This issue may be explored by considering what has been happening in the culture of the Facebook community of users. One way which SNS are involved is in the creation of social business and opportunities for marketing and innovation. Accordingly, there has been a call for business organizations as networks of communities interacting with clients to ensure that there is alignment between their leaders and their culture to facilitate this role for SNS.

Studying Culture in Facebook

Kuo et al.'s (2013) study investigated three social information affordances for expressive information control, privacy information control, and image information control in Facebook. The results demonstrated gender differences among users. Commenting on this outcome, the researchers noted

The results showed that the three affordances can significantly explain how Facebook's interface designs facilitate users' self-presentation activities. In addition, the findings reveal that males are more engaged in expressing information than females, while females are more involved in privacy control than males. A practical application of our study is to compare and contrast the level of affordances offered by various social network sites (SNS) like Facebook and Twitter, as well as differences in online self-presentations across cultures. Our approach can therefore be useful to investigate how SNS design features can be tailored to specific gender and culture needs (p. 635).

Thus, Kuo et al.'s (2013) study exemplifies a method for investigating the cultural dimension on Facebook.

A THEORETICAL FRAMEWORK FOR STUDYING CULTURE AND CONFLICT WITHIN AN ONLINE CLOSED COMMUNITY

Social Presence

Social presence (SP) has emerged as an area of interest related to culture and conflict in studying online closed communities such as Facebook (Rourke, Anderson, Garrison, & Archer, 2000). It consists of affective, interactive and cohesive components. The affective component is indicated by emotional expression, the use of humor, and disclosure behaviors. The interactive component is indicated by behaviors such as continuing or making links to previous conversation such as a reply to a thread, quoting from others' messages, referring explicitly to others' messages, asking questions, complimenting or expressing appreciation, and expressing agreement. The cohesive component consists of vocatives or direct ways of addressing participants by name, addressing a group using inclusive pronouns, using phatic communication and salutations that fulfil a social function, and using greetings and closures.

Conflict Messages

Conflict messages are embodied in posts among users. They may occur as elements within a post. These conflict messages may have integrative and disintegrative effects (Horton & Hunt, 1984). Participation in conflict messages could involve the creation and response to messages. Conflict messages are indicated by statements of mutually incompatible goals and are characterised by cognitive, behavioral and affective behaviors (Barki & Hartwick, 2004). These messages may be reflective of integrative and disintegrative outcomes (Horton & Hunt, 1984) and a range of conflict styles (Euwema, van der Vliet, & Bakker, 2003; Rahim, 1983). The degree and extent of participation are worth exploring. The production of conflict messages can be evident in the frequency and type of conflict style handling expressed in posts and responses to posts.

In searching the literature, the results of the search strategies, keywords such as culture and conflict were combined with Facebook and focused on experimental/theoretical studies and social network studies were reviewed for thematic patterns.

SOLUTIONS AND RECOMMENDATIONS:

Purpose, Objectives, Research Questions, and Method

This methodological approach utilises a systematic literature review to explore concepts and characteristics of culture and conflict in Facebook use among members of closed communities. The main objective is to identify patterns of concerns and research findings in relation to these variables. This approach seeks to answer the emergent research question focusing on the major themes in the literature review which offer perspectives on reconceptualization of new media such as Facebook. Details of the method adopted were provided in the first section.

Findings

1. **Social Business/Marketing Potential and Threats Emerged as a Major Theme**: The first aspect of this theme focuses on the role of the culture within organizations that seek to benefit from the use of social media to capitalize on opportunities for capturing value in marketing and innovation, as well as operations and leadership. Thus for online communities, it is recommended that the leadership and the culture of the communities should be aligned (Kiron, Palmer, Phillips, & Kruschwitz, 2012). A potentially negative dimension to the reliance on social media is posed by threats to a brand. These threats are referred to as "collaborative brand threats" which are planned, deliberate attacks on brands by large numbers of social media users (Rauschnabel, Kammerlander, & Ivens, 2016). In this regard, research is being developed to anticipate what can signal or anticipate these attacks (triggers), how these attacks can develop momentum (amplifiers) and how brand and reputation managers can respond effectively (reaction strategies) (Rauschnabel, Kammerlander, & Ivens, 2016). These two aspects of social business have implications for how online communities think of, and use social media. The first aspect, the social business/marketing potential, helps us to think of the positive uses to which online creators and users of content might put social media, and the role of organizational culture in facilitating marketing and innovation, especially. The second aspect alerts us to the potential danger and the strategic ways in which brand management can be challenged to be more resilient and adaptive in dealing with new arenas of conflict during interactions with users within their communities. This theme reflects a focus on culture as a critical variable in studying Facebook.

2. **Online Communities:** There were several aspects of this theme, not surprisingly, owing to the presence of online communities as a keyword among 26% or roughly 1 in 4 of the 956 studies found. First, the formation and development of online communities has attracted attention among researchers. In one study (Goggins, Laffey, & Gallagher, 2011) researchers investigated the formation of patterns of interaction and the development of online group practices using six case studies. This study suggests another key role for culture as a key variable.

Second, another study (Ch'Ng, 2015) explored the formation, maintenance and disintegration of a fringe Twitter community to understand whether offline community structure applies to online communities – laboratory case using Big Data to track user-generated content to assess the significance of "particular user nodes" with centrality measures and to track "ego centralities" with time –series analysis. This method was used to determine whether online communities of this type are sustained by specific ego characteristics of users that support opposing ideologies and the creation of resilience among "desperate online users" who find ways to overcome social media limitations. This focus emphasizes both cultural and conflict variables.

Third, the role of brand love and social identity on Facebook was addressed in another study (Vernuccio, Pagani, Barbarrosa, & Pastore, 2015). This study identified the value of leveraging customers' social identity with experiences that engage them in a social-interactive manner to strengthen their emotional bond with a brand among online communities such as Facebook. Such engagement was further explored and confirmed in an experiential study (Wondwesen, 2016). This third aspect reflects a focus on culture.

Fourth, this research highlights members' contribution of knowledge to online communities (Chou, 2010). This emphasis suggests the value of taking into account individual differences, extrinsic and intrinsic motivation, and how they relate to the knowledge members might wish to contribute in building online communities. Culture is once more accentuated in this aspect of online communities. Fifth, the focus is on the role of country of origin (COO) and how that relates to image and brand loyalty when globally recognized sports teams, for example, are associated positively with brands from that country (White & Absher, 2013). Culture is again reflected in this fifth aspect. Sixth, this example relates to how our perception of how the Other judges us (based on Sartre's social communication framework) is often influential in online communities (Lopato, 2016). Culture and identity are reflected in this aspect of research on online communities. Seventh, another aspect of online community research addresses social media's potential for supporting virtue friendship based on Aristotle's work (Elder, 2014). This aspect reflects the perspective of culture and its link to philosophy. Thus, these five aspects of research on online communities (examples 3-7) reflect a focus on culture as a key variable.

The eighth aspect of this research focuses on collaborative learning (Borstnar, 2012). This focus embraces both culture and conflict as key variables. The ninth aspect of online community research explores the role of intergroup intractable conflicts and the implications for social media (Bar-Tal, Abutbul-Selinger, & Raviv, 2014), with a focus on conflict as a variable. Altogether, these nine aspects of online community research, five focusing on culture and four on both culture and conflict, suggest that this is a fertile and generative area of research. Such interest implies that a potentially useful avenue for exploring and developing reconceptualizations of new media may exist in this line of research.

3. Approaches to studying uses of social media platforms include the data on user statistics, and their motivations for using specific aspects of online platforms that focus, for example, on understudied areas such as Twitter hashtags and Facebook favorites and more "destructive" activities as unfollowing (Weller, 2016). Both culture and conflict are reflected in this theme.

4. Organizational members' use of social networks has generated debate over its value (Moqbel, Nevo & Kock, 2013). This debate can be explored by investigating the role of organizational members' use of SNS and its effect on job satisfaction, perceived organizational commitment and job performance. Similar research has been conducted in relation to supervisor-subordinate communication (Steele & Plenty, 2015) but not with a focus on the context of SNS. Moqbel, Nevo and Kock (2013) contend that SNS rather than promoting presenteeism, or being at the workplace but working below peak capacity, can foster work-life balance, and demonstrate organizational commitment. Another aspect of members' contribution of knowledge to SNS lies in concerns about employee ignorance. One study found employees' ignorance could have a negative impact on their intention to share knowledge. This results in poor decision-making and communication in organizations, and can "limit the organizational ability to repel external threats, implement innovation and manage future risks" (Israilidis, Siachou, Cooke, & Lock, 2015, p. 1109). This research focus suggests the key role of culture as a variable in studying an online community such as Facebook.

5. Another interesting research theme lies, firstly, in comparing young users of social media. In one such comparison in France social platform use and cyber bullying was investigated and the researchers' findings recommended educating young users about a positive and safe use of the Internet seriously, and providing appropriate guidance, especially for primary school children (Blaya & Fartoukh, 2016). Secondly, the adolescent perspective is taken into account in proposing a "a conceptual model of social media consumption" to help them "identify positive and negative outcomes and

the behavioral strategies of media selection and differentiation used to cope with them" (Hübner Barcelos & Vargas Rossi, 2014, p. 275). This theme reflects culture and conflict.

6. Online privacy (a component of the culture variable) is another critical research theme relating to SNS. There are two dimensions worth noting. There is a distinction between types of online privacy. In the context of online social networks (OSN), privacy between users is different from privacy between a user and a third party. Researchers explain the difference between interpersonal and third-party disclosure. In the first instance, based on symbolic interactionist accounts of privacy, "users are performing dramaturgically for an intended audience" (Heyman, De Wolf, & Pierson, 2014, p. 18). In the second instance, "third-party privacy is based on the data that represent the user in data mining and knowledge discovery processes, which ultimately manipulate users into audience commodities" (Heyman, De Wolf, & Pierson, 2014, p. 18). When these distinctions were applied to the privacy settings of Facebook, LinkedIn and Twitter the findings indicated "that users are granted more options in controlling their interpersonal information flow towards other users than third parties or service providers" (Heyman, De Wolf, & Pierson, 2014, p. 18). Related to online privacy is the issue of self-disclosure. Research on self-disclosure, (another component of the culture variable) focuses on personality factors which influence SNS users' motivation to disclose information about themselves as well as share information (Chen, Pan, & Guo, 2016).

7. **Social Information Behavior (SIB):** Various aspects of social information behavior have been researched. Six of them are described and are linked to issues of tension; fake identities, treats and attacks; the extent of national cultural influence; photo sharing; restrictions on occupational use of social media; and benefits and dangers. They reflect the culture and conflict perspectives.

    a. Serendipity and disruption (conflict): The rise in popularity of social media has led to its promotion as a platform for serendipity, but ironically this feature has been accompanied by disruption (Skågeby, 2012). According to Skågeby (2012), there are five prevalent tensions relating to social disruption: market logic and social logic; public and private; work and non-work; individual and collective; and IRL (In Real Life) or AFK (Away From Keyboard). These tensions reflect the conflict variable.

    b. Fake identities, threats, attacks (conflict): Modern challenges to security are posed by the use of fake identities, threats and attacks on SNS such as Facebook (Hoehle, Zhang, & Venkatesh, 2015; Krombholz, Merkl, & Weippl, 2012). This theme reflects the conflict variable.

    c. National culture has little effect on the relationship between usability constructs and continued intention to use mobile social media applications (Hoehle, Zhang, & Venkatesh, 2015). The culture variable is reflected in this theme.

    d. Facebook photo sharing especially among adolescent users emerged as a popular activity on Facebook since its launch in 2005, and requires research (Malik, Dhir, & Nieminen, 2015). The culture variable is reflected in this theme.

    e. As an example of occupational use, certified public accountants tend to never use Facebook, LinkedIn, Twitter, and chat rooms. They prefer traditional communication channels such as written documents and telephone call and electronic mail is used frequently with a few significant differences among gender, age, education level achieved, and number of employees in the firm (Rollins & Lewis, 2012). Culture is reflected in this theme.

    f. The benefits and dangers of enjoyment of social networking sites were predicted (Turel & Serenko, 2012), but this has become an increasingly important area of research interest on new media. Culture is reflected in this theme.

Overall, these six aspects of social information behavior (SIB) reflect the underlying influence of conflict (examples 1-2) and culture (examples 3-6) on social media and SNS, and suggest six subthemes of SIB for reconceptualising new media.

FUTURE RESEARCH DIRECTIONS

Seven broad thematic areas have emerged from an analysis based on a systematic literature review of research on culture, conflict and Facebook focusing on selected studies. In some themes there are extensive subsections or subtopics associated with them, for example, online communities, and social information behaviour. These clusters suggest that these two areas have attracted much interest and perhaps reflect the most developed aspects of research. Perhaps they signal the potential significance of these themes and subtopics as areas for emphasis which may have implications for the reconceptualization of new media. Next, the implications for online communities and SIB, as two major themes, are discussed in some detail and reference is made to the other five.

In the case of online communities their formation, maintenance and dissolution can influence how new media develop and the trajectories of knowledge that are being developed. Reflection on this observation suggests that both culture and conflict exert considerable influence and are influenced by a focus on online communities on Facebook. In the case of closed communities, there are prospects for using current understandings and new knowledge to study and gain a better grasp of how such online communities are being shaped as cultural phenomena and may function as sites of mediatized conflict. These insights have relevance for users, co-creators of content, and managers and researchers studying new media. However, issues of access, privacy and ethical and practical issues related to insider research can create new, but not insurmountable challenges.

The focus on social information behaviour alerts researchers assessing and studying new media to the complexity and range of issues that have emerged. Again culture and conflict offer contextual groundings for this line of research. For example, issues relating to the potentially serendipitous and disruptive nature of new media, the related benefits and dangers of enjoying social media, and other issues such as privacy, disclosure, fake identities and threats indicate that these variables are likely to play a significant role in how new media are engaged, and are shaped, even as they shape cultural connections and conflict interactions on a platform such as Facebook, the largest SNS.

The influence of social media in changing the way persons connect or reconnect with others, entertain themselves, pursue leisure activities, shop and find jobs is recognized (Yusuf, Al-Banawi, & Rahman Al-Imam, 2014), but several challenges exist which can have implications for the reconceptualization of new media. A review and research agenda for understanding Generation Y and their use of social media (Bolton et al., 2013) acknowledged that prior research on Generation Y's social media use raised more questions than it answered. Bolton et al.'s (2013) critique of such research argued that its primary focus was on the USA and perhaps one or other country, "ignoring other regions with large and fast-growing Generation Y populations where social-media use and its determinants may differ significantly"; tended to "study students whose behaviors may change over their life cycle stages"; relied on "self-reports by different age groups to infer Generation Y's social media use"; and did "not examine the drivers and outcomes of social-media use". These reviewers noted that their paper provided a conceptual framework for considering the antecedents and consequences of Generation Y's social media usage. This chapter argues that one problematic consequence or impact relates to the use of social media in negative ways.

One particularly problematic and negative impact is that social media may be used to perpetuate and promote online threats such as cyber bullying, bullying and victimization. These practices pose risks to children and young people and more generally to persons in workplace settings. These risks include cyber bullying, privacy breaches, reputational damage and assault on personal dignity on SNS, in addition to hazards associated with geo-tagging, facial recognition techniques and the spreading of viruses using social media (Haynes & Robinson, 2015). In critiquing commonly used definitions of risk such as "a situation involving exposure to danger" or "the possibility that something unpleasant or unwelcome will happen", Haynes and Robinson observed that these examples are "not very specific and need to be pinned down (Pearsall & Hanks, 1999, p. 1602)." Haynes and Robinson (2015, p. 97) offered this definition: "risk is defined as an uncertain event which has an adverse impact on an activity or outcome. Applied here, risk is an event of unknown probability of occurrence involving personal data on an SNS that has a negative impact on that person". Haynes and Robinson recommended that for regulatory purposes concerned with the management and mitigation of risk, an analysis of the occurrence of risk events and their consequences can provide a basis for evaluating different regulatory approaches. This approach offers a way to reconceptualize treating with cyber bullying and bullying on SNS and via social media.

One consequence of the negative use of new media is workplace bullying. An examination of whether job satisfaction and work-related depression played a role in mediating the relationship between workplace bullying and job satisfaction, and work-related depression, play a role in mediating the relationship between workplace bullying 'and three forms of employee performance or behaviors: task performance, individual-targeted citizenship behavior (OCB-I), and interpersonal counterproductive work behavior (CWB-P)" in a small developing Caribbean country found that "job satisfaction alone partially mediated the relationship between workplace bullying and task performance, whereas work-related depression alone partially mediated the relationship between workplace bullying and OCB-I. Both job satisfaction and work-related depression partially mediated the relationship between workplace bullying and CWB-P." (Devonish, 2013).

Another consequence is the impact on children and youth. Using self-report survey data from over 3000 middle and high school students in a Midwest US city, Baker and Pelfrey (2016) explored the effect of experiencing the strains of traditional bullying victimization and cyber bullying victimization on adolescents' self-reported soft drug use, hard drug use, and weapon carrying behavior among both frequent and infrequent users of social networking sites. The results indicated that cyber bullying victimization and the anticipated strain of feeling unsafe at or on the way to or from school were significantly and positively associated with the three ways of delinquent coping among both sets of social network users (Baker & Pelfrey, 2016). This finding suggests there are similar negative consequences of traditional bullying and cyber bullying via social media and confirms an earlier finding (Lampert & Donoso, 2012). Given this finding of similar negative consequences, it would be useful to explore the impact of strategies used to counteract traditional bullying when applied in new media environments. It raises the possibility of reconceptualizing new media as parallel or complementary vehicles for social support for victims.

Social support affords victims of bullying a recourse to help from family and friends in (77% of online cases, or about four out of five children), but the most common responses were solving the problem on one's own (31%) or hoping the problem would go away (24%) (Livingstone, Haddon, Görzig, & Ólafsson, 2011, p. 71). Interestingly "children who experience more psychological difficulties are more likely to be victims or perpetrators of cyberbullying" (Lampert & Donoso, 2012, p. 146). Despite the acknowledged value of social support in helping bullying victims to cope, there is some inconsistency in what kind of social support is actually helpful and a lack of understanding of why there is inconsistency

(Matsunaga, 2011). Possible theoretical ways of understanding such inconsistency include learning about the extent of victims' positive appraisal, and to a lesser extent, esteem support or network support, and the gap between desired and received support. To date these issues have been studied in the context of post bullying adjustment in a retrospective (recall-based) study of four face-to-face bullying situations (collectively, physical, indirect, material harm, and online) among college students under 20 (Matsunaga, 2011), but not specifically in a separate social media or SNS context using actual *in situ* online bullying experiences. Conceivably, just as cyber bullying and bullying can occur via social media and SNS, bullied victims can also seek support from their online networks to cope with this phenomenon, but the extent to which they do so and the outcomes of such efforts are largely unknown. Some important questions for the reconceptualization of new media include developing an understanding of whether social support provided through social media has the same or different impact and variation in outcomes on bullied victims and bullies.

A third consequence of the use of social media in negative ways is found in social groups in various cultural contexts. Using multilevel analysis of data from four racial/ethnic groups, Williams and Peguero (2013) found that bullying is more frequent among blacks who are higher achievers, but is just as harmful on later achievers among all groups studied. In a study of rural African American youth, where the incidence rates for bullying, victimization and aggressive victimization paralleled other population groups, bullies are often rated as aggressive, hyperactive and manipulative, and are likely to be members of both aggressive and non-aggressive groups and popular and unpopular groups (Estell, Farmer, & Cairns, 2007). Bullies tend to use humiliation, intimidation, and terrorization to target persons and may do so repeatedly and systematically with the intention of inflicting an emotional burden on the victim, and are successful, innovative, informed and trained persons (Altinöz, et al., 2010).

An analysis of European gymnasium students' perceptions of online threats such as cyber bullying, bullying abuse, sexual harassment, revealing of personal information and the sharing of harmful content, indicated that social networks are widely used for social and leisure purposes (Žibėnienė & Brasienė, 2013). In that study, while most young persons thought that they were aware of these threats and knew how to protect themselves, they revealed information that could put them at risk such as their surnames (94.5%), uploaded photos in which their faces are visible (87.2%), identified their school (84.1%) and their real age (72.2%). More boys than girls tended to set their profiles as public and were more likely to receive abusive messages but other studies suggested girls were more likely to be targeted and to report being targeted (Lampert & Donoso, 2012; Livingstone, Haddon & Görzig, 2012). Only 1 in every 5 students would opt not to seek help if their rights were violated. A study of pre-school teachers' perceptions of online risks for EU children found similar results with 85% of the sample being concerned about the revelation of sensitive information, encountering inappropriate sexual content (13%), and cyber bullying (3%) as noted previously (Dönmez, Odabaşi, Yurdakul, Kuzu, & Girgin, 2017; Kabakçı, Odabaşı, & Çoklar, 2008; Odabaşı, Kabakçi, & Çoklar, 2007). Even when there are existing legal and regulatory frameworks the risk persists. It has been recommended that a useful approach stresses the "importance of multi-stakeholder involvement, proportionality of measures, procedural guarantees (such as transparency) and the careful combination of regulatory strategies targeted at illegal as well as harmful conduct and content risks for a balanced protection of minors in social networks" (Lievens, 2011, p. 43).

Another study, this time of Taiwanese 7th graders found that boys compared to girls were more likely to be both bullies and victims (Wei & Lee, 2014). Employing social network analysis Wegge, Vandebosch and Eggermont (2014) found that cyber bullying is a reflection of traditional bullying among adolescents in Europe, may occur mutually, and is more likely to occur in same-gender and same-class contexts.

Using secondary qualitative data, Ephraim (2013) found that children and youth aged 13-30 in Africa are the largest users of social networks. This study, having found that SNS are used in cyber bullying and violence against girls and women, proposes a culture –centered approach that stresses ethical use of these media and respect for the dignity and rights of other users. Based on an in depth survey of 25,000 children in Europe, it was found that, contrary to popular expectations, children were developing the skills to cope with and counteract bullying and sexual exploitation but certain challenges remained and some were still vulnerable (Livingstone, Haddon & Görzig, 2012).

Based on a review of the literature that showed bullying is a group process that is dependent on context (Sentse, Kiuru, Veenstra, & Salmivalli, 2014), researchers used statistical procedures and found that levels of bullying were inversely related to likability among Finnish adolescents in evaluating an anti-bullying program "in grades 7-9 (N = 9,183, M age at wave 1 = 13.96 years; 49.2% boys; M classroom size = 19.47) from 37 intervention and 30 control schools". Higher levels of bullying were related to lower levels of likability. This effect also held in cases of lower levels of bullying and greater likability after controlling for perceived popularity and gender. Finally, higher levels of bullying predicted higher levels of likability among peers also after controlling for popularity and gender. Social network positions based on peer nominations such as being an isolate or a clique member, for example, often relates to bullying experiences (physical, verbal or relational) (Lin, Wu, Lee, Lin, & Chiang, 2014). These findings suggest that indicators such as likability, perceived popularity, and social position indices are related to social networks and bullying. Thus, if social media are employed in cyber bullying or bullying, it would be interesting to explore whether these influences are impacting social media use or whether social media use are impacting the role of these influencers. Theoretically one might posit the view that social media, when used as tools for cyber bullying and bullying, may be investigated further in the case of Facebook using likability and dislikability metrics. In this vein an interesting issue is whether the indices are related to conflict situations that exist in cyber bullying and bullying, and whether these indices could be used to anticipate, predict and better understand and manage online conflict behaviors.

An investigation into whether adolescents learn to become morally disengaged or practice self-justifying behavior as a result of socialization found that gender, bullying and perceived popularity did not moderate the influence of friends on moral disengagement over time except in early adolescence (Sijtsema, Rambaran, Caravita, & Gini, 2014). The implication of this finding is that by the time persons use social media in conflict situations cyber bullying, gender and perceived popularity may not have influential roles. Adopting a social network perspective to study cyber bullying in classroom-based friendships of young people, investigators found that more cyber bullying occurs in high closeness concentration in offline and online friendship networks but there was less cyber bullying in high global clustering settings (Heirman et al., 2015).

Changing the public behavior of a randomly selected group of social referents, who exert influence over their peers in everyday social interaction, changes their peers' perceptions of collective norms and their harassment behavior (Paluck, Shepherd, & Smith, 2012). A follow-up study based on network analyses of peer-to-peer influence found that social referent students or students who attract more student attention can be incorporated into anti-bullying programs to spread perceptions of conflict as less socially normative among their peers (Paluck, Shepherd, & Aronow, 2016). This finding confirms an earlier suggestion by other researchers (Mouttapa, Valente, Gallaher, Rohrbach, & Unger, 2004) that when bullying and aggression prevention efforts target highly aggressive students, this may have a positive influence on their friends, in conjunction with assertiveness training in handling aggressive situations.

The other five themes, though not as evenly represented as the foregoing ones discussed, offer possibilities for identifying new areas for research exploration and growth. If the research on comparisons of users, online privacy, approaches to studying uses of social media platforms, organizational members' use of SNS, social business/marketing potential applications across the range of uses and preferences for SNS such as Facebook, appears to be less prevalent, this may signal that these five themes may not be active areas of interest or are understudied areas, or may be exciting new areas to be explored. Asking questions about the current status and future implications of these issues and why they have come to be so, pose several avenues for interrogation of new media. They offer opportunities for exploring taken for granted assumptions about these five themes and critiquing both popular wisdom and scientific inquiry on new media.

Growing interest in incivility in the US and elsewhere (Anderson, Brossard, Scheufele, Xenos, & Ladwig, 2014) is increasingly being associated with new media online discourse and rhetoric. Referring to a world characterised as increasingly volatile, uncertain, complex, and ambiguous (VUCA), International Communication Association President Peng Hwa Ang (2017) appropriated a post-Cold War term to express the view that populist sentiments are reversing the trends began almost 30 years ago in removing barriers and promoting freedom and movement. He noted the work of communication scholars, communicated powerfully, is one way of addressing the VUCA challenge by shining a light and clarifying what is not known in a VUCA world. This can be achieved, not by making issues more difficult to understand or by being unquestioning, for the people and the world they inhabit.

New media have a role to play in defining and shaping the world in which humans communicate. The challenge is to ask the right questions, critiquing assumptions, in searching for new meanings and new interpretations in reconceptualizing new media. The seven themes identified and linked to culture and conflict on Facebook, discussed earlier, offer possible avenues for further research and making sense of how new media are being reconceptualized and how they impact human communication. They also offer further exciting opportunities to understand, embrace and learn more about humanity and what makes communication, despite the presence and affordances of new media, a fundamentally human phenomenon.

CONCLUSION

This chapter explored cultural connections and conflict interactions using research conducted on Facebook. A systematic literature review spanning several databases identified, analysed and discussed seven major themes that present perspectives on the reconceptualization of new media. The emergent findings and discussion offer possibilities for better understanding, challenging and further investigating issues pertaining to culture and conflict on one SNS platform such as Facebook.

REFERENCES

Agger, B. (2015). *Oversharing: Presentations of self in the internet age*. London: Routledge.

Altinöz, M., Parildar, C., Çakiroglu, D., Barlas, M., Çaliskan, G., & Özdil, G. (2010). Bullying encountered during workplace training: Comparison of bullying level perceived by trainees whose workplace managers are women and men (Sample of Hacettepe University). *Selcuk Üniversitesi Sosyal Bilimler Enstitüsü Dergisi, 24*, 63-74. Retrieved from dergisosyalbil.selcuk.edu.tr/susbed/article/download/212/196

Anderson, A. A., Brossard, D., Scheufele, D. A., Xenos, M. A., & Ladwig, P. (2014). The "nasty effect:" Online incivility and risk perceptions of emerging technologies. *Journal of Computer-Mediated Communication, 19*(3), 373–387. doi:10.1111/jcc4.12009

Anderson, B., Fagan, P., Woodnutt, T., & Chamorro-Premuzic, T. (2012). Facebook psychology: Popular questions answered by research. *Psychology of Popular Media Culture, 1*(1), 23–37. doi:10.1037/a0026452

Ang, H. P. (2017). *Communicating with Power in a VUCA World*. Retrieved from http://www.icahdq.org/blogpost/1523657/272158/Communicating-With-Power-in-a-VUCA-World

Arno, A. (2009). *Alarming reports: Communicating conflict in the daily news*. Oxford, UK: Berghahn Books.

Baker, T., & Pelfrey, W. Jr. (2016). Bullying victimization, social network usage, and delinquent coping in a sample of urban youth: Examining the predictions of general strain theory. *Violence and Victims, 31*(6), 1021–1043. doi:10.1891/0886-6708.VV-D-14-00154 PMID:28661374

Bar-Tal, D., Abutbul-Selinger, G., & Raviv, A. (2014). The culture of conflict and its routinization. In P. Nesbitt-Larking, C. Kinnvall, T. Capelos, & H. Dekker (Eds.), *The Palgrave handbook of global political psychology* (pp. 369–387). London: Palgrave Macmillan.

Barki, H., & Hartwick, J. (2004). Conceptualizing the construct of interpersonal conflict. *International Journal of Conflict Management, 15*(3), 216–224. doi:10.1108/eb022913

Blaya, C., & Fartoukh, M. (2016). Digital uses, victimization and online aggression: A comparative study between primary school and lower secondary school students in France. *European Journal on Criminal Policy and Research, 22*(2), 285–300. doi:10.100710610-015-9293-7

Bolton, R., Parasuraman, A., Hoefnagels, A., Migchels, N., Kabadayi, S., Gruber, T., ... Solnet, D. (2013). Understanding Generation Y and their use of social media: A review and research agenda. *Journal of Service Management, 24*(3), 245–267. doi:10.1108/09564231311326987

Borstnar, M. (2012). Towards understanding collaborative learning in the social media environment. *Organizacija, 45*(3), 100–106. doi:10.2478/v10051-012-0010-8

Boyd, D., & Ellison, N. B. (2008). Social network sites: Definition, history, and scholarship. *Journal of Computer-Mediated Communication, 13*(1), 210–230. doi:10.1111/j.1083-6101.2007.00393.x

Castells, M. (2013). *Communication power* (2nd ed.). Oxford, UK: Oxford University Press.

Ch'Ng, E. (2015). The bottom-up formation and maintenance of a Twitter community: Analysis of the #FreeJahar Twitter community. *Industrial Management & Data Systems, 115*(4), 612–624. doi:10.1108/IMDS-11-2014-0332

Chen, X., Pan, Y., & Guo, B. (2016). The influence of personality traits and social networks on the self-disclosure behavior of social network site users. *Internet Research, 26*(3), 566–586. doi:10.1108/IntR-05-2014-0145

Chou, S.-W. (2010). Why do members contribute knowledge to online communities? *Online Information Review, 34*(6), 829–854. doi:10.1108/14684521011099360

Conboy, M. (2006). *Tabloid Britain: Constructing a community through language.* London: Routledge.

Couldry, N., & Curran, J. (Eds.). (2003). *Contesting media power: Alternative media in a networked world.* Oxford, UK: Rowman and Littlefield.

Devonish, D. (2013). Workplace bullying, employee performance and behaviors. *Employee Relations, 35*(6), 630-647.doi:10.1108/ER-01-2013-0004

Dönmez, O., Odabaşi, H., Yurdakul, I., Kuzu, A., & Girgin, U. (2017). Development of a scale to address perceptions of pre-service teachers regarding online risks for children. *Kuram Ve Uygulamada Egitim Bilimleri, 17*(3), 923-943. doi:10.12738/estp.2017.3.0022

Elder, A. (2014). Excellent online friendships: An Aristotelian defense of social media. *Ethics and Information Technology, 16*(4), 287–297. doi:10.100710676-014-9354-5

Ephraim, P. (2013). African youths and the dangers of social networking: A culture- centered approach to using social media. *Ethics and Information Technology, 15*(4), 275–284. doi:10.100710676-013-9333-2

Estell, D., Farmer, T., & Cairns, B. (2007). Bullies and victims in rural African American youth: Behavioral characteristics and social network placement. *Aggressive Behavior, 33*(2), 145–159. doi:10.1002/ab.20176 PMID:17441015

Euwema, M. C., van de Vliert, E., & Bakker, A. B. (2003). Substantive and relational effectiveness of organizational conflict behavior. *International Journal of Conflict Management, 14*(2), 119–139. doi:10.1108/eb022894

Fisher, E. (2015). 'You media': Audiencing as marketing in social media. *Media Culture & Society, 37*(1), 50–67. doi:10.1177/0163443714549088

Goggins, S., Laffey, J., & Gallagher, M. (2011). Completely online group formation and development: Small groups as socio-technical systems. *Information Technology & People, 24*(2), 104–133. doi:10.1108/09593841111137322

Haynes, D., & Robinson, L. (2015). Defining user risk in social networking services. *Aslib Journal of Information Management, 67*(1), 94–115. doi:10.1108/AJIM-07-2014-0087

Heirman, W., Angelopoulos, S., Wegge, D., Vandebosch, H., Eggermont, S., & Walrave, M. (2015). Cyberbullying-entrenched or cyberbully-free classrooms? A class network and class composition approach. *Journal of Computer-Mediated Communication, 20*(3), 260–277. doi:10.1111/jcc4.12111

Heyman, R., De Wolf, R., & Pierson, J. (2014). Evaluating social media privacy settings for personal and advertising purposes. *Info, 16*(4), 18–32. doi:10.1108/info-01-2014-0004

Hoehle, H., Zhang, X., & Venkatesh, V. (2015). An espoused cultural perspective to understand continued intention to use mobile applications: A four-country study of mobile social media application usability. *European Journal of Information Systems*, *24*(3), 337–359. doi:10.1057/ejis.2014.43

Horton, P. B., & Hunt, C. L. (1984). *Sociology* (6th ed.). New York: McGraw Hill.

Hübner Barcelos, R., & Alberto Vargas Rossi, C. (2014). Paradoxes and strategies of social media consumption among adolescents. *Young Consumers*, *15*(4), 275–295. doi:10.1108/YC-10-2013-00408

Israilidis, J., Siachou, E., Cooke, L., & Lock, R. (2015). Individual variables with an impact on knowledge sharing: The critical role of employees' ignorance. *Journal of Knowledge Management*, *19*(6), 1109–1123. doi:10.1108/JKM-04-2015-0153

Kabakçı, I., Odabaşı, H. F., & Çoklar, A. N. (2008). Parents' views about Internet use of their children. *International Journal of Education and Information Technologies*, *4*(2), 248–255. http://www.naun.org/main/NAUN/educationinformation/eit-75.pdf

Kiron, D., Palmer, D., Phillips, A., & Kruschwitz, N. (2012). Social business: What are companies really doing? *MIT Sloan Management Review*, *53*(4), 1–32. Retrieved from http://sloanreview.mit.edu/article/what-managers-really-think-about-social- business/

Köhl, M. M., & Götzenbrucker, G. (2014). Networked technologies as emotional resources? Exploring emerging emotional cultures on social network sites such as Facebook and Hi5: A trans-cultural study. *Media Culture & Society*, *36*(4), 508–525. doi:10.1177/0163443714523813

Krombholz, K., Merkl, D., & Weippl, E. (2012). Fake identities in social media: A case study on the sustainability of the Facebook business model. *Journal of Service Science Research*, *4*(2), 175–212. doi:10.100712927-012-0008-z

Kuo, F.-Y., Tseng, C. Y., Tseng, F.-C., & Lin, C. S. (2013). A study of social information control affordances and gender difference in Facebook self- presentation. *Cyberpsychology, Behavior, and Social Networking*, *16*(9), 635–644. doi:10.1089/cyber.2012.0345 PMID:23849000

Lampert, C., & Donoso, V. (2012). Bullying. In S. Livingstone, L. Haddon, & A. Görzig (Eds.), *Children, risk and safety on the internet* (pp. 141–150). Bristol, UK: Policy Press at the University of Bristol. doi:10.1332/policypress/9781847428837.003.0011

Lievens, E. (2011). Risk-reducing regulatory strategies for protecting minors in social networks. *Info*, *13*(6), 43–54. doi:10.1108/14636691111174252

Lin, Y., Wu, W., Lee, C., Lin, D., & Chiang, Y. (2014). Effects of social network indicators and positions in class on bullied experiences among junior high school students in Taiwan. *Taiwan Gong Wei Sheng Za Zhi*, *33*(4), 397- 409. https://search.proquest.com/docview/1561743546

Livingstone, S., Haddon, L., & Görzig, A. (Eds.). (2012). *Children, risk and safety on the internet*. Bristol, UK: Policy Press at the University of Bristol. doi:10.1332/policypress/9781847428837.001.0001

Livingstone, S., Haddon, L., Görzig, A., & Ólafsson, K. (2011). *Risks and safety on the internet. The perspective of European children. Full findings*. London: London School of Economics and Political Science.

Lopato, M. (2016). Social media, love, and Sartre's look of the Other: Why online communication is not fulfilling. *Philosophy & Technology, 29*(3), 195–210. doi:10.100713347-015-0207-x

Malik, A., Dhir, A., & Nieminen, M. (2015). Uncovering Facebook photo tagging culture and practices among digital natives. *Global Media Journal, 13*(24), 1-21. Retrieved from http://www.globalmediajournal. com/open-access/uncovering-facebook-photo-tagging-culture-and-practices-among-digital-natives.pdf

Matsunaga, M. (2011). Underlying circuits of social support for bullied victims: An appraisal-based perspective on supportive communication and postbullying adjustment. *Human Communication Research, 37*(2), 174–206. doi:10.1111/j.1468-2958.2010.01398.x

Meng, J., Martinez, L., Holmstrom, A., Chung, M., & Cox, J. (2017). Research on social networking sites and social support from 2004 to 2015: A narrative review and directions for future research. *Cyberpsychology, Behavior, and Social Networking, 20*(1), 44–51. doi:10.1089/cyber.2016.0325 PMID:28002686

Moqbel, M., Nevo, S., & Kock, N. (2013). Organizational members' use of social networking sites and job performance. *Information Technology & People, 26*(3), 240–264. doi:10.1108/ITP-10-2012-0110

Mouttapa, M., Valente, T., Gallaher, P., Rohrbach, L. A., & Unger, J. B. (2004). Social network predictors of bullying and victimization. *Adolescence, 39*(154), 315–335. PMID:15563041

Odabaşı, H. F. I., Kabakçı, I., & Çoklar, A. N. (2007). *İnternet, aile ve çocuk* [The internet, family and children]. Ankara, Turkey: Nobel Yayıncılık.

Paluck, E., Shepherd, H., & Aronow, P. (2016). Changing climates of conflict: A social network experiment in 56 schools. *Proceedings of the National Academy of Sciences of the United States of America, 113*(3), 566–571. doi:10.1073/pnas.1514483113 PMID:26729884

Paluck, E., Shepherd, H., & Smith, E. R. (2012). The salience of social referents: A field experiment on collective norms and harassment behavior in a school social network. *Journal of Personality and Social Psychology, 103*(6), 899–915. doi:10.1037/a0030015 PMID:22984831

Rahim, A. (1983). A measure of styles of handling interpersonal conflict. *Academy of Management Journal, 26*(2), 368–376. doi:10.2307/255985 PMID:10263067

Rauschnabel, P., Kammerlander, N., & Ivens, B. (2016). Collaborative brand attacks in social media: Exploring the antecedents, characteristics, and consequences of a new form of brand crises. *Journal of Marketing Theory and Practice, 24*(4), 381–410. doi:10.1080/10696679.2016.1205452

Rollins, M., & Lewis, S. (2012). Communication practices of certified public accountants. *Journal of Organizational Culture, Communications and Conflict, 16*(1), 107-112. Retrieved from https://search. proquest.com/docview/1037693138

Ross, K., Fountaine, S., & Comrie, M. (2015). Facing up to Facebook: Politicians, publics and the social media(ted) turn in New Zealand. *Media Culture & Society, 37*(2), 251–269. doi:10.1177/0163443714557983

Rourke, L., Anderson, T., Garrison, D. R., & Archer, W. (2000). Assessing social presence in asynchronous text-based computer conferencing. *International Journal of E-Learning and Distance Education, 14*(2), 50–71. Retrieved from http://www.ijede.ca/index.php/jde/article/view/153/341

Sentse, M., Kiuru, N., Veenstra, R., & Salmivalli, C. (2014). A social network approach to the interplay between adolescents' bullying and likeability over time. *Journal of Youth and Adolescence, 43*(9), 1409–1420. doi:10.100710964-014-0129-4 PMID:24752280

Sijtsema, J. J., Rambaran, J. A., Caravita, S. C. S., & Gini, G. (2014). Friendship selection and influence in bullying and defending: Effects of moral disengagement. *Developmental Psychology, 50*(8), 2093–2104. doi:10.1037/a0037145 PMID:24911569

Skågeby, J. (2012). The irony of serendipity: Disruptions in social information behavior. *Library Hi Tech, 30*(2), 321–334. doi:10.1108/07378831211239988

Steele, G. A., & Plenty, D. (2015). Supervisor-subordinate communication competence and job and communication satisfaction. *International Journal of Business Communication, 52*(3), 294–318. doi:10.1177/2329488414525450

Turel, O., & Serenko, A. (2012). The benefits and dangers of enjoyment with social networking websites. *European Journal of Information Systems, 21*(5), 512–528. doi:10.1057/ejis.2012.1

Vernuccio, M., Pagani, M., Barbarossa, C., & Pastore, A. (2015). Antecedents of brand love in online network-based communities. A social identity perspective. *Journal of Product and Brand Management, 24*(7), 706–719. doi:10.1108/JPBM-12-2014-0772

Wegge, D., Vandebosch, H., & Eggermont, S. (2014). Who bullies whom online: A social network analysis of cyberbullying in a school context. *Communications- European Journal of Communication Research, 39*(4), 415-433. doi:10.1515/commun-2014-0019

Wei, H., & Lee, W. (2014). Individual and social network predictors of physical bullying: A longitudinal study of Taiwanese early adolescents. *Violence and Victims, 29*(4), 701–716. doi:10.1891/0886-6708. VV-D-12-00173 PMID:25199395

Weller, K. (2016). Trying to understand social media users and usage. *Online Information Review, 40*(2), 256–264. doi:10.1108/OIR-09-2015-0299

White, D., & Absher, K. (2013). Red Devils, Royals, and the River Thames. *Sport, Business and Management, 3*(4), 312–326. doi:10.1108/SBM-05-2013-0011

Williams, L., & Peguero, A. (2013). The impact of school bullying on racial/ethnic achievement. *Race and Social Problems, 5*(4), 296–308. doi:10.100712552-013-9105-y

Wondwesen, T. (2016). An experiential model of consumer engagement in social media. *Journal of Product and Brand Management, 25*(5), 424–434. doi:10.1108/JPBM-05-2015-0879

Yusuf, N., Al-Banawi, N., & Rahman Al-Imam, H. (2014). The social media as echo chamber: The digital impact. *Journal of Business & Economics Research (Online), 12*(1). Retrieved from https://search.proquest.com/docview/1477975226

Žibėnienė, G., & Brasienė, D. (2013). Using the Internet, online social networks and potentially incurred risk: Student opinions. *Social Technologies, 3*(1), 53-67. Retrieved from https://search.proquest.com/docview/1426562879

KEY TERMS AND DEFINITIONS

Closed Community: A private group of persons who use social platforms and web-based infrastructure and service and networking or connections to create personal profiles that have restricted access.

Conflict: A situation in which at least two parties have perceived mutually incompatible goals and interests and which can be managed using strategies ranging from integrative or win-win to competitive or win-lose approaches.

Conflict Interactions: Behaviors of parties whose goals and interests are perceived to be mutually incompatible. These interactions may include cognitive (thought), behavioral (action), and affective (feeling) dimensions.

Culture: The characteristic visible and invisible ties that bind its members and which are reflected in the shared assumptions, beliefs, interests, practices, and patterns of behavior.

Facebook: A social networking site that facilitates interactivity and connectivity, immediate and instantaneous content creation and sharing, and supports user updated private and public profiles.

Intercultural Connections: Social relationships facilitated by social media platforms that allow users to match their interests and preferences based on the online profiles they create.

Social Networking Sites (SNS): A term that refers to both networks or web-based infrastructure and services, and networking or connections among users of SNS.

Social Presence: Consists of affective (feeling, emotion, humour, disclosure), interactive (connecting or linking or replying), and cohesive (forms of address, salutations, greetings, and closures fulfilling a social function) components of behavior.

This research was previously published in Reconceptualizing New Media and Intercultural Communication in a Networked Society; pages 198-222, copyright year 2018 by Information Science Reference (an imprint of IGI Global).

Chapter 25
Online Self–Disclosure:
Opportunities for Enriching Existing Friendships

Malinda Desjarlais
Mount Royal University, Canada

ABSTRACT

Due to their audiovisual anonymity and asynchronicity, social media have the potential to enhance self-disclosure, and thereby facilitate closeness among existing friends. In this chapter, the author highlights findings relating to the beneficial social connectedness outcomes that can be linked to online self-disclosure, synthesizes relevant literature that addresses who reaps the most benefits from online self-disclosure, and makes suggestions to direct future research in this area. Theoretical perspectives are identified throughout the chapter that are relevant to understanding the benefits of online self-disclosure, the relation between personal characteristics as predictors of online self-disclosure, and moderating factors of the effect of online self-disclosure on social connectedness. Empirical findings support both social compensation and social enhancement perspectives.

INTRODUCTION

Learning to maintain close relationships is a central developmental task of adolescence and young adulthood. Intimate friendships have implications for psychosocial adjustment and the quality of adult relationships. A lack of close friends is associated with feelings of loneliness, alienation, depression, and low self-esteem (Baumeister & Leary, 1995; Buhrmester, 1990; Jose, Ryan, & Pryor, 2012; Marion, Laursen, Zettergren, & Bergman, 2013). Among adolescents and young adults, a key component of intimate interpersonal relationships is self-disclosure, or the sharing of personally relevant thoughts, feelings, and experiences (Bauminger, Finzi-Dottan, Chaston, & Har-Even, 2008). It is essential then to explore venues that facilitate self-disclosure among friends.

DOI: 10.4018/978-1-6684-6307-9.ch025

Adolescents and young adults are increasingly turning to social media to connect with others (Davis, 2012; Reich, Subrahmanyam, & Espinoza, 2012). Social media are online platforms that allow users to create a profile about oneself, as well as connect and exchange information with other members (Boyd & Ellison, 2007; Henderson, Snyder, & Beale, 2013). Social media includes, but is not limited to, social networking sites (e.g., Facebook, Instagram, and SnapChat), instant messaging services (e.g., Facebook Messenger), text messaging, blogging sites (e.g., Twitter, and Tumblr), and multiplayer online games (e.g., Mindcraft, and Fortnite) (Ryan, Allen, Gray, & McInerney, 2017). According to a Pew Research Center survey of Americans in 2018, approximately 88% of 18- to 29-year-olds indicated they use some form of social networking, and a large proportion of these social media users visit the site daily (74% of Facebook users, 82% of Snapchat users, and 81% of Instagram users) (Smith & Anderson, 2018).

Social media has the potential to enhance self-disclosure, and thus facilitate closeness among existing friends and ultimately intimacy development. In an attempt to evaluate the potential of the virtual world for positive psychosocial development, the current chapter: summarizes the findings related to the beneficial social connectedness outcomes that can be linked to social media use in general and specifically to online self-disclosure; synthesizes relevant literature that addresses who reaps the most benefits from online self-disclosure; and provides suggestions to direct future research in this area. Although the focus of the chapter is on the benefits of online self-disclosure, in order to provide an unbiased portrait of online interactions, the author also highlights some of the drawbacks of sharing personal information online in general. Finally, considerations when using social media and posting information online are discussed, which can influence users' behaviours or be included in conversations with youth by parents, educators, and clinicians.

BACKGROUND

According to the interpersonal process model of intimacy, intimacy is the product of a transactional, interpersonal process in which two fundamental components of intimacy are self-disclosure and partner responsiveness (Laurenceau, Barrett, & Pietromonaco, 1998; Reis & Patrick, 1996; Reis & Shaver, 1988). According to this perspective, intimacy develops on an interaction-by-interaction basis, where an individual discloses personally relevant information, thoughts and feelings to a partner, and receives a response, which is interpreted as the partner's understanding, validating, and caring (Reis & Patrick, 1996). Mutual disclosure leads to greater liking and feelings of closeness and contributes to healthy social development (Chan & Lee, 2014; Sprecher, Treger, Wondra, Hilaire, & Wallpe, 2013). Over time, individuals interpret and assimilate their experiences in these interactions, and form a general perception of the degree to which the friendship is intimate and meaningful (Reis, 1994). Recently, adolescents and young adults have turned to the Internet to help meet their need for self-disclosure.

When considering social media, there are numerous venues for sharing information about oneself with others, including private and public channels. Instant messaging systems provide a more private mode of communication, where messages (pictures, text, web links, and so on) are shared only with the recipient(s). On the other hand, social networking sites are a relatively public channel for which users can share information with their social network, including pictures (which can be tagged with the individual's identity), videos, web links, status updates, and a profile of the user him/herself (which may include user demographics, likes/dislikes, contact information, and educational/work information). Users also can respond to other members' posts through posting comments and/or sending a virtual like, which is shared with the poster's social network. Information such as age, religion, political views, and sexual preference are often viewed as non-private matters among young adolescents and are commonly shared on social network profiles (Livingstone, 2008). Although users have relative control over the information shared with members, with the option of presenting a false or real self, most emerging adults present their real self (Michikyan, Dennis, & Subrahmanyam, 2015).

Although social media may be propitious for friendships, face-to-face interactions seem to be preferred when interacting with existing friends. While self-disclosure is typically greater online than offline among strangers (Antheunis, Valkenburg, & Peter, 2007; Yang, Yang, & Chiou, 2010), adolescents and young adults report greater self-disclosure with friends in person compared to online exchanges (Huang & Yang, 2013; Schiffrin, Eldeman, Falkenstern, & Stewart, 2010; Valkenburg, Sumter, & Peter, 2011). Casual exchanges online with friends (e.g., discussing homework, offline plans, jokes, interests, funny videos, and events from the day) are three times more common than intimate disclosures (e.g., personal problems, opinions, and exactly what they are feeling) (Davis, 2012). Although self-disclosure may be less frequent online compared to offline, meaningful conversations between friends do still occur online. Indeed, users turn to social media to discuss sensitive topics or personal issues individuals find hard to discuss face-to-face with friends (Schouten, Valkenburg, & Peter, 2007; Yang et al., 2010). In interviews, adolescents indicated instant messaging their personal problems with their friends (Davis, 2012).

When considering the social consequences of using social media in general, two opposing hypotheses have been formulated: the displacement hypothesis and the stimulation hypothesis (Kraut et al., 1998; Valkenburg & Peter, 2011). The displacement hypothesis states that social media hinders the quality of existing friendships because online interactions, which are considered superficial, displaced time spent with friends and more meaningful interactions (Valkenburg & Peter, 2011). Prior to the turn of the century, much of the research examining outcomes associated with social media use has reported negative consequences, such as elevated levels of loneliness, social isolation, depression, and stress (Kraut et al., 1998; Nie & Erbring, 2000). In contrast, the stimulation hypothesis postulates that social media users primarily spend time online with existing friends, and that these interactions facilitate the maintenance and closeness of these relationships (Valkenburg & Peter, 2011). More recently, social media use predominantly has been associated with positive social consequences. Specifically, greater use is related to enhanced friendship quality (Blais, Craig, Pepler, & Connolly, 2008; Desjarlais & Willoughby, 2010; Subrahmanyam & Šmahel, 2011; Valkenburg & Peter, 2011), social connectedness (Bessiere, Kiesler, Kraut, & Boneva, 2008), social support (Wolak, Mitchell, & Finkelhor, 2003), number of friends (Antheunis et al., 2007), diversity of friends (Koutamanis, Vossen, Peter, & Valkenburg, 2013), and social capital (Antheunis, Schouten, & Krahmer, 2016), in addition to decreased feelings of loneliness (Deters & Mehl, 2013; Pittman & Reich, 2016).

Only a few recent studies reported negative effects of online social interaction. Some researchers suggest that already lonely and depressed individuals are drawn to the Internet rather than engagement in social media causing loneliness and depression (Amichai-Hamburger & Ben-Artzi, 2003; Caplan, 2003; Sun et al., 2005; van den Eijnden, Meerkerk, Vermulst, Spijkerman, & Engels, 2008). In contrast, it has also been argued that the time spent communicating online is related to increased loneliness because online communication is essentially a solitary activity, and although users are in contact with others, they are still physically alone (Stepanikova, Nie, & He, 2010; Turkle, 2011). And others indicate that the relation between loneliness and social media use may be related to its purpose of use. One study revealed that adolescents who actively used Facebook to compensate for poor social skills showed increases in loneliness, whereas adolescents who used Facebook to supplement offline interactions exhibited reductions in loneliness (Teppers, Luyckx, Klimstra, & Goossens, 2014).

The shift from negative to primarily positive social consequences of social media use over the years of research can be explained by the drastic increase in Internet use for social purposes among adolescents and young adults since the initial studies. Kraut and colleagues (1998) examined social media use among first time Internet users, and thus none of the participants' existing friends were online at the time. As such, time spent chatting online with unacquainted partners detracted quality time from interactions with existing offline friends. More recently, however, much of adolescents' social media friends consist of people who they interact with in the real world (Reich et al., 2012). Adolescents today embrace social media as a tool for socialization, using it predominantly to supplement rather than replace offline interactions with friends (Valkenburg & Peter, 2011). There is consensus among researchers that the positive social outcomes associated with today's social media use is a result of self-disclosure. Therefore, the next section will focus on the benefits associated with personal disclosure via social media and consider who may benefit most from online self-disclosure.

BENEFITS OF ONLINE SELF-DISCLOSURE

Much attention has been devoted to understanding why social media is attractive for disclosing personal information. According to Valkenburg and Peter's (2009b) Internet-enhanced self-disclosure hypothesis, online communication creates a comfortable context that facilitates self-disclosure, which in turn enhances the quality of friendships. Specifically, the anonymity and asynchronization afforded by social media enhance controllability of self-disclosure. When communicating with friends, users are afforded opportunities for audiovisual anonymity, which refers to the lack or reduction of nonverbal (visual or auditory) cues conveyed (Valkenburg & Peter, 2011). Users can choose the richness of the cues they wish to convey when interacting online, including the use of static images, video-conferencing, and voice messaging. In most social platforms, users also can reflect on and revise what they type before they send their message (Walther, 2007). Even with more synchronous conversations, such as instant messaging, users are still able to pause before pressing the send button.

For the most part, online self-disclosure does enrich friendships. Empirical research shows increased online self-disclosure is related to increases regarding closeness to friends (Desjarlais & Joseph, 2017; Pornsakulvanich, Haridakis, & Rubin, 2008; Valkenburg & Peter, 2009a), perceived support (Iacovelli & Johnson, 2012), social capital (Ellison, Steinfield, & Lampe, 2007), trust, understanding, commitment (Yum & Hara, 2005), and well-being (Joseph, Desjarlais, & Herceg, 2019; Valkenburg & Peter, 2007; Valkenburg et al., 2011). Furthermore, online self-disclosure has been positively related to offline self-disclosure, which in turn was associated with enhanced quality of communication among existing friends (Desjarlais & Joseph, 2017). Although empirical evidence supports the Internet-enhanced self-disclosure hypothesis, Valkenburg and Peter (2009b) suggest that the effects of online self-disclosure may be contingent upon situational and dispositional factors. Therefore, the question arose: who reaps the greatest benefits from online self-disclosure?

Within the literature, there are two main methods to assess factors that may influence online self-disclosure effects, including identifying and testing: (a) antecedents to online self-disclosure, and (b) moderating variables in the relation between online self-disclosure and friendship quality. First, since online self-disclosure is associated with positive outcomes for users, researchers argue that identifying characteristics of individuals who predominantly engage in online self-disclosure sheds light on whose friendships benefit the most from intimate online interactions (Valkenburg & Peter, 2009b). Within the literature, age, gender, and social competence have received much attention as predictors of online self-disclosure. In terms of age and gender, cross-sectional and longitudinal studies support that older adolescents disclose more information online compared to younger adolescents (Bonetti, Campbell & Gilmore, 2010; Bryce & Fraser, 2014), and typically girls disclose more than boys (Peter, Valkenburg, & Schouten, 2005; Punyanunt-Carter, 2006; Schouten et al., 2007; Valkenburg et al., 2011). Although these findings suggest greater benefits for both older and female adolescents, the author suggests that differences in self-disclosure are attributable to developmental differences among adolescents. In offline social situations, older adolescents disclose more personal information to friends than their younger peers (Bauminger et al., 2008; Schouten et al., 2007). In addition, adolescent girls report engaging in discussion and personal disclosure as a means of developing intimacy with their friends, whereas adolescent boys typically develop and sustain friendships through shared activities and interests (Mathur & Berndt, 2006). Since greater offline self-disclosure is associated with heightened online self-disclosure (Chiou & Wan, 2006; Schouten et al., 2007), online interactions may simply mimic offline interactions rather than being especially advantageous for older or female adolescents.

Next, the audiovisual anonymity and asynchronicity characteristics of social media can be particularly beneficial for adolescents who exhibit shyness and anxiety in offline interactions (Chan, 2011). In accordance, two opposing hypotheses were established based on differences in the relationship between social anxiety and online self-disclosure. The social compensation hypothesis postulates that a fear of evaluation may lead socially anxious individuals to turn to the Internet to communicate with peers to a greater extent than those with lower levels of social anxiety, resulting in greater positive outcomes for friendships among socially anxious users (Amichai-Hamburger, 2007; Kraut et al., 2002; Valkenburg, Peter, & Schouten, 2006). The reduced audiovisual cues associated with social media may alleviate inhibitions and shyness individuals typically experience in face-to-face interactions, and thus adolescents can more easily disclose themselves online, which enriches friendships. Indeed, people with higher levels of social anxiety were more likely to report using Facebook to compensate for personal inadequacies (Bodroža & Jovanović, 2016), perceive online communication as valuable for self-disclosure (Valkenburg & Peter, 2007; Weidman et al., 2012), and exhibit a greater decrease on average in social anxiety in online interactions (Yen et al., 2012) compared to less socially anxious peers. Similarly, introverted adolescents more frequently turned to social media to compensate for lacking social skills than extroverted individuals, and adopting this social compensation motive was associated with increased online self-disclosure (Peter et al., 2005; Schouten et al., 2007). Furthermore, people reporting higher social anxiety (Bonetti et al., 2010; Wang, Jackson, & Zhang, 2011; Weidman et al., 2012) or lower self-esteem (Hollenbaugh & Ferris, 2014) reported greater online self-disclosure.

In contrast, those who already have strong social skills may consider social-based technologies as another venue to interact with friends. The rich-get-richer (aka social enhancement) hypothesis proposes that adolescents who already have strong social skills in real life use online communication platforms as an additional method to interact with others, which provides them with additional opportunities to engage in meaningful interactions with existing friends and thereby greater social benefits than their less socially competent peers (Schouten et al., 2007; Valkenburg et al., 2006). Empirical evidence also supports this perspective. Findings from a cross-sectional survey show that increases in loneliness are related to decreases in online self-disclosure (Leung, 2002). Similarly, extroverted individuals who used social media to make connections disclosed more intimate personal information than others (Hollenbaugh

& Ferris, 2014), leading to increases in emotional, social and physical support from close online relationships (Weiqin, Campbell, Kimpton, Wozencroft, & Orel, 2016). Furthermore, longitudinal research supports a reciprocal relationship between adolescents' ability to initiate offline relationships and online self-disclosure with a close friend (Koutamanis et al., 2013). In other words, those with already strong social skills disclose more online which further strengthens their social skills.

It should be noted that some other studies have provided empirical evidence for both social compensation and enhancement perspectives, or no evidence for either perspective. For example, when considering curvilinear associations, the relationship between extroversion and frequency of leaving comments (a form of online self-disclosure) appeared as a U-shaped curve (Wang, Lv, & Zhang, 2018). This means that both low and high levels of extroversion engaged in heightened levels of self-disclosure, supporting both perspectives. On the other hand, researchers have reported no association between social anxiety and the following: Facebook self-disclosure (Green, Wilhelmsen, Wilmots, Dodd, & Quinn, 2016; Liu, Ang, & Lwin, 2013; McCord, Rodebaugh, & Levinson, 2014; Shaw, Timpano, Tran, & Joormann, 2015), number of status updates (Deters, Mehl, & Eid, 2016; Weidman & Levinson, 2015), and perceptions of Facebook social support (Indian & Grieve, 2014). Potentially, these studies may have missed important relationships by examining only linear relationships. In conclusion, there is empirical support for both the social compensation and rich-get-richer perspectives when considering antecedents for increased online self-disclosure.

Instead of examining antecedents for online self-disclosure, it has been argued that identification of whose friendships benefit most from intimate online interactions requires exploration of moderating variables (Desjarlais & Willoughby, 2010; Valkenburg & Peter, 2009b). In other words, research needs to shed light on the group of individuals for whom the relationship between online self-disclosure and closeness to friends, for example, is strongest. The few researchers who have adopted this perspective in the context of online self-disclosure have focused on people who struggle to make social connections, including social anxiety and self-esteem.

Desjarlais and Willoughby (2010) suggest that support for the social compensation hypothesis and the rich-get-richer hypothesis stems from identifying whether the positive association between social media use and friendship quality is stronger for adolescents with strong social skills (social enhancement) or are socially inept (social compensation). Therefore, they extended the frameworks of the social compensation and rich-get-richer hypotheses. In effect, the social compensation hypothesis postulates that adolescents with high levels of social anxiety who engage in online communication exhibit enriched friendships compared to their highly anxious peers who do not chat with their friends online. Conversely, the rich-get-richer hypothesis assumes that, as a result of strong social skills, less socially anxious adolescents who communicated with friends online exhibit more positive friendships compared to less socially anxious peers who engage less in online communication.

To directly test the reframed compensation and enhancement perspectives, Desjarlais and Willoughby (2010) examined whether the relation between engaging in online chat and friendship quality was dependent on social anxiety among adolescent girls and boys. Chatting online was associated with enhanced levels of friendship quality for adolescent girls, regardless of their level of social anxiety; which supported both the social compensation and rich-get-richer hypotheses. However, adolescent boys with higher levels of social anxiety reported more positive friendship quality if they engaged in online communication than if they did not, whereas, at low levels of social anxiety, engaging in online communication had no effect on friendship quality; supporting only the social compensation hypothesis (Desjarlais & Willoughby, 2010). The findings suggest that opportunities for self-disclosure benefit adolescent girls, socially anxious or not; whereas socially anxious adolescent boys may find it especially difficult to engage in meaningful discussions with friends and thus benefit most from the comfort of communicating online.

Social media may also be especially beneficial for people with low self-esteem. Individuals with low self-esteem possess a relatively low liking for themselves and are more socially anxious and introverted than those with high self-esteem (Leary & MacDonald, 2003). Although individuals with low self-esteem desire social connection (Anthony, Wood, & Holmes, 2007), they tend to have lower quality relationships and self-disclose less than their peers with higher self-esteem (Gaucher et al., 2012; Wood, Hogle, & McClellan, 2009). Similar to those with high social anxiety, sharing thoughts and feelings online may be more comfortable and less embarrassing for those with low self-esteem.

Forest and Wood (2012) compared the relationship between online self-disclosure and social rewards between young adults with high versus low self-esteem. In one of their experiments, undergraduate Facebook users provided their 10 most recent status updates, which were rated by three external blind coders for positivity and negativity. They also indicated the number of likes and the number of different people who commented on each of the posts (which were combined as an indicator of social reward). The effect of valence of posts on social reward did depend on participants' level of self-esteem. The more positivity participants with low self-esteem expressed in their status updates, the more comments/ likes they received from their Facebook friends. In contrast, participants with high self-esteem received more comments/likes from friends for their more negative updates compared to positive posts. According to Forest and Wood (2012), while friends may have been providing encouragement and support when individuals with high self-esteem seemed down, friends of users with low self-esteem may respond more for positive over negative posts in order to encourage this atypical behavior. Since likes and comments from friends and followers can indicate affirmation and support for another (Metzler & Scheithauer, 2017; Zhang, 2017), social media does have the potential to benefit adolescents with both low and high self-esteem, just in different situational contexts. However, given that negative updates are more common for people with low self-esteem, they may be less likely to reap the benefits social media has to offer in comparison to those with high self-esteem (Forest & Wood, 2012).

Empirical support for the social compensation hypothesis also emerges from research that examines whether social competence characteristics moderate the relationship between social media use in general (rather than self-disclosure specifically) and positive social outcomes. Socially anxious social media users benefit more in terms of connectedness with unfamiliar partners (Lundy & Drouin, 2016) and subjective well-being (Indian & Grieve, 2014) compared to those low in social anxiety. Young adults with lower self-esteem in particular benefit from Facebook use for the formation of casual relationships (Ellison et al., 2007; Steinfield, Ellison, & Lampe, 2008). Similarly, at low levels of social competence, more text messaging on the previous day was associated with less current day stress; whereas, there was no association between text-messaging and stress at high levels of social competence (Ruppel, Burke, Cherney, & Dinsmore, 2017).

Overall, there is mixed support for the social compensation and rich-get-richer perspectives when considering predictors of online self-disclosure. On the other hand, there is substantial support for the social compensation hypothesis when examining social competence characteristics of social media users as moderators for the relationship between online self-disclosure and social consequences. Adolescents and young adults with social anxieties or weak social skills, on average, exhibit more positive friendship quality the more they disclose personal information to friends online or compared to less socially anxious peers. Despite the increasing attention researchers have devoted to understanding the effects of social media use in general, and for online self-disclosure specifically, social media research is still in its infancy. As such, suggestions for future research are provided in the next section.

DIRECTIONS FOR FUTURE RESEARCH

Although knowledge pertaining to the social effects of social media use has rapidly grown, there are areas that still require additional attention. First, research on the social compensation perspective primarily has focused on those who exhibit difficulties in social situations, including social anxiety, low self-esteem, and loneliness. Given the centrality of self-disclosure to friendship quality, it is plausible that the benefits of online self-disclosure may extend to anyone who has limited opportunities for intimate discussions offline. In addition to dispositional traits, stress, school commitments, work schedules, and home responsibilities also may limit opportunities young adults have to spend with their friends, and thereby strain existing friendships. Since social media is used to supplement rather than replace offline interactions with friends (Valkenburg & Peter, 2011), online self-disclosure may not only compensate for those who struggle in social situations, but also for those who struggle to find time to arrange in person interactions with friends. Future research is required to assess whether friendships are better maintained in the latter situation if individuals engage more in online self-disclosure.

Second, most support for the social compensation hypothesis has been from cross-sectional studies, and of the few longitudinal studies included most only followed participants for a year (e.g., Valkenburg et al., 2011). There is an obvious call for more longitudinal research to more fully understanding the long-term consequences of social media use for adolescents and young adults. Although empirical evidence supports that social benefits are accrued from online self-disclosure for socially anxious individuals, these benefits appear to be relatively small. For example, engaging in online chat accounted for 3% of the variance in friendship quality whereas social anxiety accounted for 16% of the variance (Desjarlais & Willoughby, 2010). However, there is the potential that benefits may accumulate over time for those with high social anxiety. Continued use of social media may provide those with high social anxiety with opportunities to make meaningful connections with friends and practice social skills they otherwise may have missed out on because of their tendency to shy away from social situations. The added self-disclosure moments may eventually lessen the gap in the quality of friendships between socially anxious and socially competent adolescents over time, through increased meaningful interactions and/or practice of social skills. Overall, online communication does influence offline social competence (Desjarlais & Joseph, 2017; Koutamanis et al., 2013), and this may be especially beneficial for those with low social competence.

On the other hand, there is concern that the control social media provides over self-disclosure could severely impact face-to-face interactions in the long-term (Turkle, 2011). Although in the short-term social media appears beneficial for friendships, heavy social media users may engage in less and less face-to-face interactions over time, which may be particularly damaging for those with already weak friendships or social skills. Using path analysis, Kim, LaRose, and Peng (2009) showed that young adults who were lonely or with deficient social skills adopted a stronger preference for online interaction, which in turn was related to compulsive or problematic Internet use. Also, problematic Internet use resulted in negative life outcomes (e.g., harming significant interpersonal relationships), which led to more loneliness. If social media use begins during pre-adolescence, then many interactions with friends will occur in a virtual space during a critical period of social development. Opportunities to develop interpersonal competence (e.g., initiating relationships, asserting displeasure with others' actions, self-disclosure of personal information with the presence of audiovisual cues, and managing interpersonal conflict) may be impeded, which could have detrimental effects when adolescents grow up. Currently, adolescents are expressing challenges for carrying on a synchronous conversation (Turkle, 2011). Therefore, longitudinal studies are required to identify the positive and negative effects of adolescents' online self-disclosure for their adult relationships.

DRAWBACKS OF ONLINE SELF-DISCLOSURE

When considering the effects of online self-disclosure between existing friends specifically, research emphasizes opportunities for adolescents and young adults. However, considering that disclosures on social networking sites, such as Facebook or Instagram, reach beyond the user's close social network, the sharing of personal information can be risky. Therefore, the purpose of the current section is to highlight the literature regarding drawbacks to sharing personal information on social networking sites so readers have enough information to make an informed decision (or can provide advice to others) regarding what they post on public channels.

Deciding what to share on social networking sites comes with its challenges. As a consequence of the low source anonymity (i.e., information can be attributed to a specific individual) in a relatively pubic context consisting of multiple audiences (i.e., friends, family members, relatives, colleagues, acquaintances), social network users typically are cautious about how they present themselves (Marder, Joinson, Shankar, & Houghton, 2016). According to the 'chilling effect', because of the high surveillance on social networking sites, users carefully manage their online self to meet perceived expectations of their social network (Marwick & boyd, 2011). This often includes users holding back to avoid an undesirable impression (Marwick & boyd, 2011). Indeed, youths admit to self-censorship of posts (Das & Kramer, 2013; Xie & Kang, 2015), untagging their identify from undesirable photos uploaded and tagged by others (Lang & Barton, 2015), altering posts to impress others (Chua & Chang, 2016), and refrain altogether from certain topics of conversation (Marwick & boyd, 2011). The presence of a diverse Facebook network is related to greater online tension (Binder, Howes, & Sutcliffe, 2009), posting regret (Xie & Kang, 2015), and presenting a desirable rather than completely true portrayal of oneself (Chua & Chang, 2016). This may have negative implications for adolescents' developing self-concept (Reid, 1998).

In addition, when personal information is accessible by people or groups other than the intended audience, there is the potential and real risk of victimization. Greater disclosure increases chances of identity theft, trafficking, cyber stalking, and privacy invasion (Hasebrink, Livingstone, Haddon, & Olafsson, 2009; Li, Lin, & Wang, 2015). In one study of online bullying, 72% of adolescent respondents experienced at least one incident in the past year (Juvonen & Gross, 2008). Furthermore, one's postings can be incriminating, sometimes resulting in social or psychological risks. Posting stories about engagement in risky behaviors, including underage drinking, drug experiences, and involvement in illegal activities, can result in school suspensions or criminal charges (Peluchette & Karl, 2008). In addition, conflicts with parents (Youn, 2005), declines for job offers from employers (Schultz, Koehler, Philippe, & Coronel, 2015), and feelings of jealousy in response to ambiguous information posted by a romantic partner (Muise, Christofides, & Desmarais, 2009) have occurred from information shared on social media. Finally, users have experienced regret for posting about sensitive topics, lies, and personal secrets on social networking sites (Wang et al., 2011b), and in an attempt to rectify the situation have deleted pictures or comments, or posted fake information (Das & Kramer, 2013). People may not think about the consequences of what they post or how the posts will be perceived by the target audience, are emotional when posting, or consider that posts may be seen by unintended audiences (Wang et al., 2011b). Therefore, while posting personal information may facilitate connections with friends, at the same time the information has the potential to be socially and psychologically damaging if used in unintended ways by unintended recipients.

RECOMMENDATIONS

In order to experience benefits associated with online connections, one must share information with friends. It is important then for users, parents, educators, clinicians, and policymakers, to consider the following to promote healthy use of social media. First, social media provides opportunities for those with low social competence to interact with friends that they may have opted out of otherwise. Youth who struggle in social situations and turn to social media can be encouraged to share information about themselves with friends through private (safer) channels in attempt to enrich social skills and intimacy development. At the same time, however, it is imperative to acknowledge the limitations of the benefits associated with online self-disclosure. The literature suggests small effects for connectedness between friends, even for those who struggle in real life social situations. And although online communication has the potential to afford users with opportunities to practice social skills (Koutamanis et al., 2013), online interactions tend to be disjointed from real life (Davis, 2012) and there is no evidence for long-term improvements in social competence. Thus, while online disclosure can facilitate social situations it not should replace key real-life socialization. Furthermore, heavy social media use can impede other areas of life that are also essential for psychosocial development, including sleep (Tavernier & Willoughby, 2014), family connection (Padilla-Walker, Coyne, & Fraser, 2012), and academic success (Jacobsen & Forste, 2011). Youths or parents can monitor social media use and set limits on times and contexts appropriate for use.

Second, considerations of the benefits associated with online self-disclosure must be paired with acknowledgement of the potential risks. Encouraging users to consider privacy settings, appropriate channels for sharing personal information (i.e., private over public channels), and thinking about the consequence about what they post prior to sharing may mitigate the risk of online self-disclosure. Adolescents and adults who are knowledgeable of the consequences of disclosing online are less likely to share personal information and more likely to protect their privacy (Christofides, Muise, & Desmarais, 2012).

CONCLUSION

Level of social competence, in itself or that which stems from social anxiety, self-esteem, or loneliness, does predict online self-disclosure as well as changes in the level of benefit experienced by users when disclosing online. People who struggle with offline interactions tend to exhibit the greatest benefits from social media use and online self-disclosure for social connections. Audiovisual anonymity and asynchronous conversation style afforded by social media appear to create a comfortable environment for those experiencing social awkwardness or discomfort. However, it should be noted that although greater benefits are observed for those struggling in social situations, online self-disclosure does not completely dissolve differences observed in ratings of friendship quality between socially competent and socially anxious individuals. Instead, socially anxious individuals exhibit less poor friendships compared to those more socially competent when using social media. In conclusion, social media should not be perceived as the solution for those struggling with face-to-face social interactions, but rather as a potential aid that produces some short-term benefits for interpersonal relationships. This recommendation, however, is cautioned as the opportunities afforded by online disclosure for relationship development are paired with potential and real social and psychological risks when personal information is used in an unintended fashion or seen by unintended audiences.

ACKNOWLEDGMENT

This research received no specific grant from any funding agency in the public, commercial, or not-for-profit sectors.

REFERENCES

Amichai-Hamburger, Y. (2007). Personality, individual differences and Internet use. In A. Joinson, K. McKenna, T. Postmes, & U. D. Reips (Eds.), *The Oxford handbook of Internet psychology* (pp. 187–204). Oxford, UK: Oxford University Press.

Amichai-Hamburger, Y., & Ben-Artzi, E. (2003). Loneliness and Internet use. *Computers in Human Behavior*, *19*(1), 71–80. doi:10.1016/S0747-5632(02)00014-6

Antheunis, M. L., Schouten, A. P., & Krahmer, E. (2016). The role of social networking sites in early adolescents' social lives. *The Journal of Early Adolescence*, *36*(3), 348–371. doi:10.1177/0272431614564060

Antheunis, M. L., Valkenburg, P. M., & Peter, J. (2007). Computer-mediated communication and interpersonal attraction: An experimental test of two explanatory hypotheses. *Cyberpsychology & Behavior*, *10*(6), 831–836. doi:10.1089/cpb.2007.9945 PMID:18085973

Anthony, D. B., Wood, J. V., & Holmes, J. G. (2007). Testing sociometer theory: Self-esteem and the importance of acceptance for social decision-making. *Journal of Experimental Social Psychology*, *43*(3), 425–432. doi:10.1016/j.jesp.2006.03.002

Baumeister, R. F., & Leary, M. R. (1995). The need to belong: Desire for interpersonal attachments as a fundamental human motivation. *Psychological Bulletin*, *117*(3), 497–529. doi:10.1037/0033-2909.117.3.497 PMID:7777651

Bauminger, N., Finzi-Dottan, R., Chason, S., & Har-Even, D. (2008). Intimacy in adolescent friendship: The roles of attachment, coherence, and self-disclosure. *Journal of Social and Personal Relationships*, *25*(3), 409–428. doi:10.1177/0265407508090866

Bessiere, K., Kiesler, S., Kraut, R., & Boneva, B. S. (2008). Effects of Internet use and social resources on changes in depression. *Information Communication and Society*, *11*(1), 47–70. doi:10.1080/13691180701858851

Binder, J., Howes, A., & Sutcliffe, A. (2009, April). The problem of conflicting social spheres: effects of network structure on experienced tension in social network sites. In *Proceedings of the SIGCHI conference on human factors in computing systems* (pp. 965-974). ACM. 10.1145/1518701.1518849

Blais, J. J., Craig, W. M., Pepler, D., & Connolly, J. (2008). Adolescents online: The importance of Internet activity choices to salient relationships. *Journal of Youth and Adolescence, 37*(5), 522–536. doi:10.100710964-007-9262-7

Bodroža, B., & Jovanović, T. (2016). Validation of the new scale for measuring behaviors of Facebook users: Psycho-Social Aspects of Facebook Use (PSAFU). *Computers in Human Behavior, 54*, 425–435. doi:10.1016/j.chb.2015.07.032

Bonetti, L., Campbell, M. A., & Gilmore, L. (2010). The relationship of loneliness and social anxiety with children's and adolescents' online communication. *Cyberpsychology, Behavior, and Social Networking, 13*(3), 279–285. doi:10.1089/cyber.2009.0215 PMID:20557247

boyd, d. m., & Ellison, N. B. (2007). Social network sites: Definition, history, and scholarship. *Journal of Computer-Mediated Communication, 13*, 210-230. doi:10.1111/j.1083-6101.2007.00393.x

Bryce, J., & Fraser, J. (2014). The role of disclosure of personal information in the evaluation of risk and trust in young peoples' online interactions. *Computers in Human Behavior, 30*, 299–306. doi:10.1016/j.chb.2013.09.012

Buhrmester, D. (1990). Intimacy of friendship, interpersonal competence, and adjustment during preadolescence and adolescence. *Child Development, 61*(4), 1101–1111. doi:10.2307/1130878 PMID:2209180

Caplan, S. E. (2003). Preference for online social interaction: A theory of problematic Internet use and psychosocial well-being. *Communication Research, 30*(6), 625–648. doi:10.1177/0093650203257842

Chan, A. T., & Lee, S. K. (2014). Education plans, personal challenges and academic difficulties: An empirical study on self-disclosure among post-90s teens in Hong Kong. *International Journal of Adolescence and Youth, 19*(4), 468–483. doi:10.1080/02673843.2012.751042

Chan, M. (2011). Shyness, sociability, and the role of media synchronicity in the use of computer-mediated communication for interpersonal communication. *Asian Journal of Social Psychology, 141*, 84–90. doi:10.1111/j.1467-839X.2010.01335.x

Chiou, W. B., & Wan, C. S. (2006). Sexual self-disclosure in cyberspace among Taiwanese adolescents: Gender differences and the interplay of cyberspace and real life. *Cyberpsychology & Behavior, 9*(1), 46–53. doi:10.1089/cpb.2006.9.46 PMID:16497117

Christofides, E., Muise, A., & Desmarais, S. (2012). Risky disclosures on Facebook: The effect of having a bad experience on online behavior. *Journal of Adolescent Research, 27*(6), 714–731. doi:10.1177/0743558411432635

Chua, T. H. H., & Chang, L. (2016). Follow me and like my beautiful selfies: Singapore teenage girls' engagement in self-presentation and peer comparison on social media. *Computers in Human Behavior, 55*, 190–197. doi:10.1016/j.chb.2015.09.011

Das, S., & Kramer, A. (2013, June). Self-censorship on Facebook. In *Proceedings of the Seventh International AAAI Conference on Weblogs and Social Media* (pp. 120–127). Washington, DC: Association for the Advancement of Artificial Intelligence.

Davis, K. (2012). Friendship 2.0: Adolescents' experiences of belonging and self-disclosure online. *Journal of Adolescence*, *35*(6), 1527–1536. doi:10.1016/j.adolescence.2012.02.013 PMID:22475444

Desjarlais, M., & Joseph, J. J. (2017). Socially interactive and passive technologies enhance friendship quality: An investigation of the mediating roles of online and offline self-disclosure. *Cyberpsychology, Behavior, and Social Networking*, *20*(5), 286–291. doi:10.1089/cyber.2016.0363 PMID:28418718

Desjarlais, M., & Willoughby, T. (2010). A longitudinal study of the relation between adolescent boys and girls' computer use with friends and friendship quality: Support for the social compensation or the rich-get-richer hypothesis? *Computers in Human Behavior*, *26*(5), 896–905. doi:10.1016/j.chb.2010.02.004

Deters, F. G., & Mehl, M. R. (2013). Does posting Facebook status updates increase or decrease loneliness? An online social networking experiment. *Social Psychological & Personality Science*, *4*(5), 579–586. doi:10.1177/1948550612469233 PMID:24224070

Deters, F. G., Mehl, M. R., & Eid, M. (2016). Social responses to Facebook status updates: The role of extraversion and social anxiety. *Computers in Human Behavior*, *61*, 1–13. doi:10.1016/j.chb.2016.02.093

Ellison, N. B., Steinfield, C., & Lampe, C. (2007). The benefits of Facebook 'friends': Social capital and college students' use of online social network sites. *Journal of Computer-Mediated Communication*, *12*(4), 1143–1168. doi:10.1111/j.1083-6101.2007.00367.x

Forest, A. L., & Wood, J. V. (2012). When social networking is not working: Individuals with low self-esteem recognize but do not reap the benefits of self-disclosure on Facebook. *Psychological Science*, *23*(3), 295–302. doi:10.1177/0956797611429709 PMID:22318997

Gaucher, D., Wood, J., Stinson, D., Forest, A., Holmes, J., & Logel, C. (2012). Perceived regard explains self-esteem differences in expressivity. *Personality and Social Psychology Bulletin*, *38*(9), 1144–1156. doi:10.1177/0146167212445790 PMID:22711742

Green, T., Wilhelmsen, T., Wilmots, E., Dodd, B., & Quinn, S. (2016). Social anxiety, attributes of online communication and self-disclosure across private and public Facebook communication. *Computers in Human Behavior*, *58*, 206–213. doi:10.1016/j.chb.2015.12.066

Hasebrink, U., Livingstone, S., Haddon, L., & Olafsson, K. (2009). *Comparing children's online opportunities and risks across Europe: Cross-national comparisons for EU Kids Online*. EU Kids Online.

Henderson, M., Snyder, I., & Beale, D. (2013). Social media for collaborative learning: A review of school literature. *Australian Educational Computing*, *28*(2). Available at http://journal.acce.edu.au/index.php/AEC/article/view/18

Hollenbaugh, E. E., & Ferris, A. L. (2014). Facebook self-disclosure: Examining the role of traits, social cohesion, and motives. *Computers in Human Behavior*, *30*, 50–58. doi:10.1016/j.chb.2013.07.055

Huang, C. L., & Yang, S. C. (2013). A study of online misrepresentation, self-disclosure, cyber-relationship motives, and loneliness among teenagers in Taiwan. *Journal of Educational Computing Research, 48*(1), 1–18. doi:10.2190/EC.48.1.a

Iacovelli, A. M., & Johnson, C. (2012). Disclosure through face-to-face and instant messaging modalities: Psychological and physiological effects. *Journal of Social and Clinical Psychology, 31*(3), 225–250. doi:10.1521/jscp.2012.31.3.225

Indian, M., & Grieve, R. (2014). When Facebook is easier than face-to-face: Social support derived from Facebook in socially anxious individuals. *Personality and Individual Differences, 59*, 102–106. doi:10.1016/j.paid.2013.11.016

Jacobsen, W. C., & Forste, R. (2011). The wired generation: Academic and social outcomes of electronic media use among university students. *Cyberpsychology, Behavior, and Social Networking, 14*(5), 275–280. doi:10.1089/cyber.2010.0135 PMID:20961220

Jose, P. E., Ryan, N., & Pryor, J. (2012). Does social connectedness promote a greater sense of well-being in adolescence over time? *Journal of Research on Adolescence, 22*(2), 235–251. doi:10.1111/j.1532-7795.2012.00783.x

Joseph, J. J., Desjarlais, M., & Herceg, L. (2019). Facebook depression or Facebook contentment: The relation between Facebook use and well-Being. In R. T. Gopalan (Ed.), Intimacy and Developing Personal Relationships in the Virtual World (pp. 104–125). Hershey, PA: IGI Global. doi:10.4018/978-1-5225-4047-2.ch007

Juvonen, J., & Gross, E. F. (2008). Extending the school grounds? - Bullying experiences in cyberspace. *The Journal of School Health, 78*(9), 496–505. doi:10.1111/j.1746-1561.2008.00335.x PMID:18786042

Kim, J., LaRose, R., & Peng, W. (2009). Loneliness as the cause and the effect of problematic Internet use: The relationship between Internet use and psychological well-being. *Cyberpsychology & Behavior, 12*(4), 451–455. doi:10.1089/cpb.2008.0327 PMID:19514821

Koutamanis, M., Vossen, H. G., Peter, J., & Valkenburg, P. M. (2013). Practice makes perfect: The longitudinal effect of adolescents' instant messaging on their ability to initiate offline friendships. *Computers in Human Behavior, 29*(6), 2265–2272. doi:10.1016/j.chb.2013.04.033

Kraut, R., Kiesler, S., Boneva, B., Cummings, J., Helgeson, V., & Crawford, A. (2002). Internet paradox revisited. *The Journal of Social Issues, 58*(1), 49–74. doi:10.1111/1540-4560.00248

Kraut, R., Patterson, M., Lundmark, V., Kiesler, S., Mukopadhyay, T., & Scherlis, W. (1998). Internet paradox: A social technology that reduces social involvement and psychological well being? *The American Psychologist, 53*(9), 1017–1031. doi:10.1037/0003-066X.53.9.1017 PMID:9841579

Lang, C., & Barton, H. (2015). Just untag it: Exploring the management of undesirable Facebook photos. *Computers in Human Behavior, 43*, 147–155. doi:10.1016/j.chb.2014.10.051

Laurenceau, J. P., Barrett, L. F., & Pietromonaco, P. R. (1998). Intimacy as an interpersonal process: The importance of self-disclosure, partner disclosure, and perceived partner responsiveness in interpersonal exchanges. *Journal of Personality and Social Psychology*, *74*(5), 1238–1251. doi:10.1037/0022-3514.74.5.1238 PMID:9599440

Leary, M. R., & MacDonald, G. (2003). Individual differences in trait self-esteem: A theoretical integration. In M. Leary, & J. Tangney (Eds.), *Handbook of self and identity* (pp. 401–418). New York, NY: Guilford Press.

Leung, L. (2002). Loneliness, self-disclosure, and ICQ ("I Seek You") use. *Cyberpsychology & Behavior*, *5*(3), 241–251. doi:10.1089/109493102760147240 PMID:12123247

Li, K., Lin, Z., & Wang, X. (2015). An empirical analysis of users' privacy disclosure behaviors on social network sites. *Information & Management*, *52*(7), 882–891. doi:10.1016/j.im.2015.07.006

Liu, C., Ang, R. P., & Lwin, M. O. (2013). Cognitive, personality, and social factors associated with adolescents' online personal information disclosure. *Journal of Adolescence*, *36*(4), 629–638. doi:10.1016/j.adolescence.2013.03.016 PMID:23849657

Livingstone, S. (2008). Taking risky opportunities in youthful content creation: Teenagers' use of social networking sites for intimacy, privacy and self-expression. *New Media & Society*, *10*(3), 393–411. doi:10.1177/1461444808089415

Lundy, B. L., & Drouin, M. (2016). From social anxiety to interpersonal connectedness: Relationship building within face-to-face, phone and instant messaging mediums. *Computers in Human Behavior*, *54*, 271–277. doi:10.1016/j.chb.2015.08.004

Marder, B., Joinson, A., Shankar, A., & Houghton, D. (2016). The extended 'chilling' effect of Facebook: The cold reality of ubiquitous social networking. *Computers in Human Behavior*, *60*, 582–592. doi:10.1016/j.chb.2016.02.097

Marion, D., Laursen, B., Zettergren, P., & Bergman, L. R. (2013). Predicting life satisfaction during middle adulthood from peer relationships during mid-adolescence. *Journal of Youth and Adolescence*, *42*(8), 1299–1307. doi:10.100710964-013-9969-6 PMID:23771820

Marwick, A. E., & Boyd, D. (2011). I tweet honestly, I tweet passionately: Twitter users, context collapse, and the imagined audience. *New Media & Society*, *13*(1), 114–133. doi:10.1177/1461444810365313

Mathur, R., & Berndt, T. J. (2006). Relations of friends' activities to friendship quality. *The Journal of Early Adolescence*, *26*(3), 365–388. doi:10.1177/0272431606288553

McCord, B., Rodebaugh, T. L., & Levinson, C. A. (2014). Facebook: Social uses and anxiety. *Computers in Human Behavior*, *34*, 23–27. doi:10.1016/j.chb.2014.01.020

Metzler, A., & Scheithauer, H. (2017). The long-term benefits of positive self-presentation via profile pictures, number of friends and the initiation of relationships on Facebook for adolescents' self-esteem and the initiation of offline relationships. *Frontiers in Psychology*, *8*, 1–15. doi:10.3389/fpsyg.2017.01981 PMID:29187827

Michikyan, M., Dennis, J., & Subrahmanyam, K. (2015). Can you guess who I am? Real, ideal, and false self-presentation on Facebook among emerging adults. *Emerging Adulthood, 3*(1), 55–64. doi:10.1177/2167696814532442

Muise, A., Christofides, E., & Desmarais, S. (2009). More information than you ever wanted: Does Facebook bring out the green-eyed monster of jealousy? *Cyberpsychology & Behavior, 12*(4), 441–444. doi:10.1089/cpb.2008.0263 PMID:19366318

Nie, N. H., & Erbring, L. (2002). Internet and society: A preliminary report. *IT & Society, 1*, 275-283.

Padilla-Walker, L. M., Coyne, S. M., & Fraser, A. M. (2012). Getting a high-speed family connection: Associations between family media use and family connection. *Family Relations, 61*(3), 426–440. doi:10.1111/j.1741-3729.2012.00710.x

Peluchette, J., & Karl, K. (2008). Social networking profiles: An examination of student attitudes regarding use and appropriateness of content. *Cyberpsychology & Behavior, 11*(1), 95–97. doi:10.1089/cpb.2007.9927 PMID:18275320

Peter, J., Valkenburg, P. M., & Schouten, A. P. (2005). Developing a model of adolescent friendship formation on the Internet. *Cyberpsychology & Behavior, 8*(5), 423–430. doi:10.1089/cpb.2005.8.423 PMID:16232035

Pittman, M., & Reich, B. (2016). Social media and loneliness: Why an Instagram picture may be worth more than a thousand Twitter words. *Computers in Human Behavior, 62*, 155–167. doi:10.1016/j.chb.2016.03.084

Pornsakulvanich, V., Haridakis, P., & Rubin, A. M. (2008). The influence of dispositions and Internet motivation on online communication satisfaction and relationship closeness. *Computers in Human Behavior, 24*(5), 2292–2310. doi:10.1016/j.chb.2007.11.003

Punyanunt-Carter, N. M. (2006). An analysis of college students' self-disclosure behaviors on the internet. *College Student Journal, 40*, 329–331.

Reich, S. M., Subrahmanyam, K., & Espinoza, G. (2012). Friending, IMing, and hanging out face-to-face: Overlap in adolescents' online and offline social networks. *Developmental Psychology, 48*(2), 356–368. doi:10.1037/a0026980 PMID:22369341

Reid, E. (1998). The self and the internet: Variations on the illusion of one self. In J. Gackenbach (Ed.), *Psychology and the Internet: Intrapersonal, Interpersonal, and Transpersonal Implications* (pp. 29–41). San Diego, CA: Academic Press.

Reis, H. T. (1994). Domains of experience: Investigating relationship processes from three perspectives. In R. Erber, & R. Gilmore (Eds.), *Theoretical frameworks in personal relationships* (pp. 87–110). Hillsdale, NJ: Erlbaum.

Reis, H. T., & Patrick, B. P. (1996). Attachment and intimacy: Component processes. In E. T. Higgins, & A. W. Kruglanski (Eds.), *Social psychology: Handbook of basic principles* (pp. 523–563). New York, NY: Guilford.

Reis, H. T., & Shaver, P. (1988). Intimacy as an interpersonal process. In S. Duck (Ed.), *Handbook of personal relationships* (pp. 367–389). Chichester, UK: Wiley.

Ruppel, E. K., Burke, T. J., Cherney, M. R., & Dinsmore, D. R. (2017). Social Compensation and enhancement via mediated communication in the transition to college. *Human Communication Research, 44*(1), 58–79. doi:10.1093/hcr/hqx003

Ryan, T., Allen, K. A., Gray, D. L., & McInerney, D. M. (2017). How social are social media? A review of online social behaviour and connectedness. *Journal of Relationships Research, 8*, e8. doi:10.1017/jrr.2017.13

Schiffrin, H., Edelman, A., Falkenstern, M., & Stewart, C. (2010). The associations among computer-mediated communication, relationships, and well-being. *Cyberpsychology, Behavior, and Social Networking, 13*(3), 299–306. doi:10.1089/cyber.2009.0173 PMID:20557249

Schouten, A. P., Valkenburg, P. M., & Peter, J. (2007). Precursors and underlying processes of adolescents' online self-disclosure: Developing and testing an "Internet-Attribute-Perception" model. *Media Psychology, 10*(2), 292–315. doi:10.1080/15213260701375686

Schultz, M. D., Koehler, J. W., Philippe, T. W., & Coronel, R. S. (2015). Managing the effects of social media in organizations. *S.A.M. Advanced Management Journal, 80*, 42–47.

Shaw, A. M., Timpano, K. R., Tran, T. B., & Joormann, J. (2015). Correlates of Facebook usage patterns: The relationship between passive Facebook use, social anxiety symptoms, and brooding. *Computers in Human Behavior, 48*, 575–580. doi:10.1016/j.chb.2015.02.003

Smith, A., & Anderson, M. (2018). Social media use in 2018: A majority of Americans use Facebook and YouTube, but young adults are especially heavy users of Snapchat and Instagram. *Pew Research Center.* Retrieved from http://www.pewinternet.org/wp-content/uploads/sites/9/2018/02/PI_2018.03.01_Social-Media_FINAL.pdf

Sprecher, S., Treger, S., Wondra, J. D., Hilaire, N., & Wallpe, K. (2013). Taking turns: Reciprocal self-disclosure promotes liking in initial interactions. *Journal of Experimental Social Psychology, 49*(5), 860–866. doi:10.1016/j.jesp.2013.03.017

Steinfield, C., Ellison, N. B., & Lampe, C. (2008). Social capital, self-esteem, and use of online social network sites: A longitudinal analysis. *Journal of Applied Developmental Psychology, 29*(6), 434–445. doi:10.1016/j.appdev.2008.07.002

Stepanikova, I., Nie, N. H., & He, X. (2010). Time on the internet at home, loneliness, and life satisfaction: Evidence from panel time-diary data. *Computers in Human Behavior, 26*(3), 329–338. doi:10.1016/j.chb.2009.11.002

Subrahmanyam, K., & Šmahel, D. (2011). Intimacy and the Internet: Relationships with friends, romantic partners, and family members. In K. Subrahmanyam, & D. Šmahel (Eds.), *Digital youth* (pp. 81–102). New York, NY: Springer. doi:10.1007/978-1-4419-6278-2_5

Sun, P., Unger, J. B., Palmer, P. H., Gallaher, P., Chou, C. P., Baezconde-Garbanati, L., ... Johnson, C. A. (2005). Internet accessibility and usage among urban adolescents in Southern California: Implications for web-based health research. *Cyberpsychology & Behavior, 8*(5), 441–453. doi:10.1089/cpb.2005.8.441 PMID:16232037

Tavernier, R., & Willoughby, T. (2014). Sleep problems: Predictor or outcome of media use among emerging adults at university? *Journal of Sleep Research, 23*(4), 389–396. doi:10.1111/jsr.12132 PMID:24552437

Teppers, E., Luyckx, K., Klimstra, T. A., & Goossens, L. (2014). Loneliness and Facebook motives in adolescence: A longitudinal inquiry into directionality of effect. *Journal of Adolescence, 37*, 691–699. doi:10.1016/j.adolescence.2013.11.003 PMID:24321573

Turkle, S. (2011). *Alone together: Why we expect more from technology and less from each other*. Philadelphia, PA: Basic Books.

Valkenburg, P. M., & Peter, J. (2007). Preadolescents' and adolescents' online communication and their closeness to friends. *Developmental Psychology, 43*(2), 267–277. doi:10.1037/0012-1649.43.2.267 PMID:17352538

Valkenburg, P. M., & Peter, J. (2009a). The effects of instant messaging on the quality of Adolescents' existing friendships: A longitudinal study. *Journal of Communication, 59*(1), 79–97. doi:10.1111/j.1460-2466.2008.01405.x

Valkenburg, P. M., & Peter, J. (2009b). Social Consequences of the internet for adolescents: A decade of research. *Current Directions in Psychological Science, 18*(1), 1–5. doi:10.1111/j.1467-8721.2009.01595.x

Valkenburg, P. M., & Peter, J. (2011). Online communication among adolescents: An integrated model of its attraction, opportunities, and risks. *The Journal of Adolescent Health, 48*(2), 121–127. doi:10.1016/j.jadohealth.2010.08.020 PMID:21257109

Valkenburg, P. M., Peter, J., & Schouten, A. P. (2006). Friend networking sites and their relationship to adolescents' well-being and social self-esteem. *Cyberpsychology & Behavior, 9*(5), 584–590. doi:10.1089/cpb.2006.9.584 PMID:17034326

Valkenburg, P. M., Sumter, S. R., & Peter, J. (2011). Gender differences in online and offline self-disclosure in preadolescence and adolescence. *British Journal of Developmental Psychology, 29*(2), 253–269. doi:10.1348/2044-835X.002001 PMID:21199497

van den Eijnden, R. J. J. M., Meerkerk, G. J., Vermulst, A. A., Spijkerman, R., & Engels, R. C. M. E. (2008). Online communication, compulsive internet use, and psychosocial well-being among adolescents: A longitudinal study. *Developmental Psychology, 44*(3), 655–665. doi:10.1037/0012-1649.44.3.655 PMID:18473634

Walther, J. B. (2007). Selective self-presentation in computer-mediated communication: Hyperpersonal dimensions of technology, language, and cognition. *Computers in Human Behavior, 23*(5), 2538–2557. doi:10.1016/j.chb.2006.05.002

Wang, J. L., Jackson, L. A., & Zhang, D. J. (2011a). The mediator role of self-disclosure and moderator roles of gender and social anxiety in the relationship between Chinese adolescents' online communication and their real-world social relationships. *Computers in Human Behavior*, *27*(6), 2161–2168. doi:10.1016/j.chb.2011.06.010

Wang, K., Lv, Y., & Zhang, Z. (2018). Relationship between extroversion and social use of social networking sites. *Social Behavior and Personality*, *46*(10), 1597–1609. doi:10.2224bp.7210

Wang, Y., Norcie, G., Komanduri, S., Acquisti, A., Leon, P. G., & Cranor, L. F. (2011b, July). I regretted the minute I pressed share: A qualitative study of regrets on Facebook. In *Proceedings of the seventh symposium on usable privacy and security* (p. 10). ACM. 10.1145/2078827.2078841

Weidman, A. C., Fernandez, K. C., Levinson, C. A., Augustine, A. A., Larsen, R. J., & Rodebaugh, T. L. (2012). Compensatory internet use among individuals higher in social anxiety and its implications for well-being. *Personality and Individual Differences*, *53*(3), 191–195. doi:10.1016/j.paid.2012.03.003 PMID:22791928

Weidman, A. C., & Levinson, C. A. (2015). I'm still socially anxious online: Offline relationship impairment characterizing social anxiety manifests and is accurately perceived in online social networking profiles. *Computers in Human Behavior*, *49*, 12–19. doi:10.1016/j.chb.2014.12.045

Weiqin, E. L., Campbell, M., Kimpton, M., Wozencroft, K., & Orel, A. (2016). Social capital on Facebook: The impact of personality and online communication behaviors. *Journal of Educational Computing Research*, *54*(6), 747–786. doi:10.1177/0735633116631886

Wolak, J., Mitchell, K. J., & Finkelhor, D. (2003). Escaping or connecting? Characteristics of youth who form close online relationships. *Journal of Adolescence*, *26*(1), 105–119. doi:10.1016/S0140-1971(02)00114-8 PMID:12550824

Wood, J. V., Hogle, A., & McClellan, J. C. D. (2009). Self-esteem and relationships. In H. Reis, & S. Sprecher (Eds.), *Encyclopedia of human relationships* , (vol. 3, pp. 1422–1425). Thousand Oaks, CA: Sage. doi:10.4135/9781412958479.n464

Xie, W., & Kang, C. (2015). See you, see me: Teenagers' self-disclosure and regret of posting on social network site. *Computers in Human Behavior*, *52*, 398–407. doi:10.1016/j.chb.2015.05.059

Yang, M., Yang, C., & Chiou, W. (2010). Differences in engaging in sexual disclosure between real life and cyberspace among adolescents: Social penetration model revisited. *Current Psychology (New Brunswick, N.J.)*, *29*(2), 144–154. doi:10.100712144-010-9078-6

Yen, J. Y., Yen, C. F., Chen, C. S., Wang, P. W., Chang, Y. H., & Ko, C. H. (2012). Social anxiety in online and real-life interaction and their associated factors. *Cyberpsychology, Behavior, and Social Networking*, *15*(1), 7–12. doi:10.1089/cyber.2011.0015 PMID:22175853

Youn, S. (2005). Teenagers' perceptions of online privacy and coping behaviors: A risk–benefit appraisal approach. *Journal of Broadcasting & Electronic Media*, *49*(1), 86–110. doi:10.120715506878jobem4901_6

Yum, Y. O., & Hara, K. (2005). Computer-mediated relationship development: A cross-cultural comparison. *Journal of Computer-Mediated Communication, 11*(1), 133–152. doi:10.1111/j.1083-6101.2006. tb00307.x

Zhang, R. (2017). The stress-buffering effect of self-disclosure on Facebook: An examination of stressful life events, social support, and mental health among college students. *Computers in Human Behavior, 75,* 527–537. doi:10.1016/j.chb.2017.05.043

ADDITIONAL READING

Desjarlais, M., Gilmour, J., Sinclair, J., Howell, K. B., & West, A. (2015). Predictors and social consequences of online interactive self-disclosure: A literature review from 2002 to 2014. *Cyberpsychology, Behavior, and Social Networking, 18*(12), 718–725. doi:10.1089/cyber.2015.0109 PMID:26652672

Forest, A. L., & Wood, J. V. (2012). When social networking is not working: Individuals with low self-esteem recognize but do not reap the benefits of self-disclosure on Facebook. *Psychological Science, 23*(3), 295–302. doi:10.1177/0956797611429709 PMID:22318997

Green, T., Wilhelmsen, T., Wilmots, E., Dodd, B., & Quinn, S. (2016). Social anxiety, attributes of online communication and self-disclosure across private and public Facebook communication. *Computers in Human Behavior, 58,* 206–213. doi:10.1016/j.chb.2015.12.066

Laurenceau, J. P., Barrett, L. F., & Pietromonaco, P. R. (1998). Intimacy as an interpersonal process: The importance of self-disclosure, partner disclosure, and perceived partner responsiveness in interpersonal exchanges. *Journal of Personality and Social Psychology, 74*(5), 1238–1251. doi:10.1037/0022-3514.74.5.1238 PMID:9599440

Nguyen, M., Bin, Y. S., & Campbell, A. (2012). Comparing online and offline self-disclosure: A systematic review. *Cyberpsychology, Behavior, and Social Networking, 15*(2), 103–111. doi:10.1089/cyber.2011.0277 PMID:22032794

Turkle, S. (2011). *Alone together: Why we expect more from technology and less from each other.* Philadelphia, PA: Basic Books.

Valkenburg, P. M., & Peter, J. (2009b). Social Consequences of the internet for adolescents: A decade of research. *Current Directions in Psychological Science, 18*(1), 1–5. doi:10.1111/j.1467-8721.2009.01595.x

Valkenburg, P. M., & Peter, J. (2011). Online communication among adolescents: An integrated model of its attraction, opportunities, and risks. *The Journal of Adolescent Health, 48*(2), 121–127. doi:10.1016/j.jadohealth.2010.08.020 PMID:21257109

KEY TERMS AND DEFINITIONS

Antecedent Variable: An independent variable that precedes other independent variables in time. It comes earlier in an explanation or chain of causal links.

Asynchronicity: The exchanges of messages intermittently rather than in real-time. Delays between receiving and sending messages can occur.

Audiovisual Anonymity: A lack or reduction of nonverbal (visual or auditory) cues conveyed during a conversation with one or more partners.

Moderating Variables: A third variable that affects the strength of the relationship between two or more variables.

Online Communication: The use of social media to send messages to other users.

Online Self-Disclosure: The sharing of intimate information about the self on social media.

Self-Disclosure: The sharing of personally relevant thoughts, feelings, and experiences.

Social Media: Online platforms that permit users to create a profile, as well as connect and exchange information about oneself with other members. Examples include social networking sites, instant messaging services, blogging sites, and multiplayer online games.

This research was previously published in The Psychology and Dynamics Behind Social Media Interactions; pages 1-27, copyright year 2020 by Information Science Reference (an imprint of IGI Global).

Chapter 26
Trial by Social Media:
How Do You Find the Jury, Guilty or Not Guilty?

Jacqui Taylor
Bournemouth University, Poole, UK

Gemma Tarrant
Bournemouth University, Poole, UK

ABSTRACT

Social media makes it easier than ever to access information and opinions associated with criminal proceedings and viewing or discussing these pre-trial could reduce juror impartiality. This study explored whether viewing social media comments influenced mock juror verdicts. Seventy-two participants formed 12 six-person 'mock juries'. All participants received information regarding a murder trial. Nine groups were exposed to social media comments, manipulated to be negative, positive or neutral towards the defendant. The remaining three groups only received trial information (control condition). Results showed that prior to group discussion, exposure to negatively-biased comments significantly increased the number of guilty verdicts, however these effects disappeared after group discussion. Therefore, although jurors may be unable to remain impartial before a trial, jury discussion can remove these prejudices, supporting previous group research. Further research is suggested where participants interact actively with social media, rather than passively viewing comments.

INTRODUCTION

The rapid growth in the use of the internet and social media have made it easier to gain access to information and opinions relating to the people involved in and the circumstances of legal proceedings. The influence of pre-trial publicity via traditional mass media has been thoroughly researched (e.g. Studebaker & Penrod, 1997), however, there is less research focusing on the influence of social media. Information is now instantly accessible and on a global scale, often making it difficult to avoid; indeed Bakhshay & Haney (2018) report on the difficulty finding jurors who have not been exposed to potentially biased extra-legal information.

DOI: 10.4018/978-1-6684-6307-9.ch026

The Role of the Jury

In the UK, juries are made up of twelve individuals aged between 18 and 70 selected randomly from the electoral register and their role is to arrive at a verdict on the charge facing the defendant by considering questions of fact and applying the law to these facts (Herring, 2018). This random selection is intended to ensure that the twelve members of the jury represent a wide range of individuals in society. Every individual who is charged with a criminal offence within the European Union has the right to a fair trial by an impartial jury, under the Human Rights Act (1998). An impartial juror is free from bias and prejudice and is free from the influence of knowledge acquired outside of the courtroom (Surette, 1998). Pre-trial publicity surrounding criminal investigations can potentially destroy a defendant's rights to a fair trial and if a court decides that the jury is prejudiced due to exposure to pre-trial publicity, proceedings may be adjourned or there may be a re-trial. Jurors are instructed that they are to decide the case based solely on the evidence presented within the courtroom, and that they must not conduct any independent research or discuss the case with any other person outside of the courtroom until deliberations are complete (Judicial Conference Committee, 2012). Mock jury studies involve participants acting as jurors and are used to research aspects of the judicial system where it is not possible or ethical to conduct research using jurors involved in real trials. Although mock jury studies have contributed much to the understanding of the judicial system, they have received some criticism relating to low ecological validity (O'Connell, 1988). However, a recent review argues that they can produce valid and reliable findings (Bornstein, Golding, Neuschatz, Kimbrough, Reed, Magyarics, & Luecht, 2017).

Pre-trial Publicity: Negative and Positive

Pre-trial publicity can adversely influence the juror decision making process in both positive (pro-defendant) and negative (anti-defendant) ways (Fein, McCloskey & Tomlinson, 1997). Moran & Cutler (1991) found that the greater the amount of publicity, the greater the tendency of jurors to find the defendant guilty, regardless of whether publicity was negative or positive. The majority of research explores the effects that negative pre-trial publicity can have on juror decision making and highlights ways in which information is portrayed as anti-defendant and incriminating (Fein, Morgan, Norton & Sommers, 1997). Positive pre-trial publicity generally occurs less frequently than negative, but occurs more often in high profile cases in which the defendant is wealthy and/or well known to the public (e.g., Martha Stewart as cited in Ruva & McEvoy, 2008). Ruva (2010) found that people pay more attention to negative information compared to positive information and relate this to the negativity bias identified in social psychology (Baron & Branscombe, 2016). Steblay, Besirevic, Fulero and Jimenez-Lorente (1999) conducted a meta-analytic review of 44 empirical studies and found that participants exposed to negative pre-trial publicity were significantly more likely to give guilty verdicts compared to those not exposed to this pre-trial publicity. Additionally, Ruva, McEvoy & Bryant (2007) found that exposure to negative pre-trial publicity significantly affected the number of guilty verdicts, and also the sentence length awarded and perceptions of defendant credibility. While Ruva, Guenther & Yarbrough (2011) found that mock jurors exposed to positive pre-trial publicity were significantly more likely to vote not guilty and rate the defendant as more credible.

Jacquin & Hodges (2007) conducted mock juror research using the murder investigation of Andrea Yates, who in 2001 was found guilty of the murder of her five children. Yates was suffering from severe post-partum psychosis when she systematically drowned her five children. The researchers provided participants with either sympathetic (positive) or unsympathetic (negative) media about the murder and found that those who were exposed to unsympathetic media were significantly more likely to convict Yates of murder, compared to those who received no media, unbiased media or sympathetic media. However, exposure to media about this high-profile case prior to the experiment could have confounded the results and also only traditional media were used, not social media.

Psychological processes related to decision-making are important to consider. It has been reported that a third of jurors consciously or subconsciously decide on a verdict before the opening arguments of a trial, and consequently this bias affects how subsequent evidence is processed (Carlson & Russo, 2001). Social psychological research has shown that first impressions of people are formed as quickly as one-tenth of a second (Willis & Todorov, 2006) suggesting that exposure to negative pre-trial publicity can lead to rapid formations of negative impressions of the defendant. Within a criminal trial, the prosecution are required to present their case against the defendant first. The defence subsequently presents any contrary evidence or provides arguments to counter the evidence presented by the prosecution. The trial concludes with the closing arguments at which point the prosecution will present after the defence have addressed the court. Cognitive psychology has demonstrated that information we receive first and last are much better remembered, compared to information presented in between these. Drawing on an understanding of these so-called 'primacy' and 'recency' effects, jurors may be able to remember more information presented at the beginning and at the conclusion of the trial, that is, the evidence and information of the prosecution.

Pre-trial social media comments are often the first sources of information available to jurors and details can be magnified by retweets and likes. The primacy effect explains that information we receive first strongly influences our views and perceptions, which can lead to a confirmation bias amongst those involved in a trial (Baron & Branscombe, 2016). A confirmation bias occurs when information consistent with a person's belief is sought, and consequently information supporting the other side of the argument is disregarded. In terms of negative pre-trial publicity, this means that information supporting the defendants' guilt is favoured over information suggesting innocence (Rassin, Eerland & Kuijpers, 2010). Ruva et al. (2011) found that jurors exposed to pre-trial publicity (both positive and negative) distorted witness testimony in the direction consistent with the pre-trial publicity bias. Hope, Memon & McGeorge (2004) found that jurors exposed to negative pre-trial publicity reported significantly higher pre-decisional distortion in support of the prosecution, resulting in an increased incidence of guilty verdicts.

Although individual jurors may succumb to memory errors and biases, research and practice shows that jury deliberation will at least partially or wholly correct these errors and biases. For example, if an individual juror mistakes pre-trial publicity as court evidence and attempts to use it during deliberations, another jury member will usually correct the error. Pritchard & Keenan (2002) found that jury deliberation resulted in a slight memory improvement, corrected errors and did not introduce distortions. However, Ruva & LeVasseur (2012) conducted a content analysis of 30 mock juror deliberations and found that exposure to pre-trial publicity influenced the interpretation and discussion of trial evidence during deliberations. They found that jurors exposed to negative pre-trial publicity were significantly more likely to discuss ambiguous trial facts in a manner that supported the prosecution. The researchers also found that jurors were either unwilling or unable to adhere to instructions forbidding them from discussing extra-legal information and that those jurors who mentioned pre-trial publicity during the deliberations were rarely corrected. These findings suggest that jury deliberations may not always correct errors and biases.

Research has also explored whether pre-trial publicity can affect jurors ability to discriminate between sources of information. This is known as source memory and is the ability to accurately attribute information to its source. Ruva and Hudak (2013) found that pre-trial publicity had significant effects on source memory judgements, with those exposed to pre-trial publicity being less accurate. Pre-trial publicity also had a significant effect on critical source memory errors (misattributing pre-trial publicity as trial information), with those exposed to negative pre-trial publicity making more of these errors. These findings suggest that jurors who have been exposed to pre-trial publicity may find it difficult to discriminate between information heard in the court room and information they have received from pre-trial publicity.

Social Media

The growth of social media poses new challenges for the criminal justice system. Social media enables users to communicate their views and opinions anonymously, or with a reduced level of identifiability. The wider diversity of views and anonymous conditions can lead to a greater level of opinion polarisation (at the extreme ends of the continuum); a phenomenon highlighted in previous online decision making research (Taylor & MacDonald, 2002). This polarising effect could potentially lead to an even greater level of pre-trial influence, as more extreme views are expressed.

Social media sites such as Facebook (now with 2250 million active users) and Twitter (with over 326 million active users) (Statista, 2019) allow individuals to post their views to a global stage and receive replies almost instantaneously, anywhere and at any time. Jurors can consult online social media sources in order to aid decision making, despite court instructions not to do this. This was demonstrated during a child abduction and sexual assault case, when a female juror was removed from the jury after posting on her Facebook page "I don't know which way to go, so I'm holding a poll" (reported in Mastro, 2011). By searching in this way, the juror becomes at risk of 'informational social influence' which is the desire to be correct and possess accurate perceptions of the world (Baron & Branscombe, 2016). Other people's actions and opinions define social reality and these are used as a source of information in order to shape our own actions and opinions. Informational social influence is a powerful source of conformity, particularly in situations in which individuals are highly uncertain about what is correct or accurate (Baron & Branscombe, 2016).

The trial of Casey Anthony has been cited by Cloud (2011) as the first murder trial of the social-media age. Anthony was suspected of involvement in her 2 year old daughter's death when the young child's body was found near the family home in America. By posting comments onto social networking websites, the public aired their opinions; the majority were convinced of Casey Anthony's guilt. The prosecution sought the death penalty but the trial controversially resulted in Casey Anthony being acquitted of murder. Cloud suggested that the jurors were able to base their verdict solely on information heard within the court room and ignored the pre-trial publicity and unsubstantiated opinions. In 2012, during the investigation into the murder of Jill Meagher, Australian police issued a statement via Twitter instructing people to refrain from posting comments which could endanger the presumption of innocence. Another example where a juror had already formed views and opinions as a result of publicity on social media was shown in the case of R v Huhne and Pryce (BBC, 2013) where the judge was asked directly by the jury: *"Can a juror come to a verdict based on a reason that was not presented in court and has no facts or evidence to support it either from the prosecution or the defence?"* (BBC, 2013). This question resulted in the following negative comments by the judge: *"The answer to that question is firmly 'no' ...that is because it would be completely contrary to the directions I have given you for anyone to return a verdict except a true verdict according to the evidence".* The jury was later dismissed by the judge and a retrial ordered.

Experimental Rationale and Hypotheses

This study explores whether biased social media comments influence mock jurors in their decision making and the following hypotheses will be tested.

H_1: There will be no difference in verdicts between those participants viewing neutral social media comments and those viewing no social media (the control condition).

H_2: Viewing negatively biased social media comments will produce more guilty verdicts, compared to verdicts given by participants viewing positive comments, neutral comments or no comments.

H_3: Viewing positively biased social media comments will produce more not guilty verdicts, compared to verdicts given by participants viewing negative comments, neutral comments or no comments.

H_4: Group discussion will reduce the impact of social media influence on juror decision making.

H_5: Jurors will report higher confidence in their individual verdict post-deliberation, compared to pre-deliberation.

METHODOLOGY

Design

A between-groups experimental design was used with four conditions: no social media, negative bias, positive bias and neutral. The dependent variables included: pre-discussion and post-discussion verdicts (guilty or not guilty), and confidence in decision rating (pre-discussion and post-discussion).

Participants

Seventy two participants (16 males, 56 females) aged between 18 and 33 ($M=20.43$, $SD=2.11$) and from a range of courses were recruited from a UK University via opportunistic sampling. Participants volunteered through an advertisement posted on an experimental participant software system which informed participants of the nature of the experiment, the requirements of participation, an ethics statement and the course credits available. Participants were randomly assigned to a 6-person mock jury, in one of four conditions. Gender was not controlled for and inevitably most groups contained more female members. Social media use was not controlled for; the majority of participants had an active social media account ($N=71$) of which most used daily ($N=61$).

Materials

Participants received instructions outlining how the experiment was to be conducted in an information sheet and signed an informed consent form. Individuals allocated to the control condition received instructions stating that they would be exposed to information from a real court trial regarding a murder investigation. Participants within the experimental conditions received the same instructions however, in addition it was stated that they would receive social media comments relating to the trial.

The information relating to a murder trial was based on a real murder investigation (R v Boreman and others, 1999), however, names and events were changed for ethical reasons. Some evidence from post-mortem examinations remained in order to ensure that evidence presented to participants was realistic. This case was selected from a number of potential cases as the defendant's guilt was unclear and therefore participants would need to make their own decision based on the evidence presented to them.

Fictional social media comments (from Twitter and Facebook) were created for use within the experimental conditions. Social media comments were either positive towards the defendant, negative towards the defendant, or neutral. Spelling, grammar and punctuation errors were introduced in order to reflect real comments posted onto social media websites. Social media searches were conducted on recent murder investigations to help construct the comments.

Pre- and post-discussion questionnaires asked participants to record their individual verdicts as well as confidence in their verdict, measured on a 6-point Likert scale. The post-discussion questionnaire also collected information relating to social media use and whether participants would search social networking sites for information relating to a defendant should they become a member of a real jury. A separate answer sheet was supplied to the group after the discussion, on which to record the group verdict. A debrief form was provided on completion of the study.

Procedure

Participants were given details about the study along with a consent form, which notified them of their right to withdraw at any time during the study and that they could request the withdrawal of their data after the study. If participants agreed to participate in the experiment, the consent form was signed. Participants allocated to the control condition received a copy of the court transcript and were asked to complete a pre-discussion questionnaire. They were then asked to discuss the evidence as a mock-jury and reach a collective verdict. Participants were instructed that the verdict given should be based on the evidence heard within the courtroom and not outside of the courtroom. The mock-jury recorded their verdict on a separate answer sheet. Participants were then required to complete the post-discussion questionnaire which involved giving a second individual verdict and answering questions on social media use. Participants allocated to the experimental conditions experienced the same procedure however, they were also given social media comments about the trial, presented at the same time as the court transcript. A debrief form was given to all participants on completion of the study.

RESULTS

The verdicts given by mock-jurors prior to deliberations are shown in Table 1, which shows that 'guilty' verdicts were more frequently expressed from mock-jurors who were exposed to negatively biased social media, while 'not guilty' verdicts were more frequently expressed by mock-jurors exposed to positively biased social media. Verdicts expressed by participants in the control and neutral conditions are very similar, supporting H_1.

Table 1. Cross-tabulation of observed frequencies, bias of social media and the individual verdict given by mock-jurors prior to deliberations

Verdict		No comments (Control)	Positively biased comments	Negative biased comments	Neutral comments
		Condition			
Guilty		5	1	8	3
Not Guilty		13	17	10	15
Total		18	18	18	18

As the data is at a categorical level a Pearson's chi-squared was conducted and this resulted in a significant difference across conditions (χ^2 (3, N =72) = 8.24, p = .041, φ = .338, odds ratio = 13.56). The adjusted residual indicated that mock-jurors exposed to negative social media comments were significantly more likely (2.4) to produce a guilty verdict compared to mock-jurors exposed to neutral, positive or no social media, supporting H_2. The adjusted residual also indicated that mock-jurors who were exposed to positive social media comments were significantly more likely (2.1) to produce a not guilty verdict, compared to mock-jurors exposed to negative, neutral or no social media, supporting H_3.

Statistical tests were conducted on jurors' individual verdicts after the deliberations, in order to determine whether the biasing effects of social media remain. The frequencies of verdicts given by mock-jurors after jury deliberations are shown in Table 2 which shows that despite juror exposure to biased social media, 'not guilty' was the most frequent verdict expressed across all conditions.

Table 2. Cross-tabulation of observed frequencies, bias of social media and the individual verdict given by the mock-juror after deliberations

Verdict		No comments (Control)	Positively biased comments	Negative biased comments	Neutral comments
		Condition			
Guilty		1	0	0	2
Not Guilty		17	18	18	16
Total		18	18	18	18

A Pearson's χ^2 test of mock-jurors individual verdicts after deliberations indicated no significant difference between conditions (χ^2 (3, N=72) =3.83, p= .281, φ = .231), supporting H_4 that the biasing effects of social media were reduced by the deliberation process. Regardless of their exposure to social media, the collective verdicts given by all groups after deliberation found the defendant 'not guilty'; also supporting H_4.

In the post-discussion questionnaire, participants were asked whether they would conduct a social media search of a defendant if they were serving as a member of a real jury and 46% of participants (N=33) reported that they would. The differences between confidence ratings pre and post jury deliberations were examined to test H_5: that jurors will report higher confidence in their verdict post-jury deliberations, compared to pre-jury deliberations. The results showed that confidence ratings in the verdict increased after jury deliberations (mean 4.46) compared to pre-jury deliberations (mean 3.76). A Kolmogorov-Smirnov test revealed that 'confidence in verdict' data was not normally distributed (pre-discussion: D (72) = .213, p = < .001 and post-discussion: D (72) = .225, p = < .001). Therefore, a Wilcoxon signed rank test of differences was conducted and the results revealed that the confidence ratings were significantly different (W = 163; z = -5.198, p = < .001, with a strong effect size r= .576), supporting H_5.

DISCUSSION

The results support all hypotheses and found that pre-trial juror exposure to biased social media influenced the verdicts given, such that exposure to negative social media significantly increased the number of 'guilty' verdicts and exposure to positive social media significantly increased the number of 'not guilty' verdicts given (H_2 and H_3). These findings are consistent with previous findings regarding the effects of pre-trial publicity on juror decision making (Fein et al, 1997; Jacquin et al, 2007; Ruva & LeVassear, 2012; Steblay et al, 1999).

The trial selected for this study was chosen as there was insufficient evidence and it was unclear whether the defendant started the fire and therefore committed murder, or whether the fire was the result of an accident. This should have therefore resulted in the defendant being found 'not guilty' of murder due to the lack of proof. The findings could reflect the process of informational social influence (Baron & Branscombe, 2016). Jurors who were unsure of a verdict may have consulted the social media comments in order to shape their own opinions in order to reach a verdict. It would be interesting therefore in future research to examine different types of trial (e.g. where there is clear evidence to support a guilty or non-guilty verdict).

The study found that following jury deliberations there was no significant difference in the verdicts given by jurors, supporting H_4 which hypothesised that the biased nature of social media comments would be reduced by the deliberation process. Subsequently, it was found that all mock-juries across all conditions reached a verdict of 'not guilty', further suggesting that the biasing effects of social media can be significantly reduced by the deliberation process. Therefore, although mock-jurors individually were affected by the social media bias, collectively they are not likely to be influenced by social media. Interestingly, despite instructions to base the verdict solely on information given within the transcript, social media was repeatedly discussed by two juries during deliberations and when discussing the final verdict. This finding is consistent with that of Ruva & LeVasseur (2012) who found that jurors were either unwilling or unable to adhere to instructions forbidding them from discussing extra-legal information. A possible explanation for this finding could be that jurors either did not fully understand the instructions given to them or that the instructions were not read carefully, rather than assuming that jurors had simply chosen to disregard the instructions. In a real criminal investigation, these instructions would be given verbally to jurors by a judge and jurors would be expected to confirm that they had understood the instructions and the consequences of breaching these instructions. Of concern, it was found that almost half of the participants reported that they would conduct a social media search on a defendant if they were serving as a juror in a real criminal trial. This is concerning for the criminal justice system where the defendants' rights to a fair trial by an impartial jury could be deemed to have been violated.

Finally, the results support H$_5$ (the confirmatory hypothesis), as jurors confidence in their verdicts were rated higher following jury deliberation compared to before deliberation. This finding is consistent with previous literature on the impacts of group discussion on individual decisions.

Implications of the Findings

The finding that exposure to biased social media comments has a significant influence on the verdicts given by jurors has implications for the criminal justice system. These findings suggest that jurors may be unable to remain impartial to the biasing effects that social media can have on decision making. Every individual who is charged with a criminal offence in the European Union has the right to a fair trial by an impartial jury under the Human Rights Act (1998) and a biased juror would therefore contravene these rights and potentially result in an incorrect outcome or claims for a mistrial. Biased jurors could result in the conviction of an innocent defendant and vice versa which is contrary to the aims and fundamental principles of the criminal justice system. Should the jury return a guilty verdict and a member of the defence believes that this decision was made by biased jurors then the defence are entitled to appeal the outcome of the trial. In trials where the outcome is flawed due to a biased jury, the verdict can be overturned and the defendant acquitted of an offence.

In order to protect defendants' rights, methods have been implemented in an attempt to reduce the impact of pre-trial publicity. *Voir dire* is the preliminary questioning of potential jurors by a judge to determine whether a juror has biased beliefs or opinions and is therefore unable to remain impartial. This questioning can determine whether prospective jurors have already conducted prohibited activity and whether they agree to follow the rules prohibiting any independent research regarding the case (Simpler, 2012). In the case of R v Huhne and Pryce (BBC, 2013), *voir dire* could potentially have identified the issues and negated the need for a retrial. Further research exploring the effectiveness of *voir dire* in reducing the bias caused by exposure to social media is required. Fein et al. (1997) found that despite instructions from the judge to disregard incriminating evidence in the form of pre-trial publicity, jurors' verdicts were significantly affected. However the researchers found that if jurors were given reason to be suspicious about why such incriminating evidence was presented to the media, their verdicts were similar to those given by jurors who were not exposed to such media. Despite finding that social media significantly influences jurors pre-discussion decisions, this study found that the biasing effects of social media disappeared after the deliberation process. Further research is needed to explore the way deliberation reduces bias amongst jurors.

Strengths and Limitations

As with other mock jury studies, there are some methodological issues regarding their ecological validity (Bornstein et al., 2017) and this study was similarly limited in group size, sample size and participant make-up. In the United Kingdom juries are comprised of 12 members, while this study used 6 member juries and group size can significantly affect decision-making. Future research needs to increase both the size of the groups and also the size of the sample. Participants were from the student population, which affects the generalisability of the findings. Keller and Weiner (2011) found that student mock jurors were more lenient in assigning guilt to murder cases, compared to community members in mock jury trials. Also, students are more likely to use social media than the general population; a higher use of social media would increase the opportunity for an individual to be exposed to and be influenced by comments and information relating to criminal investigations posted onto social networking websites. Further research could explore jurors' perceptions of the quality of information available via social media and a variety of age groups with varied experience of social media could be included to more accurately represent the demographic composition of a real jury. In this study exposure to social media was restricted within a controlled environment, while in real criminal trials jurors may have access to a variety of posts, which may or may not be influential. Jurors could also be exposed to hundreds of posts as opposed to the ten used in this study. Further research could expose participants to a larger number and variety of social media and also ask them to interact with posts.

CONCLUSION

This study has added to the literature exploring juror decision making and pre-trial information. The findings are in line with previous research regarding negative pre-trial publicity and suggest that social media should be considered as a significant threat to juror impartiality and the legitimacy of the verdicts derived from the trial process. Further research should be conducted to explore methods to identify and manage or reduce these biases.

REFERENCES

Bakhshay, S., & Haney, C. (2018). The media's impact on the right to a fair trial: A content analysis of pre-trial publicity in capital cases. *Psychology, Public Policy, and Law*, *24*(3), 326–340. doi:10.1037/law0000174

Baron, R. A., & Branscombe, N. R. (2016). *Social Psychology* (15th ed.). Boston: Pearson.

BBC. (2013). *Ten questions posed by the Vicky Pryce jury*. Retrieved from http://www.bbc.co.uk/news/uk-21521460

Bornstein, B. H., Golding, J. M., Neuschatz, J., Kimbrough, C., Reed, K., Magyarics, C., & Luecht, K. (2017). Mock juror sampling issues in jury simulation research: A meta-analysis. *Law and Human Behavior*, *41*(1), 13–28. doi:10.1037/lhb0000223 PMID:27762572

Carlson, K. A., & Russo, J. E. (2001). Biased interpretation of evidence by mock jurors: A meta-analysis. *Journal of Experimental Psychology. Applied*, *7*(2), 91–103. doi:10.1037/1076-898X.7.2.91 PMID:11477983

Cloud, J. (2011). Fascination with the Casey Anthony case has made it the first major murder trial of the social-media age. *Time*, *177*(26), 42–45.

Dexter, H. R., Cutler, B. L., & Moran, G. (1992). A test of *voir dire* as a remedy for the prejudicial effects of pre-trial publicity. *Journal of Applied Social Psychology*, *22*(10), 819–832. doi:10.1111/j.1559-1816.1992.tb00926.x

Fein, S., McCloskey, A. L., & Tomlinson, T. M. (1997). Can the jury disregard that information? The use of suspicion to reduce the prejudicial effects of pre-trial publicity and inadmissible testimony. *Personality and Social Psychology Bulletin, 23*(11), 1215–1226. doi:10.1177/01461672972311008

Fein, S., Morgan, S. J., Norton, M. I., & Sommers, S. R. (1997). Hype and suspicion: The effects of pre-trial publicity, race, and suspicion on jurors' verdicts. *The Journal of Social Issues, 53*(3), 487–502. doi:10.1111/j.1540-4560.1997.tb02124.x

Herring, J. (2018). *Criminal Law: text, cases and materials* (8th ed.). Oxford, UK: OUP. doi:10.1093/he/9780198811817.001.0001

Hope, L., Memon, A., & McGeorge, P. (2004). Understanding pre-trial publicity: Pre-decisional distortion of evidence by mock jurors. *Journal of Experimental Psychology. Applied, 10*(2), 111–119. doi:10.1037/1076-898X.10.2.111 PMID:15222805

Jacquin, K. M., & Hodges, E. P. (2007). The influence of media messages on mock juror decisions in the Andrea Yates trial. *The American Journal of Forensic Psychology, 25*(4), 21–40.

Johnson, M. K. (1997). Source monitoring and memory distortion. *Philosophical Transactions of the Royal Society of London. Series B, Biological Sciences, 352*(1362), 1733–1745. doi:10.1098/rstb.1997.0156 PMID:9415926

Johnson, M. K., Hashtroudi, S., & Lindsay, D. (1993). Source monitoring. *Psychological Bulletin, 114*(1), 3–28. doi:10.1037/0033-2909.114.1.3 PMID:8346328

Judicial Conference Committee. (2012). *Proposed model jury instructions. The use of electronic technology to conduct research on or communicate about a case.* Retrieved from: http://www.uscourts.gov/news/2012/08/21/revised-jury-instructions-hope-deter-juror-use-social-media-during-trial

Keller, R. S., & Wiener, L. R. (2011). What are we studying? Student jurors, community jurors, and construct validity. *Behavioral Sciences & the Law, 29*(3), 376–394. doi:10.1002/bsl.971 PMID:21766327

Kelly, A., Carroll, M., & Mazzoni, G. (2002). Meta-memory and reality monitoring. *Applied Cognitive Psychology, 16*(4), 407–428. doi:10.1002/acp.803

Kiernan, M. K., & Cooley, S. E. (2012). Juror misconduct in the age of social networking. *Federation of Defense & Corporate Counsel Quarterly, 62*(2), 179–193.

Mastro, F. J. (2011). Preventing the "Google Mistrial": the challenge posed by jurors who use the internet and social media. *Litigation, 37*(2), 23-27. Retrieved from http://media.wix.com/ugd/a36d16_8626fd696d5f43f9b2eb81fc6d336540.pdf

Moran, G., & Cutler, B. L. (1991). The prejudicial impact of pre-trial publicity. *Journal of Applied Social Psychology, 21*(5), 345–367. doi:10.1111/j.1559-1816.1991.tb00524.x

Moran, G., & Cutler, B. L. (1997). Bogus publicity items and the contingency between awareness and media-induced pre-trial prejudice. *Law and Human Behavior, 21*(3), 339–344. doi:10.1023/A:1024846917038

Nietzel, M. T., & Dillehay, R. C. (1983). Psychologists as consultants for changes of venue. *Law and Human Behavior*, *7*(4), 309–355. doi:10.1007/BF01044735

O'Connell, P. D. (1988). Pre-trial publicity, change of venue, public opinion polls: A theory of procedural justice. *University of Detroit Law Review*, *65*, 169–197.

Pritchard, M. E., & Keenan, J. M. (2002). Does jury deliberation really improve jurors' memories? *Applied Cognitive Psychology*, *16*(5), 589–601. doi:10.1002/acp.816

R. Boreman (1999). Retrieved from http://netk.net.au/UK/Boreman.asp

Rassin, E., Eerland, A., & Kuijpers, I. (2010). Let's find the evidence: An analogue study of confirmation bias in criminal investigations. *Journal of Investigative Psychology and Offender Profiling*, *7*(3), 231–246. doi:10.1002/jip.126

Ruva, C. L. (2010). *How Pre-trial Publicity Affects Juror Decision Making and Memory*. Hauppage, NY: Nova Science Publishers.

Ruva, C. L., Guenther, C. C., & Yarbrough, A. (2011). The roles of impression formation, emotion and pre-decisional distortion. *Criminal Justice and Behavior*, *38*(5), 511–534. doi:10.1177/0093854811400823

Ruva, C. L., & Hudak, E. M. (2013). Pretrial publicity and juror age affect mock-juror decision making. *Psychology, Crime & Law*, *19*(2), 179–202. doi:10.1080/1068316X.2011.616509

Ruva, C. L., & LeVasseur, M. A. (2012). Behind closed doors: The effect of pre-trial publicity on jury deliberations. *Psychology, Crime & Law*, *18*(5), 431–452. doi:10.1080/1068316X.2010.502120

Ruva, C. L., McEvoy, C., & Bryant, J. (2007). Effects of pre-trial publicity and jury deliberation on juror bias and source memory errors. *Applied Cognitive Psychology*, *21*(1), 45–67. doi:10.1002/acp.1254

Simpler, M. F. (2012). The unjust "web" we weave: The evolution of social media and its psychological impact on juror impartiality and fair trials. *Law and Psychology Review*, *36*, 275–296.

St. Eve, A. J., & Zuckerman, M. A. (2012). Ensuring an impartial jury in the age of social media. *Duke Law & Technology Review*, *11*, 1–29. doi:10.1080/02763877.2014.982316

Statista. (2019). Retrieved from http://www.statista.com/

Steblay, N., Besirevic, J., Fulero, S. M., & Jimenez-Lorente, B. (1999). The effects of pre-trial publicity on juror verdicts: A meta-analytic review. *Law and Human Behavior*, *23*(2), 219–235. doi:10.1023/A:1022325019080

Studebaker, C. A., & Penrod, S. D. (1997). Pre-trial publicity: The media, the law, and common sense. *Psychology, Public Policy, and Law*, *3*(2-3), 428–460. doi:10.1037/1076-8971.3.2-3.428

Studebaker, C. A., Robbennolt, J. K., Pathak-Sharma, M. K., & Penrod, S. D. (2000). Assessing pretrial publicity effects: Integrating content analytic results. *Law and Human Behavior*, *24*(3), 317–336. doi:10.1023/A:1005536204923 PMID:10846375

Surette, R. (1998). *Media, Crime, and Criminal Justice* (2nd ed.). London: Wadsworth Publishing Company.

Taylor, J., & MacDonald, J. (2002). The effects of asynchronous computer-mediated group interaction on group processes. *Social Science Computer Review*, *20*(3), 260–274. doi:10.1177/089443930202000304

Willis, J., & Todorov, A. (2006). First impression: Making up your mind after a 100-ms. exposure to a face. *Psychological Science*, *17*, 592–598. doi:10.1111/j.1467-9280.2006.01750.x PMID:16866745

This research was previously published in the International Journal of Cyber Research and Education (IJCRE), 1(2); pages 50-61, copyright year 2019 by IGI Publishing (an imprint of IGI Global).

Chapter 27
Classifying the Influential Individuals in Multi-Layer Social Networks

Ruchi Mittal

https://orcid.org/0000-0001-6818-2355
Netaji Subhas Institute of Technology, New Delhi, India

M.P.S Bhatia

Computer Engineering Department, Netaji Subhas Institute of Technology, New Delhi, India

ABSTRACT

Nowadays, social media is one of the popular modes of interaction and information diffusion. It is commonly found that the main source of information diffusion is done by some entities and such entities are also called as influencers. An influencer is an entity or individual who has the ability to influence others because of his/her relationship or connection with his/her audience. In this article, we propose a methodology to classify influencers from multi-layer social networks. A multi-layer social network is the same as a single layer social network depict that it includes multiple properties of a node and modeled them into multiple layers. The proposed methodology is a fusion of machine learning techniques (SVM, neural networks and so on) with centrality measures. We demonstrate the proposed algorithm on some real-life networks to validate the effectiveness of the approach in multi-layer systems.

INTRODUCTION

Social media is one of the fastest growing areas among users for communication and sharing information. It grows with an exponential rate due to advancement in technologies. For example, Twitter, Instagram, Facebook and so on are few social networking platforms where millions of users connected. Analysis of social networking platforms is one of the popular areas among researchers. The set of users and relationships between users are modeled in the form of a network, where each user is a node, and edge denotes the relationship (Breza & Chandrasekhar, 2019). Analyzing social network unveils diverse knowledge

DOI: 10.4018/978-1-6684-6307-9.ch027

about users, their behavior and relationships (Newman, 2003). There exist several methods like centrality measures, community detection and so on, which helps in the analysis of such networks. The purpose of measuring centralities is to find the influential power of nodes in the system. There are several types of centrality measures like eigenvector, degree, betweenness and each having a different purpose, which we will discuss later in the next section. Community detection is identifying a set of nodes, which are highly connected compare to other nodes (Kuncheva & Montana, 2015).

Influential individuals are impactful users with loyal audiences, and other users tend to trust their recommendations. In social networks, Influential individuals could be highly connected and reachable nodes of the systems. For example, in social networking site Twitter, a user having a high number of followers could be marked influencer because they are trusted the source of information and their message is reachable to a large number of the audience (Watanabe & Kabashima, 2014; Mallipeddi, Kumar, Sriskandarajah, & Zhu, 2018).

Most of the existing research work for finding influential users from the social network is considering only one type of relationships between users, i.e., single layer networks are involved in the study whereas we are targeting to include multiple types of relationships between users, which is further modeled as multi-layer social networks (Domenico, Granell, Porter, & Arenas, 2018).

The primary purpose of finding such influential users is to achieve large cascades and full reachability. The high reachability is easily attaining in multi-layer systems because of the topology of the network. Identification of influential users is a crucial task, and in this paper, we propose a methodology to find such users from the multi-layer system by collaborating machine learning techniques with centrality measures and community detection (Sadri, Hasan, Ukkusuri, & Lopez, 2018).

Our proposed approach starts by computing the betweenness centrality, closeness centrality and degree centrality of each node of the multi-layer network. The purpose of finding centrality values is to check how much a node is central in the network. Next, we identify the communities in the system. Community detection helps us in the classification process when we introduce machine-learning algorithms for finding influential individuals from the system. The proposed model uses the influence capabilities of the target user and his/her friends to see how prone the friends are to getting influenced by the target user and user characteristics.

The significant benefactions of the paper are:

- We empirically try to find influential users in multi-layer networks;
- We propose a novel methodology to find influencers who can cascade information to a broad audience in a social network;
- We use some standard multi-layer network datasets for our study.

Paper Outline

In the next section, we discuss the work done in the related area of multi-layer networks, centralities and so on. In part 3, we talk our proposed approach for measuring the influential power of users, in section 4, we discuss the datasets, and at last, we enlighten the experiment results.

BACKGROUND

Influential Users in Social Networks

Measuring the influential power of a user in the social networks helps in digging out exciting findings from the systems, which are further used in many applications. For instance, influential users are a great source of information distribution. A theory related to influence is trust, and in social networks, it involves in advertisements, promotions and so on. Bacha and Zin (2018) and Cha, Haddadi, Benevenuto, and Gummadi (2010) finds the influential users from the Twitter dataset from the users having a large number of followers. Shin, Xu, and Kim (2008) give different definitions of influence and depending on the application it varies. Wadhwa and Bhatia (2015, 2016) proposed an algorithm for finding the radicalization in social networks using a Markov chain algorithm and implement the same on twitter datasets. Mittal and Bhatia (2018) proposed an algorithm based on gradient descendent to find anomalous users exist in multi-layer networks. Mittal and Bhatia (2017) proposed a methodology to find structural holes in multi-layer social networks. Structural holes are the nodes, which are helping to connect multiple sub-groups of the network.

Centralities and Community Detection in Multi-Layer Social Networks

Much initial research on social networks mainly focuses on community detection and centrality measurements. Newman (2004, 2001) present many algorithms used for analyzing the structural properties of the social network community detection, centrality measurements and so on. Later on, these algorithms are used to dig information about users, their behavior and so on. For example, in the social networking site, Facebook likes & replies features are marked as influence features and are used to find the influential power of a user (Lin, Wu, Chen, & Yang, 2015). Considering multiple functions at a time encourage the new form of the social network called multi-layer social networks, where each layer represents a different kind of relationship among users. Battison and Nicosia (2014) proposed algorithms for computing the communities, degree distributions, measuring centralities for multi-layer networks.

Wadhwa and Bhatia (2012, 2014) discuss social networks, community detection and classify community detection algorithms based on the usage and applications. Mittal and Bhatia (2017) proposed a methodology to see the behavior of social network in terms of community structure formed in the social network. Mittal and Bhatia (2018) analyze the different structural properties of multi-layer systems to see how multi-layer social networks are different from traditional social networks. (Mittal, & Bhatia, 2018) find prominent authors from the scientific collaboration multi-layer network by applying community detection and centrality algorithms. Huang, Shao, Wang, Buldyrev, Stanley, and Havlin (2013) and Shao, Huang, Stanley, and Havlin (2014) proposed algorithm for finding clusters in social networks and check the robustness of those clusters with other techniques.

In this paper, we are aiming to find influential individuals based on the computed instrumental score, which are calculated using centralities and machine-learning techniques. Centrality measures are one of the best ways to see the importance of nodes in networks. There exist numerous centrality algorithms such as degree, Katz, closeness, eigenvector, page rank and so on. Mittal and Bhatia (2018) proposed a new formulation for measuring the closeness centrality of nodes in multi-layer networks. Mittal and Bhatia (2018) proposed algorithms for measuring centralities in multi-layer systems using few nature-inspired algorithms such as ant colony algorithm. Mittal and Bhatia (2019) Proposed algorithms for measuring bottleneck centrality of nodes in multi-layer networks. We discuss these algorithms in the next section.

Machine Learning Techniques

Recently, machine learning develops a great interest among researchers. In general, there are two types of machine learning techniques: supervised and unsupervised learning. Supervised learning means learning a function based on example input-output pairs where mapping of input to the output takes place Nigam (2001) and Ghani, Jones, and Rosenberg (2003) upgrade the supervised learning by considering both the input and output at the same time. Similarly, in unsupervised learning inferences are drawn from information without considering the output (Kolog, Montero, & Toivonen, 2018).

In this paper, we use supervised learning techniques like SVM classification method, Random forest method, Naive Bayes Method (Escudero, Màrquez, & Rigau, 2000) and Neural networks methods for classifying the influential users form the social networks. We discuss these methods later in the next section.

METHODOLOGY OF THE PROPOSED APPROACH

Here, we discuss the proposed approach for fining the influential users from multi-layer social networks. The proposed method starts by calculating the degree centrality, betweenness centrality, closeness centrality and bottleneck centrality for each node of the system. Next, we estimate the communities by applying the Infomap community detection algorithm defined for multi-layer networks.

Next, centralities values and communities are processed in machine learning techniques for predicting the values for all nodes. At last, to validate the proposed approach, we find the accuracy in the results using precession, recall, and f1-score methods. A brief introduction of the proposed plan is shown in Figure 1.

Figure 1. Workflow of proposed approach

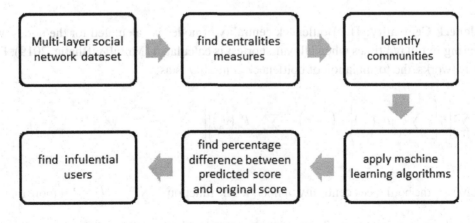

Centrality Measures

As discussed earlier, centrality algorithms find the significance or status of each node in a given network. In this paper, we include the following centrality algorithms for the proposed work:

- **Degree Centrality:** Degree centrality is one of the more straightforward and popular centrality measures, which finds the score based on the connection of nodes, i.e. with how many nodes a node, is connected. It is the summation of the amount of the incoming and outgoing links of a node to other neighboring nodes (Watanabe, & Kabashima, 2014). It is formally defined as, for an undirected network N having node set X and edge set Y is given as:

$$D(x) = \deg(x)$$

In this paper, we find the influential users of the system. A user having high degree centrality means that user is quite popular in the network and can be marked as the prominent user.

- **Closeness Centrality:** In multi-layer networks, the closeness centrality of nodes is found the reachability of nodes to all other nodes (Mittal & Bhatia, 2018). In simple systems, the closeness centrality is given as the sum of the shortest paths between nodes to all other nodes (Mittal, & Bhatia, 2018):

$$CCC\left(i\right) = \gamma \frac{1}{\Sigma d * \left(p_{i^a \to j^a}\right)} + \left(1 - \gamma\right) \frac{1}{\Sigma d * \left(p_{i^a \to j^\beta}\right)}$$

The function $d * \left(p_{i^a \to j^a}\right)$ is the shortest path between nodes i & j of same layer and $\Sigma d * \left(p_{i^a \to j^a}\right)$ is the shortest path between nodes i & j of different layers. γ is a tuning parameter used for balancing the importance within the layer or across layers.

- **Bottleneck Centrality:** The Bottleneck centrality of nodes is calculated for the nodes, which are appearing in full n/4 times when all pair shortest is calculated (Mittal & Bhatia, 2019). For multi-layer networks, the formulation of bottleneck centrality is as:

$$BN_s\left(v\right) = \sum_{\substack{s,t \epsilon V \\ s \neq t}} \left[\gamma \left(\sum_{s \neq t \neq v_\alpha \in N_m} P_{st}\left(v_\alpha\right)\right) + \left(1 - \gamma\right) \left(\sum_{s \neq t \neq v_\alpha \in N_m} P_{st}\left(v_\alpha\right)\right)\right]$$

Here, $BN(v)$ is the bottleneck centrality of node v. The function $\sum_{s \neq t \neq v_\alpha \in N_m} P_{st}\left(v_\alpha\right)$ 1 if more than $|V(T_s)|/4$ paths from node s to other nodes in T_s meet at the vertex v, otherwise $P_s(v) = 0$.

Community Detection

The term community means a sub-group of nodes having strong connections compare to other nodes of the network. Here, we use a multiplex Infomap algorithm for calculating communities in multi-layer networks (Domenico, Lancichinetti, Arenas, & Rosvall, 2015). This method partitions the system based on the interconnected topology and information flow.

Supervised Machine Learning Techniques

In this article, we use following machine learning techniques:

- **SVM Classification:** SVM stands for "Support Vector Machine" is a supervised machine-learning algorithm, which is, used in both classification and regression problems. In this algorithm, each data item is plot into an n-dimensional region with the value of each feature being the value of a distinct coordinate. It is a binary classifier having two classes marked as the true class or false class (Fei, & Liu, 2006);
- **Naive Bayes:** Naive Bayes is a probabilistic technique, which follows the statistical approach to find the set of probabilistic features and express the shared probability patterns of categories (Escudero, Màrquez, & Rigau, 2000). Naïve Bayes technique uses Bayes theorem to find the strong ties between the features. This technique is beneficial for large datasets and follows sophisticated classification methods. The basic formulation of this method is given as follow:

$$P\left(c|x\right) = \frac{P(x \mid c)P\left(c\right)}{P\left(x\right)}$$

Here, P(c|x) is the posterior probability, P(x|c) is the likelihood priority, P(c) is the class of prior probability and the P(x) is the predictor prior probability.

- **Decision Trees:** The decision tree is a sense-tagged algorithm in which the training is done for prediction (Navigli, 2009). In this algorithm, yes-no types of rules are used for classification and dividing the training dataset. In the topology of the decision tree, internal nodes are the features and edges represent feature value and leaf nodes as the sense;
- **Neural Networks:** The interconnection of artificial neurons evolves the concept of neural networks. Such networks consist of multiple hidden layers, and with the help of these layers, the input is processed. There are two types of neural network techniques: backpropagation and feedforward. In both the techniques input and expected output are used for learning. Such approaches aim to make use of input features to divide the training set into non-overlapping sets by considering the expected outputs. (Azzini, da Costa Pereira, Dragoni, & Tettamanzi, 2008).

Figure 2. Neural network algorithm basic working

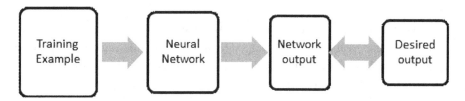

Compute Influential Score

The influential score is calculated by getting the difference between the original score of the nodes with the predicted score of the nodes, i.e. before and after applying machine-learning algorithms. The nodes having value and least change in the expected value are marked as influential users. A snippet of the proposed algorithm is shown in Algorithm 1.

Algorithm 1: Classifying influential individuals in multi-layer social network

```
Data: Graph G
Result: iu: set of influential users
Initialization:
1.          Identify communities in network
2.          For each node i
3.          Calculate various centrality value
4.          Apply SVM, Naïve Bayes, Decision Tree, Neural Networks
5.          Calculate Influential Score for each node i
6.          Put high valued nodes in set iu
7.          iu is the desired output.
```

EXPERIMENTAL RESULTS

Datasets Used

The proposed methodology is implemented on two multi-layer networks: Vickers Chan 7th-grade dataset and London transport dataset. Both the dataset consist of 3 layers and each layer describes the different relation between nodes. A brief description of both the dataset is given below:

- **Vickers Chan 7th Graders:** Vickers composes this dataset after analyzing the behavior of 29 7th grade students in a school in Victoria, Australia (Vickers, & Chan, 1981). The dataset consists of 3 layers and each layer defines the relation between students by asking the following questions:
  Who do you get on within the class?
  Who are your best friends in the class?
  Who would you prefer to work with?

There are 29 nodes in the network out of which 1-12 are boys and rest are girls. The total numbers of edges in the network are 740, which shows the network is highly connected.

- **London Transport Dataset:** This dataset is collected from the official website of Transport for London for the year 2013. It consists of 369 nodes (each train station denotes a node of the network) and 441 edges (each route between stations denotes edge). Underground, over ground and DLR stations indicate the different layers of the system (Domenico, Solé-Ribalta, Gómez, & Arenas, 2014).

Implementation Details

The proposed methodology is implemented using the muxViz tool, Python and R programming language. In muxViz, we find degree centrality, betweenness centrality, and communities of the network (Domenico, Porter, & Arenas, 2015). Using R programming, we see the bottleneck centrality of nodes of the net. The Machine learning algorithms and performance analysis are done using python programming. We implement our proposed methodology on the system having 8GB RAM and 2.3 GHz Intel processor.

Performance Metrics

Calculating the precision, recall, and f1-score checks the performance of the proposed methodology. The precision metric finds the ratio of correctly predicted positive values with the total predicted the positive value for each node of the network. The recall metric calculates the rate of accurately predicted positive benefit to all computed values of nodes in the system. F1 Score is the weighted average of Precision and Recall, and this score takes both false positives and false negatives into account.

Results

In this section, we discuss our findings on both the multi-layer dataset after applying the proposed algorithm. In figure 3 and figure 4, we demonstrate the performance of the proposed methodology on both the datasets. We calculate the precision, recall, and f1-score individually machine-learning algorithms and estimate the variation in values of precision and recall. London Transport dataset, The neural network algorithm doesn't perform well for almost all the centrality values, whereas naïve Bayes and decision trees are the vice versa. From the performance, we can see that the choice of the machine learning algorithm is an important aspect.

We also find the accuracy for the machine learning algorithms for both the datasets to check the overall performance of each of the classification. In the table below, we conclude that the Naïve Bayes algorithm holds high accuracy and neural networks have less accuracy in results. From these results, we find that the neural network algorithm is not best suited for such applications.

At last, we compute the influence score for all the nodes of both the datasets. We found that only 20% of nodes in London transport network have less percentage of difference in the predicted vs. original score. This happens because the system is sparse. So, we mark such nodes as the influential individual of the networks and such influential stations are busiest stations and have more train traffic compare to others.

Figure 3. Precision, recall, F1-score and support metrics London transport dataset for various machine learning algorithms and centrality methods

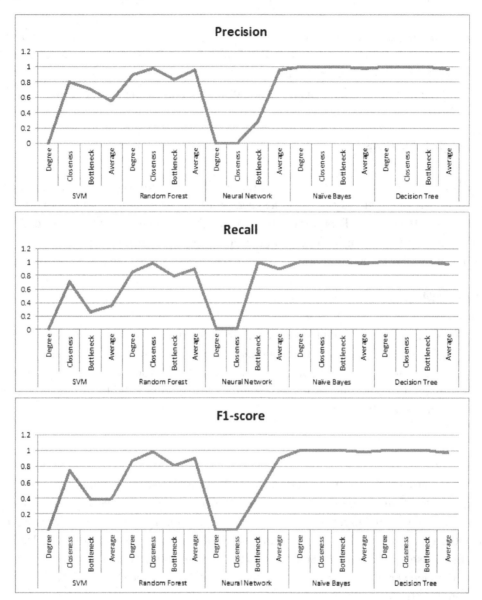

Table 1. Accuracy metrics of proposed model for both dataset

Machine Learning Algorithm	Accuracy (Vicker Chan Dataset)	Accuracy (London Transport Dataset)
SVM	97%	96%
Random Forest	93%	94%
Naive Bayes	97%	97%
Neural Networks (200 hidden Layers)	83%	80%
Decision Tree	97%	95.5%

Figure 4. Precision, recall, F1-score and support metrics for Vicker Chan dataset for various machine learning algorithms and centrality methods

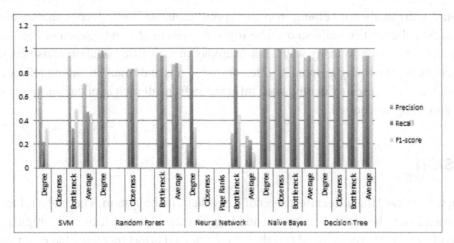

Figure 5. Accuracy metrics of proposed model for both dataset

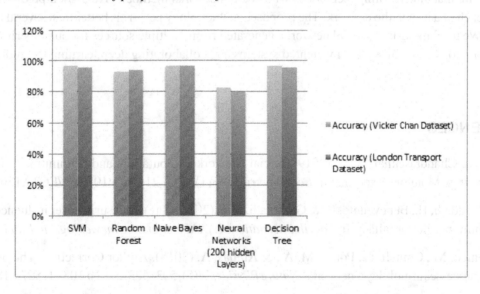

For Vicker Chan dataset, we compute the influential score for the nodes and found that 35.5% of nodes have less percentage of difference in the predicted vs. original score. This happens because the network is dense. So, we mark such nodes as the influential individual of them, and such prominent students are quite popular in the class. From these results, we conclude that collaborating machine learning techniques with multi-layer social networks techniques provides us some interesting findings, which are used to identify and classify influential users in the networks.

Implementation in Cyber Hack Applications

The Influential individuals are helping in many applications such as advertisements, election campaigns, scientific collaborations and so on. The roles of Influential users in each of these applications are different but are helping in many ways. For example, in scientific collaborations network, finding influential scientists are helping in spreading new technologies and research among fellow researchers. The proposed approach is used to identify such influencers from all such application, where information diffusion or spreading is required.

CONCLUSION

In this paper, we analyzed the influential power of individuals in the system. The analysis includes different types of correlations between users by considering the network in the form of multiple layers. When all the properties of a user were studied together, the combined effort increases the reach value further. Here, we built a model to find the influential individuals in the networks. We empirically showed that collaborating machine learning techniques with social networks methods give a good prediction of the average reach of a user in the network. The proposed methodology performs better than several baselines systems. We used multi-layer social networks generated from multiple sources for our experiments. We are planning to extend our work on weighted systems and collaborating deep learning techniques in the future.

REFERENCES

Breza, E., & Chandrasekhar, A. G. (2019). Social Networks, Reputation, and Commitment: Evidence From a Savings Monitors Experiment. *Econometrica*, 87(1), 175–216. doi:10.3982/ECTA13683

Cha, M., Haddadi, H., Benevenuto, F., & Gummadi, K. P. (2010, May). Measuring user influence in twitter: The million follower fallacy. In *Fourth international AAAI conference on weblogs and social media*.

De Domenico, M., Granell, C., Porter, M. A., & Arenas, A. (2018). Author Correction: The physics of spreading processes in multilayer networks. *Nature Physics*, 14(5), 523–523. doi:10.103841567-018-0065-4

De Domenico, M., Lancichinetti, A., Arenas, A., & Rosvall, M. (2015). Identifying modular flows on multilayer networks reveals highly overlapping organization in interconnected systems. *Physical Review X*, 5(1), 011027. doi:10.1103/PhysRevX.5.011027

De Domenico, M., Porter, M. A., & Arenas, A. (2015). MuxViz: A tool for multilayer analysis and visualization of networks. *Journal of Complex Networks*, 3(2), 159–176. doi:10.1093/comnet/cnu038

De Domenico, M., Solé-Ribalta, A., Gómez, S., & Arenas, A. (2014). Navigability of interconnected networks under random failures. *Proceedings of the National Academy of Sciences of the United States of America*, 111(23), 8351–8356. doi:10.1073/pnas.1318469111 PMID:24912174

El Bacha, R., & Zin, T. T. (2018, May). A Survey on Influence and Information Diffusion in Twitter Using Big Data Analytics. In *International Conference on Big Data Analysis and Deep Learning Applications* (pp. 39-47). Springer Singapore.

Escudero, G., Màrquez, L., & Rigau, G. (2000). Naive Bayes and exemplar-based approaches to word sense disambiguation revisited. arXiv preprint cs/0007011

Fei, B., & Liu, J. (2006). Binary tree of SVM: A new fast multiclass training and classification algorithm. *IEEE Transactions on Neural Networks, 17*(3), 696–704. doi:10.1109/TNN.2006.872343 PMID:16722173

Huang, X., Shao, S., Wang, H., Buldyrev, S. V., Stanley, H. E., & Havlin, S. (2013). The robustness of interdependent clustered networks. *Europhysics Letters, 101*(1), 18002. doi:10.1209/0295-5075/101/18002

Kolog, E. A., Montero, C. S., & Toivonen, T. (2018, January). Using machine learning for sentiment and social influence analysis in text. In *International Conference on Information Theoretic Security* (pp. 453-463). Cham: Springer. 10.1007/978-3-319-73450-7_43

Kuncheva, Z., & Montana, G. (2015). Community detection in multiplex networks using locally adaptive random walks. Retrieved from http://arxiv.org/abs/1507.01890

Lin, K. C., Wu, S. H., Chen, L. P., & Yang, P. C. (2015, August). Finding the key users in Facebook fan pages via a clustering approach. In *2015 IEEE International Conference on Information Reuse and Integration* (pp. 556-561). IEEE. 10.1109/IRI.2015.89

Mallipeddi, R., Kumar, S., Sriskandarajah, C., & Zhu, Y. (2018). A Framework for Analyzing Influencer Marketing in Social Networks: Selection and Scheduling of Influencers. Fox School of Business.

Mittal, R., & Bhatia, M. P. S. (2017, July). Mining top-k structural holes in multiplex networks. In *2017 8th International Conference on Computing, Communication and Networking Technologies (ICCCNT)* (pp. 1-6). IEEE. 10.1109/ICCCNT.2017.8204129

Mittal, R., & Bhatia, M. P. S. (2018). Anomaly Detection in Multiplex Networks. *Procedia Computer Science, 125*, 609–616. doi:10.1016/j.procs.2017.12.078

Mittal, R., & Bhatia, M. P. S. (2018, July). Cross-Layer Closeness Centrality in Multiplex Social Networks. In *2018 9th International Conference on Computing, Communication and Networking Technologies (ICCCNT)* (pp. 1-5). IEEE. 10.1109/ICCCNT.2018.8494042

Mittal, R., & Bhatia, M. P. S. (2018). Characterizing the Properties of the Multiplex Social Networks. In *IEEE conference Indiacom.*

Mittal, R., & Bhatia, M. P. S. (2019). Analysis of Multiplex Social Networks Using Nature-Inspired Algorithms. In *Nature-Inspired Algorithms for Big Data Frameworks* (pp. 290–318). IGI Global. doi:10.4018/978-1-5225-5852-1.ch012

Mittal, R., & Bhatia, M. P. S. (2019). Identifying Prominent Authors from Scientific Collaboration Multiplex Social Networks. In *International Conference on Innovative Computing and Communications* (pp. 289-296). Springer Singapore. 10.1007/978-981-13-2324-9_29

Mittal, R., & Bhatia, M. P. S. (2019). Discovering bottlenecks entities in multi-layer social networks. *Journal of Discrete Mathematical Sciences and Cryptography*, 22(2), 241–252. doi:10.1080/0972052 9.2019.1582870

Newman, M. E. J. (2003). The structure and function of complex networks. *SIAM Review*, 45(2), 167–256. doi:10.1137/S003614450342480

Sadri, A. M., Hasan, S., Ukkusuri, S. V., & Lopez, J. E. S. (2018). Analysis of social interaction network properties and growth on Twitter. *Social Network Analysis and Mining*, 8(1), 56. doi:10.100713278-018-0533-y

Shao, S., Huang, X., Stanley, H. E., & Havlin, S. (2014). Robustness of a partially interdependent network formed of clustered networks. *Phys. Rev. E*, 89(3), 032812. doi:10.1103/PhysRevE.89.032812 PMID:24730904

Shin, H., Xu, Z., & Kim, E. Y. (2008, December). Discovering and browsing of power users by social relationship analysis in large-scale online communities. In *Proceedings of the 2008 IEEE/WIC/ACM International Conference on Web Intelligence and Intelligent Agent Technology* (Vol. 1, pp. 105-111). IEEE Computer Society. 10.1109/WIIAT.2008.391

Vickers, M., & Chan, S. (1981). *Representing classroom social structure*. Melbourne: Victoria Institute of Secondary Education.

Wadhwa, P., & Bhatia, M. P. S. (2012). Social networks analysis: trends, techniques and future prospects.

Wadhwa, P., & Bhatia, M. P. S. (2014). Community detection approaches in real world networks: A survey and classification. *International Journal of Virtual Communities and Social Networking*, 6(1), 35–51. doi:10.4018/ijvcsn.2014010103

Wadhwa, P., & Bhatia, M. P. S. (2014). Classification of radical messages in Twitter using security associations. In *Case studies in secure computing: Achievements and trends* (pp. 273-294).

Wadhwa, P., & Bhatia, M. P. S. (2014). Discovering hidden networks in on-line social networks. *International Journal of Intelligent Systems and Applications*, 6(5), 44–54. doi:10.5815/ijisa.2014.05.04

Wadhwa, P., & Bhatia, M. P. S. (2015). Measuring radicalization in online social networks using Markov Chains. *Journal of Applied Security Research*, 10(1), 23–47. doi:10.1080/19361610.2015.972265

Wadhwa, P., & Bhatia, M. P. S. (2015). An approach for dynamic identification of online radicalization in social networks. *Cybernetics and Systems*, 46(8), 641–665. doi:10.1080/01969722.2015.1058665

Wadhwa, P., & Bhatia, M. P. S. (2016). New Metrics for Dynamic Analysis of Online Radicalization. *Journal of Applied Security Research*, 11(2), 166–184. doi:10.1080/19361610.2016.1137203

Watanabe, S., & Kabashima, Y. (2014). Cavity-based robustness analysis of interdependent networks: Influences of intranetwork and internetwork degree-degree correlations. *Phys. Rev. E*, 89(1), 012808. doi:10.1103/PhysRevE.89.012808 PMID:24580282

This research was previously published in the International Journal of Electronics, Communications, and Measurement Engineering (IJECME), 8(1); pages 21-32, copyright year 2019 by IGI Publishing (an imprint of IGI Global).

Chapter 28
The Culture of Volunteerism and the Role of Social Media in its Development

Maged Akel
Tishreen University, Lattakia, Syria

Osama Mohammad
Tishreen University, Lattakia, Syria

ABSTRACT

Volunteering is one of the various social activities that human societies have known and practiced since their inception. It is not the outcome of the last decades of the life of these societies, but it was present in almost every human civilization in its various forms and methods. Voluntary work is of great importance as far as individuals and societies are concerned. It is a symbol of solidarity among the members of the community and all its institutions. It positively affects people's lives as well as the community at large. It symbolizes the meanings of good, giving, and help. Accordingly, volunteering has become a cornerstone in building society and social cohesion among its members. In this regard, voluntary work is of great importance. It necessitates the need to spread this culture in the society and to promote and develop volunteerism among young people using all available and possible methods.

INTRODUCTION

Volunteerism is considered one of the most important social activities that accompanied the emergence of human society. It evolved through its development through the ages. The impact of various types and methods of spontaneous volunteerism is dominant in almost every human civilization.

As the human society developed, voluntary work has developed in terms of size and impact. It had a specific methodology and mechanisms of action. This has led the societies of the world to pay more attention to volunteerism, and to spread the culture that supports it as well as to develop the mechanisms that make it possible to benefit most from volunteers, their skills and expertise which they wish to har-

DOI: 10.4018/978-1-6684-6307-9.ch028

ness in the developmental field. Moreover, the mechanism harnessed should implant in their minds the culture of voluntary work and incite them to practice it in all its forms.

The best of these mechanisms is that promotes and develops the culture of volunteering can be social media networks. They have two advantages as far as the field of volunteering is concerned. The first is that they can address a large number of people through participating in voluntary initiatives. The second is publicity for these initiatives so that the idea of voluntary work becomes popular, and then turns to developmental initiatives having supporters of financial and cultural capabilities who would help develop and support these initiatives.

RESEARCH PROBLEM

Volunteering work plays a crucial role in building and developing society through its many activities, projects and services which are characterized by smoothness, flexibility and speed of movement. Voluntary work today is one of the outstanding works in the lives of people and societies at peace and war times and at times of crisis. It is an essential element in achieving social cohesion among individuals of society, especially with crises and tribulations afflicting humanity. But voluntary work as an important humanitarian practice is not one in all human societies. It differs from a society to another in terms of form, size, motives, trends, and from time to time. It becomes important and increasingly needed as the societies progress and their life getting more and more complex in all fields and aspects of life.

Volunteering, in this context, has become a vital area for important cultural, social and economic activities. The modern concept of development gives particular importance to the voluntary sector.

In view of this paramount importance for volunteerism, societies ought to pay attention to volunteering, disseminate and reinforce this culture in society, and find appropriate mechanisms and means for the development and promotion of this culture. Perhaps one of the most important means and mechanisms that develop and promote voluntary work within the community are social media networks. These networks represent the new generation of the Internet. They provide new opportunities to communicate through the network using social networking sites, and their impact on people, and how these social media sites can be exploited by some institutions and organizations.

Almost every organization and establishment have a page or an account on social media networking sites, where the big role of this site is shown through contribution to the construction of social virtual networks.

The Facebook site is in the forefront; it is the most important because of its great impact in supporting the idea of communication. It is possible to promote the culture of voluntary work among young people, and to demonstrate its role in society, and the need to engage in it. This is due to the benefits it offers to members or users and their community, providing opportunities to exchange videos and photos and share files and conduct instant conversations and achieve direct communication and interaction, which plays a significant role in influencing the youth using it.

It also might contribute to the development of the culture of volunteerism, which will enable the community to benefit from the energies and capabilities of volunteers and their skills.

The culture of voluntary work reflects a national will that springs from the desire of individuals in society to progress, develop and participate in confronting the challenges and crises that afflict society to minimize their effects and guarantee a better standard of living. Volunteers and voluntary associations have become a criterion showing the degree of the progress and sophistication of a society.

Accordingly, the problem of this research is thus the following main questions:

- What is the culture of voluntary work?
- What is the role of social media networks in the development of voluntary work within society?

THE IMPORTANCE OF THE STUDY

The importance of the study springs from the society's urgent need for voluntary work and the need to spread its culture among young people as a way to fill the gaps and put an end to present deficiencies, as well as to address the problems that the government sector cannot handle alone. Voluntary work plays a great role in the overall development process in society.

The importance of this study stems from the great importance of the social media networks in the life of each person as a modern means of communication that ensures constant and direct communication between individuals. These sites contribute to the promotion of human thought because they are easy to use, a feature these sites enjoy making them much more powerful than other means of communication.

Of course, this can pave the way for the development of the culture of volunteerism and spread it everywhere, especially among the youth, who represent the power and source of energy for the society.

RESEARCH GOALS

The present study aims at:

1. Recognizing the concept of voluntary work, its importance, and the need to spread its culture in society;
2. Identifying the role of social media networks in the development of the culture of volunteering within the community.

Previous studies:

- Youth and voluntary work in Palestine (Rahal, 2006).

The problem of the study:

- The main problem here is the lack of active participation in voluntary work in Palestine. This is reflected in the low participation and limited participation in the public sphere.

The researcher adopted the historical approach in addition to using the analytical descriptive approach in analyzing the crisis of voluntary work and the comparative approach in studying the experiences of some countries.

THE MAIN FINDINGS OF THE STUDY

- The decline of voluntary work in Palestine with the formation of the Palestinian National Authority;
- Another reason which caused the decline in voluntary work in Palestine is the decline in the positive values and the lack of interest of various socialization institutions in enhancing this value in children;
- The prevailing economic conditions and the weak financial resources of the voluntary organizations led to the decline in voluntary work in Palestine;
- Male and female volunteers do not often participate in decision-making within voluntary institutions (Social Impact of Volunteerism, 2011).

The problem of the study:

- The problem of this study is the social impact of voluntary work. This is a secondary, independent study that assesses whether the national and community service affects society as a whole. This study adopted the descriptive and historical approach.

The main findings of the study are:

- Volunteerism promotes social relations between different sectors;
- Volunteerism helps build a more cohesive, safer and stronger society. It also helps in reinforcing the social network between local communities and the neighborhoods;
- Volunteerism encourages people and those interested in citizenship to be more active in civic engagement;
- Volunteerism provides some public services, pushing sustainable development forward, and solving environmental problems;
- The role of social media networks in serving the humanitarian work (Al Harbi, 2014).

THE PROBLEM OF STUDY

The problem of the study in the main question:

What is the role of social media networks in the service of humanitarian work?

The researcher used a descriptive approach based on collecting, organizing and arranging data to reach the results.

The main findings of the study are:

- Humanitarian action is a form of human solidarity, which provides good for others;
- Some of the fields of humanitarian work: advocacy, relief, health and media;
- Social media networks play an internal and external role in case of disturbances and disasters;
- Their internal roles are to clarify the truth and highlight the damage and losses and to suggest ways and methods of support and assistance;

- Their external role includes religious education, health and security in addition to the coordination of charitable support and assistance.

CONCEPTS AND TERMINOLOGY

Work

Work is defined as an occupation or a profession for which the individual acquires skills, experience and knowledge usually associated with a long experience and practice. It can also be considered a skill since it necessitates certain knowledge and abilities. It can also be considered as an activity of the individual from which he or she derives the meaning of existence and livelihood as well as bread wining (Arab Women Organization, 2011, p. 16).

Volunteerism

Volunteerism is idiomatically defined as applying this term to that characteristic of social theory which aims at interpreting the act that lies in the intentions of its doer, that is, the volunteers acting voluntarily and their actions are not determined according to their organic or social structure (Bruce & Yearly, 20, 2006, p. 315).

Voluntary Work

It is "the work that is done by some persons who voluntarily choose to do it, without asking for any compensation" (Hornby, 2010, p. 1709).

Culture

It is all that the human hand has made and all the human mind has created in all areas of the natural, social and intellectual aspects of the environment, which includes his inventions, discoveries and social heritage of customs, traditions and customs. It has a role in the social process that is passed from generation to another (Ibrahim, 2003, p. 49).

Social Media Networks

It is a system of electronic networks which allows the subscriber to create a site of his own, and then connects it through an electronic social system with other members who have the same interests and hobbies, or it connects the subscriber with friends of the university or high secondary (Radi, 2003, p. 23).

Study Approach

The descriptive approach will be adopted in this study based on gathering organizing and arranging information to reach the results.

The Concept and Importance of Volunteerism

The concept of voluntary work is not a recent concept. It is found in all civilizations and religions. Volunteerism is divided into general volunteerism, and voluntary work. The general volunteerism means that the volunteer does a voluntary act which is not directly related to his or her scientific or practical background.

In the voluntary work, the volunteer is volunteering through his or her knowledge and expertise specialized in the field gained through his or her academic studies and work so that organizations and bodies which work in this field benefit from his or her experience.

Volunteerism, linguistically speaking, is defined as a form of obedience. It is a kind of donation. It is not a must (Al Safar, 2004. p. 8).

Idiomatically, Volunteerism is defined as a social activity carried out by individuals individually or collectively through an association or an institution, without asking for something in return. It aims satisfying the needs and solving the problems of society and contributing to the consolidation of the development process in it. (Al-Rashoud, 2007, p. 328).

Volunteering is therefore a non-profit work. It is not a professional work. It is carried out by individuals in order to help and develop the standard of living of others.

Sociologists have defined volunteerism as an effort based on skill, experience or expertise, which is exerted on a desire or choice, for the purpose of performing a social duty without necessarily expecting financial reward (Aswad, 2011, p. 272).

The Importance of Voluntary

Voluntary work is an integral part of the government's efforts and a support for its efforts as well. It is characterized by flexibility and speed of movement, which enables it to overcome some of the difficulties and solve problems that government institutions may not be able to handle.

Volunteering is an appropriate field for conscious and responsible youth. It is also the key that opens the horizon for communication with others, builds bridges of brotherhood and generates generosity. It is one of the most important means of strengthening social ties and promoting human values.

The significance of voluntary work springs from the fact that it seeks to serve the community and satisfy the needs of people because it develops human's mental abilities, skills and behavioral qualifications, which strengths his or her personality. Experience and expertise can also be gained from voluntary work can also make man well aware of the reality of community where he lives. It might also show the individual his or her prestige in society. It expands the circle of his or her relations and connections, and shows his talents and competencies (Al-Zaffar, 2007, p. 16).

Moreover, voluntary work is viewed as a measure of progress and development among nations. It plays a vital role in the process of comprehensive development in society in collaboration with other sectors in the society.

In view of the importance of volunteerism, it is necessary to pay more attention to it and to ensure that the culture of voluntary work among young people is constantly supported, observed and encouraged.

Volunteering Culture

The level of culture in any society is a sign of the vitality or stagnation of this society. If the culture of the prevailing society is productive and flexible, it is an advanced dynamic society and vice versa. If culture is a negative, then society will be stagnant and inefficient.

At present day, volunteerism has become an approach, a work method that requires abilities and skills that volunteers have to acquire and practise them practically. If the culture of volunteering is an integral part of the culture of developed societies representing the system of values, principles, standards and practices that encourage initiative and positive action done for the good and benefit of others.

Therefore, the extent of volunteering and involvement in it depends on the extent of the culture of volunteerism in the social sphere. Accordingly, it was necessary to activate the culture of volunteering at the theoretical and practical levels in the social environment through:

1. Formulating a new discourse on the culture of volunteering in a new manner capable of influencing contemporary generations;
2. Focusing on the benefits and gains achieved by the voluntary work for volunteers to convince them of the importance of participating in it;
3. Attracting new voluntary work for breathing a new spirit in society, and producing new ideas and programs;
4. Overcoming the problems and obstacles which hinder voluntary work, and encouraging volunteers and offering financial and spiritual support (Al Yosif, 2005, pp. 21-22).

Thus, the culture of volunteerism comes as one of the necessary needs to be strengthened and developed in the personality of the individual, which evolves through the processes of socialization and cultural formation by the educational institutions.

Types of Volunteer Work

Types of voluntary work vary depending on the organization, whether public, private or non-profit. It also depends on whether that organization engages in voluntary work for a fixed or long period of time, or according to its program. In general, two forms of volunteerism can be distinguished.

Individual Voluntary Work

It is a social act or behavior done by the individual spontaneously, willingly and without any financial gain, based on ethical, social, humanitarian or religious considerations. Individual volunteerism is, however, can stop at any time when facing obstacles unlike the second type.

Institutional Voluntary Work

It is more advanced than individual voluntary work, more organized and more influential in society. In society, there are many institutions in which voluntary work is of great importance. Institutional volunteerism contributes to all social efforts and energies, making them effective if these efforts are incorporated and coordinated (Amer, 2011, p. 9).

It gives the group more respect and strength and thus makes its members immune against individualism or selfishness or deviation from the goals set, and makes them stronger when facing difficulties and challenges during the exercise of voluntary work. Other kinds of voluntary work is donating money and to a body to do something, and volunteering through consultation or research and study.

Benefits of Volunteering

Voluntary work allows people to be involved in the lives of their local and national communities. It gives them a sense of belonging and integration. It also gives them the chance to participate directly in change processes and to support new developments. Thus, it becomes a tool to control their lives and fulfill their responsibilities.

Impact of Voluntary Work on the Individual and Society

Voluntary work has many positive effects both at the individual and community levels.

The Most Important Effects on the Individual Volunteer

First, feeling a kind of psychological comfort when doing any voluntary work.

Second, getting new life experience and knowledge in life. Third, acquiring abilities and capabilities to help improve the behavior of the volunteer.

Fourth, filling in leisure times in a useful way and strengthening the sense of national belonging and making the individual well aware of his or her value and social status. (Al Maliki, 2010, p. 44).

It is worth noting that values of solidarity and the sense of empathy, sympathy and cooperation are a common denominator of all voluntary activities. As these values play an essential role in promoting the physical, economic and social well-being of the most vulnerable and poorest classes in the society, voluntary work can contribute to reducing slavery. Social cohesion and confidence are greater and stronger where voluntary activities take place.

The Positive Effects of Voluntary Work on Society

The positive effects of volunteering on society are:

1. Increasing and reinforcing solidarity and human relations among the members of the society;
2. Developing society in all respects of life;
3. Eliminating destitution as much as possible. Volunteerism often launches campaigns for raising financial donations;
4. Promoting positive competition between individuals and groups;
5. Spending money that would otherwise be spent uselessly in voluntary service projects of paramount importance in society, such as building a school for war-displaced people or refugees (Mashalah, 2017).

It, is therefore, clear that voluntary work must be taken into consideration in every development plan, where it is essential to expand volunteerism and support it, and to promote and reinforce its culture within society.

SOCIAL MEDIA

Social Media sites and networks are one of the most prominent manifestations of the new mass media of the Internet revolution. It depends on new technologies like forums and social networking programs.

Social media has the advantage of being a non-intermediary media, because unlike traditional mass media, (which is an intermediary media that starts as institutional broadcast directed toward public reception), everyone here can be a journalist and a spectator or follower at the same time.

Social media networking can be defined as a set of web sites that have emerged with the second generation of the Internet. It enables people to communicate in a virtual community environment where account holders are grouped according to interest groups or affiliation networks through direct communication services such as sending messages, viewing others' profiles following others' news, the news they themselves want to make public. Social media offers writings, pictures, films, chats and definitions. (Alsaid & Abdelal, 2009, p. 7).

Social Media networks have become an effective means of communication in everyday events, providing an opportunity for all young people, researchers and politicians to convey their ideas and discuss their social, economic and political issues whatever they like to convey thus going beyond natural borders to new and uncensored spaces.

Advantages and Disadvantages of Social Media

Advantages of Social Media Networks

Social media has many benefits like:

1. Ongoing communication among users of these networks with each other. This communication might reinforce social cohesion and improve relations in the community. Social media can also be a means to exercise cultural and social activities that aim at bringing people closer;
2. Social Media also facilitates the process of communication. It allows citizens to have the ability to express themselves, their community and issues;
3. Another advantage of social media networking is that it is global, going beyond time and space barriers and facilitating communication easily in a virtual technical environment;
4. It also offers the possibility of interactivity where the interactive user is an active player because he or she is the receiver, the sender, the writer and the participant;
5. Social media is also a channel that enables people to launch their innovation and creativity. It can also help spread the culture of volunteering and encourage young people to engage in it through the promotion and publicity displayed on its websites about its importance and its benefits for individuals and society;
6. It also helps to exchange ideas, views and getting to know the culture of people of other nations (Al Dodi, 2011, p. 8).

Despite the importance of social media networks, but like any other technological means they have their disadvantages and shortcoming. Some of the disadvantages of social media can be summed up as follows.

Disadvantages of Social Media Networks

1. Excessive use has a negative impact on the health of individuals, which makes them more vulnerable to tension and depression and other psychological disorders;
2. Wasting youths' surfing through the pages of those sites and talking about trivial matters;
3. Overuse can cause social isolation, lack of integration of the individual with his or her family and detachment from the problems and concerns of the family as well as lack participation in social events;
4. Social media can a fertile soil for the emergence of abnormal.

Ideas as well as rumors. All new events are echoed and exchanged on social media sites by different and sometimes contradictory groups (Yaqob, 2015, p. 35).

The Role of Social Media Networks in Spreading the Culture of Voluntary Work in Society

Volunteerism was not far from the state of human consciousness in its new nature in social media networks.

Many institutions and associations took advantage of the new media in spreading the culture of volunteering in all its forms by establishing pages on social media networks .They made their activities public on social media sites. This helped a lot to spread the culture of voluntary work and to attract more volunteers.

Social media networks provided an unprecedented opportunity to address people from all walks of life in different regions.

It is worth noting that social media are mostly used by the young people. This group of people is the most important resource. It the pillar of the voluntary workforce.

Therefore, it was necessary to reach them and speak their language and thus attract and encourage them to volunteer and plant the culture of voluntary work in their minds. It is not always necessarily to use social media networks to publish pictures, news or videos about the activities of associations or voluntary organizations. It is enough to write about topics which have something to do with voluntary work showing its benefits as far as individuals and society are concerned.

In addition to the above mentioned, the role of social networks in promoting and reinforcing the culture of voluntary work within society can be achieved by:

1. Making use of technology as an activity that contributes to the development of volunteerism;
2. Collecting, storing, retrieving and analyzing voluntary work information, because using such networks in information systems management makes information available in a timely and efficient manner based on the efficiency of available data;
3. Improving the quality of the internal processes of volunteerism and providing effective information systems to facilitate the efficiency of planning and organization across the networks of social media;

4. It is also possible to receive and study complaints and urgent cases electronically and analyze them to verify the credibility of the urgent situation (Kirdi, 2011, p. 44).

CONCLUSION

Social media networks are of great importance as far as their users are concerned. They have progressed from being a means of communication to a tool used to promote and support voluntary work, which is crucial and vital for society and its members. Social media is indispensable to promote the culture of voluntary work in society, especially among the youth.

Voluntary work associations and organizations have been used to serve and achieve the general and specific objectives for which they were found.

REFERENCES

Al-Maliki, S. (2010). The extent of the awareness of postgraduate students at Umm Al-Qura University of the fields of voluntary work for women [Master's Thesis].

Al-Rabihat, S. (1993). Citizen Participation in Social Volunteerism and Prevention of Crime and Deviation. Arab Center for Security Studies and Training.

Al Saffar, H. (2004). *Voluntary work at community service*. Saudi Arabia: Dar Atyaf for Publishing and Distribution.

Al Seid, A. & Abdel-Al, H. (2009). Social networks and their impact on the specialist and library. Egyptian Association of Libraries and Information, Shawki Salem Library, Egypt.

Al-Yousef, A. (2005). *Culture of Voluntary Work*. Jeddah: Al-Raya Development Center.

AlDowei, I. (2011). *Social Networking. Makom Magazine*.

Amer, N. (2011). Participation in voluntary work, a study presented to the centers of social development.

Arab Women Organization. (2011). Gender and Sociology of Work and Institution.

Aswad, M. A. R. (2011). *Fields of Voluntary Work*. Egypt: Center for Research and Studies.

Bruce, S., & Yearley, S. (2006). The Sage Dictionary of Sociology. London, UK: SAGE Publications. Retrieved from https://rfdvcatedra.files.wordpress.com/2014/08/sage-dictionary.pdf

Hornby, A. S. (2010). *Oxford Advanced Learner's Dictionary* (7th ed.). China: Oxford University Press.

Jacob, S. (2015). Impact of Social Networking Sites on Political Awareness [Master's Thesis]. Postgraduate College, An-Najah University, Palestine.

Kirdi, A. (2011). *Skills of the Department of Charitable Work*. Egypt: Al-Hadi Foundation for Printing.

Mashala, F. (n.d.). The Benefits of Volunteering in the Life of the Individual and Society. Retrieved from http://mawdoo3.com

Radi, Z. (2003). Use of social networking sites in the Arab world. *Journal of Education*, 15.

Rahal, O. (2009). *Youth and voluntary work in Palestine.*

VSO International. (2014). Valuing volunteering the role of volunteering in sustainable development. Retrieved from https://www.vsointernational.org/sites/default/files/the_role_of_volunteering_in_sustainable_development_2015_vso_ids.pdf

This research was previously published in the International Journal of Information Systems and Social Change (IJISSC), 10(3); pages 14-23, copyright year 2019 by IGI Publishing (an imprint of IGI Global).

Chapter 29
Detection and Prevention of Twitter Users with Suicidal Self–Harm Behavior

Hadj Ahmed Bouarara

(iD) https://orcid.org/0000-0002-4973-4385

GeCoDe Laboratory, Saida, Algeria

ABSTRACT

Recently, with the development of communication means such as 4G and the rapid growth of the use of mobile devices (smartphones and tablets) the number of twitter users has increased exponentially. By the end of 2018 Twitter had 321 million active users with over 600 million tweets every day. However, all this information will have no use if we cannot access the meaning it carries. The authors' idea is to identify Twitter users with suicidal or self-harm behaviors by analyzing their tweets using an algorithm inspired from the social life of Asian elephants. The objective is to prevent the situations of depressions, threats of suicide or any other form of self-destructive behavior that exists on Twitter.

INTRODUCTION AND PROBLEMATIC

Twitter strives to provide an environment where users can feel free to express themselves. People's anxiety is reported to have increased 70% since the advent of the internet, according to a study published in 2018 by UK-based Royal Society of Public Health (Araque, 2019). Social networks are a vector of anxiety, sleep problems and depression. Twitter receives in this study, the palm of the worst network for morale.

In 2017, an event prompted them to react: an 18-year-old man posted a tweet explaining his desire to end life on twitter, it was April 24, 2017. The next day, he put an end to his days. A shock for users and a bad buzz for twitter. Since 2017, social networks have been working with suicide prevention associations around the world to provide support to persons in distress (Alaei, 2019).

It is difficult to interpret online publications. Even so, there are some warning signs that can help us to identify people who are suicidal or have a risk of self-harm such as:

DOI: 10.4018/978-1-6684-6307-9.ch029

- Does this person show a sense of depression or hopelessness in his publications?
- Does this person publish morbid comments? Does she evoke death unequivocally?
- Does this person post comments about past suicide attempts?
- Does this person describe or publish photos of self-harm?

In this context our goal is to develop a new system to detect depressive persons with self-harm or self-suicidal behavior using an algorithm inspired from the social life of Asian elephants. This system aims to analyze the feelings of twitter users based on the interpretation of their publications to prevent situations of depression by signaling a self-destructive post.

The general structure of this paper will be as follows: we start with a state of the art for presenting the essential works in this topic, after we go on with a section detailing our approach and proposed components then an experimental and comparative study will be carried out for presenting the best results obtained. Finally, we will finish with a conclusion and describing some lines of thought that remain open and that we want to share them with you.

LITERATURE REVIEW (RELATED WORK)

Our people detection problem with self-harm or suicidal behavior is registered in sentiment analysis field. In what follows we will mention the different works to realize in this context:

The work of Mohammad et al In (Mohammad, 2013) have described two state-of-the-art of SVM classifiers, one to detect the sentiment of messages such as tweets and SMS (message-level task) and one to detect the sentiment of a term within a message (term-level task) followed by the contributions of researcher Nasukawa and his team in 2003 (Nasukawa, 2003) who proposed a new method for extracting associated concepts from segments and summing the orientations of the opinion vocabulary present in the same segment.

In 2018 Mauro Dragoni et al proposed a commonsense ontology for sentiment analysis based on SenticNet, a semantic network of 100,000 concepts based on conceptual primitives (Dragoni, 2018). In 2006, researchers Kanayama and Nasukawa (Kanayama, 2006) as well as Ding and Liu (Ding, 2008) in 2008 proposed, for their part, a learning-based approach that uses the coordination conjunctions present between a word already classified and a word unclassified.

A new Approach using deep learning was proposed by Cicero Nogueira dos Santos in 2014 for the analysis of tweets, the authors applied their idea on the corpus STS and they have obtained an accuracy of more than 80% (Dos Santos, 2014). A Multimodal sentiment analysis is a very important growing field of research. A promising area of opportunity in this field is to improve the multimodal fusion mechanism in (Majumder, 2018) Majumder et al have developed a Hierarchical Fusion with Context Modeling based on a Multimodal Sentiment Analysis.

In (Alaei, 2019) different approaches to sentiment analysis applied in the field of data analysis and evaluation of metrics. The paper concludes by outlining future research avenues to further advance sentiment analysis in tourism as part of a broader Big Data approach.

In (Xiang, 2018) a new methodology has been adopted using a machine learning approach with which textual documents are represented by vectors and are used for training a polarity classification model. Several documents' vector representation approaches have been studied, including lexicon-based, word embedding based and hybrid vectorizations. The competence of these feature representations for the sentiment classification task is assessed through experiments on four datasets containing online user reviews in both Greek and English languages, in order to represent high and weak inflection language groups. In (Zheng, 2018) Zheng et al had the idea of sentimental feature selection for sentiment analysis of Chinese online reviews and also in (Proksch, 2019) the authors create a multilingual sentiment-based approach that can effectively capture different types of parliamentary conflict.

In (Araque, 2019), Araque et Zhu proposed a sentiment classification model that uses the semantic similarity measure in combination with embedding representations. In order to assess the effectiveness of this model, the authors perform an extensive evaluation. Experiments show that the proposed method can improve Sentiment Analysis performance over a strong baseline, being this improvement statistically significant.

PROPOSED APPROACH: THE SOCIAL LIFE OF ASIAN ELEPHANT

Generally, each Asian elephant lives in a group led by a matriarch1 (aged and experienced), who coordinates the movements of the herd. Elephants in each group may be temporarily divided to search for sources of water or food while maintaining contact (pool, 1999).

Elephants communicate with each other directly and discreetly up to 10 km away with an inaudible infrasound for humans (Bates, 2007). The experiments shown that elephants are able to recognize and follow their family members (Bates, 2008). They will join the contact calls sent by his friends from the same group.

The organization of the elephants social life has a practical advantage: when resources are scarce, in the case of drought, for example, links become tighter and elephants in the same group (family) come closer together. Each elephant in a drought situation looks for water points and follows the choice of its congeners. When he finds water points, he sends signals to inform his friends of the place of water. Elephants maintain close ties even after a separation of more than one year (McComb, 2001).

A scenario that summarizes the social phenomenon of Asian elephants in search of food or water points in case of drought is: Initially, a set of elephants are looking for a water point in the space randomly. Elephants do not know where is the water point but they know exactly how far away is and the positions of their elephant friends, then the question that arises: what is the strategy followed to find the water in good conditions? The best solution is to follow the elephants having best position relative to the water point with which have a strong bond of friendship thus to follow the laws of the matriarch who guide the direction of the group.

PASSAGE FROM NATURAL TO ARTIFICIAL

This part is dedicated to the passage of the natural life of social Asian elephants to artificial life as shown in Table 1.

Table 1. Passage from social life to artificial life of social Asian elephants' algorithm

Natural life of Asian social elephants	Algorithm of social Asian elephants
An elephant joins the water point found by his family group	**Each user is classified in the most appropriate class (depressive or non-depressive)**
Suppose the case where there are only two water points in the search space	**Two classes (depressive and no-depressive)**
Environment	Search space (twitter)
Elephant	Twitter user
Group of elephants	The users tweets (corpus)
Matriarch (oldest female)	Represents the message of the person with the highest score in the learning base
Best individual of each elephant group (initialization)	For each class it is the Person who has the best correlation with the centroid (barycenter)
Best individual (in process)	Best fitness function
Friendship link between elephant i and the best individual	α: link between each user and the best individual of each class (depressive or non-depressive)
Friendship link between the elephant I and the matriarch	β: link between each user and the matriarch of each class (depressive or non-depressive)
Communication between the elephant and the best individual	$\left| ME_T^g - E_T^i \right|$
Communication between the elephant i and the matriarch	$\left| PE_T^g - E_T^i \right|$

THE ARTIFICIAL LIFE OF SOCIAL ASIAN ELEPHANTS' (SAE) ALGORITHM

We have imitated the social life of Asian elephants and their water points search phenomenon in case of drought to formulate a new algorithm to detect depressive behavior by analyzing the users of twitter network. In our problem we have two classes depressive and no-depressive. The user status will be transformed to vectors. Each user with a velocity V is classified according to a fitness function based on his experience, the experiences of other users, the friendship relation that exists with the users of each class and the directives received by the matriarch of each class. The input of the algorithm is a set of twitter users' vectors (corpus), divided into two parts the learning basis and the test basis. The general process is detailed in Figure 1 and the stages of its operation are discussed later:

Initialisation

Initially, the position E_0^i and the velocity V_0^i of each user relative to each class g are calculated by the next equations (1) et (2):

$$VE_0^i = score\left(i\right) \tag{1}$$

$$E_0^i\left(g\right) = \text{the linear correlation between instance i and the centroid of class g} \tag{2}$$

Figure 1. General architecture of social Asian elephants (SEA) algorithm for depressive person detection

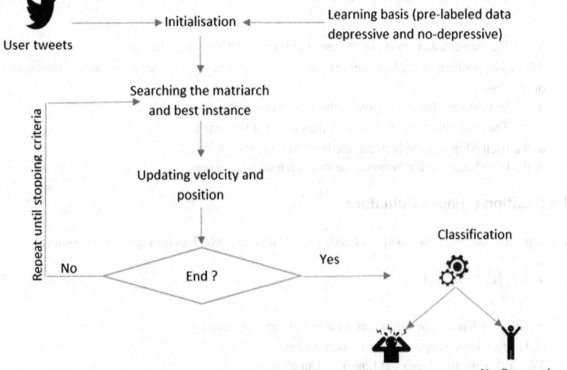

- $VE_0^i(g)$: The initial movement velocity of the user i.
- $E_0^i(g)$: The initial position of the instance t relative to the class g.
- *Score(i)*: The weights sum of the components user vector i.

For the classification of a new instance (of the test database) the following process is launched:

Matriarch

We are looking for the matriarch of each class (depressive or no-depressive) that is the user with the highest score (the elephant female, the oldest and the most experienced).

$$Mt(g) = (max(score(i)))g \tag{3}$$

- *Mt(g)*: The matriarch user at time t in class g.
- (max(*score(i)*))g: the user that has the highest score in the class g.

Velocity

The movement velocity of each user changes from time t to t + 1 by the equation (4):

$$VE_{T+1}^i(g) = \frac{VE_T^i}{\alpha\left(\left\|ME_T^g - E_T^i\right\|\right) + \beta\left(\left\|PE_T^g - E_T^i\right\|\right)} \tag{4}$$

- VE_T^i : The movement velocity of the user i at time t relative to the class g.
- ME_T^g : The position of the best user at time t in class g (initially it is the closest user to the centroid of the class).
- E_T^i : The position of user i at time t relative to the class g.
- PE_T^g : The position of the matriarch of the class g at the time t.
- α: the friendship relation between the best user and the user i.
- β: the friendship relation between the matriarch and the user i.

The Position (Fitness Function)

This step calculates the new position of each user relative to each class through the equation (5):

$$E_{t+1}^i(g) = E_t^i(g) + VE_{t+1}^i(g) \tag{5}$$

- E_t^i (g): position or fitness function of user i at time T in class g.
- G: has two values depressive or no-depressive.
- VE_{t+1}^i (g): velocity of user i at time T + 1 in class g

Evaluation (Classification) and Update

Each user is classified in the class (depressive or no-depressive) with the lowest fitness function. After each iteration the parameters of the algorithm are updated. The same process will be repeated until stopping criterion (number of iteration).

Procedure

The next pseudo code summarizes the functioning of the social elephant algorithm for the detection of depressive people in twitter network.

Social elephants algorithm.

1: Elephant: twitter user
2: input:
3: - corpus (learning basis, test basis)
4: - Initialisation $\left(E_{T=0}^i, V_{T=0}^i\right)$
5: $T \leftarrow 0$
7: while not CD do
8: for each tweets user to be classified do
9: for each class g do

10: calculate

11: $Mt(g) = (\max(score(i)))g$

12: find best user ME: with smaller position E

13: $VE_{T+1}^{i}(g) = \dfrac{VE_{T}^{i}}{\alpha\left(\left\|ME_{T}^{g} - E_{T}^{i}\right\|\right) + \beta\left(\left\|PE_{T}^{g} - E_{T}^{i}\right\|\right)}$

14: $E_{t+1}^{i}(g) = E_{t}^{i}(g) + VE_{t+1}^{i}(g)$

15: end for

16: L'instance$(i) \leftarrow$ the class with the smallest fitness function

17: end for

18: update (ME, M, V)

19: $T \leftarrow T + 1$

20: end while

21: output: the class of each user from the test basis.

For the vectorization of user tweets we use: i) text cleaning by eliminating special characters and numbers. ii) transforming tweets to a set of terms using bag of words, stemming or n-gram characters. ii) coding using TF (Term Frequency) or TF * IDF (term frequency * inversed document frequency).

Tweets2011 Corpus (Tweets)

Table 2. General statistical dataset Tweets2011

Category	Depressive	not depressive
Cinema	85	62
Policy	49	33
War	64	13
Sport	33	58
Music	119	56
Science	19	58

In our experiments we used the Tweets2011 corpus that was used in information retrieval famous competition called TREC 201. This specialized body built to keywords. The authors of this corpus have used the API to retrieve Twitter4J 649 tweets where they used keywords (politics, cinema, sport, music, war, science). After TREC in 2012 these tweets were classified in two class (depressive tweet, tweet not depressed) (McCreadie, 2012). The following table summarizes the classification of tweets.

Validation Measures

To validate our results, we have used different metrics that exist in literature such as recall, precision, f-measure, kapa static true positive, false positive, false negative and true negative (Oksuz, 2018).

Results and Discussion

In order to validate the quality of our proposal we have applied an experimental protocol by varying:

- Text representation methods.
- We set the parameters Alpha = 1 and beta = 1.
- Number of iteration.

with objective is to identify the sensitive parameters, we have fixed in each test one parameters and varying the others. We calculate the f-measure, entropy, recall precision kappa static. The best results are illustrated in the following tables.

NB: The boxes colored in blue represent the best results and the boxes colored in red represent the bad results.

Result with Variation of Text Representation:

As a result of the different languages that exist in the world, finding the best message representation technique is a very important task. In this part, we set each time the technique of representation of text (N-grams-characters with N of 2 to 5 and bag of words) and we vary the other parameters. The results are shown in the next table and figures.

Table 3. The results of analysis using the Asian elephant's algorithm for detecting depressive person in twitter with variation of representation techniques

		Evaluation measures						Confusion matrix	
		Precision	Recall	f-measure	TS (%)	TE(%)	static kappa		
Text representation techniques	Bag of words	0. 724	0. 699	0.7	67.79%	32.21%	0354	258	98
								111	182
	Stemming	0. 786	0617	0.6913	68.72%	31.28%	0386	228	62
								141	218
	2-gram characters	0.819	0.7235	0.769	75.19%	24.81%	0.5038	267	59
								102	221
	3-gram characters	0.86	0.764	0811	79.81	20.19	0.596	282	44
								87	236
	4-gram characters	0.918	0.791	0.854	84.12%	15.86%	0688	292	26
								77	254
	5-gram characters	0844	0.764	0802	78.58	21.42	0.56	282	52
								87	228

Figure 2. Number of tweets depressive and not-depressive obtained by the Asian elephants algorithm classified by categories

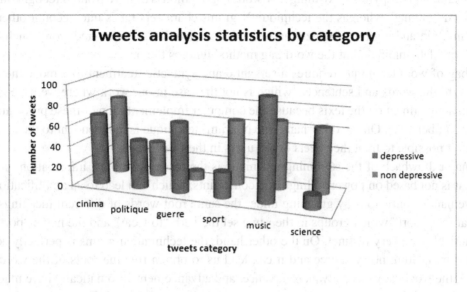

Figure 3. Comparison of text representation techniques results using the Asian elephants algorithm

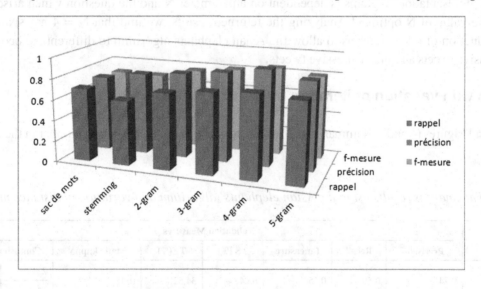

By observing the Table 3 and the previous Figures (2 and 3) we found that the technique N-grams characters (the blue boxes) allows to obtain the best results compared to the representation bag of words with a F = 0.85, TS = 84% and kappa static = 0.68. A discussion and interpretation of the different results is detailed below:

- The n-gram representation is tolerant to the problems of copy-and-paste technology and especially when copying a tweet from a PDF document, a Word document or from a web page.

- Some characters of the copied words will be imperfect for example, it is possible that the word "text-mining" is copying "text-ining". A word bag method will have trouble recognizing that it is the word "mining" whereas the technique N-grams characters takes into account other N-grams like 'ini', nin and ing to recognize the word. It can also detect compound words such as "united state" or "data mining", but the word bag method ignores them.

- The bag of word technique requires a semantic and syntactic treatment to remove the ambiguity related to the words and sentences, which is not the case in our work where we have not applied linguistic treatment on the texts because the computer implementation of these procedures is relatively cumbersome. On the other hand, the N-grams technique is independent to the language and makes it possible to treat the tweets of the users in their raw states

- the major drawback of the stemming technique is the loss of complete information on the terms since it is not based on powerful linguistic constraints, which can lead to an amplification of noise and semantic confusions by grouping under the same root words of different meanings. Like the lexical root "port" which groups in the same set the verb "to wear" and the name "port" whereas semantically are very distinct. On the other hand, the technique n-grams is perfectly adapted for texts coming from noisy source and it can lead us to obtain free the roots of the words. For example, the words advance, advance, advance, and advancement automatically have much in common when considered as sets of N-grams. Another advantage is its ability to work with both short and long documents.

- The representation N-grams is dependent on a parameter N and the question which arises: What is the value of N optimal? Analyzing the returned results, we find that N = 4 has spawned the production of relevant terms to allow the Asian elephants algorithm to differentiate between depressive tweets and not-depressive tweets.

Results with variation of iteration number:

Table 4 and Figures (4 and 5) summarize the influence of the parameter iteration number in the obtained results.

Table 4. The analysis results using the Asian elephants' algorithm and variation of distance measures

| | | **Validation Measures** | | | | | | **Confusion matrix** | |
		Precision	Recall	f-measure	TS (%)	TE(%)	static kappa		
Distances measures	10	0.74	0.59	0.654	65.48%	34.52%	0313	221	76
								148	204
	40	0.918	0.791	0.854	84.12%	15.86%	0688	292	26
								77	254
	80	0.781	0715	0.745	72.41%	27.59%	0.45	264	74
								105	206
	120	0.7217	0674	0.699	66.71	33.29	0347	249	96
								120	184

Figure 4. The results of analysis using the Asian elephants algorithm for detecting depressive person in twitter with variation of iterations number

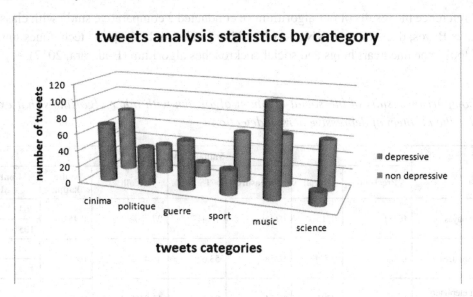

Figure 5. Comparison of distance measurements using Asian elephants

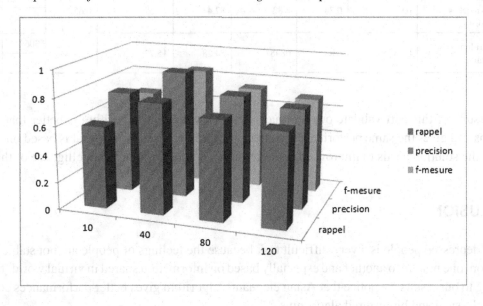

The results clearly show that the stopping criterion is a sensitive parameter because the quality of results of the social elephant algorithm change with the variation of the iterations number.

Comparative Study

in order to reference the results of our algorithm we conducted a comparative study with classical techniques (Naive Bayes, decision tree, KNearest Neighbor) and with bioinspired techniques integrated in the EBIRI tool (machine heart lungs and social cockroaches algorithm (Bouarara, 2017).

Table 5. Comparison results of the social elephant algorithm with other algorithms that exist in the literature for the problem of depressive person detection

<table>
<thead>
<tr>
<th rowspan="3">Algorithms</th>
<th colspan="2"></th>
<th colspan="8">Valuation Measures</th>
</tr>
<tr>
<th colspan="2"></th>
<th>Precision</th>
<th>Recall</th>
<th>f-measure</th>
<th>TS (%)</th>
<th>Recall(%)</th>
<th>static kappa</th>
<th colspan="2">Contingency Matrix</th>
</tr>
</thead>
<tbody>
<tr>
<td colspan="2" rowspan="2">Naive bayes</td>
<td rowspan="2">0.781</td>
<td rowspan="2">0715</td>
<td rowspan="2">0745</td>
<td rowspan="2">72.41%</td>
<td rowspan="2">27.59%</td>
<td rowspan="2">0.45</td>
<td>264</td>
<td>74</td>
</tr>
<tr>
<td>105</td>
<td>206</td>
</tr>
<tr>
<td colspan="2" rowspan="2">Decision tree</td>
<td rowspan="2">0608</td>
<td rowspan="2">0.51</td>
<td rowspan="2">0558</td>
<td rowspan="2">53.62%</td>
<td rowspan="2">46.48%</td>
<td rowspan="2">0.09</td>
<td>190</td>
<td>122</td>
</tr>
<tr>
<td>179</td>
<td>158</td>
</tr>
<tr>
<td colspan="2" rowspan="2">Asian elephants algorithm</td>
<td rowspan="2">0918</td>
<td rowspan="2">0791</td>
<td rowspan="2">0854</td>
<td rowspan="2">84.12%</td>
<td rowspan="2">15.86%</td>
<td rowspan="2">0688</td>
<td>292</td>
<td>26</td>
</tr>
<tr>
<td>77</td>
<td>254</td>
</tr>
<tr>
<td colspan="2" rowspan="2">Social cockroaches Algorithm</td>
<td rowspan="2">0.92</td>
<td rowspan="2">0.74</td>
<td rowspan="2">0.82</td>
<td rowspan="2">82.43</td>
<td rowspan="2">17.57</td>
<td rowspan="2">0.65</td>
<td>276</td>
<td>21</td>
</tr>
<tr>
<td>93</td>
<td>259</td>
</tr>
<tr>
<td colspan="2" rowspan="2">Heart lung machine</td>
<td rowspan="2">0.88</td>
<td rowspan="2">0.82</td>
<td rowspan="2">0848</td>
<td rowspan="2">84.28</td>
<td rowspan="2">15.72</td>
<td rowspan="2">0.68</td>
<td>306</td>
<td>39</td>
</tr>
<tr>
<td>63</td>
<td>241</td>
</tr>
</tbody>
</table>

The results of this part validate our originally set goal where our algorithm is better than the like algorithms and gives the same performance as the algorithm because our proposal is based on the principle that the solution needs to improve from iteration to another through the intelligence of the group.

CONCLUSION

detecting depressed people is a very difficult task because the feelings of people are not stable and can change from one minute to another and especially based on information shared in virtual world (tweeter). According to our results we notice that Asian elephant's algorithm gives better performances compared to others classical and bioinspired algorithms.

Finally, we propose that Social network owners must add an option to analyze the status of each user to say that a person is in a normal or depressive situation by suggesting those users to:

- Consult a doctor or psychologist because There are many effective treatment modalities against depression, including medications (eg antidepressants) and psychotherapy.
- Get as much information as possible about depression and how it is treated. This will allow you to understand what is happening to you and make informed decisions.

- Adopt a healthy lifestyle and Work less if necessary, avoid sources of unnecessary stress, allow yourself hours of rest and sleep, and eat well are all measures that can help you get back on your feet quickly.

FUTURE WORKS

We will apply the algorithm to the problem of suspicious person detection, spam filtering, DNA classification, information retrieval, sentiment analysis in video, plagiarism detection, and all classification problem supervised or unsupervised.

REFERENCES

Alaei, A. R., Becken, S., & Stantic, B. (2019). Sentiment analysis in tourism: Capitalizing on big data. *Journal of Travel Research*, *58*(2), 175–191. doi:10.1177/0047287517747753

Araque, O., Zhu, G., & Iglesias, C. A. (2019). A semantic similarity-based perspective of affect lexicons for sentiment analysis. *Knowledge-Based Systems*, *165*, 346–359. doi:10.1016/j.knosys.2018.12.005

Bouarara, HA, & Hamou, RM (2017). *Bio-Inspired Environment for Information Retrieval (Ebiri): innovations from nature*. European academic editions.

Bouarara, H. A., Hamou, R. M., & Amine, A. (2015). New Swarm Intelligence Technique of Artificial Social Cockroaches for Suspicious Person Detection Using N-Gram Pixel with Visual Result Mining. *International Journal of Strategic Decision Sciences*, *6*(3), 65–91. doi:10.4018/IJSDS.2015070105

Ding, Y., Liu, X., Zheng, Z. R., & Gu, P. F. (2008). Freeform LED lens for uniform illumination. *Optics Express*, *16*(17), 12958–12966. doi:10.1364/OE.16.012958 PMID:18711534

Dos Santos, C., & Gatti, M. (2014). Deep convolutional neural networks for sentiment analysis of short texts. In *Proceedings of COLING 2014, the 25th International Conference on Computational Linguistics* (pp. 69-78). Academic Press.

Dragoni, M., Poria, S., & Cambria, E. (2018). OntoSenticNet: A commonsense ontology for sentiment analysis. *IEEE Intelligent Systems*, *33*(3), 77–85. doi:10.1109/MIS.2018.033001419

Finegold, J. A., Asaria, P., & Francis, D. P. (2013). Mortality from ischaemic heart disease by country, region, and age: Statistics from World Health Organisation and United Nations. *International Journal of Cardiology*, *168*(2), 934–945. doi:10.1016/j.ijcard.2012.10.046 PMID:23218570

Kanayama, H., & Nasukawa, T. (2006, July). Fully automatic lexicon expansion for domain-oriented sentiment analysis. In *Proceedings of the 2006 conference on empirical methods in natural language processing* (pp. 355-363). Association for Computational Linguistics. 10.3115/1610075.1610125

Kumar, J., & Selvan, T. (2019). Management Efficiency and Profitability of Selected Indian Public and Private Sector Banks. *International Journal of Knowledge-Based Organizations*, *9*(1), 26–35. doi:10.4018/IJKBO.2019010103

Lohikoski, P., Kujala, J., Haapasalo, H., Aaltonen, K., & Ala-Mursula, L. (2016). Impact of trust on communication in global virtual teams. *International Journal of Knowledge-Based Organizations*, 6(1), 1–19. doi:10.4018/IJKBO.2016010101

Majumder, N., Hazarika, D., Gelbukh, A., Cambria, E., & Poria, S. (2018). Multimodal sentiment analysis using hierarchical fusion with context modeling. *Knowledge-Based Systems*, *161*, 124–133. doi:10.1016/j.knosys.2018.07.041

McComb, K., Moss, C., Durant, S. M., Baker, L., & Sayialel, S. (2001). Matriarchs as repositories of social knowledge in African elephants. *Science*, *292*(5516), 491–494. doi:10.1126cience.1057895 PMID:11313492

McCreadie, R., Soboroff, I., Lin, J., Macdonald, C., Ounis, I., & McCullough, D. (2012, August). One building has reusable Twitter corpus. In *Proceedings of the 35th International ACM SIGIR conference on Research and development in information retrieval* (pp. 1113-1114). ACM.

Mohammad, S. M., Kiritchenko, S., & Zhu, X. (2013). NRC-Canada: Building the state-of-the-art in sentiment analysis of tweets.

Nasukawa, T., & Yi, J. (2003, October). Sentiment analysis: Capturing favorability using natural language processing. In *Proceedings of the 2nd international conference on Knowledge capture* (pp. 70-77). ACM. 10.1145/945645.945658

Oksuz, K., Can Cam, B., Akbas, E., & Kalkan, S. (2018). Localization recall precision (lrp): A new performance metric for object detection. In *Proceedings of the European Conference on Computer Vision (ECCV)* (pp. 504-519). Academic Press. 10.1007/978-3-030-01234-2_31

Pathak, S., & Agrawal, R. (2019). Design of Knowledge Based Analytical Model for Organizational Excellence. *International Journal of Knowledge-Based Organizations*, *9*(1), 12–25. doi:10.4018/IJKBO.2019010102

Poole, J. (1999). Signals and assessment in African elephants: Evidence from playback experiments. *Animal Behaviour*, *58*(1), 185–193. doi:10.1006/anbe.1999.1117 PMID:10413556

Proksch, S. O., Lowe, W., Wäckerle, J., & Soroka, S. (2019). Multilingual sentiment analysis: A new approach to measuring conflict in legislative speeches. *Legislative Studies Quarterly*, *44*(1), 97–131. doi:10.1111/lsq.12218

Xiang, R., Long, Y., Lu, Q., Xiong, D., & Chen, I. H. (2018, October). Leveraging Writing Systems Change for Deep Learning Based Chinese Emotion Analysis. In *Proceedings of the 9th Workshop on Computational Approaches to Subjectivity, Sentiment and Social Media Analysis* (pp. 91-96). Academic Press. 10.18653/v1/W18-6214

Yücenur, G. N., Atay, İ., Argon, S., & Gül, E. F. (2019). Integrating Fuzzy Prioritization Method and FMEA in the Operational Processes of an Automotive Company. *International Journal of Knowledge-Based Organizations*, *9*(3), 14–32. doi:10.4018/IJKBO.2019070102

Zheng, L., Wang, H., & Gao, S. (2018). Sentimental feature selection for sentiment analysis of Chinese online reviews. *International Journal of Machine Learning and Cybernetics*, 9(1), 75–84. doi:10.100713042-015-0347-4

ENDNOTE

[1] The matriarch: she can be a big sister, mother, aunt, grandmother or grand aunt for all the members of her group. She has knowledge of the group; she knows the migratory routes, the rhythm of the seasons and the important places to find water and vegetation.

This research was previously published in the International Journal of Knowledge-Based Organizations (IJKBO), 10(1); pages 49-61, copyright year 2020 by IGI Publishing (an imprint of IGI Global).

Chapter 30
Recurrent Neural Network (RNN) to Analyse Mental Behaviour in Social Media

Hadj Ahmed Bouarara
https://orcid.org/0000-0002-4973-4385
GeCoDe Laboratory, Algeria

ABSTRACT

A recent British study of people between the ages of 14 and 35 has shown that social media has a negative impact on mental health. The purpose of the paper is to detect people with mental disorders' behaviour in social media in order to help Twitter users in overcoming their mental health problems such as anxiety, phobia, depression, paranoia. The authors have adapted the recurrent neural network (RNN) in order to prevent the situations of threats, suicide, loneliness, or any other form of psychological problem through the analysis of tweets. The obtained results were validated by different experimental measures such as f-measure, recall, precision, entropy, accuracy. The RNN gives best results with 85% of accuracy compared to other techniques in literature such as social cockroaches, decision tree, and naïve Bayes.

1. INTRODUCTION AND PROBLEMATIC

The human beings are under unprecedented competition pressures. Unavoidably, growing teenagers have to experience various adolescent psychological pressures, coming from study, communication, affection, self-recognition, etc. Facing the radical reform of society and economy, lot of persons get confused and become over-stressed due to their immature development of self-cognition and discrimination ability towards things (Koenig, 2018).

Instagram, Twitter, Facebook and Snapchat: these platforms attract the attention of 91% of 16-24 year olds. Between narcissism and harassment, creativity and self-expression, social networks are at the origin of a social revolution, especially among "millennials" (born between 95 and the early 2000s). Unfortunately the conclusion of StatusOfMind is that: social networks are, for the most part, bad for the morale

DOI: 10.4018/978-1-6684-6307-9.ch030

of its young users. Thus, twitter is considered to be the most harmful followed closely by Snapchat, then Facebook and finally Instagram (Dragoni, 2018). According to a study by the public health foundation (Mental Health Foundation, 2015), the rate of anxiety and depression has jumped 70% among young people in the last 25 years when it correlated these figures with the increased use of social media. The study established a list of the negative consequences of social networks: cyber-harassment, Addiction (or the feeling of anxiety about missing something), Anxiety, depression, the feeling of loneliness, lack of sleep, physical ill-being. more than one in two (55%) say they have been embarrassed in their daily life by "symptoms of mental difficulty" (anxiety, phobia, depression, paranoia). Even more worrying: one in five young people (22%) say they have felt this discomfort significantly (HO, 2018).

In recent years, we are in a digital world where information is available in large quantities and in various forms. 80% of this mass of information was in textual form. It has only been recently that psychologists, interested in the psychological underpinnings of word usage, have begun using similar analyses of text to understand what words reveal about how people think and feel. For this reason, we need specific tools to access sentiments and meanings hidden in these data (Kazemian, 2018).

In this paper, we have applied the recurrent neural network in order to detect persons with abnormal mental behaviour through twitter analysis. The general structure of this paper will be as follows: we start with a state of the art for presenting the essential works in this topic, after we go on with a section to detail the adaptation of Recurrent Neural Network then an experimental and comparative study will be carried out for presenting the best results obtained. Finally, we will finish with a conclusion and describing some lines of thought that remain open and that we want to share them with you.

2. LITERATURE REVIEW (RELATED WORK)

Microblogging websites have evolved to become a source of varied kind of information. This is due to nature of microblogs on which people post real time messages about their opinions on a variety of topics, discuss current issues, complain, and express positive sentiment for products they use in daily life. In fact, companies manufacturing such products have started to poll these microblogs to get a sense of general sentiment for their product.

The work of Hatzivassiloglou and McKeown in 1997 (Hatzivassiloglou, 1997) consists in using the coordinating conjunctions present between a word already classified and an unclassified word, followed by the contributions of researcher Nasukawa and his team in 2003 (Nasukawa, 2003) who proposed a new method for extracting associated concepts from segments and summing the orientations of the opinion vocabulary present in the same segment.

In the same year, researchers Yu and Hatzivassiloglou (Yu, 2003) used the probability of ranking a word to measure the strength of the orientation of the named entities. In 2006, researchers Kanayama and Nasukawa (Kanayama, 2006) as well as Ding and Liu (Ding, 2008) in 2008 proposed, for their part, a learning-based approach that uses the coordination conjunctions present between a word already classified and a word unclassified (Antonius, 2016).

The approaches of Pang et al introduced in 2002, and that of Charton and Acuna-Agost published in 2007 (pang, 2002) consist of classifying the texts according to a global polarity (positive, negative and neutral). These methods were optimized by Wilson and his research team in 2005 (Wilson, 2005). However, the difficulty lies in the constitution of these corpora of learning, which is a manual process to perform for each area studied. Finally, Vernier and his team (Vernier, 2009), have relied on a method of detection and categorization of the evaluations locally expressed in a corpus of multi-domain blogs. The second Dictionary-based Approach has had a lot of work. In 2015, Rosenthal and his team (Rosenthal, 2015) built General Inquiry which contains 3596 words labeled positive or negative. In Nakov and al work published in 2016 (Nakov, 2016), they use only adjectives for the detection of opinions. They manually build a list of adjectives they use to predict sentence direction and use WordNet to populate the list with synonyms and antonyms of polarity-known adjectives.

Another significant effort for sentiment classification on Twitter data is by Barbosa and Feng (2010). They use polarity predictions from three websites as noisy labels to train a model and use 1000 manually labeled tweets for tuning and another 1000 manually labeled tweets for testing. They however do not mention how they collect their test data. They propose the use of syntax features of tweets like retweet, hashtags, link, punctuation and exclamation marks in conjunction with features like prior polarity of words and POS of words.

In Hu and Liu's work published in 2004 (Hu, 2004), they use only adjectives for detecting opinions. They manually build a list of adjectives that they use to predict sentence orientation and use WordNet to populate the list with synonyms and antonyms of adjectives whose polarity is known. In the work of Liu et al introduced in 2007 (Jingjing, 2007), the authors count the number of occurrences of each entity in the section expressing a positive opinion and that of negative opinions. In the work of Zhang and his team accompanied in 2010 (Zhang, 2010), the authors have shown that the noun phrases and the noun can also contain opinions. They count the number of positive and negative sentences for each feature of the product using the opinion lexicon prepared by Ding and his research team in 2008 (Ding, 2008). The strength (intensity) of opinion is also necessary. In 2005, Pang and Lee (Bo PANG, 2005) focus on sensing public opinion and use the work of Pang and Lee (Bo PANG, 2002) and Turney (TURNEY, 2002) to classify documents as "thumbs up "Or" thumbs down ", depending on the opinion they convey.

3. RECURRENT NEURAL NETWORK FOR ANALYZING PSYCHOLOGICAL TROUBLING PROBLEM

Considering the input vectors of tweets which vary over time. We used the recurrent connections generally connect all the outputs of the neurons of a layer to all the inputs of these same neurons. As shown in Figure 1 where the x_i^t and x_i^t respectively designate the inputs (weighting of the components of each tweet vector) and the outputs of the layer at time t (psychologically normal class or not).

The recurrent connections reinject the previous outputs y_j^{t-1} at the input of the layer at time t. the network traverses the entered tweet of size T according to the direction of reading, and produces an output y, as illustrated in Figure 2.

The RNN "reads" the input tweet, and produces its output at the last step of time. In this case, the output is a label (psychologically normal or not). Ex: 1) "This stay was wonderful" normal class. 2) "We had a terrible night our neighbor snored all night" psychologically not normal. The network learning consists in learning these three matrices on the basis of labeled examples. W, R and V:

- The w_{ji} are the weights connecting the ith entry to the jth neuron of the recurrent layer.
- The r_{jj} are the weights of the recurrence, connecting the output of the jth recurrent neuron to the input of the jth recurrent neuron.
- The v_{kj} connecting the jth neuron of the recurrent layer to the kth neuron of the output layer.

Figure 1. A simple RNN layer with three inputs and two outputs. The weights w_{ji} connecting the inputs to the output, and the weights r_{jj} (recurrent connections) between the output and the input of the layer.

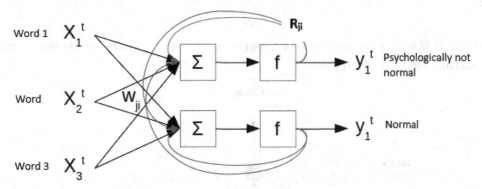

Figure 2. General architecture for detecting users with psychological disorders through the analysis of tweets

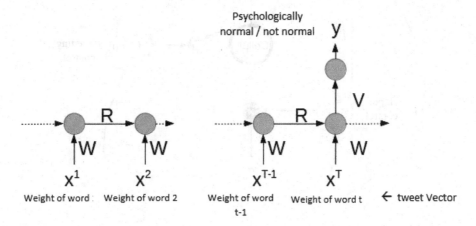

To allow the RNN to maintain a state over a long period of time we used the LSTM (Long Short-Term Memories) as illustrated in Figure 3.

As can be seen in the diagram, the memory cell can be controlled by three control doors that can be seen as valves:

- The input control part: decides whether the input should modify the contents of the cell.
- The forgetting control part: decides whether to reset the cell contents to 0.
- The output control part: decides whether the contents of the cell should influence the exit of the neuron.
- F: sigmoid function applied to the weighted sum of the inputs (in blue), the outputs (in green) and the cell (in orange).
- x_i et z_h: inputs and outputs of cell.
- s_c: the value of the cell.
- $\iota, \omega, c\iota, \omega, c$: the indices respectively describing the results from the input control, forgetting and the cell.

- w_{il}: the weights connecting the inputs to the input cell.
- $wh\phi$: the weights connecting the outputs to the forget door.

Figure 3. The LSTM neuron comprising an internal memory (cell) controlled by the three input (input), forget (forget) and output (output) doors

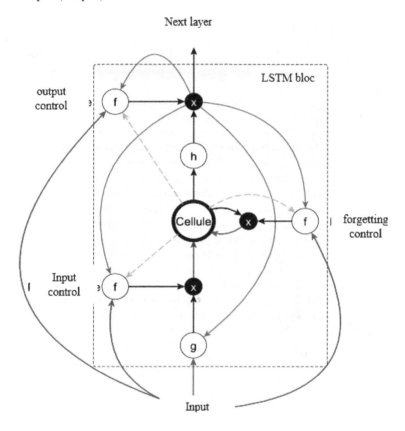

The equations governing the three control parts are therefore as follows; they are the application of the weighted sum followed by the application of an activation f:

- Input control:

$$a_i^t = \sum_{i=1}^{I} w_{il} x_i^t + \sum_{h=1}^{H} w_{hl} z_h^{t-1} + \sum_{c=1}^{C} w_{cl} s_c^{t-1} \tag{1}$$

$$b_i^t = f(a_i^t) \tag{2}$$

- Forgetting control:

$$a_\phi^t = \sum_{i=1}^{I} w_{i\phi} x_i^t + \sum_{h=1}^{H} w_{h\phi} z_h^{t-1} + \sum_{c=1}^{C} w_{c\phi} s_c^{t-1} \tag{3}$$

$$b_\phi^t = f(a_\phi^t) \tag{4}$$

- Output control:

$$a_\omega^t = \sum_{i=1}^{I} w_{i\omega} x_i^t + \sum_{h=1}^{H} w_{h\omega} z_h^{t-1} + \sum_{c=1}^{C} w_{c\omega} s_c^{t-1} \tag{5}$$

$$b_\omega^t = f(a_\omega^t) \tag{6}$$

Regarding the memory cell, its content Sc can be updated or reset to 0. A weighted sum of the inputs and outputs is first applied:

$$a_c^t = \sum_{i=1}^{I} w_{ic} x_i^t + \sum_{h=1}^{H} w_{hc} z_h^{t-1} \tag{7}$$

The content of the cell at time t is then recalculated as the sum of two terms:

$$s_c^t = b_\phi^t s_c^{t-1} + b_i^t g\left(a_c^t\right) \tag{8}$$

- The first term takes the previous value of the cell s_c^{t-1}, which can be canceled by the value of the oblivion control b_ϕ^t ;
- g: Sigmoid function;
- The second term is the influence of the weighted sum, driven by the value of the front door b_i^t.

Finally, the output of the LSTM neuron is calculated by an activation h applied to the value of the memory cell s_c^t, driven by the value of the output control b_w^t :

$$y_c^t = b_w^t h\left(s_c^t\right) \tag{9}$$

- h: Hyperbolic tangent function

For the learning phase of LSTM we used the BPTT algorithm (Backpropagation Through Time) as for classic recurrent networks, by unfolding the recurrent network over time. In our work. We have used Keras which has provide a very nice wrapper called bidirectional that make the implementation of LSTM effortless.

4. TWEETS2011 CORPUS (TWEETS)

In our experiments, we used the Tweets2011 corpus that was used in information retrieval famous competition called TREC 201. This specialized body built to keywords. The authors of this corpus have used the API to retrieve Twitter4J 649 tweets where they used keywords (politics, cinema, sport, music, war, science). After TREC in 2012 these tweets were classified in two class (depressive tweet, tweet not depressed) (McCreadie, 2012). Table 1 summarizes the classification of tweets. One advantage of this data, is that the tweets are collected in a streaming fashion and therefore represent a true sample of actual tweets in terms of language use and content.

Twitter is a social networking and microblogging service that allows users to post real time messages, called tweets. Tweets are short messages, restricted to 140 characters in length. Researchers have used hashtags related to emotions to create and using a combination of rules to generate an emotion score for each tweet in this corpus.

Table 1. General Statistical Dataset Tweets 2011

Category	Depressive	Not Depressive
Cinema	85	62
Policy	49	33
War	64	13
Sport	33	58
Music	119	56
Science	19	58

5. VALIDATION MEASURES

To validate our results, we have used different metrics that exist in literature such as recall, precision, f-measure, kapa static true positive, false positive, false negative and true negative (Oksuz, 2018).

6. RESULTS AND DISCUSSION

In order to validate the quality of our proposal we have applied an experimental protocol with objective is to identify the sensitive parameters. Firstly, we have fixed in each test one parameter and varying the others. We have calculated the f-measure, recall precision loss and accuracy. The best results are illustrated in Tables 2-3 and Figure 4.

We have noticed that the precision and the efficiency of the RNN clearly change with the change of the theme of each tweat. The results show that we had a success rate of 85% and an accuracy of 85%, Recall of 89%, f-measure of 87%. The increase in the number of epochs a allows the performance of the RNN to be improved as shown in the curves in the Figure 4.

Figure 4. The loss and accuracy of analysis using RNN-LSTM approach for detecting person with abnormal mental behavior over twitter by varying of epoch number

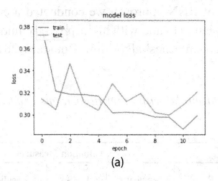

(a)

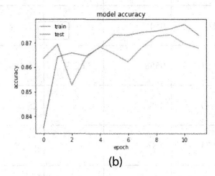

(b)

Table 2. The results of analysis using RNN-LSTM approach for detecting person with abnormal mental behavior over twitter

	Precision	Recall	F measure
Psychologically normal	0.92	0.89	0.91
Psychologically abnormal	0.83	0.89	0.83
Average	0.85	0.89	0.87

Table 3. The results of analysis using RNN-LSTM approach for detecting person with abnormal mental behavior over twitter in different categories

Category	Precision	Recall	f-measure
cinema	0.837	0.865	0.85
Politic	0.849	0.894	0.871
War	0.848	0.915	0.88
sport	0.982	0.911	0.945
music	0.887	0.929	0.908
science	0.864	0.882	0.873

7. COMPARATIVE STUDY

in order to reference the results of RNN approach we conducted a comparative study with classical techniques (naive bayes and decision tree) and with bioinspired techniques integrated in the EBIRI tool (machine heart lungs and social cockroaches' algorithm (Bouarara, 2017) (Table 4).

Table 4. Comparison results of our model with other algorithms existed in literature for the problem of depressive person detection

Algorithms	Valuation Measures							
	Precision	Recall	f-measure	TS (%)	Recall(%)	static kappa	Contingency Matrix	
Naive bayes	0.781	0715	0745	72.41%	27.59%	0.45	264	74
							105	206
Decision tree	0608	0.51	0558	53.62%	46.48%	0.09	190	122
							179	158
RNN-LSTM	0.85	0.89	0.87	85%	25%	/	329	59
							40	221
Social cockroaches Algorithm	0.92	0.74	0.82	82.43	17.57	0.65	276	21
							93	259
Heart lung machine	0.88	0.82	0848	84.28	15.72	0.68	306	39
							63	241

The results of this part validate our goal where our algorithm is better than the others algorithms.

8. CONCLUSION

Under the rapid social and economic development and intensive competition pressures, adolescents are experiencing different psychological pressures coming from study, communication, affection, and self-recognition. If these psychological pressures cannot properly be resolved and released, it will turn to mental problems, which might lead to serious consequences, such as suicide or aggressive behaviour. The detection of person with psychological problem over twitter is a very difficult task because the feelings of users are not stable and can change rapidly especially in virtual world (twitter). We have adapted the Recurrent Neural Network (RNN) to this problem and obtained a result of 85% accuracy and 0.87 f-measure. The obtained results demonstrate that our proposition outperform others classical techniques existed in literature.

Finally, we propose that Social network owners must add an option to analyse the status of each user to say that a person is in a normal or depressive situation by suggesting those users to:

- Consult a doctor or psychologist because There are many effective treatment modalities against depression, including medications (eg antidepressants) and psychotherapy.
- Get as much information as possible about depression and how it is treated. This will allow you to understand what is happening to you and make informed decisions.
- Adopt a healthy lifestyle and Work less if necessary, avoid sources of unnecessary stress, allow yourself hours of rest and sleep, and eat well are all measures that can help you get back on your feet quickly.
- The analysis of Twitter data can further our understanding of how health behaviours are affected by social media discourse.

For Future works, we will apply the algorithm to the problem of suspicious person detection, spam filtering, DNA classification, information retrieval, sentiment analysis in video, plagiarism detection, and all classification problem supervised or unsupervised.

REFERENCES

Alaei, A. R., Becken, S., & Stantic, B. (2019). Sentiment analysis in tourism: Capitalizing on big data. *Journal of Travel Research*, *58*(2), 175–191. doi:10.1177/0047287517747753

Antonius, N., Gao, X., & Xu, J. (2016). Applying enterprise social software for knowledge management. *International Journal of Knowledge and Systems Science*, *7*(4), 19–39. doi:10.4018/IJKSS.2016100102

Bo, P., & Lillian, L. (2005). Seeing stars: Exploiting class relationships for sentiment categorization with respect to rating scales. In *Proceedings of the 43rd annual meeting on association for computational linguistics*. Association for Computational Linguistics.

Bo, P., Lillian, L., & Shivakumar, V. (2002). Thumbs up? Sentiment classification using machine learning techniques. In *Proceedings of the ACL-02 conference on Empirical methods in natural language processing-Volume 10*. Association for Computational Linguistics.

Bouarara, HA, & Hamou, RM (2017). *Bio-Inspired Environment for Information Retrieval (Ebiri): Innovations from nature*. European Academic Editions.

Bouarara, H. A., Hamou, R. M., & Amine, A. (2015). New Swarm Intelligence Technique of Artificial Social Cockroaches for Suspicious Person Detection Using N-Gram Pixel with Visual Result Mining. *International Journal of Strategic Decision Sciences*, *6*(3), 65–91. doi:10.4018/IJSDS.2015070105

Ding, X., Liu, B., & Yu, P. S. (2008, February). A holistic lexicon-based approach to opinion mining. In *Proceedings of the 2008 international conference on web search and data mining* (pp. 231-240). 10.1145/1341531.1341561

Ding, Y., Liu, X., Zheng, Z. R., & Gu, P. F. (2008). Freeform LED lens for uniform illumination. *Optics Express*, *16*(17), 12958–12966.

Dragoni, M., Poria, S., & Cambria, E. (2018). OntoSenticNet: A commonsense ontology for sentiment analysis. *IEEE Intelligent Systems*, *33*(3), 77–85. doi:10.1109/MIS.2018.033001419

Hatzivassiloglou, V., & McKeown, K. R. (1997, July). Predicting the semantic orientation of adjectives. In *Proceedings of the 35th annual meeting of the association for computational linguistics and eighth conference of the European chapter of the association for computational linguistics* (pp. 174-181). Association for Computational Linguistics.

Ho, T., & Do, P. (2018). Social network analysis based on topic model with temporal factor. *International Journal of Knowledge and Systems Science, 9*(1), 82–97. doi:10.4018/IJKSS.2018010105

Hu, M., & Liu, B. (2004, July). Mining opinion features in customer reviews. In AAAI (Vol. 4, No. 4, pp. 755-760). Academic Press.

Kanayama, H., & Nasukawa, T. (2006, July). Fully automatic lexicon expansion for domain-oriented sentiment analysis. In *Proceedings of the 2006 conference on empirical methods in natural language processing* (pp. 355-363). Association for Computational Linguistics.

Kazemian, S. (2018). The Role Micro-Blogging Plays in Informal Communication and Knowledge Sharing Activities Within Universities: A Review of The Literature. [*International Journal of Knowledge and Systems Science, 9*(3), 18–31. doi:10.4018/IJKSS.2018070102

Kiss, I. M., & Buzás, N. (2015). Who Tweets About Technology?: Investigating the Role of Twitter in the Diffusion of Technological Information. *International Journal of Knowledge and Systems Science, 6*(1), 46–59. doi:10.4018/ijkss.2015010104

Koenig, A., & McLaughlin, B. (2018). Change is an emotional state of mind: Behavioral responses to online petitions. *New Media & Society, 20*(4), 1658–1675. doi:10.1177/1461444817689951

Liu, J., Cao, Y., Lin, C. Y., Huang, Y., & Zhou, M. (2007, June). Low-quality product review detection in opinion summarization. In *Proceedings of the 2007 Joint Conference on Empirical Methods in Natural Language Processing and Computational Natural Language Learning (EMNLP-CoNLL)* (pp. 334-342). Academic Press.

McCreadie, R., Soboroff, I., Lin, J., Macdonald, C., Ounis, I., & McCullough, D. (2012, August). One building has reusable Twitter corpus. In *Proceedings of the 35th International ACM SIGIR conference on Research and development in information retrieval* (pp. 1113-1114). ACM.

Nakov, P., Ritter, A., Rosenthal, S., Sebastiani, F., & Stoyanov, V. (2016). SemEval-2016 task 4: Sentiment analysis in Twitter. In *Proceedings of the 10th international workshop on semantic evaluation (semeval-2016)* (pp. 1-18). Academic Press.

Nasukawa, T., & Yi, J. (2003, October). Sentiment analysis: Capturing favorability using natural language processing. In *Proceedings of the 2nd international conference on Knowledge capture* (pp. 70-77). ACM.

Oksuz, K., Can Cam, B., Akbas, E., & Kalkan, S. (2018). Localization recall precision (lrp): A new performance metric for object detection. In *Proceedings of the European Conference on Computer Vision (ECCV)* (pp. 504-519). 10.1007/978-3-030-01234-2_31

Peter, D. (2002). Thumbs up or thumbs down?: semantic orientation applied to unsupervised classification of reviews. In *Proceedings of the 40th annual meeting on association for computational linguistics*. Association for Computational Linguistics.

Rosenthal, S., Nakov, P., Kiritchenko, S., Mohammad, S., Ritter, A., & Stoyanov, V. (2015). Semeval-2015 task 10: Sentiment analysis in twitter. In *Proceedings of the 9th international workshop on semantic evaluation (SemEval 2015)* (pp. 451-463). Academic Press.

Vernier, M., Monceaux, L., Daille, B., & Dubreil, E. (2009). Catégorisation des évaluations dans un corpus de blogs multi-domaine. *Revue des nouvelles technologies de l'information*, 45-70.

Wang, W. M., Cheung, B. C., Leung, Z. C., Chan, K. H., & See-To, E. W. (2019). A social media mining and analysis approach for supporting cyber youth work. In Multigenerational Online Behavior and Media Use: Concepts, Methodologies, Tools, and Applications (pp. 1737-1753). IGI Global.

Wilson, T., Wiebe, J., & Hoffmann, P. (2005, October). Recognizing contextual polarity in phrase-level sentiment analysis. In *Proceedings of the conference on human language technology and empirical methods in natural language processing* (pp. 347-354). Association for Computational Linguistics.

Yu, H., & Hatzivassiloglou, V. (2003, July). Towards answering opinion questions: Separating facts from opinions and identifying the polarity of opinion sentences. In *Proceedings of the 2003 conference on Empirical methods in natural language processing* (pp. 129-136). Association for Computational Linguistics.

Zhang, L., Liu, B., Lim, S. H., & O'Brien-Strain, E. (2010, August). Extracting and ranking product features in opinion documents. In *Proceedings of the 23rd international conference on computational linguistics: Posters* (pp. 1462-1470). Association for Computational Linguistics.

Zheng, L., Wang, H., & Gao, S. (2018). Sentimental feature selection for sentiment analysis of Chinese online reviews. *International Journal of Machine Learning and Cybernetics*, 9(1), 75–84. doi:10.100713042-015-0347-4

This research was previously published in the International Journal of Software Science and Computational Intelligence (IJSSCI), 13(3); pages 1-11, copyright year 2021 by IGI Publishing (an imprint of IGI Global).

Chapter 31

The Rise of Professional Facebook Content Generators in Vietnam:
A Fake News Campaign Against the Betibuti Founder

Le Thu Mach
Monash University, Australia

ABSTRACT

This case study is empirical research. It highlights the fact that the dynamic and complex Facebook content generators involve actively in the formulation and dissemination of fake news in Vietnam. Professional Facebook content generators include not only the paid online commentators, being hired by the government or business sector but also the professional journalists, who can earn for their living by promoting certain ideas and products on Facebook. As journalism functions as a tool for propaganda in Vietnam, even some governmental officers engage in the formulation of fake news, as long as the fake news serves the propaganda purposes. Through the analysis of the engagement of each group of Facebook content generators in fake news, this chapter contributes to the identification and elimination of fake news, and therefore, it is especially significant for journalists in reflexive truth-seeking practice.

INTRODUCTION

The media landscape in Vietnam during 2014-2019 has witnessed a rise of professional content generators on Facebook, including journalists and paid online commentators. The pre-mature legal system can be the reason for this phenomenon. Legal framework for social media management in Vietnam has not yet fully developed. In addition, Vietnamese does not have law for doing lobbying. As the consequences, using media, particularly the prominent social media platform, Facebook, to promote ideas and policies becomes a common practice. Doing propaganda is a norm for Vietnamese journalism. Thus, authorities

DOI: 10.4018/978-1-6684-6307-9.ch031

can sometimes prioritise shaping the public viewpoints, rather than truth seeking and verification. This chapter investigates the roles and characteristics of those who produce and deliver content on Facebook for professional purposes, and elaborates their performance in a case study of the fake news against Le Nhat Phuong Hong, the founder of Betibuti, the breastfeeding community in Vietnam.

The first section of this chapter analyses the media context in Vietnam, from the measles outbreak in April 2014 to the approval of the Cyber Security Law in June 2018. The measles outbreak stimulated an unprecedented wave of using Facebook to call for the resignation of the Minister of Health. Responding to this wave, the Minister of Health began to use Facebook for public communication and, as of October 2018, she was the first and only minister managing a ministerial Facebook account in Vietnam. The government and business sector started to establish so-called 'cyber troops' and paid online commentators to manipulate social-media contents. Professional journalists engage in Facebook across a spectrum of three categories: social-media refuters, hybrid-media producers, and social-media leaders. Notably, journalists have formed a system of professional content generators on Facebook, doing advocacy for the business sector. The intensive engagement of journalists on Facebook blurs the boundary between professional journalism and manipulated communication. In June 2018, the National Assembly of Vietnam passed the Cyber Security Law, which requests proof of identification from social-media users. Before that, social-media accounts could be unverified and unidentifiable. These developments in the context of Vietnamese media have caused the mushrooming of fake news on Facebook, as well as degradation of journalistic quality.

The latter section of this chapter analyses a case study of fake news used against the Betibuti breast-feeding advocacy group. As of early March 2018, the group had 250,000 followers. In mid-March 2018, starting from a rumour on Facebook that 'a mother and an infant died during home-based labour in Ho Chi Minh City', the Ministry of Health of Vietnam (MoH) organised a press conference to deliver the MoH's charges against the group. Some MoH officers confirmed that the rumour was true, which provoked public scrutiny of the group. Journalists and Facebook became platforms for character assassination and defamation of the group's founder. Facebook deleted the founder's account, resulting in the removal of the group from social media and cancellation of group events. MoH then confirmed that the story about a mother and an infant dying was not true. However, this fake news stopped the expansion of breast-milk promotion and advocacy. The reputation of the group founder was severely damaged and had not yet been restored by the end of October 2018. The positive media notice she had earned before was removed or blacked-out by mainstream journalism.

BACKGROUND CONTEXT FOR THE RISE OF PROFESSIONAL FACEBOOK CONTENT GENERATORS

This section explores the rise of professional Facebook content generators in Vietnam from 2014 to 2019. It identifies the measles outbreak in April 2014 as the beginning of using Facebook for public-opinion expression and manipulation. Following this change in the media landscape, a shift has occurred among state-controlled journalists from publishing on mainstream media to publishing on Facebook. Notably, journalists stopped working for the state-run media house and started earning by posting advertorial contents on Facebook, marking the formation of a new media system on Facebook parallel to that of the mainstream media system. Besides journalists, paid online commentators are joining the network generating Facebook contents. Although posting on Facebook was becoming a highly organised profession, the law associated with social media had not yet sufficiently reacted until the legislative enactment of the Cyber Security Law in June 2018.

Legal Framework

According to Article 14 of the Vietnamese Press Law (Government, 2016), only the entities belonging to the Communist Party of Vietnam (CPV) and the Government can establish journalism organisations. The private sector is not permitted to establish and run journalism organisations. The CPV and the Government control all aspects of journalism, including licensing, patrolling, staffing, training, material supplies, access to information, distribution of media products, and TV and radio frequency control (Palmos, 1995, pp. 7-37). Vietnamese professional journalists must apply for the government-issued press cards (Government, 2016). Violation of the press law results in press-card withdrawal and a ban from professional journalism practice. In this milieu, journalism organisations are the governmental units and journalists are the governmental information officials. Huu Tho (1997), a well-known Vietnamese journalism commentator, in his textbook for journalism education and training *Công việc của người viết báo* (The jobs of journalists), states, 'Since journalists are the spokespeople for the [Vietnamese Communist] Party, the first and foremost truth for journalists is the Party's truth' (p. 25). From this analysis, it could be asserted that journalism coverage is verified by the party-certified journalists and aligns with the guidance from that authority.

The regulations of social media in Vietnam have been elaborated in Decree number 72, the Penal Code and the newly introduced Cyber Security Law. First, Decree number 72 (72/2013/ND-CP, 2013) requires Vietnamese social-media providers to register their services under the governmental provision. However, the decree applies to Vietnamese social media and social networks, and is not applied to international counterparts, such as Facebook, YouTube and Google. Second, the sections numbered 79, 88 and 258 of the Vietnamese Penal Code 1999 (which were renumbered accordingly as 109, 117 and 343 in the new 2015 Penal Code) were often applied to violation of the state's interests, anti-state propaganda and actions aimed at overthrowing the government. However, privately owned businesses, nongovernmental organisations and individuals who do not work for the government are marginalised by the protective boundary of these code sections. Third, in June 2018, the Cyber Security Law was approved. Item 2a of Article 26 in this law requires the information of Vietnamese Internet users to be identifiable and physically accessible on Vietnamese territory. Item 1đ of Article 27 in this law announces that the Government can invest in research and development to trace online sources. Before the Cyber Security Law, there had been a legislative hollow in source identification and traceability. This created the favourable conditions for the rise of fake news on social media.

Measles Outbreak Marks the Rise of Facebook

There is evidence of Facebook blockage in Vietnam during 2009-2012 (Gallup, 2015; ITC News, 2012). However, since October 2012, Facebook has one million new accounts from Vietnam per month, and in March 2013, the number of Vietnamese Facebook users was 12 million (BBC, 2013). As of January 2018, Facebook was the top social-media platform in Vietnam. Sixty-one percent of Vietnamese Internet users were active on Facebook. With 55 million Facebook accounts, Vietnam ranked seventh globally in terms of the number of Facebook users (We-are-social, 2018).

In April 2014, a measles outbreak occurred in Hanoi, an extraordinary milestone in Vietnam media history. With this event, Facebook entered the realm of agenda setting, resulting in the unprecedented social-media embedded strategy among governmental officials.

Facebook Goes Mainstream

For the first time, Vietnamese journalism reported that Facebook had become the source for the top CPV leader. At the start of the measles outbreak, the Deputy Prime Minister, Mr Vu Duc Dam, confirmed that he got the news from a doctor's Facebook page, and not from state-run journalism. On April 16, 2014, Tuoi Tre newspaper published:

During the hospital inspection in the afternoon of April 15, the Deputy Prime Minister Vu Duc Dam said he would like to thank a doctor working in the National Paediatric Hospital who posted on Facebook about the fact that many children died of measles. After the post, the Deputy Prime Minister knew the fact and paid the hospital inspection visit. (Lan-Anh, 2014)

In this news article, Tuoi Tre newspaper covers both the Deputy Prime Minister and the source on Facebook. Stuart Hall discussed this practice: 'The media do not only simply "create" the news . . . [by reproducing the definitions of those who have privileged access] the media stand in a position of structured subordination to the primary definers' (Hall, Critcher, Jefferson, Clarke, & Roberts, 1979, p. 59). This opens up the ideological role of the media. Hall et al. (1979) cited Marx's basic proposition that 'the ruling ideas of any age are the ideas of its ruling class' (p. 59). He asserts:

Because this class owns and control the means of material production, the class also owns and controls the means of 'mental production'. In producing their definition of social reality, and the place of 'ordinary people' within it, they construct a particular image of society which represents particular class interests as the interests of all members of society. (Hall et al., 1979, p. 59)

In this example, by reporting that the top national leader used Facebook, the media produces a 'way-of-life' perception that Facebook is an accredited source for the ruling class, and as such, the society could also trust the source on Facebook.

Facebook for Online Mass Protest

The measles outbreak marked the first time the public used Facebook to protest the national leaders. A Facebook Page titled *Bộ trưởng Y tế hãy từ chức* (Call for the resignation of the Minister of Health https://www.facebook.com/botruongytetuchuc/) was established in October 2013. However, not until the measles outbreak in April 2014 did the page get public notice. On April 18, 2014, 24 hours after Tuoi Tre newspaper published the news article about the hospital inspection by the Deputy Prime Minister, over 2,000 people joined this page. The number of likes dropped sharply on May 3, 2014, because on that day, public attention shifted to the Chinese oil rig Hai Yang Shi You 981, which entered the disputed sea of Vietnam. Between 2013 and 2018, this period of two weeks from April 16 to May 3, 2014 attracted the most significant number of likes and followers to the page (The data was provided by the admin(s) of the Facebook Page call for the resignation of Minister of Health, in April 2015).

It is noteworthy that, according to the administrator(s) of the page, these are the organic likes, not the paid likes. An organic interaction on social media is defined as interacting with certain content shared through unpaid distribution (Chandler & Munday, 2016). From this definition, social media users who make organic like must be interested in the topic of the page. They may do some online searching around the issue before being navigated to the page. Interestingly, from observation of the author, many people used real names with real profiles to join this protesting Facebook page, an unprecedented protest on social media in the one-party state of Vietnam.

Facebook for Public Mobilisation

From April 17 to April 20, 2014, a fundraising campaign arose on Facebook and reached 500 million Vietnamese dongs (USD 25,000). This charity was for the purchase of new respiration aid equipment for the measles patients in children's hospitals. ZingNews described the campaign:

The donation was sent to a bank account. The senders transfer money to the bank account, and then leave comments under a post to notify Minh Do [the campaign leader] of the amount and contact details. After the calculation at the end of each day, the total amount and the spending plan will be publicly posted on the personal page [of Minh Do]. (ZingNews, 2014)

Facebook Embedded in Governmental Communication Strategy

In response to the anti-fan page, Minister of Health Madam Nguyen Thi Kim Tien launched her official Facebook account in October 2014: one personal account (https://www.facebook.com/kimtien1102) and one professional account, managed by the Ministry of Health (https://www.facebook.com/botruongboyte.vn/). As of October 2018, the former has over 45,000 followers, while the latter has over 350,000 followers. The Ministry of Health is the pioneer among Vietnamese governmental organisations for embracing social media in the communication strategy.

Journalists' Engagement on Facebook

A survey conducted in 2017 indicates 96.89% of Vietnamese journalists are using Facebook (Mach, 2017). The journalists are fragmented according to the intensity of their engagement on Facebook for professional practice. There are three categories of journalists, differentiating to each other by journalists' engagement on Facebook. They are social-media influencers, hybrid-media producers, and social-media refuters. The data for this spectrum of categories is acquired from observation of Facebook of the well-known former journalists from 2014 to 2017, and from the survey conducted with 227 journalists to examine how they use Facebook (Mach, 2017).

Social-Media Influencers

They have the high commitment to Facebook, and the low commitment to journalism. These journalists do not identify themselves as working for any media house although previously they were working as journalists of mainstream media houses. They are no longer having the press-cards or governmental professionally certified licenses. They construct real profiles on Facebook to brand themselves as influential non-affiliated journalists. Truong Huy San (Facebook Osin Huy Duc), Le Nguyen Huong Tra (Facebook Co Gai Do Long), Bach Hoan, Truong Duy Nhat, and Tran Dang Tuan, are some of the typical social-media leading journalists. Osin Huy Duc was a journalist of Tuoi Tre newspaper before being a Facebook-influencers journalist. During a period in 2016-2017, Osin Huy Duc was considered an alarm bell ringing to notify of corruption, because he often posted on his Facebook page the stories of corruption investigations before the policemen and the court released the reports. The formulation of the group of social-media influencers-journalists highlights the fact that there exists a system of highly organised journalistic professional practice on Facebook. This system is independent from the state in term of governance and finance; however, it depends on the inter-personal relationship between journalists and their sources of confidential information that they post on Faebook.

Hybrid-Media Producers

Journalists in the group of hybrid-media producers practice intensive engagement with both social media and journalism. These journalists identify themselves as permanent members of mainstream media organisations. They use social media to share links to their media organisations' websites. Besides sharing professional notes, their posts also cover personal perspectives, such as their families and friends, travelling and hobbies. Although using social media, they tend to set priorities for mainstream media and publish on mainstream media first. Abiding by regulations of their media organisations, they can reduce the level of engagement with social media if there are potential conflicts with their professional practice in mainstream media houses. The author has copies of some contracts, in which journalists were paid by business to promote certain products and services on their Facebook. According to a PR Manager who provided the author such copies of contracts in 2018, it was a common practice for Vietnamese journalists to earn money by posting advertorial content on Facebook.

One of the typical examples for the hybrid-media producers is *Tổ ngàn lai* (One thousand like) group. It is an unofficial name for a group of journalists who are still working at state-run newspapers. Their Facebook posts often attract thousands of interactions (like, share, comments), and as such they identify themselves as a KOL (key opinion leaders) group. The term *Tổ ngàn lai* was coined by NHS, a founding member of the group, in a post on his Facebook in 2015, in which he promised to write a book about profiles of journalists who get a lot of interaction on Facebook. According to NHS (2017), on their Facebook posts, these journalists do not associate themselves with any media house, although they are working as senior managers of media houses. The content of *Tổ ngàn lai*'s posts is often advertorial. They are considered as inappropriate for publication on mainstream media because they lack concrete evidence and use slang and lewd language for many instances, which is unsuitable for the mainstream media.

Social-Media Refuters

These journalists engage in state-run journalism only and keep a very low profile or no profile on social media. Although they demonstrate key attributes of performing well on social media, such as technically savvy and skilful creative writing, these journalists deny using social media for professional purposes. They establish strong bonds with their media organisations and adhere to Press Law and regulations.

A journalist can be listed in different category, depending on his/her engagement on social media from time to time. For example, Do Doan Hoang, a well-known journalist of Lao Dong Newspaper was a social-media refuter in 2015 (DDH, 2015), but he became a hybrid-media producer from late 2018. Dinh Duc Hoang, a well-known journalist of VnExpress Newspaper was one of the members of *One thousand like* group, and was a hybrid-media producer before 2016, but deactivated (closed down) his Facebook and became a social-media refuter from 2016 to late 2018.

Paid Commentators

The media landscape of Vietnam recorded the emergence of paid commentators, of which there are two major types: government-based and business-based.

Government-Based Commentators

Since 2012, the government-based online commentators have been increasing in quantity. The chairman of Hanoi Propaganda and Training Committee, Mr Ho Quang Loi, revealed in an annual media meeting on December 9, 2012:

There are 900 online commentators in Hanoi, working as propagandists in sensitive circumstances. Hanoi also runs a 'fast click and react' journalists club. The authority even establishes an 'expert group' to direct fight in debates and writing wars. The group constructs 19 online websites and over 400 social media accounts. (Dao-Tuan, 2013)

Nationwide, members of national and CPV-based associations, such as the Elder People Association, Youth Union, Women Association and Veterans' Association, are also trained to use social media to protect the government and CPV (Truong-Son, 2015). In December 2017, in a conference of Central Propaganda and Training Commission in Ho Chi Minh City, Lieutenant General Nguyen Trong Nghia, Deputy Head of the Military's Political Department, confirmed that the Ministry of Defence had been using a military-based cyber troop called the '47th force'. It took this name after decision number 47-QD/TW in 2011, which required the army to protect the CPV and the State in cyberspace. As of late 2017, the 47th force was confirmed to have over 10,000 people. These government-based commentators receive instruction from their organisations to use social-media accounts to leave comments that 'correct the wrong views' on the Internet (Mai-Hoa, 2017).

Business-Based Commentators

A director of a social-media marketing company in Hanoi said in July 2018 that online marketing had evolved to a new branch of corporate communication (Cuong, 2018). The social-media service companies generate hundreds of thousands of fake Facebook accounts to meet the quantification ends of the online marketing campaigns. As consequences, interactions such as like, share, views, report and especially comments can be sold and bought as Facebook commodities. Many online groups exist for Facebook interaction exchange, allowing Facebook users to call for likes and shares. Many applications have been developed to create and maintain fake social-media accounts automatically. Astroturf became a prevalent practice when large numbers of fake social-media accounts could like and comment on Facebook, so that the opinions on Facebook are easy to manipulate. Dissident contents are quickly reported by the mass of fake accounts and quickly removed from the Facebook space. The industry adheres to the regulations of Facebook and Google and takes full advantage of the social-media algorithms to increase the reach of Facebook contents to the target audience.

THE FAKE NEWS AGAINST THE FOUNDER OF THE BREASTFEEDING COMMUNITY

The Rising Momentum of Breastfeeding Tendency

Betibuti is a breastfeeding community founded by Mrs. Le Nhat Phuong Hong in September 2013. According to Mrs. Hong (LNPH, 2018) initially, the community opened a Facebook group (https://www.facebook.com/groups/betibuti/), on which new mothers shared experiences of how to breast feed their new-born babies. The community then expanded its charters to different cities and provinces in Vietnam and the Vietnamese oversea communities, as well as its clubs for new dads and new grandmothers, who supported their wives and daughters in labour and baby care. These grassroots charters and clubs also established their own Facebook pages and groups. The main Facebook group, opened and administered by the founder, grew at the rate of over a thousand new members a week. As of March 2018, the Facebook group had 250,000 members helping each other in various online and offline programs, including breastfeeding, complement feeding, tandem nursing and a small-scale human-milk bank. Le Nhat Phuong Hong and the Betibuti community took part in the breastfeeding policy-making process and policy implementation in Vietnam. According to Mrs. Hong (LNPH, 2018), Betibuti was invited as a representative for community participants to the inauguration of the first breast milk bank in Da Nang city in 2017. While there is insufficient data to confirm the correlation between the development of the breastfeeding movement and the shrinking of the market for dairy products in Vietnam, there is an apparent decline in the sale of dairy products. Market research by Nielsen in six cities in Vietnam indicates the decrease in the retail unit value and volume of milk-based products (Nielsen, 2015). As the consequences, the growth of Betibuti could pose a shrink in the market share of milk companies.

In February 2018, the founder of the breastfeeding community, Mrs. Le Nhat Phuong Hong, advertised for a course on prenatal motions, described as helping pregnant women to practice dancing and squat so that it would be easier to deliver the baby. On its Facebook page, the breastfeeding community discussed that such motions help the pregnant women to avoid the risk of caesarean sections, with the result that the mother and baby would not be separated after the surgery, and the babies could be breast-fed within the first hours of life. The course was scheduled to take place in four days in June and July 2018, and cost 15 million dongs. This was expected to be the first training for the trainers, with the participation of one Australian birth-motion expert and 30 Vietnamese trainers. According to Mrs. Hong, the course was considered as the first in series of Bebibuti community initiatives to reduce the formal medical treatment on mothers and babies, helping them less dependent on doctors and hospitals. From this point, Betibute started to have conflicts with the viewpoints of the MoH, who always advice the public to visit doctors and hospitals for medical treatment. At the time of February 2018, the breastfeeding community led by Mrs. Hong had conflicts of interests to both business of milk products and the governmental public health sector.

FAKE NEWS CAMPAIGN AGAINST THE FOUNDER OF BETIBUTI

The Story on Facebook Goes Mainstream

On March 14, 2018, a story started from a Facebook account named Minh Phuong and went viral. The story was about a woman and her new born baby, died in labour at home in Ho Chi Minh City. The woman in the story studied a course on 'obeying the nature in birth' which costed 15 million VND (equivalent to 640 USD in March 2018). Many photos of a screen-shot capturing the story were shared on Facebook and picked up by journalism. The following section is the text translated from the photo of some screenshots, published on 2Sao, a website of the *VietnamNet* newspaper (Moc, 2018).

- Text in the Facebook status:

  Ho Chi Minh City, 1 hour ago

  Hi everyone, let me share a story.

  15 million [Vietnam]dongs, 2 people died, after studying the course "Obeying the nature in birth". Can she [Mrs. Hong – the founder of Betibuti] compensate? Will she accuse people of not doing what she teaches? Will she deny the dead woman studied her course?

- Text in the first screenshot:

  My friend died because of her [Mrs. Hong], she died at home, not enough energy to push [the baby out] and exhausted to death. The new born baby died of being stuffed up. I don't know my friend follows her [Mrs. Hong's course]. Just got to know about this story 20 minutes ago. I'm crying for my friend and her baby.

  Oh my God. Poor her. The old woman [Mrs. Hong] should be in jail because of unintentionally manslaughter.

  You should write the story in full. We will share it. Poor the kids.

- Text in the second screenshot:

  My friend died. She paid 15 million [Vietnam Dong] to study the course "Obeying the nature in birth", and she wanted to give birth at home like the westerners do. But in the west people have home doctor. We in Vietnam don't [have home doctors]. The mother died of exhausting. The baby died of being stuffed up. The husband got mad. People have to tie him up at home.

  Oh my God. Why no one stayed beside her during the labour…

  Her husband was at work. She didn't phone him. He found her after she died.

- Text in the third screenshot:

  Her husband is still screaming and doesn't believe she died. He swears to find the house of LNPH. He urged his wife to stay in hospital, but the wife insisted to have home labour. And she squatted to push to baby out. Her husband called me just right now. They are too young and too stupid. How can she breathe if she squats and puts pressure on her heart?

  This story had two items of correct information. First, the course fee 15 million VND. Second, the squatting motions dancing course was for pregnant women. However, it mixed up with two items of incorrect information. First, the course was scheduled in June 2018 and had not yet taken place by the time of the story in March 2018. Second, the course was for the trainers, not for pregnant women.

MoH Confirmed the Unverified Story

By the end of business hours on the day, March 14, 2018, before the evening news, Mr. Nguyen Duc Vinh, the Head of the Department of Mothers' and Children's Health, a unit of MoH, confirmed that the authority had found the dead mother and child. The mother's name was T.V.M., living in Thao Dien Ward, District 2, Ho Chi Minh City. About 10:30 pm on March 14, 2018, MoH sent an official letter to the Department of Health of Ho Chi Minh City and to Tu Du Hospital of Obstetrics and Gynaecology, assigning these two organisations to further investigate the case. Mr. Vinh promised the details about the story would be revealed at a MoH press conference in on March 15, 2018. These developments of the story were reported in the news articles "Controversy around the pregnant woman obeying the nature in birth", published on Tuoi Tre newspaper website at night on March 14, 2018. Thus, by the end of the day March 14, 2018, the news was confirmed by an accredited source and the source promise further details in the following morning.

Facebook Became the Platform for Character Assassination

There was a gap of 12 hours from the confirmation by the MoH manager on the evening of March 14, 2018, to the press conference on the morning of March 15, 2018. The night became the prime time for the story to go viral on Facebook. The character assassination on Facebook against Mrs. Hong was conducted using the following approaches.

First, the naming and shaming approach: On the Facebook discussion, the name of the founder was no longer associated with the name of the breastfeeding group Betibuti. Instead, she was featured as the religious leader of a new group titled 'Obeying the nature'. This group was accused of practising extreme self-reliance in birth delivery, refusing doctors and medical aids, anti-vaccine, anti-medicine, and over-worshipping the benefits of human milk (LNPH, 2018).

Second, the use of memes: Some pieces of text that Mrs. Hong posted on Betibuti group were copied, cut out of context, and spread rapidly on Facebook with cynical comments. The most-spread memes were the screen-shot photos in which the following text was highlighted: 'breastfeeding can help the new knuckle grows again on a cut finger of a baby', 'sore-eyes on babies can be healed by dropping mothers' milk', 'like animals, human beings can deliver the babies without medical interference'. Another type of meme is the photo of Mrs. Hong placed together with the photo of a new-born baby whose umbilical cord was uncut, and placenta was attached to the baby (LNPH, 2018). The creation of these memes required professional skills and it was time consuming, which might be produced long before the news.

Third, defamation by highlighting asymmetric knowledge: According to Mrs. Hong (LNPH, 2018) several doctors posted on their Facebook criticising the "Obeying the nature" life-style, creating contrast between the knowledge provided by qualified doctors and the experience shared by the breastfeeding community. Her resume was retrieved, provoking another topic for criticism. She had postgraduate qualification in IT, working experience in the banking sector, and the certifications for the short courses on breastfeeding. It was discussed that she was underqualified and ineligible to share knowledge of maternity.

Fourth, the massive report: Pursuant to Facebook policy and algorithms, an account is deleted if many other accounts submit a report to Facebook. Many Facebook accounts reported that Le Nhat Phuong Hong was using someone else's name for her Facebook account. As a result, Facebook deleted Le Nhat Phuong Hong's account on the night of March 14, 2018. Le Nhat Phuong Hong then sent to Facebook her proof of identification and eventually recovered the Facebook account on March 28, 2018. During two weeks of waiting for verification, she was unable to use Facebook to respond to the attack (LNPH, 2018).

The Fake News as an Excuse for Propaganda

According to Le Nhat Phuong Hong, she was travelling to Australia in March 2018. Thus, she could not physically attend the press conference. In the early morning of March 15, 2018, before the press conference, Le Nhat Phuong Hong sent an email to one of the leaders of MoH. In the email, she explained the prenatal motion course had not yet taken place. Therefore, it would be unreasonable to claim that the mother and the baby died because of practising what the mother learnt from the course. The email was replied by the leader's assistant about one hour before the press conference (the author was allowed to access to these emails for the purpose of doing research).

The press conference was broadcast live and livestreamed on Facebook. At the beginning of the press conference, Mr. Nguyen Duc Vinh corrected his announcement made on March 14, 2018. He said the story of a mother and a baby dying in birth delivery was not yet verified. He promised MoH would further survey in Ho Chi Minh City and neighbourhood provinces to find the mother and the baby. The address of the dead mother and baby he mentioned the day before, which was in Thao Dien Ward, District 2, Ho Chi Minh City, was actually the home address of Le Nhat Phuong Hong.

The rest of the press conference turned out to be propaganda against developments in the 'Obeying the nature in birth' lifestyle. The press conference was hosted by the Head of the Legal Compliance Department of MoH, the Head of the Professional Committee of the Ho Chi Minh City Department of Health, and the Vice Director of Tu Du Hospital of Obstetrics and Gynaecology. The main message delivered during the conference was recommending professional medical treatment and warning against the risk of practising the community-based maternity initiatives.

On March 19, 2018, MoH sent an official request to the Ministry of Policemen for an investigation on the identification of the Facebook account Minh Phuong, who started the fake story. The Facebook account named Minh Phuong was deleted, and no longer found after March 15, 2018. As of March 2019, there had been no further media report or police report about the identification of Facebook account of Minh Phuong.

Consequences of Fake News

The Betibuti breastfeeding community has not grown since the fake news. Nine thousand members abandoned the Facebook group from March to October 2018, on which 2,000 members abandoned in the first week after the fake news. The course on prenatal dancing, which was scheduled in June and July 2018, was cancelled. This fake news is the starting point for a campaign 'correcting' the view point of the breastfeeding community toward 'Obeying the nature in birth'. With expertise in communication management in public health, the Deputy Minister of Health, Doctor Nguyen Thanh Long, was appointed to become the Deputy Chairman of the Central Propaganda and Training Commission starting in October 2018.

State-run journalism removed the name of Le Nhat Phuong Hong from the previously published news article. An example for the practice of removal can be observed in the news article 'Caution when using bio salty water for babies'. Data from the Content Management System of the *Health and Life* newspaper website indicated that the article was published twice—the first time at 1:27pm, February

23, 2016, and the second time at 11:05am, June 30, 2018. The first version was deleted from the website of *Health and Life* and is no longer accessible. However, it was picked up and republished on Baomoi and Zing News. The first version was published before the fake news. It used Le Nhat Phuong Hong as the source with indirect quotation. The second version of this news article was published after the fake news, in which the name of Le Nhat Phuong Hong and the indirect quotation were deleted. In this way, positive journalism coverage she had earned before the fake news was removed from the Internet. Le Nhat Phuong Hong was not quoted in any news article on mainstream media from the fake news to the end of October 2018.

SOLUTIONS AND RECOMMENDATIONS

To help journalists and audience in fake news identification in Vietnamese media landscape, it is necessary to figure out the elements composing the fake news in the country. This section discusses six typical elements involved in the generation of the fake news, particularly in the context of the rise of using Facebook for professional communication in Vietnam. The elements are presented in the sequence of their appearance in the fake-news process.

Unverified Sources

The fake news starts from an unverified Facebook account whose identification is unclear. The account neither posts any personal photos nor 'friends' verified persons. The person(s) behind the Facebook account tell(s) the story in a Facebook group where members may not know each other. Conversations about the story are made up between unverified accounts. Then the made-up story is captured and shared as screen-shot photos. After the screen-shot photos spread on the Internet, the source Facebook account is permanently deleted and untraceable. In the example of the fake news against Le Nhat Phuong Hong, the Facebook account 'Minh Phuong' was unverifiable, nor could the group in which Minh Phuong posted the story be identified. Only the photos capturing the screen-shot story were shared on Facebook and published by newspapers.

Half-Truth

The story shared on Facebook is made up from some correct information, such as the course fee of 15 million dongs, and the address in District 2 of Ho Chi Minh City, which is also the home address of the Betibuti founder. The story on Facebook is often a mixture of truth and falsehood, which requires much effort to be fact-checked.

Confirmation by Authority

The information shared on Facebook is just the story. When the story is confirmed by the authority, and published by the mainstream media, it becomes fake news. In this case, the MoH official confirmed the information about the dead mother and baby and promised to provide a detailed investigation the next day. The 12-hour gap between the confirmation and detailed investigation was long enough for the fake news to go viral and exaggerated by mainstream media. In this case, the authority confirmed the fake news because it might help the MoH to criticise the Betibuti community initiatives of being self-helped and dependent from hospitals and doctors. The authority can alter their answer later, but it was long enough for the fake news to be widespread.

Paid Commentators

As discussed previously, paid commentators can be the anonymous business-paid, or the government-based commentators. The online troop uses hundreds of anonymous Facebook accounts to make a massive report, so that the Facebook account of the victim is blocked or removed from the Internet. The paid commentators also post misleading and hate-speech contents. The government-based commentators (in this case, they are doctors) generate seeding comments against the victim of the fake news.

Removal From Journalism

The worst consequence of the fake news occurred when it created a new meaning for the previous events. Reputation was ruined, and the presence of the fake news victim was removed from the state-run journalism. It is very common in Vietnam journalism to rewrite and repost articles published years before. In the new version of articles, the names, the citations and the photos relating to the fake-news victims are deleted. Since the fake news can lead to a new version of history, fake news sometimes is employed as an excuse for erasing the old conception and making the new meaning.

From Fake News to New Policy

In some cases, the new sense made of the fake news becomes the foundation for the proposal of new policies and procedures. In these cases, the fake news is the good news. MoH made it a chance to correct the viewpoints around home-birth, that are considered wrong or opposite to the mainstream.

The Journalists

This element was not involved in the fake news against Betibuti founder. However, social-media influencers, and hybrid-media producers sometimes involve in fake news generating. For example, in the protest of the Cybersecurity Law in Binh Thuan province in June 2018, Mai Thanh Hai, a journalist of Thanh Nien newspaper, posted on his Facebook that two policemen died in the protest because of nail and gas bombs. Because Mai Thanh Hai was a professional press-carded journalist working in Binh Thuan province, his story on Facebook was considered verified news. Before it was detected as the fake news, it had been used as an excuse for the mobilization of heavily armed forces to Binh Thuan to stop the protesters (Journalist's Mai Thanh Hai and the fake news around the developments of the protest in Binh Thuan was analysed in the post "Revisit the story in Binh Thuan" on BoxitVN blogs on June 15, 2018).

FUTURE RESEARCH DIRECTIONS

The chapter investigate just one case study of the fake news on Facebook environment. It is necessary to study more cases, to identify the models of fake news and the involvement of the professional Facebook content generators. More case studies would help to consolidate the validity of the formula of the elements of fake news, improving the possibility of fake news detection. One of the extensions for this case study is to investigate the impacts of the fake news on its victims. How the viewpoints created by the fake news affect the fake news victim? What are their re-actions? And what is the optimal re-actions against the fake news that is intentionally and professionally created?

CONCLUSION

In conclusion, the fake news against the founder of the breastfeeding community is typical show case for the involvement of the professional Facebook content generators in fake news. It reflects the complexity of the fake news actors in the Vietnamese media landscape during 2014-2019 in general, and in public-health areas in particular. Journalists and audience are recommended to use seven above-mentioned elements to judge whether the news is genuine or made up. The Cybersecurity Law, legislated in June 2018 and becoming effective in January 2019, is believed to enable identifying, verifying and improving the traceability of a story on Facebook. However, when the law sets the priority as protecting the Party and State in Vietnam, it would create a legal gap and the mushrooming of the defamation against entities and individuals in the private sector. For the ultimate fake news prevention in Vietnam, the function of propaganda should be eliminated from journalism, which is problematic in the one-party country.

REFERENCES

72/2013/ND-CP. (2013). Decree No.72 on management, provision and use of Internet and online information services. Hanoi: The Parliament of Vietnam.

BBC. (2013). Thủ tướng 'xây mạng xã hội cho giới trẻ' [Prime Minister "build a social network for the youth"]. BBC Vietnamese. Retrieved from https://www.bbc.com/victnamese/vietnam/2013/03/130325_viet_nam_xay_mang_xa_hoi

Blessing, K., & Marren, J. (2013). Is the PR-ization of media...B.S.? *Media Ethics*, 24(2).

Chandler, D., & Munday, R. (2016). Organic reach. In D. Chandler & R. Munday (Eds.), *A Dictionary of Social Media. Online*. Oxford University Press.

Cuong, L. T. (2018). Interview: The rising industry of paid online commentators and contents. In L. T. Mach (Ed.), *RepuDigital Company, Hanoi city, July 23, 2018*.

Dao-Tuan. (2013). Tổ chức nhóm chuyên gia bút chiến trên Internet/Establish the expert groups for pen-fighting on the Internet. Lao Dong. Retrieved from http://www3.laodong.com.vn/chinh-tri/to-chuc-nhom-chuyen-gia-but-chien-tren-internet-98582.bld

DDH. (2015, June 9). I Interview: Investigating journalism about environment. Lao Dong Newspaper.

GALLUP. (2015). The changing media landscape in Vietnam. Retrieved from http://www.bbg.gov/wp-content/media/2015/06/Vietnam-Event-Final.pdf

Vietnamese Government. (2016). Press Law. Retrieved from http://www.wipo.int/wipolex/en/text.jsp?file_id=447052

Hall, S., Critcher, C., Jefferson, T., Clarke, J., & Roberts, B. (1979). *Policing the crisis: Mugging, the state, and law and order.* Great Britain: The Macmillan Press Ltd.

ITCNews. (2012). Facebook bị chặn do nhà mạng cân nhắc lợi ích kinh tế [Facebook was blocked because of economic reasons]. ICTNews. Retrieved from https://www.thongtincongnghe.com/article/31972

Lan-Anh. (2014). 108 trẻ chết do sởi và biến chứng: Bộ Y tế giấu dịch? [108 children died of measles: Does the Minister of Health conceal the epidemic?]. Tuoi Tre. Retrieved from https://tuoitre.vn/108-tre-chet-do-soi-va-bien-chung-bo-y-te-giau-dich-602991.htm

Mach, L. T. (2017). *How Vietnam Journalists use social media. Vietnam Journatists.* Hanoi: Vietnam Journalists Association.

Mai-Hoa. (2017). Hơn 10.000 người trong 'Lực lượng 47' đấu tranh trên mạng [Over 10 000 people in 'the 47th force' fight online]. Tuoi Tre. Retrieved from https://tuoitre.vn/hon-10-000-nguoi-trong-luc-luong-47-dau-tranh-tren-mang-20171225150602912.htm

Moc. (2018). Người cổ vũ sinh con thuận tự nhiên bỗng "mất tích" sau thông tin sản phụ tử vong vì áp dụng bài học [The leader of Obeying the nature in birth suddenly "disappear" after the news that a mother died because applying what she learnt in home-birth]. 2Sao. Retrieved from https://2sao.vn/sinh-con-thuan-tu-nhien-2-me-con-san-phu-chet-o-tp-hcm-n-148686.html

NHS. (2017) An interview by the author about To ngan lai [One thousand like group] (Interviewer: L. T. Mach).

Nielsen. (2015). Nielsen Vietnam Market Pulse 2015.

LNPH. (2018). An Interview by the author with Nhat-Le Phuong-Hong about the fake news. In L. T. Mach (Ed.), *On-phone interview, October 19, 2018.*

Palmos, F. (1995). *The Vietnamese press: The unrealised ambition.* Western Australia: Edith Cowan University.

Pike, D. (1970). North Vietnam Theory of Communication. In V. C. a. Archieve (Ed.), *Douglas Pike Collection: Unit 3 - Insurgency Warfare.* Texas Tech University.

Tho, H. (1997). *Cong viec cua nguoi viet bao.* Vietnam: Education Publishing House.

Truong-Son. (2015). Công an Hà Nội đang xác minh về lực lượng 'dư luận viên' tự phát [Hanoi investigates the self-emerged online 'opinion shapers']. Thanh Nien. Retrieved from https://thanhnien.vn/thoi-su/cong-an-ha-noi-dang-xac-minh-ve-luc-luong-du-luan-vien-tu-phat-542332.html

We-are-social. (2018). Digital Report 2018 in Southeast Asia. Retrieved from https://www.slideshare.net/wearesocial/digital-in-2018-in-southeast-asia-part-1-northwest-86866386

WHO. (2014). Measles Rubella Bulletin. *World Health Organisation, 8*(12), 10.

ZingNews. (2014). Cộng đồng mạng quyên góp mua máy thở cho trẻ bị sởi [The online community donate to buy aspiratory aids for measles children]. ZingNews. Retrieved from https://news.zing.vn/cong-dong-mang-quyen-gop-mua-may-tho-cho-tre-bi-soi-post409720.html

ADDITIONAL READING

Adam, G. S. (1993). Notes towards a Definition of Journalism: an old craft as an art form. St Petersburg, Florida, The Pyonter Institute for Media Studies.

Albarran, A. B. (2013). The Social Media Industries. London, Routledge.

Mach, L.T. (2019). Vietnam. In D.L. Merskin (Ed.), The SAGE International Encyclopedia of Mass Media and Society. USA: SAGE.

Mcnair, B. (2018). Fake news: falsehood, fabrication and fantasy in journalism, Abingdon, Oxon: Routledge.

Nash, C. (2016). What is Journalism? The Art and Politics of a Rupture. London: Palgrave Macmillan.

Nguyen, N. (2015). Bài học từ khủng hoảng truyền thông về dịch sởi của Bộ Y tế [Social Listening: Lessons learnt for the Ministry of Health from the communication crisis in the measles outbreak]. Hanoi: Brands Vietnam.

Tho, H. (1997). Cong viec cua nguoi viet bao Vietnam: Education Publishing House.

KEY TERMS AND DEFINITIONS

Business-Based Commentator: A person who gets paid from social-media marketing service company to generate content on social media as requested by the clients of the company.

Government-Based Commentator: A person who works for governmental organisation, maybe a doctor, a student, a scientist, etc., and generates content on social media as requested by government to protect governmental interests.

Half-Truth: The truth elements marking parts of the news and often be used to deceive the audience that whole of the news is the truth.

Hybrid-Media Producer Journalist: A journalist who is working full-time for mainstream media and at the same time earns money for publishing on social media.

Paid Commentator: A person who gets paid to generate contents and interaction on social media.

Social-Media Influencer Journalist: A journalist who used to work for mainstream media before but no longer had a license to work in mainstream media anymore, but still earn great public attraction by publishing on social media.

Social-Media Refuter Journalist: A journalist works for mainstream media and intentionally avoid using social media for professional purposes.

Chapter 32
Commercial Use of Mobile Social Media and Social Relationship:
The Case of China

Li Zhenhui
Communication University of China, China

Dai Sulei
Communication University of China, China

ABSTRACT

China is well known for its wide and increasing commercial use of mobile social media for various purposes in different areas, ranging from online shopping to social networking. Such a popular commercial use was insightfully examined in relation to social relationship in the age of mobile internet, which enables people of either weak or strong connections to socialize anywhere anytime, leading to scenarios where mobile social media can be leveraged for profits. In what way can user experiences be guaranteed while platforms' value-added targets be achieved at the same time? In addressing that question, the authors of this chapter examined the commercial use of mobile social media in the context of complicated social networks. It is expected from the editor that further studies are to be carried out to comprehensively and comparatively examine the same topic in different countries or cultures.

INTORDUCTION

In the Internet age, especially in the age of mobile Internet, online social networks are making the connection, interaction, and relationship among people even more complicated. The social relationship of the younger generation is also being made more complicated, in which individual roles are being constantly transformed (Luo, 2017). In the past, mechanistic logic and reductionism were applied to analyze the problems of social networks from social sciences perspectives. In fact, the strength of weak

DOI: 10.4018/978-1-6684-6307-9.ch032

ties (Granovetter, 1973) could play a more important theoretical role in explaining social networks in the Internet age, which argued that the weak ties in social networks could satisfy some social needs, with those who have favorable resources play a key connecting role as bridges.

Before studying changes in social networks, technical factors should be first taken into consideration. Information technology is clearly the fundamental factor for social reshaping, and in an era where strength and efficiency surpass any source of power, the technical logic has begun to replace the functions of social regulation and cultural traditions in certain areas, which changes people's cognitive and action frameworks. To make people's connection more convenient and meet people's social needs, mobile social media are growing more mature with technology, and developers spare no efforts to strive to occupy every single market. Even though mobile users are so different in their perceptions and expectations of mobile social media, mobile social media have gradually been transformed a communication tool to a living necessity. This development has been driven by business and user traffic, regardless of platforms, channels or media, which in turn would attract more attention and capital. When mobile social media and commercial capital are becoming more maturely integrated, interacted, interconnected, or even interdependent, how mobile social media have been commercially leveraged in the context of the mobile Internet and in the presence of the strength of weak ties of social networking. That is an imperative topic to be fully investigated from mixed perspectives in relation to communication and economics studies.

RESEARCH PURPOSE

Based on the view of strength of weak ties of social networking, the research on mobile social software, driven by Internet technology, is deconstructing the power structure and communication pattern. And when audiences have more power, they will have their own commercial value and they are likely to pay for channels and contents.

Mobile Internet, firstly, is to deconstruct the power structure of traditional society. Fei (2006) proposes 'Differential mode of association' of agricultural society and he thought blood relationship is the basis of agricultural social relations where egoism occupies personal emotions and there is on obvious distinction between public and private, also, violent ruling, without democracy; Industrial society appears *'Group pattern'*, where nation controls rare resources and builds a new organizational framework with production materials, employment position and living space, so that it can eliminate the differential mode of association based on the blood relationship. Internet society has brought elimination of those power structures. The decentralization and fragmentation of state power, and the opening and connection of the Internet have changed the scarcity of resources, and the mobile Internet has made information sharing easier, and even the marginal cost of surplus social resources is close to zero. The essence of *"sharing"* makes the Internet burst out with greater energy. Sun (1993) argues that the basic unit of social control and resource allocation gradually loses the power to monopolize social resources and to control social relations. The society becomes a relatively independent source of resources and opportunities, and individual dependence on the state is significantly weakened (Sun, 1993).

Mobile Internet then deconstructs the dependence of traditional media on content and channels and the content is not the key point anymore and channels are not the only choice. In the internet system, Yu (2016) proposes a new developing direction which is 'Relationship Empowerment'. He argues that 'relationship empowerment gives the public right and ability to discuss and participate in public affairs, by stimulating individual value and relationship networking. Hence, the environment and pattern of social governance are undergoing unprecedented changes (Yu, 2016). This way of empowerment could also be seen as a paradigm for the reconstruction of the value of the media in the Internet age. The Six Degree Separation theory nowadays can even become to Three Degree. It is very important for every transformation of media form whether the vital hint which hided among everyone could be accurately controlled and stimulated or spread forms could be strengthened with activation and scene technology.

Another important reason for supporting the theory of strong-weak ties theory is the technology and means provided by the Internet, which increases the scenes of users. When new scenes appear, people can play different roles in a variety of scenes. For example, virtual reality technology can create a versatile field to make people enter a scene that connects many people's social connections and feelings to achieve the immersive experience. Once these technologies are widely used, users can generate emotional experiences, and personal emotions are fully driven. This is the best mobilization and utilization of relational resources and emotional resources. The emergence of multiple situations is a key point which can become a strong relationship between social media and audience.

Information technology surpasses the supreme power source in efficiency and intensity, showing its own logic, and even in some areas has been or has replaced the functions of social regulation and cultural traditions, reshaping people's cognitive, behavior, and perception frameworks. Therefore, the social relationship is being reshaped, and the allocation system of social resource is transformed. Mobile social applications are clearly closely related to users. And user relationship is vital to social media.

LITERATURE REVIEW

User-centric relationship network covers various application scenes. SoLoMo (Social, Local, Mobile) has deeply changed internet user's habit to obtain information. In internet age, mobile internet changes the whole relation structure from the bottom of society, and various mobile social media nearly have occupied all social networking nodes of people. Developers are also constantly occupying market gaps, and the business model of social applications is being promoted by capital. Now, the business model of mobile social media is mainly built from two ways. The one is that application itself can realize cash storage or income and another one is to attract flow to external applications for cash achieving. No matter which way, it is reusing the weak ties which are already gathered. From the strong-weak ties theory, interpreting the social relationship changes in the era of mobile internet and the meaning behind it, and paying attention to the commercial phenomena appearing in social applications, to support some viewpoints are the purpose of this chapter.

Research on Strong-Weak Ties of Social Relationships

The relationship between the strengths and weaknesses of the audience is related to the changes in social relations. 'Free flow resource' and 'Free Space' both promote structural differentiation between societies. For the performance of the audience on social media, social structure differentiation is the underlying reason. Sun (1993) describes the manifestation of structural differentiation in his article. Firstly, he argues that society becomes a relatively independent source of resources and opportunities and the dependence of individuals on the state are evidently weakened. Then, relatively independent social power would be developed and formed. Lastly, the intermediary organization would appear, which is a civil organization between the state and family and these organizations do not target social services and profitability. Because of the 'Free flow resource' and 'Free space', the re-division and structuring between the state and society has brought far-reaching significance to all aspects of Chinese society. For individuals, changes in identity and status will naturally lead to more independence.

Yu (2016) mentions one concept called 'Relationship Empowerment' in his paper that the most prominent trait of the Internet society is that information technology has become the basic power shaping society. In internet society normal people are given by some power which transcends any age and their (internet celebrities and opinion leaders) value and influence hardly came from administration, capital or force (Yu, 2016). Internet, especially social media, not only gives individuals the speaking and executive power, but also meets individuals needs of social resources and materials in basic survival and longer-term development. Personal internal needs and value system are being re-arranged.

Based on the development of technology, the emergence of mobile terminals actually realizes the switching of scenes at any time. Peng (2015) argues that the mobile Internet includes three areas that is content, social and service, and mobile media has made a leap in the three directions of content media, relationship media and service media. She also mentions that in the analysis and application of mobile scenes, the current focus is on the location and significance of users here and now, but in the long run, the analysis and application of mobile scenes need to involve three stages (Peng, 2015). In addition to here and now, mobile scenes also need to extend to two different space-times of 'Before here and after here'. Our research on social software is to explore all aspects of the various situations, such as causes, conditions, and impacts. Once the audience have become dependent on the scene, it means that the fixed relationship is highlighted, or briefly, the strong relationship is established.

Actually, defining the transformation of strong-weak ties in social media can be described in terms of very vivid words, which is from 'Masked Internet' to 'Face-seeing internet'. Masked internet brings great freedom based on anonymity. Face-seeing internet is constantly updating social platform functions of social media. Social attributes lead to a strong tie with a limited scope, but this transformation needs many activate factors, such as multiple interactions which brought by social users' common concerns and providing real-time communication and advancement of sticky communication mobile platforms. This layer of conversion implementation would make the Internet more and more close to interpersonal communication, and of course, it would be the basis for mobile social media to expand business applications.

Research on the Business Application of Social Mobile Media

The development of mobile technology brought about the rapid growth of mobile data. As of December 2017, the number of mobile Internet users in China reached 753 million (CNNIC, 2018). The report (2018) points out the proportion of Internet users using mobile terminals s increased from 95.1% in 2016 to 97.5%. Moreover, there is a change about mobile terminals. Smart devices represented by mobile phone have become the basis of 'Internet of Everything'. Smart lights for cars and home appliance have begun to enter personalized and intelligent application scenarios. This is also consistent with 'scenarios that bring strong connections'. Business application research for the mobile social industry has gradually become a hot topic. Data output is mainly concentrated in industry reports. Some scholars interpret the attributes of mobile social media from the perspective of communication. Some scholars analyze the innovation of social media from the field of marketing.

On the whole, the business model on mobile social media has few refining results. All of them are based on case studies. Cheng (2014) uses SWOT analysis to expound the commercialization of Tencent WeChat. He proposes that the WeChat business model components include proposition, network, maintenance and realization of value. Liu (2015) conducts a business form analysis on social networking sites, Weibo, and instant messaging. But it lacks systematic summaries and improved views. Zhao and Luo (2015) use the 'street-side network' as an example to obtain the optimization steps of social network application software through the research methods of questionnaires. It includes 'person', 'machine', 'material', 'law' and 'ring'. In five aspects, the product is iterated. But providing personalized services, securing user information and improving the user experience can provide a precedent for other social media. Li (2014) analyzes that WeChat's profit points include user payment, advertising revenue, value-added services, profit sharing, e-commerce and game revenue. It points out that WeChat's profit direction is mainly focused on value-added services, marketing platforms, games and e-commerce platforms. Zhao (2014) points out that the core business model of WeChat is 'platform business model'. But the content of the discussion still focuses on four types of modules: value-added, games, marketing and e-commerce.

In terms of review, the scholars' research focuses on the case study of the representation. The power structure and relationship network behind the mobile social platform are not mentioned. The expression of the viewpoint is not refined enough. The discussion on the profit model only stays at present, not highlighting the changes of mobile social which resulted from the changes of mobile internet. So what are the changes of advertising, value-added, game and e-commerce in future? Will there be new profitable revenue points? This chapter attempts to propose a new profit model.

Research Methods and Research Problem Design

This chapter mainly adopts the investigation method with a systematic understanding of case, industry data and existing research results. It also conducts text analysis on the survey data. It shows the current development status and prospects of the deep logic and profit model of current mobile social media by reading the relevant documents. At the same time, in order to make the arguments more sufficient, the case analysis method is introduced to analyze the commercialization method of mobile social software.

DATA ANALYSIS AND DISCUSSION

Mobile Social Media From the Perspective of Social Relations

Technological Change Makes Mobile Internet Become the Dominant Technology

Mobile Internet is the technological change firstly. It breaks through the barriers of time and space from the technical level. It also brings the possibility of sending and receiving information anytime and anywhere. The individual has become a small tower. With the continuous development of technology, the speed of information dissemination and the expansion of information storage, the audience has gradually gained a new understanding of their own roles. Under the drive of subjective initiative, they have made adjustments in the era of mobile internet. The ''empowerment'' function of mobile internet technology even surpasses the Internet. Because the conditions for changing the scene at any time are realized, people become more active actors. The emergence of scenes means the deconstruction of traditional rights structure, as well as society redistribution of resources.

Based on technologies such as Internet of Things, big data, cloud computing and high-frequency information transmission, on one hand, mobile internet inherits the characteristics of PC terminal interaction and the advantage of crossing the information gap. On the other hand, it breaks down the barriers of time and space. It adds meaningful 'instant' communication to users. In addition, in the diversity of information, it is more creative. It can meet the transmission of various types of information such as text, voice, pictures, video, etc. With the help of high-frequency communication technologies such as 4G, 5G and Wi-Fi, users can even make up for the shortcomings of mass communication - 'lacking of interpersonal communication interaction' under the carrier of the Internet APP.

Especially on various smart phone applications, it covers almost every corner of the user's life, such as social, shopping, entertainment and knowledge sharing by satisfying the needs of users at all levels. All things that users can think of and hope to use are developed. It's better to say that the mobile Internet is connected by multiple small fields instead of a large of field. It is precisely because of the technology that the relationship between these small fields is complicated. In the case of social software, the crowds gathered on the same social software. It means that the recognition of the software interaction, whether it is interpersonal communication between people, or group communication within a small group, or the organization and dissemination of social software are gathered on this platform. Individuals become the center of platform maintenance. Multiple individuals are connected together to provide a continuous source of power for social software. It provides cumulative users and further profitability.

Mobile Social Media's Role Changes

From a personal point of view, it is a change in personal roles. Internet pioneer Negroponte (1997) once predicted that digital survival naturally has the essence of 'empowerment', which would lead to positive social changes. And in the digital future, people will find new dignity. We can see that this prophecy has become a reality today. The Internet empowers ordinary people more than any era. It has dealt a blow to any source of power. Both the opinion leaders in Internet and people who influence the surrounding people pass on their information to others. When some creative and influential mobile Internet users use those apps with non-social attributes, they will make them socialized. It can be seen that under the level of technological innovation, the way of social interaction has changed significantly. Specifically, individuals have such performance in the mobile Internet.

Individuals become the direct productivity of social networks. In other words, the wisdom of individuals provides the raw materials for social networks. The operational logic of Web 2.0 makes everyone a relatively independent 'propagation base station (Peng, 2013). On the basis of data, individuals can maintain the passive acceptance of information in the past, as well as actively control the data production. Through the shaping of data, Internet people have gradually formed a way to survive and perform in this era. In the traditional sense, the 'background' has been moved to the 'front desk'. People are no longer constrained by whether they need to take into account the image, but play a role in the massive wave of information. Based on the 'performance' and 'relationship' of data, individuals are gradually exposed to form a 'data memory' about this era. As far as social networks are concerned, based on the use and satisfaction of individual contributions, attention resources, knowledge reserves and user data support for social platforms can even become the basic driving force for the existence of the platform. Zhihu, as a platform for user knowledge collection, the way of rationally treating problems has become a gathering place for a large number of outstanding intellectuals. It is precisely because this platform provides a relatively rational communication environment that it can stand out among many social platforms. The power of users brings together a steady stream of content for the platform.

Individuals assume the responsibility of spreading nodes. And the network of individual connections becomes a new place for public opinion. When the technical conditions satisfy the individual's ability to act as a small mobile tower, we can regard the individual as a node in the communication network. Of course, this node will be based on the individual's grasp of the information, the social status of the individual and the reason of the opinion leader. But the common point is that the entire process of 'coding, decoding, decoding' can be completed. Mobile social software is very easy to become a new 'public opinion generation and fermentation platform' when it acts as a life communication assistant. In the public opinion event, the individual is continuously coding as an information node, releasing the code at a relatively fast speed and then decoding. Sending and promoting the process of public opinion events has become a new place for public opinion fermentation.

The habits of personalized usage are obvious. Mobile social software is also tending to introduce personalized customization services. Different people have different software usage habits. People's information 'experience domain' is different in size. So the performance is different in the process of socialization. Users use mobile social media to obtain information and experience knowledge. They use it as a medium to interact with people in the society to generate information flow. On the one hand, it is to understand the surrounding environment. It can be called the 'environmental radar' function of Lasswell's three functions. On the other hand, it is better to integrate into society and complete the socialization process. With the advancement of Web3.0 technology, social software has also showed different needs in the process of socialization between people, paying more attention to personalized customization and creating private scenes.

'Mobile Community': Scenarioization of Mobile Social Media Mimicry Environment

The Internet platform combines the breadth of mass communication and the depth of interpersonal communication. The mobile social application restores the communication advantages of interpersonal communication. It includes the comprehensive meaning of transmitting information, the strong two-way, the high feedback, and the flexible method. It also broadens the types, time and space of interpersonal communication on a technical level. On the one hand, it is no longer limited by time and place. People who are not in the same situation can also interact. On the other hand, it developed multiple ways of paralleling sound and picture in the ways of communication. Then a private imaginable discourse space can be built.

'Relationship' plays a fundamental role in mobile social applications and it embodies in two aspects. First of all, strong connections are based on the users' trust. Mobile social software has numerous complex functions and has accumulated a large amount of users' information. Besides, it can record users' normal life and even analyze such behavioral characteristics like reading and consumption habits. In this case, if it is not built on a high degree of trust between users, it will not be easy to obtain data. In other words, the essence of the existence of mobile social networks is based on the users' trust in sharing information, including sharing their hobbies, interests, status, activities and locations online. Network topology varies, and mobile social network is a tool to connect nodes of users. Interpersonal trust manifests the interactive generation of value conception, attitude, mood, and even personal charm between the users. The word ''network trust'' has initiated many research by scholars when it was put forward in the 20th century. Lu (2003) has concluded network trust into three categories: the trust relationship between the users and the websites in the electronic commerce activities, the 'trust system' of technology, the trust relationship in the process of online interpersonal communication and the network trust among the users in the mobile social networking platform.

In addition, the relationship between the platform and users is also worth studying. Unlike WeChat as a social software, there are also many platforms maintaining a light connection with users and rarely being used unless when they are needed. This kind of trust is based on the theory of 'Uses and Gratifications', the theory shows that whether in mental or in action, once the platform has the characteristics which the users need and could bring a certain degree of satisfaction for users, it may obtain basic trust. What's more, if users feel the platform is coordinated with their own using habits, the reliability will be enhanced. This is also why the platforms will make a difference in the competition. To focus attention on the commercial realization of mobile social application, only if users are confident with security and privacy of the platform may the consuming behavior or the 'payment' action can be generated, which means users confident with the platform and willing to pay attention and money for support.

From the perspective of social scenes, all communication activities are carried out under specific scenes. Merowitz(2010) believes that it takes a long time for the traditional development of society to form a universal connotation of any scene. Electronic media also create a scene in the development and become a situational factor which will influence the human behaviors. Lippmann(2010) believed that the communication behavior of modern people is not in the real environment, but in the 'pseudo-environment' rendered by mass communication. In English, words like situation, context, settings and field are used to express the semantics of a situation, and in Chinese, there are also synonyms words like situation, background, and environment, which are not easy to distinguish.

From the perspective of space-time dimension, Goffman (2009) believes that a scene is 'a place that is limited to a certain extent by the perceptible boundary'. In a specific time and place, only people who face each other in the same three-dimensional space can perceive the same information. Merowitz (2010) and Goffman (2009) also stressed from the situational perspective, 'places create information system of live communication, and other channels create many other types of situation.' One of the most conspicuous signs is the birth of the television which created a new situation for people directly. People sitting in front of the TV to watch the content on the screen and their mood going up and down with the plot as if they are one part of the virtual world.

Some scholars believe that the elements of scene in the mobile era include space and environment, users' real-time state, their habits and social atmosphere based on the perspective of compound latitude of new era. These scenes become the entrance of data for mobile media.

Despite of the dimensions, the emergence of the scene is ultimately oriented to the deconstruction of the traditional power structure. In a macroscopic view, information technology disintegrates the operation mechanism of power structure in traditional society. First of all, the interaction between different scenes become more common when a new social scene has emerged, and the word 'decentralization' can best represent the disperse of traditional social rights. In the past, the privileged shapes their authority through clearly defined scenes which could sustain their uniqueness and mystique. Network platform becomes more open and full of information hybridity. Due to Internet technology, network platform has greatly filled the chasm between ordinary people and power center caused by information asymmetry, so that people from different social classes are placed in a unified scene. French philosopher Foucault (2012) proposed that information asymmetric is equivalent to a low-cost and efficient tool for social governance, just like the pyramid prison in ancient Rome: prisoners are kept in different cells and the jailer can monitor them at the top meanwhile the other prisoners could not see him. It is known as 'Panopticon' while Internet technology has generated a new social structure described as ''common view prison'' which is completely relative to 'Panoticon'. The later, as an 'onlooker' structure, concentrates on many-to-one model. In this way, information is relatively symmetrical. The information in this time is relatively symmetrical, managers will no longer have absolute control of the information resources and almost every manager are in the surveillance of ordinary citizens thus the role has exchanged between the two. Quantitatively, managers are less outnumbered, and moreover, the protections which new information technology has brought to the democracy have become more rampant, such as anonymous, hint, group-behavior-infection.

Microscopically, the mechanism of power granting has broken through the previous mode of ''institutional appointment''. Toffler (2006) believes that force, wealth, and knowledge constitute the triangle cornerstone of different power frames based on the criterion of the evolution of human society. The early human society need force to penalize but with the rise of the capital market, a part of power has changed from force to wealth, money can make a clear distinction between reward and penalty and more flexible; As the industrial civilization declines, knowledge became the dominant force and people from all social stratification has an opportunity to grasp, it could violate the violence if applied appropriately so that it has been called 'high-grade right'.

However, there is no one such as web celebrity, influential WeChat official accounts, Taobao celebrities could obtain the position from international agencies for it comes from their own relationship resources. The social status in today's market-oriented society will be relatively easy to obtain when every individual and every institution has channels to obtain attentions and financial support.

A deeper reason is that those groups such as marginal groups and isolated individuals who are easily neglected in traditional society, are also 'empowered' in the era of mobile Internet. Different from the superposition of order in the period of institutional empowerment and the pursuit of maximization of economic interests in the period of industrial capitalism, however, mobile Internet is different, it has changed the paradigm of individual empowerment and fundamentally changed the rules of the game of power. Those who have traditionally been kept out of the empowerment sphere have deservedly stepped into the center of the stage. Moreover, there is no upper or lower level of empowerment. For the web celebrities and their fans, they are all the consensual subjects participated and no one is forced. 'Mutual benefit, mutual respect and mutual identity' are necessary conditions for the existence of cooperation mechanism. After scaling up to the entire society, interpersonal cooperation will be enhanced exponentially instead of growing layer by layer in the pattern of hierarchy.

For social resources, it also breaks through the dominance of 'scarce resources' in the past and advocates 'sharing economy' now. The characteristics of internet such as open, interactive and complex have changed the endorsement of trust among various subjects. Nowadays the core of trust construction is the capacity of connecting, integrating and applying relational resources. As Tencent Charity for example, in August 2017, it launched a charity activity called 'one yuan purchasing a painting', it chose to advertise in the WeChat moments, and turning the paintings created by mental disorder children into electronic ones selling on 1 yuan. Each work has a simple introduction and summary of status of the children. People could scan the QR code to pay and sending the blessings, writing the messages meanwhile. This activity spread widely on WeChat platform. Different from the past form of donating money on the spot and large amount of the remittance, the form of 'Internet and commonweal' has made charity no longer just a process of mobilization, dissemination of information, donating money, but can widely obtain the effect of emotional resonance among the public. The conception of 'charity is nearby' and 'everyone could become a commonweal' will become more down to earth. In this micro public welfare platforms, common strangers are connected with each other due to consensus and trust. Together, each person's puny effect will confluence into huge power.

The change that the mobile internet brings to the social environment, is connecting everyone in every corner of the world, letting them abandon their suffering in the real life and be connected together. It gives confidence to everyone to integrate into the society, because common resources are shared and various ethnic groups, all kinds of demands are included within a framework to interact, so that people could be harmonious yet different.

Changes in Communication Content and Forms of Mobile Social Media

After mobile network successfully enter the market, all kinds of applications have showed carrying out by smart phones. Among numerous of mobile applications, instant-messaging software is on the top of downloads ranks in mobile application market for replacing text function and integrating social circle. For now, this software is mature after development and the problems of adhesiveness of users has been resolved, the only problem left is how to break through the bottleneck problem of user experience. Besides, there is no doubt that for the emergence of new social software, the requirement of attracting attention is still necessary.

Though the content of mobile social media still follows the mode of user-generated content, it is developing towards the direction of professional, depth and precision. Meanwhile, many content producers that are widely concerned have emerged. With the era of live broadcasting and short video has come, more ordinary people become a popular star. Those content provides a new subculture environment for the new generation of young Internet users who admire the secular pleasure and their spiritual satisfaction are related to the short-time value, so that they could compete with the mainstream culture. Of course, with the further evolution of the Internet, those subcultures will eventually be integrated after the process of compromise. From the view of professional communicators, precision is the main feature for the users can get information exactly right what they need, and the analysis tools are needed to produce accurate delivery and production. In this way, under the support of multiple forms of contact, that fragmented information actually has a rule to follow, which is accorded with information personalized and customized.

In terms of communication form, due to the flexibility of mobile terminals, the form setting must conform to the reading characteristics of mobile intelligent devices, which is, flexible switching, short text, light reading, multi-text and so on. Compared with traditional social media, the function of browsing and searching of mobile social media are less important. However, in recent years, public accounts and other community functions have been opened and searching functions have been added to expand the functions of social media. It has changed the 'treelike' information flow mode of traditional media into the 'network' information flow mode of the new media era and increased the subjective initiative of the audience, finally strengthened the 'interaction' and 'feedback' effect. With the further development of interactive media, the future media environment will be more immersive.

Theoretical Basis of Commercialization of Mobile Social Media

Mobile social media owns a huge number of users, it is also a way of communication based on social relations. This means that mobile social media holds huge social capital and has the ability to carry out business transformation. Massive users accumulated by strong relationships can provide a great marketing space. By using aggregation effect, information can be aggregated, and the essence of attention economy can be shown.

Three Degrees of Separation- Strong and Weak Ties- Structural Hole- SoLoMo

The theory of 'Six Degrees of Separation' is a well-known social theory, also known as the 'Small World Theory'. The theory shows that weak relationships are ubiquitous in society and play a very powerful role. At the beginning, the theory is closely linked to the Internet, and then lead to emergence of 'social software' that support people to establish a close and mutual trust relationship. These are also what we are familiar today as the social software. Blog took the lead in popularity at the initial period, thanks to its equipped features of posting feelings, communicating with ease and personalized displaying. After a while of gradual evolution, there came these chatting software with purpose of making friends which were built on direct social relations. And more innovative social interaction cases were then springing up. Domestically, platforms such as Renren, Qzone, Douban.com and Zhihu were all role models, who knew well how to use games, knowledge discussions as ways to better communicate with their users. With development of mobile network, 'Six Degrees of Separation' was upgraded into 'Three Degrees of Separation'. That's where mobile social network was built on the basis of a 'strong relationship', as compared to the Internet, mobile web can bring people much closer to burst out more concentrated capabilities. Hence in an era of mobile social media, people often find that it is easier to get acquainted with strangers who share common interests or hobbies, or whom they are more willing to get to know. And the function of location sharing makes users feel much closer.

Based on Granovetter (1973) 's 'The Strength of Weak Ties' theory, American sociologist Burt(1995) proposed the theory of 'Structural Holes' in his study on what hinders interpersonal communications. A structural hole is understood as a gap between two individuals who have complementary sources to information. The theory suggests that some individuals in a social network hold certain positional advantages/disadvantages from how they are embedded in neighborhoods or other social structures. And if we see the network as a whole, it seems that there are gaps in the network structure (Dong & Li, 2011, p.40-43). Coleman (1988)'s theory of social capital has the greatest impact on the theory of structural holes. Only by participating in social groups and establishing group ties can people gain social capital. Heterogeneity is significant among weak ties and the feasibility of sharing scarce resources between the two sides is also greater. People who do not have a strong relationship with each other are not able to communicate smoothly because of objective or subjective barriers. The hypothesis of weak ties can be regarded as the foundation of structural holes theory. On the contrary, strong ties are shaking this foundation. It believes that if people are closely connected in mobile social networks, the holes will shrink or even disappear.

The concept of mobile social networking that based on strong ties is SoLoMo, which means Social, Local, Mobile. Since the concept was put forward by John Doerr, a partner of a well-known venture capital firm in February 2011, technology companies started to consider it as the development trend of future Internet marketing. In fact, this is indeed a keyword of mobile internet. In order to obtain real services in the virtual Internet, people can achieve their goals through shifting. LBS applications (positioning services) have been pushed into people's vision. Virtual networks can react to the real human society through this application technology. LBS applications (Location service) have been pushed into people's vision. Virtual networks can react to the reality through this technology. Mobile social media knows that it's not enough for social users to just record where they've been. What's more important is how different LBS applications can make, that is, 'geographic location information can provide what services'. In November 2010, Renren became the biggest LBS service provider in China after the launch of the 'Everyone Check-in' product based on mobile Renren's clients. Users are willing to 'check in' because the product integrates the real social relationship in Renren, which makes it possible to increase the opportunities for interaction between friends. Businessmen are always sensitive, and advertisers always pay attention to what users care about. In order to promote the new flavor of beverage, Tingyi (Cayman Islands) Holding Corp launched campaign through LBS services, 'Everyone Check-in' and 'Sina Wei Territory', which brought direct profit growth offline.

Attention Economy and Community Shared Economy

'...In an information-rich world, the abundance of information means the lack of information consumption. Now, the object of information consumption is the attention of its recipients. The abundance of information leads to a lack of attention. Therefore, attention needs to be allocated effectively in an excessive amount of consumable information resources,' said Herbert Simon, the Nobel Prize Winner for Economics in 1978. Because attention is a psychological concept, therefore, a psychologist named Thorngate put forward 'attention economy'. Zhang (2009) mentions that the so-called attention economy is human interaction mode of production, processing, distribution, exchange and consumption of attention resources. In the Internet era, the attention economy is more obvious, the group of internet celebrities is the example. In the era of mobile social networking, information tends to be more fragmented, so it is hard to gather up the attention from audience. But at the same time, delivering information accurately becomes easier. Users can customize the information based on their preferences. Mobile social media has huge marketing potential in allocating users' attention.

Felson and Spaeth (1978) mentioned the concept of 'Collaborative Consumption'. But sharing economy did not become popular until recent years. Under the background of mobile social networking, the essence of sharing economy is based on the interpersonal relationship, and economic value is realized by detonating a certain scale of user groups. The greatest value of mobile internet lies in the network effect. Sharing economy is more like a community economy on mobile social software. People stop hiding their name in social network communities, mutual trust starts to increase, and then value got generated from it, together to form a self-operating, self-cycling economic system. In these community systems, any need or interest may eventually evolve into a business purpose. And both extensive networking resources and business development are worth noting and exploring. In a many-to-many relationship, information, resources and creativity are stimulated by the interaction, and then they will reproduce content and value. Therefore, social interaction will be self-operating and self-enhancing once it develops to a certain extent.

Social Virtual Currency and Fan Economy

According to mUserTracker (2017), a monitoring product of iResearch, a provider of online audience measurement and consumer insights in China, the monthly number of mobile devices that contain social APPs reached nearly 590 million in May 2017. Among the mobile netizens, the social communication APP usage rate is the highest, namely 91.8%.(Figure 1) There are many ways to use the interpersonal relationship in the mobile social era for marketing. Based on some common understandings, social platforms produce many virtual gifts to replace money for fans to interact with their idols, which is essentially word-of-mouth communication. From the Stealing Vegetables game in the Qzone.com to giving out gifts during live-streaming, those actions are all aimed at increasing the activeness of fans through using social virtual currencies on mobile social platforms. From a certain point of view, it is the monetization of fans, apart from letting fans to consume directly, it also involves the deep interaction between individuals and brands. There is an important feature of social currency, which is the ability to arouse users' emotional resonance by presenting interesting content, and in turn stimulating their sharing behaviors. That is a typical communication process of transforming the influence from thoughts to actions. With the development of live-streaming, the scale of users has increased dramatically, and social dividend has increased. Under the external push of technology support and capital boost, the scale of live-streaming industry keeps expanding.

Figure 1. China mobile social app monthly independent device number trend map during June 2016-May 2017
Note: China's social network includes independent network communities like Baidu's social product Baidu Tieba, social products of portal websites like Sina Weibo and Qzone, and excludes instant messaging APPs.

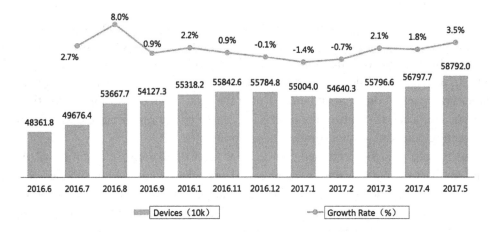

Mobile social networking offers the opportunities for people to have the decision-making power, to release them from the shackles of society. Social virtual currency becomes the carrier of time consumption in social networking, it also carries emotions and thoughts. It is a common asset held by consumers and enterprises, which helps to enhance user's recognition and loyalty to the brand, and also helps to realize the rapid marketing promotion of the brand in a short time, that is, word of mouth.

Ways to Commercialize Mobile Social Media: A Case Study of Communication Social Media

Mobile social media is a combination of mobile internet, smart terminal and media service. CIC(2015) introduced the different categories that mobile social media applications fall into, including Weibo/blog, dating networking, entertainment social networking, instant messaging, community social networking, anonymous social networking and workplace social networking. In the above categories, instant messaging applications can play a role comparable to mobile phone in people's daily life. With the largest cumulative user traffic, mature user experience and greater stickiness of users, the foundation for cash revenue is becoming increasingly solid. This is also the focus of this chapter.

The Current Profit Model of Mobile Social Media

The commercial practice on mobile social media in recent years are mainly focus on internal cash flow, drainage to external APP and advertising.

Turing Internal Value-Added Flow Into Cash

Mobile social media can usually bring a group of core users together. They are able to maintain daily activity and overlap the communication between users invisibly. Under the background of three-degree segmentation, it is less difficult to connect two strangers. For platforms, it has the basis to user operation and the ability to bring value-added products through internal flow.

The most important way of realizing internal flow is to use social virtual currency to complete the value-added closed-loop within the media. As mentioned in the previous article, virtual currency is sold by catering for people's psychological social needs. And with the development of social software algorithms, these virtual currencies are dressed up with aesthetics. From QQ space decoration in the early years to sending presents in live-streaming, they have become the media of user communication. Taking anonymous social media Momo as an example, Momo announced its unaudited financial statements for the third quarter of 2017. Quarterly growth in paid subscribers brought in total revenue of value-added services of $26.3 million, up 45% year-on-year, mainly concentrated on members' subscription revenue and virtual gift revenue. The products ordered by members include recording visitors, quiet viewing, voice self-introduction, group online reminder, exclusive membership logo and personalized information pages, etc.

Figure 2. The utilization rate of China netizens' mobile application in May 2017
Source: mUserTracker 2016.11. Based on data of 4 million mobile phones and tablet mobile device software on a daily basis, as well as communication data from over 100 million mobile devices plus joint computing research.

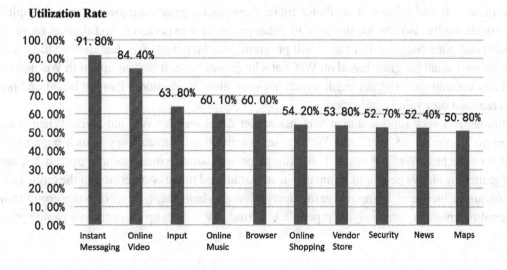

Table 1. Momo 2017 First three quarters earnings

	Total net revenue ($ one hundred million)	Gross Revenue of Value-added Services ($ Ten thousand)	Mobile Game Revenue ($ Ten thousand)	Mobile Marketing Revenue ($ Ten thousand)
2017 Q3	3.545	2630	800	1740
2017 Q2	3.122	2460	910	1900
2017 Q1	2.652	2290	1160	1790

Value-added service means mobile social media transforming their social attributes and user resources into real wealth. It also creates a more interesting social environment for users. In addition, there is also the form of liquidation which is developing downstream products within mobile social media.

Ding Talk is a working APP, the main functions are providing smart office phone, recording office attendance, etc. The registered users climbed after the APP becoming an internal office communication platform. In order to highlight its workplace function, it started to focus the function of recording attendance. By accumulating users online and developing hardware products offline, the company used the platform to publicize and sell, and achieve its goal to revenue.

Using Internal Flow to Attract External Flow

Flow has great potential for adding values. Social media will naturally attract capital attention on the basis of such huge traffic and share with other offline enterprises. On the one hand, it can achieve a win-win situation on using resource; on the other hand, it can add a new way to create cash flow. This is also a widely used way of making profits in mobile social media

Social Game Mode: Rich Benefits, Promising Prospects

Adding the game section in social media to trigger multi-user participation has been commonly used in early non-mobile social media. It is represented by various small games in QQ space. Fast, interactive, interesting, simple and relational attributes make these social games unique and make people happy. Mobile social media also choose this way to enhance the user experience, and it takes more effort in game form and page design. After the 'small program' was launched, WeChat allowed the company to develop its own small program based on WeChat's huge user base. It was equipped in WeChat platform and directly entered the program page, which not only directly promoted its own brand and products, but also realized user value conduction.

'Jumping' is a very representative WeChat applet developed by WeChat team. When it was first launched on December 28, 2017, the WeChat team introduced a mandatory launch page and recommended it to the huge WeChat users. This little game with smart voices, simple operations, and challenging gameplay allows people to 'jump up' in an instant and make competition in the circle of friends. A continuous influence of 'jumping' game decryption and being able to send to the group to hold an invitational tournament can easily help people kill time. By setting up an exclusive game springboard for the brand, WeChat has also achieved the function of advertising, in order to obtain advertising fees, and gain more.

Lao Yue Gou is a social APP that uses games to attract users. In May 2017, Lao Yue Gou announced that it had 45 million registered users in China. The main ways to promote themselves are using joint live-streaming platforms and the fan communities. Inside the APP, user's behavior data are generated around the game. Through the settings of different game types, users can get a more authentic display of their self-state. For a game social platform, it will have a higher matching efficiency if it can present user portraits more realistic and comprehensive, compare with the settings that matching friends with strangers. In the process of mining user's value, Lao Yue Gou has developed value-added services such as providing accompanies, opening self-owned internet cafes and table games shops. All those actions form a closed-loop with online games and other value-added services. Lao Yue Gou's revenue reached 40 million yuan in 2017 (36Kr, 2017).

'Social Media + E-Commerce' Model

This is a reliable way to mature development and to commercialize at present, and transaction sharing can be a significant profit point for social media. First of all, for the e-commerce platforms such as Taobao, Tmall, and JD.com, cooperation with social media can introduce sufficient traffic into e-commerce. In addition, they can use the user data obtained from social media to enhance fan marketing and content marketing, so as to make the shopping mall recommendation more accurate and improve the shopping experience. JD-WeChat shopping, mobile QQ shopping and other social e-commerce provide businesses and consumers with another platform to directly establish a trust relationship, which is a new entry for consumers to mobile shopping. Secondly, for social media, e-commerce has a payment logistics system that is complementary to the social media O2O closed-loop and realizes commercialization by diverting traffic to the e-commerce platform.

In 2014, Sina weibo announced the launch of Alipay's payment tool, "Weibo payment" on its platform. It opened a receiving function to the users who is has enterprise qualification certification, this means that the platform where the fans gather is going to employ fan economy. After Sina Weibo announced its cooperation with Taobao in 2013, Weibo started to imported flow to Taobao and obtained transaction share. It has taken another step on the road of commercialization. By using marketing strategy with social elements and the word-of-mouth to spread the brand and to improve brand recognition, it changed the weak ties in the past into strong ties which have multi-direction links. It shows that the 'marriage' of e-commerce and social media can bring win-win relation.

Secondary Sale Model

The secondary sale we know is to sell time and space from TV to advertisers, the essence is to sell the audience's attention to advertisers. When audience's attention shifts to internet platform, internet advertising has gradually replaced television advertising, and capital tends to be attracted to most people's attention. As audiences divert their attention to mobile social media, the profit-seeking nature of capital completes for the secondary sale. The products are still the audience's attention, and in the era of mobile internet, audience's attention is more focused on the content than in the era of television.

Social media has an advantage which cannot be found in the traditional content era. It can be well targeted at a particular type of consumers to improve the conversion rate of advertisements. The big data provide accurate information on age, gender, income, and interest, and individualized environment creates a sense of personal identity. The connection between the strong relationship and the weak relationship also invisibly constructs the user's social identity, thereby distinguishing the complete virtual anonymity of the internet era, so that advertisers are more targeted in the promotion to provide better services.

In 2016, the scale of social advertising in China was 23.96 billion yuan. China is also following the global trend of rapid growth of social networks, with the development of advertising technology, the original information stream advertisement, video advertisement, H5 advertisement and soft text marketing advertisement based on social media have pushed social advertisement to a high-speed development period.

The Efficiency of Social Media's Cash Conversion Under Social Scene

Although mobile social networking has more flexibility and business opportunities, there are also shortcomings in various ways of cash conversion.

Internal Cash Conversion is Easy to Reach Saturation Point

Each social media has its own characteristics and target users, which limits the main direction of one social media in the process of turning flow into cash. Both social and media attributes require social media to consider both the strength and weakness of the relationship between users. It relies on the relationship chain for business development, but also need to convey certain information to users, whether through pictures, videos, or text.

Being the one-to-one dating APP, Momo was initially turning flow into cash through ads. Now it put video social networking as its main business and most of its revenue comes from live-streaming services. According to Momo, in the third quarter of 2017, the proportion of live-streaming business increased from 80% in the first quarter to 85.36%. However, making money from live-streaming subscribers has entered into a stagnation period, which means that Momo has encountered the predicament of saturation. The solution is either to maintain the existing cash conversion way and enhance media content, or to continue to seek the next business opportunity to develop new business.

The Limited Ability of Turning Flow Into Cash

However, consumers are difficult to fully adjust to. For different types of advertisements, the level of audience attraction varies. Therefore, advertising has become a relatively mature one in all commercialization channels, but it cannot monopolize all channels. The advertisers will use the benefit as the standard, and the audience will also pay attention to some advertisements.

WeChat's 'Moments' function is a form of precise delivery of advertisement based on big data analysis. However, from the perspective of existing WeChat advertising technology, it is impossible to achieve the target of investment, let alone precise marketing. In the context of WeChat 'Moments', information tends to be redundant and complicated. People rarely discuss topics in income, consumption, and living standards in 'moments'. Even if so, the revealed information could be misleading, such as the act of showing off wealth, and the desire to seek weird ideas. The strategy of topic marketing in social media is nothing more than a notion. The hot topics can always attract people's attention and have the advantage of viral spreading. But there are also problems, such as poor controllability, fast propagation speed, and rapid update of public opinion trends. There are not many brands that can accurately predict public opinion. Hence, this kind of topic marketing has its limitations and faces difficulties.

The Strong Ability to Attract External Flow and Turning It Into Cash

Shareaholic (2015), a foreign content marketing platform published a report announcing that social media has become the biggest source of recommendation traffic for websites, targeting the huge traffic that Facebook and Twitter have brought into blogs.

Taking shopping as an example, although social media has constructed social and shopping scenarios, it would be friction if the entrance is not packaged and publicized to cultivate users' habit of using scenario entrance. It attracts users by using discounts. Meanwhile, it strengthens users' memory of scene entrance by triggering scene memory, such as sending short messages and APP messages.

The Social Game Model Works Well

For the user experience in the social context of strong-weak ties, scene is the most emotional alternative to enable users to have a stronger immersive experience. Games can compensate for simple social media attributes and provide users with a perfect scene. By providing tips and plots to stimulate users' willingness to consume in the game, using interesting social functions to improve users' activities, game developers, advertisers and online payment systems can all benefit from the industry chain.

"Face to Lite" is a typical APP that integrates games into mobile strangers' social networking. After users' registration, there will be a various types of dating game. These functions can create a romantic scene, which can offer opportunities to chat with strangers at any time and can also transfer weak ties between strangers into a strong connection.

CONCLUSION

To analyze the strong and weak relationship in the context of a mobile social era is aimed to solve social relationship development behind the technical level. It doesn't matter if it's a weak connection among strangers created by network attributes, or it's a strong connection built upon social communities and scenes. Both are based on people's instinct to socialize anywhere and anytime. This is also the basis for social media to develop into multiple branches and make profits. In what way can user experiences be guaranteed while platforms' value-added targets be achieved at the same time? This chapter attempts to summarize commercial application rules of mobile social media for communication.

Build a Scene to Maintain User Activity

Attracting users to retain is the primary condition for communication social media to survive as a functional software. The drawback of the tool will be remembered by users only when certain scenes are present. For example, all mobile phones have a call and text message function, which leads to the condition that the tool solves the user's just need problem. But it is still limited by the frequency of use, which requires further active users.

The reason why WeChat is regarded as a 'dependency' by people is its multi-faceted scene setting. First of all, group scenes are very easy to stimulate the gathering of people. The first group breaks through the limits of time and distance and regroups together. The collection of occasional groups can also be guaranteed. The community plays the role of the media, releasing information and exchanging information, it becomes a distribution center for information. Secondly, the circle of friends is a big social platform. Self-information sharing at any time and the function of comment, like, sharing makes it a place for information diffusion. It also has the saying that 'We can know the world in the circle of friends'. These functions are all creating an image scene for the user, allowing the user to experience the feeling of 'a lot of information and high social frequency' in WeChat. Construction of scenarios help to open up space for new products, and also means there is commercial potential.

Games and E-Commerce Access to Increase Profit Points

Communication-based social media is targeting the communications space, but it can also increase profit margins by accessing games and e-commerce. The game can realize the scene substitution, and the scene of socialization is the part that every enterprise is trying to build. In the past, the relationship between enterprises and users was not equal. The majority of users were eager for getting quality content but it's not available, and there was almost no relationship between users. In this context, Tencent's QQ, which does not create content, has made great strides. The most successful part of this social software is established a perfect membership system that allows users to create themselves through interaction, when most companies focus on production content. The more active Zhihu (Chinese network Q&A community) and Douban (Chinese community website) in the Chinese market also follow this principle. QQ has developed the user's payment habits, and the game sector in Tencent has also brought real benefits to the company. In 2003, Tencent released a series of games prefixed with QQ, 'QQ Fantasy' and 'QQ Tang' became the childhood memories of the older generation of QQ. In 2006, Tencent officially entered the field of online games and embarked on the development of highways. Until now, it has accounted for half of China's game industry. Tencent Games, which carries the QQ scene, has given itself a well-performing advertisement and helped Tencent possess a stable revenue channel.

The traditional e-commerce platform relies on its own platform to carry users, and also uses traditional advertising methods in publicity and promotion. In May 2016, think tank Analysys and JD.com jointly released 'the China Mobile Social E-Commerce Development Special Research Report'. It showed that domestic mobile e-commerce transactions reached 2.07 trillion yuan in 2015. This is not only a quantitative accumulation, but also a qualitative change. Looking at the development of e-commerce platforms over the years, there is a place worthy of attention: the cooperative relationship with social media.

In 2014, JD.com teamed up with instant communication social media like QQ's mobile phone app and WeChat to tap into mobile e-commerce industry. Among all the social media, those in the communication category have the largest user base and are used most frequently as they fit better into mobile social communication's features. Therefore, they become the e-commerce platforms' first choice.

For e-commerce platforms, the first move to realize their purpose of gaining traffic is promotion. Social media has such advantages in concentrating dispersed traffic and improving users' engagement. It's the most reliable way to reach a large number of users in a short time through mobile social media. Most consumers will refer to other buyers' reviews to make purchases. But such relation between consumers themselves and other users belongs to the 'weak tie' category. Sharing information among friends based on social media platforms is able to enhance users' trust in products. Moreover, the opening of mobile social e-commerce platforms also improves overall operational efficiency of both sides. Take JD.com as an example, after joining hands with WeChat and QQ, these two mobile social applications have launched many public platforms in addition to instant messaging and social entertainment. It has also opened interfaces to third parties. All these have enhanced users' consumption experiences and provided richer user data for companies, making it easier for precision marketing.

Invest in High Quality Advertising to Attract Attention

The significance of advertising is to attract attention. The advantage of mobile social media is that it can reach large-scale users. In recent years, social marketing has continued to develop, and advertising creativity combined with life is also easily accepted by the public, but the disadvantage of social media is that technology is not enough to achieve precision marketing.

Mobile social users have obvious likes and dislikes of advertising forms, which results in completely different recommendation effects of various advertisements. Those attracting the highest attention are video advertising, QR code advertising, feeds and APP recommendations. While those with the most selective attention are screen ads or pop-up advertising. All these stems from users' experiencing effects. Based on the theory of Usage and Satisfaction, users seek attention according to their own needs. Mobile social users pay more attention to product performances introduced by advertisements, while also have the desire to further understand high-quality audio-visual effects of advertisements and advertising discount information.

For mobile social platforms, high-quality advertising means having the effect of reaching users, but also stimulating users' desire to view and pay attention. The goal of all advertising is to motivate public action. The Moment advertisements in WeChat are collected through open appraisal to reach the attention information. The convergent advertisement method is close to the user's habits, but there are often cases of inaccurate promotion. A good social advertisement can instantly capture the user's eyes, trigger the desire to explore, allow users to think that they have a real need for such information or items from their own perspective. Or it pushes public join the purchase list in the future, and make people actively talk about brands with friends to form a share path, not simply conduct rude closure or rushing through.

REFERENCES

Burt, R. S. (1995). *Structural Holes: The Social Structure of Competition*. Cambridge, MA: Harvard University Press.

Cheng, J. F. (2014). *Research on business models of mobile social media* (Master Thesis). Northwestern University.

CNNIC. (2018). *China Social Media Overview' released by CIC*. Available at: http://www.cac.gov.cn/2018zt/cnnic41/index.htm

Coleman, J. S. (1988). Supplement: Organizations and Institutions: Sociological and Economic Approaches to the Analysis of Social Structure. *American Journal of Sociology*, *94*, S95–S120. doi:10.1086/228943

Dong, X. M., & Li, F. Y. (2011). Research on rural private lending on structural hole theory. *South China Finance*, *8*, 40–43.

Fei, X. T. (2006). *Local China*. Shanghai People's Publishing House.

Felson, M., & Spaeth, J. L. (1978). Community Structure and Collaborative Consumption: A Routine Activity Approach. *The American Behavioral Scientist, 21*(4), 614–624. doi:10.1177/000276427802100411

Feng, L. (2004). Social scene: Psychological field of the communication subject. *China Communication Forum*.

Foucault, M. (2012). *Discipline and Punishment: the birth of prison*. Life, Reading and New Knowledge SanLian Bookstore Press.

Goffman, E. (2009). The presentation of self in everyday life. *Threepenny Review, 21*(116), 14–15.

Granovetter, M. S. (1973). The Strength of Weak Ties. *American Journal of Sociology, 78*(6), 1360–1380. doi:10.1086/225469

Harwit, E. (2017). WeChat:social and poitical development of China's dominant messaging app. *Chinese Journal of Communication, 10*(3), 312–327. doi:10.1080/17544750.2016.1213757

Lippmann, W. (2010). Public opinion and the politicians. *National Municipal Review, 15*(1), 5–8. doi:10.1002/ncr.4110150102

Liu, C.Z. (2015). Discussion on profit models of mobile social media. *News World*, (8),188-189.

Lu, X. H. (2003). *Network reliance: Challenges between virtual and reality*. Shanghai: Southeast University Press.

Luo, J. D. (2017). *Complex: Connections, Opportunities and Layouts in the Information Age*. CITIC Publishing Group Co., Ltd.

Meyrowitz, J. (2010). Shifting worlds of strangers: Medium theory and changes in "them" versus "us". *Sociological Inquiry, 67*(1), 59–71. doi:10.1111/j.1475-682X.1997.tb00429.x

Negroponte, N. (1997). *Being Digital*. Hainan Press. doi:10.1063/1.4822554

Peng, L. (2013). Evolution of "Connection": The Basic Clue of the Development of Internet. *Chinese Journal of Journalism & Communication*, (2), 6-19.

Peng, L. (2015). Scene: new elements of media in the mobile age. *Journalism Review*, (3), 21-27.

Sun, L. P. (1993). Free flow resources and free activity space --- China's social structure changes during its reform. *Probe*, (1): 64–68.

Sun, L.P.(1996). Relations, social network and social structure. *Sociological Studies*, (5), 20-30.

Yu, G. (2016). *Social currency- The road to business monetizing in the era of mobile social networking*. Posts and Telecom Press.

Yu, G.M. (2009). Media revolution: From panorama prison to shared-scene prison. *People's Tribune, 8*(1), 21.

Yu, G.M. (2016). Reconstruction of media influence under the paradigm of relationship empowerment. *News and Writing*, (7), 47-51.

Yu, G.M., & Ma, H. (2016). New power paradigm in digital era: Empowerment based on relation network in social media --- Social relation reorganization and power pattern dynamics. *Chinese Journal of Journalism & Communication,* (10), 6-27.

Yu, G.M., & Ma, H. (2016). Relationship empowerment: a new paradigm of social capital allocation --- The logical change of social governance under network reconstruction of social connection. *Editorial Friend,* (9), 5-8.

Yu, G.M., Zhang, C., Li, S., Bao, L.Y., & Zhang, S.N. (2015). The era of individual activation: Reconstruction of communication ecology under the logic of the Internet. *Modern Communication,* (5), 1-4.

Zhang, L. (2009). *The research of the western attention economy school.* China Social Sciences Press.

This research was previously published in Impacts of Mobile Use and Experience on Contemporary Society; pages 128-149, copyright year 2019 by Information Science Reference (an imprint of IGI Global).

Chapter 33

The Important Role of the Blogosphere as a Communication Tool in Social Media Among Polish Young Millennials:
A Fact or a Myth?

Sylwia Kuczamer-Kłopotowska

https://orcid.org/0000-0003-4781-0118
University of Gdańsk, Poland

Anna Kalinowska-Żeleźnik
University of Gdańsk, Poland

ABSTRACT

This chapter proposes and discusses the hypothesis that the blogosphere is a relatively well-developed and independent social media communication tool used by millennials. The first part of the study concentrates on the theoretical aspects of social media communication as presented in the literature, and the way blogs and the whole blogosphere function. The communicational and social profile of Generation Y is presented as it is this cohort that constitutes the major portion of the Polish blogging community. The prevailing trends in the Polish blogosphere are discussed, following a desk research into reports and professional studies. Moreover, some comments and findings are presented regarding an experiment conducted by the authors in which some representatives of younger millennials ran personal, non-profit blogs on a subject of their choice.

DOI: 10.4018/978-1-6684-6307-9.ch033

INTRODUCTION

The social media market is characterised by the dynamic growth of various platforms and possible communication tools. Still, the research shows the blogosphere – with its communicational, marketing, and advertising potential – remains an important part of the world wide web. The global blogosphere is in its maturity stage, which means it is stable but growing at a slower pace. Blogs are a commonplace phenomenon with a significant impact on the way individuals function in their societies. The Polish blogosphere, too, is growing steadily. Just like everywhere else, with time and the permanent development of new social media forms and tools, the Polish blogosphere is changing: new trends emerge, and various aspects of the art of blogging and online presence take the spotlight.

One of the most prevailing trends – which is a subject of research – is the increase in the importance and the frequency of using social media channels to communicate blog contents. More and more often, bloggers make use of various social media to provide a permanent communication channel for their readers, which makes obsolete the original means of communication that is the comment section. The length of an average blog entry increases, which may be the reason for the decrease in posting frequency. In order to keep the readers interested and engaged, bloggers frequently make use of the shorter and easier social media formats (e.g. Facebook, Snapchat, Instagram, Twitter) to accompany the main contents of their blogs. As a natural consequence, a question may be raised here whether blogs remain an independent communication tool within social media or whether their role was slightly aberrated. And if blogosphere is not the independent communication tool, can we talk about its important role in Generation Y communication at all?

For the reasons mentioned above, the authors decided to describe the phenomenon from the perspective of Polish millennials, who constitute the major portion of the Polish blogging community. This study describes blogs as an integral part of constantly developing social media communication, defining the characteristic features of this form of communication among millennials, and discussing the validity of the hypothesis that the blogosphere is a relatively mature and independent social media communication tool for Polish younger millennials.

The discussion in the study is based on a literature review and desk research. Moreover, some comments and findings are presented regarding an experiment conducted by the authors in which some representatives of younger millennials ran personal, non-profit blogs on a subject of their choice.

POLISH BLOGOSPHERE PROFILE AND CREATING COMMUNICATION CHANNELS

In the broad range of online communication tools, social media are doubtless one of the most important ones. Due to their dynamic growth, the specific character, the scope of functionalities available through the services, and the continuous increase in the number of users, they have become an important communication channel. They demand continuous and careful attention, as well as quick adaptation to new circumstances, which is to say they entail creating new ways of surviving in an evolving and dynamic environment which is continuously discovered anew (Cross, 2011, pp. 3-4; Szewczyk, 2015, p. 120; Couldry, 2012).

The term 'social media' refers to using online and mobile technologies to transform communication into interactive dialogue. The media are used for social interaction in the form of an elaborate set of electronic (online) communication tools which go far beyond what we used to know as social communication (Allmer, 2015, pp. 44-45). Usually, social media are divided into several different categories: blogs and microblogs (Twitter, WordPress, Blogger), social networks (Facebook, LinkedIn, nk.pl, MySpace), content services (YouToube, Instagram, Pinterest), virtual games (World of Warcraft), virtual worlds (Second Life), and social bookmarking web services (delicious.com).

Social media are an extremely dynamic phenomenon. Research shows that it may take only several month to significantly change the design, the character, or the scope of functionalities of a given service (Pruszyński, 2012). The dynamics of such changes, i.e. the growth rate of social media services, has constantly been increasing. Complementary apps and services are transformed to eventually make their scopes of functionalities relatively similar (Wagner, 2014). Such initiatives are meant to ensure loyalty of current users and win new ones through better quality and competitiveness of services (Somers, 2014).

Blogs are one of the most dynamic forms of participation in online communication. They are online services with chronological entries called 'posts' (Drezner, Farrell, 2007, p. 2). Once, they used to be diaries or memoires written by Internet users. Nowadays, they concentrate on many various topics, which depends on many different factors, e.g. the preferences, the goals, and the abilities of their authors, as well as on profiles of given blogs (Cass, 2007, pp. 4-7; Pedersen, 2010, pp. 16-17).

Recent studies show that this form of social communication has been developing in Poland. The Polish blogosphere is dominated by women (84.2%). The most popular blog categories are: lifestyle (15.2%), cooking (14.4%), beauty (12%), art and culture (9.5%), personal (7.7%), family (5.8%), fashion (5.3%), and crafts (4.8%). That general disproportion is not, however, reflected in specific blog categories. Women are found most often in the beauty and the crafts categories (98.8% and 98.4%, respectively). Men dominate the following categories: cars (98.4%), money (71.4%), and sports (70%). Analyses of blog contents against the age of their authors show that in the younger millennials cohort the following categories are most common: fashion, beauty, lifestyle, health and fitness, and personal (see report *Badanie Polskiej Blogosfery 2016*, 2016, p. 10).

Blogging platforms are characterised by their interactivity. Usually, blogs grant open access for everyone, and both entries and comments can be read by the authors and the readers alike (Zygmunt, Koźlak, Krupczak, Małocha, 2009, p. 673). The informal and personal character of the opinions, the ability to interact and comment, and the opportunity to impact opinions and emotions make blogs a form of expression and inspiration which influences people's attitudes, behaviours, and decisions, as well as giving readers a chance to develop relationships (Li, Bernoff, 2009, cited in: Gregor, Kaczorowska-Spychalska, 2014, p. 18).

However, the interactivity and the two-way real-time communication between authors and readers are not limited to a given blogging platform (Dean, 2010, pp. 33-37; Cass, 2007, pp. 199-201; Cross, 2011, pp. 5-13). With time, social media are becoming more and more important in communicating blog contents. There is only little research available confirming – indirectly – that hypothesis. The only evidence is the fact that the previous research into the Polish blogosphere had not identified using social media channels for communicating blog contents, nor had it attempted to define the scope of the phenomenon (see report *Badanie Polskie Blogosfery 2014*, 2014). Earlier studies provide no relevant data. We can therefore assume that social media have for long been used to communicate blog contents, but the frequency and the scope of the phenomenon must have been more limited than what is currently happening as evidenced in recent studies (see report *Badanie Polskiej Blogosfery 2016*, 2016, pp. 19-20).

The studies of blog traffic patterns show a great diversity of traffic sources, e.g. Google organic entries, direct entries, and using aggregator websites and social channels. The research shows varied results for each traffic source and regularities pertaining to blog categories. Organic traffic is most common for cooking, art and culture, and crafts blogs. Least common is the lifestyle category, and – again – art and culture[1]. The relation is reversed for the traffic from social media channels. The largest share of traffic from the channels go to lifestyle, and art and culture blogs; the smallest – to the cooking, travel, and beauty categories (see report *Badanie Polskiej Blogosfery 2016*, 2016, p. 19).

The report presents a detailed analysis of the social media communication channels used by bloggers (p. 19). It concentrates on three dimensions:

- Using various social platforms for communicating blog contents,
- Sizes of blog communities,
- Importance of each channel for bloggers.

The analysis shows two interesting correlations between:

- The increase in PV blog stats and the increase in the proportion of blogs with Facebook fan pages, Instagram and Pinterest profiles, or Snapchat accounts; and
- The increase in PV blog stats and the decrease in the proportion of blogs with Google+ profiles.

The analysis of the average values for all the subjects of the study made it possible to define the two social channels most often used for communicating blog contents. They are Facebook and Instagram (used by 91.1% and 88.9% of Polish bloggers, respectively). The least important for them are Snapchat (16.3%), Pinterest (16.8%), and Twitter (28.6%) (see report *Badanie Polskiej Blogosfery 2016*, 2016, p. 20).

DIGITAL CHARACTERISTICS OF GENERATION Y COMMUNICATION PROCESSES

Generation Y is also often referred to as 'Millennium Generation', 'millennials', 'Generation whY', 'Echo Boomers', 'Generation Net' (Tapscott, 2010), 'Generation Next', Search Generation', 'Me Generation', 'iPod Generation', and even 'Flipflop Generation'. Generation Y consists of people born between 1980 and 1996 (van den Bergh, Behrer, 2012), or 1977 and 2004, or maybe between 1980 and 2000. Some authors emphasise the fact that the term should only be used when referring to people from the USA or Canada (see *Webster's II New College Dictionary*, 2005). The nomenclature is, however, accepted in Poland, too, although there are no precise dates in the literature for when the cohort starts and ends.

The traits which are most often associated with the entire millennial generation are: using all the possibilities that communication technologies gives us and a sort of a life impatience resulting in fast and intensive existence, multitasking, and looking for new stimuli and challenges. The members of Generation Y belong to numerous online communities, and have many acquaintances – not only in the virtual reality (Tapscott, 2010).

Polish publications on the subject most often claim that the 'Generation Y' moniker refers to people born between 1983 and 1997 (Oleszkowicz, Senejko, 2013), who are now 20—35 years old. For them, the twenty first century marks the beginning of their exploration of the job market. The temporal shift, in comparison with the USA and Canada, results from the fact that the new technologies came to the countries of the post-Soviet bloc with a certain delay. Polish millennials are a large cohort (about 11 million people), yet so diverse that they can be divided into two subgroups with both common and differentiating features. The younger millennials are people born between 1990 and 2000, whereas the older ones were born between 1977 and 1989. The former are most often still studying; the latter have jobs. It means that the opinions of the two subgroups may and will often be poles apart (especially as regards their purchasing power, preferences, and shopping behaviours).

The older millennials are attributed with some traits of the preceding Generation X[2]; however, the new social, political, and technological reality – mostly, the growth of communication technologies – forced them to adapt quickly to the new conditions and to use the Net effectively for communication, spending free time, and online shopping.

The younger millennials in Poland are a group of about 5 million. Just like their older siblings, they share some traits with Generation X, as well as resembling Generation Z[3] – with their smartphones giving them immediate access to the Internet, communication with their friends, music, films, and numerous apps. Their high digital literacy should not however be treated in terms of the communication technologies only, as it is about their lifestyle and self-expression.

The younger millennials put a lot of emphasis on their image. They use all the Internet has to offer in this regard, all the newest tools, social media, and the blogs they run (see *Raport Odyseja Public Relations 2014*, 2014). The studies conducted on the Polish blogosphere in 2016 show that the majority of bloggers are members of Generation Y. We can see two distinct age groups there: 1) between 26 and 35 years old (40.7% of the subjects), and between 20 and 25 years old (25.6% of the subjects), which more or less reflects the age range for Polish millennials. Similar results were obtained in the earlier study from 2014 in which the two major groups were individuals between 26 and 35 years old (34%) and between 20 and 25 years old (34%) (see report *Badanie Polskiej Blogosfery 2014*, 2014, p. 6; report *Badanie Polskiej Blogosfery 2016*, 2016, p. 6).

AIMS, METHODOLOGY, AND CONCLUSIONS OF THE STUDY

The experiment conducted by the authors, in which some representatives of younger millennials ran personal, non-profit blogs on a subject of their choice, may be deemed as a continuation of the discussion of the blogs as a relatively mature and independent communication tool in social media.

The experiment was carried out for five consecutive years (2013-2017). Its aim was to record changes, trends, and specific behaviours in blogosphere of Generation Y[4], that is the largest cohort in the Polish blogging community. The subjects were to create and run for at least four months a free and non-profit blog. In order to make sure the experimental situations were as similar as possible to what would have happened in real life, the authors gave the bloggers the freedom to choose any subject and any blogging platform. The results of the experiment were assessed against several criteria: 1) general appearance (aesthetics, images and content compatibility); 2) layout (template, font, content presentation); 3) content (topics, originality, factuality, works presented, photos, etc.); 4) writing style; 5) the profiles of the communities.

During the five-year experiment, thirty nine blogs were created and run. Their subject matters were: lifestyle (25.6%), hobbies (20.5%), fashion and beauty (20.5%), and healthy lifestyle (15.4%) – which reflected the general tendencies in the age group. Next, there were blogs devoted to travelling (7.7%), cooking (5.1%), and art and culture (5.1%) – which also reflects the recent popularity of the categories in the Polish blogosphere (see report *Badanie Polskiej Blogosfery 2016*, 2016, p. 10).

As was mentioned above, the following aspects of running a blog were analysed: the size and the profile of a blog community, as well as its specific behaviours; the authors' attempts to support building such communities; and continuous activating the communities' engagement. At that stage, the statistics were analysed showing the structure of traffic sources. The data obtained reflect the general tendency in the Polish blogosphere, i.e. the considerable diversity of the sources and the prevalence of Google organic entries. In the five years of the experiment, their share varied from 48% to 56%. The organic traffic volume varied depending on how active the bloggers were in building and engaging their communities. The use of social media channels increased steadily from 5% at the beginning to nearly 40% at the end of the experiment. The figures obtained in the last instalment of the experiment were slightly higher than the average for the Polish blogosphere in general. That was probably due to the specific communication practices of Polish millennials, who tend to use social media every day. The sharp increase in the number of social media channels generating traffic coincided with the steady increase in the number of social media used for communicating blog contents. While in the first year of the experiment, out of the eight blogs, only two were supported through another social medium communicating blog contents and activating the communities, with time, the number grew to reach seven out of seven blogs that were run at that time.

Apart from the year-to-year increase described above, two other tendencies can be seen.

- The steady increase in the number of social media used for communicating contents of blogs to readers. Whereas in the first year of the study, only two blogs used one, additional social medium (which was a Facebook fan page), in the last year all the bloggers enriched their communication with their readers through social media (the average was 2.4 additional channels). The first choice was always Facebook; then, they activated Instagram, Twitter, and Pinterest accounts.
- The increase in the scope, the diversity, and the intensity of actions undertaken by bloggers in social media to keep their readers interested and engaged, with simultaneous decrease in the intensity of conversation on blogs.

Briefly speaking, social media are more and more often being used for communicating blog contents at the expense of conversations held directly on blogs, and the results of the experiment reflect the general tendencies observed in the Polish blogosphere. The inconsequential deviations from the average values for the entire blogging community in Poland may result from the aforementioned specific character of the communication patterns of younger Generation Y in Poland and the prevalence of social media in this cohort. The observations may contribute to the discussion of blogs as independent communication tools in social media. It appears that building a vast, active, and loyal community around a blog, attractive content is not enough. Bloggers need to actively create a broad portfolio of social media accounts which will be used for communicating blog contents.

CONCLUSION

In this study, the authors discuss the hypothesis of the blogosphere as a mature and independent communication tool in social media. The reports describing the Polish blogosphere provide evidence supporting the opinion that nowadays blogs are an insufficient means of communicating content. They do not come up with conclusions literally supporting the claim that social media are more and more often being used for communicating blog contents at the expense of conversations held directly on blogs. There are, however, reasons why it may be assumed that such process is taking place. This tendency appears to be confirmed by the observations and conclusions of the experiment conducted by the authors in which some representatives of younger millennials ran personal, non-profit blogs on a subject of their choice. In the context of the above considerations, it is difficult to confirm the thesis about the important role of the blogosphere as a communication tool in social media among Polish young millennials.

Since the research referred to in this study was selective, i.e. its focus was the younger millennials cohort, it must not be treated as exhausting and conclusive as to the scale of the process in the entire Polish blogging community. It may, however, be a starting point for further, more comprehensive research into the phenomenon, including other generations.

An electronic tool of social communication, blogs are a relatively mature phenomenon which still makes effective use of new possibilities and growth opportunities. Apart from the trend towards changing the hierarchy of the channels for communicating blog contents and conversing with users, various studies focus on other aspects of the current dynamics in the blogosphere. The most common tendencies are: decentralisation of activity (as a result of decrease in the importance of the user/blogger conversations on blogs), higher value of engaged users, decreasing value of comments, lower community migration rate, lack of content recycling, or growing importance of vloggers and influencers (using mostly Facebook and Twitter) at the expense of bloggers (Hunt, 2016). They all deserve a closer look and appropriate research efforts which will help us better understand how the Polish blogosphere works.

REFERENCES

Allmer, T. (2015). *Critical Theory and Social Media. Between emancipation and commodification*. New York, NY: Routledge. doi:10.4324/9781315750491

Badanie Polskiej Blogosfery 2014. (2014). Retrieved on 6 Jan 2018 from http://brief.pl

Badanie Polskiej Blogosfery 2016. (2016). Retrieved on 6 Jan 2018 from http://www.blog-media.pl

Behrer, M., & van den Bergh, J. (2012). *Jak kreować marki, które pokocha pokolenie Y*. Warszawa: Wydawnictwo Samo Sedno.

Cass, J. (2007). *Strategies and Tools for Corporate Blogging*. New York, NY: Elsevier. doi:10.4324/9780080481173

Couldry, N. (2012). *Media, Society, World. Social Theory and Digital Media Practice*. Cambridge, UK: Polity Press.

Coupland, D. (1991). *Generation X: Tales for an Accelerated Culture*. New York, NY: St. Martin's Press.

Cross, M. (2011). *Bloggerati, Twitterati. How Blogs and Twitter Are Transforming Popular Culture*. Santa Barbara, CA: Praeger.

Dean, J. (2010). *Blog Theory. Feedback and Capture in the Circuits of Drive*. Cambridge, UK – Malden, MA: Polity Press.

Drezner, D. W., & Farrell, H. (2007). Introduction: Blogs, politics and power: a special issue of Public Choice. New York, NY: Springer Science+Business Media.

Gregor, B., & Kaczorowska-Spychalska, D. (2014). *Blogi jako element strategii promocji on-line. Zeszyty Naukowe Uniwersytetu Szczecińskiego Nr 829, Studia Informatica Nr 35*. Szczecin: Wydawnictwo Naukowe Uniwersytetu Szczecińskiego.

Hunt, J. (2016). *Trendy w blogosferze na rok 2016*. Retrieved on 10 Jan 2018 from http://jasonhunt.pl

Li, Ch., & Bernoff, J. (2009). *Marketing technologii społecznych*. Warszawa: Wydawnictwo MT Biznes.

Oleszkowicz, A., & Senejko, A. (2013). *Psychologia dorastania. Zmiany rozwojowe w dobie globalizacji*. Warszawa: Wydawnictwo Naukowe PWN.

OMG! Czyli jak mówić do polskich milenialsów. (2014). Retrieved on 11 Dec 2017 from http://mobileinstitute.eu

Pedersen, S. (2010). *Why Blog? Motivations for blogging*. Oxford, UK: Chandos Publishing. doi:10.1533/9781780631714

Pruszyński, J. (2012). *Pijaru Ficzery #19*. Retrieved 15 Dec 2017 from http://pijarukoksu.pl

Singh, A. (2014). Challenges and Issues of Generation Z. *IOSR Journal of Business and Management, 16*(7).

Somers, R. (2014). *Instagram Video vs. Vine: Which Is the Video Marketing Champ?* Retrieved on 15 Oct 2017 from http://marketingprofs.com

Szewczyk, A. (2015). *Marketing internetowy w mediach społecznościowych. Zeszyty Naukowe Uniwersytetu Szczecińskiego Nr 863, Studia Informatica, Nr 36*. Szczecin: Wydawnictwo Naukowe Uniwersytetu Szczecińskiego.

Tapscott, D. (2010). *Cyfrowa dorosłość. Jak pokolenie sieci zmienia nasz świat*. Warszawa: Wydawnictwo Akademickie i Profesjonalne.

Törőcsik, M., Szűcs, K., & Kehl, D. (2014). How Generations Think: Research on Generation Z. *Acta Universitatis Sapientiae Communicatio, 1*, 23–45.

Troksa, L. M. (2016). *The Study of Generations: A Timeless Notion within a Contemporary Context*. Retrieved from https://scholar.colorado.edu

Wagner, K. (2014). *Messaging Wars: Vine vs. Instagram, Facebook, Twitter, Snapchat*. Retrieved on 15 Dec 2017 from http://mashable.com

Webster's II New College Dictionary. (2005). Boston, MA: Houghton Mifflin Reference Books.

Zygmunt, A., Koźlak, J., Krupczak, Ł., Małocha, B. (2009). Analiza blogów internetowych przy użyciu metod sieci społecznych. *Automatyka, 13*(2).

ENDNOTES

[1] It is due to the diversity of the art and culture blogs included in the study that they are found at both ends of the scale.

[2] Generation X (the 'Indifferent Generation' or 'Ghost Generation') includes people born between 1965 and 1981, even though in some sources the cohort ends as late as in 1986. The X in the moniker referring to individuals reacting to the chaotic reality with individualism and pessimism was popularised by D. Coupland's study *Generation X* (Coupland, 1991).

[3] 'Generation Z' describes young people born after 1995 (opinions vary as to when the cohort starts – some mention 2000). The generation is commonly thought to treat new technologies as something natural because they have always been here even before they were born. They are also described as Generation C (from 'connected to the Net'). Experts focus in their definitions on change (that is the state the generation likes best) as continuous experimentation implies growth and is stimulating. The members of the generation most often concentrate on the reality and the material aspects of life, as well as being creative and ambitious. They want it all and they want it now. The have a different attitude towards knowledge – they value fast searches and creative ways of obtaining knowledge. They know the world is changing, and deem knowledge as something that may lose its value. They are mobile. They know other languages and often have friends in different parts of the world (Troksa, 2016; Törőcsik, Szűcs, Kehl, 2014; Singh, 2014).

[4] The experiment described in the publication involved members of the younger millennials cohort.

Section 4
Utilization and Applications

Chapter 34
Adolescents, Third–Person Perception, and Facebook

John Chapin
Pennsylvania State University, USA

ABSTRACT

The purpose of this chapter is to document the extent of Facebook use and cyberbullying among adolescents. It is based on a study theoretically grounded in third-person perception (TPP), the belief that media messages affect other people more than oneself. As Facebook establishes itself as the dominant social network, users expose themselves to a level of bullying not possible in the analog world. The study found that 84% of adolescents (middle school through college undergraduates) use Facebook, and that most users log on daily. While 30% of the sample reported being cyberbullied, only 12.5% quit using the site and only 18% told a parent or school official. Despite heavy use and exposure, adolescents exhibit TPP, believing others are more likely to be negatively affected by Facebook use. A range of self-protective behaviors from precautionary (deleting or blocking abusive users) to reactionary (quitting Facebook) were related to decreased degrees of TPP. Implications for prevention education are discussed.

INTRODUCTION

Consider the numbers:

- 800 million: Number of active Facebook users (Lyons, 2012).
- 49: Percentage of Americans using Facebook (Lyons, 2012).
- >50: Percentage of American teens who have been cyber-bullied (Bullying Statistics, 2012).
- 10 to 15: Percentage of bullied teens who tell their parents (Bullying Statistics, 2012).
- 4,400: Number of teen suicides in the U.S. each year (CDC, 2012).

The National Crime Prevention Council (2012) defines cyber bullying as "the process of using the Internet, cell phones or other devices to send or post text or images intended to hurt or embarrass another person." This may include sending nasty messages or threats to a person's email account or cell phone,

DOI: 10.4018/978-1-6684-6307-9.ch034

spreading rumors online or through texts, posting hurtful or threatening messages on social networking sites or web pages, stealing a person's account information to break into their account and send damaging messages, pretending to be someone else online to hurt another person, taking unflattering pictures of a person and spreading them through cell phones or the Internet, sexting or circulating sexually suggestive pictures or messages about a person.

The use of Facebook and other social media can be especially problematic, because once something is shared, it replicates and may never disappear, resurfacing at later times. Cyber bullying can be damaging to adolescents and teens. It can lead to depression, anxiety and suicide (Bullying Statistics, 2012).

The purpose of the study is to document the extent of Facebook use and cyber bullying among a sample of adolescents. The study is theoretically grounded in third-person perception, the belief that media messages affect other people more than oneself. Exploring third-person perception, Facebook use and cyber bullying may shed light on the extent of the problem and may also explain why adolescents do not report cyber bullying and do not take self-protective measures online.

THE STUDY

Procedures and Participants

Participants were recruited through school-based programs about bullying offered by Crisis Center North, a Pennsylvania women's center. Multiple school districts and universities participated. The sample (N = 1,488) was 51% male, with an average age of 15 (range = 12 (middle school) to 24 (college undergraduate)). These age ranges were selected because they coincide with reported cases of cyber bullying and dating/relationship violence.

Results

Participants believed they were less likely than others to be affected by Facebook use. This is classic Third-person perception (TPP). As predicted, participants who believed they are less influenced than others by Facebook use also believed they are less likely than others to become the victim of cyber bullying. This misperception is called optimistic bias.

Most of the participants (84%) said they use Facebook. When controlling for non-users, the average adolescent logs on daily. Enjoyment of Facebook ranged from zero (uncommon among users) to "LOVE it." Use and enjoyment emerged as the strongest predictor of TPP.

TPP increased as perceived social norms reject cyber bullying as normal. Responses to the statement, "my friends think cyber bullying is funny," ranged from strongly agree (4%) to strongly disagree (55.6%). Over half of the adolescents (64%) disagreed or strongly disagreed with this statement, indicating the subjective norm for cyber bullying is perceived to be more supportive of victims than bullies. Age emerged as a weak predictor, with TPP increasing with age. There were no differences attributable to gender or race.

Table 1 shows the percentage of adolescents who have taken steps to prevent harm on social media. Deleting friends or blocking peers was the most common action taken (50.8%). Nearly one-third of the sample (30%) said they have been electronically bullied, so an additional 20% of the sample has taken this action as a precautionary measure. The remaining behaviors are each below the 30% (affected) range, suggesting 12% to 25% of adolescents who experience cyber bullying take no action. Participants scored an average of 70% on a knowledge pre-test. Responses to individual items ranged from 89% correctly responding that deleted posts and photos from Facebook can be recovered, to 59% incorrectly responding that drug and alcohol abuse are reasonable explanations for bullying and violence.

Table 1. Percentage of adolescents who have taken self-protective behaviors

Behavior	% Taken
Deleted "friends" or blocked someone from Facebook	50.8%
Told a parent or school official about a cyber bullying incident	18.0%
Saved comments or posts to document the abuse.	17.5%
Quit using Facebook or another social networking site	12.5%
Changed cell phone number	5.7%

Discussion

As Facebook establishes itself as the dominant social network, approaching 1 billion users world-wide, adolescents expose themselves to a level of bullying not previously possible in the analog world. Facebook has a minimum age requirement of 13, but 12-year-olds in the current sample reported daily use. Adolescents over share personal information and photos on their own and have no control over what peers share on their behalf. The national statistics on teen suicide speak for themselves.

The current study found that 84% of adolescents (middle school through college undergraduates) use Facebook, and that most users log on daily. While 30% of the sample reported being cyber bullied, only 12.5% quit using the site, and only 18% told a parent or school official about the abuse. Informal discussions within the school-based sessions suggest the 30% figure may be under reported. Students routinely talked about behaviors that meet the legal definition of stalking as "normal," saying things like, "If I didn't want people to know where I am all the time, I wouldn't post it," and "That's what Facebook is for." Between the GPS tracking capabilities embedded in posted photos and literally posting locations in status updates and in applications like Foursquare and Runkeeper, escalating from cyber stalking to in-person stalking would be easy.

A possible explanation for bullied adolescents' failure to report harassment is a form of third-person perception; they believe the impact on themselves is minimal when compared to their peers. Despite heavy use and exposure, adolescents exhibit third-person perception (TPP), believing others are more likely to be affected by Facebook use. A range of self-protective behaviors from precautionary (deleting or blocking abusive users) to reactionary (quitting Facebook) were related to decreased degrees of TPP. TPP was also related to optimistic bias; adolescents who believe others are more influenced by Facebook also believe others are more likely to become the victims of cyber bullying. This information is useful to schools, parents and anti-bullying programs, suggesting a media literacy approach to prevention education may decrease TPP and increase self-protective behaviors.

The remaining predictors of TPP flesh out a better understanding of the interplay between TPP and cyber bullying. The strongest predictor of TPP was liking of and use of Facebook. TPP only decreased with experience. The more adolescents use Facebook, without experiencing cyber bullying first-hand, the more they enjoy the experience, believe they will not be adversely affected and larger the perceived gap between themselves and others. Beliefs about peers' perceptions of cyber bullying (subjective norm) widen the perceived self/other gap. Facebook can provide a positive experience for adolescents, a place to establish an identity and maintain relationships with peers. Unfortunately, it also establishes a platform for name calling, harassment and abuse. Adolescents need to be aware of the dangers, so they can take appropriate precautions and be aware of resources, if they do become victimized electronically. Partnerships between school systems and women's centers may offer a viable solution.

BACKGROUND/LITERATURE REVIEW

Outline

The study described in this chapter draws together a number of related literatures. After grounding the work in adolescents and social media, a number of studies in communications and health psychology are explored. Authors in these two disciplines don't often draw equally from the other. This is unfortunate, as the following review of the literatures shows they are clearly related and the preceding study documents the relationship. The second section introduces the reader to third-person perception (TPP), a communications theory about perceived influence of the media. The next section introduces optimistic bias, a health psychology theory that explains why people believe they are invulnerable to harm. Each of these are misperceptions that result in behaviors: People act on their perceptions, not on reality. The last section reviews the literature on subjective norms: How adolescents' perceive the attitudes of their peers impacts their own perceptions of social media and ultimately their uses and abuses of social media platforms.

Adolescents and Social Media

A report issued by the American Academy of Pediatrics (2011) outlined the benefits and risks of social media use by children and adolescents. On the positive side, staying connected with friends and family, exchanging ideas, and sharing pictures. Adolescent social media users find opportunities for community engagement, creative outlets, and expanded social circles. According to the report, the risks fall into these categories: peer-to-peer (bullying), inappropriate content, lack of understanding of privacy, and outside influences (social and corporate). The report also refers to "Facebook Depression," which emerges when adolescents spend too much time on social media and start exhibiting classic signs of depression.

A number of social media apps were designed specifically for finding sexual contacts or the "hook-up culture." Apps like Grindr and Tinder allow users to find potential sexual partners locally, using the GPS in their smart phones. The popular app Snapchat began as a means to quickly share explicit photos for a set period of time, without the receiver saving a copy of the image. Use of the app has evolved, with some users sharing benign photos and videos and others using it for more explicit purposes. Facebook also began as a hookup app limited to college students. As other users (including parents) were permitted to use the app, the social media giant evolved, becoming many things to over one billion users worldwide.

A recent study (Stevens, Dunaev, Malven, Bleakley & Hull, 2016) outlined how adolescents use social media in their sexual lives. Adolescents seek out sexual content (sexually explicit material, information about sexual health, sexual norms). Social media platforms provide an opportunity for sex-related communication and expression; According to the study, 25%-33% of adolescent social media users post or distribute provocative images, seeking feedback on their appearance or connection with other users. Finally, social media provide adolescents with tools for seeking out romantic or sexual partners, which may result in risky behaviors.

The National Academies of Sciences, Engineering, and Medicine issued a review of a decade of research on bullying (Flannery et al., 2016). According to the report, bullying and cyberbullying prevalence rates reported vary from 17.9 to 30.9% of school-aged children for the bullying behavior at school and from 6.9 to 14.8% for cyberbullying. Much of the variance can be attributed to sexual orientation, disability, and obesity. Physical consequences can be immediate (injury) or long-term (headaches, sleep disturbances). Psychological consequences include low self-esteem, depression, anxiety, self-harming, and suicide. There is some evidence to suggest links between being bullied in adolescence and perpetration of violence in adulthood.

Third-Person Perception and Social Media

Third-person perception (TPP) is the belief that negative media message influence others more than oneself. The phenomenon has been well-documented over a variety of contexts, which recently include news coverage of election polls (Kim, 2016), deceptive advertising (Xie, 2016), and the impact of religious cartoons (Webster, Li, Zhu, Luchsinger, Wan & Tatge, 2016). A third-person effect emerges when the misperception causes a behavior or attitude change. The most common third-person effect reported in the literature is support for censorship (Chung & Moon, 2016; Webster et al., 2016).

A growing literature is documenting TPP regarding social media (Antonopoulous, Veglis, Gardikiotis, Kotsakis & Kalliris, 2015; Wei & Lo, 2013). Facebook users believe they are less likely than other users to suffer negative consequences to their personal relationships and privacy (Paradise & Sullivan, 2012). Adolescents believe others are more harmed by sexting, and, in turn, support restrictions for others.

TPP and Optimistic Bias

Of the many theoretical frameworks thought to contribute to third-person perception, optimistic bias is the most promising. Optimistic bias is the belief that "bad things happen to other people" (Weinstein, 1980). More than 100 studies have documented optimistic bias in a range of health issues, including cancer (Jansen, Applebaum, Klein, Weinstein, Cook, Fogel & Sulmasy, 2011), natural disasters (Trumbo, Lueck, Marlatt & Peek, 2011), and sexually transmitted diseases (Wolfers, de Zwart & Kok, 2011). The first to link the two literatures (Chapin, 2000) found that adolescents exhibiting optimistic bias regarding risky sexual behaviors also exhibited TPP regarding the influence of safer sex (HIV) advertisements. Adolescents who exhibited first-person perception, believing they were more influenced by the TV spots than were their peers, reduced their optimistic bias to a more realistic risk perception. A number of later studies have linked the literatures in a number of contexts, including bird flu (Wei, Lo & Lu, 2007), computer knowledge (Li, 2008), and domestic violence (Chapin, 2011).

The Behavioral Component

Optimistic bias and third-person perception are both misperceptions about risk. Misperceptions are interesting in their own right, but they become more important, because people act on their misperceptions. Both literatures include a behavioral component (Behaviors and attitude changes brought about by the misperceptions). In a recent optimistic bias study of adolescents in the Netherlands, participants exhibited optimistic bias regarding sexually transmitted diseases (STDs): Adolescents believed they were less likely than their peers to contract an STD (Wolfers, de Zwart & Kok, 2011). It is well documented that people who exhibit optimistic bias are less likely to take precautions. In this case, adolescents who believed they were less likely to contract a STD were also less likely than peers to get tested. Recent studies have also linked optimistic bias with failure to use sun screen (Roberts, Gibbons, Gerrard & Alert, 2011), failure to vaccinate children (Bond & Nolan, 2011), and diminished mental health (O'Mara, McNulty & Karney, 2011).

People exhibiting TPP are also predicted to act on their perceptions, but what is described in the literature as a behavioral component is more often measured as an attitude or support for restriction. A study of video games found heavy gamers exhibited higher degrees of TPP (Schmierbach et al., 2011). TPP was related to less support for censorship of violent video games. Recent studies have also linked TPP with support for censorship (Lim & Golan, 2011), willingness to restrict product placement in film (Shin & Kim, 2011) and increased information seeking (Wei, Lo & Lu, 2011). The study of TPP and Facebook use among college students (Paradise & Sullivan, 2012) failed to document a relationship between TPP and support for enhanced regulation of the social networking site.

Subjective Norms

Subjective norm is our perception that most people (friends, family, etc.) take a particular position on a particular topic (Fishbein & Ajzen, 1975). Consider the example of college students and gambling. College students are at an age that is highly impressionable, experimental and conducive to risk-taking. Not surprisingly, college students are three times as likely as adults to gamble. The advent of Internet gambling brings the high stakes of Las Vegas to dorm rooms across America. Students' parents likely view gambling as economically irresponsible, so personal attitudes and subjective norms are at odds. A study of 345 mid-western college students (Thrasher, Andrew & Mahony, 2007) found that both positive attitudes about gambling and perceived positive subjective norms predicted increased gambling among college students. The researchers suggest that gambling-themed campus events (casino nights, poker clubs) help create positive subjective norms that may differ from students' family perspectives, and thus may increase gambling among students.

While it has yet to be applied to violent crime, one study (Woolley & Eining, 2006) examined the applicability of subjective norms to one of the most common non-violent crimes among college students: Software piracy. Students routinely download music (mp3 files) illegally; the same principles apply to sharing software. For instance, the Microsoft Office Suite costs hundreds of dollars. "Free" versions are available online and sharing or copying CDs is commonplace. The study focused on accounting students and the expensive software packages required for coursework. The study split subjective norm into two categories: peer and authority (A business professor may not approve of piracy, but peers may be routinely engaging in the behavior). Both categories predicted piracy among accounting students. Compared to previous studies, Woolley and Eining found that students today are more aware of copyright restrictions, but also have greater access to computers, making piracy easier than ever. The study also found that students were more likely to pirate software than adults. The belief that software developers charge too much for their product and the belief that "everybody does it" support continued infractions. There have been no previous TPP studies using subjective norms as a predictor.

FUTURE RESEARCH DIRECTIONS

Understanding how children and adolescents use social media and their misperceptions about potential harms is an important first step. Addressing the problem is the next step. This information is useful to schools, parents and anti-bullying programs, suggesting a media literacy approach to prevention education may decrease optimistic bias and TPP, thereby increasing self-protective behaviors. It's important that children and adolescents have realistic perceptions of their vulnerability online, ways they can protect themselves, and the available resources once a harm has taken place. This study resulted from a collaboration between a university (Penn State) and a local women's center (Crisis Center North). Each brought specific areas of expertise resulting in free services to area schools. At the end of the school year, the partners meet to review the results and improve the curriculum specific to the needs of the schools. This model is easily replicated in other communities.

REFERENCES

American Academy of Pediatrics. (2011). *Clinical report: The impact of social media on children, adolescents, and families*. Retrieved from www.pediatrics.org/cgi/doi/10.1542/peds.2011-0054

Antonopoulous, N., Veglis, A., Gardikiotis, A., Kotsakis, R., & Kalliris, G. (2015). Web third-person effect in structural aspects of the information on media websites. *Computers in Human Behavior, 44*, 48–58. doi:10.1016/j.chb.2014.11.022

Bond, L., & Nolan, T. (2011). Making sense of perceptions of risk of diseases and vaccinations: A qualitative study combining models of health beliefs, decision-making and risk perception. *BMC Public Health, 11*(1), 1471–2458. doi:10.1186/1471-2458-11-943 PMID:22182354

Bullying Statistics. (2012). *Cyberbullying statistics*. Retrieved from http://www.bullyingstatistics.org/content/cyber-bullying-statistics.html

Centers for Disease Control and Prevention. (2012). *Youth suicide*. Retrieved from http://www.cdc.gov/violenceprevention/pub/youth_suicide.html

Chapin, J. (2000). Third-person perception and optimistic bias among urban minority at-risk youth. *Communication Research, 27*(1), 51–81. doi:10.1177/009365000027001003

Chapin, J. (2011). Optimistic bias about intimate partner violence among medical personnel. *Family Medicine, 43*(6), 429–432. PMID:21656399

Chung, S., & Moon, S. (2016). Is the third-person effect real? A critical examination of the rationales, testing methods, and previous findings of the third-person effect on censorship attitudes. *Human Communication Research, 42*(2), 312–337. doi:10.1111/hcre.12078

Fishbein, M., & Ajzen, I. (1975). *Belief, attitude, intention and behavior: An introduction to theory and research*. Reading, MA: Addison-Wesley.

Flannery, D., Todres, J., Bradshaw, C., Amar, A., Graham, S., Hatzenbuehler, M., ... Rivara, F. (2016). Bullying prevention: A summary of the report of the National Academies of Sciences, Engineering, and Medicine. *Prevention Science*, *17*(8), 1044–1053. doi:10.100711121-016-0722-8 PMID:27722816

Jansen, L., Applebaum, P., Klein, W., Weinstein, N., Cook, J., & Sulmasy, D. (2011). Unrealistic optimism in early-phase oncology trials. *Ethics and Human Research*, *33*(1), 1–8. PMID:21314034

Kim, H. (2016). The role of emotions and culture in the third-person effect process of news coverage of election poll results. *Communication Research*, *43*(1), 109–130. doi:10.1177/0093650214558252

Li, X. (2008). Third-person effect, optimistic bias, and sufficiency resource in Internet use. *Journal of Communication*, *58*(3), 568–587. doi:10.1111/j.1460-2466.2008.00400.x

Lyons, G. (2012). *Facebook to hit a billion users in the summer. Analytics and Insights*. Retrieved from http://connect.icrossing.co.uk/facebook-hit-billion-users-summer_7709

National Crime Prevention Council. (2012). *Cyber bullying law and legal definition*. Retrieved from http://definitions.uslegal.com/c/cyber-bullying/

O'Mara, E., McNulty, J., & Karney, B. (2011). Positively biased appraisals in everyday life: When do they benefit mental health and when do they harm it? *Journal of Personality and Social Psychology*, *101*(3), 415–432. doi:10.1037/a0023332 PMID:21500926

Paradise, A., & Sullivan, M. (2012). (In)visible threats? The third-person effect in perceptions of the influence of Facebook. *Cyberpsychology, Behavior, and Social Networking*, *15*(1), 55–60. doi:10.1089/cyber.2011.0054 PMID:21988734

Roberts, M., Gibbons, F., Gerrard, M., & Alert, M. (2011). Optimism and adolescent perception of skin cancer risk. *Health Psychology*, *30*(6), 810–813. doi:10.1037/a0024380 PMID:21688914

Stevens, R., Dunaev, J., Malven, E., Bleakley, A., & Hull, S. (2016). Social media in the sexual lives of African American and Latino youth: Challenges and opportunities in the digital neighborhood. *Media and Communication*, *4*(3), 60–70. doi:10.17645/mac.v4i3.524

Thrasher, R., Andrew, D., & Mahoney, D. (2007). The efficacy of the Theory of Reasoned Action to explain gambling behavior in college students. *College Students Affairs Journal*, *27*(1), 57–75. PMID:20803059

Trumbo, C., Luek, M., Marlatt, H., & Peek, L. (2011). The effect of proximity to Hurricanes Katrina and Rita on subsequent hurricane outlook and optimistic bias. *Risk Analysis*, *31*(12), 1907–1918. doi:10.1111/j.1539-6924.2011.01633.x PMID:21605150

Webster, L., Li, J., Zhu, Y., Luchsinger, A., Wan, A., & Tatge, M. (2016). Third-person effect, religiosity and support for censorship of satirical religious cartoons. *Journal of Media and Religion*, *15*(4), 186–195. doi:10.1080/15348423.2016.1248183

Wei, R., & Lo, V. (2007). The third-person effects of political attack ads in the 2004 U.S. presidential election. *Media Psychology*, *9*(2), 367–388. doi:10.1080/15213260701291338

Wei, R., & Lo, V. (2013). Examining sexting's effects among adolescent mobile phone users. *International Journal of Mobile Communications*, *11*(2), 176–193. doi:10.1504/IJMC.2013.052640

Weinstein, N. (1980). Unrealistic optimism about future life events. *Journal of Personality and Social Psychology*, *39*(5), 806–460. doi:10.1037/0022-3514.39.5.806

Wolfers, M., de Zwart, O., & Kok, G. (2011). Adolescents in the Netherlands underestimate risk for sexually transmitted infections and deny the need for sexually transmitted infection testing. *AIDS Patient Care and STDs*, *25*(5), 311–319. doi:10.1089/apc.2010.0186 PMID:21542726

Woolley, D., & Eining, M. (2006). Software piracy among accounting students: A longitudinal comparison of changes and sensitivity. *Journal of Information Systems*, *20*(1), 49–63. doi:10.2308/jis.2006.20.1.49

Xie, G. (2016). Deceptive advertising and third-person perception: The interplay of generalized and specific suspicion. *Journal of Marketing Communications*, *22*(5), 494–512. doi:10.1080/13527266.2 014.918051

This research was previously published in Analyzing Human Behavior in Cyberspace; pages 28-38, copyright year 2019 by Information Science Reference (an imprint of IGI Global).

Chapter 35
Application and Impact of Social Network in Modern Society

Mamata Rath

https://orcid.org/0000-0002-2277-1012

Birla Global University, India

ABSTRACT

Social network and its corresponding website permits a client to make a profile, set up an authorized account to create a digital representation of themselves, to select other members of the site as contacts, make connections with them, communicate and engage with these users in different social activities, etc. So, social network includes details of persons, group details, their friends list, contact list, business, affiliations, personal data, personal preferences, and historical information. In this age of smart communication and technology, most of the time people are connected with mobile smart telephones in their work culture, home, office, or any other related places. As they are constantly associated with social systems for long time, they get new posts, messages, and current refreshed news readily available in a flash. This is the constructive part of social networking that individuals consistently remain refreshed with most recent news and innovation. This chapter presents an overview of social network design, various issues, and emerging trends that are evolved simultaneously with modern age. It also presents a detail study on application and impact of social network in modern society as well as exhibits an exhaustive review of security measures in social sites.

INTRODUCTION

Different Social Network Sites (SNS) such as facebook, MySpace, YouTube and Bebo etc. got maximum user appreciation and became very prominent during the period and primary decade of the twenty-first century. But it was challenging to know who are their clients, how are they utilized and are social network locales a passing trend or will they be a generally lasting feature of the Internet- all these were difficult to handle. In the meantime, various pro locales have developed many social networking features, including digg.com (news separating), YouTube (video sharing) and Flickr (picture sharing): Are these

DOI: 10.4018/978-1-6684-6307-9.ch035

the future as in social networking will end up installed into different applications as opposed to keeping up a moderately free presence? Social network destinations have pulled in noteworthy media intrigue due to their fast ascent and wide client base, particularly among more youthful individuals, and as a result of different terrifies, for example, the posting of unseemly material by minors and the potential SNS use in personality extortion. There is likewise a justifiable worry from guardians about their kids investing a lot of energy in an obscure online condition (M.Rath et. al, 2018) Be that as it may, there is a little methodical examination into social network destinations to look at the pervasiveness of attractive and bothersome features and to get solid proof of examples of clients and employments. This chapter audits such research and numerous subjective and blended strategy examinations concerning explicit parts of SNS use or into explicit gatherings of clients. One of the issues with social occasion information about SNSs is that they are benefit making endeavours and data about angles, for example, client socio-economics and use designs are commercial privileged insights. Notwithstanding the usage of security approaches to ensure individuals' data, this makes deliberate investigations troublesome. MySpace is a fractional special case, in any case, and this part exploits to exhibit a few examinations of MySpace clients to supplement the writing surveys(M.Rath et.al, 2018).

Social system information can help with acquiring significant understanding into social practices and uncovering the fundamental advantages. New huge information advances are developing to make it less demanding to find important social data from market examination to counter fear based oppression. Sadly, both various social datasets and huge information advancements raise stringent security concerns. Enemies can dispatch surmising assaults to anticipate delicate idle data, which is reluctant to be distributed by social clients. Along these lines, there is a trad eoff between information advantages and security concerns. It has been examined in some examination work about how to improve the exchange off between idle information protection and modified information utility. We propose an information sanitation system that does not significantly decrease the advantages brought by social system information, while delicate inactive data can in any case be secured. Notwithstanding considering intense foes with ideal deduction assaults, the proposed information sanitation procedure (Z. He et.al, 2018) can at present protect the two information advantages and social structure, while ensuring ideal idle information security.

A social system is a description of the social structure including individuals, for the most part people or affiliations. It speaks to the manners by which they are associated all through different social familiarities extending from easygoing social contact to close natural bonds (J. Jiang et.al, 2018). The casual association is a caught structure made out of social people and associations between them. Huge scale online relational associations like Sina Weibo, Tencent Wechat and Facebook have pulled in a substantial number of customers starting late People should need to use relational associations to pass on or diffuse information. For example, an association develops another thing, they have to advance the thing in a particular casual network. The association has a limited spending so they can simply give free precedent things to couple of customers (Rath et.al, 2018). Four major applications of social networks are as follows.

- Multimedia – Photo-sharing: Flickr – Video-sharing: YouTube – Audio-sharing: imeem
- Entertainment – Virtual Worlds: Second Life – Online Gaming: World of Warcraft
- News/Opinion – Social news: Digg, Reddit – Reviews: Yelp, epinions
- Communication – Microblogs: Twitter, Pownce – Events: Evite – Social Networking Services: Facebook, LinkedIn, MySpace. Figure 1 shows Four important applications of social networks.

Figure 1. Four important applications of social networks

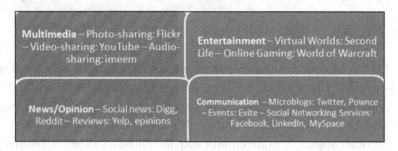

They assume that the fundamental customers could influence their buddies to use the things, and their friends could affect theirs colleagues. Through the verbal effect, incalculable finally get the items. Impact help is a basic research issue in relational associations. It picks a course of action of k centers as seeds with a particular ultimate objective to help the inducing of considerations, ends and things.

Section one presents the introduction part. Segment 2 shows Exigent features in Social Networking and utility devices utilized in social system for improvement and support, for example, context of big data, delicate registering methods and so on. Segment 3 presents applications and Impact of Social Networking in Modern Society and at last section 4 concludes the chapter.

Exigent Features in Social Networking

Many challenging issues should be tended to execute plan of social system design. Most of them are as per the following:

1. Representation of learning - Although different ontologies catch the rich social ideas, there is no need many "persuasion" ontologies characterizing a similar idea. How might we advance toward having few normal and exhaustive ontologies?
2. Control and administration of learning - Semantic Web is, relative the whole Web, genuinely associated at the RDF diagram level however inadequately associated at the RDF archive level. The open and circulated nature of the Semantic Web likewise presents issues. How would we give productive and powerful components to getting to learning, particularly social systems, on the Semantic Web. There are different types of social network sites that are used by many people now a days in cyber space. They are used for various purposes such as entertainment, education, friendship, lifestyle, business etc. .
3. Analysis, extraction and joining of data from social system Even with all around characterized ontologies for social ideas, separating social systems accurately from the loud and fragmented learning on the (Semantic) Web is exceptionally troublesome. What are the heuristics for incorporating and intertwining social data and the measurements for the validity and utility of the outcomes?
4. Derivation and honesty in dispersed impedance Provenance partners certainties with social elements which are between associated in social system, and trust among social elements can be gotten from social systems. How to oversee and lessen the multifaceted nature of circulated induction by using provenance of learning with regards to a given trust show?.

Applications and Impact of Social Networking in Modern Society

Inoculation and Security in Social Network

W. Yang et.al (2015) recommend how to keep the engendering of social network worms through the immunization of key nodes. Not at all like existing control models for worm proliferation, a novel immunization methodology is proposed dependent on network vertex impact. The procedure chooses the basic vertices in the entire network. At that point the immunization is connected on the chosen vertices to accomplish the maximal impact of worm control with insignificant expense. Diverse calculations are executed to choose vertices. Reenactment tests are introduced to break down and assess the execution of various calculations.

Social Set Identification and Analysis

In view of the human science of affiliations and the arithmetic of set hypothesis, R. Bhatrapu et. al, (2016) presents another way to deal with huge information investigation called social set analysis. Social set analysis comprises of a generative system for the methods of insight of computational social science, hypothesis of social information, applied and formal models of social information, and a systematic structure for consolidating huge social informational indexes with authoritative and societal informational indexes. Figure 2 shows example of some social media available in internet.

Figure 2. Example of some social media

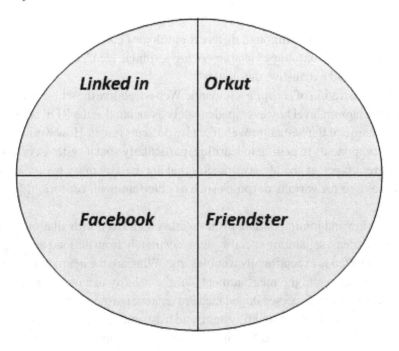

Table 1. Represents various impact and issues of social network on society

Sl.No	Literature	Year	Impact of Social Network
1.	M.Davidekova et.al	2017	Emergency social network approach that uses emergency posting through Application Program Interface.
2.	C.Marche et.al	2017	Object navigation in social network as per distance from one node to other
3.	Merini et.al	2017	Image tracing in social network using CNN approach
4.	P.Santi et.al	2012	Analysis of mobile social network based on mobility model for the purpose of next generation network
5.	L.Nie et.al	2016	Learning and Teaching from Multiple Social Networks
6.	E. Hargitai et.al	2016	Investigation on Social network analysis based on big data, big problems and Internet Log Data
7.	Z.Zhao et.al	2018	Recommendation of movie for social awareness through multi modal network learning
8.	A.Mitra et.al	2016	Analytical study of dynamic models in social network
9.	Rachael P. et.al	2017	Focus on positive aspects of social security measures
10.	Md.S. Kamal et.al	2016	An automated system for Monitoring of facebook data

Longitudinal Mobile Telephone Dataset:

An enormous, longitudinal mobile telephone dataset has been explored that comprises of human versatility and social network data at the same time, enabling us to investigate the effect of human portability designs on the basic social network. D. Wang et.al (2015). Fig.3 shows few prominent social web sites.

Figure 3 shows few prominent social web sites . Important Social Networking Websites are – MySpace – Facebook – Hi5 – Orkut – Bebo – Friendster – LinkedIn – StudiVZ – Xing. Worldwide top 10 websites as per August 2008 survey are given is fig.4 (Source: comScore). With an objective to build up a methodical comprehension of mobile social networks Device to Device (D2D) communication are conveyed by X. Chen et. al, (2015) who use two key social question, to be specific social trust and social correspondence, to advance effective collaboration among gadgets. With this understanding, an alliance diversion theoretic structure has been produced to devise social-tie-based collaboration techniques for D2D interchanges. Table 2 shows details of various issues in social networking in modern society.

Social network analysis (SNA) is becoming increasingly concerned not only with actors and their relations, but also with distinguishing between different types of such entities. For example, social scientists may want to investigate asymmetric relations in organizations with strict chains of command, or incorporate non-actors such as conferences and projects when analyzing coauthorship patterns. Multimodal social networks are those where actors and relations belong to different types, or modes, and multimodal social network analysis (mSNA) is accordingly SNA for such networks. S. Ghani et.al (2013) present a design study that we conducted with several social scientist collaborators on how to support mSNA using visual analytics tools. Based on an openended, formative design process, a visual representation called parallel node-link bands (PNLBs) has been devised that splits modes into separate bands and renders connections between adjacent ones, similar to the list view in Jigsaw. We then used the tool in a qualitative evaluation involving five social scientists whose feedback informed a second design phase that incorporated additional network metrics. Finally, a second qualitative evaluation has been conducted with social scientist collaborators that provided further insights on the utility of the PNLBs representation and the potential of visual analytics for mSNA.

Figure 3. Few prominent social web sites

```
Google
Microsoft
Yahoo!
AOL
Wikimedia
eBay
CBS
Fox Interactive Media
Amazon Sites
Facebook
```

Impact of Social Network on Education

A most noticeable resources for Universities are the information and must be shielded from security break. Security dangers and prevention (C. Joshi et.al, 2017) particularly develop in University's network, and with thought of these issues, proposed data security structure for University network condition. The proposed structure decreases the danger of security rupture by supporting three stage exercises; the primary stage surveys the dangers and vulnerabilities with a specific end goal to distinguish the frail point in instructive condition[8], the second stage concentrates on the most noteworthy hazard and make significant remediation design, the third period of hazard appraisal display perceives the helplessness administration consistence necessity so as to enhance University's security position. The proposed structure is connected on Vikram University Ujjain India's, processing condition and the assessment result demonstrated the proposed system upgrades the security level of University grounds network. This model can be utilized by chance investigator and security administrator of University to perform dependable and repeatable hazard examination in practical and reasonable way. W. Chen et. al (2015) propose associating the secluded administration islands into a global social administration system to improve the administrations' friendliness on a global scale. In the first place, connected social administration particular standards are proposed dependent on connected information standards for distributing administrations on the open Web as connected social administrations. At that point, another system has been proposed for building the global social administration organize following connected social administration particular standards dependent on complex system speculations. Table 3 describes Social networking design and focused challenges in society.

Table 2. Details of various issues in social networking in modern society

Sl. No	Literature	Year	Social Network Issues/ Challenges
1	W.Yang et.al	2016	Immunization Strategy for Social Network
2	R. Vatrapu et.al	2016	Social set analysis with big data analysis
3	D.Wang et.al	2015	Impact of human mobility on social network
4	X. Chen et.al	2015	Mobile social networking – D2D communication
5	M. Trier et.al	2009	Exploring and searching social architecture
6	L. Meng et.al	2016	Interplay between individuals evolving interaction patterns
7	S. Ghani et.al	2013	Visual analysis for multi-modal social network analysis
8	W. Chen et.al	2015	Global Service network for web service discovery
9	Y. Song et.al	2015	Friendship influence on mobile behaviour of location based social network users
10	Y. Wang et.al	2015	Epidemic spreading model based on social active degree in social network
11	H. Zhao et.al	2015	Social discovery and exploring the correlation among 3D serial relationship
12	Y. Wu et.al	2018	Challenges of Mobile social device cashing
13	Y. Zhu et.al	2013	A survey of social based routing in delay tolerant network
14	T. Silawan et.al	2017	Sybilvote: Formulas to quantify the success probability
15	L. Zhang et.al	2018	Social networks public opinion propagation influence models
16	B.Schneier	2010	Taxonomy of social networking data
17	C.Yu et.al	2014	Collective learning for the social norms
18	V.K.Singh et.al	2014	Online and physical network with social implications
19	Z. Yan et.al	2015	Trustworthy pervasive social networking
20	Z. Wang et.al	2013	Peer-assisted social media streaming with social receprocity
21	A.M. Vegni et.al	2015	Social network with vehicular communication
22	F. Xia	2014	Exploiting social relationship to enable ad-hoc social network
23	M. Yuan et.al	2013	Security in social network with sensitive labels protection scheme
24	C. Timmerer	2014	Social multimedia in social network

In mobile figuring research zone, it is very alluring to comprehend the attributes of client development with the goal that the easy to understand area mindful administrations could be rendered successfully. Area based social systems (LBSNs) have thrived as of late and are of incredible potential for development conduct investigation and information driven application plan. While there have been a few endeavors on client registration development conduct in LBSNs, they need exhaustive examination of social effect on them. To this end, the social-spatial impact and social-fleeting impact are broke down artificially by Y. Song et. al (2015) in light of the related data uncovered in LBSNs. The registration development practices of clients are observed to be influenced by their social fellowships both from spatial and fleeting measurements. Besides, a probabilistic model of client mobile conduct is proposed, joining the thorough social impact display with degree individual inclination show. The trial results approve that the proposed model can enhance expectation precision contrasted with the best in class social recorded model thinking about fleeting data (SHM+T), which for the most part ponders the transient cyclic examples and utilizations them to show client versatility, while being with reasonable unpredictability.

Table 3. Social networking design and focused challenges

Sl. No	Literature	Year	Highlighted Topics
1	R. M. Bond *et.al*	2017	Effect of social networks on academic outcomes
2	S.Rathore *et.al*	2017	Survey of security and privacy threats of social network users
3	J.Zhu *et.al*	2017	Influence maximization in social networks
4	F.Meng *et.al*	2017	Data communication between vehicle social network
5	W.Wang *et.al*	2017	Crowd sourcing complex tasks by team formation in social network
6	V.Amelkin *et.al*	2017	Polar opinion dynamics in social network
7	R. Schlegel *et.al*	2017	Privacy preservation location sharing
8	C.Joshi *et.al*	2017	Security threats in Educational Social network
9	J.Kim *et.al*	2018	Social network in disaster management
10	A.Ahmad *et.al*	2017	Authentication of delegation of resource use in social networking
11	B.Tarbush *et.al*	2017	Dynamic model of social network formation
12	R.Rau *et.al*	2017	Financial outcome of social networks
13	D.Quick *et.al*	2017	Pervasive social networking forensic
14	S.Janabi *et.al*	2017	Privacy as a concern among social network users
15	L.C.Hua *et.al*	2017	Cooperation among members of social network in VANET

An enhanced Susceptible-Infected-Susceptible (SIS) plague spreading model is proposed (Y. Wang et.al, 2015) with the end goal to give a hypothetical technique to examine and foresee the spreading of illnesses. As a moving station in a city, a vehicle has its own dataset of directions. On every direction, remote connections can be worked between various clients and the vehicle Since every vehicle is related with a particular territory that covers certain potential client gatherings, such portable vehicles have turned into the premise of a Vehicle Social Network (VSN) for prescribing items to potential clients in present day society .However, little research has concentrated on publicizing through a VSN . For VSN-based publicizing, the advertiser normally situated in a remote Central Office (CO)chooses certain vehicles to go about as recommenders as indicated by their scope territories. Data about the vehicles' scope zones will be sent from the VSN to the advertiser working at the CO i.e., information backhauling. Moreover, the advertiser will sent the outcomes in regards to the picked recommenders to all vehicles in the VSN, i.e., information front hauling. Naturally, a compelling correspondence framework is desperately required to help information transmission.

CONCLUSION

From the study above, it can be summarised that there are many positive impact of social networking systems on current society. Communicating with people and making friendship is a very natural method of connecting people, moreover who are of different age groups and different backgrounds. It was never been less demanding to make companions than it is at the present time. Furthermore, that is primarily on account of social networking locales. Only a couple of decades back it was really hard to associate with individuals, except if you were the excessively cordial sort ready to make discussion with anybody at a gathering. The increasing use of mobile smart phones among people helped change this, associating individuals recently. It's completely conceivable to have groups, friendship and communication among several companions on Facebook. They may not be companions you know on an individual dimension and invest energy with in reality on a week after week premise. Be that as it may, they're companions regardless. There are a few people I consider companions who I have never met — actually, I may never meet them — yet that doesn't decrease the association we have because of social networks. They for the most part do mind, and will let you know so. They will tune in to what you need to state, and help you manage any issues you might confront. In the event that this isn't the situation, you might need to discover new companions. The fact of the matter is that on social networking destinations, we're ready to sympathize with one another. A companion may have experienced a comparative difficulty that you are right now experiencing, and they will have the capacity to enable you to get past it. Social networks support sparing of quality time because of quick correspondence among friends and group members. Our time is being extended more trim and lesser by work and family duties. In any case, social networking sites offer an opportunity to impart in a rapid and productive way. Composing a relaxed comment for twitter takes only few seconds, and one can finalise a business deal, an appointment, an interview, a conference, a business meeting through these social sites very easily. So, there are many positive impact of social networks on people.

REFERENCES

Ahmad, A., Whitworth, B., Zeshan, F., Bertino, E., & Friedman, R. (2017). Extending social networks with delegation. In *Computers & Security* (Vol. 70, pp. 546–564). Elsevier.

Al-Janabi, Al-Shourbaji, Shojafar, & Shamshirband. (2017). Survey of main challenges (security and privacy) in wireless body area networks for healthcare applications. *Egyptian Informatics Journal, 18*(2), 113-122.

Amelkin, V., Bullo, F., & Singh, A. K. (2017). Polar Opinion Dynamics in Social Networks. *IEEE Transactions on Automatic Control, 62*(11), 5650–5665. doi:10.1109/TAC.2017.2694341

Bond, Chykina, & Jones. (2017). Social network effects on academic achievement. *The Social Science Journal, 54*(4), 438-449. doi:10.1016/j.soscij.2017.06.001

Chen, W., Paik, I., & Hung, P. C. K. (2015). Constructing a Global Social Service Network for Better Quality of Web Service Discovery. *IEEE Transactions on Services Computing, 8*(2), 284–298. doi:10.1109/TSC.2013.20

Chen, X., Proulx, B., Gong, X., & Zhang, J. (2015). Exploiting Social Ties for Cooperative D2D Communications: A Mobile Social Networking Case. *IEEE/ACM Transactions on Networking, 23*(5), 1471–1484. doi:10.1109/TNET.2014.2329956

Dávideková, M., & Greguš, M. (2017). Social Network Types: An Emergency Social Network Approach - A Concept of Possible Inclusion of Emergency Posts in Social Networks through an API. *2017 IEEE International Conference on Cognitive Computing (ICCC)*, 40-47. 10.1109/IEEE.ICCC.2017.13

Ghani, S., Kwon, B. C., Lee, S., Yi, J. S., & Elmqvist, N. (2013). Visual Analytics for Multimodal Social Network Analysis: A Design Study with Social Scientists. *IEEE Transactions on Visualization and Computer Graphics, 19*(12), 2032–2041. doi:10.1109/TVCG.2013.223 PMID:24051769

Hargittai, E., & Sandvig, C. (2016). *Big Data, Big Problems, Big Opportunities: Using Internet Log Data to Conduct Social Network Analysis Research. In Digital Research Confidential:The Secrets of Studying Behavior Online* (p. 288). MIT Press.

He, Z., Cai, Z., & Yu, J. (2018). Latent-Data Privacy Preserving With Customized Data Utility for Social Network Data. *IEEE Transactions on Vehicular Technology, 67*(1), 665–673. doi:10.1109/TVT.2017.2738018

Hua, L. C., Anisi, M. H., Yee, P. L., & Alam, M. (2017). Social networking-based cooperation mechanisms in vehicular ad-hoc network—a survey. In *Vehicular Communications*. Elsevier. doi:10.1016/j.vehcom.2017.11.001

Jiang, J., Wen, S., Yu, S., Xiang, Y., & Zhou, W. (2018). Rumor Source Identification in Social Networks with Time-Varying Topology. IEEE Transactions on Dependable and Secure Computing, 15(1), 166-179. doi:10.1109/TDSC.2016.2522436

Joshi, C., & Singh, U. K. (2017). Information security risks management framework – A step towards mitigating security risks in university network. *Journal of Information Security and Applications, 35*, 128-137.

Kim, J., & Hastak, M. (2018). Social network analysis: Characteristics of online social networks after a disaster. *International Journal of Information Management, 38*(1), 86-96.

Mady & Blumstein. (2017). Social security: are socially connected individuals less vigilant? *Animal Behaviour, 134*, 79-85.

Marche, Atzori, Iera, Militano, & Nitti. (n.d.). Navigability in Social Networks of Objects: The Importance of Friendship Type and Nodes' Distance. *IEEE Globecom Workshops (GC Workshops)*, 1-6.

Meng, F., Gong, X., Guo, L., Cai, X., & Zhang, Q. (2017). Software-Reconfigurable System Supporting Point-to-Point Data Communication Between Vehicle Social Networks and Marketers. *IEEE Access: Practical Innovations, Open Solutions, 5*, 22796–22803. doi:10.1109/ACCESS.2017.2764098

Meng, L., Hulovatyy, Y., Striegel, A., & Milenković, T. (2016). On the Interplay Between Individuals' Evolving Interaction Patterns and Traits in Dynamic Multiplex Social Networks. IEEE Transactions on Network Science and Engineering, 3(1), 32-43. doi:10.1109/TNSE.2016.2523798

Merini, T. U., & Caldelli, R. (2017). Tracing images back to their social network of origin: A CNN-based approach. *IEEE Workshop on Information Forensics and Security (WIFS)*, 1-6.doi: 10.1109/WIFS.2017.8267660

Mitra, A., Paul, S., Panda, S., & Padhi, P. (2016). A Study on the Representation of the Various Models for Dynamic Social Networks. *Procedia Computer Science, 79*, 624-631.

Nie, L., Song, X., & Chua, T.-S. (2016). *Learning from Multiple Social Networks. In Learning from Multiple Social Networks*. Morgan & Claypool.

Quick, D., & Choo, K.-K. R. (2017). Pervasive social networking forensics: Intelligence and evidence from mobile device extracts. *Journal of Network and Computer Applications, 86*, 24-33. doi:10.1016/j.jnca.2016.11.018

Rath, Pati, & Pattanayak. (2018). An Overview on Social Networking: Design, Issues, Emerging Trends, and Security. *Social Network Analytics: Computational Research Methods and Techniques*, 21-47.

Rath, M. (2017). Resource provision and QoS support with added security for client side applications in cloud computing. *International Journal of Information Technology, 9*(3), 1–8.

Rath, M., & Panda, M. R. (2017). MAQ system development in mobile ad-hoc networks using mobile agents. *IEEE 2nd International Conference on Contemporary Computing and Informatics (IC3I)*, 794-798.

Rath, M., & Pati, B. (2017). *Load balanced routing scheme for MANETs with power and delay optimization. International Journal of Communication Network and Distributed Systems, 19*.

Rath, M., Pati, B., Panigrahi, C. R., & Sarkar, J. L. (2019). QTM: A QoS Task Monitoring System for Mobile Ad hoc Networks. In P. Sa, S. Bakshi, I. Hatzilygeroudis, & M. Sahoo (Eds.), *Recent Findings in Intelligent Computing Techniques. Advances in Intelligent Systems and Computing* (Vol. 707). Singapore: Springer. doi:10.1007/978-981-10-8639-7_57

Rath, M., Pati, B., Panigrahi, C. R., & Sarkar, J. L. (2019). QTM: A QoS Task Monitoring System for Mobile Ad hoc Networks. In P. Sa, S. Bakshi, I. Hatzilygeroudis, & M. Sahoo (Eds.), *Recent Findings in Intelligent Computing Techniques. Advances in Intelligent Systems and Computing* (Vol. 707). Singapore: Springer. doi:10.1007/978-981-10-8639-7_57

Rath, M., Pati, B., & Pattanayak, B. K. (2016). Inter-Layer Communication Based QoS Platform for Real Time Multimedia Applications in MANET. Wireless Communications, Signal Processing and Networking (IEEE WiSPNET), 613-617. doi:10.1109/WiSPNET.2016.7566203

Rath, M., Pati, B., & Pattanayak, B. K. (2017). Cross layer based QoS platform for multimedia transmission in MANET. *11th International Conference on Intelligent Systems and Control (ISCO)*, 402-407. 10.1109/ISCO.2017.7856026

Rath, M., & Pattanayak, B. (2017). MAQ:A Mobile Agent Based QoS Platform for MANETs. *International Journal of Business Data Communications and Networking, IGI Global, 13*(1), 1–8. doi:10.4018/IJBDCN.2017010101

Rath, M., & Pattanayak, B. (2018). Technological improvement in modern health care applications using Internet of Things (IoT) and proposal of novel health care approach. *International Journal of Human Rights in Healthcare*. doi:10.1108/IJHRH-01-2018-0007

Rath, M., & Pattanayak, B. (2018). Technological improvement in modern health care applications using Internet of Things (IoT) and proposal of novel health care approach. *International Journal of Human Rights in Healthcare*. doi:10.1108/IJHRH-01-2018-0007

Rath, M., & Pattanayak, B. K. (2014). A methodical survey on real time applications in MANETS: Focussing On Key Issues. *International Conference on, High Performance Computing and Applications (IEEE ICHPCA)*, 1-5, 22-24. 10.1109/ICHPCA.2014.7045301

Rath, M., & Pattanayak, B. K. (2018). Monitoring of QoS in MANET Based Real Time Applications. Smart Innovation, Systems and Technologies, 84, 579-586. doi:10.1007/978-3-319-63645-0_64

Rath, M., & Pattanayak, B. K. (2018). SCICS: A Soft Computing Based Intelligent Communication System in VANET. Smart Secure Systems – IoT and Analytics Perspective. *Communications in Computer and Information Science, 808*, 255–261. doi:10.1007/978-981-10-7635-0_19

Rath, M., Pattanayak, B. K., & Pati, B. (2017). *Energetic Routing Protocol Design for Real-time Transmission in Mobile Ad hoc Network. In Computing and Network Sustainability, Lecture Notes in Networks and Systems* (Vol. 12). Singapore: Springer.

Rathore, S., Sharma, P. K., Loia, V., Jeong, Y.-S., & Park, J. H. (2017). Social network security: Issues, challenges, threats, and solutions. *Information Sciences, 421*, 43-69. doi:10.1016/j.ins.08.063

Rau, R. (2017). Social networks and financial outcomes. *Current Opinion in Behavioral Sciences, 18*, 75-78.

Rtah, M. (2018). Big Data and IoT-Allied Challenges Associated With Healthcare Applications in Smart and Automated Systems. *International Journal of Strategic Information Technology and Applications, 9*(2). doi:10.4018/IJSITA.201804010

Sajadi, S. H., Fazli, M., & Habibi, J. (2018). The Affective Evolution of Social Norms in Social Networks. IEEE Transactions on Computational Social Systems, 5(3), 727-735. doi:10.1109/TCSS.2018.2855417

Santi. (2012). Mobile Social Network Analysis. In *Mobility Models for Next Generation Wireless Networks: Ad Hoc, Vehicular and Mesh Networks*. Wiley Telecom. doi:10.1002/9781118344774.ch19

Sarwar Kamal, M. (2017). De-Bruijn graph with MapReduce framework towards metagenomic data classification. *International Journal of Information Technology, 9*(1), 59–75. doi:10.100741870-017-0005-z

Schlegel, R., Chow, C. Y., Huang, Q., & Wong, D. S. (2017). Privacy-Preserving Location Sharing Services for Social Networks. *IEEE Transactions on Services Computing, 10*(5), 811–825. doi:10.1109/TSC.2016.2514338

Schneier, B. (2010). A Taxonomy of Social Networking Data. *IEEE Security and Privacy, 8*(4), 88–88. doi:10.1109/MSP.2010.118

Silawan, T., & Aswakul, C. (2017). SybilVote: Formulas to Quantify the Success Probability of Sybil Attack in Online Social Network Voting. IEEE Communications Letters, 21(7), 1553-1556.

Singh, V. K., Mani, A., & Pentland, A. (2014). Social Persuasion in Online and Physical Networks. *Proceedings of the IEEE, 102*(12), 1903–1910. doi:10.1109/JPROC.2014.2363986

Song, Y., Hu, Z., Leng, X., Tian, H., Yang, K., & Ke, X. (2015). Friendship influence on mobile behavior of location based social network users. *Journal of Communications and Networks (Seoul), 17*(2), 126–132. doi:10.1109/JCN.2015.000026

Tarbush, B., & Teytelboym, A. (2017). Social groups and social network formation. *Games and Economic Behavior, 103*, 286-312.

Timmerer, C., & Rainer, B. (2014). The Social Multimedia Experience. Computer, 47(3), 67-69.

Trier, M., & Bobrik, A. (2009). Social Search: Exploring and Searching Social Architectures in Digital Networks. *IEEE Internet Computing, 13*(2), 51–59. doi:10.1109/MIC.2009.44

Vatrapu, R., Mukkamala, R. R., Hussain, A., & Flesch, B. (2016). Social Set Analysis: A Set Theoretical Approach to Big Data Analytics. *IEEE Access: Practical Innovations, Open Solutions, 4,* 2542–2571. doi:10.1109/ACCESS.2016.2559584

Vegni, A. M., & Loscrí, V. (2015). A Survey on Vehicular Social Networks. *IEEE Communications Surveys and Tutorials, 17*(4), 2397–2419. doi:10.1109/COMST.2015.2453481

Wang, D., & Song, C. (2015). Impact of human mobility on social networks. Journal of Communications and Networks, 17(2), 100-109.

Wang, W., Jiang, J., An, B., Jiang, Y., & Chen, B. (2017). Toward Efficient Team Formation for Crowdsourcing in Noncooperative Social Networks. IEEE Transactions on Cybernetics, 47(12), 4208-4222.

Wang, Y., & Cai, W. (2015). Epidemic spreading model based on social active degree in social networks. *China Communications, 12*(12), 101–108. doi:10.1109/CC.2015.7385518

Wang, Z., Wu, C., Sun, L., & Yang, S. (2013). Peer-Assisted Social Media Streaming with Social Reciprocity. *IEEE eTransactions on Network and Service Management, 10*(1), 84–94. doi:10.1109/TNSM.2012.12.120244

Wu, Y. (2016). Challenges of Mobile Social Device Caching. IEEE Access, 4, 8938-8947.

Xia, F., Ahmed, A. M., Yang, L. T., Ma, J., & Rodrigues, J. J. P. C. (2014). Exploiting Social Relationship to Enable Efficient Replica Allocation in Ad-hoc Social Networks. *IEEE Transactions on Parallel and Distributed Systems, 25*(12), 3167–3176. doi:10.1109/TPDS.2013.2295805

Yan, Z., Feng, W., & Wang, P. (2015). Anonymous Authentication for Trustworthy Pervasive Social Networking. IEEE Transactions on Computational Social Systems, 2(3), 88-98. doi:10.1109/TCSS.2016.2519463

Yang, W., Wang, H., & Yao, Y. (2015). An immunization strategy for social network worms based on network vertex influence. *China Communications, 12*(7), 154–166. doi:10.1109/CC.2015.7188533

Yu, C., Zhang, M., & Ren, F. (2014). Collective Learning for the Emergence of Social Norms in Networked Multiagent Systems. *IEEE Transactions on Cybernetics, 44*(12), 2342–2355. doi:10.1109/TCYB.2014.2306919 PMID:25415942

Yuan, M., Chen, L., Yu, P. S., & Yu, T. (2013). Protecting Sensitive Labels in Social Network Data Anonymization. *IEEE Transactions on Knowledge and Data Engineering, 25*(3), 633–647. doi:10.1109/TKDE.2011.259

Zhang, L., Wang, T., Jin, Z., Su, N., Zhao, C., & He, Y. (2018). The research on social networks public opinion propagation influence models and its controllability. *China Communications, 15*(7), 98–110. doi:10.1109/CC.2018.8424607

Zhao, H., Zhou, H., Yuan, C., Huang, Y., & Chen, J. (2015). Social Discovery: Exploring the Correlation Among Three-Dimensional Social Relationships. IEEE Transactions on Computational Social Systems, 2(3), 77-87.

Zhao, Z., Yang, Q., Lu, H., Weninger, T., Cai, D., He, X., & Zhuang, Y. (2018). Social-Aware Movie Recommendation via Multimodal Network Learning. *IEEE Transactions on Multimedia, 20*(2), 430–440. doi:10.1109/TMM.2017.2740022

Zhu, J., Liu, Y., & Yin, X. (2017). A New Structure-Hole-Based Algorithm For Influence Maximization in Large Online Social Networks. IEEE Access, 5, 23405-23412. doi:10.1109/ACCESS.2017.2758353

Zhu, Y., Xu, B., Shi, X., & Wang, Y. (2013). A Survey of Social-Based Routing in Delay Tolerant Networks: Positive and Negative Social Effects. IEEE Communications Surveys & Tutorials, 15(1), 387-401.

This research was previously published in Hidden Link Prediction in Stochastic Social Networks; pages 30-49, copyright year 2019 by Information Science Reference (an imprint of IGI Global).

Chapter 36
Unemployment, Personality Traits, and the Use of Facebook:
Does Online Social Support Influence Continuous Use?

Dandison C. Ukpabi
iD https://orcid.org/0000-0002-5081-354X
University of Jyväskylä, Finland

Olayemi Olawumi
University of Eastern Finland, Finland

Oluwafemi Samson Balogun
iD https://orcid.org/0000-0002-8870-9692
University of Eastern Finland, Finland

Chijioke E. Nwachukwu
iD https://orcid.org/0000-0002-7982-2810
Horizons University, Paris, France

Sunday Adewale Olaleye
University of Oulu, Finland

Emmanuel Awuni Kolog
Business School, University of Ghana, Ghana

Richard O. Agjei
Centre for Multidisciplinary Research and Innovation (CEMRI), Abuja, Nigeria

Frank Adusei-Mensah
iD https://orcid.org/0000-0001-8237-5305
University of Eastern Finland, Finland

Luqman Awoniyi
University of Turku, Finland

Donald Douglas Atsa'am
University of the Free State, South Africa

Oluwafikayo Adeyemi
University of Illinois at Urbana-Champaign, USA

DOI: 10.4018/978-1-6684-6307-9.ch036

ABSTRACT

Different personality traits respond differently to unfavourable life situations. Unemployment can have several negative social, economic, and domestic consequences. Many people use social media for a variety of reasons. The aim of this study is to examine the way different personality traits respond to Facebook in the period of unemployment. Data was obtained from 3,002 unemployed respondents in Nigeria. The study used regression model to analyse the data. Among the five personality traits, results indicated that the relationship between neuroticism and online social support was negative. However, the relationship between online social support and satisfaction was positive. The study highlights several theoretical and practical implications.

INTRODUCTION

Unemployment is a pervasive economic condition. Authorities at the international, national and municipal levels are all trying to keep the unemployment figure down to the minimum. It is a concern because when people are unemployed, it leads to several negative consequences such as social (e.g., crimes), economic (e.g., poverty) and domestic (e.g., relationship and family breakup) (Hooghe et al., 2010; Song et al., 2011; Siwach, 2018). Unemployment can lead to negative personality change (Boyce et al., 2015), thus, the individual's disposition to life begins to take a downward turn. Generally, a coping strategy is to resort to the encouragement of others in the period of misfortune with some personality traits more adaptable to change than others (Merema et al., 2013). Interestingly, self-disclosure, which is the art of disclosing one's personal information to others (Bazarova & Choi, 2014) plays a crucial role on the level of trust that communicating partners have with each other, and the amount of information they share. Accordingly, the more revealing information that the communicating partners provide to others, the more they will be trusted with confidential information.

To the best of our knowledge, there have been no study done to establish how these personality traits adopts coping strategies during unemployment. Thus, the objective of this study is to understand how the different personality traits respond to online social support and whether the social support provided leads to satisfaction and continuous use of Facebook among the unemployed. Specifically, this study (a) examines the influence of personality traits on online social support in unemployment; (b) evaluates the role of online social support on satisfaction with Facebook, and (c) evaluates the role of satisfaction on continuous use of Facebook during the time of unemployment. Theoretically, our study is important because it contributes to the social media literature by explicating the psychological role of Facebook during unemployment. Additionally, our study extends the online social support in relation to unemployment and social media use. The rest of paper is structured as follows: next section addresses the literature review. This is followed by the methodology, analysis and results. The discussion section is presented, before providing the implications as the study concludes with the limitations and avenues for future research.

LITERATURE REVIEW

Personality Traits

A summary of each of these personality traits is provided below.

Conscientiousness

Conscientiousness is defined as individual differences in the propensity to follow socially prescribed norms for impulse control, goal-directed, able to delay gratification, and to follow norms and rules (Roberts et al., 2009). People with high degree of conscientiousness are reliable and prompt. A number of studies have been conducted to gain insight into the characteristics of conscientiousness. Notable of the attributes of conscientiousness in extant literature are avoidance of work, organization, impulsivity, antisocial, cleanliness, industriousness, laziness, appearance, punctuality, formality, and responsibility. Searching for jobs and the success in finding one, is largely dependent on individual's personality (Kanfer et al., 2001). Also, in the online platform, Giota and Kleftaras (2014) found a positive relationship between conscientiousness and online social support. Thus, it is argued that during period of unemployment, individuals are likely to turn to Facebook as an escape route to seek social support. It is thus hypothesized that:

H1. Individuals with conscientious personality trait will respond positively to online social support in the period of unemployment.

Neuroticism

Neuroticism is one of the 'Big Five' factors in the study of personality in psychology (Hassan et al., 2019). This mirrors one's propensity to experience psychological ordeal, as well as high levels of the trait are associated with a sensitivity to threat (Friedman and Schustack, 2016). Neuroticism is measured on a continuum, ranging from emotional stability to emotional instability thus from low neuroticism (Toegel and Barsoux, 2012) to high neuroticism (Dwan and Ownsworth, 2017).

Studies show that high levels of stress (Frost & Clayson, 1991) and high levels of depression (Dooley et al., 2000) can be associated with unemployment. This is because neuroticism involves stress and depression at the dispositional level (Abitov, 2018 et al., 2018; Widiger et al., 2009). Therefore, unemployment will trigger higher neuroticism. Demographic factors like age and gender, have been discovered to mediate neuroticism levels such that neuroticism scores progressively decrease as people advance in age and become more comfortable with their situation in life (Oishi et al., 2007). Research suggests that the neuroticism levels of females usually are higher than those of males, notwithstanding, however, as they advance in age, this gender disparity decreases (Weisberg et al., 2011). Absence of social support may result in loneliness (Heinrich & Gullone, 2006) and low self-esteem (Waters & Moore, 2002). Similarly, lack of social support and low self-esteem induce negative emotions, cognitions, and behaviours (Cohen et al., 2000; Sedikides & Gregg, 2003).

H2. Individuals with neurotic personality trait will respond positively to online social support in a period of unemployment.

Agreeableness

It is the trait that reflects tendency to be cooperative, trusting and compassionate. Agreeable personalities are believed to be agreeable, friendly and good-natured, sympathetic and warm. Individuals with agreeable traits are easy to get along with as they are generally kind, friendly and considerate (Amichai-Hamburger et al., 2010). An individual who is known to be hostile is less likely to receive social support from his or her social network. An extraverted individual is likely to have many of his or her social networks to turn to for support, when he or she is under stress (Swickert et al., 2010). In addition, various research studies have shown that individuals with high agreeableness personality, respond positively to social support while those with low agreeableness personalities do not show a significant change to social support (Hoth el al. 2007; Swickert et al., 2010). Thus, in a period of unemployment, the study contends that individuals with agreeable personality traits will seek online social support.

H3. Individuals with agreeable personality trait respond positively to online social support in a period of unemployment.

Openness

Openness is a personality trait that measures flexibility in individual's imagination, openness to new ideas, culture and experience (Amichai-Hamburger et al., 2010). It reflects the ability to be flexible, tolerant and open-minded. Also, open individuals are liberal, like novelty, focus mainly on practical things and eschewed imagination (Heinström, 2003). According to O'Súilleabháin et al. (2018), openness facilitate ability of an individual to respond to stress in an adaptive manner. In other words, individuals with a high level of openness trait have tendency to withstand and adapt to new stress. As a result, openness correlates positively with stress response. Open individuals respond positively to social support and they tend to reciprocate any emotional support they received (Leary and Hoyle, 2009). Thus:

H4. Individuals with openness personality trait will respond positively to online social support in a period of unemployment.

Extraversion

Extraverts are "outward-turning" enjoy more frequent social interactions, feel energized after spending time with other people. They are also believed to be attention-seekers, easily distracted, and unable to spend time alone. According to the Myers-Briggs Personality Type Indicator (MBPTI), extroverts have more of the following traits: sensing, thinking and judging and less of intuition, feeling and perceiving (Yoo and Gretzel, 2011). Extraverts air their grievances rather than letting them sink or fester. They are believed to enjoy better social support from, electronic networks, religious communities, local communities, rehabilitation groups and other organizations. Because they do not allow the problems to sink in but rather share it in support groups, they are believed to have a better psychological health and are protected against psychological stress. They are more likely to use support forums to discuss personal struggles, and disclose emotions and thoughts pertaining to their struggles than introverts.

H5. Individuals with extraversion personality trait will respond positively to online social support in a period of unemployment.

Online Social Support and Satisfaction

Job satisfaction is the degree to which one is content with their activity, consequently a worker's readiness to perform at an ideal dimension (Hoffman-Miller 2013). Some underlying assumption of Job Satisfaction according to Taye (2018) includes theoretical review, contemporary theories, theories of job satisfaction, types of job satisfaction measurement scale, empirical review and conceptual framework. The antecedence of job satisfaction: Motivation (Sohail et al., 2014; Nyantika et al., 2015), Working environment (Rasiq & Maulabakhsh, 2015; Jain & Kaur, 2014), Employees' salary (Saeed et al., 2013), level of fairness (Saeed et al., 2013), Promotion and Job security (Saeed et al., 2013) and thriving at work and fairness perception. The consequences are financial indicators (Batokic, 2016) and Repeat-purchase intension (Kuo et al., 2013)

Continuous use of Social networks is defined according to how much a user reads or posts, messages, photos, or links, utilizing different channels including cell phones and personal data assistants as well as personal computers (Kim et al., 2010). Some of the factors that precipitate the continuous usage are: creating awareness (Wu et al., 2018), it promotes sharing of lectures (Royall et al., 2017), encourages easy communication (Chen & Liu, 2017; Cheng et al., 2017), it helps to maintain contacts (McLean et al., 2017), easy access to books thereby the cost of purchasing books (Kim & Kim, 2018), It boosts self-esteem (Turel et al., 2018), it helps to improve social and communication skills (Charoensukmongkol & Sasatanun, 2017) and it intensify knowledge (Leonardi, 2017; O' Connor et al., 2016).

H6. Online social support is positively related to satisfaction.
H7. Satisfaction is positively positively related to continuous use

METHODOLOGY

Data for this study was obtained from Nigeria. Nigeria is the largest country in Africa with a population size of about 200 million (InternetWorld Stat, 2018). Unemployment rose from 16.74 million in 2011 to 20.9 million in 2018 (NBS, 2018). Similarly, Facebook subscription rose from 4.3 million in 2011 to 17 million in 2017 (Vanguard, 2012; InternetWorld Stat, 2018). Thus, as unemployment increased, so did the number of Facebook subscription. Survey was administered via face-to-face contact to respondents with focus on those who have lost their jobs or those that are willing to change their jobs. A screening question such as (a) student but looking for part-time job; (b) uunemployed; (c) employed but looking for a better job; and (d) employed and not looking for another job, was used. Out of 3,021 responses received, 19 were removed during data cleaning. Accordingly, 3,002 were used for the data analysis. Similarly, the items for measuring the constructs were obtained from extant studies. As such, items measuring personality traits comprising conscientiousness, neuticism, agreeableness, openness and extraversion were obtained from Yoo and Gretzel (2011); online social support (Chung, 2014); self-disclosure and satisfaction (Kim et al., 2014) and continuous use (Chen, 2014). These items were measured using 7-pointLikert scale. Please see Appendix 1 for the items.

Data Analysis and Results

Linear regression analysis is used to show the linear relationship between a dependent (or response) variable and an independent (or predictor) variable. The linear regression models are of the form:

$$y = b_0 + b_1 + e \tag{1}$$

where Y is the dependent variable; X_i are the independent variables; b_i are the regression coefficients; e is the random error. To test if the regression model significantly fits the data, the study considers the hypothesis: H_0. The regression model does not significantly fit the data; vs; H_1. The regression model significantly fits the data. Also, H_0 is rejected if the p-value is less than or equal to the level of significance

$$y = b_0 + b_1 X$$

Where

$$b_0 = \bar{y} - b_1\bar{x} \quad and \quad b_1 = \frac{\sum xy - \sum x \sum y}{\sum x^2 - (\sum x)^2}$$

b_0= intercept

b_1= slope

x= independent variable

y= dependent variable.

Table 1. Descriptive statistics for unemployment

Descriptive	Frequency	Percentage	Mean	Std. Deviation
Gender			1.49	0.51
Male	1523	50.8		
Female	1475	49.2		
Age			1.97	1.01
18 - 28	1220	40.7		
29 – 31	967	32.2		
32 – 41	553	18.4		
42 – 51	213	7.1		
52 and above	47	1.6		
Marital Status			1.54	0.53
Single	1409	47		
Married	1573	52.4		
Others	20	0.6		
Education			1.69	0.84
High school/diploma	1498	49.9		
Bachelor's degree	1073	35.8		
Master's degree	317	10.6		
Doctorate degree	77	2.6		
Others	35	1.1		

In Table 1, among the participants, male participants (1523=50.8%) are more than the female (1475=49.2%) participants. For gender, the mean and standard deviation was (M=1.49, SD=0.51). Additionally, different age groups participated in the study. Age bracket 18 – 28 was the highest with (1220=40.7%), 29 – 31 account for 29 – 31 (967=32.2%), 32 – 41 (553=18.4%), 42 – 51 (213=7.1%), 52 and above (47=1.6%). The age mean and standard deviation is (M=1.97, SD=1.01). The frequency of single was (1409=47%), married participants excel single and others (1573=52.4%), while others only account for (20=0.6%). The mean and standard deviations of marital status are (M=1.54, SD=0.53). Regarding education, High school/diploma records the highest participants with (1498=49.9%), Bachelor's degree (1073=35.8%), Master's degree (317=10.6%), Doctorate degree (77=2.6%), and others (35=1.1%). The mean and standard deviations of education are (M=1.69, SD=0.84) respectively.

Table 2. Reliability test result

(n=2993)	Mean	Std. Deviation	A	(n=2993)	Mean	Std. Deviation	A
CON1	4.01	0.97	0.82	EXT2	3.71	1.03	0.82
CON2	4.11	0.87	0.82	EXT3	3.69	1.06	0.82
CON3	4.07	0.86	0.82	EXT4	3.83	1.03	0.82
CON4	4.01	0.93	0.82	EXT5	3.69	1.11	0.82
CON5	3.83	1.01	0.82	OSS1	3.63	1.13	0.81
NEU1	2.3	0.90	0.82	OSS2	3.69	1.08	0.81
NEU2	2.05	0.77	0.82	OSS3	3.7	1.07	0.81
NEU3	2.75	1.19	0.83	OSS4	3.66	1.12	0.81
NEU4	2.8	1.20	0.83	OSS5	3.71	1.14	0.81
NEU5	2.82	1.17	0.83	SED1	3.55	1.19	0.81
AGR1	3.86	0.99	0.82	SED2	3.61	1.13	0.81
AGR2	3.94	0.94	0.82	SED3	3.73	1.03	0.81
AGR3	3.97	1.00	0.82	SED4	3.8	1.06	0.81
AGR4	3.78	1.06	0.82	SAT1	3.67	1.12	0.81
AGR5	3.3	1.14	0.82	SAT2	3.81	1.01	0.82
OPE1	3.95	0.95	0.82	SAT3	3.94	0.96	0.82
OPE2	3.88	0.95	0.82	SAT4	4	0.95	0.82
OPE3	3.95	0.95	0.82	SAT5	4.01	0.96	0.82
OPE4	3.88	0.96	0.82	CONT1	3.85	1.01	0.81
OPE5	3.77	1.00	0.82	CONT2	3.9	0.92	0.81
EXT1	3.6	1.11	0.82	CONT3	4.09	0.84	0.82

In Table 2, the study conducted reliability test with SPSS and the Cronbach Alpha test was between 0.81 to 0.83. Alpha calculation is suitable for multiple-items measurement and Alpha result for this study was above the boundary of 0.7 as stipulated by the earlier authors (Tavakol and Dennick, 2011). The study also used SPSS for regression analysis and the main effect for conscientiousness yielded an F ratio of $F(1, 300) = 40.66$, $p<.05$, Neuroticism $F(1, 300) = 0.95$, $p>.05$, agreeableness $F(1, 300) = 70.50$, $p<.05$, openness $F(1, 300) = 84.73$, $p<.05$, extraversion $F(1, 300) = 43.44$, $p<.05$, online social support $F(1, 300) = 52.86$, $p<.05$, satisfaction $F(1, 300) = 85.04$, $p<.05$. To compare group means, the study used Stata to conduct discriminant analysis (Table 3). The result shows that the p-value (0.000) is less than 0.05. The study concludes that there is difference in the group 1 (male) and group2 (female) using the variables marital status, extraversion and there is no difference in the group 1 (male) and group2 (female) using the variables educational status, employment status, conscientiousness, agreeableness, openness, neuroticism, online social support, self-disclosure, satisfaction and continuous use of Facebook. The variables used do not contribute to discriminant function since it is not close to zero. And since p-value (0.000) is less than 0.01, the study can conclude that the corresponding function explain the group membership well (male and female). 57.0% of the group cases were correctly classified while 43.0% were wrongly classified. The study constructed a discriminant score that (1) for detecting the variables marital status, educational status, age, conscientiousness, online social support, self-disclosure, neuroticism, openness, agreeableness, extraversion, and continuous use of Facebook which allows discrimination between male and female and (2) for classifying cases into different groups (Table 4).

Table 3. Test of equality of group means

	Wilks' Lambda	F	df1	df2	Sig.
Marital	0.982	54.337	1	2996	0
Education	1	0.005	1	2996	0.945
Employ	1	0.004	1	2996	0.951
Avegcon	1	0.167	1	2996	0.682
Avegneu	1	0.962	1	2996	0.327
Avegagr	0.999	2.521	1	2996	0.112
Avegope	1	0.223	1	2996	0.637
Avegext	0.998	5.29	1	2996	0.022
Avegoss	1	0.601	1	2996	0.438
Avegsed	0.999	3.822	1	2996	0.051
Avegsat	1	0.085	1	2996	0.77
Avegcont	0.999	1.571	1	2996	0.21

Note: Wilks' Lambda test is to test which variable contribute significance in discriminant function. The closer Wilks' lambda is to 0, the more the variable contributes to the discriminant function. The table also provides a Chi-Square statistic to test the significance of Wilk's Lambda. If the p-value is less than 0.05, the study concludes that the corresponding function explains the group membership well.

Table 4. Classification of group

			Gender	Predicted Group Membership		Total
				1	**2**	
Original	Count	1		827	696	1523
		2		593	882	1475
		Ungrouped cases		1	1	2
	%	1		54.3	45.7	100
		2		40.2	59.8	100
		Ungrouped cases		50	50	100

*57.0% of original grouped cases correctly classified.

Table 5. Hypothesized relationships

Models (OSS)	B	SE	T	p-value	R²	Hypothesis	Confirmation
CON	0.083	0.013	6.4	0.000	0.013	H1	Accepted
NEU	0.011	0.011	0.97	0.330	0.000	H2	Rejected
AGR	0.104	0.012	8.4	0.000	0.023	H3	Accepted
OPE	0.119	0.013	9.2	0.000	0.028	H4	Accepted
EXT	0.299	0.014	20.8	0.000	0.126	H5	Accepted
Models (SAT)							
OSS	0.49	0.022	22.8	0.000	0.148	H6	Accepted
Models (FCU)							
SAT	0.44	0.015	29.2	0.000	0.221	H7	Accepted

*CON: Conscientiousness, NEU: Neuroticism, AGR: Agreeableness, OPE: Openness, EXT: Extraversion,
OSS: Online Social Support, SAT: Satisfaction, FCU: Facebook Continuous Use.
Note: Since Eigen value is small (0.024), the less variance the function explains in the dependent variables.

From Table 5, as p-value (0.000) is less than 0.01. The study concludes that the regression model significantly fits for the data. This implies that 1.31% of the variability in the conscientiousness is explained by online social support. Conscientiousness is positively related to online social support, that is, conscientiousness → online social support (β=0.09, t=6.4, P Value = <.01). Also, since p-value (0.3300) neuroticism is greater than 0.05. The study concludes that the regression model does not significantly fits the data. This implies that 0.03% of the variability in neuroticism is explained by online social support. This result indicates that neuroticism is negatively related to online social support, that is, neuroticism → online social support (β=0.01, t=0.97, P Value = >.05). Regarding agreeableness, the p-value (0.0000) is less than 0.01. The study concludes that the regression model significantly fits the data. This implies that 2.3% of the variability in the agreeableness is explained by online social support. Agreeableness is positively related to online social support, that is, agreeableness → online social support (β=0.10, t=8.4, p-value = <.01). With regards to openness variable, the p-value (0.0000) is less than 0.01. The study concludes that the regression model, significantly fits the data. This implies that 2.75% of the variability in openness is explained by online social support. Openness is positively related to online social support, that is, openness → online social support (β=0.12, t=9.2, P Value = <.01). As shown in

Table 5, extraversion p-value (0.0000) is less than 0.01. The study concludes that the regression model significantly fits the data. This implies that 12.61% of the variability in the extraversion is explained by online social support. Extraversion is positively related to online social support, that is, extraversion → online social support (β=0.30, t=20.8, P Value = <.01). Further, online social support p-value (0.0000) is less than 0.01. The study concludes that the regression model significantly fits the data. This implies that 14.78% of the variability in the online social support is explained by online social support, that is, online social support → satisfaction (β=0.49, t=22.8, P Value = <.01). As shown in Table 5, the p-value of satisfaction (0.0000) is less than 0.01. The study concludes that the regression model significantly fits the data. This implies that 22.09% of the variability in the satisfaction is explained by continuous use. Satisfaction is positively related to continuous use, that is, satisfaction → Facebook continuous use (β=0.44, t=29.2, P Value = <.01). In all the analyses conducted, satisfaction as a predictor of Facebook continuous use has the highest coefficient of determination and it was a little bit below weak in comparison with the threshold of 25% of R^2. Regarding online social support for unemployment, extraversion was the highest predictor. For online social support, satisfaction of the Facebook users was extremely significant while Facebook users' satisfaction exceptionally predicted Facebook continuous use. All the hypotheses proposed were accepted except H2 that had insignificant p-value.

DISCUSSION

Due to the scarcity of studies that address the role of unemployment on an indivdual's personality traits and how it influences their use of social network sites, this study fills this gap by analysing a model that explicates the interrelationships between the unemployed personality traits, online social support and continuous use of Facebook in an emerging market context. Seven hypotheses were proposed for which six were accepted while one was rejected. Thus, conscientiousness, agreeableness, openness and extraversion were all positively related to online social support. Again, online social support demonstrated a positive relationship with satisfaction with the use of facebook while satisfaction also showed a positive relationship with continuous use. Interestingly, the relationshp between neuroticism and online social support was not supported. This finding is in line with extant findings which showed negative relationship between neuroticism and Instant messaging application (Amiel and Sargent, 2004). This finding is one of the most crucial for this study because unemployment exerts social pressure on the individual because of their inability to perform statutory obligations (Raimi et al., 2015), thus leading to depressive thoughts, social withdrawal and disruption of family peace and joy (Brand, 2015).

Theoretically, our study contributes to existing knowledge by explicating how the different personality traits responds to online social support, during the period of unemployment. Majority of the studies on the relationship between personality traits and the use of social networks dwell on general experiences such as students, relationship management (Knnibbe and Luchies, 2013) and coping strategies (Lepri et al., 2016). Thus, the current study extends this body of work to unemployment as a critical social challenge. Furthermore, to the best of our knowledge there is an acute shortage of empirical studies, which examines social media use in an emerging market context in Africa. With this study, our findings shades light on a very challenging social anomie which should be of interest to both policy makers and scholars.

Finally, our study offers many insights to different stakeholders. For instance, administrators and managers of Facebook and other social media platforms can leverage on our findings to optimize the content, particularly job-related advertisements. Nigeria and other African countries are currently facing challenging times in terms of job loss. Therefore, to continue to make these platforms attractive, they need to encourage companies who are hiring to utilize social media channels as advertisement channels.

CONCLUSION

Unemployment affects all the observed temperaments, however, the degree to which they resort to online social support divers. Extraversive individuals are the most prone to resort to online social support. The next is openness. Openness is characterized by originality, independence, and intellectual curiosity. Persons high on the openness scale are full of ideas and values and may be seen by others as intelligent. This also leaves important implications for policy planners and administrators in the developing countries. It has been found that individuals with higher level conscientiousness tend to be more empathetic towards others. Thus, people with high conscientiousness could control, regulate, and direct their impulses at ease and prompt. This finding can further be explained in line with social influence. Thus, social influence shapes people's conscientiousness, thereby influencing people's thought about their social surroundings. Conversely, people with low conscientiousness are dull and often rely on others to control, regulate, and direct their impulse.

Limitation and Future Research

One of the limitations of our study was in the representativeness of the sample. Nigeria currently has about 17 million Facebook subscribers. Thus, 3000 respondents may be unsuitable for a large country like Nigeria. The data was collected in the South Western part of Nigeria which may have neglected the views of users in the South-East, South-South, North-Central, North-East and North-West alike. It is likely that a more representative sample, could offer a different result. Neuroticism normally ranges from high to low, but our study generally lumped them together without identifying these different segments. These results could also affect the interpretation of our result. In spite of these drawbacks, it is believed that this study offers interesting perspectives to the use of Facebook by the unemployed in Nigeria.

REFERENCES

Abitov, I., Gorodetskaya, I., Akbirova, R., & Sibgatullina, L. (2018). Superstitiousness and Paranormal Beliefs of Engineering Students Comparing to Students Majoring in Sciences, Arts and Humanities. *Revista ESPACIOS, 39*(10).

Amichai-Hamburger, Y., & Vinitzky, G. (2010). Social network use and personality. *Computers in Human Behavior, 26*(6), 1289–1295. doi:10.1016/j.chb.2010.03.018

Amiel, T., & Sargent, S. L. (2004). Individual differences in Internet usage motives. *Computers in Human Behavior, 20*(6), 711–726. doi:10.1016/j.chb.2004.09.002

Bogg, T., & Roberts, B. W. (2004). Conscientiousness and Health-Related Behaviours: A Meta-Analysis of the Leading Behavioural Contributors to Mortality. *Psychological Bulletin, 130*(6), 887–919. doi:10.1037/0033-2909.130.6.887 PMID:15535742

Boyce, C. J., Wood, A. M., Daly, M., & Sedikides, C. (2015). Personality change following unemployment. *The Journal of Applied Psychology*, *100*(4), 991–1011. doi:10.1037/a0038647 PMID:25664474

Boyce, C. J., Wood, A. M., & Powdthavee, N. (2013). Is personality fixed? Personality changes as much as "variable" economic factors and more strongly predicts changes to life satisfaction. *Social Indicators Research*, *111*(1), 287–305. doi:10.100711205-012-0006-z

Brand, J. E. (2015). The far-reaching impact of job loss and unemployment. *Annual Review of Sociology*, *41*(1), 359–375. doi:10.1146/annurev-soc-071913-043237 PMID:26336327

Charoensukmongkol, P., & Sasatanun, P. (2017). Social media use for CRM and business performance satisfaction: The moderating roles of social skills and social media sales intensity. *Asia Pac. Manag. Rev.*, *22*(1), 25–34. doi:10.1016/j.apmrv.2016.10.005

Chen, H.-T., & Li, X. (2017). The contribution of mobile social media to social capital and psychological well-being: Examining the role of communicative use, friending and self-disclosure. *Computers in Human Behavior*, *75*, 958–965. doi:10.1016/j.chb.2017.06.011

Chen, Y. F. (2014). See you on Facebook: Exploring influences on Facebook continuous usage. *Behaviour & Information Technology*, *33*(11), 1208–1218. doi:10.1080/0144929X.2013.826737

Cheng, X., Fu, S., & de Vreede, G.-J. (2017). Understanding trust influencing factors in social media communication: A qualitative study. *International Journal of Information Management*, *37*(2), 25–35. doi:10.1016/j.ijinfomgt.2016.11.009

Chung, J. E. (2014). Social networking in online support groups for health: How online social networking benefits patients. *Journal of Health Communication*, *19*(6), 639–659. doi:10.1080/10810730.2012.757396 PMID:23557148

Cohen, S. (2004). Social relationships and health. *The American Psychologist*, *59*(8), 676–684. doi:10.1037/0003-066X.59.8.676 PMID:15554821

Cohen, S., Gottlieb, B., & Underwood, L. (2000). Social relationships and health. In S. Cohen, L. Underwood, & B. Gottlieb (Eds.), *Measuring and intervening in social support* (pp. 3–25). Oxford University Press. doi:10.1093/med:psych/9780195126709.003.0001

Dooley, D., Prause, J., & Ham-Rowbottom, K. (2000). Underemployment and Depression: Longitudinal Relationships. *Journal of Health and Social Behavior*, *41*(4), 421–436. doi:10.2307/2676295 PMID:11198566

Dwan, T., & Ownsworth, T. (2017). *The Big Five personality factors and psychological well-being following stroke: a systematic review*. Academic Press.

Giota, K. G., & Kleftaras, G. (2014). The discriminant value of personality, motivation, and online relationship quality in predicting attraction to online social support on Facebook. *International Journal of Human-Computer Interaction*, *30*(12), 985–994. doi:10.1080/10447318.2014.925770

Goldberg, L. R. (1993). The structure of phenotypic personality traits. *The American Psychologist*, *48*(1), 26–34. doi:10.1037/0003-066X.48.1.26 PMID:8427480

Hassan, A., Zain, Z., & Ajis, M. (2019). Leadership Personality and Social Dis-integration in Somalia. *Asian Research Journal of Arts & Social Sciences*, *8*(3), 1–9. doi:10.9734/arjass/2019/v8i330101

Headey, B. W., Schupp, J., Tucci, I., & Wagner, G. G. (2010). Authentic happiness theory supported by impact of religion on life satisfaction: A longitudinal analysis with data for Germany. *The Journal of Positive Psychology*, *5*(1), 73–82. doi:10.1080/17439760903435232

Heinström, J. (2003). Five personality dimensions and their influence on information behaviour. *Information Research*, *9*(1). Available at http://InformationR.net/ir/9-1/paper165.html

Hooghe, M., Vanhoutte, B., Hardyns, W., & Bircan, T. (2010). Unemployment, inequality, poverty and crime: Spatial distribution patterns of criminal acts in belgium, 2001–06. *British Journal of Criminology*, *51*(1), 1–20. doi:10.1093/bjc/azq067

Hoth, K., Christensen, A., Ehlers, S., Raichle, K., & Lawton, W. (2007). A Longitudinal Examination of Social Support, Agreeableness and Depressive Symptoms in Chronic Kidney Disease. *Journal of Behavioral Medicine*, *30*(1), 69–76. doi:10.100710865-006-9083-2 PMID:17219057

Jain, R., & Kaur, S. (2014). Impact of work environment on job satisfaction. *International Journal of Scientific and Research Publications*, *4*(1), 1–8.

Kanfer, R., Wanberg, C. R., & Kantrowitz, T. M. (2001). Job search and employment: A personality-motivational analysis and meta-analytic review. *The Journal of Applied Psychology*, *86*(5), 837–855. doi:10.1037/0021-9010.86.5.837 PMID:11596801

Kim, J. H., Kim, M. S., & Nam, Y. (2010). An analysis of self- construal's motivations, Facebook use and user satisfaction. *International Journal of Human-Computer Interaction*, *26*(11-12), 1077–1099. doi:10.1080/10447318.2010.516726

Kim, J. Y., Chung, N., & Ahn, K. M. (2014). Why people use social networking services in Korea: The mediating role of self-disclosure on subjective well-being. *Information Development*, *30*(3), 276–287. doi:10.1177/0266666913489894

Kim, N., & Kim, W. (2018). Do your social media lead you to make social deal purchases? Consumer-generated social referrals for sales via social commerce. *International Journal of Information Management*, *39*, 38–48. doi:10.1016/j.ijinfomgt.2017.10.006

Knnibbe, T. J., & Luchies, L. B. (2013). Motivations to use Facebook for new relationships predicts poorer well-being among extraverts but better well-being among introverts. *Journal of Interpersonal Relations, Intergroup Relations and Identity, 6.*

Kuo, Y., Hu, T., & Yang, S. (2013). *Effects of inertia and satisfaction in female online shoppers. In Handbook of Individual Differences in Social Behavior.* Guilford Publications, Inc.

Leonardi, P. M. (2017). The social media revolution: Sharing and learning in the age of leaky knowledge. *Information and Organization*, *27*(1), 47–59. doi:10.1016/j.infoandorg.2017.01.004

Lepri, B., Staiano, J., Shmueli, E., Pianesi, F., & Pentland, A. (2016). The role of personality in shaping social networks and mediating behavioral change. *User Modeling and User-Adapted Interaction*, *26*(2-3), 143–175. doi:10.100711257-016-9173-y

Lowe, J. R., Edmundson, M., & Widiger, T. A. (2009). Assessment of dependency, agreeableness, and their relationship. *Psychological Assessment*, *21*(4), 543–553. doi:10.1037/a0016899 PMID:19947788

McLean, K., Edwards, S., & Morris, H. (2017). Community playgroup social media and parental learning about young children's play. *Computers & Education*, *115*, 201–210. doi:10.1016/j.compedu.2017.08.004

Nyantika, K. D., Kipchumba, K. S., Auka, O. D., & Asienyo, O. B. (2015). Effect of selected motivational factors on the job satisfaction of civil servants within government devolved functions in Nakuru County. *International Journal of Innovation and Applied Studies*, *12*(1), 287–299.

O'Súilleabháin, P., Howard, S., & Hughes, B. (2018). Openness to experience and stress responsivity: An examination of cardiovascular and underlying hemodynamic trajectories within an acute stress exposure. *PLoS One*, *13*(6), e0199221. doi:10.1371/journal.pone.0199221 PMID:29912932

Oguntunde, P. E., Okagbue, H. I., Oguntunde, O. A., Opanuga, A. A., & Oluwatunde, S. J. (2018). Analysis of the inter-relationship between students' first year results and their final graduating grade. *International Journal of Advanced and Applied Sciences*, *5*(10), 1–6. doi:10.21833/ijaas.2018.10.001

Oishi, S., Schimmack, U., Diener, E., Kim-Prieto, C., Scollon, C. N., & Choi, D. (2007). The value-congruence model of memory for emotional experiences: An explanation for cultural and individual differences in emotional self-reports. *Journal of Personality and Social Psychology*, *93*(5), 897–905. doi:10.1037/0022-3514.93.5.897 PMID:17983307

Raimi, L., Akhuemonkhan, I., & Ogunjirin, O. D. (2015). Corporate Social Responsibility and Entrepreneurship (CSRE): Antidotes to poverty, insecurity and underdevelopment in Nigeria. *Social Responsibility Journal*, *11*(1), 56–81. doi:10.1108/SRJ-11-2012-0138

Roberts, B., Hill, L., & Davis, J. P. (2017). How to Change Conscientiousness: The Sociogenic Trait Intervention Model. *Personality Disorders*, *8*(3), 199–205. doi:10.1037/per0000242 PMID:29120219

Roberts, B. W., Kuncel, N. R., Shiner, R., Caspi, A., & Goldberg, L. R. (2007). The power of personality: The comparative validity of personality traits, socioeconomic status, and cognitive ability for predicting important life outcomes. *Perspectives on Psychological Science*, *2*(4), 313–345. doi:10.1111/j.1745-6916.2007.00047.x PMID:26151971

Roberts, B. W., Walton, K. E., & Viechtbauer, W. (2006). Patterns of mean-level change in personality traits across the life course: A meta-analysis of longitudinal studies. *Psychological Bulletin*, *132*(1), 1–25. doi:10.1037/0033-2909.132.1.1 PMID:16435954

Royall, J., Isyagi, M. M., Iliyasu, Y., Lukande, R., & Vuhahula, E. (2017). From Access to collaboration: Four African Pathologists Profile Their Use of the Internet and Social Media. *Clinics in Laboratory Medicine*, *10*(5). PMID:29412885

Saeed, R., Lodhi, N. R., Iqbal, A., Nayyad, H. H., Mussawar, S., & Yaseen, S. (2013). Factors influencing job satisfaction of employees in telecom sector of Pakistan. *Middle East Journal of Scientific Research*, *16*(11), 1476–1482.

Sedikides, C., & Gregg, A. P. (2003). Portraits of the self. In M. A. Hogg & J. Cooper (Eds.), *Sage handbook of social psychology* (pp. 110–138). Sage.

Siwach, G. (2018). Unemployment shocks for individuals on the margin: Exploring recidivism effects. *Labour Economics*, *52*, 231–244. doi:10.1016/j.labeco.2018.02.001

Sohail, R. S., Saleem, S., Ansar, S., & Azeem, M, A. (2014). Effect of Work Motivation and Organizational Commitment on Job Satisfaction: (A Case of Education Industry in Pakistan). *Global Journal of Management and Business Research*, *14*(6).

Song, Z., Foo, M. D., Uy, M. A., & Sun, S. (2011). Unraveling the daily stress crossover between unemployed individuals and their employed spouses. *The Journal of Applied Psychology*, *96*(1), 151–168. doi:10.1037/a0021035 PMID:20919793

Swickert, R., Hittner, J., & Foster, A. (2010). Big Five traits interact to predict perceived social support. *Personality and Individual Differences*, *48*(6), 736–741. doi:10.1016/j.paid.2010.01.018

Tavakol, M., & Dennick, R. (2011). Making sense of Cronbach's alpha. *International Journal of Medical Education*, *2*, 53–55. doi:10.5116/ijme.4dfb.8dfd PMID:28029643

Toegel, G., & Barsoux, J. L. (2012). How to become a better leader. *MIT Sloan Management Review*, *53*(3), 51–60.

Turel, O., Brevers, D., & Bechara, A. (2018). Time distortion when users at-risk for social media addiction engage in non-social media tasks. *Journal of Psychiatric Research*, *97*, 84–88. doi:10.1016/j.jpsychires.2017.11.014 PMID:29220826

Van den Akker, A. L., Deković, M., Asscher, J., & Prinzie, P. (2014). Mean-level personality development across childhood and adolescence: A temporary defiance of the maturity principle and bidirectional associations with parenting. *Journal of Personality and Social Psychology*, *107*(4), 736–750. doi:10.1037/a0037248 PMID:25133720

Waters, L., & Moore, K. (2002). Self-Esteem, Appraisal and Coping: A Comparison of Unemployed and Re-Employed People. *Journal of Organizational Behavior*, *23*(5), 593–604. doi:10.1002/job.156

Weisberg, C. G. (2011). De Young, J.B. Hirsh (2011) Gender differences in personality across the ten aspects of the Big Five. *Frontiers in Personality Science and Individual Differences*, *2*, 178. PMID:21866227

Wu, Y., Xie, L., Huang, S. L., Li, P., Yuan, Z., & Liu, W. (2018). Using social media to strengthen public awareness of wildlife conservation. *Ocean and Coastal Management*, *153*, 76–83. doi:10.1016/j.ocecoaman.2017.12.010

Yoo, K. H., & Gretzel, U. (2011). Influence of personality on travel-related consumer-generated media creation. *Computers in Human Behavior*, *27*(2), 609–621. doi:10.1016/j.chb.2010.05.002

This research was previously published in the International Journal of E-Adoption (IJEA), 13(1); pages 56-72, copyright year 2021 by IGI Publishing (an imprint of IGI Global).

APPENDIX: EXAMPLES

Table 6. Conscientiousness (Yoo and Gretzel, 2011)

CON1	I carry out my plans
CON2	I pay attention to details
CON3	I am always prepared
CON4	I make plans and stick to them
CON5	I am exacting in my work
Neuroticism (Yoo and Gretzel, 2011)	
NEU1	I get stressed out easily
NEU2	I worry about things
NEU3	I fear for the worst
NEU4	I am filled with doubts about things
NEU5	I panic easily
Agreeableness (Yoo and Gretzel, 2011)	
AGR1	I sympathize with others' feelings
AGR2	I am concerned about others
AGR3	I respect others
AGR4	I believe that others have good intentions
AGR5	I trust what people say
Openness (Yoo and Gretzel, 2011)	
OPE1	I get excited by new ideas
OPE2	I enjoy thinking about things
OPE3	I enjoy hearing new ideas
OPE4	I enjoy looking for a deeper meaning in things
OPE5	I have a vivid imagination
Extraversion (Yoo and Gretzel, 2011)	
EXT1	I talk a lot to different people at parties
EXT2	I feel comfortable around people
EXT3	I start conversations
EXT4	I make friends easily
EXT5	I don't mind being the center of attention

Table 7. Online social support (Chung, 2014)

OSS1	I use Facebook to gather information about job opportunities
OSS2	I use Facebook to find out things I need about job opportunities
OSS3	I use Facebook to look for information I need about job opportunities
OSS4	I use Facebook to talk to a knowledgeable individual about job opportunities
OSS5	I use Facebook to get answers to specific questions about job opportunities

Table 8. Self-disclosure (Kim, Chung and Ahn, 2014)

SED1	I would like to use Facebook to let my life and news be known to others
SED2	I would like to use Facebook to share my unemployment experience
SED3	I would like to use Facebook to express my personality with my friends and my friend of friends
SED4	I would like to use Facebook to leave a record with photos and emoticon and show them to others

Table 9. Satisfaction (Kim, Chung and Ahn, 2014)

SAT1	I am satisfied with what I achieve at work
SAT1	I feel good at work
SAT1	I am satisfied with my use of Facebook
SAT1	I will keep using Facebook
SAT1	I will recommend people around me to use Facebook

Table 10. Continuous use (Chen, 2014)

FCU1	I will continue to use Facebook for my personal needs
FCU2	Using Facebook is something I would like to do to seek social support
FCU3	I see myself continuing to use Facebook for various reasons, such as getting close to others, and so on

Chapter 37
The Effect of Social Networks on Relationships Outside the Network

Tami Seifert

Kibbutzim College of Education, Technology, and the Arts, Israel

Idit Miara

Kibbutzim College of Education, Technology, and the Arts, Israel

ABSTRACT

This chapter examines the impact of three different aspects of romantic discourse on social networks: romance, identity, and privacy. Qualitative research focused on the influence of the social networks on the opinions and interpersonal behavior of 11 single academics, aged 30-45 years old, men and women who used Facebook as a means for meeting potential romantic partners. The research employed semi-structured in-depth interviews to elicit qualitative data. Results indicate that an intimate, romantic setting cannot exist on the social network. Most users enhanced their identity in order to appear more attractive online. Most of the interviewees clearly felt that they needed to control the exposure of their personal details, and there was a clear indication that privacy does not exist online: it seems to be impossible to limit exposure of the published contents to specific selected audiences. Online romantic relationships are a metonymy for rapidly changing values and social norms in a dynamic global reality.

INTRODUCTION

Technological developments have an indelible impact on the society in which we live, and their influence shapes new norms and rules. The Internet is seen as a world in which new friendships and support networks are formed, so that the user feels involved and supported. Nevertheless, this world often creates a fantastic illusion, and participants may feel a sense of alienation and loneliness.

DOI: 10.4018/978-1-6684-6307-9.ch037

The dynamics and interactions on social networks (SNs) create a new and varied world of online dating sites and "romantic" encounters. SNs have altered their original function and because of their unique features they have been used to form various types of interpersonal relations. Facebook is open to a community of users and yet it can provide the individual user with a sense of anonymity and invisibility, in other words it can seemingly maintain the user's privacy (Cooper & Sportolari, 1997).

The present study investigated how the virtual world in general and SNs in particular influence romantic interactions and interpersonal behavioral norms outside the network. The research focused on Facebook as a SN that allows the formation of social relationships between couples and investigated the opinions about the existence of romance and privacy in SNs and how SNs influence romantic relationships and social norms outside the network.

Two main questions were derived from this topic to underpin the research:

1. Which characteristics are reported by the interviewees and expressed in their Facebook texts as part of their romantic discourse in encounters between couples?
2. Do the interviewees think that the romantic discourse on Facebook influences romantic discourse outside Facebook and if so, how?

REVIEW OF RELEVANT LITERATURE

Romantic Relationships on the Internet

The last decade has witnessed a revolution in the ways that singles meet other singles. In the "era of isolation", the Internet offers displays of a wide array of eligible single men and women, allowing the user to form romantic encounters and helping to break through gender norms and to form new rules for dating.

The Creation of Romantic Relationships on the Net

The SNs help users to create a self-image (DeVito, Birnholtz & Hancock, 2017; Rettberg, 2017). Consequently, although the romantic connections acquired on the net may be intensive, this does not necessarily testify to any genuine reality. Couple relations on the net often create a fantasy for the user (Mendelson & Papacharissi, 2010). The probability that two people meet on the net is insufficient to ensure that a relationship will be formed. However, geographical space is reduced on the net and this sense of geographical vicinity combined with imagination can help two partners to develop a relationship (Mayers, 1993; Halpern, Katz & Carril, 2017).

The feeling created as a result of the use of the Internet as a tool for acquaintance and to establish a couple relationship is frequently ambivalence. Although romance is usually associated with love and leisure the romantic relationship usually becomes commercialized and practical, contributing to its endurance. Network users today are usually individual, independent persons who seek self-realization (Illouz, 1997). They choose and evaluate their partners through technological means, thus, creating a new situation. This situation allows them to get to know each other through calm conversation at a time when it is suitable and comfortable for both partners. Of course, this conversation lacks the characteristics of normative discourse including meaningful components such as: facial expressions, body language etc.

The development of face-to-face relationships undergoes metamorphosis: from the initial encounter, based on vicinity in space and physical attraction, to the revelation of the potential partner's image and self-exposure (Illouz, 1997). In contrast the development of romantic relationships on the Internet space undergoes an opposite process – while the close relations formed in the initial conversations on chats and/or on Internet pages are often deep, personal and intimate, in face-to-face relationships, physical interaction determines much of the relationship and this intensive exposure may lead to sexual consequences and renewed future search (Wysocki, 1998).

Motives for Couple Relations on Social Networks

In the Internet era, a new persona is created, in a new method for making acquaintances with several characteristics: anonymity and discretion; invisibility; escape, intimacy (Cooper & Sportolari, 1997) and imagination and difference (Amichai-Hamburger & Ben-Artzi, 2000). As a dating site, the SN creates a large alternative space for the shy and unconfident user that is less restricted. This world opens up a new window, facilitating the realization of the desire and ability to become involved. Additionally, the communications media and the technological space apparently protects the user: he/she is kept safe in their interaction with the other user since they are able to gain access to and alter their answers online. This differs from face-to-face dialogs which are conducted as oral "ping-pong" with no possibility to alter answers after they have been voiced (Amichai-Hamburger & Ben-Artzi, 2000). This process alters the acquisition of social observation and dynamic social norms are created outside the technological space (Cooper, McLoughlin & Campbell, 2000). The network user acts in a new world and can create an alternative and different identity than that which he/she holds in human reality.

Activity on the Net: Fictive Identity or Construction of a New Self?

Many philosophers and theorists have discussed the concept of the "self". Kohut (1971) defined the self as a collection of feelings, thoughts, images and ideas that the individual grants to himself/herself. Goffman (1980) claimed that we shape our self-identity according to the situation in which we find ourselves. Invisibility on the Internet has important consequences. It enhances the user's experience of success and self-evaluation (Barak, 2006). However, on the Internet the falsification of identities and unreliable behavior is accepted and even becomes a regular practice. Psychologists estimate that this re-construction of identity allow the user to shape their personality (Turkle, 1995). The persona that appears on the Internet covers itself with masks and different identities, it tries out and examines several identities until the stage when one of the identities becomes an integral and indivisible part of the real self that exists outside the net (Turkle, 1995). Additionally, the use of the network and the time spent on it create a familiarity with a better self and ability to cope with it. Thus, the user is afforded a different experience and a more intelligent ability to examine the "self" (Mckenna & Bargh, 2000). The use of the network exposes aspects of the user's personality that would not be exposed outside this world (Suler, 2004). This manner of activity has been broadened by the world of dating sites, which allows a type of invisibility and self-branding on SNs. One of the networks that has been a trailblazer in this field is a Facebook profile.

FACEBOOK

Facebook: The Privacy Dilemma

In the past, networks had a common character and concept. Today, the SNs have a decentralized character adapted to the individuals who use the network and their character (Wellman, 2003). The depth of connections and relationships on the network vary from what are known as "weak ties" to "strong ties" The substance of the relationships and their strength are defined according to the level of several parameters: (1) intimacy; (2) closeness; (3) length of acquaintance (Granovetter, 1973). It was found that closeness is the main dimension that contributes significantly to the strength of the contact.

The SNs were established in order to reinforce connections existing on the net. Recent research suggests that these networks help to create new connections and opportunities. Relations on the SN can reach a high level of intimacy and familiarity. Continuity is needed following the initial acquaintance on the Internet space to sustain a subsequent relationship between the two network users (Granovetter, 1973). Facebook users will try to find new persons in order to empower their social world in a way that they would not be able to do in actual reality.

Dating Sites

In the last decade, the world of dating sites and ANs has increased its volume and become an integral part of making acquaintances in the modern era. Search engines and SNs help singles to find their partners (Whitty & Carr, 2006). The dating sites in fact fulfill two main purposes: (1) finding romantic contacts for the long-term with a view to marriage and bringing children into the world and; (2) finding romantic sexual partners for short-term relationships for entertainment, pleasure and amusement. The sorting process that the user undergoes is comparatively simple in comparison to that which the prospective dater undergoes outside the Internet. Moreover, the abundant supply of potential partners reaches the surfer in a convenient ready-made package and they just have to leaf through forwards and backwards until they find a suitable candidate (Ben-Ze'ev, 2004).

In studies conducted in the USA, it was found that most users on the dating sites are between ages 30-49. They are mostly academics and their income is above average with greater preponderance of male users (Whitty & Carr, 2006). Studies have found that women and people with lower level education perceive the Internet as an unsafe environment, that can be dangerous and violent. Falsification of many details of the personae of users on these sites is seen by this population as fraudulent and unreliable (Shade, 2002).

In the virtual world, there are other parameters by which the potential partner can be evaluated: writing style, recklessness, spelling mistakes, imagination, creativity, nicknames, pictures etc. The Internet users try to present themselves as attractive and in demand (Connolly, Palmer, Barton, & Kirwan, 2016). It was found that men describing their personality will focus on their personality traits, while women focus on their external appearance. Women will describe themselves as: young, slim, sexy while men describe themselves as romantic and having a good sense of humor (Ben Ze'ev, 2004).

Most of the population that surfs on dating sites does so in order to find a partner for relations outside the network. Relationships that begin on the network, eventually lead to a face-to-face meeting. In some of the cases the users experience disappointment regarding the appearance of the partner during the meeting outside the technological space. Thus, falsification of identity on the net will mostly be expressed by users who do not aspire to form long-term relationships and this form of activity serves them for momentary entertainment and pleasure (Connolly, Palmer, Barton, & Kirwan, 2016). The situation is problematic since the two people do not always have the same goal, meaning that their purpose for using the network may be different. Research has also shown that there are often gaps between the desired characteristics of the partner that the surfer chooses and their prospective partner's requirements (Ben-Ze'ev, 2004).

Facebook: A Platform for Acquaintance Where Identity and Relationships Can Be Built in the Digital Space and Beyond It

Facebook brands those who use it and helps them to construct identities and profiles. In fact, it is a marketing tool for those who use it, the individuals that use the site to create and construct identities. In other words, identity-making is a public process that also includes the construction of the "self" by a person and by the others (Zhao, 2006). The users of the network clothe themselves in different online images forming a dichotomy with their real-life identities beyond the Internet space (Turkle, 1995). This space actually helps them to bypass limitations that exist in face-to-face encounters.

Facebook is actually the ideal environment to examine the construction of identity in an online environment, where relationships are anchored in online communities. It was found that in online dating there is an expectation that users will also engage in structuring identity and will adopt strategies of self-presentation that will help them to protect their anonymity (Connolly, Palmer, Barton, & Kirwan, 2016). This means that the individuals on Facebook will adopt a structured self and not necessarily their real self, which remains hidden. Thus, Facebook users are likely to emphasize things or create an exaggerated form of their possible self, appropriate for the accepted, preferred stereotype outside the online network. In contrast to networks that offer opportunities for dating on the net for those who search solely for momentary romantic relationships, Facebook allows the expansion of existing relationships and acts as an alternative for meeting new acquaintances and the establishment of a romantic couple relationship on the network that will continue outside the network (Zhao, Grasmuck & Martin, 2008). By its very structure, and special profile Facebook has created unique features for the construction of identities. Different goals have developed for identity construction offering different characteristics for its users. Facebook has become a known brand and is marketed today as a broad accessible and available tool for a global audience. Beyond its existence as an online network it has helped to develop different ethical rules that widely influence the dating world and couple hood.

METHODOLOGY

The research aimed to investigate the influence of SNs in general, and specifically of Facebook on couple relationships outside the network.

RESEARCH DESIGN

The research was a qualitative-phenomenological study, dealing with the correlation between participants' external reality, their thinking and feelings and their subjective inner world (Denzin & Lincoln,

1994). The choice of qualitative research enabled the researchers to study how the world of singles' couples is structured in Facebook discourse and the implications of this world on relationships outside the network. Qualitative research aspires to conduct deep investigation into the substance of the studied phenomenon, with an emphasis on the respondents' experiences (Denzin & Lincoln, 1994). Using this methodology, it was possible to elicit and understand the interviewees' meanings and provide interpretation for the experience of couple hood on Facebook and to understand the influence of this experience outside the network.

Sample and Sampling Procedure

The sample in this study was a "convenience sample" and included 11 male and female singles aged between 30-45 years in Israel. They expressed their consent to participate in the research. In order to attain maximum diversity, interviewees were selected from different occupational fields and different geographical regions of Israel (Patton, 1990). The respondents participated in Facebook as a platform on which they could make romantic acquaintances. The interviews were conducted in person at the respondents' homes.

TOOLS USED FOR THE STUDY

A semi-structured in-depth interview (Smith, 1995) specially created for the research by the researchers was used to collect the singles' experiences. The singles were interviewed in person about their activities on Facebook as a platform on which they could make romantic acquaintances. Interview guidelines were employed including a list of questions that served as a tool to remember to focus on the studied subject, in content and to thoroughly exhaust the participants' personal experiences (Patton, 1990). The questions relied on the fact that the Facebook reality is structured by the participants, and the responses to the questions were used to collect data and construct central generalizations that could be transformed into a theoretical attitude (Smith, 1995). The interview encompassed several main areas of interest: (1) the perception of romance, the influence of couple relations on the network on the construction and/or extinction of romance; (2) the meaning and significance of the creation of an identity on the network on the couple's relationship; (3) the Facebook privacy dilemma.

DATA ANALYSIS

The interviews were tape-recorded with the respondents' consent and transcribed. Data analysis was performed by clearly defining the units of analysis and constructing a hierarchy of the repeated contents and themes in the narrative texts, in an attempt to compose a theoretical model (Sabar Ben-Yehoshua, 2001). Qualitative analysis was conducted in stages: the first stage involved repeated holistic readings of all the interviews until the researchers felt that they were familiar with the collected materials. The second stage involved content analysis of the interviews according to "field grounded theory" (Glaser & Strauss, 1967) and main themes and categories were identified. At the third stage the categories were organized into themes with common subjects by relating to the respondents' linguistic elements and images (Lincoln & Guba, 1985). At the last stage, the researchers examined whether there were connections between the different themes through focus and comparison between the contents.

FINDINGS

Three main themes emerged from the interviews: romance, identity and privacy. Categories were derived from these themes. The themes were investigated and received responses from the qualitative interviews. The names of the interviewees reported in the findings are fictive to ensure their anonymity and privacy, for example P1, P2 or P3.

Romance on the Net: Couple or Individual

A central theme that emerged from the interviewees' narratives was their consideration for romance as part of a relationship. They reported that at each state when an intimate situation was created, romance developed. They felt that romance was lacking in SNs. They noted that: physical contact, speech and gestures exchanged between couples create an intimate situation that cannot exist in general on the Internet and in particular on Facebook. It appears from the interviewees' responses that conversations on the Internet are initial discourse that permits the individual to get to know basic identifying details of a prospective partner as a preparation for a meeting outside the Internet.

Intimacy and Privacy in a Romantic Online Conversation

When the interviewees talked about romance they invariably spoke about "intimacy". For most of the interviewees intimacy is formed in a quiet space. A complex situation is created between a couple that meet and get to know each other. According to the interviewees' responses, the intimacy component must exist so that romance can develop. In this manner, intimate cognizance becomes a partnership with someone who is known and familiar. In intimate situations symbiosis forms, allowing the "self" to be shared and bond with parts of the other. Asked about romance on the network, P1 expressed amazement:

I don't think that there is romance on the network. The relationship becomes something that is between interpersonal and publicity, I experience romance when something is intimate. If I make a contact in order to share, that's not romantic.

Thus, intimacy is formed from shared activity between partners who continue romantic discourse in confidentiality. P7 described her first meeting with her partner:

two people who do things together, going to the beach together ... holding hands, intimate things, things that you do not share with others, something personal that is not exposed.

Such intimacy was seen as impossible on the network by interviewees who think that it is only possible to perform romantic gestures on the network. P2 thought that the lack of intimacy would harm absolute romance as he sees it:

It's as though someone is making a party or someone proposes marriage during a football game, there are people who see this as something romantic, to propose marriage in front of the whole world. But it's not intimate. There can [only] be romantic gestures on the Internet.

Most of the interviewees emphasized the issue of touch, and giving and taking as conditions for the creation of romance without which romance could not exist. Intimacy was in their opinion created in a real meeting between two people who create reciprocal discourse between them and communication with special qualities.

Difficulties Involved in Creating a Romance on the Network

When the interviewees were asked to define romance, most of them gave a clear definition that included intimacy, shared gestures and containment. Nevertheless, the interviewees were hesitant to declare that romance existed on the network. They felt that there could be no romance without conversation, a face-to-face meeting and gestures of giving and reciprocity between a couple. P8 argued that it was impossible to realize a romantic relationship in the virtual space of the network:

I think that there is no true romance on the network. There is gesturing when one person writes to another, personal matters and personal greetings in posts. [But] I think that it is far more romantic to receive this in a note and not written in the post ...in my opinion the network serves to publish romantic gestures. It's like seeing pictures of diners in a restaurant menu and not really eating the meal.

In her interview, P9 opposed the use of the networks. She did not see the use of technology as an alternative for romantic relationships. P9 found it difficult to understand why she should conduct such a relationship on the network. She told us that she found herself outside the game because she did not approve of such relations. For her, romance did not and could not exist on the Internet:

I am against it, it's shocking, I personally do not like it because there is no courting here and no investment by the man in what is known as romance, it's only to make the initial contact ...when a man invests in me, courts me, invites me for a date, or meals [that can be romantic].

In contrast to P9, P4 does not believe in romantic communication on the network in general, but believes that it can exist to some extent. The network can be used for interpersonal interaction after a continuous period of relations between a couple, and P4 indicates that the network could help to sustain the relationship:

I think that if it takes place let us say after the contact is already established and they already met, for example if they have been going out together for a year, then I think it is personal, even if it's written correspondence.

Although written correspondence may be created after a relationship is established, P4 still does not believe in romantic correspondence on a SN:

there is no romance on the network, it is all shallow communication ... I think it is just a tool for initial acquaintance.

Unlike the other interviewees, P5 found that using the network was effective and efficient. The network opened a window and many possibilities for the user. P5 did not see the Internet as a place where romance developed, however she thought that the network offered many possibilities for meeting people:

I think it's wonderful, because not everyone has ways for meeting people and the network provides them with possibilities they did not otherwise have. In other times you had to go to a club or seek a match through family or friends. Today there are more possibilities on the Internet and that is amazing. Nevertheless, it is not suitable for everyone because there are some who get confused by such a large choice, and there are those who are more stable who are satisfied with what they found on the network and continue on to their real lives.

The evidence from most of the interviewees seems to indicate that there is no romance on the Internet. Romance is seen as created in meetings outside the network. The dialogs on the network provide a springboard from which to begin the relationship and as a basis for getting to know the other person. P4 explained:

[its] just a springboard to form something that will be continued afterwards in a meeting or telephone call.

The interviewees indicated that romance cannot be expressed in a shared space. One of them (P9) thought that her reservation regarding romance on the network was because she had been born and educated during the 1980s, when there was not much exposure to technology, differing from the experience of those who were born into the technological world.

There are some girls who are thrilled when they are proposed marriage and they receive 1000 likes ... I think romance is more personal and private ... perhaps those who did not grow up with the Internet relate to this as something less natural than those who grew up with it.

Initial Encounters on the Network: "Hi, Would You Like to Get to Know Me?"

Most of the interviewees intimated that romantic discourse only exists on the network at the very beginning, in order to make the initial acquaintance. P10 noted:

On the dating sites of the network it is just to make an acquaintance, not for deep conversations, and that's where a decision is made whether to get to get to know someone in more depth or not.

P7 told us:

I went into the site but didn't have any romantic discourse, only exchange of general details, a first dialog that is meant to get to know them, for example what our hobbies are.

Like those interviewees noted above P4 described her conversation on the Internet as the use of a tool to meet her future partner. She told us that she received initial details concerning the partner in the correspondence on the network, but that she had still not managed to form a real connection with someone she met on a SN. She felt that the technological screen formed a wedge between her and her partner:

The network is like a screen, it's not something real unless you channel this just for something real – to meet up ... and that's why I have never met someone new through the network.

In contrast to P4, P2 noted the advantages of a conversation on the network. He indicated that romantic correspondence on the network is advantageous for someone who is introverted and finds it difficult to express their feelings. It offers various opportunities to become acquainted with women with whom they would not talk without the use of Internet. Nevertheless, like P4, P2 only used Facebook for initial acquaintance: *On the Internet it's more a matter of initial meeting and outside the network it's something more concrete and serious*, and he added:

I wasn't good at chatting up girls in person, it requires far more courage to start to talk with a girl in a pub or discotheque ...it's far easier to send a "Hi" or something like that to a thousand girls who live in your vicinity and if ten percent answer you that is already a good start ... first you say "hi" and then you introduce yourself... and tell them something about yourself; 'I live alone ... I have my own apartment ... I am single etc. ... I am looking for something serious, or a one-night stand or something else ... and then she says yes ... and that's how the Internet conversation begins.

In contrast to most of the other interviewees, P3's conversation on Facebook did not only include initial acquaintance with the potential partner. She reported deep conversations that contained experiences and emotions that helped her to get to know her partner:

Yes, there was a guy who contacted me on the site and sent me a message: 'Hi, how are you doing? I'd like to get to know you'. I felt it was a compliment and sent him a message: 'Yes, I'd be happy to get to know you', and that was followed by a ping-pong of questions: where are you from, what do you do? etc. and very quickly we went on to a "chat" conversation and then it became a real conversation through the network and that quickly advanced.

IDENTITY ON THE NETWORK

The interviewees described their identities and the ways in which they were reflected on the dating sites and on the network. It seemed from their evidence that the description of their identity on the network differs from their real identity outside the network. Most of them published selective details for their image on the network.

"If Someone Looks at Me from Behind They Won't Know Who I Am": Basic Identity

Most of the interviewees who were asked to describe how they characterize their identity on Facebook, told us that they only publish basic information, detailing their occupation. Thus, too the pictures that they publish on their profile are selective and displayed only to friends on Facebook. P2 explained:

First of all you being with your personal details, for security reasons you are also prohibited from putting too many personal details on Facebook. You only put in the relevant details ... for example if you went to a low level school you wouldn't mention that ...just like you wouldn't put a place of work that had fired you into your Curriculum Vitae ... I think that finding work and finding a girl are the same thing.

P4 reinforced the words of other interviewees, saying that the construction of a Facebook profile is an important parameter in one's career. She added that Facebook is an accessible means, in which work partners are exposed to pictures and posts that are published there:

It is not always advantageous ... my family has a completely different political opinion so I don't always share discussions with them – on Facebook I am even more cautious, sometimes I prefer not to upload a picture from family events which are not fitting for the character of my friends from college or similar matters ... as if I make a selection and it's not always spontaneous.

Many of the interviewees saw the construction of their initial profile on Facebook as something laconic, without any imagination and providing basic information about their identity. P5 reinforced the words of P2:

I have a Facebook profile that I built from my picture, first and family names and my professional status, where I studied and what my profession is. Most of the details are rather dry ... my identity is far more interesting and complex than appears on the network. I am more reserved and closed on the network.

It seems that the image that the interviewees present on Facebook is not identical to their real identity. The Facebook image is a fantasy and presents facets of their personality that they want to present. P8 talked about his Facebook profile:

I think that it only partially resembles [my identity] since I haven't really participated in the activity for a long time. Let's suppose that I mark likes for some pictures or posts of others, from whom I can perhaps learn something about my opinions but in general it is far from reality. On Facebook I am quite passive and what others publish doesn't really interest me. If I mark likes for friends on the network this is mainly to be considered "a good guy" unless it is something that somebody from my close circle publishes, then I relate to it more seriously and give likes intentionally.

P3 feels that she can choose to present her identity on the network as she wishes. This provides her with confidence as she can choose which details will appear on her profile. She feels that she does not need to expose intimate information that she does not want to share with her network friends:

It gives me confidence since it allows me to express my opinion on subjects that are raised there, it's another platform that creates an experience of identity, where I can expose things and upload pictures from the experiences that occur around me.

The Privacy Dilemma

When the interviewees spoke about privacy, their main theme was their reluctance to share things. The interviewees testified that the right to privacy allows them to act in their private space without exposure to other people. They feel that privacy is built through their ability to selectively choose the details that they decide to expose. Most of the interviewees claimed that there is no privacy on the network. The use of the network was seen by them as an intrusion into their personal world. It seems that most of the interviewees feel that the collaborative element of the SNs clashes with what they understand by the term "privacy". Yet, their participation in SNs stems from their understanding that they are an integral part of the technological circle.

Privacy: Considerations for Controlling Exposure

For some of the interviewees privacy means the ability to control their personal space, where they can determine the rules of the game. P7 related to her desire to expose details of her life. She described "privacy" as *something of yours that you do not wish to expose to everyone … daily matters that you don't want to share.*

Like other interviewees, P6 related to the word "exposure", which she included as part of her consideration of the term "privacy". She related to the component of "perfection". P6 claimed that exposure of details of her life is influenced by the desire to show an image of perfection to her target audience on the network:

In principle, it means not exposing my feelings … the less good things. I think that when things are just perfect then there are less filters and when they are less perfect then more care is taken to maintain privacy.

The Network Exposes: Privacy Is Invaded

The interviewees were in a state of dilemma and confusion regarding the definition of the term "privacy" on the net.

You can maintain privacy on the network but you have to be on the alert all the time. Let's say if you publish a post on the iPhone there was a possibility that it would also publish your location, so I closed that possibility. Let's say that yesterday I wanted to note that I was in Tel Aviv, but then I thought, I have lots of friends in Tel Aviv and perhaps they would like to meet me and I wasn't so available for that. If I upload a picture then I flow with that … those are matters of principle for me. For example when there are articles on a book that I read that I thought of publishing, but then I thought that my family might be hurt by them so I didn't publish them, in other words, that relates more to opinions and attitudes.

Like P4, P7 also considered aspects of exposure on the network. P4 spoke about conflicts and dilemmas when she used the network. She described a situation of deliberation when a gap formed between her desire to share something on the network and her fear that her privacy would be infringed in her world. She spoke about a process that the user undergoes before publishing contents on the network.

There can't be any privacy on the network because the moment that the sites and Facebook began there is no privacy. There are things that you can expose or not expose and at the moment everyone is exposed. If you are not exposed on Facebook then you are exposed on your mobile phone ...Yes, if a picture is too exposed I block it or delete it completely. Sometimes for example I leave a picture that I took on my mobile phone and don't publish it.

P11 supported her words, adding:

There may be a sense of privacy but in practice there is no privacy, there is always someone who will analyze the data that you publish on the network and use it.

It seems from P11's words that exposure of personal contents stimulates subjective interpretation of the published contents. This interpretation is dangerous for the publishing person, if the message that they intended to impart was not understood when the contents are shared.

Publishing Contents on the Network: I Am Aware That I Am Exposed

The interviewees were asked to express their feelings concerning their knowledge that others were "nitpicking" whatever they put on their Facebook accounts. Like P4, so too P6 felt that the Facebook contents took on a collaborative dimension. This collaboration meant that the contents were visible to and open to criticism by others. P6 told us that she would choose not to publish pictures on Facebook that she did not wish to expose to a wide public, but rather upload them on to other SNs that maintain the privacy of the people photographed. P5 claimed that the problem created in the framework known as Facebook was the shared friends circle of a member telling something to another member. In this manner, their pictures would be exposed to a broad audience that she was not willing to share this information with. P6 described this:

It doesn't bother me and it doesn't interest me, I take into account that everything that I upload becomes public and I have no control of how it will look, what they will say or remark ... [but] when Tamar was born I asked everyone not to upload her photographs on Facebook ...I felt that something that this was something that was exclusively mine and not everyone should share in this ...until today I won't upload her pictures.

P11 explained that he often encountered dilemmas when he published contents on the network. He examined the materials that he wanted to upload and deliberated before leaving them for a continuous period:

It is not something private for me, sometimes I had opinions about an article that I decided to publish and then I took it down because I had second thoughts about the subject and so I deleted it. ...I'm not sure if I could say that I was afraid exactly ...like when we sometimes say something that should not be said and then rethink things and perhaps wait before saying it.

P1 supported what the other interviewees had noted. He understood that the information that he chose to publish on the network exposed information from his private life. In his opinion, the contents were open to the use of a wide community to whom he published the information. His words intimate that putting contents on the net should be considered selectively. P1 noted contents that he preferred to delete because of their implications:

I made a photographs competition together with a group of friends on the network and the pictures were silly, in retrospect I regret that they were published ...: so no, today I would not do that, I have matured, it has implications ...you have to sort things before uploading them onto the network. It actually reflects who we are.

On the other hand, he said that there was a tremendous advantage in sharing:

Everyone can know what the consequences will be, the question is whether it is possible to use the information in a bad or good way. There are good consequences, for example if you need help. But again, it is transformed from private to public. There is no privacy and users can exploit the information in a bad way.

The Network: Close Follow-Up

When the interviewees were asked about their observation of their friends' accounts on Facebook, most of them admitted that in their spare time they surf the SNs in general and especially Facebook. Their acquaintances' profiles are interesting and intriguing and the users find themselves "tracking" their friends on the network. P2 explained that with the help of the network he is exposed to the worlds of people whom he knew in the past. He learns about what has happened to them, what their occupations are, their status and sexual preferences:

All sorts of things interest me ...my 'ex's or all sorts of people ... to see if they are married and whether they have children ...someone from my class published that she was a lesbian ... all sorts of things like that.

In contrast to P2, P7 does not track down people from her past. She is occupied with the present status of her current friends. P7 spoke about an additional dimension, her she does not only follow her friends on the network, but also the reactions and feedback that her friends write on the SNs:

I love to look at pictures, [especially] family and if there are reactions to your pictures. I am not on the network everyday but I follow it.

P5 added an observation from a different angle regarding the tracking of friends on Facebook. She explained that she tends to offer friendship only after she has viewed the profile of the user that she intends to approach. She said that there are very specific parameters according to which she chooses her virtual friends, for example: their noted content, age and occupation:

I look at the profiles of other people that I know on Facebook, so I was slightly interested in what is happening to them today, what they experience and then I decide whether to offer them friendship on the network or not.

In her interview P5 said that there is professional dimension to the Facebook search. She learns about her profession by looking at the profiles of her friends on the network. In her interview, it seemed that the P5's cooperation with users creates a professional partnership that broadens the horizons of the area in which she works.

I look at it from a professional level in the field of cosmetics, where they studied and what they do and I look at how they wrote things with their content and then I offered them friendship ... and when others offer me friendship I check what they write and then decide whether to confirm their friendship.

P7 expressed anxiety regarding the exposure of her private details on the Internet and on Facebook. She explained that she does not expose private details because of her desire to maintain confidentiality. She notes that even in situations where friends look at her Facebook account, she feels that her inner world is exposed:

It is harmful, I don't expose all my personal matters ...I feel that they are intruding on my privacy although I only have my close friends on Facebook, they see the pictures and it is not revealed to people who are not my Facebook friends.

P4 talked about another dimension of the implications of personal details to other users. P4 explained that people publish and share information on the network without being aware of the implications. P4 explained that she sometimes feels discomfort about information that she publishes:

I only upload onto Facebook those contents with which I feel comfortable ... I think that each person only publishes what he feels fine to publish ... for example, my friend was once right-wing and since being in the theater she has changed her opinions and become left-wing and two of her brothers cancelled their friendship and when she talks with them they say they can't continue to be her friends on Facebook because she puts up posts that hurt their friends who are right-wing.

In contrast to P4, (P11) agrees that there is a free choice in the very fact of opening and sharing a personal Facebook account. He explained that users should be understanding and know that they expose their details on the network and are exposed:

Those who want to see, let them see, I relate to Facebook as a noticeboard so similar to a noticeboard I have to know that someone will look at it...on the one hand it is intriguing to know who looks while on the other hand I think it can be onerous.

Figure 1 provides a model of the categories and themes that emerged from the findings

Figure 1. Model of categories and themes relating to the influence of social networks on relationships outside the network

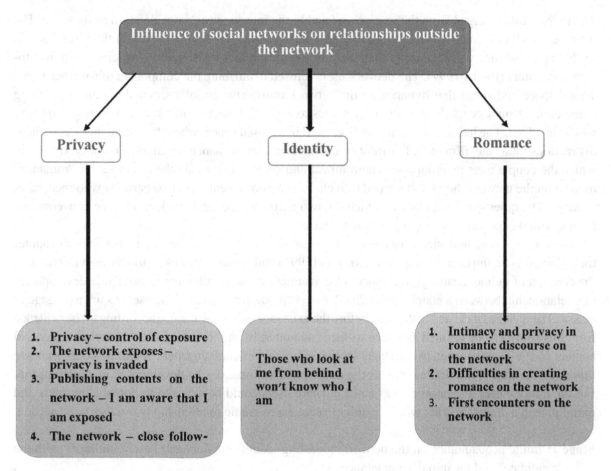

DISCUSSION

This research investigated how the virtual world in general and specifically Facebook influences romantic activities and norms outside the Internet. The main themes that emerged from the initial analysis related to the access to and development of romantic relationships on the network: romance, identity and privacy.

Romance on the Network

The network has in recent years become a key space for romantic and sexual relationships. This space allows surfers to get to know others in order to form serious relationships such as friendship and marriage on the one hand and on the other hand to form random temporary attractions (Ben-Ze'ev, 2004). The research participants were asked about the nature of the connection that was formed between them and their potential partners and they were asked to describe their experiences on the network.

Does Romance Exist on the SN?

The themes that emerged from the research related to the interviewees' consideration of romance. The most outstanding opinion voiced in the findings was that romance did not appear in the virtual space. In the past, romance was seen as a component in the formation of love and it was created in face-to-face encounters (Illouz, 1997). The network users refused to attribute the component of romance to the virtual space and stated that romance on the network transforms an interpersonal act into something commercial. Romance on the network only relates to the initial meeting in which the users get to know who is involved. The intimate context is only created in a closed space, where two partners meet without distractions (at a café, film etc.). For most of the interviewees, romance remained a fantastic dream, in which the couple meet in an intimate environment and get to know each other. In order for "romance" to exist on the network they felt it needed to include four components: (1) two partners who meet face-to-face; (2) a quiet space – a place in which the two partners meet and conduct intimate conversation; (3) a spiritual experience, and; (4) physical contact.

The interviewees emphasized that the second parameter, i.e. the "space" in which a romantic encounter took place was an important component. Mayers (1993) and Illouz (1997) saw modernism as enabling the creation of public meanings in a sphere of consumption and as allowing an authentic development of a relationship between a couple and defined this as "modern romance". The users aspire to engage in classical romance as it existed in the past, before the existence of SNs. Romance according to the evidence from this study can be defined as a face-to-face encounter, in an intimate space that includes physical contact and gestures between two partners such as *going to the beach together ...holding hands, intimate things*. According to the findings this is the only way that romance can develop within a relationship. For the interviewees, the network was a place where users could be exposed to potential partners and participate in a dialog, in other words in order to create a romantic relationship two stages were needed:

Stage 1: Initial acquaintance on the network, revealing identifying data and basic familiarity with the "candidate" and for initial acquaintance.

Stage 2: A face-to-face encounter including an intimate conversation between two partners willing to form a relationship:
what happens on the network is not real, it's just a type of courtship and preparation for romance outside the network, romance outside the network is real.

The interviewees negated the possibility of a continuous romance on the network. Dialog in a virtual space that is not shared creates an intimate, experiential and adventurous moment. Even if this acquaintance does not include any physical contact or gestures that the interviewees hoped would be included in a romantic moment, there would be a special, mysterious first meeting for the user.

The findings supported the argument of Illouz (1997) that romance and relationships on the network lack the components that were mentioned above and so there is no complete romantic relationship in the interactive space. The alternatives open to users in order to conduct a relationship are more flexible online; there are many alternatives and they create a new situation. Activities in a modern discourse on the network create a different type of interaction for love life in general and romantic discourse in particular (Illouz, 1997).

Wysocki (1996) argued that romantic relations on the network work in a single direction. The romance begins on the network and continues as interactive interaction. Face-to-face relations are intimate and physical, while romantic discourse that takes place on the Internet is an initial discussion in most cases.

Some of those who surf on the Internet in general and on dating sites in particular arrive "prepared" and motivated to arrange a first meeting. In contrast to the opinion of Wysocki (1996), the findings testify that romantic discourse does not exist on the Internet and an intimate meeting including stroking and intimate gestures are needed for romance:

romance can begin through the network, through a gesture, messages ...but it cannot remain there alone. In my opinion it can strengthen and encourage romance but you need something else beyond the network (P4).

It seems that the findings mostly contradicted and disproved the theory of Visoki. Nevertheless, it seems that after a continuous period of communication when a couple feel confident and their relationship has become more established interactive communication is formed on the SN.

Identity on the Network

The network users dress themselves in masks to create stereotypes to respond to social norms associated with both external appearance and personality characteristics. It was found that these identities develop on the network and alter. Of course, the face-to-face meeting and the path towards it are influenced by the profile and these identities acquired on the SN. However, the meeting in a space outside the network means that the user has to confront their real identity and the potential partner has to accept that real identity.

According to Barak (2006) the "invisibility" afforded by the Internet serves important purposes: the user can attain their goals in this manner. Nevertheless, the user often undergoes a process of symbiosis with the new identity, continuing to wear this mask even in a face-to-face meeting. This manner of behavior seems improper and unreliable. This may be explained because the masks that are worn by the user and the need to change them create an opportunity to examine who their real "self" is (McKenna & Bargh, 2000). In this way the user is able to cope with the search for their real self, find it and cope with it emotionally. The interviewees were asked about the process of construction and the process of coping with the construction of their identities on the network.

Facebook: Self-Presentation

Most of the interviewees altered their identity so that it would be appropriate for the partner that they wanted to "conquer" and/or for the scene for which they wanted to modify their profile. The identities published on Facebook are attractive images that undergo selection. The details that the users chose to define their "self" are subjective details intended to leave a positive impression on the surfing audience. Thus it seems that the interviewees profile is definitely their personal digital footprint.

Goffman (1980), focused his interest on an analysis of the way that people present themselves in their daily life in different social settings. He noted that when a person appears before others, they create a conscious or unconscious definition of the situation and of their identity. It was found that women more than men, tend to falsify their identities and try to adapt them to stereotypes that they think that men would see as attractive (Shade, 2002). According to the present findings, women did indeed alter their profile on Facebook in order to modify themselves to suit the situation and to impress their target audience. However, according to the interview data, it can be seen that this phenomenon also occurs among men. In other words, both sexes create a suitable personal digital footprint for themselves, which is not real, in order to "market" themselves. The users choose to present their identity in the most complimentary manner and to display a facet of their personality that will market an attractive and inviting image to surfers. The surfers understand that before they meet with the potential partner they should transmit pleasantness, beauty, seriousness, reliability, wisdom etc. This is all transmitted through dialog conducted in writing on the network (Ben-Ze'ev, 2004). The surfers understand that their presentation on the network is the first opportunity to create a continuation to a real relationship. The meeting on the network is a springboard to future dialog that will only occur if they succeed in making an impression on the user with whom they conduct an initial conversation. For them their self-presentation resembles an "entry ticket" earned for making a good impression: *you wouldn't put a place of work that had fired you into your Curriculum Vitae.*

According to Amichai-Hamburger and Ben-Artzi (2000), users do not distinguish between the identities they present in the technological space and their identity in actual reality. Nevertheless, according to the present findings the users emphasized that they consciously use fictive identities. As Goffman (1980) claims, people create complementary identities to fit the world in which they belong and the situations in which they exist. The interviewees noted that the details for the construction of their Facebook identities were selected carefully according to the message that they wanted to deliver to other users.

Amichai-Hamburger and Ben Artzi (2000) note that the use of the Internet helps introverted surfers who find it difficult to find partners and romantic relationships outside the network. These users hide and shelter themselves behind the screen. The findings show that indeed the network does provide a real advantage for these introverted surfers who find it difficult to make friendships outside the network and allows them a range of alternative opportunities to meet someone. It is easy to create identities on the Internet, using suitable pictures, a description of a fascinating life and creating a fake identity that does not resemble your true life.

Some of the findings disproved the claim of Amichai et al. (2000). The interviewees noted that they were hesitant to be extensively exposed on SNs in order to meet people. Lack of privacy and the exposure of their profile on Facebook deterred some of the interviewees and created a situation in which they consciously selected the details that they published. The users often fear the consequences of publishing their details. A situation is created in which they meet new people thanks to their Internet personal digital footprint, however the Facebook profile also has a significant disadvantage in the Internet space: *my identity is far more interesting and complex than on the network.*

Privacy on the Network

The network user is in a constant dilemma relating to the choice of details that it is suitable to expose on the network. On the network in general and on Facebook in particular the user enjoys anonymity that is not possible in a face-to-face meeting. The anonymity and privacy create a special situation suitable for introverts. Wellman (2003) assumed that because of their sophisticated technology, the networks are suitable and adapted to the personal character of each user.

Does Privacy Exist on the Network?

It seems that there is privacy on the network and it can be controlled by the user. The user has free choice to choose what to publish in the technological space and who will be the target audience that will view the materials. Brandtza (2010) calls this the "privacy conflict", the gap between efforts to maintain privacy and the desire to publish personal details on the network. The interviewees testified that they choose the details to appear in their profile, which constitutes their personal digital footprint. They decide who will be their "friends", when to react and in what manner. Facebook allows them to expose themselves as eligible singles and to market themselves as experienced professionals. To this extent it is clear that the users can enjoy privacy on the network and it is they who decide exclusively about the publication of their contents.

Nevertheless, the interviewees who used Facebook, also felt that privacy was an illusion on the SN. The network is a shared space in which privacy cannot exist in entirety. Surfers have a feeling of lack of control when their details are exposed to others that they do not know. When the interviewees were asked: "what is privacy for you?" they all expressed a need for control. According to the findings privacy only exists when two basis components exist: (1) control of the choice of contents that they expose and; (2) the ability to choose who will be able to see the contents. The exposure may be performed by a third party. The ownership of a Facebook account is only partial. The user's details can be exposed in a situation in which a friend shows the account of the user to another account holder who is not in the user's community of friends.

The anonymity that characterizes the activity on SNs differs from complex relationships in real life. Being on a SN reduces the difficult coping of persons with a passive, shy or introverted identity. The SNs undergo metamorphosis and alter their purpose, from networks serving collective needs to networks serving individual needs. This fact reflects a change that the networks are undergoing and a change in the individual's consideration of them. In the past, the networks had a common concept. Today, the SNs have a decentralized character that is suited to the user and adapted to its personal character (Wellman, 2003).

IMPLICATIONS

The findings seem to indicate that romance does not exist on the network, rather romantic signs that are expressed in written text. In the modern technological era single can create a romantic space if they adapt the modern tools (the SNs and/or online dating sites) to parameters that they consider romantic. Although the intimate space and physical contact that they expect does not exist on the network, it is possible to create a situation that aspires to intimacy during an initial conversation. The user needs to ensure that they are indeed in a "private" space where they can conduct dialog solely with the proposed partner and that there is no intervention of other partners without their knowledge during the specific conversation. The participant in the conversation should be aware that the identities on the network are built to be "attractive", attempting to create a high-quality image that will be better than those of other candidates on the SN. Awareness of this subject should prevent the user's disappointment in any future face-to-face meeting after the initial acquaintance. Moreover, romantic discourse on the network is influence by behavior outside of the network. In other words, the user will not always aspire to form a serious relationship. In the conversation, the user should define their main goals. The written word and transcription is the user's tool. The dialog should be conducted with care, the style of writing, and words that are chosen, can lead the candidate for a relationship to attain their desired goal. It should also be remembered that the ability to share and publish contents to other participants without the knowledge of the other participant in the conversation on the network limits privacy. Although the first meeting on the network can constitute a "springboard" to a relationship outside the network, the details that are provided by the user should be chosen carefully before knowing the identity of the other side in the dialog. This means that the user should continually be aware of the rules for activity on the network. The network is a space in which conversations take place for various objectives, such conversations have special characteristics that differ from conversations outside the Internet. In order to understand this issue further research should relate to the characteristics of social discourse on the Internet and its contribution to different aspects of our lives.

LIMITATIONS OF THIS STUDY

Since this was a qualitative study with a relatively small sample, the results cannot be generalized to similar circumstances. However, the reader can decide to what extent they are informative for other similar contexts.

Future research should consider a larger sample of respondents with different academic and professional characteristics. In order to derive suitable conclusions for a broader population, further research should relate to a random population of additional singles from different regions and countries. Different populations could be studied including non-academic populations and compared with populations that do not use the SNs.

To summarize, the research and findings described in this paper showed that network surfers idealize their images when presenting themselves on the network in order to be perceived as an attractive and eligible in their search for the ideal partner. The surfers adopt characteristics and attractive features from the images that they know in real life.

The interviewees were asked to define romance on the network. They found it difficult to find its existence on the network. They negated the possibility of creating a romantic situation in the virtual space.

The network personality meets its potential partner in the digital space and from there they can move on to the real world. However, the continuation of this relationship often returns to the network and exists in substance there. Nevertheless, the behavior of the couple on the network is just one of many representations of social aspects in a dynamic changing existence. Dating sites are a metonymy for a whole refreshing world that represents the society in which we live. The SNs began a novel social-personal process which has influenced our lives. At this point in time the digital networks and sites dictate new norms and rules. The open question that remains in this context is whether a long-term study over several years would reveal a different sort of couple relationships.

REFERENCES

Amichai-Hamburger, Y., & Ben-Artzi, E. (2000). The relationship between extraversion, neuroticism, and different uses of the Internet. *Computers in Human Behavior, 16*(4), 441–449. doi:10.1016/S0747-5632(00)00017-0

Barak, A. (2006). Youth and the Internet: Psychology of "as if" and "like that". [Hebrew]. *Panim, 37*, 48–58.

Ben-Ze'ev, A. (2004). *Love online: Emotions on the Internet*. Cambridge, UK: Cambridge University Press. doi:10.1017/CBO9780511489785

Connolly, I., Palmer, M., Barton, H., & Kirwan, G. (Eds.). (2016). *An Introduction to Cyberpsychology*. Routledge.

Cooper, A., McLoughlin, I. P., & Campbell, K. M. (2000). Sexuality in cyberspace: Update for the 21st century. *Cyberpsychology & Behavior, 3*(4), 521–536. doi:10.1089/109493100420142

Cooper, A., & Sportolari, L. (1997). Romance in cyberspace: Understanding online attraction. *Journal of Sex Education and Therapy, 22*(1), 7–14. doi:10.1080/01614576.1997.11074165

Denzin, N. K., & Lincoln, Y. S. (Eds.). (1994). *Handbook of qualitative research*. Sage Publications.

DeVito, M. A., Birnholtz, J. P., & Hancock, J. T. (2017). Platforms, people, and perception: Using affordances to understand self-presentation on social media. In *CSCW Proceedings of the 2017 ACM Conference on Computer Supported Cooperative Work and Social Computing* (pp. 740-754). ACM.

Glaser, B. G., & Strauss, A. L. (1967). *The discovery of grounded theory: Strategy for qualitative research*. Chicago: Aldine Publishing Company.

Goffman, A. (1980). *Presenting the self in daily life*. Tel Aviv: Reshafim. [Hebrew]

Granovetter, M. S. (1973). The strength of weak ties. *American Journal of Sociology, 78*(6), 1360–1380. doi:10.1086/225469

Halpern, D., Katz, J. E., & Carril, C. (2017). The online ideal persona vs. the jealousy effect: Two explanations of why selfies are associated with lower-quality romantic relationships. *Telematics and Informatics, 34*(1), 114–123. doi:10.1016/j.tele.2016.04.014

Illouz, E. (1997). *Consuming the romantic utopia: Love and the cultural contradictions of capitalism*. University of California Press.

Kohut, H. (1971). *The analysis of the self; a systematic approach to the psychoanalytic treatment of narcissistic personality disorders*. New York: International Universities Press.

Lincoln, Y., & Guba, E. G. (1985). *Naturalistic inquiry*. Newbury Park, CA: Sage.

Malach-Feins, A. (2002). *Falling in love: How we choose who to fall in love with?* Tel Aviv: Modan. (in Hebrew)

Mayers, G. (2003). *Social psychology*. McGraw-Hill Ryerson.

McKenna, K. Y., & Bargh, J. A. (2000). Plan 9 from cyberspace: The implications of the Internet for personality and social psychology. *Personality and Social Psychology Review, 4*(1), 57–75. doi:10.1207/S15327957PSPR0401_6

Mendelson, A. L., & Papacharissi, Z. 2010. Look at us: collective narcissism in college student Facebook photo galleries. In Papacharissi (Ed.), The networked self: Identity, Community and Culture on Social Network Sites (pp. 251–273). New York: Routledge.

Patton, N. Q. (1990). *Qualitative evaluation and research methods* (2nd ed.). Newbury Park, CA: Sage.

Rettberg, J. W. (2017). *Self-Representation in Social Media*. Academic Press.

Sabar Ben-Yehoshua, N. (2001). Ethnography in education. In N. Sabar Ben-Yehoshua (Ed.), Traditions and genres in qualitative research (pp. 100-136). Lod: Dvir. (in Hebrew)

Shade, L. R. (2002). *Gender and community in the social construction of the Internet*. Peter Lang.

Smith, J. A. (1995). Semi-structured interviewing and qualitative analysis. *Rethinking Methods in Psychology, 1*, 8-26.

Suler, J. (2004). The online disinhibition effect. *Cyberpsychology & Behavior, 7*(3), 321–326. doi:10.1089/1094931041291295 PMID:15257832

Turkle, S. (1995). *Life on the screen: Identity in the age of the Internet*. New York: Simon & Schuster.

Wellman, H., & Cross, D. (2003). Theory of mind conceptual change. *Child Development, 72*(3), 702–707. doi:10.1111/1467-8624.00309 PMID:11405576

Whitty, M., & Carr, A. N. (2006). *Cyberspace romance: The psychology of online relationships*. Hampshire, UK: Palgrave Macmillan. doi:10.1007/978-0-230-20856-8

Wysocki, D. K. (1996). *Somewhere over the modem: Interpersonal relationships over computer bulletin boards. Sociology*. Santa Barbara: University of California.

Wysocki, D. K. (1998). Let your fingers do the talking. *Sexualities, 1*(4), 425–452. doi:10.1177/136346098001004003

Zhao, S. (2006). Do Internet users have more social ties? A call for differentiated analyses of Internet use. *Journal of Computer-Mediated Communication, 11*(3), 844–862. doi:10.1111/j.1083-6101.2006.00038.x

Zhao, S., Grasmuck, S., & Martin, J. (2008). Identity construction on Facebook: Digital empowerment in anchored relationships. *Computers in Human Behavior, 24*(5), 1816–1836. doi:10.1016/j.chb.2008.02.012

Chapter 38
Online Social Capital Among Social Networking Sites' Users

Azza Abdel-Azim Mohamed Ahmed

Abu Dhabi University, UAE & Cairo University, Egypt

ABSTRACT

This research aimed to explore types of online social capital (bridging and bonding) that the Emiratis perceive in the context of social networking site (SNS) usage. A sample of 230 Emiratis from two Emirates, Abu Dhabi and Dubai, was used to investigate the hypothesis. The results showed that WhatsApp was the most frequent SNS used by the respondents. Also, a significant correlation of the intensity of social networking usage and bridging social capital was found, while there was no significant association between SNS usage and bonding social capital. The factors determined the SNSs usage motivations among the respondents were exchange of information, sociability, accessibility, and connections with overseas friends and families. Males were more likely than females to connect with Arab (non-Emiratis) and online bonding social capital. Both genders were the same in their SNSs motivations and online bridging social capital.

INTRODUCTION

Internet and Social Media Connect People

In geographic communities, people typically get to know each other in face-to-face settings, and then maintain contact via communication technologies, such as telephone and email. When geographic communities have high Internet penetration, people, groups, and organizations readily turn to email and the World Wide Web to stay in touch and exchange information (Kavanaugh, et al., 2005). Early and continuing excitement about the Internet saw it as a stimulating positive change in people's lives by creating new forms of online interaction and enhancing offline relationships. The Internet would restore community by providing a meeting space for people with common interests and overcoming the limitations of space and time (Wellman, et al., 2010: 438).

DOI: 10.4018/978-1-6684-6307-9.ch038

Gershuny (2002) argued that the Internet has changed the nature of leisure activities; the same might be said of social networking sites (SNSs). Instead of displacing leisure or communication, Facebook constitutes a new communication activity that supplements communication amongst friends. Social media provides individuals an interpersonal connection with others, relational satisfaction, and a way to learn about the surrounding cultural milieu (Croucher, 2011: 261). Online sites are often considered innovative and different from traditional media, such as television, film, and radio, because they allow direct interaction with others (Pempek, et al., 2009: 229).

To summarize, SNSs provide users with meaningful ways to make, maintain, and enhance relationships. For many "Friends", the site is the primary method through which to stay connected (Vitak, 2012: 469).

Internet Access and Social Media in the United Arab Emirates (UAE)

Social networking has spread around the world with remarkable speed. In countries such as Britain, the United States, Russia, the Czech Republic, and Spain, about half of all adults now use Facebook and similar websites (Kohut, et al., 2012: 1).

The UAE has been ranked (13) in the world in terms of individuals using the Internet, with 88% of the country's residents now online. This is just behind the United Kingdom (89.8%) and Bahrain (90%), according to the United Nations Broadband Commission report (2014), which elaborates on the number of Internet users, specifically broadband, in 191 countries. In global rankings of countries with the highest frequencies of Internet access, the UAE holds 13th place, way ahead of United States, which is in the 19th spot, and Germany, which has grabbed the 20th position (p: 102–103). It should be indicated here that the demographics of UAE residence are very unique as it includes various nationalities from Asia, Europe, USA and others. According to the National Bureau of Statistics (2010), the UAE nationals are 11.5% of the total population that exceeds 8.264.070 million and the non-national are 88.5% of it (P: 10).

Ayyad (2011) indicated that the United Arab Emirates' high percentage of Internet users makes it the "most wired nation in the Arab world and one of the top nations of the online world" (p: 43).

Al Jenaibi (2011) concluded that social media has a very strong presence in the lives of a sample of 556 Emiratis from the seven Emiratis of UAE. Most participants agreed that the use of social media is on the rise in the current teenage and adult population (Twitter, YouTube, the iPhone, Blackberry, and iPad were mentioned frequently). They had a clear conception of a wide range of uses for it, defining it as useful for contacting others, discussions, searching for information, selling products and logos, making announcements, and distributing surveys (p: 19, 20). Wiest and Eltantawy (2012) found that nearly 90% of a sample of UAE universities' students have created a profile on one of the social networking sites and 78.5% have a profile on more than one such site (p: 214). Karuppasamy, et al. (2013) found that most of a sample of the students of Ajman University of Science and Technology (n = 300) were found to be users of social networking sites, and Facebook was the most popular SNS (p: 248).

THEORETICAL FRAMEWORK AND LITERATURE REVIEW

Like traditional media, Facebook and other social networking sites consist of a one-to-many communication style, where information presented reaches many "viewers" at a time. However, with social networking sites, users are now the creators of content, and they view one another's profiles and information rather than viewing mass-produced content made by large corporations. They also become the stars of their own productions (Pempek, et al, 2009: 234).

Social networking sites are online environments in which people create a self-descriptive profile and then make links to other people they know on the site, creating a network of personal connections. Participants in social networking sites are usually identified by their real names and often include photographs; their network of connections is displayed as an integral piece of their self-presentation (Donath & Boyd, 2004: 72).

Wellman et al (2010) indicated that online interactions may supplement or replace those interactions that previously were formed offline. Some other researchers (Kavanaugh and Patterson, 2001; Hampton and Wellman, 2003; Kavanaugh, et al., 2005) have concluded that computer-mediated interactions have had positive effects on community interaction, involvement, and social capital. Social network sites now mediate a variety of human interactions for a wide spectrum of individuals, from early adolescents to adults (Ahn, 2011: 108). Donath and Boyd (2004) argued that the SNSs provide the technical features for their users to build and maintain large networks for social ties, which supplements their offline social networks. Specifically, individuals can remain in contact with more members of online networks more often than with their offline counterparts.

Social Capital and Its Types

Social capital refers to the set of resources embedded within community networks accessed and used by individuals within a network (Coleman, 1988). Putnam (2000) defined social capital as connections among individuals and the social networks and the norms of reciprocity and trustworthiness that emerge from them. Lin (2001) defined social capital as "investment in social relations with expected returns in the marketplace" (p: 19). Ellison, et al., (2014) explained that social capital is created through social interactions and the expectations of future social resources they engender (p: 856).

Some studies indicated that social capital is linked to positive social outcomes, such as better public health, low crime rates, and increased participation in civic activities (Adler & Kwon, 2002; Ellison, et al., 2007). Wellman, et al., (2010) stated that some evidence suggests that the observed decline in the offline social capital has not led to social isolation but to the community becoming embedded in social networks rather than groups, and a movement of community relationships from easily observed public spaces to less accessible private homes. If people are tucked away in their homes rather than conversing in cafes, then perhaps they are going online: chatting online one-to-one; exchanging e-mail; ranting about important topics; and organizing discussion groups or news groups (p: 437).

Although sociologists and political scientists tend to use the term "social capital", psychologists refer to a related concept using the term "social support" (Burke, et al., 2011, p: 1–2). In media literature, most scholars use "social capital" (Ellison et al. (2007; Ellison, 2008; Valenzuela, et al., 2009; Watkins & Lee, 2009).

Stevens Aubrey, Jennifer et al (2008) summarized Putnam's (2000) distinction of two kinds of social capital: bridging (characterized by weak ties) and bonding (characterized by strong ties).

- Bridging occurs when individuals from different backgrounds make connections between social networks. It is often seen as having a lot of tentative relationships ("weak ties") that provide little emotional support. Still, bridging can also be viewed as the broadening of one's social horizons or world views.

- Bonding, on the other hand, occurs when strongly tied individuals provide emotional support for one another. It occurs between individuals who have strong personal connections. The downside of bonding is its insularity; it can lead to mistrust and dislike for those outside the group (p: 2).

Johnston, et al., (2013) explained that bridging social capital occurs between individuals of different ethnic and occupational backgrounds and it provides useful information and new perspectives (p: 25). Bridging may broaden social horizons or world views, or open up opportunities for information or new resources. On the down side, it provides little in the way of emotional support. (Williams, 2006: 597).

In contrast, bonding social capital exists between family members, close friends, and other close relations and focuses on internal ties between actors. It does not provide links to individuals of differing backgrounds (Johnston, et al., 2013: 25).

Bonding social capital refers to close relationships between individuals that provide emotional support and access to scarce resources. SNSs enable members to connect with existing close friends and relatives, thus functioning as an additional means for them to interact outside of face-to-face encounters (Phua and Annie, 2011: 508). Williams (2006) stated that the individuals with bonding social capital have little diversity in their backgrounds but have stronger personal connections. The continued reciprocity found in bonding social capital provides strong emotional and substantive support and enables mobilization. Its drawback is assumed to be insularity and out-group antagonism (p: 579).

Adding further to this distinction, Johnston et al., (2013) introduced a different classification of social capital retrieved from the work of two researches (Islam et al, 2006; and Fukuyama, 2001). They suggested that social capital can be broken into two classes: cognitive and structural.

- Cognitive social capital is linked to personal aspects, such as beliefs, values, norms, and attitudes. It is also a by-product of cultural norms like religion, tradition, and shared historical experiences.
- Structural social capital is the outwardly visible features of social organizations, such as patterns of social engagement or density of social networks (p: 25).

Ellison et al. (2007) introduced a third type of social capital called "maintained social capital" that is created when individuals maintain connections to their social networks having progressed through life changes. This type of social capital supports the idea suggested by Bargh and McKenna (2004) who stated that the use of technology can assist people to maintain relationships threatened by changes in geographical location. This might be the case when university students use various types of social media to stay in touch with old high school friends and classmates who moved away to join universities in different countries or locations.

In this research, Putnam's (2000) classification of social capital (bridging and bonding) will be adapted.

Social Media and Social Capital

Social networking sites provide an important source of community and thus represent a key source of social capital in the digital age (Watkins & Lee, 2009: 16). In this context, many research efforts were spent to determine whether social media increases or decreases the level of social capital among SNS users.

SNS users were found to enjoy both the development of new relationships and the maintenance of existing relationships online (Walkins and Lee, 2009). Ahmed, Azza (2015) examined offline social support in relation to online self-disclosure. She found that the more respondents have emotional and informational offline support, the less they are likely to disclose positive matters online (p: 215). Nie (2001) argued that Internet use detracts from face-to-face time with others, which might diminish an individual's social capital. From their surveys with undergraduate Facebook users, Ellison, Steinfield, and Lampe (2007) found that Facebook usage interacted with measures of psychological well-being; Facebook intensity predicted increased levels of maintained social capital, which they interpreted as the college students' ability "to stay in touch with high school acquaintances" and possibly "offset feelings of 'friend sickness', the distress caused by the loss of old friends". However, Valenzuela, et al., (2009) found that the positive and significant associations between Facebook variables and social capital were small.

Phua and Jin (2011) suggested that SNSs naturally lend themselves to the development of large heterogeneous networks by enabling individuals to connect with people outside their immediate geographic locations (p: 506). Ahn's (2012) findings suggest that having interactions that are more positive in SNSs is related to bonding social capital but not to bridging relationships. He concluded that when one spends more time in SNSs and interacts with wider networks, one may readily keep in touch with acquaintances rather than developing close relationships, stating that the intensity of SNS use appears to influence bridging social capital development (p: 107).

Ellison, Steinfield and Lampe (2007) found that both strong and weak social ties are sustained on SNSs. Studying a sample of undergraduate university students, they concluded that intensive use of Facebook was associated with higher levels of three types of social capital: bridging capital or our "friends of friends" that afford us diverse perspectives and new information; bonding capital or "the shoulder to cry on" that comes from our close friends and family; and maintained social capital, a concept the researchers developed to describe the ability to "mobilize resources from a previously inhabited network, such as one's high school"(see also: Ellison, 2008: 22).

Greenhow and Robelia (2009) explained that the computer-mediated communication has the potential for online social interactions to enhance self-presentation, relational maintenance, and social bonding (p: 1133). Wong (2012) explained that people might be eager to present themselves in certain ways so as to manage their optimal impressions of others and get social support in return online (p: 185). Koku & Wellman (2001) argued that the Internet may be more useful for maintaining existing ties than for creating new ones. Thus, there is evidence that the Internet plays a critical role in shaping and maintaining bridging and bonding social capital (Phua and Annie, 2011: 506).

Motives of Social Networking Sites Usage and Social Capital

The uses and gratifications approach argues that different audiences use media messages for different purposes to satisfy their psychological and social needs and achieve their goals (McQuail, Blumler, & Brown, 1972). Recently, a number of researchers have employed the uses and gratifications approach in the context of new media and the social networking sites (Dunne, Lawlor & Rowley, 2010). According to Colás, et al., (2013), social network is a virtual space that is emotionally gratifying and allows young people to express their intimate feelings through the perception others have of them (p: 21).

Papacharissi (2002) identified six motives for using social networking sites: "passing time", "entertainment", "information", "self-expression", "professional advancement", and "communication with family and friends". Similar to the results pertaining to traditional media, she concluded that information and entertainment motives were most important. Banczyk, et al. (2008) found that communication and entertainment are the most important motivations for hosting a profile at MySpace, followed by passing time, providing information, and conformity (p: 15). Boyd (2008) found that teenagers were joining

SNSs because "that's where their friends are" (p: 126). Karuppasamy, et al. (2013) observed a positive association between meeting new people on SNS and an SNS addiction score; 38.2% of the moderate to high users and 21.2% of the average users used SNS for this purpose (p: 247).

Lenhart and Madden (2007) found that 91% of teen SNS users use the sites "to stay in touch with friends they see frequently and 82% to stay in touch with friends they rarely see in person", whereas only 49% use these sites "to make new friends" (p: 2).

Based on a survey of Facebook users, the findings of Villegas, et al. (2011) suggest that information and connection motives have a positive relationship with the perceived value of advertising on the site. However, when the motivation to use an SNS is moderated by bonding, perceptions toward advertising's value are negative (p: 69).

Aubrey & Rill (2013) found that those who were motivated to use Facebook for its sociability function were more likely to experience gains in online bridging and bonding. They explained that relationship-building on Facebook would be more appealing to the person who is using FB to meet people (sociability) than to the person who is using FB to create an ideal presentation of self (status) (p: 492).

Ellison, Steinfield, and Lampe (2011) found that social information-seeking behaviors, such as using FB to know more about friends and neighbors, are significantly correlated to bonding social capital.

The use of SNSs for relational purposes and the resulting social capital and relationships are culturally driven. American college students held larger but looser networks with a far greater portion of weak ties, whereas their Korean counterparts maintained smaller and denser networks with a roughly even ratio of strong and weak ties. American college students also reported obtaining more bridging social capital from their networks in SNSs than did their Korean counterparts, whereas the level of bonding social capital was not significantly different between the two groups (Choi, et al., 2011).

There is little academic work examining the online social networking and social capital in the Arab world. This study investigates the online social capital (bridging and bonding) among Emiratis using social networking sites. In other words, it investigates the type of social capital developed as a result of using SNSs. It also explores how motivation of using SNSs might make a difference in the type of the perceived social capital among respondents. The differences between males and females in their SNSs usage, type of social capital, and type of motivations are also examined.

RESEARCH QUESTIONS AND HYPOTHESES

Based on the literature, three research questions were formed:

RQ #1: What are the SNSs that are most frequently used by Emiratis?
RQ #2: What are the motives of using online social networking sites among Emiratis?
RQ #3: What is the nationality that Emiratis tend to mostly communicate with via SNSs?

In addition, five hypotheses will be examined based on the literature, as follows:

Research Hypotheses

By using the Internet, people are substituting poorer quality relationships for better relationships, substituting weak ties for strong ties (Kraut, et al, 1998: 1208). Boase, et al. (2006) in a Pew Internet survey showed that online users are more likely to have a larger network comprised of close ties compared to non-Internet users. Ellison, N. et al (2006) found that there was a strong connection between Facebook intensity and high school social capital (p: 25). Therefore, it can be hypothesized that:

H1: Intensity of SNS use is positively associated with individuals' perceived online bridging and bonding social capital.

Aubrey & Rill (2013) indicated that one of the structural properties of users' FB experiences that might predict the relationship between SNS usage and the type of online social capital is the number of relationships formed online (p: 493). Valenzuela, et al. (2009) suggested that individuals with a large and diverse network of contacts are thought to have more social capital than individuals with small, less diverse networks (p: 875). Hofer and Aubert (2013) found a negative curvilinear effect of the number of Twitter followers on bridging and the number of Twitter followees on bonding online social capital. Therefore, it can be predicted that the size of the SNS might predict the type of social capital as follow:

H2: There is a correlation between online social networking size and social capital type (bridging and bonding).

The results of Wellman, et al. (2010) suggest that the Internet is particularly useful for keeping contact among friends who are socially and geographically dispersed, concluding that communication is lower with distant than nearby friends. Also, investigating the relationship between Facebook usage and online and offline social capital, Aubrey & Rill (2013) found that Facebook habit was related to online bridging and offline network capital. They concluded that it is likely how a person uses FB, rather than how much he or she uses it, which is related to online bridging and offline network capital. This means that studying the impact of social networking on social capital should be in the light of the types of usage and patterns of SNS use. One of these patterns might be the diversity of social categories the SNS users have. Thus, it can be hypothesized:

H3: There is a correlation between diversity of social categories (various nationalities and relationships) and social capital type (bridging and bonding).

Literature on social media concluded that college students are motivated to use social media to keep in touch with old friends, sharing artifacts, learning about social events, and gaining recognition and self-expression (Ellison, et al, 2007; Papacharissi, 2002; Raacke & Bonds-Raacke, 2008). Greenhow, Christine and Robelia (2009) found that high school students from low-income families used their online social network to fulfill essential social learning functions. Ellison, et al. (2006) found that using FB to connect with offline contacts and for fun were positively associated with bridging social capital, while using it to meet new people had a negative association among a sample of high school students. These motives did not explain bonding social capital well (p: 25). Burke & Lento (2010) found a correlation between social capital and active contributions to Facebook as compared to passive consumption of other's information. Ellison, et al. (2011) found that using Facebook for information-seeking purposes were positively associated with online social capital. Therefore, it can be hypothesized that:

H4: There is a significant correlation between the motivation of using SNSs and type of social capital.

The differences between males and females have been studied by some researchers. Ayyad (2011) found that male students are more interested in using the Internet to engage in dialogue and chat with their friends and relatives, while female students are more interested in using the Internet to get information that serves their studies and to communicate with their instructors (p: 57). In the light of social capital, Colás, et al. (2013) found that online social networks are a source of resources for young people that are used to fulfill needs, both psychological and social. However, the differences between genders in these variables demonstrate that they play a compensatory role; males generally use them to cover emotional aspects ("to feel good when I am sad") and reinforce their self-esteem ("to know what my friends would say about my photos I upload"), while for young women, the relational function prevails "to make new friends" (p: 20). Therefore, it can be hypothesized that:

H5: There is a significant difference between males and females in their:
1. Motivations of using social networking sites, and
2. Online social capital.

Figure 1 illustrates the hypothesized relationships among the research variables.

Figure 1. The research variables and the related hypotheses

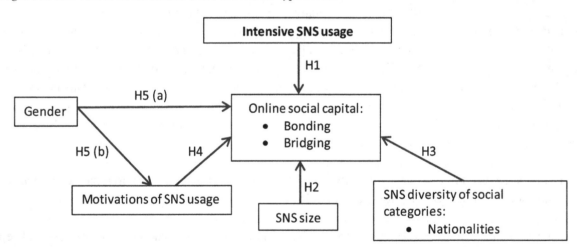

METHODOLOGY

Sampling and Data Collection

The sample is composed of only Emiratis. Two out of seven Emirates were selected to draw the sample of the study: Dubai, the leading and most modern Emirate in UAE, and Abu Dhabi, the UAE capital.

A constructed self-administrated questionnaire was used to collect the data. It included 12 questions with various kinds of measurements for the research variables which will be described later. The questionnaire was written in Arabic, as it is the native language of the respondents and it makes it easy for them to fill out the questionnaire. The questionnaire reliability was good ($\alpha = 0.851$).

The data was collected during February-March 2014. Five national students of the Mass Communication Program at Abu Dhabi University assisted in collecting data using Snowball sampling from the two Emirates where they live. The students gained extra credit in the Media Research Methods and Communication Theories courses for this extracurricular activity.

Total of (300) questionnaires were distributed and filled in by respondents. A number (70) of questionnaires were excluded due to various reasons, specifically: uncompleted sheets and inaccurate responses. Therefore, the sample was composed of (230) respondents. They were distributed equally between the two Emiratis; their characteristics are shown in Table 1.

Table 1. The demographics of the sample (n = 230)

Demographic	%
Gender	
• Males	48.3
• Females	51.7
Age (*)	
• Less than 25 years old	49.6%
• 25 to less than 35 years old	38.7%
• 35 years old and above	11.7%
Education	
• University level	67.4%,
• High school level	17.8%
• Post graduate level	10.9%
• Preparatory or less	3.9%

(*) The mean age is 26.13 & St. Deviation 8.143

MEASUREMENTS OF VARIABLES

Types of Social Networks

The respondents were asked about the social networking sites they usually use. A list of social networking sites was provided and the respondents were asked to indicate how frequently (3 "always", 2 "sometimes", 1 "rarely", and 0 "never") they use each of them (Facebook, Instagram, Kik, WhatsApp, BBM, and Twitter).

Intensity of Social Networking Connection

It refers to the frequency of using social media and the time spent on social media. Three questions were used to measure the intensity of the social networking connection adapted from Lee (2009).

The respondents were asked how many years they had been using the social networking sites. The categories were: less than a year, from 1 year to less than 3 years, from 3 years to less than 6 years, and 6 years and above. Due to the small number of respondents who chose "less than one year, this category was combined with the second one, which is "1 year to less than 3 years". The scores ranged from 1–3. The highest score (3) was for the "6 years and above" and the lowest was (1) for the "1 year to less than 3 years" category.

The second question asked about how often they use social media in the average week. The answers were almost every day, 5–6 days a week, 3–4 days a week, once or twice a week, or never. The "3–4 days a week" was combined with the "once or twice a week" due to the low number of respondents who gave this answer. The highest score (3) was for the "almost every day" and the lowest (1) was for "once or twice a week". None of the respondents expressed that they never use the SNS during an average week.

A third question asked about the number of hours the respondents use social networking sites in one day. Possible answers were: less than an hour, 1 to less than 3 hours, 3 to less than 5 hours, 5 hours and more. The first two categories were combined together; so it turned to be "1 to less than 3 hours". The highest score (3) was for the "5 or more" category, followed by 3 to less than 5 hours a day (2) and the lowest (1) was for less than 1 to 3 hours a day.

The total score of this variable was 9 and ranged from 3–9 points. Responses were divided into three categories: highly connected with SNS (8–9 points) 33.9%, moderately connected (5–7 points) 60.4%, and weakly connected (3–4 points) 5.7%. Cronbach's Alpha indicated a good internal reliability of 0.823.

Online Network Size

It refers to the size of friends the respondents have via social networking sites. The respondents were asked how many friends they have in the online social networking sites. The answers have five categories: 50 to less than 100 friends, 100 to less than 200 friends, 200 to less than 300 friends, and 300 friends and more. The results revealed that 46.5% of the sample has more than 300 friends in the SNS while 53.5% has 50 to less than 100 friends.

Diversity of Social Categories

It refers to the diversity of social categories and type of friends in terms of relationship and nationalities. It also reflects the geographical and psychological distance of SNS friends. Two questions were asked to measure this variable. The first asked how frequently the respondents communicate with the following social categories (family, colleagues, friends, relatives, work partners, and strangers). The score ranged from 3 "always", 2 "sometimes, 1 "rarely", and 0 "never". The total score for this part was 18, and respondents were divided according to their responses into three categories: high diversity of relationships (scores from 14–18) 37%, medium diversity (7–13) 60.4%, and low diversity (0–6) 2.6%.

The second question was about the nationality of the friends and followers with which the respondents communicate (Emiratis, non-Emirati Arabs, Americans and Europeans, and Asians). The total score for this question was 15, ranged from 3 "always", 2 "sometimes, 1 "rarely", and 0 "never".

The responses were divided accordingly into three categories: high diversity of nationalities (scores from 12–15) 5.2%, medium diversity (6–11) 58.7%, and low diversity (0–5) 36.1%. Cronbach's Alpha indicated good internal reliability ($\alpha = 0.851$) for the items measuring the diversity variable.

Motivation

Motives of using the online social networking sites were measured by using a 5-point Likert scale, ranging from strongly agree (4 points) to strongly disagree (0 point) for 13 different motives: "to pass time" (M = 4.03); "to connect with new friends" (M = 3.83); "to find new friends" (M = 3.13); "to have accompaniment" (M = 3.33); "to connect with my friends overseas" (M = 3.97); "to connect with my family living abroad" (M = 3.97); "to exchange opinions with friends" (M = 4.01); "to write comments on everyday events" (M = 3.62); "to upload some videos and photos" (M = 3.74); "to post some up-to-date news that might grab my friends' attention" (M = 3.82); "to read what others have posted" (M = 4.12); "because it is the best way to find the latest news" (M = 4.23); and "because it is the easiest way to connect with my friends" (M = 4.14).

Factor analysis was used to identify the factors that determine the respondents' motivations of using social media (see the results of the research).

Social Capital Measurements

The measurement of the social capital variable was adopted from Chua, Shu-Chuan and Choib, Sejung Marina (2010). Minor changes have taken place while translating the statements as a result of the pre-test and a necessity of changes to go along with the cultural differences between the western and the Arab communities.

The social capital variable consists of two sub-variables: bridging social capital and bonding social capital. The 5-point Likert Scale ranged from "strongly agree" (5) to "strongly disagree" (1 score) was used to measure the social capital variable using (10) statements for each variable as follows:

Bridging Social Capital

1. Interacting with people on the social network site makes me interested in things that happen outside of my town (M = 3.98).
2. Interacting with people on the social network site makes me want to try new things (M = 4.02).
3. Interacting with people on the social network site makes me interested in what people unlike me are thinking (M = 4.04).
4. Talking with people on the social network site makes me curious about other places in the world (M = 3.80).
5. Interacting with people on the social network site makes me feel like part of a larger community (M = 4.06).
6. Interacting with people on the social network site makes me feel connected to the bigger picture of my community (M = 4.08).
7. Interacting with people on the social network site reminds me that everyone in the world is connected (M = 4.03).
8. I am willing to spend time to support general community activities on the social network site (M = 3.82).
9. Interacting with people on the social network site provides me with a chance to connect with new people to talk to (M = 3.77).
10. I come in contact with new people on the social network site all the time (M = 3.69).

The total score was 50 and the respondents were divided according to their answers into three categories: High in bridging social capital 59.1% (scores from 39–50), moderate in the bridging social capital 39.6% (scores from 26–38) and low in bridging social capital 1.3% (scores from 10–25). The low and the moderate categories were combined because of the low percentage of the low category. The respondents then divided into two categories: high in bridging social capital (59.1%) and middle in bridging social capital (40.9%).

Bonding Social Capital

1. There are several members of the social network site I trust to help solve my problems ($M = 3.35$).
2. There is a member of the social network site I can turn to for advice about making very important decisions ($M = 3.33$).
3. There is no one on the social network site that I feel comfortable talking to about intimate personal problems (R) ($M = 3.27$).
4. When I feel lonely, there are members of the social network site I can talk to ($M = 3.39$).
5. If I needed an emergency loan, I know someone at the social network site I can turn to ($M = 2.79$).
6. I always evaluate the people I interact with on the social network site ($M = 3.47$).
7. The people I interact with on the social network site would be good job references for me ($M = 3.00$).
8. The people I interact with on the social network site would share all their money to support me if I face any financial problem ($M = 2.70$).
9. I do not know members of the social network site well enough to get them to do anything important ($M = 3.57$). (R)
10. The people I interact with on the social network site would help me fight an injustice or unfairness that I might face in my life ($M = 3.05$).

The total score of bonding social capital was 50. The respondents were categorized according to their responses into three categories: high in bonding social capital 16.5% (scores 39–50), moderate in bonding social capital 64.3% (scores 26–38), and low in bonding social capital 19.1% (scores 10–25).

Cronbach's Alpha indicated a high internal reliability ($\alpha = 0.851$) for the items measuring the social capital (bridging and bonding) variable. The respondents' age, gender, and education levels were recorded for sampling demographics.

Statistical Techniques

The SPSS statistical program was used in analyzing the data. Frequencies, Cronbach's Alpha, Pearson correlation, Factor Analysis, and T-test were used to answer the research questions and test its hypotheses.

RESEARCH RESULTS

Usage Patterns of Social Networking Sites Among the Respondents

RQ #1: What is the SNS/s that are most frequently used by Emiratis?

The results revealed that WhatsApp is the social network that got the highest percentage among SNS Emiratis users as shown in Table 2.

Table 2 shows that the SNS that is used most frequently by the sample is WhatsApp (M = 2.70), followed by the Instagram (M = 2.53), then Twitter (M = 2.08). Unexpectedly, Facebook was in fourth place among the most frequent social networking sites the respondents use. This contradicts some findings of research results in UAE and USA, as will be discussed later.

Table 2. Frequency of using SNS among respondents (n = 230)*

SNS	Frequency of Using SNS %				M	Weighted Mean %
	Always	Sometimes	Rarely	Never		
WhatsApp	81.3	12.2	2.2	4.3	2.70	90.1
Instagram	72.2	15.7	4.8	7.4	2.53	84.2
Twitter	50.9	21.7	11.7	15.7	2.08	69.3
Facebook	35.7	17.0	10.0	37.4	1.51	50.3
Kik	24.3	17.4	22.6	35.7	1.30	43.5
MySpace	11.7	6.5	11.7	70.0	0.60	20.0

(*) The respondent might choose more than one SNS

RQ #2: What are the motives of using social networking sites among Emiratis?

Factor analysis was used to identify the most factors that determine the social media usage among the respondents.

The results indicated that there are four factors identifying the motives of using social media. Table 3 presents the factor analysis rotated component matrix of SNS motivations among Emiratis.

The factor analysis reveals that there are four factors that determine the Emiratis' motivations of using SNS.

1. Exchange news, opinion and photos (items 1–5)
2. Sociability (items 6–9)
3. Accessibility (items 10–11)
4. Connecting overseas friends and families (items 12–13)

RQ #3: What is/are the nationality/ies that Emiratis tend to mostly communicate with via SNS?

Connecting to people is one of the main factors that motivate the intensive usage of SNS among various groups.

The respondents were asked with which of the nationalities they communicate most of the time through SNS. The answers are listed in Table 4.

Table 4 indicates that the Emiratis use SNS to always communicate to nationals, as Emiratis got the highest percentage compared to other nationalities, followed by the Arabs (non-Emiratis). This indicates that the SNSs are not used to extend the respondents' networking outside the Arab region.

Table 3. Factor analysis rotated component matrix of SNS motivations among Emiratis

Factors Motives	Factor 1 Exchange news, opinion, and photos	Factor 2 Sociability	Factor 3 Accessibility (new and easy way of communication)	Factor 4 Connecting to overseas friends and families
1. To exchange opinions with friends	**0.681**	-.044	0.193	0.328
2. To write comments on everyday events	**0.707**	0.239	0.109	--
3. To upload some videos and photos	**0.641**	0.292	0.102	0.160
4. To post some up-to-date news that might grab my friends' attention	**0.804**	0.123	0.217	--
5. To read what others have posted	**0.534**	0.130	0.501	--
6. To pass time	0.046	**0.614**	--	--
7. To connect with new friends	--	**0.715**	--	0.295
8. To find new friends	0.294	**0.743**	--	--
9. To have accompany	0.388	**0.636**	--	0.144
10. Because it is the best way to find latest news	0.222	0.085	**0.789**	0.065
11. Because it is the easiest way to connect with my friends	0.149	0.068	**0.820**	0.063
12. To connect with my friends overseas	0.166	0.147	0.094	**0.809**
13. To connect with my family living abroad	0.043	0.122	--	**0.836**

Table 4. Frequency of communicating with various nationalities via SNS

The Nationality	Frequency of Connecting to Various Nationalities %				Mean	Weighted Mean %
	Always	Sometimes	Rarely	Never		
Emiratis (Nationals)	81.7	15.2	2.2	0.9	2.78	92.6
Arabs (Non-Emiratis)	38.7	40.0	16.1	5.2	2.12	70.7%
Americans	10.0	16.5	22.2	51.3	0.85	28.4%
Europeans	10.0	12.6	22.2	55.2	0.77	25.8%
Asians	--	0.9	--	--	--	--

HYPOTHESES TEST

This research examines five hypotheses. The results are as follow:

H1: Intensity of SNS use is positively associated with individuals' perceived online bridging and bonding social capital.

Pearson correlation was used to test this hypothesis and the result is shown in Table 5.

Table 5. Correlation between intensive usages of SNSs and online social capital

Variables	Online Social Capital	
	Bridging	Bonding
Intensive Usages of SN Connection	.200(*)	0.100 (NS)

* $P \leq 0.001$ (2-tailed) N = 230 *(NS) non-significant*

The result showed a significant correlation between intensity of SNSs usage and bridging social capital r = .200. However, the correlation is not significant between intensive usages of SNSs and bonding social capital.

This indicates that social networking websites are effective in predicting online bridging social capital, in that the SNSs allow Emiratis to establish tentative relationships with new friends. In addition, the intensive usage of SNSs does not predict bonding social capital, which means that Emiratis tend to have weak ties via SNSs rather than strong personal connections.

H2: There is a correlation between online social networking size and the social capital types (bridging and bonding).

The result of Pearson correlation is shown in Table 6.

Pearson correlation revealed a significant weak correlation between online SNS size and bridging social capital r = .155, while there is no significant correlation between online social networking size and bonding social capital.

This means that the bigger the size of SNS, the more the bridging social capital and the lesser the online bonding will be perceived by the respondents.

Table 6. Correlation between online social networking size and the social capital type

Variables	Online Social Capital	
	Bridging	Bonding
Online social networking size	.155(*)	-0.018 (NS)

Note: * P≤ = 0.02 NS: Non significant (2-tailed) N = 230

H3: There is a correlation between diversity of social categories (nationalities and relationships) and social capital type (bridging and bonding)

The results in Table 7 showed a positive significant correlation between diversity of "relationships" connection via SNSs and both of bonding and bridging social capital. However, the diversity of "nationalities" was not significantly correlated to bonding social capital while it was significantly correlated to bridging.

Table 7. Correlation between diversity of social categories and social capital types

Variables		Online Social Capital	
		Bridging	Bonding
Diversity of social categories in SNS	Relationships	.173(**)	.139(*)
	Nationalities	.141(*)	0.028 (NS)

Note: * P≤0.03 ** P≤ 0.001 (2-tailed) N = 230 *(NS) non-significant*

H4: There is a significant correlation between motivation of using SNSs and type of social capital.

Pearson correlation revealed that there are significant correlations (*p = .000*) between respondents' motivations of using SNSs and both types of social capital (Sociability r = 0.242), (Connecting overseas friends and families r = 0.242), (Exchange news, opinions, and photos r = 0.345) and (Accessibility "new and easy way of communication", r = 0.322). The correlation between each factor of motivations and the types of social capitals were significant as shown in Table 8.

The results showed a significant correlation between all SNS motivation factors and both types of social capital: bonding and bridging. However, the correlation was stronger between motivation and bridging than bonding.

The correlation was stronger with bridging especially for both motivation factors: "exchange opinions and news" and "accessibility". The "exchange news, opinions, and photos" motive strongly predicts both bridging and bonding.

This indicates that using SNSs more for "exchanging news", "connecting families and friends", "sociability", or "accessibility" is associated with increased online bridging and bonding.

Table 8. Correlation between motivations and types of social capitals

Variables		Online Social Capital	
		Bridging	**Bonding**
SNSs Motivation factors	Exchange news, opinions, and photos	0.374(*)	0.210 (***)
	Accessibility (new and easy way of communication)	0.316(*)	0.174 (*)
	Connecting overseas friends and families	0.225(*)	0.141 (**)
	Sociability	0.241(*)	0.196 (**)

Note: * $P \leq 0.000$ ** $P \leq 0.003$ *** $P \leq 0.001$ (2-tailed) N = 230 *NS) non-significant*

H5: There is a significant difference between males and females in their:
1. Motivations of using social networking sites, and
2. Online social capital.

The T-test was used to examine this hypothesis. It showed no significant difference between males and females in their motivations of SNS usage. The results are shown in Table 9.

The T-test shows that there is no significant difference between males and females in bridging social capital in the social networking sites. The difference was significant in bonding social capital (t = 3.840, $p = 0.000$). The results show that online bonding social capital is higher among males than females.

In addition, the T-test was used to examine if there is any significant difference between males and females in their communication with various nationalities. The results revealed that there is no significant difference between males and females in their connections to Emiratis, Americans, and Europeans. However, there was a significant difference (t = 2.87, $df = 228$, $p = 0.004$) between them in their connection to Arabs (non-Emiratis). Males (M = 2.29) have more connection with Arabs (non-Emiratis) than females (M = 1.97).

Table 9. Differences between males and females in their social capital

Online Social Capital Type	Gender	Mean	Std. Deviation	t	df	Sig. (2-tailed)
Bridging	Males	2.56	0.499	-0.973	228	0.331 (NS)
	Females	2.62	0.487			
Bonding	Males	2.13	0.558	3.840		0.000
	Females	1.83	0.601			

DISCUSSION AND CONCLUSION

This research investigated the association between intensive usage of the social networking sites and online social capital. Also, the correlation between size of social networking friends/followers and the type of online social capital was investigated. The effect of diversity of relationships and nationalities on the type of online social capital was examined. The type of and effect of SNS usage motivation were tested. In this section, a discussion of the research results is presented.

In this research, it was revealed that the WhatsApp is the most frequently used SNS among the respondents. Facebook was the fourth-used SNS. This result is different from some Arab and Western research findings.

According to the Arab World Online report (2013), Facebook is the most popular social network, followed by Google+, and then Twitter. Most respondents in that report stated they have never used the other social networks listed in the AWO survey. The report also indicated 54% of respondents used Facebook more than once a day, while 30% used Google+ at the same frequency. Only 14% of respondents used Twitter more than once a day (13).

Ellison, N. et al (2007) found that university students intensively use Facebook in their everyday lives. Ahmed, Azza (2010) indicated that Facebook is the most popular online social network (65.2%) among a sample of (325) respondents from Egypt and UAE (p: 82). Mourtada and Salem (2011) found that Facebook is the most popular social media technology in the Arab world, with Twitter rapidly gaining in popularity. Al-Jenaibi, B. (2011) found that the most popular social media technologies are, for the most part, the same as in the West: Facebook, video-sharing sites like YouTube, and micro-blogging sites like Twitter. Wiest, J. and Eltantawy, N. (2012) found that Facebook is overwhelmingly the favorite social networking sites among a sample (n = 179) of UAE university students. In her quantitative and qualitative study, Ahmed, Azza (2015) found the mobile application "WhatsApp" was the most common application used among a sample of 313 Arab residents of the United Arab Emirates. Facebook and Instagram followed it. In addition, the qualitative analysis showed that Facebook is the predominant SNS among the majority of the interviewees along with WhatsApp (p: 205).

It seems that the SNS usage habits have changed rapidly throughout the past few years. The smartphone might have an impact on the frequency of using each type among many other factors, such as the culture factors and the features in each SNS.

The literature suggests that the type of relationships within the social network can predict different kinds of social capital.

The results showed that Emiratis tend to communicate with nationals and Arabs (non-Emiratis) more than people from other nationalities. This result supports the findings of Wellman et al (2010) that suggest the Internet is particularly useful for keeping contact among friends who are socially and geographically dispersed. Yet distance still matters: communication is lower with distant than nearby friends (p: 450). Also, Watkins & Lee (2009) concluded that SNS users tend to interact mostly with friends they already know well rather than be friend to complete strangers (p: 22).

Also, the research revealed that the more diverse the social categories of "relationships" and "nationalities", the more bridging social capital can be predicted. Bonding social capital is associated positively with "relationships", but negatively with "nationalities". This means that Emiratis are keen to use SNS to broaden their social networks rather than get/provide emotional support.

The results showed an association between intensity of SNS connection and bridging social capital, while no significant correlation was found between intensity of SNS connection and the bonding social capital. This result supports the Ellison, Steinfield, & Lampe (2007) findings, indicating that bridging social capital was the most valued use of Facebook. They suggested that networking through these sites may help to crystallize relationships that "might otherwise remain ephemeral" (p. 25). They explained that the intensity of Facebook usage can help students accumulate and maintain bridging social capital. This form of social capital; which is closely linked to the notion of "weak ties", seems well suited to social software applications, because it enables users to maintain such ties cheaply and easily.

Granovetter (1973) explained this process by saying that the social capital is to encourage users to strengthen latent ties and maintain connections with former friends, thus allowing people to stay connected as they move from one offline community to another.

Johnston, et al. (2013) results indicate that intensity of Facebook use plays a role in the creation of social capital, but it is particularly significant regarding the maintenance of social capital in the South African context. The Facebook intensity is positively correlated with all types of social capital.

However, Aubrey & Rill (2013) found that FB use was not associated with online bridging or online bonding; they suggested that Facebook might not be effective in facilitating bonding relationships, but it might help users to maintain already established weak ties between individuals (p: 491). Wellman, et al. (2010) concluded that the greater use of the Internet may lead to larger social networks with more weak ties and distasteful interactions with some of these ties, resulting in lower commitment to the online community (p: 494). Phua, and Jin, (2011) found that intensity of SNS usage was significantly positively associated with bonding and bridging social capital in the US college environment (p: 512). In addition, Ahn (2012) found that time spent on Facebook and MySpace was significantly related to bridging social capital, whereas there was no relationship to bonding social capital (p: 106).

In the current study, four factors were found to determine the respondents' motivations of SNS usage. These factors are: Exchange information, Sociability, Accessibility (which refers to easy way to access new information), and Connecting with overseas friends and families. This finding supports the results of Ellison (2007) who reported that Michigan undergraduate students overwhelmingly used Facebook to keep in touch with old friends and to maintain or intensify relationships characterized by some form of offline connection, such as dormitory proximity or a shared class.

In addition, the findings of the current research revealed that the four SNS motivation factors were associated with increase online bridging and bonding. This finding supports Aubrey & Rill (2013) results that found using Facebook for sociability reasons was associated with increased online bridging and bonding. Moreover, they provided evidence of the sociability motivation mediating the relationship between Facebook habits and online bonding and bridging. Ellison, et al. (2011) found that FB communication practices focused on using the site for social information-seeking purposes were positively associated with online social capital. In this context, Donath and Boyd (2004) suggested that Facebook allows users to maintain weak ties cheaply and easily. These findings suggest that intensive users of SNSs are likely to experience gains in online social capital. The results of Haythornthwaite (2000) suggest that online communicators who communicate with each other more frequently may be more likely to have closer relationships; therefore, more frequent communication with other Facebook users is necessary to build closer relationships as a first step towards bonding social capital.

LIMITATION AND SUGGESTIONS

Although the method used in this study does not allow for making a causal conclusion, it was clear that intensive usage of social networking sites is a significant predictor of online bridging social capital among Emiratis. However, the research findings are still not generalizable to the larger Emiratis population of SNS users in other Emirates.

Future studies should investigate how these variables interact among other populations of users. More research efforts should be directed to study how new generations are using the social networking websites and the mechanism used to build their social capital. More research should be conducted to investigate the differences between social capital in online and social offline settings for the two types of social capital in the Arab region. In other words, does online social capital strengthen or weaken the offline social capital? This field of research should attract more Arab scholars to investigate the impact of social media on Arab societies and whether these impacts differ from their counterparts in the US and Europe.

A longitudinal research should be conducted to investigate the habits of SNS usage among Arab societies. The findings of such research might help in planning how social media will be used to affect the Arab youth's attitude and behaviors.

In conclusion, as social network sites grow, understanding the interaction between site features and individual differences in users will become even more important and will require more attention from the media scholars.

REFERENCES

Ahmed, A. A. A. (2010). Online privacy concerns among social networks' users. *Cross-Cultural Communication, 6*, 74–89.

Ahmed, A. A. A. (2015). "Sharing is Caring": Online Self-Disclosure, Offline Social Support, and SNS in the UAE. *Contemporary Review of Middle East, 2*(3), 192–219. doi:10.1177/2347798915601574

Ahn, J. (2012). Teenagers' Experiences with Social Network Sites: Relationships to Bridging and Bonding Social Capital. *The Information Society, 28*(2), 99–109. doi:10.1080/01972243.2011.649394

Al Jenaibi, B. N. A. (2011). Use of Social Media in the United Arab Emirates: An Initial Study. *Global Media Journal Arabian Edition, 1*(2), 3-27. Retrieved from: http://www.gmjme.com/gmj_custom_files/volume1_issue2/articles_in_english/volume1-issue2-article-3-27.pdf

Aubrey, F. S., & Rill, L. (2013). Investigating Relations between Facebook Use and Social capital Among College Undergraduates. *Communication Quarterly, 61*(4), 479–496. doi:10.1080/01463373.2013.801869

Aubrey, S., Chattopadhyay, S., & Rill, L. (2008). *Are Facebook Friends Like Face-to-Face Friends: Investigating Relations Between the Use of Social Networking Websites and Social capital.* Paper presented at the annual meeting of the International Communication Association.

Ayyad, K. (2011). Internet Usage vs. Traditional Media Usage among University Students in the United Arab Emirates. *Journal of Arab & Muslim Media Research, 4*(1), 41–61. doi:10.1386/jammr.4.1.41_1

Banczyk, B., & Senokozlieva, M. (2008). *The "Wurst" Meets "Fatless" in MySpace: The Relationship Between Self-Esteem, Personality, and Self-Presentation in an Online Community.* International Communication Association, Annual Meeting.

Bargh, J., & McKenna, K. (2004). The Internet and Social Life. *Annual Review of Psychology, 55*(1), 573–590. doi:10.1146/annurev.psych.55.090902.141922 PMID:14744227

Boase, J., Horrigan, J., Wellman, B., & Rainie, L. (2006). The Strength of Internet Ties: The internet and E-mail Aid Users in Maintaining Their Social Networks and Provide Pathways to Help When People Face Big Decisions. *Pew Internet and American Life Project.* Retrieved from: http://www.pewinternet.org/files/old-media/Files/Reports/2006/PIP_Internet_ties.pdf.pdf

boyd, d. (2008). *Taken Out of Context: American Teen Sociality in Networked Publics* (PhD Dissertation). University of California-Berkeley, School of Information.

Burke, M., Kraut, R., & Marlow, C. (2011). *Social Capital on Facebook: Differentiating Uses and Users.* CHI 2011, Vancouver, Canada.

Burke, M., Marlow, C., & Lento, T. (2010). Social Network Activity and Social Well-Being. In *Proceeding of the 2010 ACM Conference on Human Factors in Computing Systems.* New York, NY: ACM.

Choi, S. M., Kim, Y., Sung, Y., & Sohn, D. (2011). Bridging or Bonding? A cross-cultural study of social relationships in social networking sites. *Information Communication and Society, 14*(1), 107–129. doi:10.1080/13691181003792624

Chua, S.-C., & Choib, S. M. (2010). Social capital and self-presentation on social networking sites: A comparative study of Chinese and American young generations. *Chinese Journal of Communication, 3*(4), 402–420. doi:10.1080/17544750.2010.516575

Colás, P., & ... . (2013). Young People and Social Networks: Motivations and Preferred Use. *Scientific Journal of Media Education, 2*(40), 15–23.

Coleman, J. S. (1988). Social Capital in the Creation of Human Capital. *American Journal of Sociology, 94*, 95–121. doi:10.1086/228943

Croucher, S. M. (2011). Social Networking and Cultural Adaptation: A Theoretical Model. *Journal of International and Intercultural Communication, 4*(4), 259–264. doi:10.1080/17513057.2011.598046

Donath, J., & Boyd, D. (2004). Public Displays of Connection. *BT Technology Journal, 22*(4), 71–82. doi:10.1023/B:BTTJ.0000047585.06264.cc

Dunne, A., Lawlor, M. A., & Rowley, J. (2010). Young People's Use of Online Social Networking Sites: A Uses and Gratifications Perspective. *Journal of Research in Interactive Marketing, 4*(1), 46–58. doi:10.1108/17505931011033551

Ellison, N. (2008). Introduction: Reshaping campus communication and community through social network sites. In The ECAR study of undergraduate students and information technology (vol. 8, pp. 19–32). Boulder, CO: Educause.

Ellison, N., Seinfield, C., & Lampe, C. (2006). *Spatially Bounded Online Social Networks and Social Capital: The Role of Facebook.* Paper presented at the Annual Conference of the International Communication Association (ICA), Dresden, Germany.

Ellison, N., Seinfield, C., & Lampe, C. (2007). The Benefits of Facebook "Friends": Social Capital and College Students' Use of Online Social Network Sites. *Journal of Computer-Mediated Communication, 12*(4), 1143–1168. doi:10.1111/j.1083-6101.2007.00367.x

Ellison, N., Seinfield, C., & Lampe, C. (2011). Connection Strategies: Social Capital Implications of Facebook-Enabled Communication Practices. *New Media & Society, 13*(6), 873–892. doi:10.1177/1461444810385389

Ellison, N., Vitak, J., Gray, R., & Lampe, C. (2014). Cultivating Social Resources on Social Network Sites: Facebook Relationship Maintenance Behaviors and Their Role in Social Capital Processes. *Journal of Computer-Mediated Communication, 19*(4), 855–870. doi:10.1111/jcc4.12078

Fukuyama, F. (2001). Social Capital, Civil Society and Development. *Third World Quarterly, 22*(1), 7–20. doi:10.1080/713701144

Gershuny, J. (2002). Social Leisure and Home IT: A Panel Time-Diary Approach. *IT & Society, 1,* 54–72.

Granovetter, M. (1973). The Strength of Weak Ties. *American Journal of Sociology, 78*(6), 1360–1380. doi:10.1086/225469

Greenhow, C., & Robelia, B. (2009). Old Communication, New Literacies: Social Network Sites as Social Learning Resources. *Journal of Computer-Mediated Communication, 14*(4), 1130–1161. doi:10.1111/j.1083-6101.2009.01484.x

Hampton, K., & Wellman, B. (2003). Neighboring in Netville: How the Internet Supports Community and Social Capital in a Wired Suburb. *City & Community, 2*(4), 277–311. doi:10.1046/j.1535-6841.2003.00057.x

Haythornthwaite, C. (2000). Online Personal Networks. *New Media & Society, 2*(2), 195–226. doi:10.1177/14614440022225779

Hofer, M., & Aubert, V. (2013). Perceived Bonding and Bridging Social Capital on Twitter: Differentiating between Followers and Followees. *Computers in Human Behavior, 29*(6), 2134–2142. doi:10.1016/j.chb.2013.04.038

Islam, K. M (2006). Social Capital and Health: Does Egalitarianism Matter?: A Literature Review. *International Journal for Equity in Health, 5*(3), 1–28. PMID:16597324

Johnston, K. (2013). Social Capital: The Benefit of Facebook 'Friends'. *Información Tecnológica, 32*(1), 24–36.

Karuppasamy, G., Anwar, A., Bhartiya, A., Sajjad, S., Rashid, M., Mathew, E., ... Sreedharan, J. (2013). Use of Social Networking Sites among University Students in Ajman, United Arab Emirates. *Nepal Journal of Epidemiology., 3*(2), 245–250. doi:10.3126/nje.v3i2.8512

Kavanaugh, A., Carroll, J. M., Rosson, M. B., Zin, T. T., & Reese, D. (2005). Community Networks: Where offline Communities Meet Online. *Journal of Computer-Mediated Communication, 10*(4). doi:10.1111/j.1083-6101.2005.tb00266.x

Kavanaugh, A., & Patterson, S. (2001). The Impact of Community Computer Networks on Social Capital and community involvement. *The American Behavioral Scientist, 45*(3), 496–509. doi:10.1177/00027640121957312

Kohut, A. (2012). *Social Networking Popular Across Globe: Arab Publics Most Likely to Express Political Views Online.* Global Attitude Project, PEW Research Center. Retrieved from http://www.pewglobal.org/files/2012/12/Pew-Global-Attitudes-Project-Technology-Report-FINAL-December-12-2012.pdf

Koku, E., Nazer, N., & Wellman, B. (2001). Netting Scholars: Online and Offline. *The American Behavioral Scientist*, *44*(10), 1752–1774. doi:10.1177/00027640121958023

Lee, S. J. (2009). Online Communication and Adolescent Social Ties: Who benefits more from Internet Use? *Journal of Computer-Mediated Communication*, *14*(3), 509–531. doi:10.1111/j.1083-6101.2009.01451.x

Lenhart, A., & Madden, M. (2007). *The Use of Social Media Gains a Greater Foothold in Teen Life*. Pew Internet and American Life Project.

McQuail, D., Blumler, J. G., & Brown, J. (1972). The television audience: A revised perspective. In D. McQuail (Ed.), *Sociology of Mass Communication* (pp. 65–135). Middlesex, UK: Penguin.

Mourtada, R., & Salem, F. (2011). Civil movements: The Impact of Facebook and Twitter. *Arab Social Media Report*, *1*(2), 1–30.

Nie, N. H. (2001). Sociability, Interpersonal Relations, and the Internet: Reconciling Conflicting Findings. *The American Behavioral Scientist*, *45*(3), 420–435. doi:10.1177/00027640121957277

Pempek, T. A., Yermolayeva, Y. A., & Calvert, S. L. (2009). College students' social networking experiences on Facebook. *Journal of Applied Developmental Psychology*, *30*(3), 227–238. doi:10.1016/j.appdev.2008.12.010

Phua, J. J., & Jin, S. A. (2011). 'Finding a Home Away From Home': The Use of Social Networking Sites by Asia-Pacific Students in the United States for Bridging and Bonding Social Capital. *Asian Journal of Communication*, *21*(5), 504–519. doi:10.1080/01292986.2011.587015

Putnam, R. D. (2000). *Bowling Alone: The Collapse and Revival of American Community*. New York: Simon & Schuster. doi:10.1145/358916.361990

Raacke, J., & Bonds-Raacke, J. (2008). MySpace and Facebook: Applying Uses and Gratifications Theory to Exploring Friend Networking Sites. *CyperPsychology & Behavior*, *11*(2), 169–174. doi:10.1089/cpb.2007.0056 PMID:18422409

The Arab World Online Report: Trends in Internet Usage in the Arab Region. (2013). Dubai School of Government.

The State of Broadband 2014: Broadband for all. (2014). A report by the Broadband Commission, United Nations: Educational, Scientific, Cultural Organization.

Tice, D. M., Butler, J. L., Muraven, M. B., & Stillwell, A. M. (1995). When Modesty Prevails: Differential Favorability of Self-Presentation to Friends and Strangers. *Journal of Personality and Social Psychology*, *69*(6), 1120–1138. doi:10.1037/0022-3514.69.6.1120

United Arab Emirates' National Bureau of Statistics. (2010). Retrieved on 24th January 2015, from: http://www.uaestatistics.gov.ae/ReportPDF/Population%20Estimates%202006%20-%202010.pdf

Valenzuela, S., Park, N., & Kee, K. F. (2009). Is There Social Capital in a Social Network Site?: Facebook Use and College Students' Life Satisfaction, Trust, and Participation. *Journal of Computer-Mediated Communication*, *14*(4), 875–901. doi:10.1111/j.1083-6101.2009.01474.x

Villegas, J. (2011). The Influence of Social Media Usage and Online Social Capital on Advertising Perception. *American Academy of Advertising Conference Proceedings*, 69.

Vitak, J. (2012). The Impact of Context Collapse and Privacy on Social Network Site Disclosures. *Journal of Broadcasting & Electronic Media*, *56*(4), 451–470. doi:10.1080/08838151.2012.732140

Walkins, S. C., & Lee, H. E. (2009). *Bonding, Bridging and Friending: Investigating the Social Aspects of Social Networking Sites.* Paper presented in the 95th Annual Convention of the National Communication Association (NCA), Chicago. IL.

Wellman, B., Haase, A. Q., Witte, J., & Hampton, K. (2010). Does the Internet Increase, Decrease or Supplement Social Capital? Social Networks, Participation and Community Commitment. *The American Behavioral Scientist*, *45*(3), 436–455. doi:10.1177/00027640121957286

Wiest, J., & Eltantawy, N. (2012). Social media use among UAE College Students One Year after the Arab Spring. *Journal of Arab and Muslim Media Research*, *5*(3), 209–226. doi:10.1386/jammr.5.3.209_1

Williams, D. (2006). On and Off the 'Net: Scales for Social Capital in an Online Era. *Journal of Computer-Mediated Communication*, *11*(2), 593–628. doi:10.1111/j.1083-6101.2006.00029.x

Wong, W. K. W. (2012). Faces on Facebook: A Study of Self-Presentation and Social Support on Facebook. *Discovery-SS Student E-Journal*, *1*, 184–214.

This research was previously published in Modern Perspectives on Virtual Communications and Social Networking; pages 90-119, copyright year 2019 by Information Science Reference (an imprint of IGI Global).

Chapter 39
Supporting Participation in Online Social Networks

Agostino Poggi

 https://orcid.org/0000-0003-3528-0260

University of Parma, Italy

Paolo Fornacciari

 https://orcid.org/0000-0002-2184-8006

University of Parma, Italy

Gianfranco Lombardo

University of Parma, Italy

Monica Mordonini

 https://orcid.org/0000-0002-5916-9770

University of Parma, Italy

Michele Tomaiuolo

 https://orcid.org/0000-0002-6030-9435

University of Parma, Italy

ABSTRACT

Social networking systems can be considered one of the most important social phenomena because they succeeded in involving billions of people all around the world and in attracting users from several social groups, regardless of age, gender, education, or nationality. Social networking systems blur the distinction between the private and working spheres, and users are known to use such systems both at home and at the work place both professionally and with recreational goals. Social networking systems can be equally used to organize a work meeting, a dinner with the colleagues, or a birthday party with friends. In the vast majority of cases, social networking platforms are still used without corporate blessing. However, several traditional information systems, such as CRMs and ERPs, have also been modified in order to include social aspects. This chapter discusses the participation in online social networking activities and, in particular, the technologies that support and promote the participation in online social network.

DOI: 10.4018/978-1-6684-6307-9.ch039

INTRODUCTION

Social networking systems represent one of the most important social phenomena involving billions of people all around the world, attracting users from several social groups, regardless of age, gender, education, or nationality. In fact, some social networking systems are become the largest information systems accessible to the general public and, because of their neutrality regarding the public-private and the work-home axes, they often assume the role of feral systems.

Social networking systems blur the distinction between the private and working spheres, and users are known to use such systems both at home and on the work place both professionally and with recreational goals. Social networking systems can be equally used to organize a work meeting, a dinner with the colleagues or a birthday party with friends. For example, the chat systems that are embedded in social networking platforms are often the most practical way to contact a colleague to ask an urgent question, especially in technologically oriented companies.

Moreover, several traditional information systems have been modified in order to include social aspects and several organizations: (*i*) allow external social networking platforms to be used (e.g., Facebook was available for Microsoft and Apple employees before the general public launch), (*ii*) have created an internal social networking platform (DiMicco & Millen, 2007), or (*iii*) allow other social platforms for specific purposes (Millen et al., 2006). However, in the vast majority of cases, social networking platforms are used without corporate blessing, maintaining their status as feral systems.

According to DiMicco (2008), most users that use social networking platforms for work purposes are mostly interested in accumulating social capital, either for career advancement or to gather support for their own projects inside the company. Given the close relation between professional usage of social media and social capital.

This chapter has the goal of discussing about the participation in online social network, about the technologies that support and promote their use by individual and organization. The next section introduces online social networks; the third section discussed about the participation in this kind of networks; the fourth section introduces the technologies the support the activities in online social network; the fifth section discusses about the use of online social network and related social media in firms and organizations; and, finally, the last section concludes the summarizing its main contributions and presenting the directions for future work.

BACKGROUND

The result of the interactions among the users in a social networking system is an online social network, i.e., a special case of the more general concept of social network. A social network is defined as a set or sets of actors and the relations defined on them (Wasserman & Faust, 1994). Social networks are typically studied using social network analysis, a discipline that focuses on the structural and topological features of the network. More recently, additional dimensions have been added to the traditional social network analytic approach (Monge and Contractor 2003; Borgatti and Foster 2003; Parkhe et al. 2006; Hoang and Antoncic 2003).

The study of structure of Online Social Networks, expressed as patterns of links among nodes, can exploit models and ideas from classical sociology and anthropology, with particular attention to contextual and relational approaches. In fact, all the results obtained in decades of studies of human networks are also at the basis of the analysis of online social networks. However, these results cannot be simply applied to the different context of online relations. Instead they have to be evaluated and adapted to the new networks, which may have significantly different structure and dynamics.

Moreover, online social networking platforms may greatly vary both technically and in their aims. They may be used by people for organizing quite diverse activities, in different types of virtual communities. In particular, virtual organizations, virtual teams, and online networks of practice are the most discussed. Although there are several differences that clearly set the concepts apart, the *trait d'union* of these virtual communities are: i) the lack of central authority, ii) their temporary and impromptu nature, and iii) the importance of reputation and trust as opposed to bureaucracy and law.

Virtual Organization

According to the definition given by Mowshowitz (1994), a virtual organization is "a temporary network of autonomous organizations that cooperate based on complementary competencies and connect their information systems to those of their partners via networks aiming at developing, making, and distributing products in cooperation." The term was then popularized by the Grid Computing community, referring to Virtual Organizations as *"flexible, secure, coordinated resource sharing among dynamic collections of individuals, institutions, and resources"* (Foster et al., 2001). The premise of Virtual Organizations is the technical availability of tools for effective collaboration among people located in different places, but their definition also emphasizes the possibility to share a large number of resources, including documents, data, knowledge and tools among interested people. Their importance is sustained by continuing trends in production and social forms, including the growing number of knowledge workers, the emergence of integrated industrial district and other aspects developing at an international level, like dynamic supply chains, just-in-time production, sub-contracting, delocalization, externalization, global logistics and mass migrations which collectively are usually named *"globalization"*.

Virtual Team

A virtual team is usually defined as a group of geographically, organizationally and/or time dispersed members connected by information and telecommunication technologies (e.g., email, video and voice conferencing services) that work together asynchronously or across organizational levels (Powell et al., 2004; Lipnack & Stamps, 2008; Ale Ebrahim et. al. (2009). Virtual teams can represent organizational structures within the context of some virtual organization, but they can also come into existence in other situations, where independent people collaborate on a project (e.g., an open source project); in these cases, they do not have hierarchy or any other common structure because member may be from different organizations.

Due to the streamlined development of information technologies, today many companies prefer to take advantage of virtual teams for the development of the work of a relevant part of their projects and more and more people work in virtual teams for at least part of the time. In fact, virtual teams allow companies to procure the best competences necessary for their projects without geographical restrictions and usually well-managed virtual teams are more productive than co-located teams (Vlaar et al., 2008). However, the success of the work of virtual team requires new skills, new ways of working and the presence of effective leaders.

Online Network of Practice

An online network of practice represents an informal and emergent virtual community that is represented by individuals connected through social relationships and that supports the exchange of information between its members in order to perform their work and sharing knowledge with each other (Brown & Duguid, 2017). The term practice represents the glue that connects individuals in the network. Usually the glue is the type of work (e.g., journalist, software developer, teacher), but often is the sharing of similar interests (e.g., common hobbies, discussing sports and/or politics). In an online network of practice, individuals may never get to know one another or meet face-to-face. Moreover, their interactions are generally coordinate through means such as blogs, microblogs, mailing lists and bulletin boards (Teigland, (2004).

Networks of practice differ from networks in several significant ways. In fact, individuals not only for their own needs, but to serve the needs of others. One of the most interesting distinctions is that in a network of practice, there is an intentional commitment to advance the field of practice, and to share those discoveries with a wider audience; in fact, its members make their resources and knowledge available to anyone, especially those doing related work (Wheatley & Frieze, 2006).

PARTICIPATION IN ONLINE SOCIAL NETWORKS

In order to understand the reasons that motivate the users in engaging in online social activities in general, and, more specifically, in sharing their valued knowledge in online communities, it is necessary to analyze the nature and the structure of their relationships in the context of a specific community, and to evaluate the possible implications for the involved users.

Social Capital

In particular, an important theoretical foundation for the analysis of participation in social networks is constituted by social capital (Maskell, 2000; Lin, 2017). Social capital represents a person's benefit due to his relations with other persons, including family, colleagues, friends and generic contacts. The concept originated in studies about communities, to underline the importance of collective actions and the associated enduring relations of trust and cooperation, for the functioning of neighborhoods in large cities (Jacobs, 1961).

Erickson (2000) argues that network variety as much as the people that someone knows, is a form of social capital valuable to both employers and employees in the hiring process. In fact, network variety is social "capital" in the same sense that education and work experience are human "capital" because all these forms of capital yield returns in the form of greater employee productivity.

Social capital has been studied as a factor providing additional opportunities to some players in a competitive scenario, and, from this point of view, it has been studied in the context of firms (Backer, 1990), nations (Fukuyama, 1995) and geographic regions (Putnam, 1995). In this sense, social capital is defined as a third kind of capital that is brought in the competitive arena, along with financial capital, which includes machinery and raw materials, and human capital, which includes knowledge and skills. Moreover, the role of social capital in the development of human capital has been studied by Loury and Coleman (Loury, 1987; Coleman, 1988).

Social capital is typically studied: (*i*) by drawing a graph of connected people and their own resources, creating a connection between each player's resources and those of his closest contacts; or (*ii*) by analyzing social structures in their own right, and supposing that the network structure alone can be used to estimate some player's competitive advantage, at the social stance.

The size of the ego-centered social network is an important factor to estimate the social capital of one individual; however, the size alone does not provide enough information. According to Burt (1992) social capital is related with the number of non-redundant contacts and not directly with the simple number of contacts. In fact, although information spreads rapidly among homogeneous, richly interconnected groups, Granovetter (1973) argues that new ideas and opportunities are introduced in the groups by contacts with people from outside the group. In order to explain this phenomenon, Granovetter distinguished among three types of ties: (*i*) strong ties, (*ii*) weak ties, and (*iii*) absent ties.

A quantitative distinction between strong and weak ties has been subject of debate, but intuitively weak ties are simple acquaintances, while strong ties are reserved for close friends and family. The "*absent ties*" indicate missing relations in the network. Burt capitalizes on Granovetter's insight, and emphasizes the importance of absent ties, that create the "*structural holes*" in the network texture. According to Burt, structural holes allow the individuals that create a weak link among two otherwise separated communities to greatly increase their social capital.

Nahapiet & Goshal (1998) discuss the role of social capital in building intellectual capital inside organizations. The authors distinguish the structural, relational, and cognitive aspects of social networks. The structural properties describe the patterns of connection among actors and regard the social system as a whole. The relational properties describe the type of ties people have developed during their interactions, including relationships like friendship, trust, and respect. The cognitive properties refer to basic knowledge, representations, languages and other systems of meaning, shared among actors. Moreover, they focus on the development of intellectual capital, which is essentially an aspect of human capital, but may also be owned by a social collectivity. In fact, they classify knowledge as (*i*) either implicit or explicit, and (*ii*) either individual or social. In the case of social knowledge, they argue that social capital facilitates the creation of intellectual capital primarily by creating conditions for exchange and combination of knowledge.

Evolution of Network Connections

Monge and Contractor (2003) proposed a multi-theoretical and multilevel model for analyzing the evolution of network connections in online social networks. Their analysis considers the following theories: self-interest, mutual interest and collective action, homophily and proximity, exchange and dependency, co-evolution, contagion, balance and transitivity, and cognition.

According to the theories of self-interest, people create ties with other people and participate in team activities in order to maximize the satisfaction of their own goals. The most known theories of self-interest are based on the notion of social capital (Burt, 1992). Another foundation of these theories lies on transaction cost economics (Williamson, 1991).

The mutual interest and collective action theories study the coordinated action of individuals in a team. They explain collective actions as a mean for reaching outcomes which would be unattainable by individual action (Fulk et al., 2004). Thus, individuals collaborate in a community because they share mutual interests.

The principle at the basis of homophily and proximity theories is that connections are mostly structured according to similarity (McPherson et al., 2001). Moreover, connections between dissimilar individuals break at a higher rate.

Another founding motivation for the emergence of groups can be the exchange and dependency theories (Cook, 1982). These theories explain the creation of communities by analyzing the network structure together with the distribution and flow of resources in the network. Example of exchange networks vary from data analysts to bands of musicians.

The underlying principle of co-evolution theories is that evolution based on environmental selection can be applied to whole organizations, and not only to individuals. Thus, they study how organizations compete and cooperate to access limited resources, and how communities of individuals create ties both internally and towards other communities (Campbell, 1985; Baum, 1999).

For explaining the spread of innovations, contagion theories study how people are brought in contact trough the social structure (Burt, 1987). Social contagion is described as a sort of interpersonal synapse through which ideas are spread. Conversely, some sort of social inoculations may prevent ideas from spreading to parts of the network.

Since macroscopic patterns originate from local structures of social networks, balance and transitivity theories cope with the study of the distribution of triads in digraphs and socio-matrixes (Holland & Leinhardt, 1975). In particular, the first applications of these studies identified the most typical distributions of triads configurations in real social networks and from such distributions showed that individuals' choices have a consistent tendency to be transitive.

Finally, cognitive theories explore the role that meaning, knowledge, and perceptions play in the development of teams and the impact of increasing specialization over collaboration. In this sense, the decision to form a collective depends on what possible members know (Hollingshead et al. 2002). These studies are grounded on the concept of transactive memory.

Social Capital and Knowledge Contribution

Chow & Chan (2008) present a study that was one of the first to provide empirical evidence about the influence of a social network, social trust, and shared goals on employees' intention to share knowledge. This study offers insights to practitioners on the value of social capital and reasons why people are or are not willing to engage in knowledge sharing within an organization. Moreover, it found that social network and shared goals directly influenced the attitude and subjective norm about knowledge sharing and indirectly influenced the intention to share knowledge. Finally, this study argues that social trust does not play a direct role in sharing knowledge and that organizational members do not differentiate between tacit and explicit knowledge when they share it.

Wasko & Faraj (2005) present a study that tries to better understand knowledge flows by examining why people voluntarily contribute knowledge and help others through electronic networks. This study starts from the theoretical model proposed by Nahapiet and Ghoshal (1998) and reports on the activities of an online network supporting a professional legal association. Using archival, network, survey, and content analysis data, it empirically tests a model of knowledge contribution. One of the result is that people usually contribute their knowledge when they perceive that it enhances their professional reputations, when they have the experience to share, and when they are structurally embedded in the network. Surprisingly, contributions occur without regard to expectations of reciprocity from others. Moreover, this study attempts to address the question of why people nevertheless contribute knowledge to others in online networks of practice. The study takes the following features into account, as possible enablers of participation: individual motivations, relational capital, cognitive capital and structural capital.

One key aspect of social contribution is given by individual motivations. In fact, an individual's expectation that some new value will be created, as result of his participation in the network. The individual should expect to receive some benefits from his contribution, even in the absence of direct acquaintance with other members of the community and without mechanisms enforcing or encouraging reciprocity. Increasing the reputation is one of the most important forms of return of investment, especially if the online reputation is believed to have a positive impact on the professional reputation.

Another enabling factor for contributions to an online community is represented by the personal relationships among individuals, as members of that community. Relational capital is directly related to the level of an individual's identification with the community, trust with other members, perception of obligation to participate and reciprocate, acceptance of common norms. In particular, commitment can be associated with a community, apart from individuals.

Any meaningful interaction between two members of a community requires some basic shared understanding. All those common semantic resources, including languages, interpretations, narratives, contexts and norms, are usually described as cognitive capital. In fact, an individual can participate in community activities only if he possesses the required knowledge and, more in general, the required cognitive capital.

Communities characterized by dense internal connections are dialectically correlated with collective actions (Structural capital). In fact, individuals who are strongly embedded in a social network, have many direct ties with other members and a habit of cooperation. On the other hand, an individual's position in the network influences his willingness to contribute, thus increasing both the number and quality of interactions.

Those factors have different weight in different social contexts. In the case study analyzed by Wasko & Faraj (2005), reputation plays a crucial role, since it also affects professional reputation. Other factors, though, also have significant correlation with the number and usefulness of contributions in the online community. The final results compare both the level and helpfulness of contributions against the following factors: (*i*) reputation, (*ii*) willingness to help, (*iii*) centrality in the network structure, (*iv*) self-rated expertise, (*v*) tenure in field, (*vi*) commitment, (*vii*) reciprocity.

With regard to individual motivations, results for the case at hand show a stronger influence of reputation over intrinsic motivations, like willingness to help. Social capital, assessed by determining each individual's degree of centrality to the network, is confirmed to play the most significant role in knowledge exchange. Also cognitive capital, assessed by self-rated expertise and tenure in the field, shows a strong influence over participation, but this is mostly limited to the individual's experience in the field, while self-rated expertise is not quite significant. Finally, in the analyzed network of practice, relational capital, assessed by commitment and reciprocity, is not strongly correlated with knowledge contribution, suggesting that these kinds of ties are more difficult to develop in an online network.

TECHNOLOGIES FOR SOCIAL ONLINE SOCIAL NETWORKS

One of the goals motivating the participation in online communities is the benefit of team work over solo work. Various studies (Van de Ven et al., 1976; Malone & Crowstone, 1994) describe the advantages and costs of coordinating team activities. In fact, while an increase in coordination can lead to greater effectiveness, typically it also produces a faster growth of coordination costs. As a consequence, a lot of effort is being devoted in creating tools and technologies that make group work more effective by containing the costs of their coordination (Bergenti et al. 2011; Franchi & Poggi, 2011; Franchi et al., 2016a). Virtual Teams assembly is another problem that online social platforms can help to solve. In fact, the success of a team depends largely on its assembly process, for identifying the best possible members.

Social collaboration platforms should also help to model and manage multidimensional networks. In fact, apart from direct relationships among people, such platforms should also include other resources. For example, in the area of academic research, a network model could include both people and the events they attend (Wasserman & Faust, 1994), thus creating a bimodal network. Su and Contractor (2011) propose a more complex multi-dimensional network model, including people, documents, data sets, tools, keywords/concepts, etc.

Additionally, in some online communities, participation may also strongly depend on adopted mechanisms and policies for preserving privacy, including confidentiality of messages and identity (Mordonini el al., 2017). For personal identity privacy, stable pseudonyms could be assigned at registration (Andrews, 2002). Moreover, in online communities and Virtual Teams, acquaintance may happen online, without previous connection in real life. In those cases, a member's reputation is directly related to his pseudonym, and ratability of his online activities may be more important than his real world identity for creating trust. Complete anonymity may also have a value in some activities of Virtual Teams, apart from encouraging participation in general. For example, an anonymous brainstorm activity may help opening a conversation about trust and ground rules for online meetings (Young, 2009).

For reaching wider and more effective adoption in open and dynamic online communities, including virtual organizations, virtual teams and online networks of practice, we argue that social networking platforms should embrace an open approach (Franchi et al. 2013). In fact, many isolated sites could not satisfy the need for an inter-organizational collaborative environment. On the other hand, organizations are not keen to rely on a single centralized site, which may pose risks to privacy and may control published data. Moreover, openness is important for participation, too. In fact, a closed environment can hardly reach the minimal dimension and variety required for activating the typical dynamics at the basis of the different theories taken into consideration by the multi-theoretical and multilevel model (Su & Contractor, 2011), for explaining participation in online social networks.

Requirements

In online social networks there are at least three distinct functional elements: (*i*) profile management, (*ii*) social graph management and (*iii*) content production and discussion. In fact, by definition, a social network cannot lack social graph management and self-presentation, no matter how minimal. On the other hand, virtually no modern online social network lacks the content generation features. According to these three main functional areas, it is also possible to draw a classification of the online social networks in three main categories: (*i*) systems where the profile and social graph management is prevalent; (*ii*) systems where the content has a prominent role with respect to social networking activities and there are frequent interactions with people not closely related; and (*iii*) systems where the two aspects have roughly the same importance.

The archetypal examples of the first category of systems are business-related and professional online social networks, like Linkedin. People pay a great deal of attention in creating their profile. In this type of systems there are usually various relationships among users, representing the variety of relationships that members may have in real life. Most users do not visit the site daily and do not add content to the system often (Skeels & Grudin, 2008).

The second type include blogging, micro-blogging and media sharing web sites, like Twitter. The "follow" relationships, which are typical for a system of this kind, are usually not symmetric. The focus is in information transmission; often the system does not support a proper profile and sometimes even the contacts may be hidden. Often weak semantic techniques such as Twitter hash-tags are used, in order to read content by subject instead than by author. Through collaborative tagging, the actors of the system may develop a sort of emergent semantics (Mika, 2007), possibly in the form of so-called "folksonomies". Considering that tags usage is a heavy tailed power-law like distribution, i.e., most people actually uses very few tags, collaborative tagging usually produce a good classification of data (Halpin et al., 2007).

The third category includes the personal online social networks, like Facebook. In this type of systems, users have a profile, partly public and partly confidential. Frequently, there is only one kind of relation, "friendship", which is symmetric and requires approval by both users. These sites have extremely frequent updates: a noticeable percentage of users perform activities on the system at least on a daily basis.

Interoperability

Among the open protocols and data formats for conveying profiles and contacts, Portable Contacts (http://portablecontacts.net/) shows some benefits, especially from the point of view of interoperability. In fact, it is quite simple and well supported by existing large social networks and mail systems, to manage lists of "friends" and address books, respectively. It also allows to associate tags and relationship types with each user, thus paving the way for semantically annotated social networks. In order to let users to express their profile, Friend of a Friend (FOAF) is another sensible choice (Brickley & Miller, 2005). In fact, it provides a descriptive vocabulary that allows the definition of profiles that can be searched and filtered through semantic engines.

Content publication and distribution is another important requirement of online social networks. Atom and RSS emerged as two similar technologies, intended to help readers to receive automatic updates of their favorite websites, and possibly from online acquaintances. RSS and Atom protocols use a pull strategy, i.e., the observer periodically checks the observed resource for updates.

As an alternative, online social networks could adopt a push strategy, i.e., the update is automatically announced to the subscribers. The OStatus protocol (http://status.org/) is a minimal HTTP-based specification for realizing a publish-subscribe mechanism designed around a huh that allows an efficient notification of news to the subscribers.

An on-going and well-supported effort to standardize typical users' activities in social networks is Activity Streams (http://activitystrea.ms/). It is an open format specification for the syndication of activities taken in social web applications and services. The activities of a user are represented as a flow and followers can get it through a subscription.

Finally, OpenSocial (http://opensocial.org/) is a set of common APIs, defined in the form of RESTful Web services, that allow developers to access core functions and information at social networks: (*i*) information about a user's profile, (*ii*) information about the social graph connecting users, and (*iii*) activities occurring in the network, including status updates, publishing of new content and media, commenting and tagging. Moreover, OpenSocial also allows the development of social applications by composing gadgets for collecting and organizing data from different services in a single user interface.

For verifying authorization across different applications, OAuth is often used. An OAuth security token can be used to grant access to a specific site (e.g., a video editing site) for specific resources (e.g., just videos from a specific album) and for a defined duration (e.g., the next 2 hours). This approach allows different social-aware systems to cooperate, and to reduce the necessity for users to maintain and use too many different passwords (Tomaiuolo, 2013; Franchi et al., 2015).

ORGANIZATIONS AND ONLINE SOCIAL NETWORKS

The initial adoption of online collaboration tools and social networking platforms in the work environment has occurred largely on an individual basis. Faced with an increasingly decentralized, expanded and interconnected environment, workers and members of organizations began adopting social networking platforms as better tools for connecting and collaborating with colleagues and partners (Einwiller & Steilen, 2015; Ellison et al., 2015). Thus, social media made their first appearance in firms and organizations mostly without indications from the management and without integration with internal information systems. In this sense, they took the form of feral systems. In fact, (*i*) they were not "part of the corporation's accepted information technology infrastructure", and (*ii*) they were "designed to augment" that infrastructure, along with the definition of Feral Information Systems provided by Houghton & Kerr (2006).

Challenges

In a study published by AT&T (2008), ten main challenges are listed for the adoption of social media by businesses. In fact, these challenges can be grouped in three main areas: (*i*) organizational costs, (*ii*) risks of capital loss, and (*iii*) technical challenges.

About organizational costs, the first issue is that social networking have indirect benefits, which often are not fully appreciated. It is probably the main area of resistance, due to the perceived costs of networking time, not seen as cost efficient activity, and the necessity to allow employees to manage their working time with more freedom. However, traditional ROI methods make it difficult to incorporate all the benefits of social media, both direct and indirect. Thus new performance indicators will be needed. Another issue is the definition of an effective plan to reach the critical mass for the social network to be functional. In fact, common figures of users creating content and collaborating through social media are pretty low, typically from 1% to 20%. Resistance to adoption can come from both regular employee and cadres, possibly including managers and executives. Such a plan would also face the problem of timeliness. In fact, developments in the Web 2.0 environment occur very fast: successful applications may reach millions of users in a couple of years, sometimes creating a new market.

Other challenges are related to the risk of loss of capital, faced by organizations in the adoption of social media. The capital at risk can include intellectual property, as well as human and social capital. In fact, organization members may easily and inadvertently leak sensible and protected content on social media, and such content may face rapid diffusion by "word of mouth" mechanisms. An even greater risk, however, may come from the increased mobility of organization members and employees. This risk is increased by the exposure of members' profiles to the outside world, including other organizations and competitors.

Finally, the adoption of online social networks implies technical costs for creating and maintaining a more complex and open infrastructure. Some important challenges regard security, which is harder to enforce as intranets need to open to the external world, for enabling social collaboration. The risks include the malicious behavior of users, as well as the proliferation of viruses and malware. Also on the technical front, social media applications require increased levels of bandwidth, storage and computational capacity, to support interactions through videos and other form of rich content. Moreover, the increased and differentiated use of social media will pose challenges for the interoperability of different applications, especially with regard to security and authentication schemes.

While the study of AT&T is formulated in reference to the business context, it is interesting to notice that similar considerations are also referred to government agencies and other types of organizations. For example, Bev et al. (2008) describe the case of government agencies. Among other issues, the study underlines the problems of (*i*) employees wasting time on social networks, (*ii*) risk of malware and spyware coming from high traffic sites, and (*iii*) bandwidth requirements. About the first issue, that we described as one aspect of the organizational costs, the authors of the document argue that the problem is not specific to Web 2.0 technologies. In fact, a similar argument was used with respect to mobile phones, emails, etc. For this reason, it is better treated as a management problem instead of a technology problem. About security, efforts should be dedicated to at least mitigate the risks, if they cannot be canceled. Finally, with regard to bandwidth and other technological issues, enough resources should be deployed, to allow at least some selected employees to use rich-content media to communicate with the public, in the most effective way.

Augmenting Information Systems

Although often social networking technologies are not condoned as part of the official information system, yet people use them routinely, at least on an individual basis. In fact, many work activities, in many different sectors, benefit from social media. The use of social media can help workers in their activities (Isari et al., 2011). Social media are a suitable means for coordination among people. Usually it happens across firm boundaries, but they can help in the coordination of activities within a same firm with a big help when employees work in different sites. In this last case, they can provide a complete environment to enable employees to self-organize online, report their status, and stay aware of the status of the other employees of course, considering all the information necessary for coordinating or helping their work. Moreover, the access to social media and, in particular, to community discussing about the technologies and the business of the company can help in the distribution of knowledge within the company and minimizing misunderstandings between colleagues who do not meet face-to-face frequently. Of course, the use of corporate microblogs, either feral or officially supported, can help in the previous cited tasks, but also it allows employees to spread knowledge, ideas, and suggestions about the ways of improving their work.

It is quite easy to find many concrete cases of use of social media for work activities, adopted at first on an individual basis. Just as examples, we will briefly cite the two quite different cases of (*i*) journalism, and (*ii*) software development.

In the field of journalism, social media have already acquired an important role, especially for reporting on breaking news. In those cases, when journalists lack direct sources, social media can guarantee an alternative flow of information, produced by eyewitnesses and other non-professional reporters, who happen to be on the scene at the right moment. However, this new flow of information poses new challenges, as professionals have to discern interesting and trustworthy sources and pieces of content in a magma of information overflow. Professional journalists, in particular, should be wary of rumors and misinformation which are easy to spread on social networks. They should avoid to augment their epidemic potential, to provide credible reports to the public and protect their own professional reputation. For this reason, some research works are targeting specifically the problem of filtering and assessing the veracity of sources found through social networks (Diakopoulos et al., 2012).

Another, very different, example is software development, where Virtual Teams are quite a common practice. In fact, individual developers increasingly use social networks to self-organize both with colleagues in the same organization, and across organizational boundaries. Also, some large communities have emerged as a grassroots process, empowered by new social media and motivated by common interests and emerging attractive targets. In particular, Begel (2010) apply a specific model of teaming to the process of software development. The teaming problems are central in the process, and thus it is highly dependent on developers' abilities to connect and relate with colleagues with similar interests and sufficient skills. The role of social media can then be analyzed in the various aspects of teaming: (*i*) forming, i.e., to select and organize developers into a team; (*ii*) storming, i.e., to reach consensus about the team's goals; (*iii*) norming, i.e., to define guidelines and development methodologies; (*iv*) performing, i.e., to actually develop the new product, through coordinated activities; (*v*) adjourning, i.e., to evaluate accomplishments and failures and improve the team's functioning.

More in general, social media are appreciated by individuals and organizations as they improve collective thinking a thus foster innovation. In fact, creativity and innovation have long been the subjects of organizational studies and social network analysis. Though not all creative ideas lead to innovation, yet it is from creativity that innovation may arise, if followed by successful implementation. Fedorowicz et al. (2008) note that creative ideas rarely come from individuals. More often, they come from teams and groups. Today, this frequently happens in Virtual Teams, through social media and e-Collaboration. Studies focus on various important aspects, such as: (*i*) the impact collaborative tools; (*ii*) the impact of e-Collaboration processes; and (*iii*) the design requirements for tools supporting creativity and innovation. Dwyer (2011) argues that, apart from the number of collaborators, it is also important to measure the quality of collaboration. In fact, various collaborator segments can be identified, with significant differences in the value of contributed ideas and the timing of participation. Thus, new metrics should be used, taking those differences into account and being based on information content. Hayne & Smith (2005) note that groupware performance depends on the fit between the structure and task of the group. However, they argue that an important role may also be played by the cognitive structure, which also maps to the group structure. In fact, collaborative tasks may push human cognitive capabilities to their limits, in terms of perception, attention and memory. Thus, the authors argue for the integration of different areas of study, such as: psychology, especially with regard to abilities and limitations; theories of social interactions, with regard to group communication and motivation; studies of groupware structures and human interactions mediated by artifacts.

To leverage the advantages of social networking, organizations and firms should support their transition from the individual adoption as feral systems to the formal incorporation into existing information systems. To achieve this goal, knowledge management professionals should act as social networking architects, in conjunction with other managers and IT professionals. In fact, social network analysis can highlight the patterns of connection among individuals and the main knowledge flows in a whole organization. Thus, it can be used by managers as a basis for reshaping the organization and advancing towards the business goals. Anklam (2004) describes three main types of intervention, to conduct after a social network analysis: (*i*) structural/organizational, i.e. change the organigrams to improve the knowledge transfer; (*ii*) knowledge-network development, i.e. overcome resistance to action on the basis of evidence, instead of intuition; (*iii*) individual/leadership, i.e. resolve problems with the particular role of individuals, for example acting as factual gatekeepers and resulting in a knowledge bottleneck. More in general, social network analysis can be useful to cope with common business problems, including: launching distributed teams, retention of people with vital knowledge for the organization, improve access to knowledge and increase innovation.

Along the same lines, Roy (2012) discusses the profile of leaders in Virtual Teams. In fact, apart from usual technical and leadership capacities, to work effectively in a virtual environment, they also need abilities to build relationships among participants and to defuse frustrations. In fact, on the one hand, they need particular communication skills, as well as good knowledge for operating video conferencing software and other CSCW tools. On the other hand, they must be able to establish trust, embrace diversity, motivating team members and fostering the team spirit.

Adaptation

The trend toward introducing social media systems in the work environment has seen a massive increase in importance in recent years. At their first appearance, without indications from the management and without integration with internal information systems, social media took the form of feral systems. However, organizations and firms are finally becoming to accept this situation as a matter of fact, trying to gain benefits from the same features that drove the introduction of social platforms in the first place. Thus, information systems are moving from the communication level, to the coordination and collaboration levels, increasingly acknowledging and leveraging the various dimensions of social relations among people, both internally and across organization boundaries.

A first strategy, that some organizations and brands are adopting, is to use social media for improving their Customer Relationship Management (CRM). In fact, social media can be a means for firms and organizations to listen to customers and to cope with the difficulties in collecting data through interviews (Murphy et al., 2011). Social media allow the use of online sources of information, sometimes for free. So firms and organizations are moving to reduce costs and time needed by traditional survey researches. Moreover, in the last years several social media monitoring tools and platforms have been developed to listen to the social media users, analyze and measure their content in relation to a brand or enterprise business and so it is reducing the time necessary for extracting the useful information through the huge data provided by social media (Stavrakantonakis et al., 2012). However, this quite popular trend towards so-called "*Social CRM*" has not always been satisfactory. A study by IBM (2011) shows that there's a quite large gap between the expectations of brand managers and social media users. In fact, only the 23% of users are keen to engage with brands on social media, and only 5% of users declare active participation. The majority, instead, limit their communications and shares with parents and relatives. Among the potentially interested people, many expect tangible benefits, including discounts, services, additional information and reviews about products. The study is in accordance with the difficulties that brands face to engage with users and to launch viral campaigns. Nevertheless, businesses continue to be greatly interested in using social media for rapid distribution of offers and content, reaching new people trough trusted introducers, but also for improving customer care and research.

A second type of effort is directed to augment internal tools, in particular Knowledge Management (KM) systems, with explicit and rich data about relationships among involved people. The long term goal of KM, in fact, is to let insights and experiences existing in implicit way into an organization emerge and become easily accessible for wider internal adoption. Such knowledge can be either possessed by individuals or embedded into common practices. To provide effective access to valuable internal knowledge and expertise, it is essential to recognize and value the particular knowledge possessed by different persons, and then to have means to contact the relevant persons in a timely manner, thus making information-seeking an easier and more successful experience. In many regards, such a scenario can be fully developed only on the basis of the evolution of existing ICT tools and the creation of new ones, by making some typical features of social networking applications available in tools for daily activities.

This trend regards existing Information Systems and also, for some aspects, platforms for Enterprise Resource Planning (ERP). In fact, some aspects of traditional ERP systems are integrating features of social networking platforms, fostering collaboration among people on the basis of direct interpersonal links and simple knowledge sharing tools. The centralized and inward approach of early systems is being challenged also in the core area of production management software. The drift towards network of integrated enterprises is testified by an increasingly dynamic production environment, arranged in the form of complex Virtual Organizations and Virtual Enterprises. In this context, the tasks of supply chain management, project and activity management, data services and access control management require the participation of actors of different organizations and possibly different places and cultures.

Finally, a third type of effort is directed to offer a large-scale knowledge sharing inside an organization through an enterprise social network (Ellison, 2015). This kind of site includes the fundamental features of online social network, but is implemented within an organization and have the ability to restrict membership or interaction to members of a specific enterprise.

FUTURE RESEARCH DIRECTIONS

The importance of online social network and the importance of the data that can be extracted from them determined a strong need of research on new techniques and models for their analysis. Our idea is agent-based techniques can easily deal with the modelling and the analysis of online social networks that represent a massive number of individuals and organizations with different behaviors and behaviors changing over time. In fact, agents are suitable to model and simulate both the low level and complex interactions among the parties. Moreover, agent-based applications can be easily executed in a distributed computing environment that can scale with the size of the online social network. We are working for some year on the use of agents for modelling and analyzing online social networks (Bergenti et al, 2013). In particular, we developed a software framework, that will be the basis for an easy and fast development of distributed applications working on online software networks (Bergenti et al., 2014), and started a first experimentation oriented to the analysis on their data (Fornacciari et al., 2017). Of course, we still working on it with the goal of providing interesting results by extending the experimentation to the modelling of online social network and involving in the experimentation two of the most known and used online social network (i.e., Facebook and Twitter).

CONCLUSION

This chapter discussed about social networking systems and how they assumed a fundamental role in both the private and working spheres. In fact, individuals use them both at home and on the work place both professionally and with recreational goals. Moreover, the chapter discussed about the importance of social capital in online social networks and showed how it or at least the idea of being able to accumulate it, either directly or indirectly, is an important factor in the participation in online social networking activities. Finally, the chapter discussed how social elements have been introduced into more traditional business systems.

The most known and used social networking platforms utilize a traditional client-server architecture. This means that all the information is stored and administered on central servers. Although this approach supports highly mobile user access since users can log-in from any web browser, it also presents many drawbacks, e.g., lack of privacy, lack of anonymity, risks of censorship and operating costs. The integration between peer-to-peer technologies and multi-agent systems may be used for developing social networks that do not present the previous drawbacks Moreover, the use of m multi-agent systems is the right solution to offer strong coordination techniques to the users of social networks and provide them more sophisticated and usable services. In the last years, we worked to study and to develop prototypes to support an evolution in this new direction, we achieved some interesting results (Franchi et al., 2016b; Bergenti, et al., 2018), but we are still working to improve such first results and to experiment some new prototypes in a real setting.

REFERENCES

Ale Ebrahim, N., Ahmed, S., & Taha, Z. (2009). Virtual R&D teams in small and medium enterprises: A literature review. *Scientific Research and Essays, 4*(13), 1575–1590.

Anklam, P. (2004, May). KM and the Social Network. *Knowledge Management Magazine*, 24-28.

AT&T. (2008). *The Business Impacts of Social Networking*. Retrieved 2012-10-20 from http://www.business.att.com/content/whitepaper/WP-soc_17172_v3_11-10-08.pdf

Baker, W. E. (1990). Market networks and corporate behavior. *American Journal of Sociology, 96*(3), 589–625. doi:10.1086/229573

Baum, J. A. (1999). Whole-part coevolutionary competition in organizations. *Variations in organization science*, 113-135.

Begel, A., DeLine, R., & Zimmermann, T. (2010). Social media for software engineering. In *Proceedings of the FSE/SDP workshop on Future of software engineering research* (pp. 33-38). ACM. 10.1145/1882362.1882370

Bergenti, F., Franchi, E., & Poggi, A. (2011). *Agent-based social networks for enterprise collaboration. In 20th IEEE International Workshops on Enabling Technologies: Infrastructure for Collaborative Enterprises* (pp. 25–28). IEEE.

Bergenti, F., Franchi, E., & Poggi, A. (2013). Agent-based interpretations of classic network models. *Computational & Mathematical Organization Theory, 19*(2), 105–127. doi:10.100710588-012-9150-x

Bergenti, F., Poggi, A., & Tomaiuolo, M. (2014). An actor based software framework for scalable applications. In *International Conference on Internet and Distributed Computing Systems* (pp. 26-35). Springer. 10.1007/978-3-319-11692-1_3

Bergenti, F., Poggi, A., & Tomaiuolo, M. (2018). Agent-Based Social Networks. In Encyclopedia of Information Science and Technology, Fourth Edition (pp. 6950-6960). IGI Global. doi:10.4018/978-1-5225-2255-3.ch602

Bev, G., Campbell, S., Levy, J., & Bounds, J. (2008). *Social media and the federal government: Perceived and real barriers and potential solutions*. Federal Web Managers Council.

Borgatti, S. P., & Foster, P. C. (2003). The network paradigm in organizational research: A review and typology. *Journal of Management, 29*(6), 991–1013. doi:10.1016/S0149-2063(03)00087-4

Burt, R. S. (1987). Social Contagion and Innovation: Cohesion versus Structural Equivalence. *American Journal of Sociology, 92*(6), 1287–1335. doi:10.1086/228667

Burt, R. S. (1995). *Structural holes: The social structure of competition*. Harvard University Press.

Campbell, J. H. (1985). An organizational interpretation of evolution. *Evolution at a crossroads*, 133.

Chow, W. S., & Chan, L. S. (2008). Social network, social trust and shared goals in organizational knowledge sharing. *Information & Management, 45*(7), 458–465. doi:10.1016/j.im.2008.06.007

Coleman, J. S. (1988). Social capital in the creation of human capital. *American Journal of Sociology, 94*, 95–120. doi:10.1086/228943

Cook, K. (1982). Network Structures from an Exchange Perspective. In *Social Structure and Network Analysis*. Sage Publications.

Diakopoulos, N., De Choudhury, M., & Naaman, M. (2012, May). Finding and assessing social media information sources in the context of journalism. In *Proceedings of the 2012 ACM annual conference on Human Factors in Computing Systems* (pp. 2451-2460). ACM. 10.1145/2207676.2208409

DiMicco, J. (2007). Identity management: multiple presentations of self in facebook. *6th International Conference on Supporting Group Work (GROUP'07)*, 1–4. 10.1145/1316624.1316682

DiMicco, J., Millen, D., & Geyer, W. (2008). Motivations for social networking at work. *Conference on Computer Supported Cooperative Work*, 711–720.

Dwyer, P. (2011). Measuring Collective Cognition in Online Collaboration Venues. *International Journal of e-Collaboration, 7*(1), 47–61. doi:10.4018/jec.2011010104

Ellison, N. B., Gibbs, J. L., & Weber, M. S. (2015). The use of enterprise social network sites for knowledge sharing in distributed organizations: The role of organizational affordances. *The American Behavioral Scientist, 59*(1), 103–123. doi:10.1177/0002764214540510

Erickson, B. H. (2017). Good networks and good jobs: The value of social capital to employers and employees. In *Social capital* (pp. 127–158). Routledge.

Fedorowicz, J., Laso-Ballesteros, I., & Padilla-Meléndez, A. (2008). Creativity, Innovation, and E-Collaboration. *International Journal of e-Collaboration*, *4*(4), 1–10. doi:10.4018/jec.2008100101

Fornacciari, P., Mordonini, M., Poggi, A., & Tomaiuolo, M. (2017) Software actors for continuous social media analysis. In *18th Workshop on Objects to Agents, WOA 2017* (pp. 84-89). CEUR.

Foster, I., Kesselman, C., & Tuecke, S. (2001). The anatomy of the grid: Enabling scalable virtual organizations. *International Journal of High Performance Computing Applications*, *15*(3), 200–222. doi:10.1177/109434200101500302

Franchi, E., & Poggi, A. (2011). *Multi-agent systems and social networks. Business social networking: Organizational, managerial, and technological dimensions*. Academic Press.

Franchi, E., Poggi, A., & Tomaiuolo, M. (2013). Open social networking for online collaboration. *International Journal of e-Collaboration*, *9*(3), 50–68. doi:10.4018/jec.2013070104

Franchi, E., Poggi, A., & Tomaiuolo, M. (2015). Information and Password Attacks on Social Networks: An Argument for Cryptography. *Journal of Information Technology Research*, *8*(1), 25–42. doi:10.4018/JITR.2015010103

Franchi, E., Poggi, A., & Tomaiuolo, M. (2016a). Social media for online collaboration in firms and organizations. *International Journal of Information System Modeling and Design*, *7*(1), 18–31. doi:10.4018/IJISMD.2016010102

Franchi, E., Poggi, A., & Tomaiuolo, M. (2016b). Blogracy: A peer-to-peer social network. *International Journal of Distributed Systems and Technologies*, *7*(2), 37–56. doi:10.4018/IJDST.2016040103

Fukuyama, F. (1995). *Trust: The social virtues and the creation of prosperity*. Free Press.

Fulk, J., Heino, R., Flanagin, A. J., Monge, P. R., & Bar, F. (2004). A test of the individual action model for organizational information commons. *Organization Science*, *15*(5), 569–585. doi:10.1287/orsc.1040.0081

Goldschlag, D., Reed, M., & Syverson, P. (1999). Onion routing. *Communications of the ACM*, *42*(2), 39–41. doi:10.1145/293411.293443

Granovetter, M. S. (1973). The strength of weak ties. *American Journal of Sociology*, *78*(6), 1360–1380. doi:10.1086/225469

Hayne, S. C., & Smith, C. (2005). The Relationship Between e-Collaboration and Cognition. *International Journal of e-Collaboration*, *1*(3), 17–34. doi:10.4018/jec.2005070102

Hoang, H., & Antoncic, B. (2003). Network-based research in entrepreneurship: A critical review. *Journal of Business Venturing*, *18*(2), 165–187. doi:10.1016/S0883-9026(02)00081-2

Holland, P., & Leinhardt, S. (1974). The Statistical Analysis of Local Structure in Social Networks. *National Bureau of Economic Research Working Paper Series, 44*.

Hollingshead, A. B., Fulk, J., & Monge, P. (2002). Fostering intranet knowledge sharing: An integration of transactive memory and public goods approaches. *Distributed Work*, 335-355.

Houghton, L., & Kerr, D. V. (2006). A study into the creation of feral information systems as a response to an ERP implementation within the supply chain of a large government-owned corporation. *International Journal of Internet and Enterprise Management*, 4(2), 135–147. doi:10.1504/IJIEM.2006.010239

IBM Institute for Business Value. (2011). *From social media to Social CRM*. Retrieved 2012-10-20 from http://public.dhe.ibm.com/common/ssi/ecm/en/gbe03391usen/GBE03391USEN.PDF

Isari, D., Pontiggia, A., & Virili, F. (2011). *Working Together in Organizations Using Social Network Sites: A Laboratory Experiment on Microblog Use for Problem-Solving*. Available at SSRN 1875924.

Jacobs, J. (1961). *The death and life of great American cities*. Vintage.

Jones, B. F., Wuchty, S., & Uzzi, B. (2008). Multi-university research teams: Shifting impact, geography, and stratification in science. *Science*, 322(5905), 1259–1262. doi:10.1126cience.1158357 PMID:18845711

Lin, N. (2017). Building a network theory of social capital. In *Social capital* (pp. 3–28). Routledge.

Lipnack, J., & Stamps, J. (2008). *Virtual teams: People working across boundaries with technology*. John Wiley & Sons.

Loury, G. C. (1987). Why should we care about group inequality? *Social Philosophy & Policy*, 5(1), 249–271. doi:10.1017/S0265052500001345

Malone, T. W., & Crowstone, K. (1994). The Interdisciplinary Study of Coordination. *ACM Computing Surveys*, 26(1), 87–119. doi:10.1145/174666.174668

Maskell, P. (2000). Social capital, innovation, and competitiveness. In *Social capital* (pp. 111–123). Oxford University Press.

McPherson, M., Smith-Lovin, L., & Cook, J. M. (2001). Birds of a Feather: Homophily in Social Networks. *Annual Review of Sociology*, 27(1), 415–444. doi:10.1146/annurev.soc.27.1.415

Millen, D. R., Feinberg, J., Kerr, B., Rogers, O., & Cambridge, S. (2006). *Dogear : Social Bookmarking in the Enterprise*. Academic Press.

Monge, P. R., & Contractor, N. (2003). *Theories of communication networks*. Oxford University Press.

Mordonini, M., Poggi, A., & Tomaiuolo, M. (2016). Preserving Privacy in a P2P *Social Network. In International Conference on Smart Objects and Technologies for Social Good* (pp. 203-212). Springer.

Mowshowitz, A. (1994). Virtual organization: A vision of management in the information age. *The Information Society*, 10(4), 267–288. doi:10.1080/01972243.1994.9960172

Murphy, J., Kim, A., Hagood, H., Richards, A., Augustine, C., Kroutil, L., & Sage, A. (2011). Twitter Feeds and Google Search Query Surveillance: Can They Supplement Survey Data Collection? *Shifting the Boundaries of Research*, 228.

Nahapiet, J., & Ghoshal, S. (1998). Social capital, intellectual capital, and the organizational advantage. *Academy of Management Review*, 23(2), 242–266. doi:10.5465/amr.1998.533225

Parkhe, A., Wasserman, S., & Ralston, D. A. (2006). New frontiers in network theory development. *Academy of Management Review*, *31*(3), 560–568. doi:10.5465/amr.2006.21318917

Powell, A., Piccoli, G., & Ives, B. (2004). Virtual Teams: A Review of Current Literature and Directions for Future Research. *The Data Base for Advances in Information Systems*, *35*(1), 7. doi:10.1145/968464.968467

Putnam, R. D. (1995). Bowling alone: America's declining social capital. *Journal of Democracy*, *6*(1), 65–78. doi:10.1353/jod.1995.0002

Roy, S. R. (2012). Digital Mastery: The Skills Needed for Effective Virtual Leadership. *International Journal of e-Collaboration*, *8*(3), 56–66. doi:10.4018/jec.2012070104

Stavrakantonakis, I., Gagiu, A. E., Kasper, H., Toma, I., & Thalhammer, A. (2012). An approach for evaluation of social media monitoring tools. *Common Value Management*, 52.

Su, C., & Contractor, N. (2011). A multidimensional network approach to studying team members' information seeking from human and digital knowledge sources in consulting firms. *Journal of the American Society for Information Science and Technology*, *62*(7), 1257–1275. doi:10.1002/asi.21526

Teigland, R. (2004). Extending richness with reach: Participation and knowledge exchange in electronic networks of practice. In *Knowledge networks: Innovation through communities of practice* (pp. 230–242). IGI Global. doi:10.4018/978-1-59140-200-8.ch019

Tomaiuolo, M. (2013). dDelega: Trust Management for Web Services. *International Journal of Information Security and Privacy*, *7*(3), 53–67. doi:10.4018/jisp.2013070104

Van de Ven, A., Delbecq, A., & Koenig, R. (1976). Determinants of coordination modes within organizations. *American Sociological Review*, *41*(2), 322–338. doi:10.2307/2094477

Vlaar, P. W., van Fenema, P. C., & Tiwari, V. (2008). Cocreating understanding and value in distributed work: How members of onsite and offshore vendor teams give, make, demand, and break sense. *Management Information Systems Quarterly*, *32*(2), 227–255. doi:10.2307/25148839

Wasko, M. M., & Faraj, S. (2005). Why should i share? examining social capital and knowledge contribution in electronic networks of practice. *Management Information Systems Quarterly*, *29*(1), 35–57. doi:10.2307/25148667

Wasserman, S., & Faust, K. (1994). *Social network analysis: Methods and applications* (Vol. 8). Cambridge University Press. doi:10.1017/CBO9780511815478

Wheatley, M., & Frieze, D. (2006). Using emergence to take social innovation to scale. The Berkana Institute.

Williamson, O. E. (1991). Comparative Economic Organization: The Analysis of Discrete Structural Alternatives. *Administrative Science Quarterly*, *36*(2), 219–244. doi:10.2307/2393356

Wuchty, S., Jones, B. F., & Uzzi, B. (2007). The increasing dominance of teams in production of knowledge. *Science*, *316*(5827), 1036–1039. doi:10.1126cience.1136099 PMID:17431139

ADDITIONAL READING

Ardichvili, A., Page, V., & Wentling, T. (2003). Motivation and barriers to participation in virtual knowledge-sharing communities of practice. *Journal of Knowledge Management, 7*(1), 64–77. doi:10.1108/13673270310463626

Chang, H. H., & Chuang, S. S. (2011). Social capital and individual motivations on knowledge sharing: Participant involvement as a moderator. *Information & Management, 48*(1), 9–18. doi:10.1016/j.im.2010.11.001

Chiu, C. M., Hsu, M. H., & Wang, E. T. (2006). Understanding knowledge sharing in virtual communities: An integration of social capital and social cognitive theories. *Decision Support Systems, 42*(3), 1872–1888. doi:10.1016/j.dss.2006.04.001

Coleman, J. S. (1988). Social capital in the creation of human capital. *American Journal of Sociology, 94*, S95–S120. doi:10.1086/228943

Dubos, R. (2017). *Social capital: Theory and research.* Routledge.

Li, C. (2010). Groundswell. Winning in a world transformed by social technologies. Strategic Direction, 26(8).

Valenzuela, S., Park, N., & Kee, K. F. (2009). Is there social capital in a social network site? Facebook use and college students' life satisfaction, trust, and participation. *Journal of Computer-Mediated Communication, 14*(4), 875–901. doi:10.1111/j.1083-6101.2009.01474.x

Wellman, B., Haase, A. Q., Witte, J., & Hampton, K. (2001). Does the Internet increase, decrease, or supplement social capital? Social networks, participation, and community commitment. *The American Behavioral Scientist, 45*(3), 436–455. doi:10.1177/00027640121957286

KEY TERMS AND DEFINITIONS

Online Network of Practice: A group of people who share a profession or an interest, whose main interactions occur through communication networks and tools.

Privacy: The right to be secluded from the presence or view of others.

Social Capital: Is a form of economic and cultural capital derived from interpersonal relationships, institutions, and other social assets of a society or group of individuals.

Social Network: Social structure made by individuals and organizations that are connected by relationships; relationships that may represent various kinds of ties between member and that can be either symmetrical or asymmetrical.

Social Networking System: A software system that allows users to manipulate a representation of their online social networks and to interact with the other users in the system, especially collaboratively discussing user-produced resources.

Virtual Organization: A network of autonomous organizations and individuals, typically with the main aim of sharing resources in a coordinated fashion.

Virtual Team: A group of workers connected mainly through information and communication technologies that is often temporary and exists only until the achievement of a specific goal.

Chapter 40

Frugal Living for Our Collective and Mutual #Bestlife on a Distributed and Global Electronic Hive Mind

Shalin Hai-Jew

Kansas State University, USA

ABSTRACT

What is not as commonly identified as an optimal life #bestlife is living #frugal, and yet, there is a global electronic hive mind about how to live sparingly based on highly variant local realities. There are blogs about living on a shoestring, stretching funds, cooking in, engaging in a DIY economy (bartering with like-minded others), living off the grid, taking low-cost and simple vacations, maintaining a food garden, raising food animals, and forgoing the more spendy aspects of modern living. The narrative goes that saving up and retiring early enables low-pressure and intentional lifestyles (and an ability to focus on family and friends), low-carbon footprints (with low impacts on the environment), and the embodiment of a frugal virtue. This chapter explores what a #frugal living EHM looks like and how it brings together people around shared values and lifestyle practices for personal peace of mind, social justice, and long-term sustainability.

INTRODUCTION

Without frugality none can be rich, and with it very few would be poor. - Samuel Johnson

Many people take no care of their money till they come nearly to the end of it, and others do just the same with their time. - Johann Wolfgang von Goethe

DOI: 10.4018/978-1-6684-6307-9.ch040

In terms of most people's #bestlife (that leads to others' jealousy and plenty of FOMO) in the materialistic West, there are various sorts of selfie-shared (or paparazzi-captured) depicted acts:

- The pursuit of ostentatious and expensive pleasure (jets, parties, high fashion, luxury bling, spa vacations, and shopping sprees),
- Having the perfect family (well set and not a hair out of place),
- Dating up (and often),
- Experiencing various acts of daring (jumping out of planes, buildering, bungee jumping, and other risk-taking),
- Hanging out with friends in various exotic locations, and
- Simply being famous, among others.

And yet, there is a narrative of frugal living on social media that has attracted adherents from around he world. Some human behaviors involve personal decisions and actions at a ground level that taken together have a larger impact on the environment and on others. There is an "emergent" aspect to individual actions taken collectively and writ large. Sometimes, the individual actions are merely individual choices, and others are somewhat coordinated. Some electronic hive minds (EHMs) can speak into such collective spaces and encourage collective awarenesses and behaviors of various types (Hai-Jew, 2019). "Frugality" or a kind of resourcefulness and avoidance of waste (of money or material resources) is one of these phenomena. People choose how they want to use their moneys and resources, and their consumption affects others' livelihoods, the respective product and service supply chains, the natural environment, and other outcomes.

Being frugal (or frugal living) goes against some of the core assumptions of economics: that people's appetites are insatiable and unlimited in a resource-constrained environment. No amount fully satisfies people's appetites, so some constraints have to be applied—such as people's financial wherewithal.

There are some "stars" (personalities) and "models" in this space:

- A "zero-waste" young woman becomes well known for apparently being able to condense all her garbage for four years in a small glass jar (East, July 6, 2016). Everything else, she says, has been composted or recycled. She is working hard on maintaining a light "carbon footprint." Her achievements have sparked a "zero-waste" movement with others working towards similar goals.
- Two young men host a podcast about frugal living in the finance realm. (They advertise themselves as "frugal dudes.")
- Several different families share on social media about their living off-the-grid and simply, while raising children. For some of the families, they have a rental that they use for funding; others have a retirement fund, built up during years of intense and often lucrative careers (and ensuing burnout). Their stories are similar in that they live in nature, raise their own food, hunt in-season, and provide for themselves through sparse resources.
- Some have stories of leaving high-powered careers in order to live off savings in urban environments, with some traveling globally and sharing their adventures.
- Others are living carefully off of their social media presences. They use advertising funds and company-provided funds for their travels and then provide reviews and evaluations to their huge populations of followers. Various world travelers visit different locales, and they share photos of

their travels and low-cost adventures. They further share stories of those who are running taxi, tourist, food, and other scams.

- A farmer buys a used truck for $100, and he video records other people wanting to sell their used trucks for a lot more money and calls them out for daring to ask for more moneys. He has clearly gotten a deal, but subsequent tales of truck breakdowns and other challenges fill his video channel.

How people present on social media may be part of a social performance. It may be "cheap talk" vs. "costly signaling," the latter of which requires actual commitments and actual sacrifices. Certainly, there has been no shortage of "reveals" of people's fictions shared widely on social media. Superficially, a simple walk-through on social media provides some snapshots of frugality, via stories that people tell about themselves (in a form of *sousveillance*):

- **People will not let usable goods go to waste. (They will somewhat make up for some of their less frugal compatriots.)**
  - ○ A search of "dumpster diving" (as a seeding term) on Google Images shows intrepid individuals hip deep in discarded contents looking for valuables. There are people with boxes of fruits and vegetables, print goods, canned goods, plastic wrapped foods, and other resources. There are signs advertising an art to dumpster diving. On Google Scholar, "dumpster diving for food" results in some 5,470 results. In mass media, there are articles that share the art to dumpster diving: in order to track what goods are dumped when and the best times to collect them (and which dumpsters are locked and which are accessible) and how to stay safe while collecting others' undesirables. Dumpster diving is now not just a practice of starving college students but of organized groups that collect goods for distribution to the hungry through food banks and other organizations.
  - ○ Second hand shopping (thrift shopping) in second hand stores and garage sales and yard sales is a global phenomenon. Social videos share various shopping adventures and finds. Some social videos unwrap the finds in others' storage units, which are auctioned off after non-paying customers stop paying rent on their storage units. Mainstream media shares stories of treasures found. Some mainline television shows feature experts who evaluate various used and antique objects for their market value to collectors.
- **They work to have small carbon footprints, and they can make do with less than others.**
  - ○ Individuals and sometimes families live in micro houses, which are just a portion of the sizes of mainstream houses. These are portable, and they have many of the affordances of other houses, but in miniature.
  - ○ Major news outlets have carried stories of landfills and the multi-generational persistence of plastics and other discarded items. There are stories of electronic goods graveyards where computers and electronic equipment is retired and salvaged for anything usable. A pioneering family who is living "plastic-free" is spotlighted and lauded. Anything left over (most of the device) is left to leach toxins into the soil and environment.
  - ○ People develop skills to grow their own food, repair their own homes and cars, cook home meals, and engage the world differently than in the mainstream. They sew their own clothes. They create their own soaps and toothpaste.
  - ○ They engage in trade with like-minded individuals. They learn to keep their bills to a bare minimum. They are creating an alternative lifestyle to the material-driven ones. Some work

intense careers and then choose to retire in their late 20s, their 30s, their 40s…and show how they can guarantee sufficient funds skimmed off of their savings.

- **They will manage finances and invest with care.** Frugal people will have a working budget that makes sense in relation to their earnings. They will have a financial plan and follow through on their savings. They will be aware of the compounding expenses of even small fees by their investors.

Frugality is not quite a coalesced movement or even really a trend yet. It reads like a general drifting phenomenon that has captured the interest of some on the periphery. The effort feels counter-cultural (because of the focus on non-materialism), and frugality is certainly not in the mainstream. In terms of people's spending, at least in the U.S., people are mostly at the limits of what their earnings enable (and beyond, for many, living on debt).

In many senses, the frugality endeavor is told from a Western point of view, and for many, the lifestyle is somewhat by choice and by purposeful expression of preferred values and behaviors (of non-wastage of material and other resources). As a construct, "frugality" is seen as more of a composite of various values than an entity alone except as a "lifestyle choice" (Todd & Lawson, 2003, p. 8). [A quote attributed to Cicero reads: "Frugality includes all the other virtues."]

As an EHM, "frugality" thinking and its thinkers seem distributed (geographically dispersed) with a mix of local interests and local realities. As a consumer phenomenon, it is studied by companies that want to know how to market to "frugal" individuals and to encourage them to spend. Some of the social imagery captured as part of this work show businesses that have arisen around "frugal" but with the idea of low-cost and discounts. Frugality is also studied by environmentalists who have an interest in encouraging people to live differently and more sustainably. One other aspect of interest with the frugality EHM is that it evokes private individual choices that have an emergent collective quality, with theoretically measurable impacts on expenditures and the natural ecosystem.

REVIEW OF THE LITERATURE

A core assumption of the "frugal living" EHM is that "endless growth" to meet insatiable human needs is infeasible. There is an ethos of "de-growth" that practitioners share, with the "politics of scarcity," so people may live in "responsible togetherness" (Natale, Di Martino, Procentese, & Arcidiaconom, 2016, p. 50). The authors explain:

The degrowth paradigm offers a possible solution to the negative effects of capitalistic and consumeristic culture. This lies in curbing the unbridled production and consumption of commodities—along with the values attached to them—and downshift towards what Latouche (2011) has named 'frugal abundance', that is, a relational and economic system freed from the myth of endless growth (Natale, Di Martino, Procentese, & Arcidiacono, 2016, p. 49).

Those who pursue "voluntary simplicity" avoid "clutter" (Gregg, 1936, as cited in Leonard-Barton, Dec. 1981, p. 243). A draft behavioral index to measure individuals' tendencies towards voluntary simplicity "characterized by ecological awareness, attempts to become more self-sufficient, and efforts to decrease personal consumption of goods" (Leonard-Barton, Dec. 1981, p. 243) includes elements like making gifts instead of purchasing them, riding bicycles for exercise and commuting, recycling (newspapers, jars, cans, and others), doing oil changes at home, developing skills "in carpentry, car tune-up and repair, or plumbing" for self-reliance, eating "meatless main meals," buying clothes from second hand stores, setting up a compost pile, making "furniture or clothing for the family," and bartering "with others in lieu of payment with money" (Leonard-Barton, Dec. 1981, pp. 250 - 251).

These values are often translated to actions, with frugality as a "pervasive consumer trait" (Lastovicka, Bettencourt, Hughner, & Kuntze, 1999, p. 85). Such approaches have been a part of "day-to-day American life" beginning in colonial times (Witkowski, 1989, as cited in Lastovicka, Bettencourt, Hughner, & Kuntze, 1999, p. 85). What are some basic observed traits of people who are frugal?

Empirically, the frugal are less susceptible to interpersonal influence, less materialistic, less compulsive in buying, and more price and value conscious. Being frugal does not correspond with being ecocentric nor with being prone to using coupons. A motivation to save the planet and being frugal are found unrelated. Further, it seems, being frugal means no necessary interest in the coupons used so often to promote convenience goods. Frugality consistently explains consumer usage behaviors. The data show the frugal use products and services resourcefully; this ranges from timing their showers to eating leftovers for lunch at work. Being frugal empirically affects purchasing. In a mental accounting experiment examining how the source of income influences spending, only the less frugal are manipulated into spending more. Scale norms from a general population survey, combined with data from Tightwad Gazette subscribers, show Gazette subscribers are on average at the top two deciles on the frugality scale. (Lastovicka, Bettencourt, Hughner, & Kuntze, 1999, p. 96)

Frugality is a part of social movements. As a "social innovation," defined broadly as "new ideas that address unmet social needs—and that work" (Mulgan, Tucker, Ali, & Sanders, 2007, p. 2, as cited in Nicholls, Simon, & Gabriel, 2015, p. 2), frugal living may lead to individual-level (micro), group level (meso), and societal and global level (macro) changes.

World-scale religious ideas and philosophies have also been harnessed for the avoidance of overconsumption through frugality, including Eastern philosophies of Confucianism, Jainism, Buddhism, Daoism, and other traditions (Roiland, 2016). Various world religious systems (including "American Indian, Buddhist, Christian/Jewish, Taoist, (and) Hindu") speak to frugality and its importance (Lastovicka, Bettencourt, Hughner, & Kuntze, 1999, p. 86). These evocations speak to spiritual dimensions in electronic hive minds, a Zen aspect with particular balanced decisions and practices.

There are arguments against lifestyles in "industrial societies and people (who) spend too much in goods and items when a majority only tries to survive" (Roiland, 2016, p. 571). And yet, frugality has to be balanced against practical considerations: "Frugality is a concept that forces (us) to redefine our priorities in life, in economy in a global system. An Ethic of frugality on different levels appears essential to face the actual challenges. However frugality cannot be presented in opposition with creativity and economic growth." (Roiland, 2016, p. 583)

Other research has focused on the various types of "food wasters" (non-frugals, meant in a derogatory sense). A study conducted in Italy described this group of "food wasters" with seven profiles.

Out of seven profiles identified, four are the most representative ones in terms of size: the conscious-fussy type, who wastes because food doesn't smell or look good; the conscious-forgetful type, who forgets what is in the fridge or on the shelves; the frugal consumer who tends not to consume fruits and vegetables and declares to waste nothing (or almost nothing); and the exaggerated cook, who overbuys and overcooks (Gaiani, Caldeira, Adorno, Segrè, & Vittuari, 2018, p. 17)

The additional profiles are "the unskilled cook," "the confused type" [who is "confused about (food) labelling"], and "the exaggerated shopper" who overbuys (Gaiani, Caldeira, Adorno, Segrè, & Vittuari, 2018, p. 23). In a sense this and other works call out those who misuse available resources. Indeed, in developed countries, when food is wasted, it is usually at the "consumption stage of the food supply chain" (Gaiani, Caldeira, Adorno, Segrè, & Vittuari, 2018, p. 17).

Thrift in terms of energy usage has been associated with consumer motivations based on "multiple self-identities" with self-concepts of the self as "environmentally friendly and a frugal person" (Thøgersen, 2018, p. 1528) as contrasted against a "green" (pro-environmental) motivation in terms of engaging in energy-saving behaviors in the home (p. 1521). Research does suggest a positive correlation between the "frugal" and "green" self-identities.

One core concept in the consumption debate is that of fairness: Which populations in the world have rights to consume outsized shares of the Earth's resources? Sustainable consumption is debated at both local and more global scales.

Socially conscious consumer behavior, like its ecological counterpart, appears to be an expression of pro-social values. In contrast, frugal consumer behavior relates primarily to low personal materialism and income constraints. As such, it does not yet represent a fully developed moral challenge to consumerism. (Pepper, Jackson, & Uzzell, 2009, p. 126)

Even if the challenge is not direct to the retail-industrial complex (so to speak), the idea of living with basic necessities alone without excess may have impacts on consumption. Marketers of firms with B-to-C (business to consumer) businesses have an interest in studying "non-consumption" (Gould, Houston, & Mundt, 1997, as cited in Todd & Lawson, 2003, p. 8). Retailers trying to find the right formula to encourage more spending among the frugal who nevertheless have the means to buy and spend more. Multiple researchers have observed that "frugal consumers feel more independent than average" (Lastovicka, Bettencourt, Hughner, & Kuntze, 1999, p. 87), which may suggest that they are less suggestible to advertising. People who are frugal are thought to be "resistant to social influences" but may be induced to spend more if they are with their "high-spending networks of friends vs. low-spending networks of friends"…in "strong-tie networks" (Lee, 2016, p. 1). A countermove for frugal consumers is to avoid such social situations (Lee, 2016, p. 5). This is also not to say that there are not industries that have arisen around the concept of "frugal," as in low-cost products and services.

There is also push-back from the "politics and geographies of scarcity" as a meta-narrative that sustains "elite and capitalist power" (Mehta, Huff, & Allouche, 2018, p. 1) and enables the denial of fuller lives for many (goes the narrative).

Some research focuses on "alternative measures of frugality" (Mowen, 2000, p. 187). For example, "tightwadism" has been studied "in conjunction with impulsiveness, bargaining proneness, materialism (negative relationship), and emotional instability" (Mowen, 2000, p. 187). As a construct, frugality was found to have "poor internal reliability" as compared to "care in spending," which did have "good internal reliability" (Mowen, 2000, p. 187). Other insights were discovered:

The only construct predictive of care in spending was the need for arousal (negative relationship). Tight-wadism was inversely related to a measure of materialism and positively related to the need for arousal, the need for body resources, and present orientation. (Mowen, 2000, p. 187)

Those who do not have a high need for excitement tend to be able to show "care in spending," and those who were less materialistic tend to be able to engage in "tightwadism," among other observations.

At more macro levels, "frugal innovations" enable better meeting the needs of those "low-income consumers who live on an income that is less than $5 a day" (Vadakkepat, Garg, Loh, & Tham, 2015, p. 1) as compared to the expensive products and services designed for those "at the top of the economic pyramid" (Vadakkepat, Garg, Loh, & Tham, 2015, p. 1).

While there is a not-unfounded fear of mass-scale "digital wildfires" sparking online and wreaking havoc (Webb, et al., Sept. 2015), social media also enables the spread of constructive and prosocial ideas, including for frugal living. Several studies inform this research work.

On social media, topic communities are those "created on-the-fly by people that post messages about a particular topic (i.e., topic communities)" (Kardara, Papadakis, Papaoikonomou, Tserpes, & Varvari-gou, 2012, p. 1). The messages may be informational, advocacy-based, call-to-action, and other types. In topic communities, there are often "core influencers" or members who have outsized influences on the other members; these are "users who produce original content that is frequently retweeted" (Kardara, Papadakis, Papaoikonomou, Tserpes, & Varvarigou, 2012, p. 12). An empirical study of core influencers in a topic community found the following dimensions:

Although they are highly mentioned by other users, they avoid getting into discussions or reproducing others' opinions. When they actually do so, they mainly refer to or cite other influential members. Their messages are mostly factual, with just a negligible part of them explicitly expressing strong sentiments about the community's topic. Nevertheless, they precede their peers in expressing their feelings towards the topic in question, thus playing a major role in shaping the dominant opinion in each community. This explains the extremely high levels of correlation they exhibit with the community's aggregate senti-ment. Their high levels of influence can be attributed to their specialized activity, as they are typically focused on few, similar topics. Our large-scale experimental analysis over real-world data verified that these patterns apply particularly to core groups of size k = 50 that are defined by the Mentions influence criterion (Kardara, Papadakis, Papaoikonomou, Tserpes, & Varvarigou, 2012, p. 12)

The core influencers play important leadership roles for the distributed online community. In terms of leadership on social media, "message content, social behavior, and (social) network structure" affect followership links on Twitter over time (Hutto, Yardi, & Gilbert, 2013, p. 821), and as such, they serve as "follow predictors" (Hutto, Yardi, & Gilbert, 2013, p. 821). Given the tendency for negative messages to be shared faster and more frequently than neutral messages or positive ones (Tsugawa & Ohsaki, 2015), those shepherding social movements may have to apply messaging finesse to avoid damage to the respective causes.

Researchers also identified image patterns on "image-based social media websites" used to support social movements (Cornet, Hall, Cafaro, & Brady, 2017, p. 2473). This work also suggests the importance of identifying image patterns around image-sharing sites harnessed for particular social movements (as in the frugal living EHM).

These research works suggest the importance of identifying leaders in electronic hive minds and studying social imagery patterns, among others. Common research methods on social media include "social network analysis, sentiment analysis, trend analysis and collaborative recommendation" (Sapountzi & Psannis, 2018, p. 893), and some of these approaches will be used here as well.

"FRUGAL LIVING" AND #BESTLIFE LIFESTYLES AND DECISION MAKING IN A DISPERSED AND GLOBAL ELECTRONIC HIVE MIND

The dispersed frugal living EHM reads as a personalized space where people commit to living simply, without clutter, in green ways. These are people who are "woke" about the need to live intentionally and in ways that preserve financial and material resources. They are not obviously political, without ties to environmental activist organizations or other entities, and they are not obviously anti- the retail-industrial complex (if you will). So from the Social Web and various social media platforms, what does this EHM look like?

On Reddit

On social media, frugality as a "thing." One of the top subreddits "about personal or domestic advice" is a thread about the "frugal use of resources" with 41,911 members in the online community and identified gendered differences in the topic (Thelwall & Stuart, 2018, p. 12). This particular subreddit ranked 100 in the "subreddits about personal or domestic advice" (Thelwall & Stuart, 2018, p. 12).

On Google Search's Autocomplete

A search for "frugal" on Google Search has some insights in the autocomplete, in this order: frugal, frugal meaning, frugality, frugal house, frugal house topeka, frugalwoods, frugal male fashion, frugal house topeka ks, frugal inc, (and) frugality definition. The autocomplete does show some sensitivity to the physical location of the author during the search. (Figure 1)

Figure 1. "Frugal" auto complete in Google search

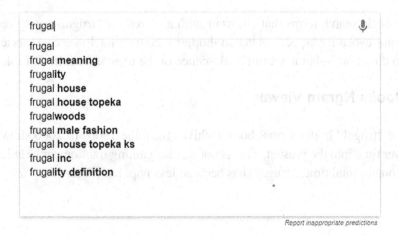

On YouTube Video Sharing Site's Autocomplete

In terms of the autocomplete on the Google YouTube platform's search, they include the following (in descending order): "frugal aesthetic, frugal living, frugal, frugal crafter, frugal gourmet, frugalwoods, frugalnista, frugal finds, frugal chic life, (and) frugal fit mom" (Figure 2).

Figure 2. "Frugal" auto complete on YouTube

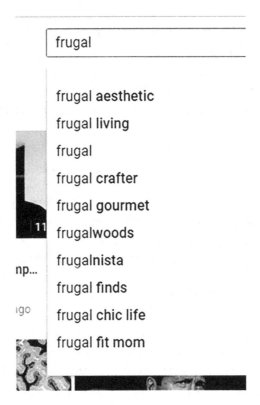

On Google Correlate

In terms of mass-scale search terms that co-occur with a search for "frugal" (on a weekly basis in the U.S.), there are some evocative aspects related to shopping, couponing, lower cost services, free services, and some how-to directions—but not a full coalescence of the idea of frugality. (Table 1)

On Google Books Ngram Viewer

An exploration of "frugal" in the formal book archives from the 1800s to 2000 show a general dropping trendline over time into the present. This is not an idea gaining traction per se at least in the formal literature. Over longitudinal time, "frugal" has become less popular. (Figure 3)

Table 1. "Frugal" on Google correlate (in the U.S., weekly mass search data)

0.7991	the frugal		0.6358	can i download
0.6815	free sheet music for piano		0.6358	adele melt my heart to stone lyrics
0.6694	docs to go		0.6355	by email
0.6653	download free		0.6355	speeddate.com
0.6546	eyebrow piercing		0.6355	download mac
0.6545	celexa		0.635	download free music
0.654	safeway coupons		0.6349	filmicity
0.6537	supras		0.6347	self shooters
0.6527	network password		0.6342	safe web
0.6515	attract women		0.6342	missouri career source
0.6513	wow robot		0.6341	screenium
0.6496	serial number mac		0.634	how to pierce
0.6491	jill cataldo		0.6339	domo games
0.6489	shop blog		0.6337	how to attract women
0.6485	coupon mom		0.6333	youtube partners
0.6485	washington state unemployment		0.6331	download cnet
0.646	melt my heart to stone lyrics		0.6329	ipod touch is frozen
0.6457	computer repair		0.6327	texts online
0.6451	where can i download		0.6326	a2z scrabble
0.6445	m1100		0.6323	canadian pharmacy
0.6438	instant watch netflix		0.6322	funniest facebook status
0.6437	r910		0.6318	melt my heart to stone
0.6427	.zip		0.6314	netflix instant play
0.6421	verizonwireless.com/backupassistant		0.6306	texting signatures
0.6417	dock app		0.6302	subimg
0.6416	dragon care		0.6301	yimmy yayo
0.6413	album list		0.63	facebook for lg
0.6413	pc free		0.63	enlarge
0.6412	number mac		0.6299	cheat o matic
0.641	westell 7500		0.6299	new @ 2
0.64	pixdrop		0.6298	goodyear eagle gt
0.6396	fupa games		0.6296	o_o
0.63953	.5 character sheet		0.6294	missouricareersource
0.6394	hats online		0.6292	netflix watch instantly
0.6373	go2ui		0.6291	bearded dragon care
0.6371	design your own shoes		0.6291	adele melt my heart to stone
0.6364	eastwestworldwide		0.6291	shepherd rescue
0.636	reviews for kids		0.6288	first federal savings bank

continues on following page

Table 1. Continued

0.6288	phone cover		0.6278	esn repair
0.6285	how to erase hard drive		0.6276	good sites
0.6285	instant watch		0.6275	blowback
0.6284	best facebook status		0.6274	eagle gt
0.6283	free printable coupons		0.6273	rock the keys
0.6283	sir pizza miami		0.6272	workforce services
0.6281	smart balance coupon		0.6271	gas blowback

Figure 3. "Frugal" trending over 200 years in the Google books ngram viewer

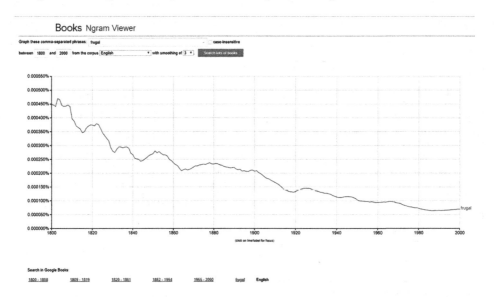

A one-degree related tags network on Flickr for "frugal" shows connections to activities like shopping and cooking. There are references to homemade and cheapfoods, recipes and vegetarianism, groceries and pasta, and DIY. (Figure 4). This network graph was laid out using the Fruchterman-Reingold Force-Based Layout Algorithm.

A 1.5 degree network graph of the "frugal" related tags network on Flickr resolves into two general groups. Group 1 at the left is more about various aspects of the frugal lifestyle, and the group to the right is more about food consumption. (Figure 5)

On Flickr Image Sharing Site

A Flickr image set (1947 items) was extracted around the seeding term "frugal." (Figure 6). The images were run through manual coding, and some themes were extracted.

Figure 4. "Frugal" related tags network on Flickr (1 deg.)

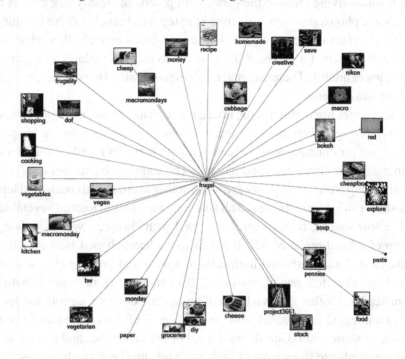

Figure 5. "Frugal" related tags network on Flickr (1.5 deg.)

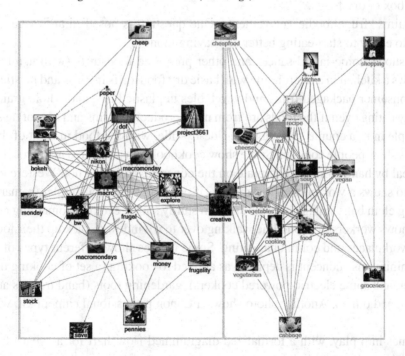

Frugal living involves living close to the earth, with photos of freshly dug carrots from the ground laid side-by-side. Some photos show various fruits growing on a branch. (There is something here about knowing where one's food actually comes from.) One image shows sparsely-flowering cauliflower, which might have illustrated a story of a garden #fail. One photo shows seedlings in paper pots. Self-grown objects need not be lower quality. There are images of prize-winning flowers, prize-winning onions, and other plants entered into contests.

There are raw vegetables highlighted in the image set, such as a close-up of garden vegetables without ends trimmed. Several images show raw chicken, with one raw chicken covered in spices.

Food displays figure prominently in this image set, with servings mostly for individuals and groups. A few close-up images show single-bite food morsels. There are cut vegetables and fruits in single serve containers. There is a soup with various leafy greens. Another soup features beans and leftover foodstuffs.

Some images show grilled fruit. There are all sorts of baked foods: roasted vegetables, baked stuffed peppers, roasted yellow squash, Brussel sprouts topped with cheese, a vegetable lasagna, and others. There is a closeup of a hand-prepared baked pie (it looks hand-shaped with its edge pressed with a fork). Some of the foods look hearty and high-carb: spaghetti and bread, a cheese pasta dish, and others. Different meals are depicted: one of miso soup, fruit and yogurt, raw carrots with dip, and a grain with vegetables mixed in. Another shows a lunch of grapes and cherries, carrots and snap peas, crackers and cheese, and an undressed green salad with carrot slices. This latter one looks like a child's packed lunch. Another several show sushi. One shows a meal of bread, cheese, and a drink in a glass (Water? Wine?). Some of the meals are suggestive of self-reportage, maybe about how closely one is adhering to a planned diet. Portion sizes seem on the smaller side, at least compared to restaurant servings. One image shows a box of dry foods.

One sign claims "frugalfoodie" movements. One question is posed in an image: "What's the one thing you can do easily to start eating better and saving money?"

One image shows home-jarred sauces and other preserved foodstuffs (with natural preservatives). One image shows a kitchen in a microhome with basic dry foodstuffs in glass and plastic containers. One image shows consumer packaged fruits and vegetables in plastic bags, and whole grains; this seems to be about healthy eating even if the foods are from mass producing farms and corporate suppliers. In one photo with people in it, a couple sits at a table side-by-side, with the food in front of them untouched.

Some photos show people cooking. Some show cookbooks. In another, a man crouches on a sidewalk and eats his meal by hand from a small plate on the concrete; he is in a non-Western country. Another far-abroad photo shows a wok on a rock stand—as if pointing back to a simpler (romanticized) time. A woman carrying cloth bags walks down the street in sturdy shoes, evoking something of a universalism. One drawing shows workers in a long line walking over to a window to pick up their food in a cafeteria; this speaks to workplaces and communal eating. Some images show different types of street food.

The "bare minimums" concept is depicted as applied to cooking (a set of cooking utensils, pots and pans, a knife set, and some electric-powered cookers), gardening tools (hand trowels and paint brushes hung on a wall), and others. Another photo shows a Canon professional camera kit, with all basic elements included.

Method comes into play, with a formalized diagrammed flowchart for a "year of living frugally," with major decision points highlighted.

"Travel hacks" come into play. One photo shows a traveler traveling light, with an image of a magazine about travel to a town in France, some bread, a bottle of Evian water, all on a plastic bag on a rock. An apparent selfie shows a man is standing on a white sand beach against a blue sky (the camera is angled upwards from the sand).

Some imagery are expressions of "splurges" and "guilty pleasures." One shows a group of musicians and the text: "I know it's ridiculously pathetic that stupid frugal things like clothes and celebrities make me happy but they do! Heck yes, they do" (in this case, the Jonas brothers). The b/w treatment gives the prior meme a retro feel. Then, there is a stacked pile of golden brownies with nuts and marshmallows, a layered cake, sweets and desserts, which also read like extravagances.

Companionship also comes into play. One photo shows two young people sitting outside on the side of a building and holding hands. This suggests appreciation for the simpler things in life. ("All the best things in life are free.") Two joggers run together, in an image about friendship and mutual health. A miniature horse as a pet is depicted in another image. There are also farm animals, like pigs in a quadtych. Toddlers and children figure in some of the photos, often in custom handmade clothing.

One theme involves low-gasoline transportation: micro cars, scooters, and others. In one, a motorcycle is parked next to a mini car. There are bicycles and two-wheeled scooters (one used for commuting for a woman in business dress). One image shows a double-decker bus. By contrast, one photo shows a stretch recreational vehicle (RV).

Some of the images tell a story; they make a statement. One photo shows a paper price tag with a 2D barcode. The printed price is $49.50, and the "sale" price added on is $49.99 or 49 cents more than the original price. This shows the fungibility of pricing and suggests the importance of paying attention and of not getting taken price-wise. Another messaging image shows a Visa credit card next to a machine button with three settings: reverse, off, auto. One can reverse usage of the credit card, turn it off, and use it automatically and without thinking. Another photo shows a closeup of a wrinkled plastic Walmart bag with the logo and the tagline "Save money. Live better." The camera is zoomed in on the first part of the tagline "Save money." Another series of multiple images shows the back panel of an electronic console, with the imprint of the location where it was assembled (Norway, in this case). This is suggestive of the importance of being aware of supply chains. Another shows various engineering blueprints for a device. A black chalkboard reads: "Make art not war," evoking a 1960s vibe. There is a photo of an empty shopping cart (except for a paper shopping circular) with a name on the cart "Mac Frugal's." Another message reads: "Our dreams and imaginations are smothered" (under the weight of monetary pursuit). A road sign reads: "SAVINGS AHEAD." Some messages contain advice: "Try to be plain in the best ways: plain truthful, plain frugal, and just plain caring." (There is an implied value system.) One image depicts a receipt, two paper bags, napkins, and an empty plastic cup to show how much wastage there is in terms of "to go" food packaging. Two images show political ads with politicians asserting that they will prevent or limit "wasteful spending." One image is a play on sparsity with words in a parking garage next to arrows, with a sign for "up" and a sign for "dn." A Snoopy cartoon shows Snoopy lying on the roof of his red dog house with Charlie Brown seated on the grass beside him with a broad smile: "The less you want, the more you love." One visual advertises "extreme couponing." A road sign reads: "Tough Decision Ahead." There are solutions promised for "Hard water stain, tips & tricks" and "RV Traveling Tips and Tricks." There is an encouraging message for living frugal, maybe even a rallying cry: "I'll go to someone cheaper."

One image shows homemade toothpaste with a highly liquid consistency in a plastic bag. A young man is using the toothpaste to brush. One photo shows a closeup of a woman receiving professional dental care (an exam). Another image shows human-made face cream. One photo shows what looks to be self-made fingernail polish, with a lumpy texture.

Another work shows an antique frog, possibly a keepsake, possibly a knick-knack. This is part of images that show antique objects. Appreciating older things is an act against a disposable economy, one in which new things are most desirable and prevail. A young boy examines an old tractor parked next to a new John Deere one. (The younger generation is bridging the two machines.) There are related photos of a wooden box and its personal contents. One photo shows an old-style instant camera. One photo shows a rusted iron handle on a wooden surface (A wooden box? A wooden drawer?), suggesting a sense of appreciation for aged objects. Old-style vintage aircraft from a prior time are shown in several "frugal" social images.

By contrast, a modern smart phone is shown with an "eco" app pulled up. In other visual depictions, there are smart phones depicted with shopping apps pulled up.

There are expressions of enthusiasm for particular elements of modern life. One image shows a bike rack with a knit "coat" with a button. Another shows an image of a low-energy long-lived spiral CFL (compact fluorescent) lightbulb.

Frugal expressions in living spaces may involve various quilts, curtains, and blankets. There are decorated dining spaces (a white kitchen table with pops of red color in the décor). There are handmade dresses and children's clothes. There are handmade shoulder bags. There are leather boots which have been hand-decorated.

Certainly, there are do-it-yourself (DIY) scenes: a table with tape and cardboard wrapped around parts of it; projects in various stages of development; some clay projects, and others. Creative expression is important. Various images depict handmade jewelry, beadwork, embroidery, knitting, crocheting, painting, and other creative endeavors. There are handmade toys. A child holds up a Lego toy creation.

There are examples of gifts wrapped in brown paper bags and tied with red yarn, depicting gifting or re-gifting. One image shows a latte on a counter in a restaurant; the drink is served in a handmade mug, giving the sense of an artisanal feel. Some photos show close-ups of hand stitching—even and skilled.

One photo shows the interior of a church. Another shows a teacher in a classroom. One visual shows a female avatar in Second Life, which open the possibility of the "immersive parasocial" and celebrity following in immersive virtual worlds (Hai-Jew, Sept. 2009).

There are examples of mutual supports—through events such as clothing swaps. There are calls for "frugal, healthy recipes" and "menu planning tips" to share. A "dumpster diving angel" preens next to a dumpster (such diving is for both individual selves and for others). Fellow home schoolers share expertise and pool their resources. Several visuals suggest the importance of frugal friends, so that there is a supportive social network.

Some of the "frugal" social imagery are commercial in nature. One business promises "coffer budget friendly portraits at an affordance price." Another touts Craigslist to "successfully sell." Various mom-and-pop business seem to be piggy-backing on this meta-narrative.

There are visual messages of engaging the public. One photo shows a man seated at a piano and performing for the public, in a park space. In several, people show off their face painted faces.

There are a miscellany of imagery, which are part of a narrative (elsewhere). There are photos of tourist sites, such as historical train cars, one showing one painted well, and another with peeling paint. There seem to be self-decoration themes, with handmade artworks (like decorative wall panels), fractal imagery (found art?), and colored pencils, fountain pens, and paint brushes. One photo shows a handmade photo album. Craftiness is highlighted, such as with a knitted handmade Christmas ornament, homemade neckties, hand-made paper decorations. A woman has highlights put into her hair at a salon (as part of a personal narrative). A woman sitting in a car shows off a toe ring. A cat lies on its back and looks toward the camera. There are several older model cars with UK license plates. One sits in a field of hay stubble against a backdrop of scattered hay bales. One photo shows a cross in front of some older stone buildings. There is a screenshot of a website with discount sales items. One photo depicts green spaces in a city where people exercise. One shows a magazine layout of an article related to frugal living. Another image shows library books in a stack (why buy when you can borrow?).

Certainly, social imagery is multi-meaninged and can be interpreted in different ways, especially when the images are de-contextualized and analyzed separately from their original contexts. Many images are also somewhat designed to be understood in a stand-alone way. Some messages are spelled out in words, which are also potentially polysemous. This is to say that such interpretations should be understood within the limits of the manual image analysis.

Figure 6. "Frugal" social imagery from Flickr

On Wikipedia

"Frugality" is an article on the crowd-sourced Wikipedia encyclopedia. An extraction of the article network around "Frugality" shows ties to a range of other values, people, concepts, and lifestyles. (Figure 7). The one-degree network graph was laid out using the Harel-Koren Fast Multiscale Layout algorithm.

A 1.5 degree article-article network around "Frugality" on Wikipedia results in 3,957 vertices (unique article pages) and 4,530 unique edges, in a network graph with a maximum geodesic distance (graph diameter) of four. An extraction of clustering using the Clauset-Newman-Moore cluster algorithm results in 19 groups. The extended article-article network graph (including article transitivity) shows links to environmental, philosophical, stewardship, faith, and nature-based implications, among others. (Figure 8)

Figure 7. "Frugality" article-article network on Wikipedia (1 deg.)

Figure 8. "Frugality" article-article network on Wikipedia (1.5 deg.)

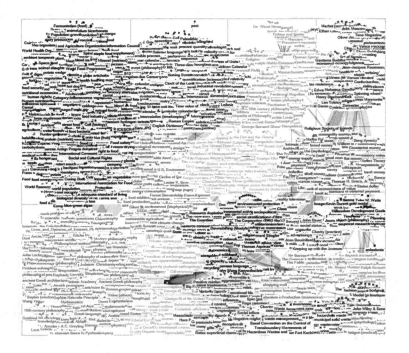

Microblogging Site

On the Twitter microblogging site, a half-dozen accounts were explored around issues of frugality. The most recent Tweets were extracted from each, excluding retweets. At the time of the data capture, here were the basic details of the respective accounts. (Table 2)

Table 2. Features of the "frugal" Twitter accounts mapped for analysis

	Tweets	Following	Followers	Likes	Lists	Start Date	Account Location
@frugalfamily https://twitter.com/frugalfamily	50,014	8,650	14,172	25,374	3	July 2009	North East, England
@TheFrugalGirl https://twitter.com/TheFrugalGirl	8,165	39	2,059	532	0	May 2009	(not shared)
@frugaldealsuk https://twitter.com/frugaldealsuk	8,007	1,378	4,538	31	1	February 2013	United Kingdom
@frugal_living1 https://twitter.com/frugal_living1	630	49	58	82	0	January 2015	United Kingdom
@frugal_Rob https://twitter.com/frugal_Rob	1,021	31	4	108	0	March 2011	(not shared)

These frugal social accounts on Twitter are both local and global (Figure 9).

A word cloud of the "frugal" account Tweetstreams show a focus on gratefulness (Figure 10). There are references to public personalities and to news sites. Days of the week also figure into the messaging, suggesting some time sensitive information.

At the top level, the most popular autocoded (machine-coded) topics include deals, frugal deals, https, things, and today, which suggests a focus on commercial interests (Figure 11).

The sentiment on the Tweetstreams of the "Frugal" social accounts on Twitter show little in the way of sentiment except for one account, which shows a high level of "Very Positive" sentiment (Figure 12).

An extracted word tree around "frugal" as the seeding term shows a lot of outlinking, which suggests the usage of Twitter to drive traffic to other websites (Figure 13).

To integrate the idea of a #bestlife and to show that that may either complement or contrast the idea of a frugal lifestyle, a single Twitter account built around the concept of "bestlife" was trawled.

On a Single Twitter Account About a #bestlife

In contrast to a frugal life, a "best life" may be somewhat understood from a Twitter account (@bestlife-online at https://twitter.com/bestlifeonline), with 2,190 Tweets, 28 following, and 6,612 followers. This account joined Twitter in January 2016. From this account, 2,145 messages were extracted, without retweets included. The social map for this account shows a global network (Figure 14).

The mapping of tweetstreams from @BestLifeOnline on Twitter shows the following word cloud on Figure 15.

Figure 9. Local and global social networks around "frugal" on Twitter microblogging site

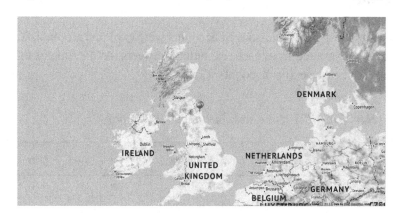

Local and Global Social Networks around "Frugal" on Twitter Microblogging Site

Figure 10. Word Cloud of tweetstreams from multiple "frugal" social accounts on Twitter microblogging site

Figure 11. Autocoded topics from mixed "frugal" social account tweetstreams on a microblogging site

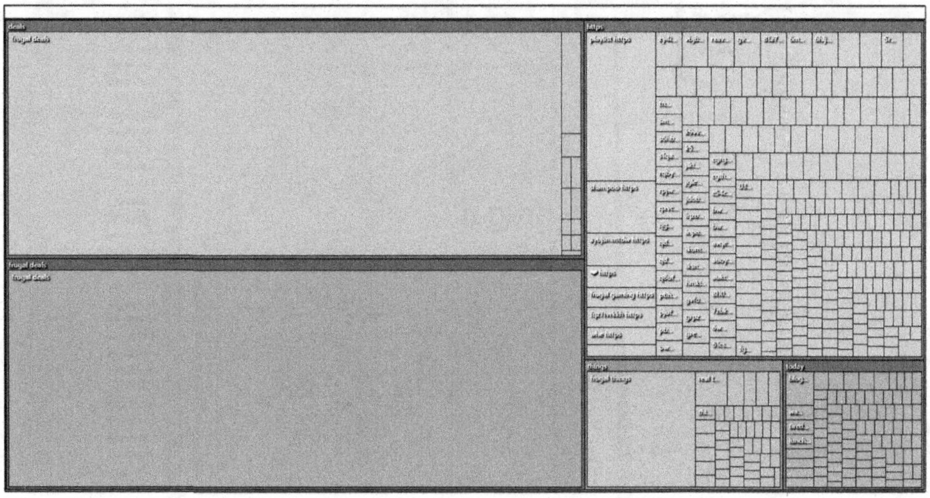

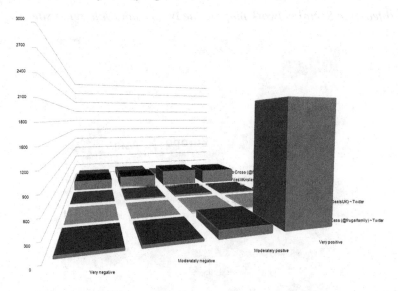

Figure 12. Autocoded sentiments from "frugal" social account tweetstreams

The sentiment of the messaging on the @bestlifeonline account does show a tendency towards moderate sentiment, both negative and positive, but more trending towards positive (Figure 16).

In terms of auto-extracted themes, a #bestlife involves lives that induce FOMO or "fear of missing out." There is royalty, the British royal family, and American Meghan Markle. There is Hollywood glamor and references to the Oscars. There is health, weddings, dating, happiness, welcoming a baby, and exercise. A subtopic is "sex life sizzle." (Figures 17 and 18) Much of social media focuses on conspicuous consumption and over-the-top lifestyles, to stand out from crowds. Very little here would be suggestive of "frugality," and yet, the general assertion in some sectors is that a "frugal" life may actually be the real #bestlife: long-lived, fulfilling, non-excessive, non-selfish, and respectful of the environment.

Figure 13. A "frugal" word tree from mixed frugal social account tweetstreams

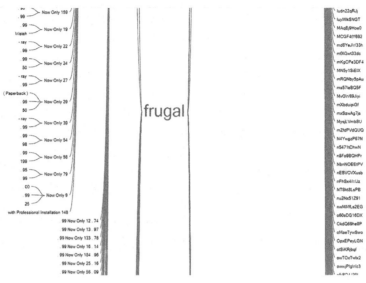

Figure 14. @Bestlifeonline Social network map on the twitter microblogging site

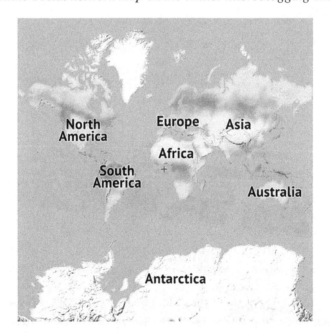

Figure 15. A Mixed sense of a #bestlife from a Twitter account

Figure 16. Sentiment related to "bestlifeonline," from a Twitter account

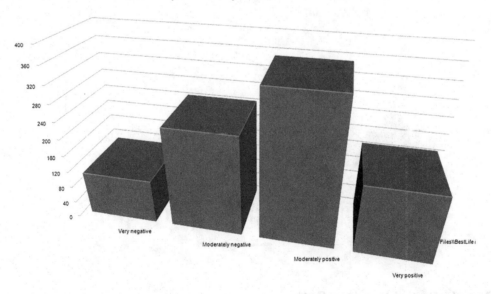

Figure 17. Autocoded themes related to "Bestlifeonline," from a Twitter account

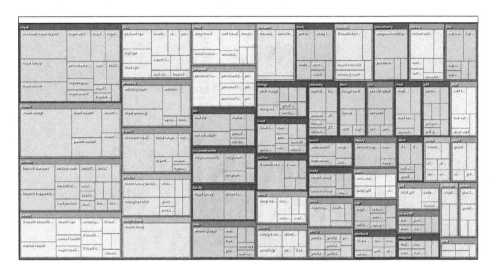

Figure 18. Auto-Extracted themes from a "Bestlifeonline" account on Twitter (pareto chart)

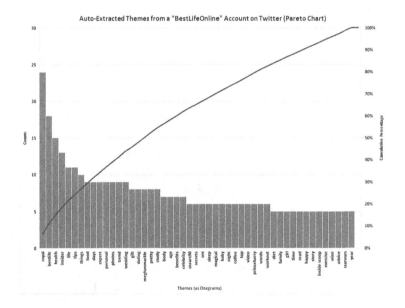

On a Google Social Imagery Set

A social imagery set from Google Images resulted in 486 images (Figure 19), using an older version of Picture Downloader Professional on Google Chrome. The image tags include the following: "living, cheap, infographic, define, money, rich, cartoon, icon, word, minimalist, clip art, scotsman, life, quote, family, family food, kids, family fun, homemaking, economides, texas, frugal living, saving, family meals, youtube, saving tips, save money, budget, activities, expenses, (and) big family." (Is the inclusion of "scotsman" a negative stereotype?) If the Flickr social image set around "frugal" focused more on image-based messaging, the Google Imagery set seems to include much more text and more "how-to's." This set was about a fourth the size of the Flickr set but seems to offer more unique and different extractable themes. Both image sets do show a bright and attractive sheen, with "join us" messaging. [Frugality is not inherently attractive to most. Communicators walk a fine line of engaging in "costly signaling" to show their commitment to a frugal lifestyle, but they risk losing their audience if they come across as too skilled, too elitist, too smug, too proselytizing, too superior, too critical, too blaming, and so on. Calling out others and casting aspersions are fast ways to alienate and lose an audience. Something that is too extreme will make it difficult for people to assume that they can make the sufficient changes. (Can you get by on $5 a day?" is a non-starter in the West.) "Frugalistas," "frugals," and their adherents are preaching to the choir in part but also engaging others considering the lifestyles and choices. Imagine how far conversations get if the conversation starters are: "So how little can you live on?" "How wasteful are you in your daily life consumption?"]

Figure 19. "Frugal" social imagery from Google images

The images show gifts, foods, clothing, makeup, household cleaners, and furniture created by skilled craft-y individuals and do-it-yourself-ers (DIYers). There are explicit messages about saving money with calculators, piggy banks, glass jars of U.S. coins, a padlock atop a man's leather wallet, and cut-up credit cards. The past is used as a basis for present living: "12 frugal lessons from the Great Depression," and "22 frugal living tips from the Great Depression." There are throwback messages and senses of retro time periods: "10 old fashioned frugal recipes from Grandma."

Some visuals show methods for saving money (and using less electricity or gas or energy). In one, a finger lowers the temperature on a thermostat, from 66 degrees to 62 degrees.

There are redefinitions of entertainment and simple pleasures. A gray-haired couple sits together companionably on a bench each reading, with something that might be suggestive of #relationshipgoals. A different older couple is seated at a round kitchen table clipping coupons together, in an indication of maybe a fixed budget and maybe working together for frugal aims.

Some of the social images tout a frugal "new you," and some suggest remorse from overspending and a lack of self-control. One image shows "6 simple ways for spenders to finally become frugal," which suggests people in transition. There are guides for "beginners." Some of the imagery indicates an awareness of the difficulty of staying disciplined. One visual advertises "ways to stay frugal" and to maintain. Another advertises "what to eat every day: a month of frugal meals" for people who prefer a more structured approach to discipline. There are "frugal living tips" calendars that may have the same effect.

Some of the language used in the visuals suggest religious motivations. One visual reads: "The frugal homeschooling mom living an abundant life on a not-so-abundant budget." Another reads: "the spiritual discipline of being frugal." Another one reads: "12 easy frugal ways to be a blessing to others." Another visual points to the desirability of "debt free living" shown with a pair of scissors being used to cut up a credit card; such living without debt is a goal described by various Christian organizations.

A particular segment of the social imagery involves messaging about how to engage with holidays (Valentine's Day, Christmas, July 4 / Independence Day, Halloween) and seasons (Fall, Autumn), with big life events (weddings, family gatherings), celebrations (parties), activities (vacations, home staycations, trips, backpacking, camping), in equivalent ways to the mainstream but with adjustments for frugality. There are directions for "12 frugal days of Christmas" and "DIY stocking stuffers." There are frugal gifts for men. (Quite a few of the gifts seem to be for the self.) There are décor ideas and decorating projects for the various holidays and seasons of the year. One visual promises an "ultimate guide to a romantic and frugal Valentine's Day." There are low-cost costume ideas for Halloween. There are "50 frugal ways to celebrate fall." A frugal wedding can involve homemade dresses for the bride and her bridal party, and there can be savings on food and photos. People who "travel at home" can practice "frugal food tips" ("For travel at home: frugal food tips"). There are "frugal gift ideas for kids." There are suggested ideas for hosting a "frugal fondue party." "Frugal backpackers" are exhorted to "spend less (and) play more," and there are even specific "frugal tips for the solo female backpacker."

A stack of gold foiled covered chocolate coins with the words "10 Frugal Living Goals You Should be Making This Year." An ambition is to be "fabulessly (sic) frugal healthy wealthy wise," reads one word mark. There are everyday ways to live frugally, such as saving money on "household expenses," "extreme couponing," building a "frugal pantry," engaging "frugal self-care tips," using "frugal living tips for single mothers," and working to "save money" without self-deprivation. Large families have "frugal living tips for large families." Eating on a budget is a common theme: "10 easy & delicious frugal dinner recipes," "family approved dinner recipes," "10 frugal weeknight dinners to make when you're broke," "10 frugal weeknight dinners to make when money's tight," "frugal Paleo" diets, and others. There are "10 frugal foods to eat for a healthy pregnancy."

Household concerns account for another tranche of social imagery from the "frugal" seeding term: "10 simple + frugal ideas to clean and organize your home…5 weeks to an organized home," different "hacks, tips & tricks" for your home, tips for "frugal homemakers," "7 ways a large family can be frugal," and others. There are creative ideas for snacks, for making low-cost ice packs, for making anti-bacterial wipes—on a budget. There are lists for "everything you need in a frugal kitchen."

There is a branch related to financial decisions: "Frugal Living: Smart Financial Decisions to Thrive!" Fashion lovers have strategies on "how to wear designer brands when you're on a budget: sale, sale, sale." Crafters can engage in "frugal crafting: how I get craft supplies and fabric for free or cheap." For basic health needs, there are low-cost options, such as for "cracked heel remedies."

"Frugal gardening" is a way to provide for a family, with potentially limited inputs, and outsized outputs. Some photos show chickens in a coop. There are idyllic images of farmhouses. Some messages advertise "eating clean" via "healthy and budget friendly meal ideas." There are descriptions of "frugal vegan" cooking, a flavor for every type of eater.

There is "frugal landscaping," which can offer lower-cost options for yard work. People can apply frugal "laundry strategies." Some of the visuals are flyers advertising frugal workshops for how to gain "frugal living skills."

Children seem to figure centrally as an important area of focus. There are "20 kids activities you wouldn't spend a dime on." There are tips on children's lunches. There are hand-sewn baby and toddler and child clothes. For those who may be anxious about frugal living, there is a visual sign that asks: "does frugal living harm kids?" Those who need to store toys have "over 15 super frugal toy storage ideas." One image shows three boys (brothers?) sitting at a counter in front of their food and ready to share a meal. All three are smiling broadly at the camera. There are "frugal family fun ideas," frugal "first birthday parties," and "frugal food favorites."

While much of the focus in the social imagery is about doing more with less ("slash spending"), some also suggest money-making from blogs and other forms of social media.

A meta-narrative "frugal millionaires" suggests that frugality has a value even for those who could choose to live otherwise. Another visual touts the "frugal habits of the super rich," by capturing single tips from globally recognizable wealthy individuals based on their life experiences. Another visual touts "frugal NBA athletes." The approach seems to be: Who do you respect, and who will you listen to, in order to promote frugal living? (It is notable that this information of wealthy frugals is second hand and broadcast by third parties. In terms of actual direct spokespeople for frugal living, most are young Caucasians and a few Asians—at least in this initial trawl of social communications data. There are mainstream media stories of billionaires who do not carry billfolds, but their reputations are sufficient that businesses will extend services and products on credit or on the promise of payment.)

Several visuals (usually Venn diagrams) compare a frugal family with a spendy one. A "frugal family" interacts with family and friends; they go hiking; they play board games; they engage in DIY; they buy index funds. A "spendy family," by contrast, has debt; they live in a McMansion; they pay for a bottle service; they care about image; they go to malls; they buy purses and shoes there. And in terms of the overlap between the spendy and frugal family, they each "breathe air, eat, go potty, (and) sleep." The visual suggests that the differences are not that extensive. Another visual (a vertical Venn diagram) suggests that frugal families drink wheat beer or India pale ale, buy Charmin, buy Honda and Toyota, shop Kirkland brands; outdoors, they engage in cooking, building and using DIY skills; use manual transmissions; invest; engage in "travel hacking" and engage in "MMM" (unclear meaning). The visual suggests that the lives of frugal families are rich. There are "frugal hacks for single living." There are frugal gifts "for new moms" and "kid-friendly autumn craft projects." There are warnings against profligate spending, such as "15 things frugal people don't pay for," "21 things frugal people don't do," and "10 habits of HIGHLY FRUGAL people that you NEED to know."

In terms of technologies, one informational graphic differentiates between "homegrown" tech and "high tech, and others suggest luddite-approaches to technologies vs. technologically savvy ones.

People need conduct their "financial affairs" with "ethics & etiquette" suggests an image, with a risqué play on the idea of "affairs." A lack of financial management skills leads to suffering. One cartoon shows a man hunched over at an ATM (automated teller machine), and one of two women observing him quips, "Withdrawal symptoms."

Another comparative informational graphic contrasts a "cheap" person vs. a "frugal" one. One data visualization asks: "Frugal vs. Cheap: Which are You?" Frugal people "care about value"; they will buy necessities at reasonable prices; they save up for things that they care about; they splurge occasionally as a reward; they "maintain good personal relationships despite their thrift." On the negative side, "cheap" individuals "care only about price" and "save money for the sake of saving money" and eschew splurging; they offend people with their cheapness. Several images warn about not being "rude" to friends because of frugality. Others visual messages warn against "being boring" in "how to be frugal without being boring." A different visual (overlapping circles on a white board or paper) addresses "frugal friends," described as "Optimists! Happy! Fun! Smart!"

Another opinion-laden visual shows "frugal" as somewhere between "miser" and "cheap," with the idea that people should not be out there shorting others or taking advantage of others. For social human beings, there are "10 frugal gift ideas." Those with children who want to impress teachers can engage "100 free or frugal teacher gift ideas" and consider "frugal & diy teacher gifts."

People not only have to engage in a social ecosystem but an environmental one. One visual shows how "frugal innovation" can increase the multiple uses of water (including gray water), to extend the life cycle uses of water, and to enhance its management as a resource. Multiple images suggest that frugality contributes to environmental conservation efforts and lessen environmental degradation.

A mind map on social media puts "frugal theory" at the center of a graph, with direct links to "food," "DIY, "shopping," "reuse/repurpose," "finance," "lifestyle," (and) "efficiency & sustainability." Another degree out are related phenomena, including "small filling meals, cheap ingredients, (and) healthy" for food; "home products, repairs, (and) home projects" for DIY, "buy it for life" for shopping, and so on. There is a network of behaviors that have implications for the individual and for the larger society. A frugal life is one that is driven by "goals & purpose."

In terms of businesses mentioned under the "frugal" label, there are book promoters, restaurants, carpenters, photography studios, and others. There is a whole other literature that deals with frugal innovations by businesses to ensure that the costs of their respective products and services are as low-cost as possible (based on smart and efficient designs). On social media, there are "frugal favorites" in terms of discount stores: Aldi's, Dollar Tree, Dollar General, and "Frugal MacDoogal beverage warehouse." There is a Frugal Kitchens & Cabinets (as a business name). Some antiques stores' storefront and internal images are also shared. Online, Craigslist is a destination site. (Some of the images show laptops being used to earn and save money.)

There are "best books" lists for those who subscribe to frugality. There are frugal bookstores. There is a free downloadable and printable resource for how to feed "a family of 7 for just $75 a week!" Some books provide angles on how to engage in "frugal innovation." Some data visualizations show book covers about frugality. There are lists of the "12 best books on budgeting, saving money, frugal living & climbing out of debt."

Some shared images seem to be "found images," such as a street sign reading "Village of Frugality." (There are faux "found images," too, with street signs made to read other messaging.)

Hunger is a real phenomenon, and it is no joke. Some headings suggest real-world challenges, such as "frugal shopping tips for when times are tight" and frugal tips "for feeding your family." For many this is about survival. One paneled illustrated work shows "handy tips for living in your car," including what essential items to have, safe places to park at night, how to keep a low profile in a neighborhood, how to maintain personal hygiene, and how to live the "mobile life." Some works offer tips on "epic frugality."

For others, there is a built-in resistance. Those who tend towards pleasure-seeking may be attracted to "frugal hedonism." There is a young woman who is a "frugal model." Frugal vagabonds live by the motto: "Life is short. Save hard. Travel far." Those who are pregnant select "10 frugal foods to eat for a healthy pregnancy," so there are mixes of considerations. There are visuals about "living well with less $$$" and "fake-it-frugal," which suggests less than full engagement. Some come-ons tease using the appeal of "secrets": "6 frugal secrets no one has told you" (with an image of a young woman whispering in another's ear). There are "9 frugal tips to finally lose 10 pounds)," for those interested in some weight loss. One image shows a crockpot; cans of beans, corn, and broth; seasonings and spices...for one-pot taco soup. There are "easy recipes from the frugal girls kitchen!" potentially building on a television comedy show about broke young women. There are ideas for "how to live frugally without feeling deprived." Those who are online socialites may engage the meme of "how to deal with the fear of missing out (FOMO) when you must live frugally." (Social media, with its focus on glamor and social brags, can be an especially hard space for those who want to be frugal. They have to give up the social one-up-manship, social comparisons, and acquisatory lifestyles portrayed on much of social media. The counter-messaging in the frugal EHM does provide an "authorizing environment" to practitioners and makes the lifestyle more appealing than it may seem on the face of things. Such encouragements may be sufficient to encourage some commitment to this path. For others, sharing on social media—impressing others—may also provide some support. Certainly, the practical information about how to maintain a family budget, how to avoid debt, how to control against financial binging, how to prepare foods in frugal ways, how to invest financially (and relatively safely), and how to avoid outsized negative impacts on the environment, are all life skills aspects of modern life.

Human nature, with its darker sides of easy jealousies and striving and judgmentalness, has to be suppressed for longer-term frugal commitments. Most people will not be satisfied with less than those around them.)

A number of the social images address issues of identity. There is a "frugal fanatic" referring to a committed individual There are frugal people and non-frugal people, based on "20 things frugal people never ever do." "Frugal entrepreneurs" engage in "low cost marketing and promotional" outreaches. Some frugal people are "minimalists," who have a preference for sparsity and simplicity. There are "tests" to assess "how frugal are you?" and "Here's how frugal you are, according to your personality type."

Counter-Messaging

In the Google image set of some 486 images, there were a few that were explicitly counter message. One read: "10 signs you're taking frugality too far and how to stop," apparently for the extremists and the obsessives. One piece of advice reads: "Be frugal with your time, not your money." Another counter viewpoint reads: "No one ever gets rich by being frugal." A meme shows an intense actor in a scene, and this reads: "One does not simply stop buying lattes"

The "frugal" electronic hive mind membership seems to draw from the conservative to the liberal continuum, from the religious to the non-religious, from the environmentally minded to the non-environmentally minded. Core impetuses range from the personal to the social. Their commitments seem to range in intensity. Some basic role types in this EHM may be understood in Table 3, from drop-in visitor to the EHM to lurker to engaged member / user-generated content contributor, and influencer. Individuals can certainly move between role types and can change their levels of commitment.

Table 3. Behavior-based role types in the "frugal" electronic hive mind

Roles	Target objectives
Drop-in visitor to EHM	• Find information • Find occasional support • Discover what the "frugal" EHM is about
Lurker to EHM	• Learn new strategies • Learn new tactics • Learn new tips • Identify new resources • Explore the online communities
Engaged member (and) User-generated content contributor in the EHM	• Create an online persona and public reputation • Interact with a virtual community • Make acquaintances, maintain relationships • Make friends, maintain relationships • Interact with community members in RL • Elicit support for self-discipline • Elicit support for problem-solving • Co-lead the EHM • Share self-generated information with others • Share other-generated information with others • Share self-generated digital contents with others • Share other-generated digital contents with others • Help in problem-solving issues raised by others • Earn moneys • Gain non-monetary resources • Build a public following • Contribute to the strength and resilience of the EHM • Create value for the community
Influencer (leader) in the EHM	• Share ideas, resources, connections, and other resources • Recognize and support others • Recruit new members • Raise the profile of the EHM • Interact with others • Engage (and occasionally change) social norms • Co-lead the EHM • Create value for the community • Create aspirational goals • Maintain an earned and outsized influence on the EHM

DISCUSSION

The frugal living movement has attracted participants from different walks of life, and it has attracted the attention of people in different verticals interested in reaching a more resistant market. The idea of living more conscientiously and mindfully and without waste is an alluring one, and the constant thinking and constant improvement approach may enable swaths of humanity to live in the world in more sustainable ways. This non-threatening approach may be appealing to many and may enable speaking into people's personal decisions and spaces in meaningful ways, peer-to-peer, friend-to-friend, given people's receptivity to close and trusted others. If people are to internalize particular values and practices, working through people's personal trust networks seems to be a winning strategy. Practical approaches at the lived level enable "small wins" and help avoid the paralysis of facing large-scale challenges (like environmental degradation). The support of an online community may enable greater encouragement of individual and small group commitments. Individual choices made individually can have widespread (even global- or planet-scale) impacts, with potential implications on human survival. What is an alternative lifestyle today can gain wider adoption and become more mainstream.

The meta-narratives are about fiscal survival, ethical living, living closer to nature, having a slower pace of modern life, non-wastage of resources, religious commitments, and environmental protections.

This research work showed only a few spokespersons—individuals, duos, and families—for this value system and lifestyle. For this effort to advance, a larger number of spokespersons and models would be needed, and more diverse spokespersons may be needed. The inventiveness of the members of this EHM seem to have been applied at low-hanging fruit (home cooking, growing vegetables, applying craftiness, sharing resources, building furniture, and so on), and it is possible that there are many other endeavors that may be adopted at micro-to-macro levels.

This work offered an early effort at modeling electronically-enabled social membership. It showed more of a cyber-physical confluence. If nothing else, this work shows that studying EHMs is not just an academic exercise but engages real-world implications.

FUTURE RESEARCH DIRECTIONS

How transferable this mix of appeals is to those in other cultures and social contexts may vary. It may well be that this lifestyle will be appealing but for a whole different set of other messaging, around community or other values. It is likely that frugality in other contexts likely will involve different sets of human-to-human innovations, given the differing cultures and contexts. Some of the social imagery are suggestive of non-Western approaches, such as "rickshaw banks" and "easy paisa" mobile banking and Grameen Bank microloans (with relatively high interest rates), and others. Some images show mini clay refrigerators (which do not require electricity) used on the African subcontinent.

This work can be built on in various ways. The main research methods here involve using publicly available data from social media platforms. These were captured at macro levels (mass search data, mass book data), meso levels (Wikipedia article networks), and at micro levels (various social media accounts based on frugality and #bestlife). Certainly, there are more direct ways to elicit responses, such as by direct online surveying. It may be interesting to map the membership of the "frugal" EHMs based on user motivations, based on self-reportage. It may be helpful to evaluate the outcomes of people's EHMs in terms of measurable behaviors and outcomes.

CONCLUSION

The meta-narrative of "frugality" is a dispersed one which does not seem to be an important challenge to mainstream material-based living. It seems to be something simultaneously aspirational as it is practical. And yet, the subjectivities of people and their intersubjectivities in interactions enable mutual encouragement in this space—for engaging with difficult challenges of living frugally in the present days. The frugal EHM does inform a range of endeavors that affect people's sparser and more mindful lifestyles, in many ways. On social media platforms, the frugality EHM involves the sharing of creative crowd-sourced ideas for living a form of a #bestlife and being in harmony with the self, with others, and with the environment. Some may be read as "trial balloons" to see how well others may accept those grassroots bottom-up approaches.

Some of the social messaging suggests extremes, with common searches for how long expired food may be consumed without severe adverse health effects. There are stories of making do on a shoestring, such as living out-of-cars and being homeless…and even travels abroad on a shoestring (hitchhiking, trading work for food, and other endeavors). Equipment, like microwaves, may be used long after their integrity has been compromised.

Perhaps Benjamin Franklin said it best in two quotes that suggests a balanced approach: "Waste neither time nor money, but make the best use of both" and "Wealth is not his that has it, but his that enjoys it." A more modern take is a quote from American industrialist Owen D. Young, who said:

We are not to judge thrift solely by the test of saving or spending. If one spends what he should prudently save, that certainly is to be deplored. But if one saves what he should prudently spend, that is not necessarily to be commended. A wise balance between the two is the desired end.

And finally, the idea of frugal living should not take away from the need for livable wages, social security nets, school nutrition programs, affordable healthcare, and policies and programs to address homelessness. Subsistence, no matter how it is dressed up and even glamorized, can be brutal and with long-term detrimental effects.

REFERENCES

Cornet, V. P., Hall, N. K., Cafaro, F., & Brady, E. (2017). How image-based social media websites support social movements. *Proceedings of the 2017 CHI Conference Extended Abstracts on Human Factors in Computing Systems*, 2473 – 2479. 10.1145/3027063.3053257

East, S. (2016, July 6). Four years' trash, one jar…zero waste. *CNN*. Retrieved Dec. 6, 2018, from https://www.cnn.com/2016/07/04/us/lauren-singer-zero-waste-blogger-plastic/index.html

Gaiani, S., Caldeira, S., Adorno, V., Segrè, S., & Vittuari, M. (2018). Food wasters: Profiling consumers' attitude to waste food in Italy. *Waste Management (New York, N.Y.)*, 72, 17–24. doi:10.1016/j.wasman.2017.11.012 PMID:29174684

Hai-Jew, S. (2009, Sept.). Exploring the immersive parasocial: Is it you or the thought of you? *Journal of Online Learning and Teaching*. Retrieved Oct. 15, 2018, from http://jolt.merlot.org/vol5no3/haijew_0909.htm

Hai-Jew, S. (2019). The electronic hive mind and cybersecurity: Mass-scale human cognitive limits to explain the 'weakest link' in cybersecurity. In *Global Cyber Security Labor Shortage and International Business Risk* (pp. 206–262). Hershey, PA: IGI Global. doi:10.4018/978-1-5225-5927-6.ch011

Hutto, C. J., Yardi, S., & Gilbert, E. (2013). A longitudinal study of follow predictors on Twitter. *Proceedings of CHI 2013*, 821 – 831. 10.1145/2470654.2470771

Kardara, M., Papadakis, G., Papaoikonomou, T., Tserpes, K., & Varvarigou, T. (2012). Influence patterns in topic communities of social media. *Proceedings of the 2nd International Conference on Web Intelligence, Mining, and Semantics (WIMS '12)*, 1 – 12. 10.1145/2254129.2254144

Lastovicka, J. L., Bettencourt, L. A., Hughner, R. S., & Kuntze, R. J. (1999). Lifestyle of the tight and frugal: Theory and measurement. *The Journal of Consumer Research, 26*(1), 85–98. doi:10.1086/209552

Lee, S.H. (M.). (. (2016). When are frugal consumers not frugal? The influence of personal networks. *Journal of Retailing and Consumer Services, 30*, 1–7. doi:10.1016/j.jretconser.2015.12.005

Leonard-Barton, D. (1981, December). Voluntary simplicity lifestyles and energy conservation. *The Journal of Consumer Research, 8*(3), 243–252. doi:10.1086/208861

Mehta, L., Huff, A., & Allouche, J. (2018). The new politics and geographies of scarcity. *Geoforum,* 1-9. (in press)

Mowen, J. C. (2000). *From frugality to modest living. In 3M Model of Motivation and Personality* (pp. 187–203). Boston, MA: Springer. doi:10.1007/978-1-4757-6708-7_14

Natale, A., Di Martino, S., Procentese, F., & Arcidiacono, C. (2016). De-growth and critical community psychology: Contributions towards individual and social well-being. *Futures,* 78 – 79, 47 – 56.

Nicholls, A., Simon, J., & Gabriel, M. (2015). Introduction: Dimensions of social innovation. In *New Frontiers in Social Innovation Research.* Basingstoke, UK: Palgrave Macmillan. doi:10.1057/9781137506801_1

Pepper, M., Jackson, T., & Uzzell, D. (2009). An examination of the values that motivate socially conscious and frugal consumer behaviours. *International Journal of Consumer Studies, 33*(2), 126–136. doi:10.1111/j.1470-6431.2009.00753.x

Roiland, D. (2016). Frugality, a positive principle to promote sustainable development. *Journal of Agricultural & Environmental Ethics, 29*(4), 571–585. doi:10.100710806-016-9619-6

Sapountzi, A., & Psannis, K. E. (2018). Social networking data analysis tools & challenges. *Future Generation Computer Systems, 86*, 893–913. doi:10.1016/j.future.2016.10.019

Thelwall, M. & Stuart, E. (2018). She's Reddit: A source of statistically significant gendered interest information? *Information Processing and Management,* 1 – 16. (in press)

Thøgersen, J. (2018). Frugal or green? Basic drivers of energy saving in European households. *Journal of Cleaner Production, 197*, 1521–1530. doi:10.1016/j.jclepro.2018.06.282

Todd, S. & Lawson, R. (2003). Towards an understanding of frugal consumers. *Australasian Marketing Journal, 11*(30), 8 – 18.

Tsugawa, S., & Ohsaki, H. (2015). Negative messages spread rapidly and widely on social media. *Proceedings of COSN '15*, 151 – 160. 10.1145/2817946.2817962

Vadakkepat, P., Garg, H. K., Loh, A. P., & Tham, M. P. (2015). Inclusive innovation: Getting more from less for more. *Journal of Frugal Innovation, 1*(2), 1–2. doi:10.118640669-015-0002-6

Webb, H., Burnap, P., Procter, R., Rana, O., Stahl, B. C., Williams, M., ... Jirotka, M. (2016). Digital wildfires: Propagation, verification, regulation, and responsible innovation. *ACM Transactions on Information Systems, 34*(3), 15. doi:10.1145/2893478

KEY TERMS AND DEFINITIONS

Autocoding: The coding of information through computational or machine means.

Electronic Hive Mind: A synchronous temporal and informal patchwork of emergent shared social consciousness (held by geographically distributed people, cyborgs, and robots) enabled by online social connectivity (across a range of social media platforms on the web and internet), based around various dimensions of shared attractive interests.

Frugality: Thrift, resourcefulness, making do with less.

Micro House: A smaller-than-regular-sized home, built often as part of the tiny house movement.

Sentiment Analysis: The analysis of language for positive or negative sentiment (without neutrality).

Zero-Waste Lifestyle: A process of making decisions and consuming in ways with as little waste as possible.

This research was previously published in Electronic Hive Minds on Social Media; pages 77-120, copyright year 2019 by Information Science Reference (an imprint of IGI Global).

Chapter 41
"Too Good to Be True":
Semi–Naked Bodies on Social Media

Anke J. Kleim
University of Strathclyde, UK

Petya Eckler
University of Strathclyde, UK

Andrea Tonner
University of Strathclyde, UK

ABSTRACT

This chapter examines how body image deception is created and understood in social media. The authors focus specifically on the beach body, which is a narrower form of bodily representation online, but where deception is especially likely to occur. Focus group discussions with young adults revealed that editing and perfecting the beach body is commonplace and even normalized on social media. However, participants distinguished between celebrities and friends in expected use of manipulation and seemed to place a limit on the acceptable types of manipulation: body tan but not body shape, for example. The authors discuss the implications of these discussions and how applying deception theory in body image research can provide useful insights.

INTRODUCTION

Media images, such as of the ideal beach body, increasingly undergo digital alteration and enhancement, so that most pictures we see online represent an idealized version of reality. This trend applies to celebrities and regular users alike. In this "online appearance culture" (Williams & Ricciardelli, 2014), users seem obsessed with posting, sharing, liking and commenting on pictures, and appearance seems to be of growing importance. Through these behaviors, users contribute to the normalization of unrealistic body and beauty ideals, which can be damaging to body image, self-evaluation and overall wellbeing (Fardouly, Diedrichs, Vartanian, & Halliwell, 2015).

DOI: 10.4018/978-1-6684-6307-9.ch041

The beach body is an especially interesting niche in the larger body image literature, due to the high expectations placed on individuals offline and online, and the likelihood that those expectations cannot be met. Thus, the mediatized beach bodies of young people online are not only photographic versions of their real bodies, but an improved and perfected representation, which agrees with the cultural standards of the day and which sometimes is quite removed from the original. Through photo manipulation, accessorizing and body positioning, these "easy lies" (Harwood, 2014) become possible.

In this chapter, we will examine mediatized images of the beach body in the context of social media through the conceptual lenses of deception, a unique combination of concepts, which has not been explored together previously, and which can expand significantly the current range and depth of research on body image and deception. We will explore what motivates young people to engage in online deception about their beach body and how they achieve it.

BACKGROUND

Body Image and the Beach Body: An Online Culture of Perfectionism

Body image is "a person's perceptions, thoughts, and feelings about his or her body" (Grogan, 2017). The dimensions, determinants and processes of body image are complex and multifaceted, given that a person's body parts and vital organs form fundamental components of the human self and identity (Belk, 1988). Cash (2012) differentiates between body evaluation, i.e. the (dis-)satisfaction with one's appearance, and body investment, i.e. the affective, cognitive and behavioral relevance of the body to a person's self-evaluation. In the context of the beach body, the behavioral component is fundamental for understanding how individuals try to control their bodies in order to look as perfect as possible during summer.

Body image attitudes form and develop throughout a person's life, starting in early childhood and changing across the lifespan (Cash, 2008). They are based upon four factors: personality traits, physical characteristics and changes, interpersonal experiences with family and peers, and cultural socialization (Cash, 2008). The latter is particularly important in the context of this chapter, as it is through acculturation that young children learn what is considered attractive and beautiful in society. To conform to society's expectations, individuals, most notably women, often invest heavily into their looks, and that may involve subtle forms of deception.

Historically, societies have focused on people's outward appearance and even considered it a symbol of a person's (dis-)ordered lifestyle (Bordo, 2013). A slim female body has been associated with positive socio-cultural qualities, such as success, social appreciation, and happiness (Grogan, 2017), and muscular male figures have been linked to strength and heroism. Overweight, in contrast, has been associated with negative attributes, such as lack of discipline and laziness (Murray, 2016). Equally, bodies that do not conform to beauty standards, such as fat, disfigured, disabled, or ageing figures, are marginalized and stigmatized (Wardle & Boyce, 2009). While slenderness has endured as the most salient bodily feature for women to aspire to over the decades, trends have also developed within body ideals. The 1990s were characterized by enlarged breasts and slender hips, while the 2000s saw a shift towards more voluptuous bottoms. Recently, muscularity has affected both men and increasingly women (Grogan, 2017).

The female beach body is typically portrayed as "slim, tanned, young, Caucasian, female and biki-nied" (Small, 2007, p. 87), which is in congruence with the common public understandings of how a (semi-naked) body ought to look.

Clothes serve as an important means to manage appearance, for instance by covering or concealing perceived bodily imperfections (Tiggemann & Andrew, 2012). When wearing swimwear, individuals' bodies are exposed and reveal details that are normally hidden from public view. The extent to which one conforms to the common beauty norms becomes visible and assessable then. Therefore, individuals try to get "beach body ready", i.e. achieve an ideal beach physique as depicted in the media through bodily preparation techniques such as dieting, exercising, hair removal and fake-tanning, which is linked to high levels of self-surveillant and controlling behaviors. This molding of one's regular body into a "beach body" is a form of body modification, which is linked to malleability beliefs and seeing the body as a project (Small, 2007; Pritchard & Morgan, 2012).

Past investigations of the beach body have been largely limited to holiday experiences and represen-tations in traditional media, such as magazines, neglecting contemporary digital culture and the visual trend of presenting bodies online. However, the beach body is no longer confined to the beach and now extends to a broad spectrum of digital platforms.

Media images, such as of the ideal beach body, increasingly undergo digital alteration and enhance-ment, so that most pictures we see online are closer to fiction than reality. Against this background, we suggest distinguishing between real bodies at the beach, i.e. semi-naked figures in swimwear in natural environments, and beach body images as displayed in media contexts, i.e. mediatized beach bodies, as they differ from each other significantly. In this chapter, we aim to look specifically into mediatized beach body images in the context of social media, a topic that has not yet been explored, but that we believe is of great importance, as it enables researchers to better understand how women mediatize images of their semi-naked bodies online.

Driven by the need to present the best possible version of themselves to others (Haferkamp & Krämer, 2011; Manago, Graham, Greenfield & Salimkhan, 2008), individuals adjust the personal information they reveal through their online profiles and the way they (inter-)act with others, much of which is visual. In this "online appearance culture" (Williams & Ricciardelli, 2014), users seem obsessed with posting, sharing, liking and commenting on pictures, and appearance seems to be of even greater importance than in offline life. On Instagram alone, approx. 95 million photos are uploaded every day (Lister, 2018), and in 2017, 54% of global Internet users reported that they shared private and sensitive photos and videos of themselves digitally (Statista, 2018). Beach body pictures are part of this trend. As of 23 October 2018, there have been 9,530,236 postings using the hashtag #beachbody, 1,747,138 postings using the hashtag #beachbodycoach and 64,670 postings under the hashtag #beachbodyready on Instagram alone. Some scholars have begun to analyze sexualized selfies (Hart, 2016; Miguel, 2016; Mascheroni, Vincent & Jimenez, 2015), but we know little about individuals who post pictures of themselves wearing swimwear.

While existing findings on social media and body image are somewhat inconsistent, photo-based online activities have been linked to poor body image (Meier & Gray, 2014). Since the publication of that study in 2014, photo-based activities on social media, including the taking and posting of "selfies" (a self-portrait, typically taken through a smartphone camera) and "usies" or "wesies" (photos that include others as well), have increased even further, particularly amongst teenagers (Grogan, Rothery, Cole, & Hall, 2018; McLean, Paxton, Wertheim, & Masters, 2015).

Similar to mass media images, photographs posted on social media are increasingly manipulated and digitally enhanced. Some 70% of 18-35-year-old women regularly edit their images before posting them

(Renfrew Foundation, 2014). Young users in particular tend to put significant effort into their pictures before uploading them. To achieve the aspired look, they often take multiple photos before carefully selecting and closely monitoring the one they find suitable to show others (Fardouly et al., 2015).

New apps and tools to modify pictures are routinely introduced and offer many ways to creatively transform ordinary photographs: re-coloring, adding polarization effects or additional elements (e.g. film scratches, picture frame), modifying film textures and tones, or retouching unwanted appearance details (Caoduro, 2014). But the most common editing strategy, as suggested in Grogan et al.'s (2018) qualitative study, is the photographic angle, through which individuals aim to present themselves as perfect. Thereby, the focus is often on the face and unwanted body parts are covered or hidden.

Through these behaviors, users contribute to the normalization of unrealistic body and beauty ideals, which can be damaging to body image, self-evaluation and overall wellbeing (Fardouly et al., 2015). Another study found that girls who shared selfies online on a regular basis and who engaged in photo manipulation were likely to feel negatively about their bodies and to show eating concerns (McLean et al., 2015).

Apart from sharing their own pictures, social media users are exposed to other users' postings. This includes private users, such as family and peers, and professional users, such as celebrities or brands. Those postings offer orientation for what other bodies look like and what is considered beautiful, while their number of likes, shares and positive comments shows what kind of pictures and bodies receive social appraisal from others. This may increase users' desire for a similar response on social media. Regular views and comments on the profiles of social media friends, i.e. social grooming, have been linked to a drive for thinness (Kim & Chock, 2015).

Besides the many studies that have focused predominantly on the negative aspects linked to social media usage and photo-based activities, some scholars have suggested that selective self-presentation through online profiles and the extra care involved may actually improve self-esteem (Gonzales & Hancock, 2010) and posting selfies might be an empowering experience for women (Tiidenberg & Cruz, 2015). Positive feedback from other users can add to the positive sensations resulting from social media behavior (Valkenburg, Peter, & Schouten, 2006). Despite these findings, most studies have uncovered negative impacts of social media usage on body image (e.g. Eckler, Kalyango, & Paasch, 2017; Fardouly et al. 2015; Kleemans, Daalmans, Carbaat, & Anschütz, 2018).

The body positivity and body neutrality movement have begun to spread online non-idealized and unfiltered images of people with more diverse body shapes and skin colors, many of whom have disfigurements and other "imperfections" that are typically excluded from thin-idealized imagery, including beach body pictures. A recent study demonstrated that being exposed to body-positive Instagram posts positively affected young women's mood, body satisfaction and body appreciation, and seeing more of this type of content might be a promising approach to trigger positive body image in social media users (Cohen, Fardouly, Newton-John, & Slater, 2019). But despite the growing attempts at showing diversity and its obvious positive effects, many social media users seem hesitant toward showing what they truly look like. One could consider that the pressure to present an idealized version of the self and to receive positive validation from others is still stronger than the bravery to show an "imperfect" self.

DECEPTION THEORY: A NEW OUTLOOK ON THE BEACH BODY

Deception has been studied from various perspectives: psychological, sociological, linguistic, etc. We will examine deception as a communication process, which involves a sender, a message and a receiver. Typical research areas include examinations of motivations for senders to engage in deception (McCornack, Morrison, Paik, Wisner, & Zhu, 2014), the deceptive message itself (Markowitz & Hancock, 2018) or the receiver and how they perceive and respond to the deceit (Levine, 2014).

Deception is often defined as "intentionally, knowingly, and/or purposely misleading another person" and messages involve "intent, awareness and/or purpose to mislead" (Levine, 2014, p. 379). Deception can include lies, omission, evasion, equivocation and generating false conclusions with true information (Levine, 2014). In terms of online communication, deception is a common focus of research. As Toma and Hancock (2012) stated, "Concerns about online deception are as old as the Internet itself" (p. 78).

Theoretical models propose that most people tend to be honest most of the time and only a few prolific liars tell most of the lies (Levine, 2014), which has been supported by evidence (Markowitz & Hancock, 2018; Serota, Levine, & Boster, 2010). As discussed previously, we can find large numbers of digitally altered photographs and optimized online profiles in the social media landscape. But does this polishing of one's online profile or photo constitute lying? Users may not perceive this behavior as lying, because they may see the lie as a low stake normative response to online codes of conduct, something Harwood (2014) called "easy lies". Such lies, also called "light", "do not cause distress, are not seen as serious, are not regretted, are more pleasant than the truth for all parties involved … and the liar would not really care if the lie was discovered" (DePaulo et al., 1996, as cited in Harwood, 2014, p. 407).

These small and harmless lies (such as commenting favorably but undeservedly on someone's cooking or praising a child's unsuccessful art project) are often situational and occur frequently in everyday interactions with friends and family. Thus, Cole (2014) argues that situational complexity can sometimes influence the creation of deceptive messages; and intent or awareness, which are often assumed to guide deception, can occur during the process of lying or even post facto. This suggests that deception may not be as rational and top-down as many scholars believe. As Cole (2014) argues, deception is "almost certainly driven by automatic and unconscious processes" (p. 396).

Some have demonstrated that in the field of online dating users lied often but subtly in order to enhance their profiles (Hancock & Toma, 2009; Toma & Hancock, 2010). Self-presentation and self-enhancement are major motives for deceiving others in the context of online/mobile dating (Markowitz & Hancock, 2018). The authors discovered that close to two-thirds of deceptive content was driven by impression management, specifically related to self-presentation and availability. The asynchronous and editable features of online dating create the perfect conditions for deception: "Users have an unlimited amount of time to create their self-presentation and the ability to revise it to make it both flattering and believable" (Toma & Hancock, 2012, p. 79). The same can be said about social media in general and how users portray their bodies and overall persona. With these media affordances at hand, users often lead a carefully orchestrated campaign of self-presentation (Toma & Hancock, 2012) and the different genders tend to value different aspects of their appearance. Men were typically found to exaggerate their height and women to underreport their weight and intentionally post less accurate photographs (Hancock & Toma, 2009; Toma & Hancock, 2010; Toma, Hancock & Ellison, 2008). This attempt at self-optimization online is an important aspect of online culture, as it contributes to unrealistic images and an atmosphere of idealized body-centered content.

These findings have direct relevance to body image and to the beach body, where a possibly flawless appearance seems as the license to expose one's semi-naked body and to receive social approval from others. Another similarity to online dating is that the ideal beach body has long been connected with romance and successful sexual relationships (Jordan 2007, Small 2016). This refers to situations at the beach and for media contexts, where women in swimwear have been portrayed as "sexually alluring decorations", i.e. sexual objects to be looked at (Jordan, 2007, p. 94). Deception thus seems likely to occur in the context of the beach body as well.

This chapter will explore two theories of deception, which address different aspects of the communication process. The Information Manipulation Theory 2 (IMT2) focuses on the creation of a deceptive message and the motivations of the sender. It "conceptually frames deception as involving the covert manipulation of information along multiple dimensions and as a contextual problem-solving activity driven by the desire for quick, efficient, and viable communicative solutions" (McCornack et al., 2014). The theory focuses on situational triggers of deception and diverges from previous models, which see deception as top-down, intentional and conscious.

Also applicable is the Truth-Default Theory (TDT) by Levine (2014), which examines the deception process from the viewpoint of the receiver. The theory posits that when people communicate with each other, they tend to presume that their conversation partner is basically honest. This presumption of honesty makes possible efficient communication and cooperation, and in most cases is correct, as most people tell the truth most of the time (Levine, 2014). This presumption also makes people vulnerable to manipulation and deception, at least in the short-term, but the theory argues that the truth default presumption is also highly adaptive to the individual and the species, and thus will improve accuracy of detection. The theory diverges from previous work in the field by focusing its detection powers not on the behaviour or nonverbal cues of the sender of communication, but on the message itself and its context. "Most lies are detected either through comparing what is said to what is or what can be known, or through solicitation of a confession" (Levine, 2014). This focus on the message and its context is especially relevant to social media, where the sender is not seen face to face and thus, they cannot provide behavioral cues of deception. However, there are plenty of opportunities to study the message itself due to the written record that remains and the asynchronous mode of communication.

The two theories have been applied to the study of politicians dodging questions and how people respond and try to detect those behaviors (Clementson, 2018a), how politicians accuse each other of evasiveness, which may affect voters' attitudes about their dishonesty (Clementson, 2016), and the role of partisan bias when detecting politicians' deception (Clementson 2018b). TDT has also been applied to various settings for the study of how people detect deception (e.g. Blair, Reimer, & Levine, 2018).

This study is the first known attempt to apply deception theories to the field of body image. While the concept of body deception has been used previously, it was linked to social comparison theory but not to any deception theories (Hildebrandt, Shiovitz, Alfano, & Greif, 2008). TDT and IMT2 are particularly useful, as together they address different aspects of the deception process and also offer a more updated and nuanced view of deception compared to some of their predecessors (Cole, 2014; Levine, 2014; McCornack et al., 2014). We will examine the sender, the message and the receiver of this communication process in an effort to discover how body image deception is created and understood in social media. We pose the following research questions:

Research Question 1: What motivates users to engage in online deception about the beach body?
Research Question 2: How do users engage in online deception about the beach body?

STUDY METHOD

This exploratory study involves 25 undergraduate international exchange students, aged 19-23, from 19 different countries and five continents: Europe, North and South America, Asia and Oceania. The students participated in four focus groups (three groups were all-female, one group was all-male) at the University of Cologne, Germany.

They discussed their perceptions of the beach body in online and offline contexts. As 92% of participants used Facebook and Instagram every day, based on a questionnaire they filled out, we could ensure that they were familiar with the usage and content posted on social media, irrespective of their home country.

Data was collected in the summer, when the beach body topic is frequently promoted in the media. Therefore, participants would likely have been recently exposed to related pictures.

The focus groups were facilitated by a fellow student who ensured that all participants were included in the discussion and that the discussion was focused on the purpose of the study. Focus groups lasted between 50 and 90 minutes. Participants were asked to discuss six broad questions about social media, two of which will be considered as a foundation for this chapter. The first question was: "What (changing) behaviors, both offline and online, have you observed amongst your female peers when it came to achieving a beach body?" The second question was: "Please think about some typical beach body postings that you can find on your social media newsfeed, e.g. published by friends or any pages/people you like or follow. How do those postings differentiate (a) from one another and (b) from real-life situations at the beach?"

Although the questions themselves aimed to evoke various comments and experiences, those often revolved around deception, as will become evident in the following section. Additionally, each participant filled in a short survey about their demographic data and social media use. All discussions were audiotaped and transcribed verbatim to allow inductive systematic analysis. See Table 1 for details on the participants.

FINDINGS

The findings below are guided by our research questions and structured around them. Based on the huge number of pictures shared online daily, one could expect users to deal with them routinely and perhaps even quickly. But our focus group discussions revealed that taking, choosing and eventually posting the "right" picture might be a lengthy process, which can involve much consideration and extra care in order to look good and receive positive feedback and appraisal from others. All groups were very clear that the ideal beach body as presented in the media, most notably on social media, differed considerably from real bodies at the beach. They thus confirmed our idea to differentiate between real and mediatized beach bodies and Grogan et al.'s (2018) suggestion that "there are disconnects between women's identity as portrayed in selfies and their 'real' offline identities" (p. 26). How exactly beach bodies are being mediatized in social media contexts and the role of deception will be discussed below.

Table 1. Focus group participants

Focus group	Name	Age	Home location	Facebook use	Twitter use	Instagram use
1	Female	n/a	Europe	Several times a day	Less than once/ twice a week	Several times a day
1	Female	22	Asia	Once/twice a day	I don't know	I don't know
1	Female	21	Europe	Several times a day	Less than once/ twice a week	Several times a week
1	Female	n/a	Asia	Several times a day	Less than once/ twice a week	Several times a day
1	Female	n/a	Europe	Once/twice a day	Less than once/ twice a week	Once/twice a day
1	Female	21	Europe	Several times a day	Less than once/ twice a week	Once/twice a day
2	Female	n/a	Europe	Several times a day	Less than once/ twice a week	Less than once/ twice a week
2	Female	22	North America	Once/twice a day	Once/twice a day	Once/twice a day
2	Female	21	Europe	Several times a day	Several times a day	Several times a day
2	Female	22	Europe	Several times a day	Several times a week	Several times a day
2	Female	21	Europe	Several times a day	Less than once/ twice a week	Once/twice a day
2	Female	n/a	Europe	Several times a day	Less than once/ twice a week	Several times a day
2	Female	n/a	South America	Several times a day	Less than once/ twice a week	Once/twice a day
3	Female	20	Oceania	Several times a day	Less than once/ twice a week	Once/twice a day
3	Female	22	Oceania	Several times a day	I don't know	Several times a day
3	Female	19	Asia	Several times a day	Several times a day	Several times a day
3	Female	20	Europe	Several times a day	Less than once/ twice a week	Once/twice a day
3	Female	n/a	Asia	Less than once/twice a week	Several times a day	Less than once/ twice a week
3	Female	23	Europe	Several times a day	Less than once/ twice a week	Once/twice a day
4	Male	n/a	South America	Once/twice a day	Less than once/ twice a week	Less than once/ twice a week
4	Male	n/a	Europe	Several times a day	Less than once/ twice a week	Several times a day
4	Male	20	Europe	Once/twice a day	Less than once/ twice a week	Less than once/ twice a week
4	Male	21	South America	Several times a day	Less than once/ twice a week	Less than once/ twice a week
4	Male	n/a	Europe	Several times a day	Several times a day	Several times a day
4	Male	21	Asia	Less than once/twice a week	Less than once/ twice a week	Less than once/ twice a week

Motives for Online Deception About the Beach Body

As discussed earlier, online self-optimization of one's body via presenting incorrect information or omission or leading to false conclusions is considered deception. Past literature has demonstrated how social media users generally try to present their best version online (Haferkamp & Krämer, 2011; Manago et al., 2008). But the focus groups revealed that posting pictures of their semi-naked appearances seemed to be exclusively reserved for women who already had a "good" body in real life:

...you need to know that your body is almost perfect, you know, to post a picture. And you don't use Photoshop to change your shape. You can change the color of your skin or something, but you still need to have a perfect body to post these pictures. (Female 1)

Having an attractive physique thus seemed to be a pre-condition for posting a beach body picture online and possible motives for doing it could be similar to those found for online dating: self-presentation and self-enhancement (Markowitz & Hancock, 2018).

Even though modern technology, such as digital photo alteration apps, could easily transform any picture into a "perfect" version, there was still the expectation to have a good-looking physique in real life and to put effort into it. However, the asynchronous nature of social media and the extended opportunity for users to gaze at each other's photos, and in this case beach bodies, meant that the stakes for online representations were higher than in offline settings.

...I think when you're posting something on Instagram, you have to look better there because it's like a picture and you can look at it for a long time. But when you're in real life, you're always like in a move. So people are not so crazy about how they look in real life because they always look better in real life than on social media because they are like in motion all the time. And the perception of people is absolutely different as well. It's like "Okay, she or he doesn't have a perfect skin or something. So what? Nobody is perfect! So what?" But on social media it's like "Oh look, no perfect skin, oh my God!" So the perception is different. You can afford for yourself not to be perfect in real life because nobody is perfect. But in social media, you have to be like all perfect. (Female 2)

However, throughout our focus groups, females were described or described themselves, as rather hesitant toward posting beach body pictures online. One reason was culture. Participants from Korea and China emphasized that acts of posing and showing off were generally disapproved of, and social media users would rarely do it. In other countries such as Russia, posting beach (body) pictures related more to stating that one could afford beach holidays rather than to exposing an ideal body. Thus, a second motivation for posting beach body pictures related to demonstrating social status. A photo from the beach may be directly about your body, but indirectly, and maybe more importantly, about showing that you can afford a beach holiday. These findings demonstrate the importance of studying body image from an intercultural perspective and the beach body is a good case study of that.

A motive for not posting beach body pictures may, however, be the explicit expectation that they should look perfect, as discussed previously. If the photos do not conform to the socio-cultural understandings of ideal beauty, girls may feel insecure about exposing their semi-naked appearances online or fear negative public feedback. The perception of the beach body in social media contexts was rather standardized and bodies that differ from the "beauty ideal" were not mentioned, even though many participants favored more realistic beach bodies when asked about different contexts.

How Users Engage in Online Deception About the Beach Body

Participants shared various techniques for enhancing their beach photos before and during the actual photography. Based on high expectations and awareness of being looked at and critically evaluated by others, picture taking at the beach was linked to females putting on make-up and choosing the right outfit, i.e. "fancy apparel," such as good looking and well-fitting (or even form-enhancing) swimwear and beach accessories, to prepare for a good shot. Some groups also mentioned last-minute exercising before taking a picture in order to increase muscle definition.

So the pictures online ... Obviously they are never as good as in life. Because you put a filter on it, you do like ten push-ups before you take the photo, you know. It's stupid. (Male 1)

Apart from the general preparations to look good on beach body pictures, participants listed some additional procedures. The most salient were mimics or posing. It seemed particularly relevant to keep smiling, look sexy and indicate good mood, but in a grown-up and serious manner, not in a childish or funny way:

And like that means that you're like sexualizing your body and it's like the main goal. It's not like 'I'm having a fun time at the beach with my friends,' it's like 'oh, look at my really skinny bikini photos.' And I'm thinking of people who do it just to take bikini photos to show off. And the whole thing that Instagram builds is the mindset that you gonna have to post pictures like that. (Female 3)

Like, I feel like I'd rather have a funny photo with my bra or with my arse not being quite as skinny as it should, but ... (Female 4)

Yeah, but then just having a good time! (Female 3)

Yes, and rather than those pictures like 'I'm serious and I'm posting', I'd rather have a funny photo. (Female 4)

As the excerpts above show, sexual objectification was perceived as normative amongst the female participants, even though they wished to differentiate from it. Showing certain mimics and moods on pictures, also described as "playing" by some participants, was perceived negatively and brings the question of why women feel the need to be smiling and in sexy poses. Reasons may be manifold and originate from each person's individual personality, but our study revealed considerable peer pressure. This supports the idea that one's body image may be influenced by family and peers through the social pressure they exert (Grogan, 2017).

This focus on mimics and poses also relates to the earlier studies on deception, which examined people's gestures, faces and other non-verbal cues for signs of cheating (e.g. Ekman, 1992). While more recent works have focused on the message rather than the sender's face to detect deception, the fact that so many young people focus on their non-verbal cues in photos and that has now become part of the deceptive message may prompt a re-examining of senders' features and cues when detecting deception.

When it came to posing, the desire to look slim and muscular dominated across cultures, which indicates a high internalization of Western ideals. To achieve this, young people would apply different poses and flex their muscles, which confirmed the aforementioned tendency toward last-minute workouts.

So many of my friends try to show the perfect body on social media. But of course they are normal people. They don't have Photoshop and these things. But I do realize they are trying their best to look thin ... like they are trying their best to look the skinniest or the strongest with lots of muscles and stuff. (Female 5)

While mimics and gestures were of particular importance, background features seemed less relevant or perhaps respondents thought of them as self-explanatory and not worth mentioning. This raises the question of whether backgrounds generally become less important if there is a (semi-naked) body in the picture and whether some kind of selective perception may occur. Future research could explore this question further.

Even with the right preparations, mimics and gestures, users may not be entirely satisfied with their pictures and optimize them further before posting. They may first pick the best shot from the series they took and then apply a filter or otherwise edit the picture. Amongst our participants, digital alteration of pictures was linked stronger to celebrities or professional advertisers than to social media "friends".

This became particularly clear in the context of advertising, where participants stated rather matter-of-factly that bikini models on adverts looked unrealistic, similar to celebrities. The digital enhancement of their social media pictures was as obvious as the fact that some of them had cosmetic surgery. Even though participants stated that it "looks like a cartoon [and] can't be real", it seemed to be accepted as part of being famous. In fact, examples were given of celebrities such as Kim Kardashian who lost many followers after posting a picture of their "real" body. Some participants felt sorry for them, whereas others made fun. Overall, it appeared that digital alteration was accepted or at least considered normal if participants did not have a personal, close relationship to the sender of the picture. These findings are in line with Grogan et al.'s (2018) qualitative study in which interviewees showed awareness of celebrities manipulating their selfies in order to look perfect.

Despite this awareness, it was repeatedly stated how comparing against better-looking people on social media made participants feel bad about their own bodies and increased their wish to look better. Our results thus support findings of previous studies on body image and social media, in which processes of upward comparison were identified as triggers of negative body image (e.g. Eckler et al., 2017; Fardouly et al. 2015; Kleemans et al., 2018).

Increased awareness of deception through digital alteration may not protect young people from negative feelings about their body or comparing against idealized images. In fact, a recent experiment on the effects of photo manipulation on Instagram showed that such photos had direct links to lower body image, even though manipulation was detected by participants (Kleemans et al., 2018). Reshaping of bodies was poorly detected, however, and the photos were still evaluated as realistic (Kleemans et al., 2018). This is an interesting finding for research aiming to identify mechanisms to trigger positive body image. It also reminds of recent findings on the use of disclaimer labels on images in traditional and social media contexts, which suggested that those had no protective effect on individuals' body dissatisfaction, even though they clearly indicated that images were edited, hence unrealistic and deceptive (Bourlai & Herring, 2014; Tiggemann, Brown, Zaccardo, Thomas, 2017; Bury, Tiggemann & Slater, 2017; Fardouly & Holland, 2018).

The differing perceptions of our respondents indicate that deception on social media is somewhat normalized and takes place in various forms.

First, some techniques to make oneself look better on pictures might be more acceptable than others. For instance, applying filters might be considered okay and even normative, whereas slimming down via a photo-editing app may be seen as unacceptable. Similarly, Grogan et al.'s (2018) study revealed, "manipulating online 'identity' through altering the appearance of selfies was seen as a legitimate, and even necessary way to enhance perceived attractiveness" (p. 25). They identified some "socially-shared rules of self-presentation" (p. 26) through which individuals tried to conform to norms and expectations of ideal beauty. These rules contained certain no-goes though, such as posting sexually suggestive pictures. It is well imaginable that the degree of digital manipulation might also be affected by those rules.

Second, idealized images were generally linked more to celebrities than to "friends", which is interesting because as discussed earlier, photo manipulation was somewhat accepted or even normalized. This leads to the question whether users tend to perceive their friends as more trustworthy and genuine than celebrities, so that they may look at them in a less critical way or whether ordinary social media users are perhaps less likely to artificially enhance their beach body images in other ways than through "basic" adjustments such as lighting or contrasts. The existing literature provides limited findings on this relatively new research topic, so more data are needed to deepen our understanding.

The last possible stage of deception is when posting pictures online. Instagram is a photo-centric platform where users can link their pictures to certain keywords using hashtags. And even though the hashtag #beachbody is a prominent one, as stated previously, beach body pictures may not always be provided with this or another beach body-related hashtag, but with different ones. In fact, respondents in all focus groups linked postings of beach body pictures to postings related to health and fitness, claiming that these were the contexts in which they were exposed to most pictures of women in bikinis/swimwear, with many being before-and-after images. To shed light onto this, future content analysis research can investigate how these hashtags correlate.

Health and fitness are frequently used terms in social media, so that they might in fact be used to disguise one's purpose to get beach body ready:

I think in America, it's like more and more like not being beach body ready, but more like being healthy, I guess. And so... it's more like "Oh, I'm..." well I don't know, I think even some of my friends are... I know that they will say: "Yeah, I just wanna be healthy. I wanna be fit." and stuff, but then like they're like "Oh my God, I need to fit in to this pair of jeans" and they're like "Oh my gosh, I really want to look good when I go to the beach in summer"... Exactly, so in the end, that's like the ultimate goal but they kind of disguise it as "No, I just wanna be fit and healthy. (Female 6)

Another participant described how young women would post pictures of themselves wearing a bikini and with a bowl of salad in front of them. He accused them of intentionally putting the focus on food, while in fact they were only interested in exposing their beach body. This might be a way of exposing one's beach body indirectly, especially in cultures where "showing off" is perceived negatively.

While our study only scratched the surface of cultural differences in deceptive social media behavior related to the beach body, it outlines many lines of inquiry in the future for more in-depth explorations.

CONCLUSION

Past body image research has emphasized normalized behaviors in several related contexts, including body dissatisfaction and dieting (e.g. Grogan, 2017). Photo-editing strategies on social media are also perceived as normal or even expected by the online community. Young users are aware that such behaviors could classify as deceptive, but did not perceive them as negative, such as Harwood's (2014) "easy lies." When discussing friends, sophisticated manipulation such as via Photoshop use was seen as uncommon, however the discussion of celebrities and influencers was more critical of deceptive practices and participants were aware of them using Photoshop prominently, which was considered a normal part of their work.

Thus, deception appears to be the ticket for acceptance and belonging into the social media community. This is in many ways worrisome. First, if deception is normative on social media, this will likely reinforce the internalization of unrealistic and unattainable beauty ideals and will further distort users' perceptions of how bodies ought to look online and offline. For instance, more young people may be taking drastic and unhealthy measures to achieve that Photoshop body offline. Second, when thin beach body ideals are disguised under hashtags such as #health, #fitness, and #detox, the lines between healthy and unhealthy behaviors continue to be blurred. In fact, many of the messages and images under these supposedly benign hashtags are neither healthy nor harmless, as they promote weight loss over health. The deception of presenting health-risking behaviors as health-promoting ones might have particularly detrimental impacts on young people's wellbeing and is something that needs to be explored in future research.

Social media users may see their manipulation of body images as "easy lies": not serious, more pleasant than the truth, inconsequential and harmless (DePaulo et al., 1996, as cited in Harwood, 2014). But we can question the harmless nature of these "small" deceptions. As millions of social media users tweak, filter and slim down their (beach) body images before posting online, deception becomes part of the cultural norm and the unrealistic thin ideal for our bodies is maintained and strengthened, with potentially damaging consequences on people's body image (Kleemans et al., 2018).

Although deception about the (beach) body on social media may be perceived as commonplace, limits on acceptability do seem to exist. The expectation that you can only post beach body photos if you are already fit, and can manipulate and enhance your tan through filters, but not change your body shape, speaks to those boundaries. These boundaries may be broken by others routinely, but seem difficult for users to detect. As Kleemans et al. (2018) showed, adolescent users trusted the photos they saw of peers and wrongly accepted them as realistic, even though they were subject to body reshaping manipulation. This brings the question of detection of deception to the forefront of body image research.

This chapter's contribution to deception theory is in connecting it for the first time with body image research and digital manipulation on social media. It builds understanding of the means and motivations for creating "small" digital lies and offers an in-depth look of how that occurs in practice. This topic could be expanded further in several directions, which are discussed below.

SOLUTIONS AND RECOMMENDATIONS

Solutions for online photo enhancement could begin with discussions of deception and the "easy lies" young people tell one another online, for instance as part of education in media literacy. The assumption of harmlessness should be challenged and real consequences of the thin ideal should continue to be emphasized online and offline. Further, young people may not even perceive their online behaviors as lying, in which case a discussion about deception, its boundaries and consequences is needed. Since most people tend to tell the truth most of the time (Levine, 2014), presenting image manipulation as deception may challenge its current normalized acceptance and users' own self-image as truthful and honest.

An overall need to build a more realistic understanding of what real bodies look like is also needed. Traditional media images, such as cosmetics advertising, have long been regulated, in many countries for truthfulness. However, this particular solution could be challenging. Research has shown that disclaimer labels on manipulated social media images have been ineffective at addressing negative consequences of exposure (Fardouly & Holland, 2018). It is thus crucial to further investigate this topic and identify efficient mechanisms to warn users about misleading and deceptive media messages.

A "code of conduct" to limit the use of digitally altered images online is another option to encourage more realism online and its creation should involve policy makers, social media companies, academics and online users. "Photoshop laws" such as in France and Israel are good examples in this direction, although just like disclaimer labels, their efficiency has not yet been empirically shown. An Industry Code of Conduct on Body Image was introduced in Australia in 2009, which required diverse sized models to be used in magazines. A content analysis a year later of young women's magazines swim suit editions showed that more than half of them were upholding elements of the code (Boyd & Moncrieff-Boyd, 2011). However, the voluntary and self-regulatory nature of the code has been criticized for being too soft on the fashion industry (Seseljia & Sakzewski, 2017).

Another recent political attempt to regulate harmful online content has been Germany's social media law, which was released on 1 January 2018 to reduce hate speech and cyberbullying on social media platforms. Content moderators have been employed at so-called deletion centers to delete or block violent comments that could be harmful to the community (Bennhold, 2018). While this approach is still a relatively young pilot project which without doubt needs continuous development based on empirical evidence, it constitutes an interesting legislative initiative to monitor and regulate content shared via social media that might negatively affect its users. It is thus conceivable to expand approaches like this to detect deceiving images. However, it must of course be acknowledged that it is potentially more difficult to identify harmful visual content relating to body image. Further understanding is thus needed of health-risking visual social media content, specifically regarding the impact of media exposure on physical and mental health.

Within an environment as vibrant and fluid as the Internet, joint forces are needed to contribute toward decisive change. Brands, celebrities and online influencers should take their share of responsibility to improve the genuine depictions of bodies and lifestyles online. A long-time belief is that thinness is the most efficient advertising strategy, but past studies have highlighted that realistic models with average-size bodies may be equally efficient (e.g. Halliwell & Dittmar, 2004). However, we must acknowledge that these attempts still run against mainstream media practices, where women are commonly objectified and the thin body ideal is used as a symbol of virtue, success, beauty, and more (Bordo, 2013; Grogan, 2017). As a result, these escapes from perfectionism may in themselves become promotional stunts and instead attract attention to the "normal" state of those celebrities, which is the touched-up, staged and deceiving self.

In this regard, parallels to Dove's Campaign For Real Beauty come to mind. The campaign did launch a mainstream conversation about authenticity and staying real, but at the same time did it within the same confines of corporate culture and consumerism, and eventually some argue that it reframed, rather than challenged, the dominant ideology of beauty in order to strengthen its own brand identity among young women (Murray, 2013). In spite of this criticism, Dove remains one of the pioneers in the attempt to promote a more diverse body image through advertising.

Corporate responsibility also relates to the advertising of potentially harmful products on social media, which many celebrities engage in. In February 2019, the medical director of NHS England, professor Stephen Powis, called for social media companies to ban "damaging" ads of weight loss aids endorsed by celebrities and urged influential celebrities to act "responsibly" (NHS England News, 2019). Right now, the rules on what can be promoted on social media are few, but in 2019, the Competition and

Markets Authority in the UK launched new guidance for social influencers (Competition and Markets Authority, 2019a). The agency has sent out warning letters to many celebrities, urging them to review any concerning practices, and has secured formal commitments from 16 of them to ensure compliant labeling, according to a recent press release (Competition and Markets Authority, 2019b).

All of the above initiatives need to be accompanied by ongoing research on positive body image and the identification of mechanisms that may eventually trigger body satisfaction to defend users against the internalization of unrealistic beauty ideals. Positive body image has been suggested as a powerful concept (Wood-Barcalow, Tylka, & Augustus-Horvath, 2010) that can be a "protective filter", used by women, to process and respond to communication in a body-preserving manner. However, there is little exploration of this positive body image in social media research. Social media can have many body positive aspects e.g. community and belonging, skill development, self-mastery, and self-acceptance. Some scholars have already argued for the importance to focus on body functionality (Alleva, Martijn, van Breukelen, Jansen, & Karos, 2015) and some recent studies suggest that yoga practices may positively affect body image (e.g. Neumark-Sztainer et al., 2018).

Body positivity and body neutrality movements may also provide solutions for unrealistic presentations, even though some have come under scrutiny for allegedly promoting obesity. The proliferation of images with people of various shapes, sizes, skin colors, and with visible blemishes that differentiate from the majority of thin-idealized bodies in the media is a crucial step on the way to fostering a more realistic depiction of how bodies actually look. The study by Cohen et al. (2019) has been a valuable academic contribution, demonstrating that exposure to body positive social media content may trigger positivity, such as higher body appreciation.

With its semi-naked and revealing appearance, the beach body is a particularly suitable theme for body positive and diversity-promoting campaigns. Fostering a more grounded understanding on social media of diverse beach bodies may be crucial in helping young people develop a more positive and self-accepting relationship to their semi-naked offline (beach) bodies. The strong connection between online and offline behavior is a particularly important aspect that needs to be explored in depth when designing new ways to diminish health-risking online deception and foster body positivity, be it in academia, policy or elsewhere.

FUTURE RESEARCH DIRECTIONS

This chapter has offered some strong initial connections between deception theory and the beach body and has raised multiple questions for future research. It demonstrated that the beach body should be studied in more depth and from various academic perspectives, as it is a prominent theme on social media, which affects people globally by sending them into annual "body panic" before summer. There is even reason to believe that body image concerns may increase during summer, when people reveal more of themselves to others. Future research should thus look more closely into individuals' body image in a seasonal context and further explore the role of social media and deception. The achievement of an ideal beach body is typically linked to a range of preparation techniques such as dieting, exercising, and hair removal. While photo manipulation might easily substitute these practices, our data showed a strong link between online and offline behavior, i.e. that there is a need to look perfect not only on social media but also in real life. Therefore, further study is needed on how online and offline behaviors relate to each another.

Future research should also increase our understanding of users' motives for manipulating their images. Self-enhancement is the logical rationale (Markowitz & Hancock, 2018) but our data indicated that further motives may be influential that relate to social status, comparisons with peer groups, need for social appraisal, peer pressure and culture-specific influences.

Another interesting line of inquiry is the assumption about truth and deception related to celebrities and friends. As our group discussions revealed, celebrities are expected to manipulate their photos constantly, but friends are perceived as more realistic and trustworthy. However, whether that is actually true remains to be confirmed through research and some studies are suggesting that this perception of the truthfulness of friends may be misleading (Kleemans et al., 2018). This also brings the question of detection of deception related to body images online, which needs further exploration.

The concept of the beach body, and related deception, could also be studied more broadly by including hashtags around fitness and health. Future content analyses can investigate how these hashtags correlate with body image photos and deception practices, and what kind of messages they communicate to users.

Finally, participants in body image research should be diversified by including more male and LGBT voices, cross-cultural aspects of research on deception and body image, especially from non-Western perspectives.

REFERENCES

Alleva, J. M., Martijn, C., van Breukelen, G. J. P., Jansen, A., & Karos, K. (2015). Expand Your Horizon: A programme that improves body image and reduces self-objectification by training women to focus on body functionality. *Body Image*, *15*, 81–89. doi:10.1016/j.bodyim.2015.07.001 PMID:26280376

Belk, R. W. (1988). Possessions and the extended self. *The Journal of Consumer Research*, *15*(2), 139–168. doi:10.1086/209154

Bennhold, K. (2018, May 19). Germany acts to tame Facebook, learning from its own history of hate. *The New York Times*. Retrieved from https://www.nytimes.com/2018/05/19/technology/facebook-deletion-center-germany.html

Blair, J. P., Reimer, T. O., & Levine, T. R. (2018). The role of consistency in detecting deception: The superiority of correspondence over coherence. *Communication Studies*, *69*(5), 483–498. doi:10.1080/10510974.2018.1447492

Bordo, S. (2013). *Unbearable weight feminism, western culture and the body*. Berkeley, CA: University of California Press.

Bourlai, E., & Herring, S. C. (2014). Multimodal communication on tumblr: "I have so many feels!" In *WebSci '14 Proceedings of the 2014 ACM Conference on Web Science* (pp. 171-175).

Bury, B., Tiggemann, M., & Slater, A. (2017). Disclaimer labels on fashion magazine advertisements: Does timing of digital alteration information matter? *Eating Behaviors*, *25*, 18–22. doi:10.1016/j.eatbeh.2016.08.010 PMID:27591965

Caoduro, E. (2014). Photo filter apps: Understanding analogue nostalgia in the new media ecology. *Networking Knowledge: Journal of the MeCCSA Postgraduate Network*, *7*(2), 67–82.

Cash, T. F. (2008). *The body image workbook: An eight-step program for learning to like your looks.* Oakland, CA: New Harbinger Publications.

Cash, T. F. (2012). Cognitive-behavioral perspectives on body image. In Encyclopedia of Body Image and Human Appearance (Vol. 1, pp. 334-342).

Clementson, D. E. (2016). Why do we think politicians are so evasive? Insight from theories of equivocation and deception, with a content analysis of U.S. presidential debates, 1996-2012. *Journal of Language and Social Psychology*, *35*(3), 247–267. doi:10.1177/0261927X15600732

Clementson, D. E. (2018a). Effects of dodging questions: How politicians escape deception detection and how they get caught. *Journal of Language and Social Psychology*, *37*(1), 93–113. doi:10.1177/0261927X17706960

Clementson, D. E. (2018b). Truth bias and partisan bias in political deception detection. *Journal of Language and Social Psychology*, *37*(4), 407–430. doi:10.1177/0261927X17744004

Cohen, R., Fardouly, J., Newton-John, T., & Slater, A. (2019). #BoPo on Instagram: An experimental investigation of the effects of viewing body positive content on young women's mood and body image. *New Media & Society*.

Cole, T. (2014). Reconsidering the role of intentionality in deceptive communication: A commentary on IMT2 and TDT From a Relational Science Point of View. *Journal of Language and Social Psychology*, *33*(4), 393–397. doi:10.1177/0261927X14534843

Competition and Markets Authority. (2019a, January 23). Social media endorsements: being transparent with your followers. Retrieved from https://www.gov.uk/government/publications/social-media-endorsements-guide-for-influencers/social-media-endorsements-being-transparent-with-your-followers

Competition and Markets Authority. (2019b, January 23). Celebrities pledge to clean up their act on social media. Retrieved from https://www.gov.uk/government/news/celebrities-pledge-to-clean-up-their-act-on-social-media

Eckler, P., Kalyango, Y., & Paasch, E. (2017). Facebook use and negative body image among U.S. college women. *Women & Health*, *57*(2), 249–267. doi:10.1080/03630242.2016.1159268 PMID:26933906

Ekman, P. (1992). *Telling lies: Clues to deceit in the marketplace, politics and marriage.* New York: Norton & Company.

Fardouly, J., Diedrichs, P. C., Vartanian, L. R., & Halliwell, E. (2015). Social comparisons on social media: The impact of Facebook on young women's body image concerns and mood. *Body Image*, *13*, 38–45. doi:10.1016/j.bodyim.2014.12.002 PMID:25615425

Fardouly, J., & Holland, E. (2018). Social media is not real life: The effect of attaching disclaimer-type labels to idealized social media images on women's body image and mood. *New Media & Society*, *20*(11), 4311–4328. doi:10.1177/1461444818771083

Gonzales, A. L., & Hancock, J. T. (2010). Mirror, mirror on my Facebook wall: Effects of exposure to Facebook on self–esteem. *Cyberpsychology, Behavior, and Social Networking*, *14*(1-2), 79–83. doi:10.1089/cyber.2009.0411 PMID:21329447

Grogan, S. (2017). *Body image: Understanding body dissatisfaction in men, women and children.* London: Routledge.

Grogan, S., Rothery, L., Cole, J., & Hall, M. (2018). Posting selfies and body image in young adult women: The selfie paradox. *The Journal of Social Media in Society, 7*(1), 15–36.

Haferkamp, N., & Krämer, N. C. (2011). Social comparison 2.0: Examining the effects of online profiles on social-networking sites. *Cyberpsychology, Behavior, and Social Networking, 14*(5), 309–314. doi:10.1089/cyber.2010.0120 PMID:21117976

Halliwell, E., & Dittmar, H. (2004). Does size matter? The impact of model's body size on women's body-focused anxiety and advertising effectiveness. *Journal of Social and Clinical Psychology, 23*(1), 104–122. doi:10.1521/jscp.23.1.104.26989

Hancock, J. T., & Toma, C. L. (2009). Putting your best face forward: The accuracy of online dating photographs. *Journal of Communication, 59*(2), 367–386. doi:10.1111/j.1460-2466.2009.01420.x

Hart, M. (2016). Being naked on the internet: Young people's selfies as intimate edgework. *Journal of Youth Studies, 20*(3), 301–315. doi:10.1080/13676261.2016.1212164

Harwood, J. (2014). Easy Lies. *Journal of Language and Social Psychology, 33*(4), 405–410. doi:10.1177/0261927X14534657

Hildebrandt, T., Shiovitz, R., Alfano, L., & Greif, R. (2008). Defining body deception and its role in peer based social comparison theories of body dissatisfaction. *Body Image, 5*(3), 299–306. doi:10.1016/j.bodyim.2008.04.007 PMID:18650136

Jordan, F. (2007). Life's a beach and then we diet: Discourses of tourism and the 'beach body' in UK women's lifestyle magazines. In A. M. Pritchard, N. Morgan, I. Ateljevic, & C. Harris (Eds.), *Tourism and gender: embodiment, sensuality and experience* (pp. 92–106). Wallingford, UK: CAB International. doi:10.1079/9781845932718.0092

Kim, J. W., & Chock, T. M. (2015). Body image 2.0: Associations between social grooming on Facebook and body image concerns. *Computers in Human Behavior, 48*, 331–339. doi:10.1016/j.chb.2015.01.009

Kleemans, M., Daalmans, S., Carbaat, I., & Anschütz, D. (2018). Picture perfect: The direct effect of manipulated Instagram photos on body image in adolescent girls. *Media Psychology, 21*(1), 93–110. doi:10.1080/15213269.2016.1257392

Levine, T. R. (2014). Truth-Default Theory (TDT): A theory of human deception and deception detection. *Journal of Language and Social Psychology, 33*(4), 378–392. doi:10.1177/0261927X14535916

Lister, M. (2017). 33 Mind-Boggling Instagram Stats & Facts for 2018. *Wordstream.* Retrieved from https://www.wordstream.com/blog/ws/2017/04/20/instagram-statistics

Manago, A. M., Graham, M. B., Greenfield, P. M., & Salimkhan, G. (2008). Self-presentation and gender on MySpace. *Journal of Applied Developmental Psychology, 29*(6), 446–458. doi:10.1016/j.appdev.2008.07.001

Markowitz, D. M., & Hancock, J. T. (2018). Deception in mobile dating conversations. *Journal of Communication, 68*(3), 547–569. doi:10.1093/joc/jqy019

Mascheroni, G., Vincent, J., & Jimenez, E. (2015). "Girls are addicted to likes so they post semi-naked selfies": Peer mediation, normativity and the construction of identity online. *Cyberpsychology (Brno), 9*(1), 5. doi:10.5817/CP2015-1-5

McCornack, S. A., Morrison, K., Paik, J. E., Wisner, A. M., & Zhu, X. (2014). Information Manipulation Theory 2: A propositional theory of deceptive discourse production. *Journal of Language and Social Psychology, 33*(4), 348–377. doi:10.1177/0261927X14534656

McLean, S. A., Paxton, S. J., Wertheim, E. H., & Masters, J. (2015). Photoshopping the selfie: Self photo editing and photo investment are associated with body dissatisfaction in adolescent girls. *International Journal of Eating Disorders, 48*(8), 1132–1140. doi:10.1002/eat.22449 PMID:26311205

Meier, E. P., & Gray, J. (2014). Facebook photo activity associated with body image disturbance in adolescent girls. *Cyberpsychology, Behavior, and Social Networking, 17*(4), 199–206. doi:10.1089/cyber.2013.0305 PMID:24237288

Miguel, C. (2016). Visual intimacy on social media: From selfies to the co-construction of intimacies through shared pictures. *Social Media + Society, 2*(2).

Murray, D. P. (2013). Investigating users' responses to Dove's "real beauty" strategy. In C. Carter, L. Steiner, & L. McLaughlin (Eds.), *The Routledge Companion to Media and Gender*. New York: Routledge.

Murray, S. (2016). *The 'fat' female body*. London: Palgrave Macmillan.

Neumark-Sztainer, D., MacLehose, R. F., Watts, A. W., Pacanowski, C. R., & Eisenberg, M. E. (2018). Yoga and body image: Findings from a large population-based study of young adults. *Body Image, 3*(24), 69–75. doi:10.1016/j.bodyim.2017.12.003 PMID:29288970

NHS England News. (2019, February 2). Top doctor calls for ban on 'damaging and misleading' celebrity social media ads. Retrieved from https://www.england.nhs.uk/2019/02/top-doctor-calls-for-ban-on-damaging-and-misleading-celebrity-social-media-ads/

Pritchard, A., & Morgan, N. (2012). 'Wild on' the beach: Discourses of desire, sexuality and liminality. In E. Waterton & S. Watson (Eds.), *Culture, heritage and representation: Perspectives on visuality and the past*. Farnham: Ashgate.

Reid Boyd, E., & Moncrieff-Boyd, J. (2011). Swimsuit issues: Promoting positive body image in young women's magazines. *Health Promotion Journal of Australia, 22*(2), 102–106. doi:10.1071/HE11102 PMID:21819351

Renfrew Foundation. (2014). Afraid to be your selfie? Survey reveals most people photoshop their images. Retrieved from http://renfrewcenter.com/news/afraid-be-your-selfie-survey-reveals-most-people-photoshop-their-images

Serota, K. B., Levine, T. R., & Boster, F. J. (2010). The Prevalence of lying in America: Three studies of self-reported lies. *Human Communication Research, 36*(1), 2–25. doi:10.1111/j.1468-2958.2009.01366.x

Seseljia, A., & Sakzewski, E. (2017, May 19). Body image: Are Australia's fashion industry standards up to scratch? *ABC News Online*. Retrieved from https://www.abc.net.au/news/2017-05-18/body-image-industry-standards-questioned/8537226

Small, J. (2007). The emergence of the body in the holiday accounts of women and girls. In A. M. Pritchard, N. Morgan, I. Ateljevic, & C. Harris (Eds.), *Tourism and gender: Embodiment, sensuality and experience* (pp. 73–91). Wallingford, UK: CAB International. doi:10.1079/9781845932718.0073

Small, J. (2016). Holiday bodies: Young women and their appearance. *Annals of Tourism Research, 58*, 18–32. doi:10.1016/j.annals.2016.01.008

Statista. (2018). Types of personal information and images shared digitally by global internet users as of January 2017. Retrieved from https://www.statista.com/statistics/266835/sharing-content-among-us-internet-users/

Tiggemann, M., & Andrew, R. (2012). Clothing choices, weight, and trait self-objectification. *Body Image, 9*(3), 409–412. doi:10.1016/j.bodyim.2012.02.003 PMID:22465473

Tiggemann, M., Brown, Z., Zaccardo, M., & Thomas, N. (2017). "Warning: this image has been digitally altered": The effect of disclaimer labels added to fashion magazine shoots on women's body dissatisfaction. *Body Image, 21*, 107–113. doi:10.1016/j.bodyim.2017.04.001 PMID:28456058

Tiidenberg, K., & Cruz, E. G. (2015). Selfies, image and the re-making of the body. *Body & Society, 21*(4), 77–102. doi:10.1177/1357034X15592465

Toma, C. L., & Hancock, J. T. (2010). Looks and lies: The role of physical attractiveness in online dating self-presentation and deception. *Communication Research, 37*(3), 335–351. doi:10.1177/0093650209356437

Toma, C. L., & Hancock, J. T. (2012). What lies beneath: The linguistic traces of deception in online dating profiles. *Journal of Communication, 62*(1), 78–97. doi:10.1111/j.1460-2466.2011.01619.x

Toma, C. L., Hancock, J. T., & Ellison, N. B. (2008). Separating fact from fiction: An examination of deceptive self-presentation in online dating profiles. *Personality and Social Psychology Bulletin, 34*(8), 1023–1036. doi:10.1177/0146167208318067 PMID:18593866

Valkenburg, D. P. M., Peter, J., & Schouten, A. P. (2006). Friend networking sites and their relationship to adolescents' well-being and social self-esteem. *Cyberpsychology & Behavior, 9*(5), 584–590. doi:10.1089/cpb.2006.9.584 PMID:17034326

Wardle, C., & Boyce, T. (2009). *Media coverage and audience reception of disfigurement on television*. London: The Healing Foundation and Cardiff University.

Williams, R. J., & Ricciardelli, L. A. (2014). Social media and body image concerns: Further considerations and broader perspectives. *Sex Roles, 71*(11-12), 389–392. doi:10.100711199-014-0429-x

Wood-Barcalow, N. L., Tylka, T. L., & Augustus-Horvath, C. L. (2010). "But I like my body": Positive body image characteristics and a holistic model for young-adult women. *Body Image, 7*(2), 106–116. doi:10.1016/j.bodyim.2010.01.001 PMID:20153990

ADDITIONAL READING

Boyd, D. (2014). *It's complicated: The social lives of networked teens*. New Haven, CT: Yale University Press.

Karsay, K., Knoll, J., & Matthes, J. (2018). Sexualizing media use and self-objectification: A meta-analysis. *Psychology of Women Quarterly*, *42*(1), 9–28. doi:10.1177/0361684317743019 PMID:29527090

Pritchard, A., Morgan, N., Ateljevic, I., & Harris, C. (2007). *Tourism and gender: embodiment, sensuality and experience*. Wallingford, UK: CAB International. doi:10.1079/9781845932718.0000

Rumsey, N., & Harcourt, D. (2012). *The Oxford handbook of the psychology of appearance*. Oxford: Oxford University Press. doi:10.1093/oxfordhb/9780199580521.001.0001

Waterton, E., & Watson, S. (2012). *Culture, heritage and representation: Perspectives on visuality and the past*. Farnham: Ashgate.

KEY TERMS AND DEFINITIONS

Beach-Body Ready: The annual and seasonal process of achieving an ideal beach physique as depicted in the media through bodily preparation techniques such as dieting, exercising, hair removal and fake-tanning.

Information Manipulation Theory 2: A theory which focuses on the creation of a deceptive message and on the motivations of the sender.

Mediatized Beach Body: Images of beach bodies displayed on social media and in mass media.

Real Beach Body: Semi-naked figures in swimwear in natural offline environments.

Truth-Default Theory: The theory posits that when people communicate with each other, they tend to presume that their conversation partner is basically honest.

This research was previously published in the Handbook of Research on Deception, Fake News, and Misinformation Online; pages 65-86, copyright year 2019 by Information Science Reference (an imprint of IGI Global).

Chapter 42

Understanding Users' Switching Between Social Media Platforms:
A PPM Perspective

Tao Zhou

School of Management, Hangzhou Dianzi University, China

ABSTRACT

Social media such as micro-blogs and social networking sites are popular among users. Due to the intense competition, it is crucial for social media platforms to attract users and retain them. The purpose of this paper is to draw on the push-pull-mooring (PPM) model to examine users' switching between social media platforms. The results indicated that identification, perceived usefulness, dissatisfaction, privacy concern, and social influence significantly affect switching intention. In addition, social influence has a positive moderation effect on switching intention. The results imply that social media platforms need to consider the effect of push, pull, and mooring factors in order to prevent users' switching behaviour.

INTRODUCTION

Social media has been popular in the world. A few social media platforms such as Facebook, WeChat, Twitter and Instagram have received wide adoption among users. For example, WeChat, the largest Chinese social media platform, has been adopted by 83.4% of internet users (CNNIC, 2019). In the US, the adoption rate of Facebook is 69% (Pew, 2019). Users can conveniently communicate with their friends, such as share, comment and like on these platforms (Xu et al., 2019). This helps strengthen social networking relationships between users, which may facilitate their continuance usage. At the same time, intense competition exists between different social media platforms. They need to expand the user base to achieve a competitive advantage. For users, they may discontinue usage of the current social media platform and switch to an alternative one. As a few platforms have similar functions and services, users may feel it relatively easy to switch to a different social media platform. This presents a great challenge to social media companies. They need to understand the factors affecting user switching and take effective measures to retain users. Otherwise, they may lose the competition.

DOI: 10.4018/978-1-6684-6307-9.ch042

Previous research has examined social media user behaviour from multiple perspectives, such as like behaviour (Xu et al., 2019), user engagement (Molinillo et al., 2019; Shen et al., 2019), impulsive purchase (Chen et al., 2019; Hu et al., 2019), and self-disclosure (Koohikamali et al., 2017; Koohikamali et al., 2019). The results advance our understanding of social media user behaviour and provide the base for future research. However, prior research has seldom considered user switch between different social media platforms. As switch represents a behaviour that is different from adoption and continuance, it is necessary to examine users' switch behaviour and identify the determinants of user switching. The results may enrich extant research on social media user behaviour.

The purpose of this research is to draw on the push-pull-mooring (PPM) model to examine users' switching between social media platforms. PPM provides a useful lens to explore user switch behaviour and it has been used to examine information systems user switching in various contexts, such as mobile payment (Wang et al., 2019a), social commerce (Li and Ku, 2018), and mobile shopping (Chang et al., 2017). In this research, we generalize it to the social media context. According to PPM, a user's switching is influenced by three types of factors: push, pull and mooring (Moon, 1995). Among them, push factors drive users away from the original platform, which include dissatisfaction and privacy concern in this research. In contrast, pull factors attract users to an alternative platform, which include perceived usefulness, perceived enjoyment and identification. Mooring factors reflect personal or social factors that prevent or facilitate user switch, which include social influence. In addition to the direct effect, we propose that social influence moderates the effects of both push and pull factors on switching intention. We expect that the results can disclose the mechanism underlying user switch and provide guidelines for social media companies on how to prevent users' switching.

RESEARCH MODEL AND HYPOTHESES

Social Media User Behaviour

As a popular service, social media user behaviour has received great attention from information systems researchers. They have examined various types of social media user behaviour, such as impulsive purchase, self-disclosure, engagement, and like behaviour. Among them, impulsive purchase is a hot topic. Xiang et al. (2016) found that parasocial interaction, which includes similarity, expertise and likeability, affects social commerce users' impulsive buying tendency. Chung et al. (2017) reported that both utilitarian value and hedonic value influence impulsive buying of restaurant products. Other research has noted that the determinants of impulse buying include affective trust (Chen et al., 2019) and social influence (Hu et al., 2019).

As users need to disclose much personal information when using social media services, self-disclosure also receives much research attention. Liu and Wang (2018) argued that boundary coordination and turbulence determine users' self-disclosure on social network sites. Koohikamali et al. (2019) noted that the trade-off between privacy concern and benefits affects self-disclosure on social network applications. Similarly, privacy concern and social support are found to influence personal health information disclosure (Zhang et al., 2018).

Other research has examined consumer engagement in social media. Shen et al. (2019) noted that technology attractiveness and community involvement affect social commerce users' engagement. Molinillo et al. (2019) reported that social support and community identification influence consumers' engagement. In addition, information technology affordance is also reported to influence users' engagement in living streaming (Sun et al., 2019).

Previous research has also examined users' switch on instant messaging and social networking services. Fang and Tang (2017) noted that network effects and regret have significant effects on users' migration between instant messaging products. Xu et al. (2014) reported that dissatisfaction and peer influence affect users' migration between social networking services. Li and Ku (2018) suggested that low transaction efficiency, social support and conformity influence users' switching from e-commerce to social commerce. These results provide foundation for our research.

As evidenced by these studies, they have examined social media user behaviour such as impulse buying, self-disclosure and engagement. They have also examined users' switch on instant messaging and social networking services. This research tries to identify the determinants of user switch between social media platforms.

PPM

PPM originates from sociology and has been traditionally used to explain human migration (Moon, 1995). The theory argues that human migration is influenced by three kinds of forces: push, pull and mooring. Push factors are those related to the original place. Pull factors are those related to the destination place. Mooring factors are those related to lifestyles and social issues that prevent or facilitate migration (Rhazali et al., 2015; Rhazali et al., 2016).

Recently, PPM has been adopted to explain information systems users' switching behaviour. Chang et al. (2017) noted that perceived value (push factor), attractiveness (pull factor) and self-efficacy (mooring factor) affect users' switching from physical stores to mobile stores. Li and Ku (2018) examined consumers' switch from e-commerce to social commerce. The push factor is low transaction efficiency, whereas pull factors include social support and social benefit. Mooring factors include conformity and personal experience. Wang et al. (2019a) explored users' switch between mobile payment applications. The push, pull, and mooring factor are privacy concern, alternative rewards and inertia, respectively. Consistent with these findings, this research applies PPM to examine social media users' switch.

Push Factors

Dissatisfaction reflects dissatisfaction with a social media platform's functions and services (Fang and Tang, 2017). Users expect to access social media platforms to effectively interact with their friends and peers. If this expectation is disconfirmed, they may feel dissatisfied and switch to an alternative platform (Sivathanu, 2019). In contrast, if they are satisfied, they may be committed to the platform and continue their usage (Bhattacherjee, 2001). Previous research has reported the effect of dissatisfaction with technical quality (Fang and Tang, 2017) and socialization support (Xu et al., 2014) on user switch. Based on these findings, we suggest:

H1.1. Dissatisfaction is positively related to switching intention.

Privacy concern reflects a user's concern on information collection and usage. Users often need to disclose much personal information on social media platforms (Moh'd Al-Dwairi and Al Azzam, 2019). They are worried whether platforms properly collect and use their information. For example, the platforms may collect too much unnecessary information about users. Platforms may also share user information with third parties without the user's consent. If users feel great privacy risk associated with self-disclosure, they may discontinue their usage and switch to other trustworthy platforms. Wang et al. (2019a) argued that privacy concern as a push factor affects users' switch between mobile payment applications. Thus:

H1.2. Privacy concern is positively related to switching intention.

Pull Factors

Perceived usefulness reflects the utility obtained from using an alternative platform. A fundamental function of social media platforms is to support users' interactions. If platforms cannot provide reliable services, users may feel lack of control (Pelet et al., 2017; Daradkeh, 2019) and perceive little utility. In addition, users may expect to access rich functions and services through a single platform. For example, WeChat, the largest Chinese social media platform, has offered payment functions to users. This provides great convenience to users and may facilitate their switching. According to the expectation-confirmation model, perceived usefulness affects a user's satisfaction and continuance intention (Bhattacherjee, 2001). Thus, we state:

H2.1. Perceived usefulness is positively related to switching intention.

Perceived enjoyment reflects the enjoyment and fun associated with using an alternative social media platform. Compared to perceived usefulness that represents an extrinsic motivation, perceived enjoyment represents an intrinsic motivation (Wang et al., 2019b). When users acquire an engaging experience, they may feel great satisfaction and continue their usage in order to obtain the enjoyment again (Zhao and Deng, 2020). In contrast, a boring experience cannot meet users' expectations and may lead to their departure. A few social media platforms have added entertainment functions to deliver more enjoyment to users. This may help improve their experience and promote their switch. Zong et al. (2019) found that perceived enjoyment affects continuance intention of social networking services. Therefore, we propose:

H2.2. Perceived enjoyment is positively related to switching intention.

Identification reflects a user's feelings of membership, belongingness and attachment to an alternative platform (Chiu et al., 2006). When users develop identification with a platform, they may build a long-term relationship with the platform and continue their usage. Social capital theory also suggests that identification represents a relational factor that promotes user behaviour (Chen et al., 2017). The emotional connections can help lock users into the current platform and prevent their switching to other platforms. Previous research has identified the effect of identification on user continuance (Lin et al., 2017; Tsai and Hung, 2019). In line with these studies, we suggest:

H2.3. Identification is positively related to switching intention.

Mooring Factor

Social influence reflects the effect of an individual user's peers and friends on his or her behaviour. It has been identified to be a significant factor affecting user adoption of an information technology (Venkatesh et al., 2003). When a user's social circle members recommend an alternative platform to the user, he or she may comply with their opinions even if he or she has not formed a positive attitude toward the platform (Al-Momani et al., 2019). This reflects a compliance process. Prior research has found the effect of social influence on impulsive buying (Hu et al., 2019) and photo tagging (Dhir et al., 2018). Consistent with these studies, we propose:

H3. Social influence is positively related to switching intention.

In addition to its direct effect, social influence may have a moderation effect on switching intention. In other words, when users receive social influence from their peers and friends, the effect of push and pull factors on their switching intention will be strengthened. This means that social influence may bias a user's self-perceptions to some extent. Thus, we state:

H4.1-4.5. Social influence positively moderates the effect of dissatisfaction, privacy concern, perceived usefulness, perceived enjoyment and identification on switching intention.

Figure 1 presents the research model.

Figure 1. Research model

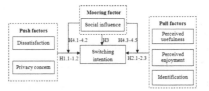

METHOD

The research model includes seven factors. Each factor was measured with multiple items. All items were adapted from extant literature to improve the content validity. These items were first translated into Chinese by a researcher. Then another researcher translated them back into English to ensure consistency. When the instrument was developed, it was tested among ten users that had social media usage experience. Then according to their comments, we revised a few items to improve the clarity and understandability. The final items and their sources are listed in the Appendix.

Items of dissatisfaction were adapted from Cheng et al. (2009) to reflect a user's dissatisfaction with the functions and information offered by a social media platform. Items of privacy concern were adapted from Wang et al. (2019a) to measure a user's concern on improper collection and usage of personal information. Items of social influence were adapted from Xu et al. (2014) to reflect the effect of friends on a user's behaviour. Items of perceived usefulness and perceived enjoyment were adapted from Hsieh et al. (2012). Items of perceived usefulness measure the utility derived from using the platform, whereas items of perceived enjoyment reflect the enjoyment and fun associated with using the platform. Items of identification were adapted from Chiu et al. (2006) to measure the feelings of belonging, closeness and membership. Items of switching intention were adapted from Fang and Tang (2017) to reflect a user's intention to switch from the current platform to an alternative one.

Data were collected through an online survey. We feel that online survey is appropriate for this research as social media users are also internet users. We posted the survey linkage in a few social media platforms such as WeChat and invited users to fill the questionnaire based on their experience of switching between competitive social media platforms, such as switch from QQ to WeChat (both have instant messaging services), or switch from Tencent Weishi to Douyin (both are live streaming products). We scrutinized all responses and dropped those that had missing values. As a result, we obtained 358 valid responses. Among them, 43.6% were male and 56.4% were female. A majority of them (80.7%) were below forty years old. Most of them (73.9%) held bachelor or higher degree. The frequently used social media platforms included WeChat (77.5%), QQ (74.2%), Weibo (48.6%), and Douyin (29.9%), which represent a few reputable Chinese social media.

We conducted two tests to examine the common method variance. First, we performed a Harman's single-factor analysis. The results indicated that the largest variance explained by an individual factor is 22.9%. Thus, none of the factors can explain the majority of the variance. Second, we modeled all items as the indicators of a factor representing the method effect, and re-estimated the model. The results indicated a poor fitness. For example, the goodness of fit index (GFI) is 0.61 (<0.90). The root mean square error of approximation (RMSEA) is 0.172 (>0.08). The results of both tests indicated that common method variance is not a significant problem in this research.

RESULTS

Data analysis includes two steps. First, we examined the measurement model to test reliability and validity. Second, we examined the structural model to test research hypotheses.

First, we conducted a confirmatory factor analysis to examine the validity. As listed in Table 1, most item loadings are larger than 0.7. Each AVE (average variance extracted) exceeds 0.5 and CR (composite reliability) exceeds 0.7. This indicated the good validity (Gefen et al., 2000). In addition, all Cronbach Alpha values are larger than 0.7, suggesting a good reliability.

Second, we adopted structural equation modeling software LISREL to estimate the structural model. The results are shown in Figure 2. Except H2.2 and H4.5, other hypotheses are supported. Table 2 lists the recommended and actual values of a few fit indices. As listed in the table, the actual values of these fit indices are better than the recommended values, indicating the good fitness (Gefen et al., 2000). The explained variance of switching intention is 93.5%.

DISCUSSION

To examine the robustness of the results, we also adopted SPSS to conduct a regression analysis. As listed in Table 3, both approaches have similar results.

Table 1. Standardized item loadings, AVE, CR and Alpha values

Factor	Item	Standardized Loading	AVE	CR	Alpha
Dissatisfaction (DS)	DS1	0.833	0.58	0.85	0.84
	DS2	0.817			
	DS3	0.645			
	DS4	0.739			
Privacy concern (PC)	PC1	0.764	0.62	0.87	0.87
	PC2	0.818			
	PC3	0.769			
	PC4	0.799			
Social influence (SI)	SI1	0.729	0.67	0.86	0.85
	SI2	0.873			
	SI3	0.853			
Perceived usefulness (PU)	PU1	0.827	0.65	0.85	0.85
	PU2	0.800			
	PU3	0.799			
Perceived enjoyment (PE)	PE1	0.833	0.66	0.85	0.85
	PE2	0.754			
	PE3	0.849			
Identification (ID)	ID1	0.834	0.71	0.88	0.88
	ID2	0.840			
	ID3	0.852			
Switching intention (SWI)	SWI1	0.810	0.71	0.88	0.88
	SWI2	0.855			
	SWI3	0.862			

Figure 2. The results estimated by LISREL

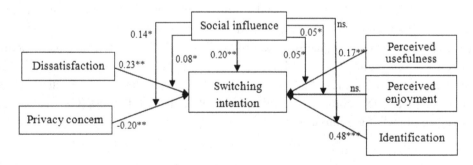

(Note: *, P<0.05; **, P<0.01; ***, P<0.001; ns, not significant)

Table 2. The recommended and actual values of fit indices

Fit Indices	χ^2/df	AGFI	CFI	NFI	NNFI	RMSEA
Recommended value	<3	>0.80	>0.90	>0.90	>0.90	<0.08
Actual value	2.74	0.838	0.981	0.971	0.977	0.070

Note: *chi²/df* is the ratio between Chi-square and degrees of freedom, AGFI is the Adjusted Goodness of Fit Index, CFI is the Comparative Fit Index, NFI is the Normed Fit Index, NNFI is the Non-Normed Fit Index, RMSEA is Root Mean Square Error of Approximation

Table 3. The results estimated by LISREL and SPSS

		LISREL	SPSS
H1.1	DS→SWI	0.23	0.18
H1.2	PC→SWI	-0.20	-0.17
H2.1	PU→SWI	0.17	0.17
H2.2	PE→SWI	ns.	ns.
H2.3	ID→SWI	0.48	0.38
H3	SI→SWI	0.20	0.23
H4.1	SI: DS→SWI	0.08	0.13
H4.2	SI: PC→SWI	0.14	0.21
H4.3	SI: PU→SWI	0.05	0.13
H4.4	SI: PE→SWI	0.05	0.09
H4.5	SI: ID→SWI	ns.	ns.

The results indicated that both push factors including dissatisfaction and privacy concern have significant effects on switching intention. Previous research has reported the effect of dissatisfaction with technical quality on user switch (Fang and Tang, 2017). This is consistent with our research. When users are dissatisfied with the current social media platform, they may have a strong urge to switch to an alternative one for better services. We found that privacy concern has a negative effect on switching intention. This is contrary to the hypothesis and previous research (Wang et al., 2019a). The mean value of privacy concern (ranging from 1 to 5) is 4.05. This suggests that users feel great privacy risk associated with using social media platforms. This may bias their evaluation and they have no intention to switch due to the potential risk derived from using a new platform. In addition, most respondents in our sample are young adults with good education. They may be sensitive to information privacy, which may affect their privacy concern on social media platforms. This in turn decreases their switching intention.

With respect to the pull factors, both perceived usefulness and identification affect switching intention. Perceived usefulness is a significant factor affecting initial adoption (Venkatesh and Davis, 2000) and post-adoption (Bhattacherjee, 2001). This research found that it also predicts users' switch. Social media platforms need to offer rich functions and services to meet users' expectations on utility. The results indicated that compared to perceived usefulness, identification has a larger effect ($\beta=0.48$) on switching intention. This demonstrates that identification is a main factor determining user switch. When users develop identification with a platform, they may be committed and attached to using it and build loyalty. This may facilitate their switch. The results did not disclose the effect of perceived enjoyment on switching intention. This suggests that users are not much concerned with the enjoyment when considering switching to an alternative platform. They pay more attention to the utility and identification. As most of our respondents have used WeChat, QQ and Weibo, they may focus on the social interactions rather than the entertainment when considering switch. Future research may validate our results in other contexts such as live streaming platforms.

As a mooring factor, social influence significantly affects switching intention. This demonstrates the effect of social circle on an individual user's behaviour. This is consistent with previous research, which has identified the effect of social influence on a user's attitude change (Tsai and Bagozzi, 2014). We also found the moderation effect of social influence on switching intention. More specifically, social influence positively moderates the effect of dissatisfaction, privacy concern, perceived usefulness and perceived enjoyment on switching intention. However, it has no moderation effect on the relationship between identification and switching intention. This shows that social circle cannot affect a user's decision to switch based on identification. When users build identification with a social media platform, they are locked into the relationship and social circle may not easily influence their behavioral decision. In addition, as identification has a relatively large effect ($\beta=0.48$) on switching intention, external social influence may not be able to further strengthen this effect.

THEORETICAL AND MANAGERIAL IMPLICATIONS

From a theoretical perspective, this research applied PPM to examine user switch between social media platforms. As noted earlier, although previous research has explored social media user behaviour such as self-disclosure, impulse buying and engagement, it has seldom examined user switch, which is different from initial adoption and post-adoption. Our results indicated that social media user switch receives the influence from three types of factors including push, pull and mooring. A majority of the variance of switching intention (93.5%) is explained by these factors. This suggests that it is appropriate to use PPM to explain social media user switch. The results enrich extant research and advance our understanding of social media user behaviour. Second, we found that among pull factors, identification has the largest effect on switching intention, whereas perceived usefulness has a relatively small effect. This indicates that users attach more importance to intrinsic motivations than extrinsic motivations when considering switch. This also extends prior research on information systems user behaviour, which has focused on the effect of perceived usefulness on user adoption (Bhattacherjee, 2001). Third, the results indicated that social influence not only directly affects switching intention, but also has a moderation effect on switching intention. These results enrich extant research that has mainly explored the direct effect of social influence on individual user attitude change (Dholakia et al., 2004). Future research may explore the moderation effect of social influence on users' other behaviors such as continuance intention.

From a managerial perspective, the results imply that social media platforms need to consider the effects of push, pull and mooring factors in order to prevent users' switching. On one hand, they need to address users' dissatisfaction. They may advance the platforms and offer rich functions and services to users. On the other hand, they need to develop users' identification with the community. They may invite a few well-known persons to act as the key opinion leaders. They may also organize offline activities to enhance the cohesion of communities. In addition, the effect of social influence cannot be neglected.

Platforms can use incentives such as points and rewards to encourage the members to invite their friends to register in the community and expand the user base.

CONCLUSION AND FUTURE WORKS

Drawing on the PPM, this research examined users' switching between social media platforms. The results indicated that user switch is influenced by the push, pull and mooring factors. These results extend extant research on social media user behaviour.

This research has the following limitations, which also provide a few directions for future research. First, we conducted this research in China, which has a typical oriental culture. Thus, future research can generalize our results to western cultures as culture may affect social influence and user behaviour. Second, besides the factors in the model, there are other factors possibly affecting user switch, such as trust, perceived value and social support. Future research may examine their effects. Third, we mainly conducted a cross-sectional study. Future research may perform a longitudinal analysis and the results may provide more insights into user behaviour development.

ACKNOWLEDGMENT

This work was supported by National Natural Science Foundation of China (71771069).

REFERENCES

Al-Momani, A. M., Mahmoud, M. A., & Ahmad, M. S. (2019). A review of factors influencing customer acceptance of internet of things services. *International Journal of Information Systems in the Service Sector*, *11*(1), 54–67. doi:10.4018/IJISSS.2019010104

Bhattacherjee, A. (2001). Understanding information systems continuance: An expectation-confirmation model. *Management Information Systems Quarterly*, *25*(3), 351–370. doi:10.2307/3250921

Chang, H. H., Wong, K. H., & Li, S. Y. (2017). Applying push-pull-mooring to investigate channel switching behaviors: M-shopping self-efficacy and switching costs as moderators. *Electronic Commerce Research and Applications*, *24*, 50–67. doi:10.1016/j.elerap.2017.06.002

Chen, X. Y., Huang, Q., & Davison, R. M. (2017). The role of website quality and social capital in building buyers' loyalty. *International Journal of Information Management*, *37*(1), 1563–1574. doi:10.1016/j.ijinfomgt.2016.07.005

Chen, Y., Lu, Y., Wang, B., & Pan, Z. (2019). How do product recommendations affect impulse buying? An empirical study on WeChat social commerce. *Information & Management*, *56*(2), 236–248. doi:10.1016/j.im.2018.09.002

Cheng, Z., Yang, Y., & Lim, J. (2009). Cyber Migration: An Empirical Investigation on Factors that Affect Users' Switch Intentions in Social Networking Sites. *42nd Hawaii International Conference on System Sciences*, 1-11.

Chiu, C.-M., Hsu, M.-H., & Wang, E. T. G. (2006). Understanding knowledge sharing in virtual communities: An integration of social capital and social cognitive theories. *Decision Support Systems*, *42*(3), 1872–1888. doi:10.1016/j.dss.2006.04.001

Chung, N., Song, H. G., & Lee, H. (2017). Consumers' impulsive buying behavior of restaurant products in social commerce. *International Journal of Contemporary Hospitality Management*, *29*(2), 709–731. doi:10.1108/IJCHM-10-2015-0608

CNNIC. (2019). *The 43rd China Statistical Report on Internet Development*. China Internet Network Information Center.

Daradkeh, M. (2019). Visual analytics adoption in business enterprises: An integrated model of technology acceptance and task-technology fit. *International Journal of Information Systems in the Service Sector*, *11*(1), 68–89. doi:10.4018/IJISSS.2019010105

Dhir, A., Kaur, P., & Rajala, R. (2018). Why do young people tag photos on social networking sites? Explaining user intentions. *International Journal of Information Management*, *38*(1), 117–127. doi:10.1016/j.ijinfomgt.2017.07.004

Dholakia, U. M., Bagozzi, R. P., & Pearo, L. K. (2004). A social influence model of consumer participation in network- and small-group-based virtual communities. *International Journal of Research in Marketing*, *21*(3), 241–263. doi:10.1016/j.ijresmar.2003.12.004

Fang, Y.-H., & Tang, K. (2017). Involuntary migration in cyberspaces: The case of MSN messenger discontinuation. *Telematics and Informatics*, *34*(1), 177–193. doi:10.1016/j.tele.2016.05.004

Gefen, D., Straub, D. W., & Boudreau, M. C. (2000). Structural equation modeling and regression: Guidelines for research practice. *Communications of the Association for Information Systems*, *4*(7), 1–70. doi:10.17705/1CAIS.00407

Hsieh, J.-K., Hsieh, Y.-C., Chiu, H.-C., & Feng, Y.-C. (2012). Post-adoption switching behavior for online service substitutes: A perspective of the push–pull–mooring framework. *Computers in Human Behavior*, *28*(5), 1912–1920. doi:10.1016/j.chb.2012.05.010

Hu, X., Chen, X. Y., & Davidson, R. (2019). Social Support, Source Credibility, Social Influence, and Impulsive Purchase Behavior in Social Commerce. *International Journal of Electronic Commerce*, *23*(3), 297–327. doi:10.1080/10864415.2019.1619905

Koohikamali, M., French, A. M., & Kim, D. J. (2019). An investigation of a dynamic model of privacy trade-off in use of mobile social network applications: A longitudinal perspective. *Decision Support Systems*, *119*, 46–59. doi:10.1016/j.dss.2019.02.007

Koohikamali, M., Peak, D. A., & Prybutok, V. R. (2017). Beyond self-disclosure: Disclosure of information about others in social network sites. *Computers in Human Behavior*, *69*, 29–42. doi:10.1016/j.chb.2016.12.012

Li, C.-Y., & Ku, Y.-C. (2018). The power of a thumbs-up: Will e-commerce switch to social commerce? *Information & Management*, *55*(3), 340–357. doi:10.1016/j.im.2017.09.001

Lin, X., Featherman, M., & Sarker, S. (2017). Understanding factors affecting users' social networking site continuance: A gender difference perspective. *Information & Management*, *54*(3), 383–395. doi:10.1016/j.im.2016.09.004

Liu, Z., & Wang, X. (2018). How to regulate individuals' privacy boundaries on social network sites: A cross-cultural comparison. *Information & Management*, *55*(8), 1005–1023. doi:10.1016/j.im.2018.05.006

Moh'd Al-Dwairi, R., & Al Azzam, M. (2019). Influences and intention of consumer's online shopping decision: Jordan as a case. *International Journal of Information Systems in the Service Sector*, *11*(1), 40–53. doi:10.4018/IJISSS.2019010103

Molinillo, S., Anaya-Sánchez, R., & Liébana-Cabanillas, F. (2019). (in press). Analyzing the effect of social support and community factors on customer engagement and its impact on loyalty behaviors toward social commerce websites. *Computers in Human Behavior*. Advance online publication. doi:10.1016/j.chb.2019.04.004

Moon, B. (1995). Paradigms in migration research: Exploring" moorings" as a schema. *Progress in Human Geography*, *19*(4), 504–524. doi:10.1177/030913259501900404 PMID:12347395

Pelet, J. E., Ettis, S., & Cowart, K. (2017). Optimal experience of flow enhanced by telepresence: Evidence from social media use. *Information & Management*, *54*(1), 115–128. doi:10.1016/j.im.2016.05.001

Pew. (2019). *Share of U.S. adults using social media, including Facebook, is mostly unchanged since 2018*. https://www.pewresearch.org/

Rhazali, Y., Hadi, Y., & Mouloudi, A. (2015). A methodology for transforming CIM to PIM through UML: From business view to information system view. *2015 Third World Conference on Complex Systems (WCCS)*, 1-6. 10.1109/ICoCS.2015.7483318

Rhazali, Y., Hadi, Y., & Mouloudi, A. (2016). Model Transformation with ATL into MDA from CIM to PIM Structured through MVC. *Procedia Computer Science*, *83*, 1096–1101. doi:10.1016/j.procs.2016.04.229

Shen, X.-L., Li, Y.-J., Sun, Y., Chen, Z., & Wang, F. (2019). Understanding the role of technology attractiveness in promoting social commerce engagement: Moderating effect of personal interest. *Information & Management*, *56*(2), 294–305. doi:10.1016/j.im.2018.09.006

Sivathanu, B. (2019). An empirical study of service quality, value and customer satisfaction for on-demand home services. *International Journal of Information Systems in the Service Sector*, *11*(4), 35–57. doi:10.4018/IJISSS.2019100103

Sun, Y., Shao, X., Li, X., Guo, Y., & Nie, K. (2019). How live streaming influences purchase intentions in social commerce: An IT affordance perspective. *Electronic Commerce Research and Applications*, *37*, 1–12. doi:10.1016/j.elerap.2019.100886

Tsai, H.-T., & Bagozzi, R. P. (2014). Contribution behavior in virtual communities: Cognitive, emotional, and social influences. *Management Information Systems Quarterly*, *38*(1), 143–163. doi:10.25300/MISQ/2014/38.1.07

Tsai, J. C.-A., & Hung, S.-Y. (2019). Examination of community identification and interpersonal trust on continuous use intention: Evidence from experienced online community members. *Information & Management*, 56(4), 552–569. doi:10.1016/j.im.2018.09.014

Venkatesh, V., & Davis, F. D. (2000). A theoretical extension of the technology acceptance model: Four longitudinal field studies. *Management Science*, 46(2), 186–204. doi:10.1287/mnsc.46.2.186.11926

Venkatesh, V., Morris, M. G., Davis, G. B., & Davis, F. D. (2003). User acceptance of information technology: Toward a unified view. *Management Information Systems Quarterly*, 27(3), 425–478. doi:10.2307/30036540

Wang, L., Luo, X., Yang, X., & Qiao, Z. (2019a). Easy come or easy go? Empirical evidence on switching behaviors in mobile payment applications. *Information & Management*, 56(7), 1–13. doi:10.1016/j.im.2019.02.005

Wang, X., Lin, X., & Spencer, M. K. (2019b). Exploring the effects of extrinsic motivation on consumer behaviors in social commerce: Revealing consumers' perceptions of social commerce benefits. *International Journal of Information Management*, 45, 163–175. doi:10.1016/j.ijinfomgt.2018.11.010

Xiang, L., Zheng, X., Lee, M. K. O., & Zhao, D. (2016). Exploring consumers' impulse buying behavior on social commerce platform: The role of parasocial interaction. *International Journal of Information Management*, 36(3), 333–347. doi:10.1016/j.ijinfomgt.2015.11.002

Xu, X., Yao, Z., & Teo, T. S. H. (2019). Moral obligation in online social interaction: Clicking the "like" button. *Information & Management*, 103249. doi:10.1016/j.im.2019.103249

Xu, Y., Yang, Y., Cheng, Z., & Lim, J. (2014). Retaining and attracting users in social networking services: An empirical investigation of cyber migration. *The Journal of Strategic Information Systems*, 23(3), 239–253. doi:10.1016/j.jsis.2014.03.002

Zhang, X., Liu, S., Chen, X., Wang, L., Gao, B., & Zhu, Q. (2018). Health information privacy concerns, antecedents, and information disclosure intention in online health communities. *Information & Management*, 55(4), 482–493. doi:10.1016/j.im.2017.11.003

Zhao, W., & Deng, N. (2020). Examining the channel choice of experience-oriented customers in omnichannel retailing. *International Journal of Information Systems in the Service Sector*, 12(1), 16–27. doi:10.4018/IJISSS.2020010102

Zong, W., Yang, J., & Bao, Z. S. (2019). Social network fatigue affecting continuance intention of social networking services The case of WeChat users in China's universities. *Data Technologies and Applications*, 53(1), 123–139. doi:10.1108/DTA-06-2018-0054

This research was previously published in the International Journal of Information Systems in the Service Sector (IJISSS), 13(1); pages 54-67, copyright year 2021 by IGI Publishing (an imprint of IGI Global).

APPENDIX

Measurement Scale and Items

Dissatisfaction (DS) (adapted from Cheng et al. (2009))

DS1. The current social media platform does not provide rich functions.

DS2. The current social media platform does not provide enough information that I need.

DS3. The current social media platform does not provide reliable information.

DS4. I cannot communicate with my friends effectively through the current social media platform.

Privacy Concern (PC) (adapted from Wang et al. (2019a))

PC1. I am concerned that the information I submit to the current social media platform could be misused.

PC2. I am concerned that others can find private information about me from the current social media platform.

PC3. I am concerned that my activities on the current social media platform could be collected without my notice.

PC4. I am concerned about providing personal information to the current social media platform because it could be used in a way I did not foresee.

Social Influence (SI) (adapted from Xu et al. (2014))

SI1. My friends are dissatisfied with the current social media platform.

SI2. My friends strongly recommend the alternative social media platform to me.

SI3. My friends have sent me invitations to sign up on the alternative social media platform.

Perceived Usefulness (PU) (adapted from Hsieh et al. (2012))

PU1. The alternative social media platform helps me be more effective in sharing information and making friends.

PU2. Using the alternative social media platform would make it easier to share information and make friends.

PU3. In general, using the alternative social media platform is more useful to my life.

Perceived Enjoyment (PE) (adapted from Hsieh et al. (2012))

PE1. Using the alternative social media platform gives me more enjoyment.

PE2. Using the alternative social media platform gives me more fun.

PE3. Using the alternative social media platform keeps me happier.

Identification (ID) (adapted from Chiu et al. (2006))

ID1. I feel a sense of belonging towards the alternative social media platform.

ID2. I have the feeling of togetherness or closeness in the alternative social media platform.

ID3. I am proud to be a member of the alternative social media platform.

Switching Intention (SWI) (adapted from (Fang and Tang (2017)))

SWI1. I intend to increase my use of the alternative social media platform in the foreseeable future.

SWI2. I intend to invest my time and effort to the alternative social media platform.

SWI3. I intend to switch from the current social media platform to the alternative one.

Chapter 43
Support for Cyberbullying Victims and Actors:
A Content Analysis of Facebook Groups Fighting Against Cyberbullying

Sophia Alim

 https://orcid.org/0000-0002-0413-3893
Independent Researcher, Bradford, UK

Shehla Khalid
Independent Researcher, Bradford, UK

ABSTRACT

This study analyses the post content and the emotions reflected in 10 open Facebook groups associated with cyberbullying, with the highest number of group members. Automated extraction via Facebook API was used to gather the data. Altogether, 313 Facebook posts were extracted and coded for content analysis. Sentiment analysis and parts of speech (POS) tagging was used to explore the emotions reflected in the content. The study findings revealed that (1) the content of the posts was mainly opinion-based in comparison to expressing personal experiences of cyberbullying. This indicated Facebook groups require stronger moderation due to digression of topics discussed. (2) Only 3% of posts in this study contained advice about cyberbullying. (3) Sentiment analysis of the posts showed that the Facebook groups focused on cyberbullying, reflected more positive sentiments in their posts. This is encouraging to cyberbullying victims to share information on cyberbullying. The findings in this study lay the foundations for more research into support for cyberbullying victims.

DOI: 10.4018/978-1-6684-6307-9.ch043

INTRODUCTION

Social media use has highlighted the issue of cyberbullying amongst society today, especially amongst young people. Between the years 2016-2017, Ditch the label (2017) surveyed 10,020 young people aged between 12-20 years old about bullying. Seven percent of young people surveyed experienced cyberbullying on a constant basis. Ten percent of young people experienced cyberbullying often.

With the younger generation growing up with the Internet, they are finding new ways to interact with technology. The field of Technoethics "recognizes technology as an intricate part of societal development which fosters change and new ethical considerations to address" (Luppicini, 2008, p. 2). The rise of cyberbullying raises concerns especially amongst parents, school staff and teachers about the ethical use of technology by young people.

Tokunaga (2010) defines cyberbullying as "any behaviour performed through electronic or digital media by individuals or groups that repeatedly communicates hostile or aggressive messages intended to inflict harm or discomfort on others." The definition mentions two criteria of traditional bullying, stated by Olweus (1993) which include repetition and intentionality. The definition of school bullying by Olweus (1993, p. 9) is that "A student is being bullied or victimised when he or she is exposed repeatedly and over time, to negative actions on the part of one or more other students."

Repetition is the repetitive nature of bullying, in that the bully can strike over and over again. The victim is on a heighted sense of worry over when the bully will strike next. Intentionality refers to the deliberate intention of the bully to harm the victim.

One of Olweus's (1993) criteria for bullying- imbalance of power is not discussed in detail in Tokunaga's (2010) definition. This highlights the difference between traditional bullying and cyberbullying, which is defined in Tokunaga, (2010) definition. The imbalance of power focuses on the feeling of a loss of power by the victim due to difficulty in defending against bullying/cyberbullying events (Smith, Mahdavi, Carvalho, Fisher, Russell & Tippett, 2008).

A number of researchers (Langos, 2012; Menesini, Nocentini, & Palladino, 2015; Slonje, Smith & Frisen, 2013; Vaillancourt, McDougall, Hymel, Krygsmen, Miller, Stiver & Davis, 2008) consensually discuss the roles of repetition, intentionality and imbalance of power as criteria for both traditional bullying and cyberbullying. Some researchers (Langos, 2014; Olweus, 1993; Menesini, Nocentini, Palladino, Frisén, Berne, Ortega-Ruiz & Naruskov, 2012; Nocentini, Calmaestra J, Schultze-Krumbholz, Scheithauer, Ortega & Menesini, 2010) also highlight two additional criteria specifically identifying cyberbullying incidents: anonymity and public versus private. Due to cyberbullying taking place online, the cyberbullies' identity is anonymous and therefore the victim can feel powerless and paranoid when communicating with people around them. If the cyberbullying attack takes place on a platform where the information is public, the attack is in the public domain. This causes stress for the victim because the impact of the attack is so prevalent for people.

There have been debates on whether the two criteria (anonymity and public versus private) are required to define a cyberbullying attack. Previous studies such as (Boyer, 2015; Menesini et al., 2012; Nocentini et al., 2010) have suggested that the two criteria are more linked to the severity of attack rather than the identification of a cyberbullying attack. Cyberbullying exists in various forms, e.g. cyberstalking, harassment, flaming, sexting, impersonation, trickery (Willard, 2007), posting/commenting on embarrassing photos or videos, aggressive messaging, and the development of hostile websites (Law, Shapka, Domene, & Gagné, 2012).

Cyberbullying can occur on a vast amount of different platforms e.g. through the use of email, text message via mobile devices, and social media. Types of social media include: social media platforms (Facebook, Google+); microblogging (Twitter); blogs; virtual worlds (Second Life); social bookmarking sites (Delicious, Digg); photo or video-sharing sites (Flickr, YouTube); and forums and discussion groups.

One of the most popular social media platforms is Facebook, with 1.79 billion active users in 2016 (Facebook, 2016). Facebook allows users to sign up and create Facebook profiles which can be made public. As well as profiles which allow users to display personal information, users can create posts as well as upload photos and videos. Interaction with other users occurs through the sharing, liking, and commenting of posts by other users.

Online communities created on social media platforms can provide a support mechanism in times of need. Cyberbullying victims, as well as other actors associated with a cyberbullying incident, e.g., parents, teachers, etc., often need support. Online communities are virtual spaces where people come together to socialise, learn, support one another and find company (Preece, 2001). The existence of online communities has benefits for both researchers and the users of the communities. Benefits include an increase in social capital, the ability to measure trust and social influence amongst humans (Wang, Singh, Zeng, King, & Nema, 2007), the exchange of information, the ability to support one another, provide entertainment, and attract attention through building a personal identity. Social capital is the drawing of resources (usually information, personal relationships, and the capacity to organise groups) from other members of the networks that he/she belongs to (Paxton, 1999).

Researchers in the field of social capital have found that users establishing strong relationships with neighbours and friends (known as bonding social capital) can lead to emotional benefits (Steinfield, Ellison&Lampe, 2008; Wenger, 1990) as well as improved physical/mental health. This is beneficial for cyberbullying victims to help them in their fight against cyberbullies. Studies by Cerna, Machackova & Dedkova (2015) and Price & Dalgleish (2010) emphasise the popularity of cyberbullying victims disclosing incidents of cyberbullying to their parents/carers and friends.

Establishing a support network enables victims to discuss how to cope with cyberbullying. Research by Alim (2015), used Twitter as a medium for content analysis of 400 tweets associated with cyberbullying and found that 33% of tweets contained advice and support for cyberbullying victims. However, there is a gap in the literature for a study which looks specifically at Facebook groups associated with cyberbullying and the post content.

A substantial amount of research: Bender, Marroquin & Jadad, 2011 (Breast Cancer); Bird, Ling & Hayes, 2011 (Floods in Queensland and Victoria) and Thoren, Metze, Bührer & Garten, 2013 (Birth of Premature Babies) shows that Facebook groups are used as an effective support tool in a variety of circumstances. For example, a study by Bender et al. (2011) used 628 Facebook groups associated with Breast Cancer and found that the groups were mainly created for fundraising, awareness, product/service promotion, or patient/caregiver support. Likewise, Thoren and et al. (2013) explored the post content from the 25 largest Facebook groups associated with premature infants and found that the groups were used for interpersonal support and information sharing.

In order to understand the types of support and information available to victims of cyberbullying and other actors associated with cyberbullying, this research study specifically examines the Facebook groups associated with cyberbullying and their post content. The aim of this study is to identify whether groups with a large number of members offers support to cyberbullying victims, and what types of support they offer. The research questions of the study detailed below, explores the content of the posts in Facebook groups and whether the groups provide a suitable platform as a support mechanism.

- RQ1: What categories of information are posted by group members in relation to cyberbullying?
- RQ2: Do posts offer support and advice to cyberbullying victims and other actors, e.g., parents?
- RQ3: What does sentiment and POS analysis of posts tell us about the sentiments and emotions reflected in the groups?

Automated data extraction is used to extract Facebook posts from the 10 groups with the highest number of group members. A combination of content and sentiment analysis as well as parts of speech (POS) tagging is used to explore the post content and the emotions that the post content reflects.

METHODOLOGY

Automated data extraction was used to extract the content of Facebook posts from 10 Facebook groups with the highest number of group members. This was in order to investigate the content of the posts. Quantitative and qualitative analysis techniques (content analysis, sentiment analysis, and POS tagging) were utilised to address the research questions.

On 16th November 2016, a search for groups using keywords such as cyberbullying, cyber bullying, and online bullying was made using Facebook. In total, 102 groups were identified, but closed groups, groups not in English, and groups relating to organisations were removed. This left 71 groups. From the 71 groups, the 10 groups with the highest number of group members were selected for analysis.

Data Extraction

Facebook posts from the ten groups were extracted using *R* and the *Rfacebook* package (created by Barbera, Piccirilli, & Geisler, 2017). The aim of the package is to provide access to the Facebook graph API within *R*. In order to connect *R* to Facebook, a Facebook application was created which generated the access token required for connection. The *Rfacebook* function *getGroup()* was used to extract Facebook posts from group pages as well as other information regarding posts, such as:

- The date that the post was posted on the group page
- The type of post, e.g., status or link
- The number of likes, comments, and shares regarding the post. In terms of exposure, 'likes' generate a minimal expression of interest, unlike commenting and sharing which require the user to get more involved with the post content.

Data Cleaning

Cleaning the data decreases noise. Social media text is known to be noisy (Baldwin, Cook, Lui, MacKinlay, & Wang, 2013). In order to prepare the posts for sentiment and POS analysis, the content was cleaned. The extracted posts were cleaned by converting all text to lower case, removing punctuation, removing numbers, stripping whitespace, removing stop words, and stemming words. Stop words are commonly used words in any language. The removal of stop words will allow the focus to fall on other words of more importance. Examples of stop words include *'how'* and *'to'* (Ganesan, 2014). Stemming words involves the removal of common word endings e.g., *'ing', 'es, 'ed',* and *'s'* to reveal the stem of the word.

Post Content

After removing the posts which were group functions, e.g., adding a user, 313 posts were analysed and coded for content by both authors of this paper using the categories in Table 1. Both authors coded each of the 313 posts. The inter-rate reliability between the two coders was 94%, which equated to high agreement between the two coders. Any discrepancies were discussed, agreed upon and refined during the coding process. Cohen's kappa (Cohen, 1960) was also used to calculate the degree of agreement. Unlike inter-rate reliability, Cohen's kappa takes the element of chance into consideration in the calculation. The kappa value for this study was 0.76, equating to substantial agreement between the coders.

The categories in which the data was coded against were derived from a similar study by Alim (2015). This study used Twitter as a social media platform to extract tweets to understand the types of support and advice provided for cyberbullying victims. The categories used for coding the data in (Alim, 2015) study included: News events; User opinions; Advertising; Advice on cyberbullying; Cyberbullying incidents; Questions about cyberbullying and Unclassified. For current study, more categories were added such as Quotes/Sayings; Other Areas linked to Cyberbullying, Experiences; group posts and legal aspects. The additional categories were added due to detailed nature of the extracted data. Additionally, subgroups were added to categories such as opinions, experiences and group posts for further differentiation.

Some posts were categorised in more than one group. Certain aspects of the post have been anonymised to protect privacy. The name of a group is annotated with [Name of Group], name of a user is annotated with [User], name of school with [Name of school], and URL link with [URL]. In Table 1, the content of the posts is presented prior to cleaning because cleaning can remove the context of the post.

Sentiment Analysis

After the posts were categorised, sentiment analysis was carried out on the posts. Sentiment analysis is the 'computational study of opinions, emotions and sentiments expressed in text' (Liu, 2010). Opinions influence our behaviour and the decisions we make. Sentiment analysis of the posts was carried out using *R Syuzhet* package and the *get_nrc_sentiment( )* function. The *get_nrc_sentiment( )* function implements (Mohammad, & Turney, 2013) NRC emotion lexicon algorithm. The emotion lexicon is a list of English words and their associations with eight emotions (fear, anger, trust, surprise, anticipation, joy, sadness, and disgust), as well as two sentiments (positive and negative) (Mohammed, 2015). Each association has a score assigned to it. Each word in the lexicon will have a score of 1 (yes) or 0 (no) for each of the emotions and sentiments. An example of the *get_nrc_sentiment( )* function, as shown in Figure1., demonstrates the emotions expressed by the sentence and gives indications of the mood.

Figure 1. Emotions expressed by using get_nrc_sentiment () function

```
> mySentiment <- get_nrc_sentiment(" the stars are shining bright")
> mySentiment
  anger anticipation disgust fear joy sadness surprise trust negative positive
1     0            1       0    0   1       0        0     0        0        1
```

Table 1. Categories for coding data

Category	Example of Facebook Posts before cleaning [all sic]
Opinions regarding Cyberbullying	hey ppl get cyberbullied all the time and some people kill them selfs so we should stick up for them and if you guys want to be jerks and get off of this then figure it out we all are proud to help others but I guess your not:/
Opinions [Empathy]	It doesnt matter how bad life may seem at the moment. God, me and everyone else still loves you and wants to see you smile. ELE <3
Opinions [Advice]	I don't think anybody needs to feel alone!! people that are being bullied, you are worth more than you will ever know, Never Give up!! you are never alone! believe in yourself !!
Opinions [Negative]	Getting bulled is fun. When you're naked. And vulnerable.
Experiences of Cyberbullying	U know i was bullied on the page called [Name of Group] they took a picture of me off a group post and harassed me and bullied me.
Experience [Advice]	We can listen to this guy. He went through the same stuff [User] did, and he felt the same way. Now he is giving people hope by posting this message.
Experience [Warning]	Remember the girl who got stabbed with a Stanley knife at [Name of School] The one who had Superglue thrown in her face? The one who got spat at on the bus? The one who got her ankles kicked in the dinner queue every day? That girl was ME. Unfortunately, I'm nearly 25 years old now. I'm not that scared child anymore, because the bullies did not beat me. I left school in 2004 with 10 Gcses, and the bullies left with nothing but their evil, stupid, naive attitudes. If anyone who bullied me reads this, you better know your card is marked. I can pretend to forgive, but I never forget. Karma is a B****... So I don't have to be!
Advertising	There is a group [Name of Group]. Go check it out!
Articles	Cyber Safety for Kids, 20 Most Useful Recommendations < #CyberSafety #Tips #Parents > What can one do about Cyber Safety for Kids? While the Internet may arguably be one of the most wonderful things invented by human beings, it is nevertheless also one of the most complicated, far-reaching, and potentially dangerous environments on earth. [URL]
Legal Aspects	Hey guys, if you could please sign this petition - [URL] The fact that youtube does not have the option to report people for horrific messages such as in the picture is terrible.
Quotes/Sayings	"Give Everything; But Up!" ~Alexis Pilkington's famous quote. Said it before every game she played to every person on her team even her coaches. Follow in her footsteps give everything but up help others and be a friend to others.
Group Posts	Just going to say, can you at least ask me before adding me to a group? I am getting really tired of people just throwing me in groups thanks for the add!!:D
Group Posts [Warning]	plz do not post dating groups in here this is a group for cyber bullying not dating
Group Posts [Negative]	Why the heck did you add me? Sure, I got bullied, but first of all, helpline is an overestimation. Friends usually only ask friends for help, second, posting all this stuff like, I'm glad you're you is cool and all, but we don't need a group to do that. And lastly, I don't want to be in half the group's I am, if you guys could NOT add anymore people without their permission, which would be great. I've been bullied long enough to know that that feel good c*** does nothing. I'm sorry if that rant seemed Jerkish, but it had to be said. And please remove me from here. *rant over*
Other Areas linked to Cyberbullying	Have you ever been told not to keep all of your passwords written down as someone can steal them? You leave your fingerprints everywhere and your fingerprint is just as easy to lift. #CyberSecurity #OnlineSafety
Not Related to Cyberbullying	Rights to Travel Explained Oct 14 City of Toledo Ore City Council[URL]

Parts of Speech Tagging (POS Tagging)

A Parts of Speech (POS) tagger is a piece of software which allocates parts of speech (e.g., noun, adjective, verb, and adverb) to words and tokens (The Stanford Natural Language Processing Group, 2016). The Facebook posts were POS tagged using *R's tagPOS()* function. The algorithm uses Penn English Treebank POS tags (Marcus, Marcinkiewicz, & Santorini, 1993). The type of tags used in sentences can highlight the tone of the sentence.

Pak and Paroukbek's (2010) study on Tweets and sentiment analysis explored the meaning of various POS tags, as well as the difference between subjective and objective text. Subjective text is more opinion-based and contains more personal pronouns. Authors of subjective text use simple past tense, write about themselves, or address the audience. Subjective text contains more utterances. An utterance is a continuous stretch of talk by one person with there being a silence before or after on the part of that person.

Objective text is based more on facts and contains more common and proper nouns. Common nouns focus on general things whereas proper nouns deal with specific things, e.g., the word city would be a common noun, but the word Chicago would be a proper noun. Verbs contained in objective text are more often in the past participle (e.g., beaten would be the past participle for the verb to beat), and in the third person. The root of the verb is coupled with modal verbs (which express possibility, e.g., shall, will, would) to express emotions. In terms of adjectives, superlative adjectives (e.g., sweetest, calmest, and brightest) are used to express emotions, whereas comparative adjectives (calmer, angrier, and sweeter) are used to state facts (Pak & Paroukbek, 2010).

POS tagging has been used in studies utilising data mining techniques to detect cyberbullying. Alakrot and Nikolov's (2015) survey of text mining techniques used in cyberbullying detection identified feature selection as having a great impact on the improved precision of text mining tools. One of the features used to detect cyberbullying was the presence of bigram tags as part of the POS tags (Dinakar et al., 2012). Bigrams are assigned tags based on a sequence of two words e.g., 'book about', 'history of'. Other features which indicate the presence of cyberbullying included the density of uppercase letters, density of bad words, number of question marks/exclamation marks, and the number of smiley faces (Huang et al, 2014).

Ethics

The data extracted for this study was from public Facebook groups. This study focuses on the content of the posts and information about the group e.g. how old the group was. Therefore, only post content and group information was extracted. Personal details of the group members were not extracted. The content of Facebook groups used in the study was publicly available information, which was available to non-Facebook members.

Studies such as (Abedin, Al Mamun, Lasker, Ahmed, Shommu, Rumana, & Turin, 2017; MacDonald, Sohn, & Ellis; 2010) utilised data from Facebook groups in their studies. Both studies didn't feel the need to seek the consent of the group participants because the data was publicly available. Research by (Kraut, Olson, Banaji, Bruckman, Cohen, & Couper, M, 2004) highlighted that breaching confidentiality of private data which could lead to identification was the greatest risk associated with online data.

Public data includes comments and posts published on pages/public groups (Wolfinger, 2016). However, there is debate on how many users realise that their public data on Facebook can be accessed by a wider audience. Some users may not read the Facebook data policy and overshare information (Madejski, Johnson, & Bellovin, 2012), believing that no one outside the stated audience will access it.

In terms of the amount of data which could be accessed and extracted, when extracting data from Facebook, the Facebook API no longer allows data extraction from the profiles of the user's friends. In order to extract from friends, they have to grant permission to the application to access their data. This makes it harder to build up big networks of data. Facebook offers users various privacy controls to dictate who has access to their profile and what information applications can access.

The extracted data for this study was stored on a password-protected computer and will be deleted once the study has been completed. Only the authors of the paper accessed the data. An issue raised by this research is the use of sensitive information found in extracted post content, i.e. the disclosure of being cyberbullied online. This may attract harm for the relevant group members and therefore the groups used in this study are anonymised and therefore will not be stated by name.

The act of cyberbullying itself brings about ethical dilemmas due to being a violation of the ethics code for information use. Subsequently this leads to consequences for the victim e.g. deterioration in mental health, low self-esteem, drugs/ alcohol issues and suicide (Ncube and Dube, 2016). All computer users have a moral responsibility to treat other users with respect and treat them how you want to be treated in the real world. However, not all users abide by this sentiment and the biggest issue associated with cyberbullying, is the identification of the perpetrator due to the issue of anonymity presented by the use of the Internet (Cross, 2009).

Once the perpetrator has been identified, the process of sanctions can raise the lack of consistency in policies regarding cyberbullying. An example being in the USA, as of August 2017, only 44 out of the 50 states had criminal sanctions in their cyberbullying laws. However, 48 states included laws covering electronic harassment which covers cyberbullying (Statista, 2018). Only a handful of states have incorporated the use of electronic communication into school bullying prevention policies. One state that has done so is New Jersey (Osborne, 2018).

Around the world, countries have different laws regarding cyberbullying. In the UK, Canada and Australia, there are no specific laws which focuses on cyberbullying solely. However, other laws can be applied to cyberbullying. An example is in the UK, laws such as the Malicious Communications Act 1988 and the Communications Act 2003 can be applied (The Cybersmile Foundation, 2017).

Research by Ncube and Dube (2016) which surveyed 60 youths from South African computer literacy engagement projects, recommended that the education department educate children about cyberbullying and cyber ethics. The study also highlighted that various technologies can be used to educate children on cyberbullying. A similar study by Harrison (2015) which explored the understanding of cyberbullying by 11-14-year-olds in the UK, found a lack of rules, monitoring and guidance in relation to cyberbullying. This finding highlights how important it is at a young age to instill skills in computer literacy and the moral responsibilities of being an online social media user.

One area not covered in studies by (Harrison, 2015; Ncube and Dube, 2016) is the role of bystanders and whether they help victims if they have witnessed a cyberbullying incident. In 2014, Canadian students aged 9-17 years old were surveyed regarding cyberbullying. From those students, 65% of them stated that they would have done something to help somebody who was experiencing unpleasant behaviour online (Steeves, 2014). However, studies such as (Kazerooni, Hardman, Bazarova & Whitlock 2018; Menesini, Zambuto & Palladino, 2017) highlighted the struggle for bystanders to intervene in cyberbullying instances, which occur on online social media platforms. The struggles centred on the relationship between the bystander, target and the cyberbullying perpetrator (Patterson, Allan, & Cross,

2017). What is highlighted in (Kazerooni et al., 2018) study is that after witnessing several offenders of cyberbullying on social media, bystanders were more likely to engage in an intervention. This finding backs Dillon and Bushman's (2015) notion that probability of a bystanders' intervention increases with the recognition of how serious cyberbullying incidents are.

Overall, the area of ethics and cyberbullying have highlighted a variety of issues which need to be considered in moving the tackling of cyberbullying forward.

RESULTS

Profiles of Groups

Table 2 presents features of the top 10 Facebook groups used in this study. The number of likes, comments, and shares tell us about the users' interactions in regard to the posted content, and the ability of users to resonate with the content (Rayson, 2015). The popularity of the 'like' function was validated by Smith (2014), who surveyed Americans about their Facebook sharing habits. He found that 44% of them liked content posted by their friends at least once a day. Users are more likely to 'like' something because it is the quickest and easiest way to show appreciation of content. It doesn't involve any writing of comments. All it takes is a click of the like button.

Utilising the groups descriptions in Table 2, the groups were categorised into three different types of groups: discussion groups; campaign groups and other groups. Groups 1, 3, 5, 7 and 9 were classed as discussion groups. Groups 6, 8 and 10 were campaign groups and groups 2 and 4 were classed as other groups.

Correlation analysis was carried out on Table 2 by calculating the correlation coefficient between variables. The variables: Number of Posts; Total number of likes; Total number of comments and Total number of shares were dependent variables. Whereas the variables Year Group Was Created and Number of Group Members were independent variables because the number of group members was not dependent on the year the group was set up, as illustrated in Table 2.

Amongst the groups in Table 2, four groups are the joint oldest, but this aspect did not translate into the posting of more material, with $R^2 = 0.05$. The same weak positive relationship occurred between the number of members and the number of posts ($R^2 = 0.14$). The average number of posts was 43, with three groups having an above average number of posts. However, despite having only 42 posts, post content from Group 1 produced the highest level of user interaction via likes, comments, and shares. Compared to the number of likes and comments, sharing wasn't popular in terms of user engagement, despite it being the greatest degree of engagement. This is due to wanting to share posts in order for other users to see it and to increase the likelihood of influencing people who follow them (Ann Voss, & Kumar, 2013).

Content Analysis

In total, 313 Facebook posts were coded using the categories in Table 2. Figures 2, 3 and 4 show the breakdown of categories.

Chi square analysis (X^2) of the variables, group type and category breakdown of the posts in the Facebook groups ($\alpha = 0.05$ or 95% confidence) found an association between the variables: ($X^2 = 3.97$, $p = 0.14$). The chi square result was statically significant at 0.05.

Table 2. Group statistics

Group ID	Year Group Was Created	Number of Group Members	Number of Posts	Total number of likes	Total number of comments	Total number of shares	Group Description
1	2011	272	42	70	218	0	Discussion group. Theme of the group is to stop cyberbullying
2	2011	155	4	11	3	0	A group set up a part of a school project
3	2011	164	36	55	56	0	Discussion group. Theme of the group is cyberbullying incidents
4	2012	146	28	46	16	0	Links to articles not related to cyberbullying.
5	2012	86	97	45	18	0	Discussion group which contains links to articles on cyberbullying and cyber security.
6	2011	450	26	30	41	0	Campaign to stop cyberbullying
7	2013	238	103	68	106	8	Discussion group. Theme of the group is methods to keep cyberbullies away
8	2012	314	60	68	73	0	Campaign against cyberbullying
9	2015	635	22	36	40	0	Discussion group. Theme of the group is how to stop protect against cyberbullying and stop bullies.
10	2014	433	14	6	6	2	Campaign to stop online bullying.

Figure 2. Number of opinion-based posts

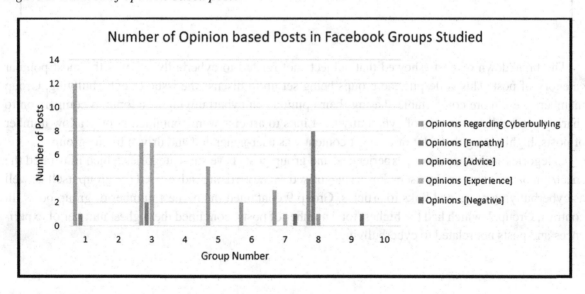

813

Figure 3. Number of Experience and Group-Based Posts

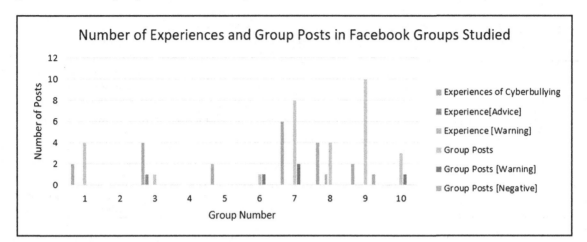

Figure 4. Number of non-experience- and group-based posts

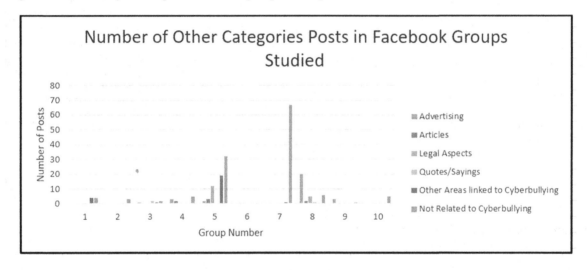

The breakdown of posts showed that subject 'not related to cyberbullying' was the most popular category of post. This is despite the groups being set up to discuss the issue of cyberbullying. Group members were more comfortable sharing their opinions on cyberbullying as a topic in comparison to sharing personal experiences of cyberbullying. Links to articles were contained in only a low number of posts, highlighting that a lot of the post content was user-generated and driven by the group.

Categories such as opinions, experiences, and group posts have sub-categories which illustrated the spectrum of emotions felt by users. Posts categorised as 'advertising' advertised the group itself as well as cyberbullying cases and links to articles. Group 9 contained the highest number of group posts. In contrast, Group 7, which had the highest total number of posts, contained the highest number of experiences and posts not related to cyberbullying.

In terms of attitudes towards cyberbullying in the post content, there was a mixture of positive and negative attitudes towards cyberbullying. The positive stances were expressed in terms of empathy, advice/suggestions, and sharing experiences. Examples of positive stance posts included:

"I promise, no matter what, no matter how busy I am. I will always be here for you (anyone) if you (anyone) needs a person to talk to. Anyday. Anytime." (Opinion/advice)

"It doesnt matter how bad life may seem at the moment. God, me and everyone else still loves you and wants to see you smile." ELE <3 (Opinion/ empathy)

"When ur being bullyed a friend will be bye ur side" (Opinion/ experience)

"There is a group [Group Name]. Go check it out!" (Advertising)

The negative stances were emphasised as warnings and negative posts. Examples included [all sic]:

"Why the heck did you add me? Sure, I got bullied, but first of all, helpline is an overestimation. Friends usually only ask friends for help, second, posting all this stuff like, I'm glad you're you is cool and all, but we don't need a group to do that. And lastly, I don't want to be in half the group's I am, if you guys could NOT add anymore people without their permission, that would be great. I've been bullied long enough to know that that feel good c*** does nothing. I'm sorry if that rant seemed Jerkish, but it had to be said. And please remove me from here. *rant over*" (Group Posts [Negative]).

"Everyone. I've made it to where i'm the only one that can post on here. So everyone that is against Cyberbullying, send me a message. If your just one of the bullys that has been starting shit on here, then stfu and get a f***ing life. This group was meant to help, but bullys got on here and started messing it up. Shows you there are too many f***ed up people. So yeah." (Opinion/ Group Posts [warning]).

"WARNING...Some of you may not like some of the things I say to these bullies but I consider this like a kind of bully boot camp... Also remember that the way I act towards these people is in no way a reflection of my true personality. I will be very blunt and arrogant.. This is a group study... Viewer discretion is advised" (Group Posts [Warning])

The posts generated a reasonable number of comments. In terms of post interaction (likes, comments, and shares), posts relating to the category opinions regarding cyberbullying generated the highest number of total comments, with 153 comments. However, posts in other categories did not generate as many comments. The categories not related to cyberbullying and opinions regarding cyberbullying also generated the highest number of likes, with 136 and 76 respectively. The first post mentioned previously generated the highest number of likes (29 likes) as well as 36 comments. In contrast, posts categorised as articles didn't produce any interaction, which indicates that resources outside Facebook were not well received by users.

Post Elements

Facebook posts were analysed to explore the elements which made up the posts. Figure 5 demonstrates the various elements.

Figure 5. Breakdown of post elements in Facebook Groups

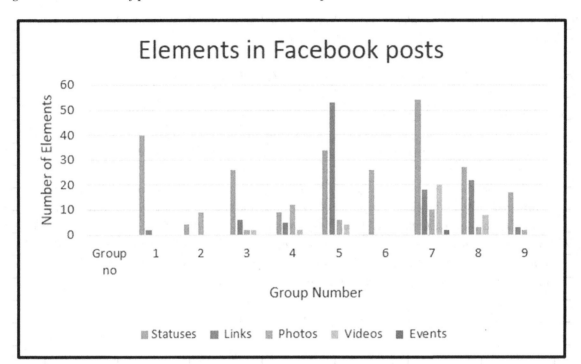

Seven of the groups contained a wide variety of elements, whereas three groups focused on certain elements. Group 7 contained a large amount of multimedia content via the use of videos, photos, and the use of events. However, not many of the posts in Group 7 were related to cyberbullying. Group 5 contained the highest amount of posts containing links to articles in areas associated with cyberbullying. Links in the posts studied ranged from articles on how to deal with computer security issues to articles about bullying experiences. Group 2, which only had a small number of posts, contained the highest number of photos. However, the posts in Group 2 were not related to cyberbullying

Sentiment Analysis

Figure 6 presents the number of sentiments bearing phrases in each group. Group 5 contains the largest number of sentiment-bearing phrases from the posts.

From all the groups, Group 5 contains the second highest amount of posts not related to cyberbullying. The trust emotion was prevalent across all the groups whereas the surprise emotion scored the least. Focusing on the groups which have post content more related to cyberbullying only (Groups 8, 5, 3 and 1), despite the presence of both positive and negative stances of cyberbullying in the content analysis, the sentiment analysis highlighted the high number of positivity-bearing phrases in comparison to negativity-bearing phrases. Groups 8, 5, 3 and 1, were a mixture of discussion and campaign groups, in terms of group type.

Figure 6. Sentiment analysis of posts

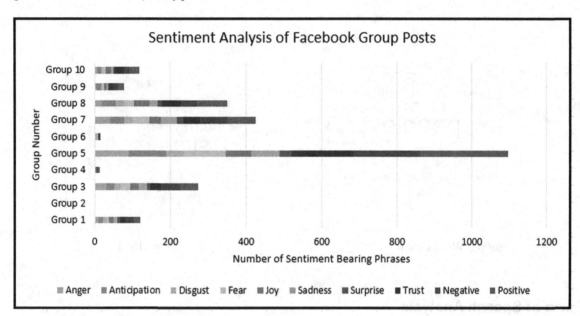

Group 3 is scored similarly in terms of number of positive and negative phrases. In contrast, Group 8's positive score is twice as much as its negative score. The most frequent words in Group 8 post content were 'bullying' and 'stop', whereas in Group 3 they were 'people' and 'don't'. This is illustrated in the word clouds in Figure 7. Word clouds have become "a standard tool for abstracting, visualizing, and comparing text documents" (University of Arizona, 2017). An example of where word clouds were used was comparing presidential debates between Trump and Clinton to find the most frequently used words. The use of the word cloud has been used in cyberbullying research e.g. Zhao, Zhou and Mao (2016) and Alim (2015).

The word clouds presented in Figure 7 which were produced for the post content of groups 3 and 8, illustrate the variety of words used in the post content for both groups as well as the difference in content posted by the users.

To explore the relationships between emotions from sentiment bearing phrases and types of groups, chi squared analysis was used. Chi square analysis of the groups whose content focused on cyberbullying (groups 1, 3, 5 and 8) and the number of negative emotions produced by the sentiment bearing phrases found no association found between the variables: ($\alpha = 0.05$ or 95% confidence) ($X^2 = 15.19$, p 0.44). Negative emotions included anger, anticipation, disgust, fear and sadness Likewise, no association was discovered between the types of groups (discussion, campaign or other) and the number of negative emotions ($\alpha = 0.05$ or 95% confidence), ($X^2 = 11.72$, p 0.30). There was no association present between types of groups and positive emotions which include joy, trust and surprise ($\alpha = 0.05$ or 95% confidence)

$(X^2 = 5.49, p\ 0.48)$. However, there was an association between the groups focused on cyberbullying and positive emotions $(\alpha = 0.05$ or 95% confidence) $(X^2 = 22.24, p\ 0.008)$. Sentiment analysis has highlighted the wide range of emotions produced in the post content and how users view cyberbullying.

Figure 7. Word clouds for Groups 3 and 8

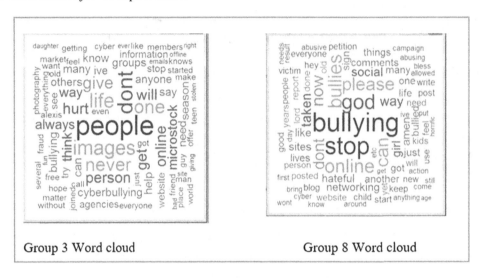

Group 3 Word cloud   Group 8 Word cloud

Parts of Speech Analysis

The text of all 313 posts were tagged for parts of speech. The results highlighted that Group 5 contained the highest number of superlative adjectives, one of the features for subjective opinionated text used to express emotions and opinions. Groups 1 and 8 contained the highest number of comparative adjectives, which are used to state facts. Group 7 had the most objective texts in terms of the number of common and proper nouns. Objective text deals with the stating of facts. Groups 1 and 8 have the highest number of utterances, which are strong predictors of subjective opinionated texts.

In terms of verbs, Group 5 had the highest number of verbs in objective texts in third person or past participles. Group 7 had the highest number of verbs in base form, but Groups 1 and 8 were not far behind. Verbs in the base form coupled with modal verbs to express emotions. Group 5 also had the highest number of authors of subjective text. Subjective text authors usually address the audience (verbs in the second person) and write about themselves (verbs in the first person), as well as using simple past tense. No groups had personal pronouns. What the POS analysis demonstrated was the balance of emotions and facts in the posts' content. Groups more centred on cyberbullying in their post content (Groups 8, 5, 3, and 1) had variations between objective and subjective texts. All groups had a high number of common and proper nouns, indicating the presence of objective texts. Groups 1, 3, and 8 contained many base form and modal verbs, which express emotions and show indications of subjective text. Groups 1 and 8 also have a high number of utterances. In terms of adjectives, Group 5 had the same number of subjective and comparative adjectives, whereas the other groups had a higher number of objective adjectives in the post content.

DISCUSSION

RQ1: What Categories of Information are Posted by Group Members in Relation to Cyberbullying?

Facebook groups can be effective for people seeking support. In this study, 9.27% of posts were advertising posts, mainly advertising events and campaigns associated with cyberbullying. Links to articles were contained in a low number of posts, highlighting that a lot of the post content was user-generated and driven by the group. Without a strict group moderator and clearly defined rules, the discussions generated by the group have the tendency to digress and this was illustrated in this study. The breakdown of posts showed that not related to cyberbullying was the most popular category of post. Despite the groups being set up to discuss cyberbullying, there were numerous posts which distracted from that, (e.g., posts on online dating.) Only four groups had content which was exclusively related to cyberbullying.

Chi squared analysis found a statically significant association between the variables, group type and different categories of posts. Discussion groups contained a large number of opinion-based posts and posts not related to cyberbullying. Campaign groups had more posts covering other areas such as advertising in contrast to number of posts not related to cyberbullying.

The content analysis of Facebook posts highlighted that users shared more opinions based on cyberbullying in comparison to personal experiences. Opinion-based posts made up 17.6% of posts, whereas personal experiences only constituted 6.39% of posts. The results are similar to Alim's (2015) content analysis of 400 cyberbullying tweets, where 28.25% of tweets were opinion-related, and 4% of tweets were discussing personal experiences. What the results of both Alim's (2015) and this study highlight is that the responses of users on platforms Twitter and Facebook focus on the sharing opinions in comparison to discussing personal experiences.

This finding is validated further by studies which has shown that cyberbullying victims, especially adolescents, choose to suffer in silence and not disclose incidents of cyberbullying to anybody. A study by Connolly (2017) into the reluctance of gifted Irish adolescents to report experiences of cyberbullying, found that the influence of gender, age and the prior experiences reporting of cyberbullying incidents were key reasons for non-reporting. In contrast, Deborah Crouch, chief executive of the Samaritans in Hong Kong, commented that due to long working hours, young people in Hong Kong had limited contact with their parents. This meant they felt alone and not able to communicate with their parents about issues affecting them including cyberbullying. Victims aged 10 years old and younger may choose not to tell their parents about cyberbullying due to cultural pressure and a sense of loneliness (Blundy, Ng, & Zheng, 2017). The use of online platforms allows cyberbullying victims to access a communication outlet where they could be potentially anonymous and not feel alone.

RQ2: Do Posts offer Support and Advice to Cyberbullying Victims and Other Actors, e.g., Parents?

In the case of current study, only 3% of posts contained advice about cyberbullying. Examples of advice included:

"Dear anyone considering suicide: Please don't give up. You are needed. You are wanted. You are important. You are loved. You are beautiful"

"We can listen to this guy. He went through the same stuff [user] did, and he felt the same way. Now he is giving people hope by posting this message."

"Cyber Bullying can be very dangerous. It kills and hurts people. Try to stop it, by standing up to it!"

The pieces of advice are mainly aimed at the cyberbullying victims. Some advice was integrated in to *opinions* and *experiences*, for example:

"Never give up. Always hold you head up. Always stay strong. Never fake a smile because you dont want people to see that your hurt. And never say that your life is over, always move on and live your life fully [sic]." (Opinion/Advice)

Despite advice not being prevalent in the posts studied in this study, advice regarding cyberbullying exists on the Internet (Fodeman & Monroe, 2009; Forward, 2014; Slonje & Smith, 2008). With cyberbullying taking place on the Internet, an opportunity for real time interventions exists. This gives the chance for the potential perpetrator to be encouraged to rescind his/hers cyberbullying message. If the victim receives the message, tailored advice can be given on how to deal with the bullying (Dinakar, Jones, Havasi, Lieberman, & Picard, 2012; Campbell, 2007).

Advice must be tailored to the relevant user groups because different age ranges use the Internet in different ways (Hargittai, Hsieh & Dutton, 2013; Nixon, Rawal & Funk, 2016). Younger users have both an online and offline presence, where older users may focus on their offline life and have less technology experience. This is one of the reasons that adults struggle with advising cyberbullying victims (Campbell, 2007). Posts which detailed experiences of cyber victims, legal aspects, and advertising may be beneficial to parents and other actors, because they bring awareness to campaigns as well as highlighting the thoughts of a cyberbullying victim.

There are various coping strategies that cyberbullying victims adopt in addition to seeking advice. School children's coping strategies centre on ignoring, retaliation, avoidance, or doing nothing (Slonje & Smith, 2008; Smith & Shu, 2000; Tokunaga, 2010). This is in contrast to victims based at university. A study by Orel, Campbell, Wozencroft, Leong, and Kimpton (2017) found that university students used a combination of offline and online strategies to help with cyberbullying. Strategies were more focused on solving the problem. The most popular strategies used were blocking, seeking help from friends, and staying away from where the cyberbullying was taking place. That can be hard where social media is involved due to the impact of social media and open boundaries. This was highlighted in research by Machackova, Cerna, Sevcikova, Dedkova, and Daneback (2013) into the coping strategies of 2,092 Czech children. Victims of cyberbullying found it hard to employ cognitive responses such as trying to mentally separate themselves from the bullying incidents. However, technical solutions such as deleting the bully from their contacts and altering their settings so that the bully couldn't contact them proved popular.

Despite Gámez-Guadix, Orue, Smith, and Calvete's (2013) notion that cyber victims can use the Internet as a coping mechanism, only 3% of posts in this study contained advice about cyberbullying. However, web-based interventions can be effective. Jacobs, Völlink, Dehue, and Lechner's (2014) on-line intervention program, called *Online Pestkoppenstoppen* (Stop Bullies Online/Stop Online Bullies), aims to promote wellbeing to cyber victims and to tackle issues such as truancy and school problems.

RQ3: What does Sentiment and POS Analysis of Posts Tells us About the Sentiments and Emotions Reflected in the Groups?

The sentiment analysis highlighted the wide range of emotions reflected in the posts' content. The groups with content more related to cyberbullying overall had more positive than negative emotions reflected in the post content as illustrated in Figure 6. The chi squared analysis highlighted the presence of a relationship between group types and positive emotions as well as groups focused on cyberbullying and positive emotions. De Jong (2016) study explored how the perception of privacy and security affects social media behaviour. The results of the study found that if the user has a positive sentiment towards Facebook use, they are more likely to share information on it because the user deems it safer. Positive sentiments in post content can encourage cyberbullying victims and other actors to see Facebook as a platform to share information on cyberbullying.

The content of the Facebook posts in this study generated numerous reactions from group members. Despite there being high levels of emotions such as anticipation and anger reflected in the posts overall, levels of joy were also reflected. This is encouraging for cyberbullying victims. Overall, the emotion '*trust*' produced the highest number of sentiments bearing phrases and presents the positivity written in the post content.

Like the sentiment analysis, POS analysis highlighted the various reactions reflected in the post content. The post content was a mixture of objective and subjective posts. However, in the groups, overall there is a higher amount of objective text in comparison to subjective text. This validates the observation in this study that Facebook groups may not be a suitable platform for victims, because the focus of the group is more likely to digress to other topic areas not always related to cyberbullying. A stronger presence by the group moderators may help keep the topic discussion on track, but even the presence of that in the Facebook groups studied has not been successful.

Sentiment analysis can prove valuable when identifying instances of cyberbullying on social media. Sintaha, Bin Satter, Zawad, Swarnaker and Hassan (2016) explored the performance of various machine learning techniques in detecting cyberbullying in social media using sentiments. The results found that the negative tweets indicated bullying tweets. In comparison, Xu, Jun, Zhu & Bellmore (2012) were successful in teaching a computer how to identify tweets regarding bullying from Twitter's daily stream of 250 million posts. More than 15,000 posts were identified as bullying related tweets per day. Sentiment analysis was then used to garner the emotions used in the tweets. The study found that "The victims and witnesses in bullying incidents often expressed sadness or anger." The bullies themselves did not have many emotional posts, but when they did, they would often be bragging. In our study, despite there being a low number of posts which detailed cyberbullying experiences, the posts contained a significant number of anger and sadness sentiment bearing phrases.

LIMITATIONS

This study focused on 10 open Facebook groups which were selected because they had the highest number of group members. A study of all Facebook groups related to cyberbullying and bullying, regardless of the number of members, would have given us a rounded view of the post content, and emotions reflected in the content, as well as the linguistic aspects of the posts. Data cannot be extracted from closed Facebook groups. In addition, the rise of privacy has impacted on the use of the Facebook API to extract Facebook data from friends. In terms of extracting profile contents from the members of a group, the members would have to grant permissions to the API application. Utilising a survey-based approach would paint a more accurate description of how cyberbullying groups work and whether they do what they say in the group description. However, the survey responses are self-reported rather than actual data.

CONCLUSION

This study has explored the post content and emotions produced from content in relation to 10 open Facebook groups associated with cyberbullying/bullying. The findings have highlighted how the post content focused more on the sharing of opinions regarding cyberbullying in comparison to writing about personal experiences of cyberbullying.

Discussions generated in some of the groups digressed as shown by the high number of posts not related to cyberbullying or bullying. This finding highlighted the need for strict group moderator and clearly defined rules. Surprisingly, only 3% of posts in this study contained advice about cyberbullying and 6.39% of posts detailed personal experiences of cyberbullying.

A positive note was the higher number of positive sentiment bearing phrases contained in the posts in contrast to negative sentiment bearing phrases. Chi squared analysis showing an association between the groups focused on cyberbullying and the number of positive emotions reflected in the posts. This is encouraging for cyberbullying victims and other actors to see Facebook as a platform to share information on cyberbullying. Further work into this area will explore what types of support cyberbullying victims look for in social media and how they utilise the support offered.

ACKNOWLDGEMENT

The author(s) declared no potential conflicts of interest with respect to the research, authorship, and/or publication of this article.

REFERENCES

Abedin, T., Al Mamun, M., Lasker, M. A., Ahmed, S. W., Shommu, N., Rumana, N., & Turin, T. C. (2017). Social Media as a Platform for Information About Diabetes Foot Care: A Study of Facebook Groups. *Canadian Journal of Diabetes*, *41*(1), 97–101. doi:10.1016/j.jcjd.2016.08.217 PMID:28126155

Alakrot, A., & Nikolov, N. S. (2015). A survey of text mining approaches to cyberbullying detection in online communication flows. In *NUI Galway-UL Alliance 5th Postgraduate Research Day*. Retrieved from: https://www.researchgate.net/publication/279173950_A_Survey_of_Text_Mining_Approaches_to_Cyberbullying_Detection_in_Online_Communication_Flows

Alim, S. (2015). Analysis of tweets related to cyberbullying. *International Journal of Cyber Behavior, Psychology and Learning*, *5*(4), 31–52. doi:10.4018/IJCBPL.2015100103

Baldwin, T., Cook, P., Lui, M., MacKinlay, A., & Wang, L. (2013). How noisy social media text, how diffrnt social media sources? In *Proceedings of the Sixth International Joint Conference on Natural Language Processing* (pp. 356-364).

BarberaP.PiccirilliM.GeislerG. (2017). *Package Rfacebook*. Retrieved from: https://cran.r-project.org/web/packages/Rfacebook/Rfacebook.pdf

Bender, J., Jimenez-Marroquin, M., & Jadad, A. (2011). Seeking support on Facebook: A content analysis of breast cancer groups. *Journal of Medical Internet Research*, *13*(1), e16. doi:10.2196/jmir.1560 PMID:21371990

Bird, D., Ling, M., & Haynes, K. (2012). Flooding Facebook-the use of social media during the Queensland and Victorian floods. *Australian Journal of Emergency Management*, *27*(1), 27.

Blundy, R., Ng, Y., & Zheng, S. (2017). Hong Kong kids suffer cyberbullying in silence amid suicide spike. *South China Morning Post*. Retrieved from http://www.scmp.com/news/hong-kong/article/2075891/cyberbullying-contributing-youth-suicides-hong-kong

Boyer, M. B. (2015). *An Examination of Catholic School Teachers' Perceptions and Legal Understanding of Cyberbullying* [Doctoral dissertation]. Loyola Marymount University.

Campbell, M. A. (2007). Cyber bullying and young people: *Treatment principles not simplistic advice*. Retrieved from http://eprints.qut.edu.au/14903/1/14903.pdf

Cerna, A., Machackova, H., & Dedkova, L. (2016). Whom to trust: The role of mediation and perceived harm in support seeking by cyberbullying victims. *Children & Society*, *30*(4), 265–277. doi:10.1111/chso.12136

Connolly, J. P. (2017). *'The silence phenomenon' an exploration of the factors influencing Irish gifted adolescents' resistance to report their experiences of cyberbullying behaviour* [Doctoral dissertation]. Dublin City University.

Cross, D., Shaw, T., Hearn, L., Epstein, M., & Monks, H. (2009). *Australian covert bullying prevalence study*. Retrieved from https://docs.education.gov.au/system/files/doc/other/australian_covert_bullying_prevalence_study_executive_summary.pdf

Dillon, K. P., & Bushman, B. J. (2015). Unresponsive or un-noticed?: Cyberbystander intervention in an experimental cyberbullying context. *Computers in Human Behavior*, *45*, 144–150. doi:10.1016/j.chb.2014.12.009

Dinakar, K., Jones, B., Havasi, C., Lieberman, H., & Picard, R. (2012). Common sense reasoning for detection, prevention, and mitigation of cyberbullying. *ACM Transactions on Interactive Intelligent Systems*, *2*(3), 1–30. doi:10.1145/2362394.2362400

Ditch the Label. (2017). The annual cyberbullying survey. Retrieved from https://www.ditchthelabel.org/wp-content/uploads/2017/07/The-Annual-Bullying-Survey-2017-1.pdf

Facebook. (2016). Company info. Retrieved from http://newsroom.fb.com/company-info/

Fodeman, D., & Monroe, M. (2009). *Safe Practices for Life Online: A Guide for Middle and High School.* International Society for Technology in Education.

Forward, C. (2014). Information and resources on Internet safety for children. *British Journal of School Nursing, 9*(3), 147–150. doi:10.12968/bjsn.2014.9.3.147

Gamez-Guadix, M., Orue, I., Smith, P., & Calvete, E. (2013). Longitudinal and reciprocal relations of cyberbullying with depression, substance use, and problematic Internet use among adolescents. *The Journal of Adolescent Health, 53*(4), 446–452. doi:10.1016/j.jadohealth.2013.03.030 PMID:23721758

Ganesan, K. (2014). *All about stop words for text mining and information retrieval.* Retrieved from http://text-analytics101.rxnlp.com/2014/10/all-about-stop-words-for-text-mining.html

Hargittai, E., Hsieh, Y. P., & Dutton, W. H. (2013). *The Oxford handbook of Internet studies.*

Harrison, T. (2015). Virtuous reality: Moral theory and research into cyber-bullying. *Ethics and Information Technology, 17*(4), 275–283. doi:10.100710676-015-9382-9

Jacobs, N., Völlink, T., Dehue, F., & Lechner, L. (2014). Online Pestkoppenstoppen: Systematic and theory-based development of a web-based tailored intervention for adolescent cyberbully victims to combat and prevent cyberbullying. *BMC Public Health, 14*(1), 396. doi:10.1186/1471-2458-14-396 PMID:24758264

Jong, N. F. (2016). *The Millennial differences regarding privacy & security perceptions on Facebook* [Bachelor's thesis]. University of Twente.

Kazerooni, F., Taylor, S. H., Bazarova, N. N., & Whitlock, J. (2018). Cyberbullying Bystander Intervention: The Number of Offenders and Retweeting Predict Likelihood of Helping a Cyberbullying Victim. Journal of Computer-Mediated Communication. Retrieved from https://academic.oup.com/jcmc/advance-article/doi/10.1093/jcmc/zmy005/4962534

Kraut, R., Olson, J., Banaji, M., Bruckman, A., Cohen, J., & Couper, M. (2004). Psychological research online: Report of Board of Scientific Affairs' Advisory Group on the Conduct of Research on the Internet. *The American Psychologist, 59*(2), 105–117. doi:10.1037/0003-066X.59.2.105 PMID:14992637

Langos, C. (2012). Cyberbullying: The challenge to define. *Cyberpsychology, Behavior, and Social Networking, 15*(6), 285–289. doi:10.1089/cyber.2011.0588 PMID:22703033

Langos, C. (2014). Regulating cyberbullying: A South Australian perspective. *Flinders Law Journal, 16*, 72–109.

Law, D. M., Shapka, J. D., Domene, J. F., & Gagné, M. H. (2012). Are cyberbullies really bullies? An investigation of reactive and proactive online aggression. *Computers in Human Behavior, 28*(2), 664–672. doi:10.1016/j.chb.2011.11.013

Liu, B. (2010). Sentiment analysis and subjectivity. In *Handbook of Natural Language Processing* (2nd ed., pp. 627–666). Chapman and Hall/CRC.

Luppicini, R. (2008). The emerging field of Technoethics. In R. Luppicini & R. Adell (Eds.), *Handbook of Research on Technoethics* (pp. 1–18). Hershey, PA: IGI Global. doi:10.4018/978-1-60566-022-6.ch001

MacDonald, J., Sohn, S., & Ellis, P. (2010). Privacy, professionalism and Facebook: A dilemma for young doctors. *Medical Education*, *44*(8), 805–813. doi:10.1111/j.1365-2923.2010.03720.x PMID:20633220

Machackova, H., Cerna, A., Sevcikova, A., Dedkova, L., & Daneback, K. (2013). Effectiveness of coping strategies for victims of cyberbullying. *Cyberpsychology (Brno)*, *7*(3). doi:10.5817/CP2013-3-5

Madejski, M., Johnson, M., & Bellovin, S. M. (2012,). A study of privacy settings errors in an online social network. In *2012 IEEE International Conference on Pervasive Computing and Communications Workshops (PERCOM Workshops)* (pp. 340-345). IEEE. 10.1109/PerComW.2012.6197507

Marcus, M. P., Marcinkiewicz, M. A., & Santorini, B. (1993). Building a large annotated corpus of English: The Penn treebank. *Computational Linguistics*, *19*(2), 313–330.

Menesini, E., Nocentini, A., & Palladino, B. E. (2015). Conceptual, theoretical and methodological issues. *Cyberbullying: From Theory to Intervention*, *15*.

Menesini, E., Nocentini, A., Palladino, B. E., Frisén, A., Berne, S., Ortega-Ruiz, R., & Naruskov, K. (2012). Cyberbullying definition among adolescents: A comparison across six European countries. *Cyberpsychology, Behavior, and Social Networking*, *15*(9), 455–463. doi:10.1089/cyber.2012.0040 PMID:22817693

Menesini, E., Zambuto, V., & Palladino, B. E. (2017). Online and school-based programs to prevent cyberbullying among Italian adolescents: What works, why, and under which circumstances. *Reducing Cyberbullying in Schools: International Evidence-Based Best Practices*, *135*.

Mohammad, S. M., & Turney, P. D. (2013). Crowdsourcing a word–emotion association lexicon. *Computational Intelligence*, *29*(3), 436–465. doi:10.1111/j.1467-8640.2012.00460.x

Mohammed, S. (2015). *NRC emotion lexicon*. Retrieved from http://saifmohammad.com/WebPages/NRC-Emotion-Lexicon.htm

Ncube, L. S., & Dube, L. (2016). Cyberbullying a desecration of information ethics: Perceptions of post-high school youth in a rural community. Journal of Information. *Communication and Ethics in Society*, *14*(4), 313–322. doi:10.1108/JICES-04-2016-0009

Nixon, P. G., Rawal, R., & Funk, A. (Eds.). (2016). *Digital Media Usage Across the Life Course*. Routledge.

Nocentini, A., Calmaestra, J., Schultze-Krumbholz, A., Scheithauer, H., Ortega, R., & Menesini, E. (2010). Cyberbullying: Labels, behaviours and definition in three European countries. *Journal of Psychologists and Counsellors in Schools*, *20*(2), 129–142.

Olweus, D. (1993) Bullying at School: What We Know and What We Can Do (Understanding Children's Worlds. Oxford: Blackwell.

Orel, A., Campbell, M., Wozencroft, K., Leong, E., & Kimpton, M. (2017). Exploring university students' coping strategy intentions for cyberbullying. *Journal of Interpersonal Violence*, *32*(3), 446–462. doi:10.1177/0886260515586363 PMID:25990383

Osborne, J. L. (2018). *The Legal Fight Against Cyber-Bullying*. Retrieved from https://www.law.com/njlawjournal/2018/02/19/the-legal-fight-against-cyber-bullying/

Pak, A., & Paroubek, P. (2010, May). Twitter as a corpus for sentiment analysis and opinion mining. In LREc, 10.

Patterson, L. J., Allan, A., & Cross, D. (2017). Adolescent perceptions of bystanders' responses to cyberbullying. *New Media & Society*, *19*(3), 366–383. doi:10.1177/1461444815606369

Paxton, P. (1999). Is social capital declining in the United States? A multiple indicator assessment. *American Journal of Sociology*, *105*(1), 88–127. doi:10.1086/210268

Preece, J. (2001). Sociability and usability in online communities: Determining and measuring success. *Behaviour & Information Technology*, *20*(5), 347–356. doi:10.1080/01449290110084683

Price, M., & Dalgleish, J. (2010). Cyberbullying: Experiences, impacts and coping strategies as described by Australian young people. *Youth Studies Australia*, *29*(2), 51.

Rayson, S. (2015). Like, comment, share? Why all Facebook interactions count. *BuzzSumo*. Retrieved from http://buzzsumo.com/blog/facebook-interactions-why-shares-likes-and-comments-all-count/

Sintaha, M., Bin Satter, S., Zawad, N., Swarnaker, C., & Hassan, A. (2016). Cyberbullying detection using sentiment analysis in social media. Retrieved from http://dspace.bracu.ac.bd/xmlui/bitstream/handle/10361/6420/13101123%2C%2013101258%2C%2013101283%2C%2013101290%20%26%2013101002_CSE.pdf?sequence=1&isAllowed=y

Slonje, R., & Smith, P. (2008). Cyberbullying: Another main type of bullying? *Scandinavian Journal of Psychology*, *49*(2), 147–154. doi:10.1111/j.1467-9450.2007.00611.x PMID:18352984

Slonje, R., Smith, P. K., & Frisen, A. (2013). The nature of cyberbullying, and strategies for prevention. *Computers in Human Behavior*, *29*(1), 26–32. doi:10.1016/j.chb.2012.05.024

Smith, A. (2014). 6 new facts about Facebook. *Pew Research Center*. Retrieved from http://www.pewresearch.org/fact-tank/2014/02/03/6-new-facts-about-facebook/

Smith, P. K., Mahdavi, J., Carvalho, M., Fisher, S., Russell, S., & Tippett, N. (2008). Cyberbullying: Its nature and impact in secondary school pupils. *Journal of Child Psychology and Psychiatry, and Allied Disciplines*, *49*(4), 376–385. doi:10.1111/j.1469-7610.2007.01846.x PMID:18363945

Smith, P. K., & Shu, S. (2000). What good schools can do about bullying: Findings from a survey in English schools after a decade of research and action. *Childhood*, *7*(2), 193–212. doi:10.1177/0907568200007002005

Statista. (2017). Number of U.S. states with state cyber bullying laws as of August 2017, by policy. Retrieved from https://www.statista.com/statistics/291082/us-states-with-state-cyber-bullying-laws-policy

Steeves, V. (2014). Young Canadians in a Wired World. Retrieved from ttps://mediasmarts.ca/sites/mediasmarts/files/pdfs/publication report/full/YCWWIII_Cyberbullying_FullReport.pdf

Steinfield, C., Ellison, N. B., & Lampe, C. (2008). Social capital, self-esteem, and use of online social network sites: A longitudinal analysis. *Journal of Applied Developmental Psychology*, *29*(6), 434–445. doi:10.1016/j.appdev.2008.07.002

Stopbullying.gov. (2014). What is cyberbullying? *StopBullying.gov*. Retrieved from http://www.stopbullying.gov/cyberbullying/what-is-it/index.html

The Cybersmile Foundation. (2017). T*he laws for cyberbullying and online abuse.* Retrieved from https://www.cybersmile.org/advicehelp/category/cyberbullying-and-the-law

The Stanford Natural Language Processing Group. (2016). *Stanford Log-linear Part-Of-Speech Tagger.* Retrieved from http://nlp.stanford.edu/software/tagger.shtml#About

Thoren, E. M., Metze, B., Bührer, C., & Garten, L. (2013). Online support for parents of preterm infants: a qualitative and content analysis of Facebook 'preemie' groups. *Archives of Disease in Childhood-Fetal and Neonatal Edition.*

Tokunaga, R. (2010). Following you home from school: A critical review and synthesis of research on cyberbullying victimization. *Computers in Human Behavior, 26*(3), 277–287. doi:10.1016/j.chb.2009.11.014

University of Arizona. (2017). Semantic Word Cloud Visualisation. Retrieved from http://wordcloud.cs.arizona.edu/description.html

Vaillancourt, T., McDougall, P., Hymel, S., Krygsman, A., Miller, J., Stiver, K., & Davis, C. (2008). Bullying: Are researchers and children/youth talking about the same thing? *International Journal of Behavioral Development, 32*(6), 486–495. doi:10.1177/0165025408095553

Voss, K. A., & Kumar, A. (2013). The value of social media: Are universities successfully engaging their audience? *Journal of Applied Research in Higher Education, 5*(2), 156–172. doi:10.1108/JARHE-11-2012-0060

Wang, W., Singh, S., Zeng, D., King, K., & Nema, S. (2007). *Antibody structure, instability, and formulation.* Retrieved from http://www.jpharmsci.org/article/S0022-3549(16)32163-3/fulltext

Wenger, G. C. (1990). The special role of friends and neighbors. *Journal of Aging Studies, 4*(2), 149–169. doi:10.1016/0890-4065(90)90012-W

Willard, N. (2007). *Cyberbullying and cyberthreats.* Champaign, Illinois: Research Press.

Wolfinger, E. (2016). "But it's already public, right?": The ethics of using online data. *News & Analysis.* Retrieved from: http://datadrivenjournalism.net/news_and_analysis/but_its_already_public_right_the_ethics_of_using_online_data

Xu, J. M., Jun, K. S., Zhu, X., & Bellmore, A. (2012, June). Learning from bullying traces in social media. In *Proceedings of the 2012 conference of the North American chapter of the association for computational linguistics: Human language technologies* (pp. 656-666). Association for Computational Linguistics.

Zhao, R., Zhou, A., & Mao, K. (2016, January). Automatic detection of cyberbullying on social networks based on bullying features. In *Proceedings of the 17th international conference on distributed computing and networking* (p. 43). ACM. 10.1145/2833312.2849567

This research was previously published in the International Journal of Technoethics (IJT), 10(2); pages 35-56, copyright year 2019 by IGI Publishing (an imprint of IGI Global).

Chapter 44
Social Media Consumption Among Kenyans:
Trends and Practices

Patrick Kanyi Wamuyu
https://orcid.org/0000-0002-4241-2519
United States International University – Africa, Kenya

ABSTRACT

Despite the growing popularity of social media among Kenyans, there is limited baseline data on the consumption of these platforms by different Kenyan communities based on demographics such as age, gender, education, income, and geolocation. The study set out to fill this gap through a baseline survey on social media consumption in Kenya. The study used a mixed-method approach, involving a survey of 3,269 respondents and 37 focus group discussions. The social media platforms in use are WhatsApp, Facebook, YouTube, Instagram, LinkedIn, and Snapchat. However, the use of social media differs by demographics. Kenyans use social media for entertainment, education, jobs, politics, sports, and social issues. Most Kenyans access social media using phones for 1-3 hours daily. Motivations for using social media include the acquisition of information, entertainment, and social interactions. Most social media users have experienced fake news, cyberbullying, and bombardment with graphic images of sex and advertisements. Kenyans consider social media to be addictive, expensive, and time-wasting.

BACKGROUND

Social Media has revolutionized how individuals, communities, and organizations create, share, and consume information. Social networks have also helped people to communicate, breaking down the geographical barriers which restricted instant communication thus permitting successful social media-facilitated collaboration. However, many social media users are also faced with emerging challenges associated with the dark side of social media use. These include ethical and privacy violation issues, data abuse and misuse, the credibility of social media content, hate speech, fake news, and bot-driven

DOI: 10.4018/978-1-6684-6307-9.ch044

interactions. Social media has also been associated with social and economic ills including family disintegration, dented reputations, and facilitation of terrorism. Social Media include SMS-based messaging platforms (e.g. WhatsApp, Facebook Messenger, WeChat), blogging platforms (e.g. WordPress, Blogger), social networking sites (e.g. Facebook, LinkedIn, Xing), Microblogs (e.g. Twitter, Tumblr), community media sites (e.g. Instagram, Snapchat, Flickr, YouTube, Dailymotion), wiki-based knowledge-sharing sites (e.g. Wikipedia), Social news aggregation sites and websites of news media (e.g. Buzzfeed, Huffington Post, Tuko News), Social Bookmarking sites (e.g. del.icio.us, Digg), social curation sites (e.g. Reddit, Pinterest) and websites by traditional news organizations, forums, mailing lists, newsgroups, social question and answer sites (e.g. Quora), user reviews (e.g. Yelp, Amazon) and location-based social networks (e.g. Foursquare).

Information and Communications Technologies (ICT) in Kenya have grown rapidly since the Internet was first launched in the early 1990s. Kenya is described as the Silicon Savanah owing to its dynamic ICT sector that has seen the development of globally acclaimed applications such as M-Pesa and Ushahidi. Ushahidi (https://www.ushahidi.com/) is an open-source platform that allows collection of distributed data via SMS, email or web and visualize it on a map or timeline from the public for use in crisis response. M-Pesa (https://www.safaricom.co.ke/personal/m-pesa) is a mobile money transfer service, payments and micro-financing service, in Kenya. Social media has become a key aspect in Kenyan public discourse, facilitating online discussions while at the same time being a key subject of scholarly, socio-cultural, economic, and political debates. Despite the growing popularity of social media platforms, there is limited baseline data on the consumption of the digital media by different Kenyan communities.

Statement of the Problem

Several studies have studied distinct use of different social media platforms including, Twitter (Tully, & Ekdale, 2014) and Facebook (Wamuyu, 2018). The Kenya Audience Research Foundation (KARF, 2020) has also been conducting media consumption audits/surveys since 2007 for their clients, with a focus on traditional media and its audiences. Nendo (Nendo, 2020) observes the use of the internet, apps, websites and social media by businesses in Kenya and providing statistical insights to enterprises in form of infographics. Studies have also explored the use of social media in different sectors of the Kenyan economy such as banking (Njeri, 2014; Njoroge & Koloseni, 2015), journalism (Nyamboga, 2014; Media Council of Kenya, 2016), community development (Murungi, 2018; Ndlela & Mulwo, 2017), advertising and marketing (Mwangi & Wagok, 2016; Aluoch, 2017) and in post-election crisis (Makinen & Kuira, 2008; Ogola, 2019).There is no data on research or a baseline survey on social media in Kenya despite its wide usage and consumption. Therefore, the study set out to fill this research gap by conducting a baseline survey on Social Media consumption in Kenya to identify the patterns of social media usage among Kenyans as well the factors motivating their use of social media.

Research Questions

The proliferation of internet-enabled mobile devices has led to the rapid development of social networking sites, resulting in a continued reconfiguration of ways in which individuals or groups access and use social media platforms. Nevertheless, little is known on how different social media platforms are relevant to diverse groups of people in Kenya based on demographics such as age, gender, education level, geographical location and income. The study was guided by the following questions: (1) what are the major Social Media sites and apps used by Kenyans?; and (2) what are the motivations behind use of social media among Kenyans? The study draws from a nationwide survey on social media consumption patterns among different demographic segments, conducted between December 2018 and March 2019. The survey sampled 3,269 respondents aged between 14 and 55 years.

Significance of the Study

The study provides the missing and much-needed baseline data on social media use among Kenyans based on different demographics. The results of this study contribute to literature on social media use in Kenya since no similar research had been carried out to measure social media use among Kenyans based on different demographics such as age, gender, education level, geographical location, and income. The study has also identified key statistics on social media users in Kenya. These statistics could be used by government, academic institutions and enterprises in the formulation of informed business strategies in order to better reach an identified target audience for improved service delivery, communication, and marketing strategies. For example, the time of the day when most Kenyans are online, could be used to identify the best time to post on social media for a target audience when the engagement rates are higher. Additionally, these statistics can be further used to develop issue-based policies, provide insights for academic inquiries, specific economic development strategies, among others.

The results also highlight the rural-urban digital divide, with most social media users in the rural areas accessing social media using cyber cafés. This could be used by the government to develop policies to address the issues pertaining to social, economic, and political empowerment. There is also a need for the government, individuals and organizations to disseminate their information through the social media, as one of the main motivations of social media use for a majority of Kenyans is the acquisition of information.

From the focus group discussions, the results indicate that individuals use social media when solving life problems. Many people have made their decisions on matters politics, personal relations, careers, and life based on social media conversations.

The paper is structured into six sections. Section 1 is the introduction, Section 2 is the literature review, and Section 3 is an elaboration on the study's research methodology, including the design and development of the survey instrument and the focus group discussion guide. Sections 4, 5, and 6 cover the study results, discussion of the study's empirical findings and the success of the study, highlighting its theoretical and practical implications, limitations and suggestions for further research, respectively.

LITERATURE REVIEW

Globally, the use of social media platforms is increasing exponentially. People use social networks such as Facebook, Twitter, and Instagram for the sole purpose of entertainment and maintaining contacts with their friends' list (Narula & Jindal, 2015). This section introduces use of social media platforms along with the motivations for using social media.

Usage of Social Media Platforms

Social media comprises of communication sites that facilitate relationship forming between users from diverse backgrounds, resulting in a rich social structure (Kapoor *et al.,* 2018). Many people are aware of the ever-mushrooming social media platforms such as Facebook, twitter, WhatsApp, LinkedIn, Instagram, TikTok, among many others (Hedman & Djerf-Pierre, 2013). According to a cross-sectional survey conducted by Alhabash and Ma (2017) among college students (N=396) which explored differences between Facebook, Twitter, Instagram, and Snapchat in terms of intensity of use, time spent daily on the platform, and use motivations, findings showed that participants spent the most time daily on Instagram, followed by Snapchat, Facebook, and Twitter, respectively. Alhabash and Ma's (2017) study also indicated that the students had the highest use intensity on Snapchat and Instagram (nearly equally), followed by Facebook and Twitter. In regard to use motivations, Snapchat took the lead in five of the nine motivations assessed by Alhabash and Ma (2017).

He, Wang, Chen, and Zha (2017) note that social media has become an online platform for businesses to market products/services and to manage customer relationships. Many small businesses have in the recent past joined the social media use bandwagon. Nawaz and Mubarak (2015) examined the adoption of social media in Sri Lankan enterprises and found that Facebook and Twitter were being used by the tourism product suppliers for advertisement and promotional purposes. Young (2017) examined how and why nonprofit human service organizations (HSOs) are using social media and found that these organizations are generally satisfied with social media use primarily to promote their organization's brand with even limited resources. Similarly, Hou and Lampe (2015) note that social media platforms are increasingly adopted by small nonprofit organizations (NPOs) to help them meet their public engagement goals. Leonardi (2015) indicates that use of enterprise social networking technologies can increase the accuracy of people's knowledge of "who knows what" and "who knows whom" at work.

Social media is known to facilitate escapism among people from some things in life. Hunt, Marx, Lipson and Young (2018) performed an experimental study to investigate the potential causal role that social media plays in the well-being of students. During the experiment, Hunt *et al.,* (2018) monitored 143 undergraduates at the University of Pennsylvania, where one group of the study participants were randomly assigned limited access to Facebook, Instagram and Snapchat and only allowed to use 10 minutes, per platform, per day, while the other group was allowed to use social media as usual for three weeks. The study results indicated that the limited use group showed significant reductions in loneliness and depression over the three-week study period as compared to the control group. A similar study conducted among secondary school students and teachers in Embu, Kenya, by Nyagah, Asatsa and Mwania (2015), showed that social media has an influence on how teenagers connect with each other and which in the long run affects their self-esteem.

The global use of social media has surpassed 3.5 billion users as of July 2019 (Social, 2019), an indication that 46 percent of the world's total population is using social media. In the Philippines, individuals spend approximately three hours and fifty-seven minutes every day on social media, making the country the global leader in social media usage (Social, 2019). In contrast, Poushter, Bishop and Chwe (2018) indicate that only less than half of Germany's population use social media. Statista's 2018 report revealed that in 2016, 38 percent of individuals in the EU-28 used social networks daily. The country with the highest share of daily social media use was Denmark, where 59 percent of the population actively engaged on social media platforms on a daily basis. Kenya has a very dynamic ICT sector, however, there is no baseline data on use of social media in Kenya despite its wide usage and consumption. Wamuyu (2017) notes that the existing digital divide, characterized by a lack of computer literacy skills, low internet access, and inadequate ICT infrastructure may be the reasons behind the low social media use among low-income urban communities. In response to this, the author sought to address the following question: Therefore, the author sought to address the following question: .

RQ1: What are the major social media platforms used by Kenyans?

Under this question, several more specific sub-questions were asked.

1.   What are the social media platforms used by Kenyans?
2.   What do Kenyans use social media platforms for?
3.   How frequently do Kenyans access social media platforms?
4.   How do Kenyans access social media platforms?
5.   Where do Kenyans access social media platforms?
6.   How much time do Kenyans spend on social media platforms per day?
7.   What time of the day do Kenyans use social media platforms?

Motivations for Using Social Media

In today's world, individuals spend several hours every day accessing and using social media platforms for social interactions, news, entertainment, and searching for information. Brandtzæg and Heim (2015) posit that people use social networks to get in contact with new people, to keep in touch with their friends, and general socializing. Studies have identified a number of factors motivating use of social media which include entertainment, information seeking, personal utility and convenience (Al-Menayes, 2015; Lampe, Ellison, & Steinfield, 2006), social surveillance or voyeurism (Mäntymäki & Islam, 2016), and self-promotion and exhibitionism (Belk, 2013; Mäntymäki & Islam, 2016). Whiting and Williams (2013) identified 10 motivations for using social media: social interaction, information seeking, passing time, entertainment, relaxation, communicatory utility, convenience utility, expression of opinion, information sharing, and surveillance or knowledge about others. Lee and Ma (2011) show that information seeking, socializing, and status seeking are the motivations for users sharing news on social media sites.

While Jung and Sundar (2016) found that people over 60 years old used Facebook for social bonding, social bridging, and as a vehicle for responding to family member requests, Joinson (2008) identified a set of eight different motivations college going students have for using Facebook, such as social connection, shared identities, photographs, content, social investigation, social network surfing, entertainment-related content, and status updates. Smock, Ellison, Lamp and Wohn (2011) studied motivations for using different features of Facebook and concluded that there are nine motives for using Facebook. These motives include habitual pastime, wanting to be part of a cool and new trend, entertainment, information sharing, escapism, companionship, professional advancement, social interaction, and meeting new people. Park, Kee and Valenzuela (2009) posit that individuals have different motivations to join Facebook groups. Some people join Facebook groups to look cooler and develop their careers, while others join the groups for socializing, entertainment needs or because they feel pressured by their friends and feel that joining these Facebook groups will boost their social standing among friends (Valenzuela, 2009).

Dhaha and Igale (2013) indicate that the motives for using Facebook among Somali youth are virtual companionship escape, interpersonal habitual entertainment, information seeking, self-expression, and passing time. In a study conducted among US adults, Lin, Lee, Jin and Gilbreath (2017) identified Facebook users' motivations as socialization, entertainment and information seeking as compared to Pinterest users whose motivations were entertainment, information seeking, and self-status seeking. Tartari (2015) identified seven motivations for Facebook use among Albanian students which included virtual companionship escape, interpersonal habitual entertainment, self-description, self-expression, information seeking, passing time, and the establishment of a new online reality that they desire, not where they actually live in.

By studying how students from University of Alabama used Twitter before, during and after a tornado disaster in April 2011, Maxwell (2020), identified four motivations for using Twitter which included the need to socialize, to entertain, to gain status or to gather information. Other studies have identified motivations to use Twitter to include information sharing and social interaction, of information seeking, mobilization, and public expression (Liu, Cheung, & Lee, 2010; Park, 2013). A review of four scholarly works done by Coursaris, Yun and Sung (2010) identified entertainment, relaxation/escape, social inter-action, and information seeking as the motivations for using Twitter. Greenwood (2013) suggests that the motives for most Twitter and Facebook users are to pursue fame and to feel valued. A study among Kuwait college students identified the motivations to use Snapchat as passing time, self-expression, self-presentation, and entertainment, while the motivations for using Twitter are self-presentation, entertainment, and social interaction, with the motivations for using Instagram including passing time, social interaction, self-presentation, and entertainment (Alsalem, 2019).

Other studies have also identified motivations for using most of the world's popular social media tools. Mull and Lee (2014) identified five motivations for Pinterest usage, which included fashion, creative projects, virtual exploration, organization, and entertainment. Huang and Su (2018) posit that motivations for using Instagram are seeking social validation, social interactions and diversion. Marcus (2015) indicates that the primary motive for Facebook posts is to establish relationships with others, whereas Instagram is more for personal use and mostly for people who are looking to get praise and likes which gives users a unique sense of satisfaction.

The motivations to use YouTube include to contribute content, including liking content, sharing a link with friends and uploading content, viewing content uploaded by others, need for relaxation and entertainment, and to meet needs for information and learning (Rosenthal, 2018; Klobas *et al.,* 2018). Klobas et al., (2018) found that Malaysian university students were strongly motivated to use YouTube for entertainment, information and learning. Myrick (2015) shows that one of the motivations to watch YouTube is to improve personal mood. Studies have also shown that the users of WhatsApp are mainly motivated by cost, entertainment, leisure, sense of community, immediacy, and intimate communication (Karapanos, Teixeira & Gouveia, 2016; Church & de Oliveira, 2013). Motivations for YouTube users also include expressing opinions and making their voice heard among their peers, entertainment and information-seeking (Hanson & Haridakis, 2008).

Zhang and Pentina (2012) identified the motivations for Chinese users of Weibo as information seek-ing, social connection, to facilitate their professional development, fulfill emotional needs, reciprocate by helping other users with advice and information, enhance their social status, express oneself, and interact with the site and other users. Hwang and Choi (2016) identified the motivations for using Sina Weibo among Chinese college students as information-gathering, followed by accessibility to celebrity, social connection, self-presentation and entertainment. Lien and Cao (2014) indicates that Chinese WeChat users' motivations are entertainment, sociality and information. Basak and Calisir (2014) identified seven motivations among LinkedIn users in Turkey which included self-promotion, group activities, job and job affairs, finding old and new friends easily, follow up, profile viewer data, and professional networking. In a study on the motives of accessing political candidate profiles on MySpace, Ancu and Cozm (2009) derived three motivations which included social interaction, information seeking and guidance, and entertainment. An online survey among the users of the social news website Reddit.com showed that the Redditors' motivations are socializing/community building, status-seeking and entertainment (Moore & Chuang, 2017).

While the above studies have identified a number of factors motivating use of social media in different countries and in diverse social, cultural and economic settings, their findings may not generalize to the Kenyan setting. The focus of this study was to examine whether the findings from past studies could be generalized to the Kenyan setting. Therefore, the author sought to address the following question:

RQ2: What are the motivations behind using social media among Kenyans?

This study investigated the following five motivations to use social media among Kenyans.

1. Acquiring information (news, knowledge, exploration);
2. Entertainment and pleasure (emotional experiences);
3. Personal identity (personal stability, social status, need for self-respect);
4. Social interactions with family members, friends and connection with the outside world;
5. To escape some things (release tension, shifting attention from unpleasant happenings).

RESEARCH METHODOLOGY

The researchers used a mixed study approach, which involved collecting both quantitative (survey) and qualitative (focus group discussions) data in two phases. Focus group discussions were used as a complementary method to the survey. Descriptive analysis was completed for the quantitative data and thematic analysis was used for the qualitative data. Use of focus group discussions resulted in the collection of in- depth data which could not have been obtained if only a survey had been used. For example, the emergence of two new motivations of using social media, namely seeking business opportunities through social media and buying and selling on social media were only realized from focus group discussions as the survey only had the commonly known motivations from the literature.

Data collection in phase one was achieved through a baseline survey to collect data on the social media usage patterns among Kenyans. The baseline survey was accomplished using a hand-delivered questionnaire. The questionnaire consisted of open-ended and closed-ended questions to measure individual social media use patterns, motivations to using social media as well as demographic questions. The participants were assured of their anonymity and confidentiality, and informed that their participation in the study was voluntary.

Phase two data was collected using focus group discussions aimed at getting the insights on the survey participants' reflections on their social media and internet use experiences and motivations. The focus group discussion sessions lasted for 120 minutes (2 hours). During each focus group meeting, 60 minutes were used for the focus group discussion guide while the other 60 minutes were for introductions, closing remarks and refreshments. Each focus group discussion had 6 to 10 participants and a moderation team (the moderator and the assistant) whose members had shared tasks.

The target population was stratified into five groups based on ages to enable a comparative analysis on social media consumption patterns. The five strata have been designed in accordance with the socio-demographic characteristics. The five strata are as follows:

- 14 to 20 years old - These constitute the high school level students that access to internet and social media during holiday period and were born in the digital media environment.
- 21 to 25 years old - These constitute college-level students and were also born in the digital media environment.
- 26 to 35 years old - These constitute early career workers and were born in a non-digital media environment but they use it.
- 36 to 45 years old - These constitute the middle-to-late career workers who mostly learnt to use digital media when they were adults.
- 46 years and above – These constitute seniors who have historically been late adopters of technology compared to the younger population.

For purposes of obtaining a representative sample, the study divided the country along the former eight administrative provinces – Nairobi, Coast, Central, Western, Nyanza, Eastern, Rift Valley, and North Eastern for purposes. From each of the former provinces, the county with the highest access to Internet was selected for data collection based on the level of internet penetration data from the Kenyan Integrated Household Budget Survey, Kenya National Bureau Statistic (KNBS, 2016). The eight counties selected were Nairobi (Nairobi Province), Mombasa (Coast), Meru (Eastern), Bungoma (Western), Mandera (North Eastern), Trans Nzoia (Rift Valley), Kisumu (Nyanza), and Nyeri (Central).

From the selected counties, one urban and one rural location with Internet penetration as per KNBS 2016 report were selected for data collection. The locations selected for data collection except Nairobi were as follows: Central (Nyeri Town and Naro Moru); Coast (Mombasa City and Changamwe); Eastern (Meru Town and Kathera); North Eastern (Mandera Town and Banissa), Nyanza (Kisumu City and Nyando); Rift Valley (Kitale Town and Kiminini); and Western (Bungoma Town and Kanduyi). However, since there is no distinction between urban and rural areas in Nairobi, the capital city was subdivided according to the socio-economic demographics used by the KNBS as follows: lower income, lower middle-income, middle-income, and high-income. Specifically, for lower income, the data was collected in (Mathare, Kangemi, Kawangware, Mukuru Kwa Njenga, Mukuru Kwa Reuben, Laini Saba, Korogocho, Kariobangi North, Dandora I through V, Kayole and Kiamaiko. For lower middle, the data was collected in Umoja I through III, Kariobangi South, Imara Daima, Riruta, Githurai, Kahawa West, Zimmerman, Mwiki, Kasarani, Njiru, Ruai, Komarock, Savannah, and Eastleigh. In middle-income, the neighborhoods were Parklands, Highridge, Mountain View, Lang'ata, South C, Nyayo Highrise, Nairobi West, Woodley, and Westlands. Runda, Kitisuru, Kileleshwa, Muthaiga, Karen, and Kilimani represented high-income neighborhoods.

RESULTS AND ANALYSIS

Baseline Survey

The nationwide survey of social media consumption patterns among different demographic segments was conducted between December 2018 and March 2019. The survey sampled 3,269 respondents aged between 14 and 55 from eight counties drawn from Kenya's former eight administrative provinces – Nairobi, Coast, Central, Western, Nyanza, Eastern, Rift Valley, and North Eastern. From the sample of 3,269, 3,166 questionnaires were fully answered – representing a health response rate of 96.9%. The data from the 3,166 respondents was used to answer research question one.

RQ1 (1): What Are the Social Media Platforms Used by Kenyans?

Use of Social Media Platforms in Kenya

Figure 1 captures a snapshot of social media platform use by Kenyans. The vast majority of Kenyans almost equally use WhatsApp (89.4%) and Facebook (89.3%). The third most used social media is YouTube (51.6%) followed by Instagram (39.4%). Both LinkedIn and Snapchat are the least popular platforms in Kenya at 9.3% and 9.1% respectively.

Figure 1. Social Media use in Kenya

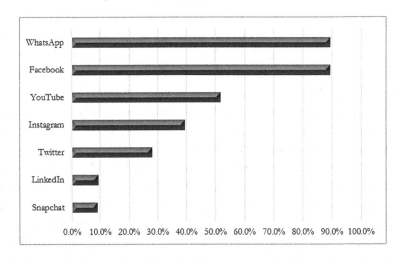

Social Media Use by Age

From Figure 2, the most active age group on social media is 26-35 years, while the least active are those aged above 46 years. Facebook is mostly used by 26-35 year-olds (34.6%) and least used by those 46 years and above (4.6%). Twitter is mostly used by those of 26-35 years (39.3%) and least used by 46 years and above (4.8%). When it comes to WhatsApp, it is also commonly used by Kenyans aged 26-35 years. Instagram is most used by 21-25 year-olds at 38.7% and least used by those beyond 46 years

(2.8%). Similarly, Snapchat is also mostly used by those aged 21-25 (36.6%). YouTube is most used by 26-35 year-olds (34.1%) and least used by 46 years and above. LinkedIn is most used by 26-35 year-olds (43.7%) and least used by those 46 years and above.

Figure 2. Social Media use by Age

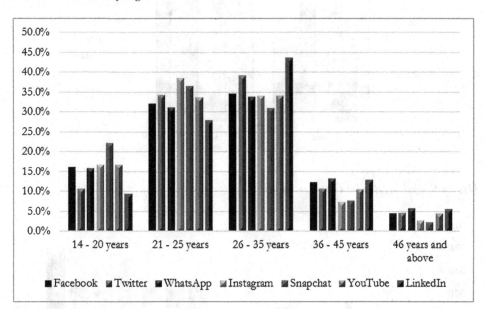

Use of Social Media by Gender

The men in Kenya are generally more active on social media platforms compared to the women (see Figure 3). They lead in all the social media platforms as active users. The preferred social media platforms among men include LinkedIn (67.8%) and Twitter (67.0%), with Snapchat being the least preferred platform, which is used by 52.5% of men, compared to 47.5% of women who had Snapchat as one of their preferred social media platforms.

The women reported the least use of LinkedIn, at 32.2%. as shown in Figure 3. It is conspicuous that while men use LinkedIn the most, women use it the least, with the reverse being true when it comes to Snapchat.

Use of Social Media by Geo-Location

Majority of Kenyans in the rural areas use Facebook (47.9%), WhatsApp (46.8%) and YouTube (44.2%), as compared to a majority of urban residents who use LinkedIn (70.3%), Snapchat (64.2%), Instagram (58.2%) and Twitter (56.8%) as shown in Figure 4.

Figure 3. Use of Social Media by Gender

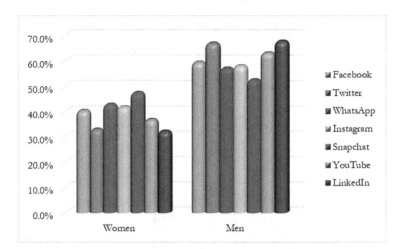

Figure 4. Use of Social Media by Geo-Location

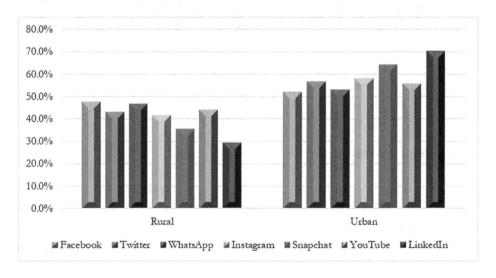

Use of Social Media by Income

A majority of low-income earners in Kenya are using WhatsApp (29.43%), YouTube (29.74%), Twitter (29.37%) and Facebook (29.28%), as compared to a majority of high-income earners who use LinkedIn (51.0%), Twitter (37.2%), YouTube (28.7%) and Instagram (27.3%), as shown in Figure 5. Most of the middle-income earners use LinkedIn (54.6%), Twitter (29.7%), Snapchat (27.8%), and YouTube (24.4%).

Use of Social Media by Income in Nairobi

In Nairobi, the majority of residents live in urban slums. Thus, those who live in informal settlements or the low-income residential areas use Facebook (30%) and WhatsApp (25%) as their social media platforms of choice as indicated in Figure 6. The middle-income residents of Nairobi mostly use LinkedIn (44.5%), Snapchat (29.8) and Twitter (29.7%). However, the lower middle-income population in Nairobi use YouTube (47.6%), WhatsApp (46.0%) and Instagram (45.6%). The high-income Nairobi residents mostly use LinkedIn YouTube and Twitter as shown in Figure 6.

Figure 5. Use of Social Media by Income

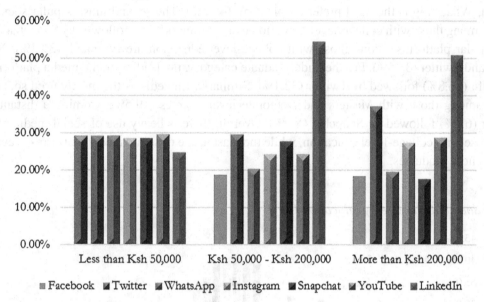

■ Facebook ■ Twitter ▨ WhatsApp ▨ Instagram ■ Snapchat ▨ YouTube ■ LinkedIn

Figure 6. Use of Social Media by income levels in Nairobi

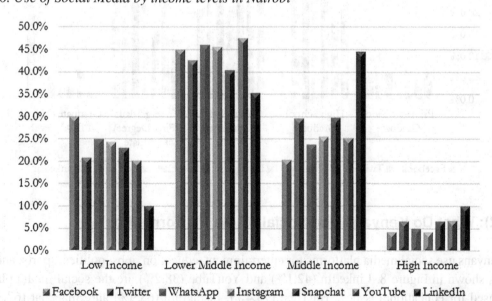

▨ Facebook ■ Twitter ■ WhatsApp ▨ Instagram ■ Snapchat ▨ YouTube ■ LinkedIn

Use of Social Media Platforms by Education Level

From Figure 7, the use of Facebook is more common among those with high school and college levels of education. Among those with higher education levels (undergraduate and graduate), the most common social media platform is LinkedIn. In the primary school category, Facebook tops at 8.5%, followed by WhatsApp and YouTube. For high school graduates, the most prevalent platform is Facebook (34.5%) followed by YouTube (32.3%). WhatsApp is third with 31.4%. However, among those with college-level education, WhatsApp is the most preferred platform (40.6%). The second most popular social media platform among those with college-level education is Instagram (40.4%) followed by Snapchat (40.0%). Other popular platforms among those with college-level education are Facebook (39.4%), YouTube (39.1%), and Twitter (38.5%). For the undergraduate category, the leading social media platform in use is LinkedIn (36.8%) followed by Twitter (32.1%). Similarly, LinkedIn is the mostly used social media platform among those with Masters and Doctorate level degrees (19.5%). Coming a distant second is Twitter (6.4%) followed by Snapchat (5.0%). Overall, there is heavy use of social media platforms among those with college-level education, while the least usage of social media platforms is among the primary school graduates.

Figure 7. Social Media Use by Education Level

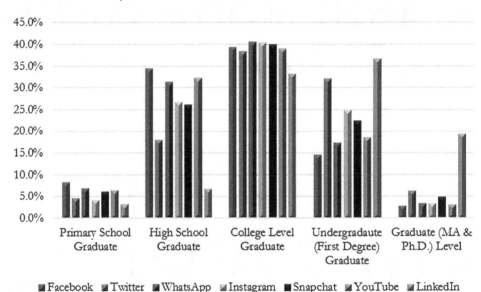

RQ1 (2): What Do Kenyans Use Social Media Platforms For?

Most Kenyans use social media platforms for entertainment, education, jobs, politics, sports, and social issues as shown in Figure 8. LinkedIn (42.1%) and YouTube (38.2%) are the social media platforms mostly used for educational issues. YouTube (74.4%), Instagram (68.9%) and Snapchat (67.3%) are frequently used for entertainment. WhatsApp is mostly used for social issues (89.4%) while LinkedIn is commonly used for job-related issues (61.9%) and education matters (42.1%). Facebook is mostly used for social (65.3%) and entertainment (60.0%) issues. Twitter is used for both social (50.2%) and political (35.1%) issues. The issues the respondents used social media for is a clear indication that people use social media to solve their life problems, make decisions and create identities.

Figure 8. Issues of Focus in Using Social Media

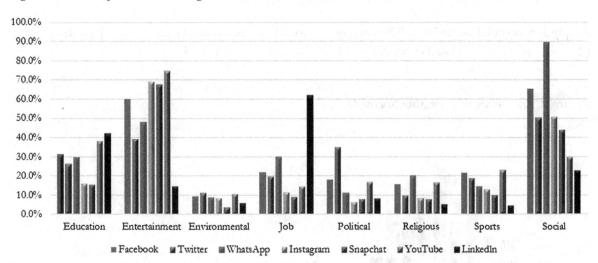

RQ1 (3): How Frequently Do Kenyans Access Social Media Platforms?

Frequency of Accessing Social Media

Social media users in Kenya are highly engaged with the platforms, with most Kenyans accessing more than one social media platform daily as indicated in Figure 9. The data on social media platform use shows that 89.3% of WhatsApp users use the platform daily, with 9.2% accessing it weekly, while 1.4% use it less often. 80.7% Facebook users visit the site daily, 15.8% use the platform weekly, while 3% say they visit the site less often. 63.6% of YouTube users visit the site daily, another 29.8% say they use it a few days a week, while 5.7% say they use the use the video-sharing platform less often. Almost half (48.7%) of Snapchat users are on the platform daily, with 27.7% who say they check in weekly, while 8.5% visit Snapchat less often than that. 54.6% of Twitter users visit the site daily, another 32.4% say they visit a few days a week, while 9.2% say they check Twitter less often. 59.8% of Instagram users visit the site every day.

RQ1 (4): How Do Kenyans Access Social Media Platforms?

Devices Used to Access Social Media

According to the survey data, most social media platform users in Kenya used their phones to access their preferred platforms. According to the survey, 78.6% of respondents stated that they accessed the platforms using mobile phones. Almost all WhatsApp (97.5%) and Facebook (96.2%) users accessed the platforms using mobile phones as shown in Figure 10. However, 40.2% and 16.5% of respondents indicated that they accessed LinkedIn using laptops and desktops respectively.

RQ1 (5): Where Do Kenyans Access the Social Media Platforms?

Physical Location of Accessing Social Media

People access social media from different physical locations, including at home (85.5%), public hotspots (23.3%), offices (22.1%) and cyber cafés (14.5%) as shown in Figure 11.

Figure 9. Frequency of Accessing Social Media

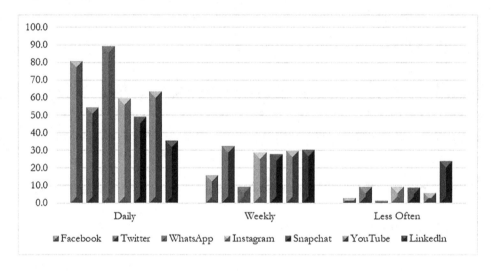

Figure 10. Devices Used to Access Social Media

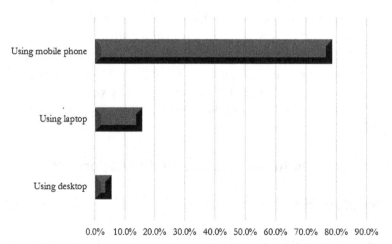

Figure 11. Physical Location of Accessing Social Media

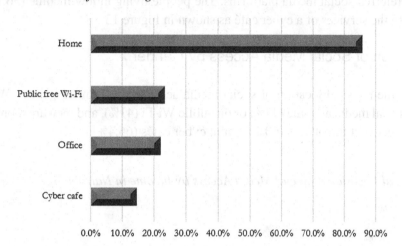

Physical Location of Accessing Social Media in Different Geo-locations

A majority of Kenyans in the rural areas and those living in low-income urban areas still value and use the services of a cyber café (53.1%). However, most of the urban population access social media from the offices (58.1%) and the public hotspots (57.7%), as indicated in Figure 12.

Figure 12. Physical Location of Accessing Social Media in different Geo-locations

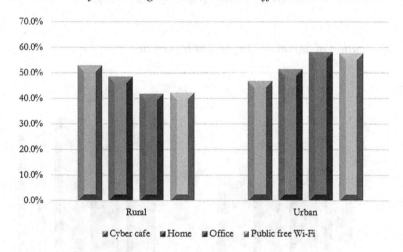

Physical Location of Social Media Access by Income in Nairobi

Even though Internet access charges are comparatively low compared to many African countries, Internet access is still expensive in Kenya. A majority of the middle-income (42.2%) Kenyan population use the office internet to access social media platforms, while the lower middle-income (49%) take advantage of readily available public Wi-Fi provided in the malls, training institutions and the entertainment spots to access their preferred social media platforms. The people living in low-income (36.1%) urban areas still value and use the services of a cyber café as shown in Figure 13.

Physical Location of Social Media Access by Gender

From Figure 14, the physical location of social media access varies among gender. Women are more likely to access social media at home (43%) or on public Wi-Fi (41%), and men are more likely to prefer accessing social media at the offices (60.1%) or at cyber cafés (66.4%).

Figure 13. Physical Location of Social Media Access by Income in Nairobi

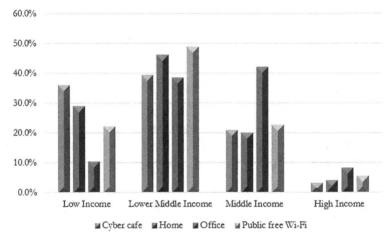

Figure 14. Physical Location of Social Media Access by Gender

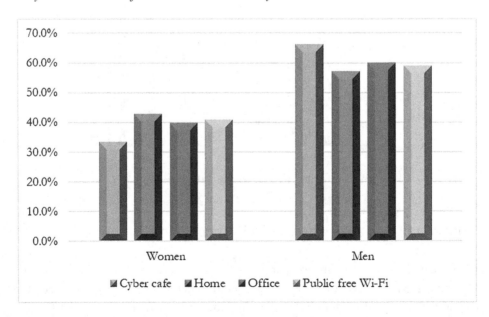

RQ1 (6): How Much Time Do Kenyans Spend on Social Media Platforms per Day?

Daily Time Spent on Social Media

On average, a vast majority of Kenyans spend more than one hour daily on social media platforms. 19.4% of social media users in Kenya spend more than three hours interacting through the social media on a daily basis as shown in Figure 15.

Figure 15. Daily time spent on Social Media

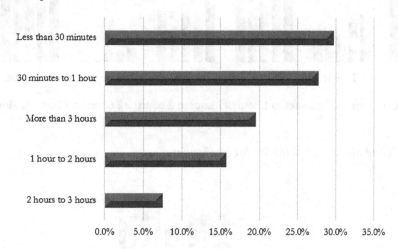

86% of WhatsApp users, 73% of Facebook users and 43% of YouTube users spend more than 1 hour online everyday as shown in Figure 16, while 60% of WhatsApp users, 46% of Facebook users and 29% of YouTube users spend more than 2 hours online everyday as shown in Figure 16.

Daily Time Spent on Social Media by Gender

Figure 17 indicates that most Kenyan men spend more time on various social media platforms available to them than women. For example, in a typical day most men (61%) spend more than two hours on social media daily as compared to 39% of women.

Daily Time Spent on Social Media by Geolocation

60% of the urban population in Kenya use social media platforms for more than 2 hours daily as compared to 40% of the people living in the rural areas who use social media for more than 2 hours on daily basis. A majority of the rural population spend between 1 and 2 hours on social media daily as shown in Figure 18.

Figure 16. Time spent online on specific platforms

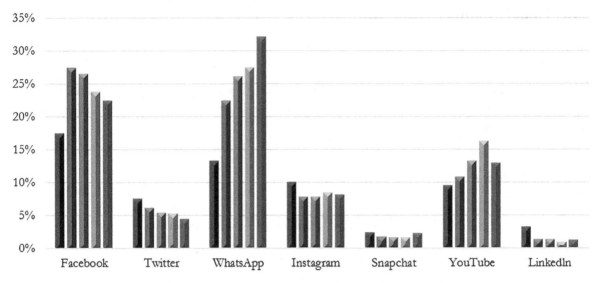

Figure 17. Daily Time Spent on Social Media by Gender

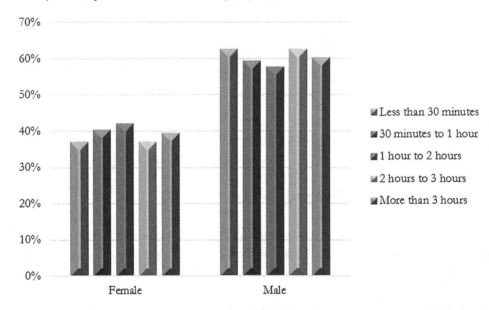

Daily Time Spent on Social Media by Age

Figure 19 shows that Kenyans of the ages between 21 and 35 (age brackets of 21-25 years and 26-35 years) are the most active users of social media available in the country. The data on the time spent on social media by age shows that the people the between the ages of 21 and 35 years spend an average of 2 hours per day on social media platforms. 37% of the 21-25 year-olds spend more than 3 hours a day on social media.

Figure 18. Daily Time Spent on Social Media by Geolocation

Figure 19. Daily Time Spent on Social Media by Age

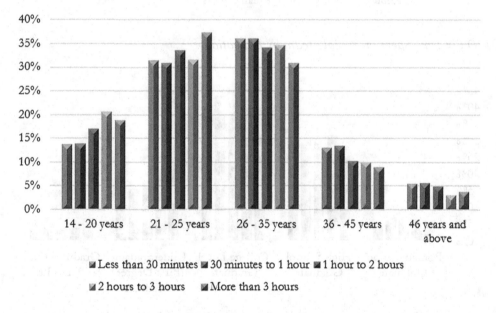

Daily Time Spent on Social Media by Income

Figure 20 shows that Kenya's middle-income group are the most active users of social media platforms in Kenya. 53% of the lower middle-class spend more than 3 hours a day on social media.

Daily Time Spent on Social Media by Education

Figure 21 shows that the college-level graduates spend much more time on social media than any other category of the education group. 41% of the respondents who were college-level graduates spent more than three hours on social media daily, while another 44% spent 2-3 hours on social media a day.

Figure 20. Daily Time Spent on Social Media by Income

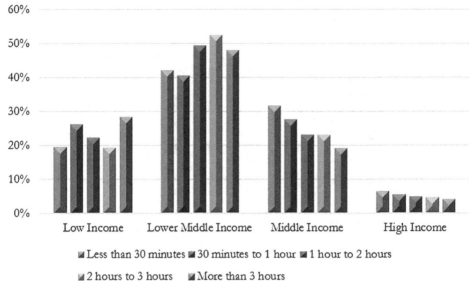

Figure 21. Daily Time Spent on Social Media by Education

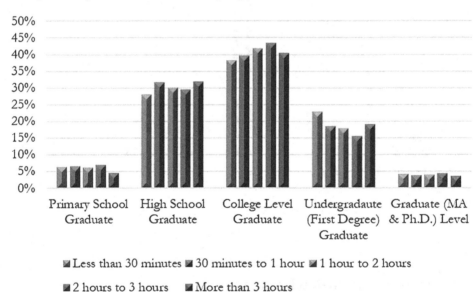

RQ1 (7): What Time of the Day Do Kenyans Use Social Media Platforms?

Time of the Day Spent on Social Media

Both night and evening hours are the times of the day when a majority of Kenyans spend most of their time on various social media platforms (see Figure 22). This could be attributed to the fact that these are the times of the day when most of Kenyans are at home after their day's work. Kenyans also spend a considerable amount of time in the morning hours on the social media platforms – which could be the period before they get busy with their daily routines.

Time of the Day Spent on Social Media by Gender

When analyzed by gender (see Figure 23), a majority of the Kenyan men (63.9%) spend more time on social media in the mornings, while most women (41.6%) spend their time on the social media platforms in the evenings.

Figure 22. Time of the day Spent on Social Media

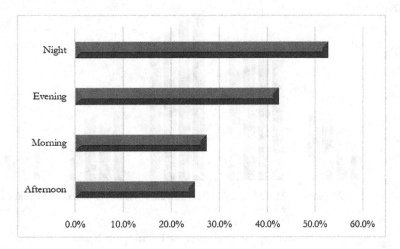

Figure 23. Time of the day Spent on Social Media by Gender

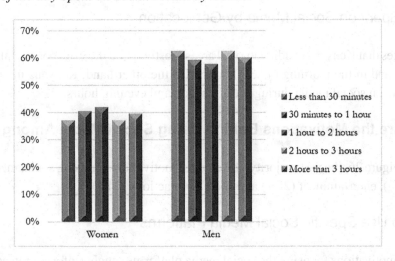

Time of the Day Spent on Social Media by Age

From Figure 24, a majority of the age groups including 26-35 years, 36-45 years and 46 years and above, spend a lot of time on various social media platforms during the morning hours. They also spend a substantial amount of time on social media during afternoon and evening hours. Kenyans in the age groups 14-20 years and 21-25 years spend most of time on social media platforms at night.

Figure 24. Time of the day Spent on Social Media by Age

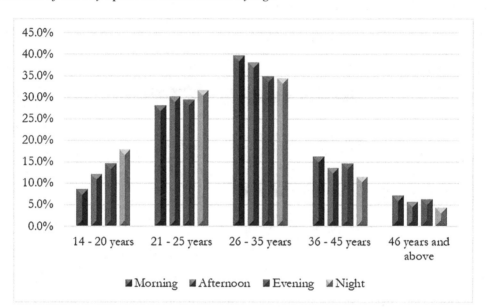

Time of Day Spent on Social Media by Geolocation

Figure 25 indicates that Kenyans residing in rural areas mostly spend their time on social media platforms at night (51.2%) and in the morning (47.3%) hours. On the other hand, Kenyans in urban areas spend most of their time on social media during the afternoon and evening hours.

RQ2: What Are the Motivations Behind Using Social Media Among Kenyans?

As indicated in Figure 26, the vast majority of Kenyans' motivations for using social media are acquiring information (31%), entertainment (28%) and social interactions (24%).

Motivations to Use Specific Social Media Platforms

Among the five motivations for using the social media platforms sought (information acquisition, entertainment, social interactions, personal identity, and escaping social realities), Facebook and WhatsApp are the mostly used for social interactions with family members, friends and connection with the outside world, while Instagram, Snapchat, and YouTube are commonly used for entertainment and pleasure (emotional experiences) and to escape societal realities (release tension, shifting attention from unpleasant happenings). On the other hand, Twitter and LinkedIn are used in creating personal identity (personal stability, social status, need for self-respect) and acquiring information (news, knowledge, exploration) as indicated in Figure 27.

Motivations to Use Specific Social Media Platforms by Different Age Groups

As shown in Figure 28, the motivations for using social media among the young people aged 14-20 years old is entertainment and pleasure (emotional experiences) while the motivations for using the internet for the 21-25 year-olds is to escape things (release tension, shifting attention from unpleasant happenings) and acquiring information (news, knowledge, exploration). For the population aged 26-35 years, the motivations to use social media are acquiring information (news, knowledge, exploration) as compared to those aged more than 36 years, whose motivations to use social media are social interactions.

Figure 25. Time of the day Spent on Social Media by Geolocation

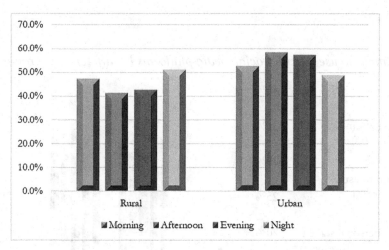

Figure 26. Motivations for using social media platforms

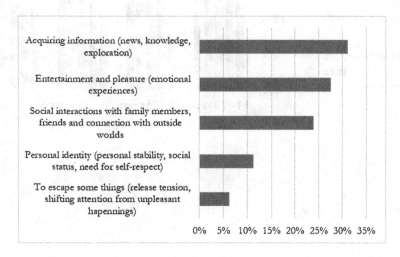

Figure 27. Motivations to use specific social media platforms

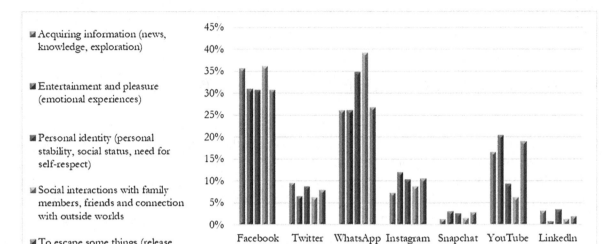

Figure 28. Motivations to use specific social media platforms by different age groups

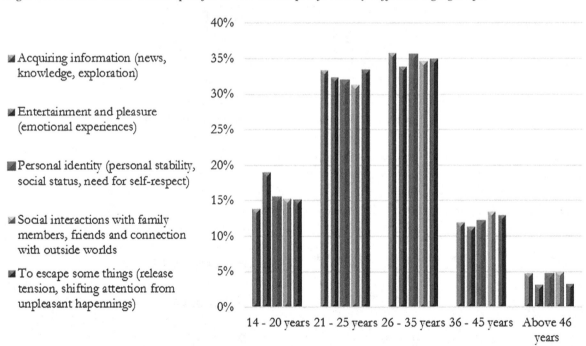

Motivations to Use Specific Social Media Platforms by Different Gender

Most men use social media for personal identity (personal stability, social status, need for self-respect) (64%), and acquiring information (news, knowledge, exploration) (62%). Kenyan women use social media to escape some things in society (release tension, shifting attention from unpleasant happenings) (44%) and entertainment and pleasure (emotional experiences) (41%), as shown in Figure 29.

Figure 29. Motivations to use specific social media platforms by different gender

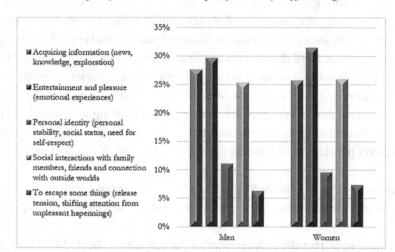

Focus Group Discussions

The study held thirty-seven focus group discussions with 258 participants in four different counties to probe participants' social media consumption. From the focus group discussions, thirteen main themes on use of internet and social media emerged: Dating (1%), Pornography (1%) Games (2%), Religion (2%), Fashion (2%), Politics (2%), Job related issues (4%), Sports (8%), Information (8%), Education (14%), Communication (15%), and Socializing (19%).

A majority of the participants indicated that at a personal level, they have experienced unpleasant experiences while using social media including fake news, cyberbullying, bombardment with graphic images of sex, and advertisements. From the focus group discussions with those aged 14-20 years and 21-25 years, the common recurring challenges associated with social media included social media being very addictive, very expensive, and time-consuming. However, the two age groups, 14-20 years and 21-25 years, also pointed out that social media creates opportunities for people to break out of boredom, to get other people's opinions on matters of interest, and to influence other people's religious beliefs.

The use of groups in social media was also a common theme among different age brackets. Social media groups are niche-specific forums where individuals share information on matters of common interest. Among the focus group discussions held in low-income areas, most social media users were members of different social media groups. The social media groups were to help the group members get updates on what is happening in their neighborhoods. One such a group is the Mathare Forum (https://web.facebook.com/Mathare-forum-773578946016362/?_rdc=1&_rdr), which had several of its members participating in three of this study's four focus group discussions held in Mathare slums. The members of social media groups such as the Mathare Forum noted that being a member of such a group is fulfilling.

Production and consumption of social media content were widespread among the focus group participants. News content consumption and contribution through social media was prevalent among the study participants. There was a high consumption of news on social media by respondents aged 26-35 years old and 36-45 years old. Video consumption and engagement on social media was the most preferred form of social media entertainment for those aged 14-20 years and 21-25 years old. Consumption of political content on social media was more common with the participants who were more than 45 years old. Among the study participants aged 14-20 years old, there were many passive consumers of social media content who were only viewing or reading social media content without contacting others or contributing.

From the focus group discussions, there was evidence of positive and negative consequences of social media content consumption. 43% of the focus group discussions' participants indicated that social media consumption has in the past influenced their actions, such as making decisions on politics, relationships and religion an indication that individuals use social media conversations to solve their life problems. The participants did draw connections between their decision making and social media consumption. The participants also indicated that creation and the consumption of social media content could lead to lose of several hours per day on less useful activities especially if one had several connections and interests online.

From the focus group discussions, two new motivations for using social media emerged. They are (i) Seeking business opportunities through social media and (ii) buying and selling on social media.

- **Seeking business opportunities:** A number of participants indicated that they use social media to reach out to potential customers and that they have been able to cultivate personal business contacts by directly messaging customers through the social media. Twenty-two study participants were using social media to promote their home businesses, to create online presence and to increase their business' visibility using Instagram, Twitter and Facebook.
- **Buying and selling on social media:** Six participants said that they have been able to directly target their customers, including their friends and followers, in a cheap and effective way and to sell their farm produce even before they harvest through Facebook and WhatsApp.

DISCUSSION

A majority of Kenyans use social media platforms on daily basis. The most commonly used social media platforms are WhatsApp, Facebook, YouTube, Instagram, LinkedIn, and Snapchat. However, the use of social media differs in platforms used by age, gender, geolocation, and levels of income. Most young Kenyans use Instagram and Snapchat while older people prefer Facebook and LinkedIn. Kenyan men use LinkedIn and Twitter while females prefer using WhatsApp and Snapchat. The people living in low-income residential areas in Nairobi use Facebook, WhatsApp, and Instagram while the residents of the middle and higher-income areas of Nairobi mostly use LinkedIn, Twitter, and YouTube. Kenyans in the rural areas mostly use Facebook, WhatsApp, and YouTube as compared to a majority of urban residents who use LinkedIn, Snapchat, Instagram, and Twitter. There are several less developed technological infrastructures in the rural areas which prevent the use of high- resource demanding social media platforms such as Snapchat and Instagram. The use of Facebook, WhatsApp, and YouTube in the rural areas could be attributed to free complimentary services offered by the telecommunications service providers.

Kenyans use social media platforms for entertainment, education, jobs, politics, sports, and social issues. LinkedIn is used for educational and job-related issues. YouTube is used for educational and entertainment issues while WhatsApp is mostly used for social issues. Facebook is mostly used for social and entertainment issues while Twitter is used for both social and political issues. More than half of the Kenyans who use WhatsApp, YouTube, Twitter, and Instagram access these platforms daily. Most of the users of these social media access the platforms using mobile phones. Most Men also access social media from cyber cafés. Most Kenyans spend 1-3 hours on social media every day. People living in urban centers access their social media platforms from their offices and public hotspots while the residents of rural areas mostly access their social media from cyber café. Most Kenyans have transitioned from accessing the internet from cyber café and offices into using mobile phones, hence most people access social media platforms at home. However, a majority of Kenyan in the rural areas and those living in low-income urban areas still value and use the services of a cyber café. Most urban population also access their social media from the offices and the public Wi-Fi. This explains why there is less activities on social media during the weekends and why most social media users post their weekend activities on Monday morning. This could be attributed to two things: One, the fact that most of the people living in urban areas are working and hence they can access the social media using the office internet; and two, in most urban areas, there is the provision and availability of open public Wi-Fi hotspots in eateries, malls and learning institutions.

Kenyans use the internet and social media platforms for dating, watching pornography, playing games, religious matters, fashion, politics, work-related issues, sports, acquiring information, education, communication, and socializing. The motivations for using social media include acquiring information, entertainment, and social interactions. Facebook and WhatsApp are the mostly used for Social interactions while Instagram, Snapchat, and YouTube are commonly used for Entertainment and to escape societal realities. Twitter and LinkedIn are used for creating a personal identity and acquiring information. Social media also influences how Kenyans make decisions on politics, relationships, and religion. Even though social media creates opportunities for people to break out of boredom, to get other people's opinions on matters of interest, and to influence other people's religious beliefs, most users have experienced unpleasant experiences such as fake news, cyberbullying, and bombardment with graphic images of sex and advertisements. Kenyans also consider social media to be addictive, expensive, and time-wasting.

CONCLUSION

This paper has provided an overview of the uses of social media platforms in Kenya and the motivations for using social media platforms among Kenyans based on diverse demographics such as age, gender, education levels, income levels, and geographical locations. The use of digital technology tends to reflect, reproduce, and amplify existing inequalities. The communities living in the rural areas and urban slums are often at a disadvantage when it comes to social media access due to infrastructural challenges such a lack of electricity and high-speed internet connectivity through the fiber cable to home or nearby rural-urban centers. This lack of infrastructure to facilitate internet and social media platforms is reflected in the number, size, and range of social media platforms accessed by the rural population, therefore, the use of social media platforms seems to reflect and amplify the existing social inequalities. But, the creation and consumption of social media content continue to be part of the Kenyan online community.

ACKNOWLEDGMENT

The author acknowledges the support of the National Research Fund, Kenya under Grant NRF/1/ MMC/418 and SIMElab Africa, a project hosted by the School of Science at USIU-Africa and funded by the US Embassy in Nairobi.

REFERENCES

Al-Menayes, J. J. (2015). Motivations for Using Social Media: An Exploratory Factor Analysis. *International Journal of Psychological Studies*, 7(1), 43–50. doi:10.5539/ijps.v7n1p43

Alhabash, S., & Ma, M. (2017). A tale of four platforms: Motivations and uses of Facebook, Twitter, Instagram, and Snapchat among college students? *Social Media+Society, 3*(1), 1-13.

Alouch, L. D. (2017). *Social Media Marketing and Business Growth of Commercial Banks in Kenya* (Master Thesis). School of Business, Department of Business Administration, University of Nairobi.

Alsalem, F. (2019). Why Do They Post? Motivations and Uses of Snapchat, Instagram and Twitter among Kuwait College Students. *Media Watch, 10*(3), 550–567. doi:10.15655/mw/2019/v10i3/49699

Ancu, M., & Cozma, R. (2009). Myspace politics: Uses and gratifications of befriending candidates. *Journal of Broadcasting & Electronic Media, 53*(4), 567–583. doi:10.1080/08838150903333064

Basak, E., & Calisir, F. (2014). Uses and Gratifications of LinkedIn: An Exploratory Study. *Proceedings of the World Congress on Engineering 2014, 2*.

Belk, R. W. (2013). Extended self in a digital world. *The Journal of Consumer Research, 40*(3), 477–500. doi:10.1086/671052

Brandtzæg, P. B., & Heim, J. (2009). Why People Use Social Networking Sites. In A. A. Ozok & P. Zaphiris (Eds.), Lecture Notes in Computer Science: Vol. 5621. *Online Communities and Social Computing. OCSC 2009*. Springer. doi:10.1007/978-3-642-02774-1_16

Church, K., & de Oliveira, R. (2013). What's up with WhatsApp?: Comparing mobile instant messaging behaviors with traditional SMS. *Proceedings of the 15th International Conference on Human-Computer Interaction with Mobile Devices and Services*, 352-361. 10.1145/2493190.2493225

Coursaris, C. K., Yun, Y., & Sung, J. (2010). *Twitter Users vs. Quitters: A Uses and Gratifications and Diffusion of Innovations approach in understanding the role of mobility in microblogging*. Paper presented at the Mobile Business and 2010 Ninth Global Mobility Roundtable (ICMB-GMR), 2010 Ninth International Conference. 10.1109/ICMB-GMR.2010.44

Dhaha, I. S. Y., & Igale, A. B. (2013). Facebook usage among Somali youth: A test of uses and gratifications approach. *International Journal of Humanities and Social Science, 3*(3), 299–313.

Greenwood, D. N. (2013). Fame, Facebook, and Twitter: How attitudes about fame predict frequency and nature of social media use. *Psychology of Popular Media Culture, 2*(4), 222–236. doi:10.1037/ppm0000013

Hanson, G., & Haridakis, P. (2008). Users Watching and Sharing the News: A Uses and Gratifications Approach. *The Journal of Electronic Publishing: JEP, 11*(3). Advance online publication. doi:10.3998/3336451.0011.305

He, W., Wang, F. K., Chen, Y., & Zha, S. (2017). An exploratory investigation of social media adoption by small businesses. *Information Technology Management, 18*(2), 149–160. doi:10.100710799-015-0243-3

Hedman, U., & Djerf-Pierre, M. (2013). The social journalist: Embracing the social media life or creating a new digital divide? *Digital Journalism, 1*(3), 368–385. doi:10.1080/21670811.2013.776804

Hou, Y., & Lampe, C. (2015, April). Social media effectiveness for public engagement: Example of small nonprofits. In *Proceedings of the 33rd annual ACM conference on human factors in computing systems* (pp. 3107-3116). 10.1145/2702123.2702557

Huang, Y., & Su, F. S. (2018). Motives for Instagram Use and Topics of Interest among Young Adults. *Future Internet, 10*, 77.

Hunt, M. G., Marx, R., Lipson, C., & Young, J. (2018). No more FOMO: Limiting social media decreases loneliness and depression. *Journal of Social and Clinical Psychology, 37*(10), 751–768. doi:10.1521/jscp.2018.37.10.751

Hwang, H. S., & Choi, E. K. (2016). Exploring Gender Differences in Motivations for Using Sina Weibo. *Transactions on Internet and Information Systems (Seoul), 10*(3), 1429–1441.

Joinson, A. M. (2008). Looking at, looking up or keeping up with people?: Motives and use of Facebook. *Proceedings of the Twenty-Sixth Annual SIGCHI Conference on Human Factors in Computing Systems 2008*, 1027-1036. 10.1145/1357054.1357213

Jung, E. H., & Sundar, S. S. (2016). Senior citizens on Facebook: How do they interact and why? *Computers in Human Behavior, 61*, 27–35. doi:10.1016/j.chb.2016.02.080

Kapoor, K. K., Tamilmani, K., Rana, N. P., Patil, P., Dwivedi, Y. K., & Nerur, S. (2018). Advances in social media research: Past, present and future. *Information Systems Frontiers, 20*(3), 531–558. doi:10.100710796-017-9810-y

Karapanos, E., Teixeira, P., & Gouveia, R. (2016). Need fulfillment and experiences on social media: A case on Facebook and WhatsApp. *Computers in Human Behavior, 55*, 888–897. doi:10.1016/j.chb.2015.10.015

Kenya Audience Research Foundation. (2020). *KARF Media Establishment Survey Highlights*. https://www.karf.or.ke/research/

Kenya National Bureau of Statistics. (2016). *Kenya Integrated Household Budget Survey (KIHBS) March 2016*. http://www.knbs.or.ke/

Klobas, J. E., McGill, T. G., Moghavvemi, S., & Paramanathan, T. (2018). Compulsive YouTube usage: A comparison of use motivation and personality effects. *Computers in Human Behavior*, *87*, 129–139. doi:10.1016/j.chb.2018.05.038

Lampe, C., Ellison, N. B., & Steinfield, C. (2006). A face(book) in the crowd: Social searching vs. Social browsing. In *Proceedings of the 2006 20th Anniversary Conference on Computer Supported Cooperative Work* (pp. 167–170). 10.1145/1180875.1180901

Lee, C. S., & Ma, L. (2011). News sharing in social media: The effects of gratifications and prior experience. *Computers in Human Behavior*, *28*(2), 331–339. doi:10.1016/j.chb.2011.10.002

Leonardi, P. M. (2015). Ambient awareness and knowledge acquisition: Using social media to learn 'who knows what' and 'who knows whom'. *Management Information Systems Quarterly*, *39*(4), 747–762. doi:10.25300/MISQ/2015/39.4.1

Lien, H. C., & Cao, Y. (2014). Examining WeChat users' motivations, trust, attitudes, and positive word-of-mouth: Evidence from China. *Computers in Human Behavior*, *41*, 104–111. doi:10.1016/j.chb.2014.08.013

Lin, J.-S., Lee, Y.-I., Jin, Y., & Gilbreath, B. (2017). Personality Traits, Motivations, and Emotional Consequences of Social Media Usage. *Cyberpsychology, Behavior, and Social Networking*, *20*(10), 615–623. doi:10.1089/cyber.2017.0043 PMID:29039699

Liu, I. L. B., Cheung, C. M. K., & Lee, M. K. O. (2010). Understanding Twitter usage: What drive people continue to tweet. PACIS 2010 Proceedings, 928–939.

Makinen, M & Kuira, W. M. (2008). Social Media and Post-Election Crisis in Kenya. *Information & Communication Technology – Africa*, 13.

Mäntymäki, M., & Islam, A. K. M. N. (2016). The Janus face of Facebook: Positive and negative sides of social networking site use. *Computers in Human Behavior*, *61*, 14–26. doi:10.1016/j.chb.2016.02.078

Marcus, S. R. (2015). 'Picturing' ourselves into being: Assessing identity, sociality and visuality on Instagram. *Proceedings of the International Communication Association Conference.*

Maxwell, M. E. (2012). *Motivations to tweet: a uses and gratifications perspective of twitter use during a natural disaster* (Master's thesis). Department of Advertising and Public Relations, University of Alabama.

Media Council of Kenya. (2016). *The Impact of Digital Technologies and Internet on Media and Journalism in Kenya*. United Nations Office at Nairobi.

Moore, C., & Chuang, L. (2017). Redditors Revealed: Motivational Factors of the Reddit Community. *Proceedings of the 50th Hawaii International Conference on System Sciences*, 2313-2322. 10.24251/HICSS.2017.279

Mull, I. R., & Lee, S. E. (2014). "PIN" pointing the motivational dimensions behind Pinterest. *Computers in Human Behavior*, *33*, 192–200. doi:10.1016/j.chb.2014.01.011

Murungi, K. M. (2018). Influence of Social Media to Community Development: Lessons from Kenya. *International Journal of Social Science and Technology*, *3*(6), 1–18.

Mwangi, M. W., & Wagok, J. (2016). Effect of Social Media on Performance of Advertisement Business in the Mainstream Media in Kenya: A Survey of Leading Media Groups in Kenya. *International Journal of Economics. Commerce and Management, IV*(4), 159–177.

Myrick, J. G. (2015). Emotion regulation, procrastination, and watching cat videos online: Who watches Internet cats, why, and to what effect? *Computers in Human Behavior, 52*, 168–176. doi:10.1016/j. chb.2015.06.001

Narula, S., & Jindal, N. (2015). Use of social network sites by AUMP students: A comparative study on Facebook, Twitter and Instagram usage. *Journal of Advanced Research, 2*(2), 20–24.

Nawaz, S. S., & Mubarak, K. M. (2015). Adoption of Social Media Marketing By Tourism Product Suppliers: A Study in Eastern Province Of Sri Lanka. *European Journal of Business and Management, 7*(7), 448–455.

Ndlela, M. N., & Mulwo, A. (2017). Social media, youth and everyday life in Kenya. *Journal of African Media Studies, 9*(2), 277–290. doi:10.1386/jams.9.2.277_1

Nendo. (2020). *Nendo 2020 Digital Report*. https://www.nendo.co.ke/2020dtr

Njeri, M. W. (2014). *Effect of Social Media Interactions on Financial Performance of Commercial Banks in Kenya* (Master Thesis). School of Business, Department of Finance, University of Nairobi.

Njoroge, C., & Koloseni, D. (2015). Adoption of Social Media as Full-Fledged Banking Channel: An Analysis of Retail Banking Customers in Kenya. *International Journal of Information and Communication Technology Research, 5*(2), 1–12.

Nyagah, V. W., Asatsa, S., & Mwania, J. M. (2015). Social Networking Sites and their Influence on the Self Esteem of Adolescents in Embu county, Kenya. *Journal of Educational Policy and Entrepreneurial Research, 2*(1), 87–92.

Nyamboga, E. N. (2014). Social Media in Kenyan Journalism: Benefits, Opportunities and Challenges. *IOSR Journal of Humanities and Social Science, 19*(12), 89–94. doi:10.9790/0837-191248994

Ogola, G. (2019). What would Magufuli do? Kenya's digital "practices" and "individuation" as a (non) political act. *Journal of Eastern African Studies: the Journal of the British Institute in Eastern Africa, 13*(1), 124–139. doi:10.1080/17531055.2018.1547263

Park, C. S. (2013). Does Twitter motivate involvement in politics? Tweeting, opinion leadership, and political engagement. *Computers in Human Behavior, 29*(4), 1641–1648. doi:10.1016/j.chb.2013.01.044

Park, N., Kee, K. F., & Valenzuela, S. B. (2009). Being immersed in social networking environment: Facebook groups, uses and gratifications, and social outcomes. *Cyberpsychology & Behavior, 12*(6), 729–733. doi:10.1089/cpb.2009.0003 PMID:19619037

Poushter, J., Bishop, C., & Chwe, H. (2018). Social media use continues to rise in developing countries but plateaus across developed ones. Pew Research Center, 22.

Rosenthal, S. (2018). Motivations to seek science videos on YouTube: Free-choice learning in a connected society. *International Journal of Science Education, 8*(1), 22–39.

Smock, A. D., Ellison, N. B., Lampe, C., & Wohn, D. Y. (2011). Facebook toolkit: A uses and gratification approach to unbundling feature use. *Computers in Human Behavior*, *27*(6), 2322–2329. doi:10.1016/j.chb.2011.07.011

Social, W. A. (2019). Global Social Media Users Pass 3.5 Billion. *Global Digital Reports*. https://wearesocial.com/blog/2019/07/global-social-media-users-pass-3-5-billion

Statista. (2018). *Social media usage in Europe - Statistics & Facts*. https://www.statista.com/topics/4106/social-media-usage-in-europe/

Tartari, E. (2015). Facebook usage among Albanian Students: A Test of uses and Gratifications Theory. *EDULEARN15 Proceedings*, 3774-3779.

Tully, M., & Ekdale, B. (2014). Sites of playful engagement: Twitter hashtags as spaces of leisure and development in Kenya. *Information Technologies and International Development*, *10*(3), 67–82.

Wamuyu, P. K. (2017). Closing the digital divide in low-income urban communities: A domestication approach. *Interdisciplinary Journal of e-Skills and Lifelong Learning, 13,* 117-142.

Wamuyu, P. K. (2018). Leveraging Web 2.0 technologies to foster collective civic environmental initiatives among low-income urban communities. *Computers in Human Behavior*, *85*, 1–14. doi:10.1016/j.chb.2018.03.029

Whiting, A., & Williams, D. (2013). Why people use social media: A uses and gratifications approach. *Qualitative Market Research*, *16*(4), 362–369. doi:10.1108/QMR-06-2013-0041

Young, J. A. (2017). Facebook, Twitter, and blogs: The adoption and utilization of social media in nonprofit human service organizations. *Human Service Organizations, Management, Leadership & Governance*, *41*(1), 44–57. doi:10.1080/23303131.2016.1192574

Zhang, L., & Pentina, I. (2012). Motivations and Usage Patterns of Weibo. *Cyberpsychology, Behavior, and Social Networking*, *6*(15), 312–317. doi:10.1089/cyber.2011.0615 PMID:22703037

This research was previously published in Analyzing Global Social Media Consumption; pages 88-120, copyright year 2021 by Information Science Reference (an imprint of IGI Global).

Chapter 45
What Are Basketball Fans Saying on Twitter?
Evidence From Euroleague Basketball's Final Four Event

Burçin Güçlü
Universitat Romon Llull, Spain

Marcela Garza
Universitat Ramon Llull, Spain

Christopher Kennett
Universitat Ramon Llull, Spain

ABSTRACT

Social media receives growing interest from sports executives. Yet, very little is known about how to make use of such user-generated, unstructured data. By exploring tweets generated during Turkish Airlines Euroleague's Final Four event, which broadcasted the four tournaments of championship among four finalist teams, the authors studied how fans respond to gains and losses and how engaged they were during games through the course of the event. The authors found that favorable reactions were received when teams won, but the magnitude of unfavorable reaction was larger when teams lost. When it came to the organizer rather than the teams, the organizer of the event received most of the positive feedback. The authors also found that main source of tweets was smartphones while tablets were not among real-time feedback devices.

DOI: 10.4018/978-1-6684-6307-9.ch045

INTRODUCTION

Society is connected on a global scale by digital communications. By year 2015, there were 3.5 billion Internet users and over 50% of the adult population around the world are said to be smartphone users (Castells, 2016). By 2017, 31% of the world's population (more than 2.3 billion people) were active social media users (Leaders, 2017).

The global population is consuming media in different ways. For instance, over the past decade the use of computers for internet access has declined rapidly and a shift to instant access through mobile devices like smartphones and tablets has occurred. For this reason, industries are adapting to new distribution channels to keep up with consumer tendencies, including the sports industry. This has led the sports ecosystem to experience dramatic changes, enabling the creation of new communication networks through emerging technologies (De Moragas et al, 2013).

How sport is watched and consumed has been disrupted in the digital era and continues to change due to technology and the emergence of various new direct-to-customer distribution channels. Fans can engage with a sports event without the need to be at venue or even watch it on television. With the advent of live or delayed streaming, instant messaging, the ability to maintain conversations in real time on social media platforms, the opportunity to review large amounts of statistics online and through applications, has created new, more complex multi-directional communication processes. These sports conversations are now happening 'on-the-go' through mobile devices and across geographic boarders on a global scale.

Social media channels receive growing interest from sports executives, politicians, and companies where the opinions of fans, voters and investors matter respectively. Given that social media allow users to build networks in an easy and timely way and to share various kinds of information (photos, videos, texts, links etc), they form an excellent platform for real-time feedback, opinion sharing and to observe fan engagement.

Social media channels have become increasing important for marketing communication because they are instant, have a global reach, are simple to use and require minimal bandwidth and device capability (Abeza et al, 2015). They have become an essential marketing tool in recent years, allowing managers, marketers, and users to interact and share information instantaneously. Advertisers use social media in sport events to generate valuable leads, get immediate feedback, post messages in real time and with the possibility to create viral effects through sharing (Beech et al, 2014). A leading example from sports is the NBA where teams provide information and content through their social media channels, while promoting their team and events, aiming to interact with their fans to receive feedback and increase the probabilities of engagement (Meng, Stavros, & Westberg, 2015).

In collaborative social media platforms such as Facebook, Instagram, Twitter or any other social media platform that allow fans to create, publish, edit or share content. Fans become co-creators of the content that is been shared, generating interactivity and increasing fans' involvement in what is happening at around the live event. Interactive content turns the fan into an active user, increasing the capacity to collaborate and manage the flow of information (Beech et al, 2014; De Moragas et al, 2013; Meng et al., 2015).

Among social media platforms, Twitter is a social networking and micro-blogging service that allows its users post real time messages and multimedia content (Kumar & Kalwani, 2012). Since Twitter was created in 2006 it has been increasingly recognized by marketing and advertisement executives as a key tool in social media-based communication campaigns, embracing the use of hashtags to share thematic content and reach diluted groups of fans with common interests (Delia & Armstrong, 2015).Twitter has become one of the most important social networks for sharing sport stories, enabling customized content to segmented target audiences, connecting fragmented audiences with other users with similar interests, helping disseminate information.

Although Twitter provides an excellent channel for fan engagement, given facilitated opinion creation and presentation, it brings newer and different challenges for researchers analyzing this content and attempting to understand its meaning. At the time of writing the 350m active Twitter users were generating around 6,000 tweets per second, creating large amounts of potential data for analysis.

While several studies explore the use of social media platforms such as Twitter around sports events, there is very limited analysis to date on the meaning of this content. By exploring tweets generated during Euroleague Basketball's Turkish Airlines Final Four event, which includes semi-finals, third and fourth place game and the championship game all played over a single weekend, the authors studied how fans respond to winning and losing, the key content in their conversations and how engaged they are during games through the course of the event. In the next section, the authors conduct a literature review. This is followed by an explanation of the research methods, results and findings, and discuss the implications of their work in the context of big data and virtual organizations. Finally, they discuss the implications and some possible directions for further research.

LITERATURE REVIEW

Fan Engagement

Sports events host an exciting mix of drama, emotion and information that attract very loyal customers: sports fans. The need to engage sports fans in meaningful ways has been an ongoing focus of sports marketing research.

The role of technology in fan engagement has become increasing important in the digital era. Geographical barriers can be crossed by online tools and social media networks creating opportunities for sport marketers to enhance engagement of fans by creating online experiences on a worldwide basis (Parganas, Anagnostopoulos, & Chadwick, 2015).

The Beijing 2008 Olympic Games was one of the first sports event where the use of digital technology enhanced successful engagement of fans from all around the world despite the geographic distance (IOC, 2009). Today, sports events such as the Olympic Games and FIFA World Cup reach large live audiences and clearly defined customer segments as part of wider marketing and communication strategies (Adıgüzel & Kennett, 2017).

Fan engagement can be achieved around a sport event time in several ways such as through the event itself, the players, the club, the venue, the media, sponsors and advertisers, online content such as websites or social media, gambling, fantasy sports, and electronic games (Foster et al, 2016).

Sports events generate conversations and sports fans seek for information and entertainment in online sources. Fans want to be informed of game results, statistics or any sports related news even without watching a game or attending to a venue. Thanks to the fragmentation of the audiences, sport marketers have had enable more choices for following sports events to allow a greater audience viewing and engagement such as watching a game on television, through online streaming or following it in social media networks (Smith & Smith, 2012).

Social media as a platform has been key to engage fans during the last decade. Sports marketers have increasingly invested time and resources to create new strategies to drive online engagement of fans enabling real-time communications and interactions (Meng et al., 2015; Smith & Smith, 2012) transforming their relationship from a passive message communication to an active message consumption, aiming to achieve the highest level of engagement by driving the fans into a participative action where they become co-creators (Vale & Fernandes, 2018) by producing and sharing their own content (Smith & Smith, 2012). Furthermore, thanks to social media networks, fans that are engaged and involved with an event, creating and sharing content, can turn into promoters of the event giving more opportunities for sports marketers to reach a bigger audience. In this matter, sports marketers and advertisers can take advantage of this behavior and communicate directly with different groups of fans through social media.

Twitter as a Fan Engagement Platform

Twitter is a social media tool that allows interaction and conversation in real-time (N. M. Watanabe, Yan, & Soebbing, 2016; Price, Farrington, & Hall, 2013; Smith & Smith, 2012). It is a platform where information such as news, opinions or up-dates are continuously shared and in a faster way than other media tools (Gibbs, O'Reilly, & Brunette, 2014). Sports leagues, teams, athletes, brands, and media aim to engage fans by developing marketing and communication strategies in Twitter. Fan engagement through Twitter can be achieved and maintained with different strategies such as communicating news, updates, or sharing live content during events (Gibbs et al., 2014), by creating marketing and communication strategies with the use of hashtags (Delia & Armstrong, 2015; Meng et al., 2015) which facilitate fans to filter, follow and participate in conversations by connecting them in virtual communities related to a specific topic but with a wider scope (Smith & Smith, 2012), by having quick interactions from sports social media manages such as click as "favorite" a user's post on Twitter (N. M. Watanabe et al, 2016), or conducting activation activities such as trivia competitions (Meng et al., 2015).

By 2013, Twitter was considered as the "most influential social media platform in sport" (Gibbs & Haynes, 2013). Later, Parganas and colleagues (2015) cite different authors that mention that sports was the highlighted conversation in Twitter with more than 40% of all tweets being sports related, especially during live events. By June 2018, Euroleague Basketball had more than 1.75 million followers in their main social media channels (Facebook, Twitter, Instagram and YouTube), almost 30% (507 thousand followers) from their Twitter account alone.

Twitter gives fans the possibility to have an active role in the online conversation through different actions such as tweeting, re-tweeting, replying, or marking as favorite other people's tweets (Parganas et al., 2015), always with the possibility of sharing their content with fans beyond their network by the use of hashtags (Smith & Smith, 2012). Twitter has become an essential tool for proliferating sports content, multiplying sports consumers' participation thanks to the real-time interaction and access to teams or athletes (N. Watanabe et al., 2015).

Even though sports marketers use Twitter as a strategic platform of engagement to connect with fans having the hashtags as a tool to identify an event or a specific topic, fan engagement strategies can be improved by knowing the fans, their motivations and actions when they actively participate in social media conversations by sharing information, cheering or criticizing a sport event, player or club. The volume of data generated around sports events creates a wealth of data for researchers to analyze and attempt to understand, and has involved the design of new methodologies and research tools amongst scholars.

Tweet Analysis

The most common methods to evaluate tweets are word clouds and sentiment analysis, A word cloud is a visual representation of word frequency (Atenstaedt, 2012). The more commonly a word appears within the raw text being analyzed, the larger the word appears in the image generated. Word clouds are increasingly being employed as a simple tool to identify the core content of, as well as to better understand the themes covered in written material, and to sketch the domains to which they pertain (Halevi & Moed, 2012).

Despite its wide use in text mining, word clouds should be interpreted with certain caveats. They often fail to group words that have the same or similar meaning. As they tend to focus only on single word frequency, they also do not identify phrases, reducing context.

In the current research, word clouds have been applied to analyze the content of tweets with specified hashtags to see whether sufficient attention is being given to the players, coaches, organization, sponsors and games and to identify outstanding factors other than the aforementioned ones.

Besides being a platform where sport marketers and advertisers can share information, Twitter is a tool where people also can share their emotions and opinions or 'sentiment'. In the sports context, Twitter can be considered a repository of emotional exchanges allowing fans to have conversations among other fans, the media or athletes (Smith & Smith, 2012).

Sports events evoke emotions in fans (Gratch et al., 2015), but fans have different levels of fandom and passion that are expressed in different ways. There are fans that cheer for their team attending to their games in a regular basis, others may prefer following their team or athlete by watching the games on television (Samra & Wos, 2014), while others will review stats and comments on social media.

Levels of fandom can be categorized in several rankings, for example Meng and colleagues (2015) mention Sutton et al (1997) who ranked fans by their level of identification in: Social fans, focused fans and vested fans; or Samra and Wos (2014) fan types classification in: temporary fan, devoted fan and fanatical fan. Each rank with specific characteristics and behaviors. It is worth noting, however, that not all sports spectators are as fans.

For sport marketers and advertisers, understanding the fans, their motivations, behavior and how they express their emotions and sentiments, can provide insights that can help to plan and execute a successful marketing campaign in social media.

Several authors agree that the uses and gratification theory is one theory that can be applied as an example to explain why people, in this case fans, use social media as a channel to satisfy human needs such as expressing their feelings and opinions joining conversations that give them the opportunity to interact with a wider audience (Santomier, Hogan, & Kunz, 2016). Other identified reasons of using social media are showing affection or negative feelings, recognition and personal identity, integration, entertainment, information seeking or sharing, and relaxation (Santomier et al., 2016; Vale & Fernandes, 2018).

A highly engaged fan is more likely to adopt an active behavior in social media (Browning & Sanderson, 2012). Twitter is nowadays a key platform where fans can express their identity and sentiment, positive or negative, towards a team, club or a specific athlete. Content in Twitter becomes interactive, co-created by the sports marketers and the fans, establishing a new level of engagement where fans aim to be heard, increasing the possibility of enhancing identification and loyalty with their team or athlete (Meng et al., 2015; Vale & Fernandes, 2018).

Greater reach in sports events is accompanied with greater fan engagement in a larger geographical context, which complicates tracking of fan engagement. Highly involved fans engage with the event experience: they use more media and longer hours to follow the games/league, they attend games more than regular sport audience; they read about sports or they practice sports (Shank & Beasley, 1998). This indicates that highly engaged fans use more social media and dispose more positive sentiments towards their teams and games.

Fan engagement can be measured in different ways and in this study refers to the total sentiments score. More recently, there have been several research projects that apply sentiment analysis to Twitter corpora in order to extract general public opinion (for a recent example, see Kim & Youm, 2017). Sentiment Analysis intends to comprehend these public opinions and distribute them into the categories like positive, negative, neutral with respect to opinion lexicons.

MAIN FOCUS OF THE CHAPTER

Fans in Silicon Valley expect more from their sports venues, and last season we scored big with our fans on innovation and engagement at the highest level. We're looking forward to partnering with Avaya to deliver even more value this season and give fans a connected, social and immersive experience unlike any other. – Dave Kaval, President of the San Jose Earthquakes

Technology is rapidly changing and shaping not only the business practices, but also the daily routines. Media coverage based solely on the game is not enough for demanding fans anymore. Sports facilities adapt to the challenges of big data by enabling more built-in data collection processes, such as high-powered wifi technologies and clouds to gather and store data from sport fans.

Despite the common conception on disruptive use of mobile phones, sports fans make use of their smart phones in order to receive real-time feedback during the different phases of the game (Lisi, 2016). As an example, Avaya Stadium in San Jose has taken a step forward by allowing fans during games the ability to get player stats as well as buy tickets and connect to social media through the Stadium App in their mobile phones (O'Connell, 2016). This is part of a broader trend in smart stadiums and it is a matter of time that the same cloud technology will become the norm at all MLS venues in United States and be exported to other sports facilities and geographic regions.

The Avaya Stadium Mobile app gives fans the opportunity to get connected to the fan experience by providing everything they need to know about their team San José Earthquakes. To be more specific, it provides a digital experience from before the game to all the way through the final seconds of the game. As a part of this unique opportunity, the stadium app contains multiple game day experiences, including a fan engagement wall, which displays fans' social media updates and other content in real time. Moreover, there are live polls and special offers, as well as information about other issues like parking, concessions and merchandise. The app also includes Quakes Digital Player Cards, fan trivia and fun facts, which allow fans to chat and post directly during a game. There are customized social media streams and information about tickets. A Wi-Fi service is powered by Avaya to make sure fans do not run into Internet malfunctions, no matter the size of the crowd. Cloud-based technologies are also implemented with "Fanalytics," a data analytics about fans' interests and activities.

METHODS

The dataset analysed in this study contains 892,852 tweets collected between May 18th and May 22nd 2017, both days inclusive, using hashtags associated with the Turkish Airlines Final Four teams and Euroleague Basketball. The four participating teams were Real Madrid, Fenerbahçe Doğuş, CSKA Moscow and Olympiacos BC, and the Final Four event took place in Istanbul from May 19-21, 2017.

The programming of the data collection and most of the analysis were done by using twitteR package in R, which provides an interface to the Twitter web API. Twitter provides free access to a sample of the public tweets posted on the platform. The platform's precise sampling method is not known, but the data available through twitteR is a good representative of the overall global public communication on Twitter at any given time (citation needed). In order to get the most complete and relevant data set, we consulted with Euroleague Basketball, and identified relevant hashtags and languages used in tweets. The following hashtags were selected for our analysis: #F4Glory, #Fener4Glory, #WeareOlympiacos, #RMBaloncesto, and #CSKAbasket. Fan engagement and use of native language required a greater variety of hashtags related to particular teams and basketball context. Thus, our sampling strategy might have missed some additional minor hashtags that referred to small or short lived conversations about particular people or issues, including tweets that may not have used our identified hashtags at all.

Selecting tweets based on hashtags has the advantage of capturing the content most likely to be about this important sport event. twitteR yields tweets which contain the keyword or the hashtag. The variables generated automatically by this package are (1) text of the tweet, (2) whether it is favorited or not, (3) number of times the tweet is favorited, (4) posted time, (5) user id, (6) whether the tweet is retweeted, (7) number of times the tweet is retweeted, (8) source of the tweet as an HTTP link, (9) user name, (10) user coordinates as latitude, and (11) user coordinates as longitude.

The method counted tweets with selected hashtags in a simple manner. Each tweet counted as one if it contained one of the specific hashtags that were being followed. If a tweet contained more than one selected hashtag, it was credited to all the relevant hashtag categories.

Contributions using none of these hashtags were not captured in this data set. It is also possible that users who used one or more of these hashtags, but were not discussing the Final Four games, had their tweets captured. Moreover, if people tweeted about the Final Four games, but did not use one of these hashtags or identify a candidate account, their contributions were not analyzed here.

Regarding the sentiment analysis, we used both a corpus based technique and a dictionary based technique (Kumar & Sebastian, 2012). We built a corpus, which is a large and structured set of text data, and preprocessed the corpus using the following standard procedures (Weiss et al., 2005). To be more specific, we first prepared the corpus by cleaning up sentences with R's regex-driven global substitute from punctuation, URLs (www), hashtags (#), targets (@) and Tweeter-specific notation (RT). Later, we converted the entire text to small caps and finally split the corpus into words. This enabled the generation of word clouds without any additional process. In order to rate the sentiment of a tweet, we defined two dictionaries which consisted of positive words and negative words lists respectively (Hu & Liu, 2004; Liu, Hu, & Cheng, 2005). The purpose of the algorithm was to assign 1 if a word was either encountered in positive words dictionary or negative words dictionary, and N/A if otherwise. We finally compared our words to the dictionaries of positive and negative terms and obtained the sum of positive and negative matches respectively. Subtracting the sum of positive matches from negative matches would return the sentiment score, which would be a positive number, negative number, or zero.

RESULTS

The communication carried out on Twitter had important characteristics. First of all, tweets in Turkish exceeded tweets in English, the common language used among basketball fans in Europe. On the other hand, the tweets in other native languages (Greek, Spanish and Russian) were far less in numbers. Consequently, the tweets in Turkish and English accounted for the greatest share of activity. Table 1 summarizes the number of tweets per hashtag in English and native languages per day.

Table 1. Number of tweets per hashtag in English and native languages per day

Hashtag	Language	May 18th	May 19th	May 20th	May 21st	May 22nd	Total
#F4Glory	Turkish	4323	49946	14614	69037	8207	146127
#Fener4Glory	Turkish	17744	168457	46034	361300	49898	643433
#F4Glory	English	1374	10923	2702	28453	6267	49719
#Fener4Glory	English	2359	9419	1048	23854	2838	39518
#WeareOlympiacos	English	148	486	118	447	43	1242
#RMBaloncesto	English	40	228	85	118	4	475
#CSKAbasket	English	45	116	10	26	2	199
#WeareOlympiacos	Greek	314	3760	538	1976	110	6698
#RMBaloncesto	Spanish	509	3403	637	795	33	5377
#CSKAbasket	Russian	4	32	2	24	5	67

The authors analyzed the discussion on Twitter in terms of (1) number of tweets in native language of Fenerbahçe (Turkish), (2) number of tweets per team in English, (3) number of tweets in native language of Olympiacos, Real Madrid, and CSKA (Greek, Spanish and Russian respectively), (4) the preferred means of communication for Turkish and international fans, and (5) sentiment analysis.

Regarding the number of tweets, the highest number of tweets was extracted from Turkish fans using #Fener4Glory hashtag in Turkish. Overall, Turkish fans tweeted for their team Fenerbahçe 643,433 times in Turkish during the span of the event. Not surprisingly, the second highest number of tweets was also extracted from Turkish fans using #F4Glory hashtag in Turkish. In total, Turkish fans tweeted for Final Four 146,127 times during the span of the event. Figure 1 summarizes the number of tweets for #Fener4Glory and #F4Glory hashtags per day in Turkish.

Regarding the number of tweets in English, the highest number of tweets was extracted from #F4Glory hashtag. In the international context, Final Four had been tweeted 49,719 times in English during the span of the event. Not surprisingly, the second highest number of tweets was extracted from #Fener4Glory hashtag with a total of 39,518 times in English during the span of the event. Compared to the aforementioned activities, Twitter activity corresponding to other teams was drastically lower. To be more specific, #WeareOlympiacos, #RMBaloncesto and #CSKABasket had been tweeted only 1242, 475 and 199 times respectively in the international context. Figure 2 summarizes the number of tweets per hashtag per day in English.

Figure 1. Number of tweets for #Fener4Glory and #F4Glory in Turkish

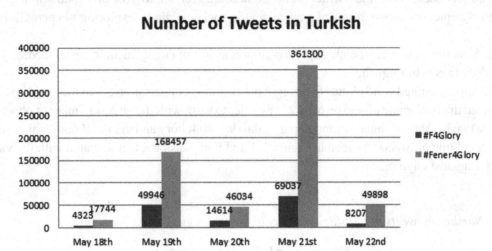

Figure 2. Number of tweets per hashtag per day in English

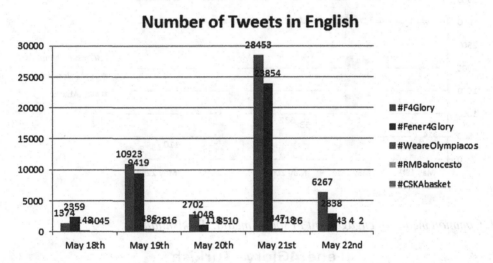

Given the low engagement of the international fans, the authors decided to conduct the same analysis for the native language of each team. Regarding the number of tweets in native language, the highest number of tweets was extracted from Greek fans using #WeareOlympiacos hashtag in Greek. Surprisingly, #WeareOlympiacos tweets in Greek outnumbered #WeareOlympiacos tweets in English, such that the former consists of 6696 tweets while the latter consists of 1242 tweets. Twitter activity concerned with #RMBaloncesto in Spanish context was lower with a total of 5377 tweets while Twitter activity concerned with #CSKABasket in Russian was lowest with 67 tweets in total. Figure 3 summarizes the number of tweets per hashtag per day in native languages of the teams.

The authors identified the common means of engagement in social media by looking at the source of the tweet. We found that the engagement pattern was same for both Turkish and international fans: Smart phones (IPhone and Android) apps account for 85% of the sources of tweets, underlining the importance of real-time feedback, while the Twitter webpage accounts for 7% to 10% and Ipad app accounts for 1%. Figure 4 depicts common means of engagement in social media by exploring #Fener4Glory tweets in Turkish.

Figure 5, on the other hand, below depicts common means of engagement in social media by exploring #F4Glory tweets in English.

The authors generated word clouds to observe the common conversation about the event. We specifically selected the final game played on May 21st in order to work with the largest number of observations. There were two hashtags of interest for that particular day, #F4Glory and #Fener4Glory which generated the highest volume of tweets. As seen in Figure 6, Final Four was largely associated with the victory of Fenerbahçe against Olympiacos.

Figure 3. Number of tweets per hashtag per day in native language

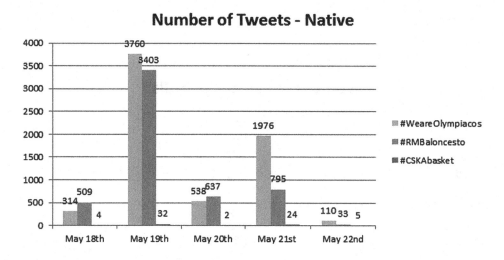

Figure 4. Common means of engagement in social media: Turkish fans

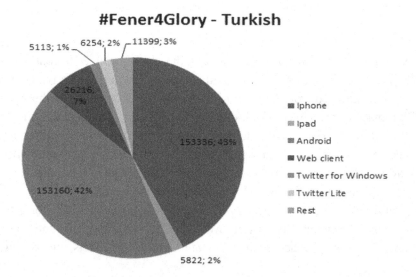

Figure 5. Common means of engagement in social media: International fans

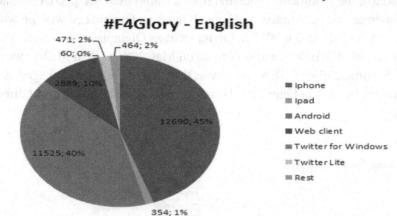

#F4Glory - English

- Iphone
- Ipad
- Android
- Web client
- Twitter for Windows
- Twitter Lite
- Rest

471; 2%
464; 2%
60; 0%
2889; 10%
12690; 45%
11525; 40%
354; 1%

Figure 6. Word Cloud for #F4Glory

Figure 7, on the other hand, indicates that Fenerbahçe's victory was largely associated with the city where the Final Four tournaments were organized – Istanbul, and the star player Bobby Dixon.

The authors quantified the sentiment inherent in tweets by applying the aforementioned algorithm and accounted for the total sentiment generated per hashtag per day. We found that the highest sentiment was generated #F4Glory hashtag, created by Euroleague Basketball as the event organizers. As seen in Figure 8, a sharp increase in sentiment was observed on the day of the games while a phase-out was observed post-games.

The authors also looked at how positive, negative and neutral sentiments evolved over the course of the game. In order to carry out this analysis, we counted positive, negative and neutral sentiments, and plotted each of these sentiments separately. As seen in Figure 9, the dominant sentiment was neutral in the beginning of the event, but positive sentiment climbed up drastically during the course of the event. The potential for sports events to generate a 'feel good' factor among fans in general was evident.

When they looked at the sentiments generated from a team-based perspective, the authors observed that the highest sentiment was generated by #Fener4Glory, as Fenerbahçe was the winner of the cup. Second highest sentiment belonged to #WeareOlympiacos as Olympiacos ranked second in Final Four. There was an increase in #RMBaloncesto sentiment on May 20th as Real Madrid won the third-place game on that day. Sentiment score CSKA was low as their fans were not as engaged as other teams' on Twitter. The results can be seen in Figure 10. Therefore, performance on the court directly affected the sentiment of fans.

Figure 7. Word Cloud for #Fener4Glory

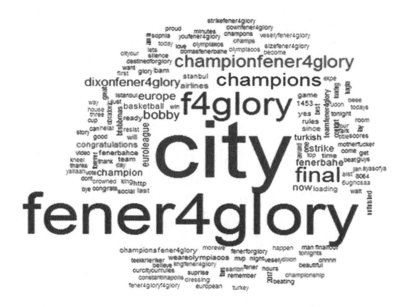

Figure 8. Evolution of #F4Glory sentiment over the event

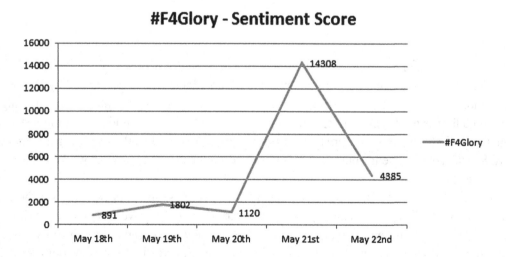

Figure 9. Evolution of #F4Glory sentiment polarity over the event

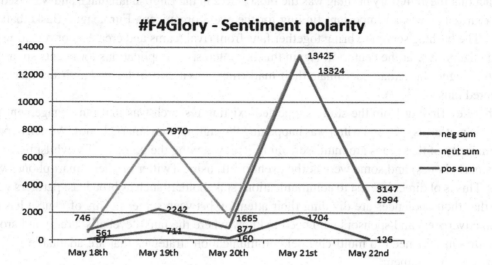

Figure 10. Evolution of team sentiments over the event

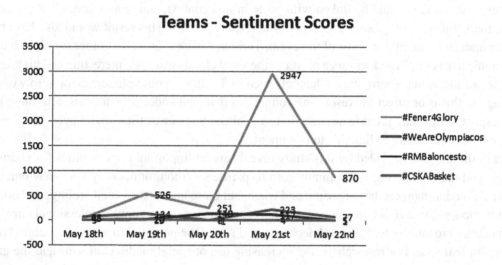

DISCUSSION

Whilst fan sentiment varies between fan groups depending largely on how their teams are performing, the overall effect of the event is positive and a general 'feel good' factor occurred in Twitter around the event. This is important for all major marketing and communications stakeholders involved in the event. For event sponsors it is important to know that whilst fan rivalries are played out on the court between teams from different geographic markets, the positive sentiment around the event transcends this. Advertisers would be interested to know how the fans are feeling in real time and how this fluctuates during a game and between games. Digital advertising tools enable advertisers to adjust their tactics in response to these changes, focusing on certain fan groups and adapting their messages accordingly to fit the mood.

The fact that the #F4Glory hashtag was the most active in the English language and was used by fans from all four teams an important finding for the event organizers, Euroleague Basketball as they created it. The hashtag served to bring together fans from rival teams and create a conversation that the event organizers were at the center of. Again this has interesting implications for events sponsors with whom Euroleague Basketball coordinate their marketing activities as it formed a virtual meeting point that gathered fans.

Another key finding from the study supported existing research was that fan engagement through social media platforms such as Twitter was happening through apps on smart phones. We can hypothesize that the majority of these fans are multi-screening (e.g. watching the game on TV whilst using Twitter on their smart phones) and some were at the event itself, using Twitter on their smart phones whilst at the arena. This is of direct interest to communications stakeholders such as broadcast partners who need to know that their audiences are dividing their attention between screens. This of course has a direct impact on advertisers and sponsors who need to know where the fans' 'eyeballs' are in and around the game, reinforcing the need to multi-channel communication strategies that are adaptable in real-time depending on fan sentiment.

In terms of the most used words and concepts used by fans, a surprising and interesting result was the prevalence of Istanbul as the host city and home to the eventual champions. The importance of place and identity among fans could be linked with pride in this context, and would have clear implications for place marketing (city, region or country) through sports events. This result would also have been of particular interest to the title sponsor of the event, Turkish Airlines, as well as other sponsors interested in geographic marketing. The focus on a player in the word clouds was also interesting and highlights the importance of individual sports stars. Channels such as Twitter become platforms for hero worshiping and yet again, this is of direct interest to the companies that sign endorsement deals with these players and the exposure this may provide not only in terms of the number of times the player was mentioned by fans, but also the ability to link this to sentiment.

Overall, the insights provided by this study reveal several important opportunities for sports event organisers and their marketing and communications partners to monitor not only fan behaviour, such as which social media channels they are using and when, but more importantly their feelings and how these are communicated through interactions with other fans. Such insights enable professionals involved in sports marketing to take better informed decisions and reveal the potential to adapt their digital marketing tactics in real time. For researchers, the increasing use of social media platforms and the growing volume of contents on them represent an unprecedented opportunity to engage in big data analysis in contexts such as sports events, and to better understand the nature and meanings of fan interactions in digital environments. This type of analysis requires new methodologies and the design of new methods to capture and analyse this data, and for researchers to undertake exploratory studies such as the one discussed in this chapter.

FUTURE RESEARCH DIRECTIONS

We see data as inevitable coming into the game. – Jeff Agoos, Vice-President for Competition at Major League Soccer (MLS)

Word cloud and sentiment analysis bring new data to the game. Live sentiment analysis is a future line of practice to check the moods of the fans pre / during / post – game. This motivated us to propose a model that retrieves tweets, calculates the sentiment orientation/score of each tweet and publishes in real-time. This recent trend for research for sentiment analysis in Twitter can be utilized and extended for many practical applications that range from applications in marketing (person marketing, event marketing), customer relationship management (customer segmentation, loyalty tracking), applications in sponsorship (sponsorship effectiveness), applications in digital media (content management, mobile app management). For example, there are new ways for fans to quantify a players' performance such as sharing of data about players in real time, even going far enough to have these data displayed on players' jersey (Lisi, 2016). The model we propose would be just another technological innovation that could make its way to fans when they watch a game on television.

Digitalization and the increasing use of social media by fans means that big data is being generated around sports events, creating an unprecedented opportunity to analyze and understand fan interaction and the nature of fan engagement. The proposed model of live sentiment analysis responds to how to make use of big data in the context of sports management and fan engagement, and how the increasing amount of data improves decision-making and fosters innovation through effective knowledge sharing practices. This model is therefore an answer to how big data in the context of sports management enhances progress and organizational performance.

CONCLUSION

Continuous monitoring is required for a multi-channel strategy, which would need to be channel-specific, team-specific, game cycle-specific and result and performance-specific. Regarding channel-specific, the authors looked at the communication on Twitter only. Regarding team-specific, the authors looked at how the number of tweets and sentimental performance changed for each team. Regarding game cycle-specific, we explored Final Four event-cycle and looked at how the number of tweets and sentimental performance changed with respect to important games. The last but not the least, the authors looked at how game results boost tweets in a performance-specific monitoring.

This comprehensive study aims to be an essential reference source for the use of Twitter data in the context of fan engagement, building on the available literature in the field of sports management while providing for further research opportunities in big data and sports management.

ACKNOWLEDGMENT

The authors thank Turkish Airlines Euroleague Basketball in Barcelona, Spain for guidance in this research project. This research received no specific grant from any funding agency in the public, commercial, or not-for-profit sectors.

REFERENCES

Abeza, G., Pegoraro, A., Naraine, M. L., & Séguin, B., & O'Reilly, N. (2015). Activating a global sport sponsorship with social media: An analysis of TOP sponsors, Twitter, and the 2014 Olympic Games. *International Journal of Sport Management and Marketing*, *154*(34), 184–213. doi:10.1504/IJSMM.2014.072010

Adıgüzel, F., & Kennett, C. (2017). *Sport event sponsorship effectiveness: A cross-cultural study*. Working Paper.

Atenstaedt, R. (2012). Word cloud analysis of the BJGP. *The British Journal of General Practice*, *62*(596), 148. doi:10.3399/bjgp12X630142 PMID:22429422

Beech, J., Kaiser, S., & Kaspar, R. (2014). *The Business of Events Management*. Pearson Education Limited.

Browning, B., & Sanderson, J. (2012). The positives and negatives of Twitter: Exploring how student-athletes use Twitter and respond to critical Tweets. *International Journal of Sport Communication*, *5*(4), 503–521. doi:10.1123/ijsc.5.4.503

Castells, M. (2016). A sociology of power: My intellectual journey. *Annual Review of Sociology*, *42*(1), 1–19. doi:10.1146/annurev-soc-081715-074158

De Moragas, M., Kennett, C., & Ginesta, X. (2013). Football and media in Europe. New sport paradigm for the global era. In Sport and the Transformation of Modern Europe. States, Media and Markets 1950-2010. London: Routledge.

Delia, E. B., & Armstrong, C. G. (2015). #Sponsoring the #FrenchOpen: An examination of social media buzz and sentiment. *Journal of Sport Management*, *29*(2), 184–199. doi:10.1123/JSM.2013-0257

Earthquakes, S. J. (2018). *Avaya Stadium - First cloud-enabled stadium in MLS*. Retrieved from https://sanjose-mp7static.mlsdigital.net/elfinderimages/170712_avaya_stadium_infographic_b_print_8-5x11.jpeg

Foster, G., O'Reilly, N., & Davila, A. (2016). *Sports Business Management: Decision Making Around the Globe*. Routledge. doi:10.4324/9781315687827

Gibbs, C., & Haynes, R. (2013). A phenomenological investigation into how Twitter has changed the nature of sport media relations. *International Journal of Sport Communication*, *6*(4), 394–408. doi:10.1123/ijsc.6.4.394

Gibbs, C., O'Reilly, N., & Brunette, M. (2014). Professional Team Sport and Twitter: Gratifications Sought and Obtained by Followers. *International Journal of Sport Communication*, *7*(2), 188–213. doi:10.1123/IJSC.2014-0005

Gratch, J., Lucas, G., Malandrakis, N., Szablowski, E., Fessler, E., & Nichols, J. (2015). GOAALLL!: Using Sentiment in the World Cup to Explore Theories of Emotion. *International Conference on Affective Computing and Intelligent Interaction (ACII)*, 898-903. 10.1109/ACII.2015.7344681

Halevi, G., & Moed, H. F. (2012, September). *The technological impact of library science research.* Paper presented at the 17th International Conference on Science and Technology Indicators (STI), Montreal, Quebec, Canada.

Hu, M., & Liu, B. (2004). Mining and summarizing customer reviews. *Proceedings of the ACM SIGKDD International Conference on Knowledge Discovery and Data.*

International Olympic Committee (IOC). (2009). *Games of the XXIX Olympiad, Beijing 2008 Global Television and Online Media Report.* IOC.

Kim, E. H., & Youm, Y. N. (2017). How do social media affect analyst stock recommendations? Evidence from S&P 500 electric power companies' Twitter accounts. *Strategic Management Journal, 38*(13), 2599–2622. doi:10.1002mj.2678

Kumar, I., & Sebastian, T. M. (2012). Sentiment Analysis on Twitter. *International Journal of Computer Science Issues, 9*(4-3), 372-378.

Leaders, R. (2017). *OTT - The shifting broadcasting landscape.* Retrieved from leadersinsport.com

Lisi, C. (2016). *Soccer's high-tech future.* Retrieved from https://ussoccerplayers.com/2016/09/soccers-high-tech-future-mls-ifab-video-referee.html

Liu, B., Hu, M., & Cheng, J. (2005). Opinion observer: Analyzing and comparing opinions on the web. *Proceedings of the 14th International World Wide Web conference (WWW2005).* 10.1145/1060745.1060797

Meng, M. D., Stavros, C., & Westberg, K. (2015). Engaging fans through social media: Implications for team identification. *Sport, Business and Management. International Journal (Toronto, Ont.), 5*(3), 199–217.

O'Connell, E. (2016). *Avaya giving San Jose Earthquakes digital boost for in-stadium fan experience.* Retrieved from https://www.sporttechie.com/avaya-giving-san-jose-earthquakes-digital-boost-for-in-stadium-fan-experience/

Parganas, P., Anagnostopoulos, C., & Chadwick, S. (2015). 'You'll never tweet alone': Managing sports brands through social media. *Journal of Brand Management, 22*(7), 551–568. doi:10.1057/bm.2015.32

Price, J., Farrington, N., & Hall, L. (2013). Changing the game? The impact of Twitter on relationships between football clubs, supporters and the sports media. *Soccer and Society, 14*(4), 446–461. doi:10.1080/14660970.2013.810431

Samra, B., & Wos, A. (2014). Consumer in Sports: Fan typology analysis. *Journal of Intercultural Management, 6*(4–1), 263–288. doi:10.2478/joim-2014-0050

Santomier, J. P., Hogan, P. I., & Kunz, R. (2016). The 2012 London Olympics: Innovations in ICT and social media marketing. *Innovation: Management, Policy & Practice, 18*(3), 251–269. doi:10.1080/14479338.2016.1237305

Shank, M. D., & Beasley, F. M. (1998). Fan or fanatic: Refining a measure of sports involvement. *Journal of Sport Behavior, 21*(4), 435–443.

Smith, L. R., & Smith, K. D. (2012). Identity in Twitter's Hashtag Culture: A Sport-Media Consumption Case Study. *International Journal of Sport Communication*, *5*(4), 539–557. doi:10.1123/ijsc.5.4.539

Vale, L., & Fernandes, T. (2018). Social media and sports: Driving fan engagement with football clubs on Facebook. *Journal of Strategic Marketing*, *26*(1), 37–55. doi:10.1080/0965254X.2017.1359655

Watanabe, N., Yan, G., & Soebbing, B. P. (2015). Major League Baseball and Twitter Usage: The Economics of Social Media Use. *Journal of Sport Management*, *29*(6), 619–632. doi:10.1123/JSM.2014-0229

Watanabe, N. M., Yan, G., & Soebbing, B. P. (2016). Consumer Interest in Major League Baseball: An Analytical Modeling of Twitter. *Journal of Sport Management*, *30*(2), 207–220. doi:10.1123/jsm.2015-0121

Weiss, S. M., Indurkhya, N., Zhang, T., & Damerau, F. J. (2005). *Text Mining-Predictive Methods for Analyzing Unstructured Information*. Springer Verlag.

KEY TERMS AND DEFINITIONS

Fan Engagement: An engagement, in social media terms, as any deliberate interaction on the fan's part, meaning that something said made them want to spend their time and take an action to show their support for.

Hashtag: A word or phrase preceded by a hash sign (#), used on social media websites and applications, especially Twitter, to identify messages on a specific topic.

Real-Time Feedback: A type of qualitative and/or quantitative data collection, received live from visitors of a website, social media platform, or mobile application.

Sentiment Analysis: A process of computationally identifying and categorizing opinions expressed in a piece of text, especially in order to determine whether the writer's attitude towards a particular topic, product, etc. is positive, negative, or neutral.

Sentiment Polarity: A basic task in sentiment analysis classifying whether the expressed opinion in a document, a sentence or an entity feature/aspect is positive, negative, or neutral.

Social Media Platform: A web-based technology that enables the development, deployment, and management of social media solutions and services. It provides the ability to create social media websites and services with complete social media network functionality.

Word Cloud: An image composed of words used in a particular text or subject in which the size of each word indicates its frequency or importance.

This research was previously published in Big Data and Knowledge Sharing in Virtual Organizations; pages 176-197, copyright year 2019 by Engineering Science Reference (an imprint of IGI Global).

Chapter 46
Navigating the Social Media Space for Māori and Indigenous Communities

Maryann Lee
Unitec Institute of Technology, New Zealand

ABSTRACT

This chapter explores how Māori and Indigenous communities are engaging in social media in ways that reflect their cultural aspirations and Indigenous ways of being. Social media provides opportunities for Indigenous people to represent an Indigenous worldview that encompasses cultural, political, and social preferences. Highlighted also in this chapter are the risks inherent within the use of social media for Māori and Indigenous communities: in ways in which the misrepresentation, commodification, and exploitation of Indigenous culture and traditions are amplified through the use of social media that support colonial ideologies and the ongoing practice of colonization.

INTRODUCTION

This chapter explores how Māori and Indigenous groups are engaging in social media in ways that reflect our cultural aspirations and Indigenous ways of being. I argue that social media provides opportunities to create new spaces to reflect an Indigenous worldview, which encompasses cultural, political and social preferences. This includes advancing an agenda of self-determination that challenges colonial ideologies and western constructs of colonization (Pihama, 2001). I also highlight the risks inherent within the use of social media for Māori and Indigenous communities; and how social media can be used to perpetuate the ongoing practice of colonization, which systematically sets out to maintain the power and control of the dominant society (Iseke-Barne, 2002).

Due to the lack of literature published on social media and Indigenous people within tertiary education (Huijser & Bronnimann, 2014), this chapter provides a Kaupapa Māori framework for better understanding Māori and Indigenous engagement in social media in general. Establishing this broader context serves to introduce some of the motivations, considerations and aspirations of Māori and Indigenous

DOI: 10.4018/978-1-6684-6307-9.ch046

people in the use of social media. In this regard, this chapter prefaces a case-study in chapter four, about the use of Facebook to support Māori doctoral scholars and academics within the New Zealand tertiary environment. For Māori, educational aspirations are not limited to educational contexts and individual success; they have much wider implications that impact on whānau (family), hapū (sub-tribe) and iwi (tribe). Therefore, understanding the context of how Māori and Indigenous groups engage in social media as a decolonizing process for the transformation of Indigenous communities is critical and relevant for all educators. This chapter begins with an introduction to a Kaupapa Māori approach, followed by a discussion on ways in which Māori and Indigenous people are using social media to support our cultural aspirations, drawing on three Kaupapa Māori principles. The final section highlights the risks associated with social media for Indigenous communities in relation to the exploitation and commodification of indigenous culture; the racial discrimination against, and misrepresentation of, Indigenous people; and the disruption of Indigenous ways of being.

A KAUPAPA MĀORI APPROACH

This analysis is underpinned by a Kaupapa Māori methodological approach that draws from a Māori knowledge base and lived experiences. Kaupapa Māori promotes the validity of Māori language, knowledge and culture (Pihama, 2001). Kaupapa Māori supports Māori academics to carry out research in ways that embrace the values and principles of our whānau, hapū and iwi (L. Smith, 2003). Linda Smith (2003) asserts that Kaupapa Māori research comes from a local Indigenous theoretical position; a philosophy that encompasses a Māori worldview including spiritual, cultural and political dimensions. The Kaupapa Māori methodological approach enables Māori academics to participate in research that draws from ontological worldviews, and embraces Māori tikanga and values (L. Smith, 2003).

Kaupapa Māori also provides a theoretical and political tool as a basis for Indigenous researchers to work as change agents and to engage in research that is transformative for Indigenous people (G. Smith, 2003). Linda Smith (2003) believes that recognizing the injustices of colonization and thinking about ways that we can resist and challenge colonial ideologies is the first step to decolonization. She argues that while there is often an illusion that colonization is no longer practiced, there are still "new forms of colonization" which have been reformed in more subtle ways and, "many of these formations are insidious, and many of them have yet to be fully explored" (L. Smith, 2003, p. 215). Social media can be considered as one of these forms that often appear neutral, a-cultural and decolonized.

Graham Smith's (2003) discussion on Kaupapa Māori emphasizes the need to uncover injustices experienced by underprivileged groups, and recognizes the powerlessness that individuals may feel about their own destinies. He points out that Māori are struggling from the injustices of the past, whether they are aware of this or not. In Graham Smith's view, Māori are located within three intervention areas: conscientization, a 'freeing' of the Indigenous mind from the dominant hegemony; resistance, or going outside the constraints of the dominant system; transformative action, or engaging in a radical pedagogy and becoming change agents (G. Smith, 2003, p. 13). These areas are not independent of each other, nor do they fall in a linear order. Instead, they represent a cyclic approach whereby all Māori can be plotted somewhere within the cycle of Kaupapa Māori praxis. This is an important critique to assist in better understanding Māori engagement in social media with a Kaupapa Māori agenda.

KAUPAPA MĀORI CONSIDERATIONS FOR SOCIAL MEDIA

Graham Smith (2003) has identified six principles as a way of understanding Kaupapa Māori theory. These principles are: Tino rangatiratanga, self determination principle; Taonga tuku iho, cultural aspirations principle; Ako, Māori, culturally preferred pedagogy principle; Kia piki ake i ng ā raruraru o te kainga, the mediation of socio-economic factors; Whānau, extended family structure principle; Kaupapa, collective philosophy principle (G. Smith, 2003). While I have drawn on three principles in this chapter to help frame a way of thinking about Māori engagement in the social media space, the Kaupapa Māori principles reflect the lived experiences as Māori. Therefore, the principles are not seen in isolation, and will often overlap within the various themes discussed.

While this chapter often refers to the use of social media by Indigenous communities in a more general way, it is important to acknowledge that these communities are hugely diverse in geographical locations, politics and cultural traditions. For example, the use of social media amongst Amazonian Indigenous people varies considerably between the urban population and the rainforest inhabitants (Virtanen, 2015). In addition, social media applications provide different tools that are used widely for a range of purposes by Indigenous groups. This section attempts to highlight some examples of the ways in which Indigenous communities are using social media, including; political activism, cultural revitalization; and building stronger relationships and connections amongst Indigenous communities.

Tino Rangatiratanga: Self-Determination Principle

'Tino rangatiratanga' is a central principle of Kaupapa Māori theory. Self-determination, autonomy and sovereignty are ways to express tino rangatiratanga, whereby Māori can make decisions and choices both individually and collectively (Pihama, 2001). Fundamental to tino rangatiratanga is the acknowledgement of Māori epistemologies that promote Māori worldviews, knowledge, language and culture as authoritative and valid. Cultural identity and aspirations of Māori can only be achieved through a Māori worldview that is defined by and for Māori. Additionally, tino rangatiratanga is often viewed as a direct protest to the Crown, and seeks to legitimize the rights of whānau, hapū and iwi. It is intrinsically linked to Te Tiriti o Waitangi, that guarantees the right for Māori sovereignty as tangata whenua (people of the land) and is seen as a binding document with the Crown (Pihama, 2001).

The notion of tino rangatiratanga aligns with an Indigenous agenda of self-determination, and provides a way of thinking about how social media can be used as a political space in pursuit of sovereignty (Waitoa, Scheyvens, & Warren, 2015). For instance, in an examination of the use of social media by the Mana Party in the 2011 New Zealand elections, Waitoa (2013) found that social media gave the Mana party greater ownership and control of their content to key audiences. This aligned with the aim of the Mana Party as articulated by Annette Sykes, to "increase political participation through the ability to acquire greater political knowledge, increase political interest, improve political self-efficacy and highlight different perspectives and political opinion on what media portrays to us" (Waitoa, 2013, p. 73). Waitoa points out that social media sites enable the Mana party to represent themselves and their perspectives directly to their key constituents - Māori communities.

Social media also enables individuals, who may not have previously seen themselves as politically active, to become strong Indigenous advocates through the re-posting of protests, sharing of images, narratives and commentaries (Duarte, 2017). In fact, political activism can take place through the 'mundane' use of social media by Indigenous people's 'self-writing' about everyday life (Petray, 2013). It can be a powerful tool to normalize Indigenous views that challenge mainstream stereotypes, allowing opportunities to create a collective online identity to support Indigenous movements (Petray, 2013).

Dr. Adrienne Keene, from the Cherokee Nation, is a strong example of how an individual blogger can contribute and connect to the much larger online community. As a Native student in an elite institution, Adrienne Keene's feelings of isolation and separation from her classmates were the catalyst for her seeking connections online. Her blog, entitled 'Native Appropriations,' examines representations of Indigenous people, focusing on issues of cultural appropriation and stereotyping. "Writing the blog gave me voice. In my semi-anonymous space on the Internet, I was free to question, be angry, and fight back-things I struggled to do in 'real life'. I watched my notoriety and influence grow online, while in my day-to-day I was still a silent girl in the back of the classroom" (Keene, 2013). Adrienne Keene now has over 100,000 followers on her Native Appropriations Facebook page, and continues to blog, as well as use Twitter and Instagram to advocate and politicize Indigenous issues.

Indigenous movements such as the EZLN, Idle No More, and the Rio Yaqui water rights, highlighted in Duarte's (2017) research, use strong social media tactics to destabilize dominant governments and neoliberal political economies. The ability to engage in social network sites, in ways that are far less regulated than other political forums, enables a range of tactics to be employed by activists. Additionally, social media offers opportunities for marginalized groups within Indigenous communities to speak out and challenge oppressive politics (Parkhurst, 2017). For example, the 'Archiving the Aboriginal Rainbow blog project' that represents the Aboriginal and Torres Strait Islander LGBTIQ peoples to assert their political positions, draw attention to their oppression and challenge violence faced by their community (Farrell, 2017). Belton (2010) supports this view, and highlights how the digital spaces enable more opportunity to articulate for political expression;

Cyberspace thus allows those who are marginalized to speak more easily in their own voices without having to go through approved representatives or channels. As a result, Indigenous peoples may demand boycotts and strikes, alert the world of human rights violations, and share political tactics and ancestral stories without having to be a present, identified body. (Belton, 2010, p. 197)

There are strong examples in New Zealand where social media networks are being used to mobilize Indigenous movements, as well as build momentum for these projects with non-Indigenous allies. The 'SOUL - Save Our Unique Landscape' Campaign exemplifies a social media articulation of tino rangatiratanga at Ōtuataua in Mangere, Auckland. Led by young Māori women, such as Pania Newton, a number of protests have taken place against the proposal for the development of 480 homes in Ihumatao on land that has historical and sacred significance to the local tribal groups and community. The use of social media platforms, including Facebook, YouTube and Twitter, has helped to galvanize support at both a local and international scale (http://www.soulstopsha.org/). Additionally, a virtual occupation of the land, with over 4000 people symbolically residing on the site to protest against the development, has drawn wide attention. Strong use of social media tactics has provided a small local protest with a much larger support base throughout New Zealand and beyond. It has also inspired other Indigenous communities experiencing similar corporate land battles.

Taonga Tuku Iho: Cultural Aspirations Principal

Taonga tuku iho is closely linked to tino rangatiratanga, and is the principle, acknowledging Māori knowledge and traditions, that continues to sustain and support whānau, hapū and iwi to live as Māori. Taonga tuku iho validates Māori ways of being and creates a space for Māori to 'be Māori', whereby cultural aspirations and identity are legitimized (G. Smith, 2003). In the face of colonization, Māori have struggled to maintain the Māori language, cultural practices and protocols. In particular, the systematic denial of the Māori language through the advancement of colonial ways has impacted negatively on Māori communities (Pihama & Cameron, 2012). The principle of taonga tuku iho is illustrated through the use of social media in a range of ways to revive and maintain Indigenous traditional culture and language, and create digital spaces that reflect cultural aspirations.

One advantage of social media is the ease with which dynamic content can be created and shared across social networks. The recording and production of spoken language, as well as music, arts and dance, enables Indigenous communities to revitalize and reinvigorate languages and cultural practices struggling to be sustained in contemporary contexts (Alexander, 2010). Social media provides an opportunity to express and represent Indigenous worldviews in ways that are responsive to Indigenous ways of being. For example, digital storytelling enables Indigenous people to control their images and narratives through their own self-representations and, in doing so, challenge the stereotypical representation by the dominant society (Iseke & Moore, 2011). Iseke and Moore (2011) state, "Collecting community stories through digital means ensures that communities honor their oral traditions and resist the dominance of texts that are prevalent in the dominant society" (p. 35). Publishing on the web can also challenge the authority of Western representations in media and texts, and disrupt the 'elite' forms of traditional publishing (Nakata, 2002). Nakata states;

The online environment has reconstituted the balance between visual, oral, and textual modes of presenting information in a way that supports cultural perspectives. Further, the Web supports publishing in ways that disrupt established 'elite' forms of publication and which 'authorize' previously excluded groups from publishing. (Nakata, 2002, p. 28)

Also highlighted in the literature are ways in which social media offers Indigenous people the ability to reflect their own identities. While social media can be a space to explore identity, Carlson (2013) suggests that those who identify themselves as Indigenous offline will tend to be no different in how they identify themselves online. Therefore, by simply engaging in social media networks, Indigenous peoples project their indigeneity and reflect their cultural interests, preferences, beliefs and practices (Carlson, 2013; Lumby, 2010). Expressing one's indigeneity on social media, Lumby (2010) argues, is not just a matter of 'being' Indigenous, but more a matter of 'doing' indigeneity. For example, in Facebook, creating member profiles, accepting 'friends', belonging to groups, liking, sharing and commenting of content etc. all directly contribute to developing a representation of one's self.

The revitalization and preservation of Indigenous languages is another cultural aspiration that supports the taonga tuku iho principle. Māori have been innovative in their approach to promoting and normalizing Māori language in its everyday use, and many are using social media as a way to support this. In 2014 Pita Paraone, the chief executive for The Māori Language Commission, called for social media to be 'swamped' with the Māori language. He states, "Social media is a new frontier for Māori language use. Māori language speakers encourage others when they use te reo Māori as their default language for tweeting and messaging" (Rotorua Daily Post, 2004). Research undertaken by Keegan, Mato and Ruru (2015) indicate this to be occurring amongst Māori in the use of Twitter. They found a vibrant community of minority language tweeters who were able to connect with each other despite their geographical distance. Keegan, Mato and Ruru (2015) identified 90,000 tweets in Te Reo Māori (Māori language), and while many were both commercial and religious tweets, there were a number of individuals using twitter to converse in Te Reo.

As discussed in chapters two and five of this book, the use of social media for teaching and learning within tertiary environments is becoming more prevalent, as teachers explore ways to engage students that encompass digital learning environments. The notion of ako as a cultural pedagogical framework is closely aligned to taonga tuku iho and is also one of Graham Smith's (1991) Kaupapa Māori principles. For Māori, ako provides a more holistic and non-linear approach to teaching and learning. Ako can also be used to define the cultural aspirations for Māori education within our society. Lee (2008) asserts that ako does not just refer to teaching and learning processes but that "ako refers to a Māori educational framework that was integral in the protection, sustenance and transmission of knowledge, shaped by what was collectively deemed necessary and important" (p. 108).

Therefore, when exploring the use of social media and online learning communities with Māori and Indigenous students, there are a number of factors to consider that contribute towards a more culturally responsive teaching and learning framework (Dashper, 2017; Tiakiwai & Tiakiwai, 2008). For example, the ITPNZ report (2004) highlights the views of Māori educators and e-learning specialists during a two-day hui which looked at the concept of ako and how it may be applied to e-learning. It was suggested that, rather than use the term e-'learning', they preferred the term 'e-ako', as it represented the holistic and aspirational nature for Māori that includes both 'teaching *and* learning'. One participant asserts, "Ako is a whole lot of interlinked concepts such as whānau. It does not stand alone ... E-ako cannot be reduced to models or rules or too strict a definition" (ITPNZ, 2014, p. 31). Such views highlight how the use of social media for teaching and learning cannot be viewed in isolation, but must incorporate the principle of taonga tuku iho that acknowledge the cultural aspirations and identity of the learner. The complexities involved in engaging in a Kaupapa Māori community of learners are highlighted and explored in the following chapter.

Huijser and Bronnimann (2014) discuss social media for Indigenous learning by drawing on Yunkaporta's 2009 'eight-way framework of Aboriginal Pedagogy'. The framework includes the following concepts: story sharing; community links; deconstruct/ reconstruct; non-linear; land links; symbols & images; non-verbal; and learning maps. Huijser and Bronnimann (2014) highlight a range of social media tools that can support each of the eight concepts and in turn provide opportunities to align with a more Indigenous learning context. They assert;

... social media allow us to start the learning process from where Indigenous students are at, and allow us to draw on existing knowledge, rather than simply imposing a knowledge set on them, because we (as in western educators) have decided that is what they should know. (Huijser & Bronnimann, 2014, p. 102)

For Indigenous students, there are benefits for engaging in social media in order to enable a more learner-centered and holistic pedagogy that aligns more strongly to an Indigenous educational framework.

Whānau: Extended Family Structure Principle

While whānau is defined as a family group or extended family which is brought together through whakapapa (genealogy), whānau can also be used metaphorically to refer to a group of people who are working to a common end. Whānau *values*, particularly if kinship connections are absent, are what governs relationships with each other and connects the group (Metge,19 95). Pihama (2001) argues that colonization has actively targeted whānau structures and presented an individualist ideological view of a 'nuclear family'. Therefore, the terms 'whānau' and 'family' are not the same and Kaupapa Māori initiatives seek to affirm the roles and responsibilities of a collective whānau group. Being part of a whānau means there is a strong commitment to provide support to other whanau members, particularly for those who cannot fend for themselves. Inherent in a whānau structure are certain rights, responsibilities and obligations that are implicit within whānau relationships (Pihama, 2001).

Social media can support the notion of whānau in ways that foster connection, sharing, and co-creating amongst online communities (Bell, Budka, & Fiser, 2007; Molyneaux et al., 2014). For Indigenous people, particularly those who have become dislocated from their tribal land and communities, social media offers a way to connect back to their homelands. Molyneaux's et al. (2014) research surveyed 633 people from geographically remote First Nation communities, in the Sioux Look Out region of north western Ontario. Amongst their findings, participants frequently used social network sites, with 72.8% reporting daily. Their research highlighted a positive correlation between how often people communicated to each other on social media outside their communities, and the frequency of traveling outside their communities. Such findings support a link between online communication and face-to-face contact (Molyneaux et al., 2014). Molyneaux et al's (2014) research also found that their participants "use the Internet or social media to celebrate and practice their culture. More than half post photographs and stories and listen to music and look at art created by Aboriginal people on SNSs" (p. 285). Through the sharing of cultural resources and exchanging of information through social media, Indigenous people are developing stronger connections amongst each other and building resilience within their communities. (Molyneaux et al., 2014).

The principle of whānau is a significant factor for Māori engagement within social media. O'Carroll (2013) examines how rangatahi (youth) use social network sites to facilitate whānau connections and communication. Her research found that many of her participants actively sought to use social network sites to engage with whānau and to increase their whānau ties and relationships. O'Carroll (2013) states, "Whanaungatanga practice in virtual spaces was underpinned with the same values and principles as those practiced in physical spaces. Enabling whānau members to connect to each other helped them to nurture their familial relationships" (p. 278). O'Carroll's research indicated that social media enabled them to maintain values of whanaungatanga, identity and tikanga, which they already experienced in a physical way, through their online engagement as well.

Additionally, the use of social media sites has enabled iwi, hapū and whānau to re-connect, communicate with and support their whānau. This is reflected in many of the Māori tribal Facebook groups that are active today. One example, The Waikato Tainui Facebook page launched in 2013, is using social media to reach out to its 65,000 descendants in Aotearoa and abroad. On their Facebook they state, "As a tribal entity we aim to empower our people by providing a range of programmes and opportunities including grants and scholarships, education and health programmes, employment and training, cultural initiatives and marae development assistance" (https://www.facebook.com/Waikato.Te.Iwi/).

CHALLENGES

While the previous section outlines some of the ways in which Māori and Indigenous are engaging in digital spaces aligned to Kaupapa Māori principles, this section draws attention to the implications and complexities that are implicit within online engagement. It also looks at some of the key challenges that social media presents to Māori and Indigenous communities. This section seeks to challenge mainstream ideologies prevalent in the Western dominant society reflected in social media sites; in particular, the exploitation and misrepresentation of Indigenous culture and traditions.

Commodification and Misrepresentation

Indigenous groups must now contend with the global digitalization of their cultural possessions being robbed and distributed for commercial gain (Iseke-Barnes & Danard, 2007). Offering even greater access to audiences as well as unrestricted commercial opportunities, the internet is participating in the commodification of Indigenous culture and knowledge. Iseke-Barnes and Danard, (2007) discuss how Indigenous symbols and representations lose all cultural significance once they become commodities. For example, the dreamcatcher, which is a spiritual symbol from the Ojibwe people, is now being sold and purchased on hundreds of thousands of websites around the world without any historical or cultural context. "The cultural significance of the dreamcatcher is erased. It simply becomes a commodity" (Iseke-Barnes & Danard, 2007, p. 29).

In addition, the misappropriation and exploitation of tribal stories via social media poses adverse risk for Indigenous people. For Māori, tribal pūrākau (stories) has been a way for Māori to retain ancestral knowledge and to portray the lives of their tupuna (ancestors). Māori can reclaim pūrākau for purposeful and pedagogical narrative, in a way that advances Māori educational aspirations and offers a counter-story to the dominant discourse (Lee, 2008). However, Lee (2008) warns of the misappropriation of pūrākau through the translation and homogenizing of myths and legends and where such stories, collated through a colonizer's perspective, portray misrepresentations of Māori.

A strong example of traditional story-telling being portrayed through a colonizer's perspective is the Walt Disney movie *Moana* that was marketed widely through social media channels in 2016. The movie presented stereotypical characters of Pacifika people, in particular Maui, who is depicted as an obese Polynesian. These representations were amplified through the sharing, liking and commenting across social networks globally. Associate Professor Leonie Pihama used social media to 'write back' and protest against the misappropriation of the movie. She asserts, "You see Moana is not our story. It is not our representation of ourselves. It does not reflect any particular nation. It is a generalised, universalised, pan-nation, colonised, exploitation that is based on what... a bunch of white men reading Gaugin" (Pihama, 2016a). Within a year of the movie coming out, advertisements were circulating on social media networks for actors who could speak the Māori language. Pihama posts again;

If this film is translated directly into te reo Māori it will contribute to the colonising beliefs about being Indigenous and will be of more danger to the ways our tamariki understand being Māori than anything else. Translations of colonial beliefs reproduce colonial beliefs. The whole script must be decolonized and rewritten before being recreated in te reo Māori. (Pihama, 2016b).

Despite Pihama's Facebook protests, the script was translated into Māori and the movie released during Māori language week in 2017. An opportunity to re-tell a traditional pūrākau in a way that reflected and honored the rich cultural beliefs and value of the Pacific and Māori people has been lost to a Walt Disney commercial venture, that was reported to have earned over $600 million at the worldwide box office (Mendelson, 2017).

Racial Discrimination

Racial discrimination and hatred exists within the Internet in many forms. While the anonymity of cyberspace enables people to engage in an indiscriminate way, without having to identify their country or culture, it can also fuel racist attitudes and actions towards ethnic groups that are perceived as a threat.

Social media platforms are not excluded from the harboring of racial attitudes and racial attacks on Indigenous peoples (Carlson, Jones, Harris, Quezada, & Frazer, 2017).

The anonymous nature of the Internet can also enable racial attacks through stolen identities and false portrayal of ethnic groups. An example of racism reported by Te Karere (Māori news programme) was a fictitious Facebook profile page that depicted a Māori "family obsessed with boozing, smoking dope and bashing women" (Te Karere NZ, 2013). The account had stolen the identity of Kimiora Webster, a secondary teacher at Rotorua Boys' High School, alongside a number of photos of other Māori identities. The page received over 58,000 likes and actively engaged its audience by posts that racialized Māori as criminals. While Webster and many other Māori made complaints about the page, at the time of reporting he had not received any response from Facebook and the false portrayal still remained accessible online. The lack of response from Facebook highlights the limited control and power users have in dealing with racial discrimination targeted through accounts and profiles created by others.

To further highlight this issue, while large social media corporations may project a position of neutrality, such a notion can hide racial discrimination. Lee (2007) discusses new forms of racism that exist within our society which do not overtly claim a hierarchy of race they speak to cultural or ethnic differences. Lee states that, "Racism often escapes recognition as such, because hegemonic discourses have secured it for a new ideological transparency, enabling dominant groups to sustain racist constructions of social difference" (p. 31).

In 2012, groups of Indigenous people were shut out of their accounts when Facebook introduced a 'real-name' policy that attempted to close any accounts that appeared to have fictitious names. The policy was created after Facebook revealed that it had 83 million fake accounts, and experienced an immediate drop in its share price (The Guardian, 2014a). The real-name policy impacted on marginalized communities that included Indigenous groups, members of the LGBT stage performers and political activists, all of whom were denied access on the basis of their names being seen as fake. The Facebook's chief product officer, "affirmed that the 'real-name' policy is meant to differentiate from other parts of the internet that accept anonymity and to protect people from trolls and abuse conducted by those protected by anonymity" (The Guardian, 2014b). However, instead it clearly highlighted the discrimination that marginalized groups continue to experience within the online social media space.

Disruption of Indigenous Ways of Being

For Indigenous communities, cultural knowledge systems, ancestry and ways of operating as a collective are interwoven through one's Indigenous experiential physical existence. The internet can be seen as a way to distance Indigenous communities from one's natural connection to life (Iseke-Barnes & Danard, 2007). Howe (1998) supports this view in his article, Cyberspace is No Place for Tribalism, and warns of the dangers that the Internet poses for Indigenous groups. He describes the Internet as a global village, whereby the irrelevance between people and landscapes further displaces Indigenous communities who are connected spiritually to land. He highlights four key dimensions – spatial, social, spiritual and experiential – that are central to tribal life and community relationships. Howe also argues that these dimensions cannot be virtualized;

Tribalism must be practiced. It must be lived and experienced. It is not merely a way of thinking or some nebulous feeling, nor is it inherent in an individual's biological makeup. Tribalism requires full sensory interaction between tribal members, on the one hand, and between tribal communities and their surrounding environments, on the other hand. (Howe, 1998, p. 24)

Issues and tensions can arise when traditional cultural practices are shifted to the online space and are incongruous with cultural values. This is evident when social media provides an alternative space to grieve the loss of a person, when people find themselves unable to physically attend ceremonies.

O'Carroll (2013) raises a number of questions around Māori engaging in customary practices and accessing tribal knowledge through social media, rather than not physically returning their tribal lands. She highlights the issues for whānau around the tikanga of virtual spaces and the appropriateness of participating in tangihanga through social network sites. The postings of photographs of tupapaku and online videos of the tangi were seen by some as inappropriate and insensitive to the whānau of the deceased. While some of the participants in her study commented on the ability to say their goodbyes, create virtual memorials online and feel part of a tangihanga back home, other participants felt an inability to connect to the wairua of tangihanga. O'Carroll re-tells an experience shared by one of her participants:

…she kissed the computer screen to say goodbye to a deceased, and found it difficult to connect to the wairua of the deceased person. Her use of the term 'sad' in this instance was to signal the sense of the emptiness of this act compared with physical presence, as she felt removed from the experience of the tangihanga ritual. (O'Carroll, 2013, p. 211)

Such an example highlights how social media cannot take the place of face-to-face engagement in such situations. Cultural practices require a physical presence for people to experience fully and connect at a more spiritual and emotional level.

CONCLUSION

It is clear that social media can create a compelling space for Māori and Indigenous groups to connect in ways that support and reflect their Indigeneity. Indigenous groups are collectively engaging in social media to assert their tino rangatiratanga both at a local and global level. Social media is a powerful tool to galvanize political change, enabling large scale Indigenous movements to directly challenge Governments over the loss of tribal land rights. Additionally, social media has the potential to capture and revitalize Indigenous language and culture in ways that honors and sustains traditional knowledge and traditions.

Social media can also bring a number of risks for Māori and Indigenous communities by offering a new mode to perpetuate the dominant ideology and further the practice of colonization. As highlighted in this chapter, the misappropriation and exploitation of Indigenous culture and practices are amplified through the digitization and use of social media. It also highlights racial discrimination, as well as new forms of covert racism through the notion of neutrality. Finally, it looks at the disruption of Indigenous ways of being that draw upon the physical, emotional and spiritual self that cannot be replicated in the online environment.

This chapter highlights ways in which Māori and Indigenous groups are engaging in social media by drawing on Kaupapa Māori principles. Kaupapa Māori responds to the changing societal forces faced by Māori and the impact on our culture, aspirations and struggles in all sectors of society. This chapter also establishes the broader context for social media use by Indigenous groups which supports the next chapter's exploration of a Facebook group for Māori doctoral students and academics. While much work is still to be done in this area, it is intended that both chapters provided a way of thinking about ways in which the use of social media can contribute to the transformation of Māori and Indigenous people's cultural and educational aspirations.

REFERENCES

Alexander, C. J. (2010). International exploration of technology equity and the digital divide: Critical, historical and social perspectives. In P. Randolpleigh (Ed.), *From igloos to iPods: Inuit Qaujimajatuqangit and the internet in Canada* (pp. 80–105). IGI Global.

Bell, B. L., Budka, P., & Fiser, A. (2007). *"We were on the outside looking in": MyKnet. org: A First Nations online social network in Northern Ontario*. Presented at the 5th CRACIN Workshop, Montréal, Canada.

Belton, K. A. (2010). From cyberspace to offline communities: Indigenous peoples and global connectivity. *Alternatives*, *35*(3), 193–215. doi:10.1177/030437541003500302

Carlson, B. (2013). The 'new frontier': Emergent Indigenous identities and social media. In M. Harris, M. Harris, & B. Carlson (Eds.), *The politics of identity: Emerging Indigeneity* (pp. 147–168). Sydney: University of Technology Sydney E-Press.

Carlson, B. L., Jones, L. V., Harris, M., Quezada, N., & Frazer, R. (2017). Trauma, shared recognition and Indigenous resistance on social media. *AJIS. Australasian Journal of Information Systems*, 21.

Dashper, M. G. (2017). *Te waha tieke: Exploring the educational potential of social networking environments for Māori students in northland schools* (Unpublished doctoral dissertation). The University of Auckland. ResearchSpace, Auckland, New Zealand. Retrieved from http://hdl.handle.net/2292/34400

Duarte, M. E. (2017). Connected activism: Indigenous uses of social media for shaping political change. *AJIS. Australasian Journal of Information Systems*, 21.

Farrell, A. C. (2017). Archiving the Aboriginal rainbow: Building an Aboriginal LGBTIQ portal. *AJIS. Australasian Journal of Information Systems*, 21.

Howe, C. (1998). Cyberspace is no place for tribalism. *Wicazo Sa Review, 13*(2), 19. doi:10.2307/1409143

Huijser, H., & Bronnimann, J. (2014). Exploring the opportunities of social media to build knowledge in learner-centered Indigenous learning spaces. *Educating in Dialog: Constructing Meaning and Building Knowledge with Dialogic Technology, 24,* 97–110.

Iseke, J., & Moore, S. (2011). Community-based indigenous digital storytelling with elders and youth. *American Indian Culture and Research Journal, 35*(4), 19–38. doi:10.17953/aicr.35.4.4588445552858866

Iseke-Barnes, J. (2002). Aboriginal and Indigenous people's resistance, the internet, and education. *Race, Ethnicity and Education, 5*(2), 171–198. doi:10.1080/13613320220139617

Iseke-Barnes, J., & Danard, D. (2007). Indigenous knowledges and worldview: Representations and the Internet. *Information Technology and Indigenous People,* 27–29.

Keegan, T. T., Mato, P., & Ruru, S. (2015). Using Twitter in an Indigenous language: An analysis of te reo Māori tweets. *AlterNative: An International Journal of Indigenous Peoples, 11*(1), 59–75. doi:10.1177/117718011501100105

Keene, A. (2013, January 28). *Native appropriations.* Retrieved from http://nativeappropriations.com/2013/01/reflections-on-3-years-at-native-appropriations.html

Lee, J. (2008). *Ako: Pūrākau of Māori teachers' work in secondary schools* (Unpublished doctoral dissertation). The University of Auckland, New Zealand.

Lumby, B. (2010). Cyber-indigeneity: Urban indigenous identity on Facebook. *The Australian Journal of Indigenous Education, 39*(S1), 68–75. doi:10.1375/S1326011100001150

Mendelson, S. (2017, March). *Box Office: Disney's "Moana" sails past $600 million worldwide.* Retrieved from https://www.forbes.com/sites/scottmendelson/2017/03/16/box-office-disneys-moana-sails-past-600-million-worldwide/#65964eab43f7

Metge, J. (1995). *New growth from old: The whānau in the modern world.* Wellington: Victoria University Press.

Molyneaux, H., O'Donnell, S., Kakekaspan, C., Walmark, B., Budka, P., & Gibson, K. (2014). Social media in remote First Nation communities. *Canadian Journal of Communication, 39*(2), 275–288. doi:10.22230/cjc.2014v39n2a2619

Nakata, M. (2002). Indigenous knowledge and the cultural interface: Underlying issues at the intersection of knowledge and information systems. *IFLA Journal, 28*(5–6), 281–291. doi:10.1177/034003520202800513

O'Carroll, A. D. (2013). *Kanohi ki te kanohi-a thing of the past? An examination of Māori use of social networking sites and the implications for Māori culture and society* (Unpublished doctoral dissertation). Massey University, Palmerston North, New Zealand.

Parkhurst, N. D. (2017). Protecting oak flat: Narratives of survivance as observed through digital activism. *AJIS. Australasian Journal of Information Systems*, 21.

Petray, T. L. (2013). Self-writing a movement and contesting indigeneity: Being an Aboriginal activist on social media. Global Media Journal: Australian Edition, 7(1), 1–20.

Pihama, L. (2001). *Tihei mauri ora: Honouring our voices: Mana wahine as a Kaupapa Māori theoretical framework* (Unpublished doctoral dissertation). The University of Auckland. Research, New Zealand.

PihamaL. (2016a, January 1). Retrieved from https://www.facebook.com/leonie.pihama

PihamaL. (2016b, January 2). Retrieved from https://www.facebook.com/leonie.pihama

Pihama, L., & Cameron, N. (2012). Kua tupu te pā harakeke: Developing healthy whānau relationships. In *For Indigenous minds only: A decolonisation handbook* (pp. 231–244). School of Advanced Research.

Rotorua Daily Post. (2004, July 22). Retrieved from http://www.nzherald.co.nz/rotorua-daily-post/news/article.cfm?c_id=1503438&objectid=11297345

Smith, G. H. (1991). *Reform & Māori educational crisis: A grand illusion.* The University of Auckland.

Smith, G. H. (2003). *Indigenous struggle for the transformation of education and schooling. Keynote Address to the Alaska Federation of Natives (AFN)* Convention.

Smith, G. H. (2003). *Kaupapa Māori theory: Theorizing transformation of education and schooling.* Presented at the Kaupapa Māori Symposium, NZARE / AARE Joint Conference, Auckland, New Zealand. Retrieved from https://pdfs.semanticscholar.org/bc1e/df21dbdf7c94cf53c13d5d0c9b132f1102cb.pdf

Smith, L. T. (2003). *Decolonising methodologies: Research and Indigenous peoples* (6th ed.). Dunedin, New Zealand: University Otago Press.

SOUL - Save Our Unique Landscape Campaign. (n.d.). Retrieved November 3, 2017, from http://www.soulstopsha.org/

Te Karere, N. Z. (2013, June). *Outrage over Facebook pages depicting fake Māori family.* Retrieved from https://www.youtube.com/watch?v=uhekwe8-xh0

The Guardian. (2014a). *Facebook quarterly report reveals 83m profiles are fake.* Retrieved November 3, 2017, from https://www.theguardian.com/technology/2012/aug/02/facebook-83m-profiles-bogus-fake

The Guardian. (2014b). *Victory for drag queens as Facebook apologises for 'real-name' policy.* Retrieved November 3, 2017, from https://www.theguardian.com/technology/2014/oct/01/victory-drag-queens-facebook-apologises-real-name-policy

Tiakiwai, S., & Tiakiwai, H. (2008). *A literature review focused on virtual learning environments (VLEs) and e-Learning in the context of te reo Māori and Kaupapa Māori education.* Ministry of Education.

Virtanen, P. K. (2015). Indigenous social media practices in Southwestern Amazonia. *AlterNative: An International Journal of Indigenous Peoples, 11*(4), 350–362. doi:10.1177/117718011501100403

Waitoa, J. (2013). *E-whanaungatanga: The role of social media in Māori political engagement* (Unpublished Master's dissertation). Massey University, Palmerston North, New Zealand.

Waitoa, J., Scheyvens, R., & Warren, T. R. (2015). E-Whanaungatanga: The role of social media in Māori political empowerment. *AlterNative: An International Journal of Indigenous Peoples, 11*(1), 45–58. doi:10.1177/117718011501100104

This research was previously published in Global Perspectives on Social Media in Tertiary Learning and Teaching; pages 51-71, copyright year 2018 by Information Science Reference (an imprint of IGI Global).

APPENDIX

Please note, some of following Māori words are not direct translations, but explanations as they relate specifically to the context in which they are used in this chapter.

Ako: Culturally preferred pedagogy principle.
Aotearoa: New Zealand.
Hapū: Subtribe.
Iwi: Tribe.
Kaupapa Māori: Māori principles.
Pūrākau: Tribal stories.
Rangatahi: Youth.
Tamariki: Children.
Tangata Whenua: Local people.
Tangihanga: Funeral protocols.
Taonga Tuku Iho: The treasure and values that are inherited by us (cultural aspirations principle).
Te Karere: Māori news program.
Te Reo Māori: Māori language.
Tikanga: Protocols.
Tino Rangatiratanga: Self-determination principle.
Tupapaku: Deceased.
Tupuna: Ancestors.
Wairua: Spirit.
Whakapapa: Genealogy.
Whānau: Extended family.
Whanaungatanga: Relationship, kinship.

Index

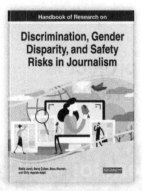

Ensure Quality Research is Introduced to the Academic Community

Become an Evaluator for IGI Global Authored Book Projects

Premier Reference Source

Stabilizing Currency and Preserving Economic Sovereignty Using the Grondona System

Patrick Collins

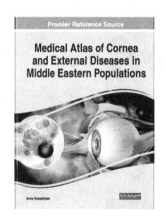

Premier Reference Source

Medical Atlas of Cornea and External Diseases in Middle Eastern Populations

Anna Hovakimyan

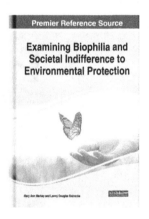

Premier Reference Source

Examining Biophilia and Societal Indifference to Environmental Protection

Mary Ann Markey and Lenny Douglas Meinecke

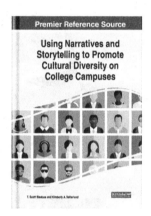

Premier Reference Source

Using Narratives and Storytelling to Promote Cultural Diversity on College Campuses

T. Scott Bledsoe and Kimberly A. Setterlund

The overall success of an authored book project is dependent on quality and timely manuscript evaluations.

Applications and Inquiries may be sent to:
development@igi-global.com

Applicants must have a doctorate (or equivalent degree) as well as publishing, research, and reviewing experience. Authored Book Evaluators are appointed for one-year terms and are expected to complete at least three evaluations per term. Upon successful completion of this term, evaluators can be considered for an additional term.

If you have a colleague that may be interested in this opportunity, we encourage you to share this information with them.

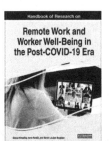

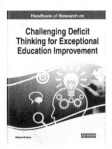

Are You Ready to
Publish Your Research ?

IGI Global
PUBLISHER of TIMELY KNOWLEDGE

IGI Global offers book authorship and editorship opportunities across 11 subject areas, including business, computer science, education, science and engineering, social sciences, and more!

Benefits of Publishing with IGI Global:

- Free one-on-one editorial and promotional support.

- Expedited publishing timelines that can take your book from start to finish in less than one (1) year.

- Choose from a variety of formats, including Edited and Authored References, Handbooks of Research, Encyclopedias, and Research Insights.

- Utilize IGI Global's eEditorial Discovery® submission system in support of conducting the submission and double-blind peer review process.

- IGI Global maintains a strict adherence to ethical practices due in part to our full membership with the Committee on Publication Ethics (COPE).

- Indexing potential in prestigious indices such as Scopus®, Web of Science™, PsycINFO®, and ERIC – Education Resources Information Center.

- Ability to connect your ORCID iD to your IGI Global publications.

- Earn honorariums and royalties on your full book publications as well as complimentary copies and exclusive discounts.

Join Your Colleagues from Prestigious Institutions, Including:

Australian National University

Massachusetts Institute of Technology

JOHNS HOPKINS UNIVERSITY

HARVARD UNIVERSITY

TSINGHUA UNIVERSITY ·1911·

COLUMBIA UNIVERSITY IN THE CITY OF NEW YORK

Printed in the United States
by Baker & Taylor Publisher Services